# MARSH GENEALOGY

## Giving Several Thousand Descendants
## *of* JOHN MARSH *of*
## Hartford, Connecticut
## 1636-1895

*ALSO INCLUDING SOME*
*ACCOUNT OF ENGLISH MARSHES, AND A*
*SKETCH OF THE MARSH FAMILY ASSOCIATION OF AMERICA*

COMPILED, EDITED AND ORIGINALLY PUBLISHED BY
### *Dwight Whitney Marsh*
—No. 5251—
OF AMHERST, MASSACHUSETTS

HERITAGE BOOKS
2008

# HERITAGE BOOKS

*AN IMPRINT OF HERITAGE BOOKS, INC.*

## Books, CDs, and more—Worldwide

For our listing of thousands of titles see our website
at
www.HeritageBooks.com

A Facsimile Reprint
Published 2008 by
HERITAGE BOOKS, INC.
Publishing Division
100 Railroad Ave. #104
Westminster, Maryland 21157

Originally published
Amherst, Massachusetts
Press of Carpenter & Morehouse
1895

International Standard Book Numbers
Paperbound: 978-0-7884-1843-3
Clothbound: 978-0-7884-7257-2

THIS BOOK IS DEDICATED

TO

## COL. LUCIUS B. MARSH

OF THE SALEM FAMILY,

PRESIDENT OF THE MARSH FAMILY ASSOCIATION, 1887–94,

Who with unwearied interest collected and published the history of his own line, John of Salem, who has given freely to collect and record facts in all our lines, and without whose sympathy and aid this volume could not have been published for several years to come.

Hardly less credit is due to John Edward Marsh of New York City and Rahway, N. J. of the New Haven Family, for entirely unsolicited and generous aid.

Let all within our lines be grateful for this outside help and unite in the hope that farther search in England may disclose for us and them a common Marsh origin.

The knights of old
Were stout and bold,
Below the sod
Their fire is cold,
Their flesh is mold,
Their doom with God.

———

All were brave and some were good.

———

This plate of arms of Sir Thomas Marsh, A. D. 1660, is from a very rare and ancient work on Heraldry (London 1679) and is "probably the ancient arms of all the Marshes with some slight variations for difference in families." It is supplied to us by the courtesy of Mr. George W. Montague, Amherst, Mass.

### ITS BLAZON :

"Gules, a horse's head couped, between three crosses bottonée fitchée, argent."

*Gules*, means a red shield.

*Couped*, cut off smoothly.

*Bottonée*, a cross that is crossed at three ends or points.

*Fitcheé*, a cross that has the lower end pointed like a dagger.

*Argent*, that the crosses are white in color (or silver)

to wit

"A red shield with a horse's head cut off smooth between three crossed crosses that are white and pointed at the foot."

Sr. Thomas Marshe of Darkes in the Parish of South Mimms in Com Middlesex Knight

To face page iv.

# THE MARSH NAME IN ENGLAND.

"REMEMBER THE DAYS OF OLD, CONSIDER THE YEARS OF MANY
GENERATIONS."

We have good reason to think that for a thousand years, men of Marsh name have been known in all parts of England. The name is found in Ireland, in a limited degree, mainly connected with the English church, but not in Scotland. As the name (common in America for over 260 years) has been distinctly English for these certainly eight, and probably ten centuries, we need not go farther back. We will here give names of definite persons for more than 20 generations, from the year 1174, 721 years ago.

> "Our days are like the shadows
> On sunny hills that lie."

From Burke's *Dictionary of the Landed Gentry of England.*

## IN NORFOLK COUNTY.

Page 247. Sir Stephen Marsh[1], Lord of Newton, Walsoken, Tid, St. Giles, etc. (These places were in the northwest corner of Norfolk Co., Eng., not far from "The Wash." D. W. M.)

His son, Jeffrey de Mariscow Marsh[2].

Jeffrey's dau. and heiress Desiderata Marsh[3], m. about 1240 Sir Roger de Colville of Newton by Leverington.

(If Desiderata Marsh[3] m. in 1240; she was b. about 1222, her father[2] about 1198 and Sir Stephen Marsh[1] about 1174. D. W. M.)

## IN SUFFOLK COUNTY, NORTHWEST CORNER.

Page 20 in supplement. Col. Marsh[1] of Mildenhall, Suffolk Co. His dau. Martha Marsh[2], m. 1706, (second wife) Jeremiah Bigsby,

Esq., Suffolk Co., and their son Thomas Bigsby[3] was A. M. and M. D. of Cambridge. (This Col. Marsh must have been b. as early as 1660, and his dau. 1684 to 1688. D. W. M.)

### IN YORK COUNTY.

Page 117 in supplement. Thomas Marsh[1] of Dey or Darton House, Darton, York Co.

His dau. Elizabeth Marsh[2] d. 1580 ; m. Roger Elmehirst of Elmehirst and Houndhill, York Co.

(If she d. 1580 after m. she was born before 1562 and her father Thomas b. before 1538. D. W. M.)

Page 405. Richard Marsh[1], D. D., Dean of York, Vicar of Halifax, York Co. m. Elizabeth Batt. Their dau. Frances Marsh[2] m. Rev. Lewis West, Archdeacon of Carlisle and Vicar of Aldenham, Cumberland Co.

Page 408. Anne Marsh m. Samuel Ferrand, bap. in Bingley Feb. 24, 1664, Rector Todwick and Vicar Rotherham (all three in York Co. D. W. M.) (If he was b. 1664, she prob. b. 1670, or 1668. D. W. M.)

### OF ENGLAND IN THE NORTHWEST.

Page 1191. Sir Edward Marsh[1] had dau. Mariana Marsh[2], m. Sir Harloven Saunders who came into England in or about 1270. He (Saunders) was descended from Robert, Lord of Innespruck, second brother of Rodolph, Count of Hapsburg and subsequently emperor. The family settled in Ireland. Their son Sir Robert Saunders, m. Dorothy, dau. Sir Edward Vickers of Lancashire.

(If Mariana Marsh m. about 1270 or 1280, she was b. about 1252 or 1262 and her father, Sir Edward, about 1228 or 1238. D. W. M.)

### OF WILTSHIRE, ENGLAND, AND OF IRELAND. .

(Narcissus Marsh, according to the Methodist Encyclopedia, was b. 1638 at Hannington, Wiltshire, England, was Archbishop 1690, and of Dublin, 1694, and of Armagh 1703, built a public library in Dublin, filled it with choice works and settled provision for two librarians. He d. 1713. We have again of the Landed Gentry :

Page 333. Francis Marsh[1], Archbishop of Dublin, his son ?

His grandson, Rev. Jeremy Marsh[3], D. D., m. Mary dau. Jeremy Taylor, Esq.

Their dau. Elizabeth Marsh[4], m. Rev. Simon Digby, Bishop of Down and Connor who d. 1824.

(The following Marshes are prob. of the same family. D. W. M.)

Page 332. Dean —— Marsh[1], his only child Mary Marsh[2], m. 1717 John Digby, Esq. of Landenstown, M. P. for Kildare, 1731 and high sheriff 1732.

Page 135 in supplement. Digby Marsh, Esq., m. Eliza, dau. Christophilus Garstein, Esq., m. Elizabeth Thompson, 1790, of Bragganstown, Louth Co., Ireland.

## OF WILTSHIRE.

(Probably same family as the Archbishop who was b. 1638. D. W. M.)

Page 1596. Samuel Marsh[1] of Clapham, M. P. for Chippenham. His dau. Annabella Marsh[2], m. (second wife) Thomas Adams, Vicar of Uske, b. Sept. 15, 1758. (Prob. his father-in-law Samuel Marsh, b. as early as 1740. D. W. M.)

### ADAMS CHILDREN.

1. Frederick.
2. Arthur, in holy orders, Vicar of Llanbaddock.
3. Annabella.
4. Frances.
5. Mary, m. *her cousin Charles Marsh*, Esq.
6. Emma, m. 1834.
7. Catherine.

Catherine Marsh[2], eldest dau. of Samuel Marsh[1], M. P., m. 1784, William Adams Williams (son Thomas above by his first wife) eight children given. (If eldest dau. m. in 1784, prob. b. 1766 and her father Samuel Marsh, M. P. prob. b. 1742. D. W. M.)

Page 1206. Gen. Marsh[1] had sister[1] who m. Robert Sealy, Esq. of Bandon, Ireland, whose father went there in beginning of the reign of Charles II. Sons "Armiger" John and George, (about 1649. D. W. M.)

### MARSH FAMILY OF KENT COUNTY, ENGLAND.

Page 831. This ancient family, styled De Marisco in ancient Latin deeds was at East Langdon near Dover, Kent, in 1326, in reign of Edward III.

In addition we have the names of over fifty members of this Marsh family in Kent, among whom was Richard Marsh, Clarke of Dover Castle and the Cinque Ports, who d. in 1626.

From other records we have Prof. Herbert Marsh of Cambridge, b. London, 1757, Bishop in 1816; Gabriel Marsh of the Admiraltie (1633) to discharge Mary and John and other vessels in the Thames; Walter Marsh who d. 1540 and his widow Eleanor m. Sir William Locke; also among "the noble army of martyrs," George Marsh, who studied at Cambridge and was curate of Deane, and martyred April 24, 1555 and Nicholas Marsh in 1532.

If we consider these persons as to time and place we have :

Sir Thomas Marsh of Middlesex Co., 1660. Near London in the heart of England.

Col. Marsh, 1660. Suffolk Co. on the east coast.

Narcissus Marsh, b. 1638, Archbishop of Dublin. Wiltshire Co., near the west coast.

The martyrs of Lancashire 1555 and Norfolk 1532.

Thomas[1] Marsh b. before 1538 and Elizabeth[2] b. before 1562, d. 1580, after marriage. Of York Co., northeast coast.

Ancient Marsh family of Kent, styled in Latin deeds " de Marisco." " Seated near Dover in the reign of Edward, 1326." South of England on the English Channel.

Sir Edward[1] Marsh, b. about 1228–38. Marianna[2] Marsh, b. about 1252–62, for she m. Sir Harloven Saunders soon after 1270. Northwest coast of England near Lancashire.

Sir Stephen[1] Marsh, b. about 1174. Jeffrey[2] de Mariscow Marsh, b. about 1198. Desiderata[3] Marsh, b. about 1222, m. 1240. East coast of England, Norfolk Co.

---

There are others claiming our notice and among them we give first honor to the printers. Their work is more valuable than that on brass or marble. And we delight to find that a printer of our name did splendid work in London more than 300 years ago. A spoken word melts on the air ; a printed word lingers down the ages.

"Among the books which formerly belonged to the kings and queens of England, and which are now in the library of the British museum, says the *American Bookmaker*, there are two which have bindings of a particularly beautiful and distinctive character. The volumes themselves are exceedingly interesting, both being presentation copies to Queen Elizabeth. The larger, a small folio, $11\frac{3}{4}$ inches by eight inches, is a copy of the "Flores Historianum," collected by Matthew of Westminster, and was printed in London by Thomas Marsh on June 2, 1570. It was published under the superintendence and at the expense of Matthew Parker, archbishop of Canterbury, and was presented by him to the Queen.

The smaller one, a quarto, eight inches and one-eighth by five inches and three-fourths, contains the Gospels in Anglo-Saxon and English, and was printed in London in the year 1571 by John Day. This most interesting volume, which was also published under the supervision of the archbishop, contains a dedication "to the Queenes Majestie," by John Fox, the Martyrologist; and we learn from a MS. note in the title page, that "This was the Dedication Book presented to the Queenes owne hands by Mr. Fox."

The bindings of these volumes are not only very charming, but they are also quite different from any others in the royal collection. They are identical, with the exception that in the smaller, a portion of the design is omitted to suit the size of the covers. The material used is a brown calf, with corners and side pieces of inlaid white leather, beautifully decorated with military trophies and musical instruments stamped in relief upon a gold ground. In the center of each cover is an ornament of very elegant design executed in the same style as the corners and side pieces, and inclosing the arms of the queen impressed in gold, her initials being placed outside; the sides are also powdered with gold dots. The larger book has brass clasps handsomely engraved, and both volumes have the edges of the leaves gilt and gauffred."

The following letter as to the Marsh family in England is of interest:

95 WHALLEY ROAD, ACCRINGTON, LANCASHIRE, ENG.
OCTOBER 4, 1888.

REV. D. W. MARSH,
    AMHERST, MASS., U. S.:

*Dear Sir:*

Having been for a series of years engaged as opportunity offered, in occasional antiquarian researches into the history, connections and origin of my family, I was somewhat interested in a circular issued by the " Marsh family of America " recently sent me by a Canadian relative.

Though a native of this town, I have lived in the early years of my childhood, in Massachusetts, my father having left Accrington and gone to the United States when I was only four months old. He, I believe, attended the ministry of the late Rev. Asa Brunson of Fall River, of whom an obituary notice, (I suppose on account of his patriarchal age ) was copied into the English newspapers. My father died in 1833 at Fall River and my mother came back here with myself and sister. My father's great uncle Thomas Marsh (son of Nicholas Marsh of Dykenook) went to America (I suppose with his wife whose maiden name was Heywood) toward the end of last or beginning of present century. So far as I know he never returned to this country.

I have not been quite successful in ascertaining to my satisfaction the origin of the name Marsh. The Lancashire Marshes to whom my family belong, are said to be of yeoman origin, and are very easily traceable for at least 400 years in this neighborhood or rather in that of Bolton Le Moors. My ancestor Nicholas Marsh came from Rivington (near Bolton) last century and became the ancestor of every person of the name of Marsh living in this town and neighborhood until within the last few years, when a very few others from Yorkshire, etc., have migrated hither.

In view of the fact that nearly every Lancashire town has its name duplicated in that of persons and families, in view also of the fact that in the vicinity of the rivers Mersey and Ribble, there are swampy lands liable to submersion in flood times, and taking into account the fact that Marsh is a geographical name, the inference seems natural that when surnames came into general use, this, like many others had a geographical origin. This however is entirely my own idea and I have not as a matter of fact found that the name has been ascribed to such a source.

The theory held by the landed gentry of the name of Marsh is this. Francis or Francisco de Marisco, a Norman, who came hither with William the Conqueror, founded the family whose patronymic has been Anglicised into Marsh. An intimate friend of mine, a Scottish landed proprietor, and Deputy Lieutenant of Lanarkshire, a noted authority in matters relating to Heraldry, alleges that the armorial bearings of the name of Marsh indicate ducal rank. So far as I have been able to ascertain, the name of Marsh, which is *certainly* and most *essentially* English, has never been associated with the English peerage except by marriage. The curious and interesting fact (supposing my friend's conclusion to be correct) referred to above, must therefore have what may be called a prehistoric or Norman reference. I have not been able to trace any relationship connection between the Marshes of the south and those of the north, except one single suggestion. In my family the distinctive and historic landmarks are the names Nicholas and Giles, these are so distinctive as to be obviously *family* names, and not merely importations from the female line.

In Fox's Book of Martyrs is given an account of the putting to death of Robert Denham, Nicholas Marsh and another at Harwich Dover Court in the County of Norfolk. My ancestor Nicholas came from the neighborhood of Horwich or Rivington about 16 or 20 miles from here. The account of Nicholas of Norfolk given also in "The Lollard," a book published by the Religious Tract Society pages 207 and 208 is to me most tremendously suggestive, albeit I am without *certain* evidence of the connection of this Nicholas of the southeast coast with my family.

There is not the same want of evidence of the connection of my family with another member of "the noble army of martyrs" George Marsh to wit. He was Curate of Deane near Bolton and was burned at the stake for his faithfulness to Christ and his doctrine, in the reign of Mary of bloody memory. His life is also given in extent in Fox's book of Martyrs, and it has also been written again somewhat more fully by the Rev. Alfred Hewlett recently deceased. My copy of this work I gave to my relative the Rev. David Marsh of Quebec who died in February last.

William Marsh, Churchwarden of Deane, invited me over there
some years since and he took me through Deane church and up to
the pulpit from which the martyr it is said preached and which has
been transposed from the now demolished ancient church into its
modern successor.  Only somewhere about 30 or 35 years separated
the martyrdom of Nicholas of Harwich in Norfolk from that of
George of Deane near Horwich in Lancashire.

My aunt stated to me that we are the descendants of George, but
I think had it been so, the tradition would have been more vivid
than it is.  That he left a family is evident however and that we are
of the same stock is well nigh certain.  There have been a good
many Irish Marshes, but these are certainly of the English stock.
Among them there have been several prelates of the Episcopal
church.  There was a Bishop Jeremy Taylor Marsh whose close
relationship to Bishop Jeremy Taylor is thus plainly indicated.

The late Rev. William Marsh of Beckenham of blessed memory
was of this stock.  He was the son of Sir Charles Marsh an Indian
soldier.  He, the Rev. William Marsh, was an Evangelical Episcopal-
ian, one of the most saintly men of his, or any other generation, and
a man most marvelously used of God in conversions.  He was married to the Lady Elizabeth Cadogan a daughter of the Earl of Cadogan.  His daughter (by his first wife), is an authoress, whose name
and works are doubtless more or less known in America.  Among
other works she wrote the life of Capt. Hedley Vicars who was
slain in the Crimean war.  Some years ago when residing for a short
time at the marine village of Lytham, I met a clergyman who acosted
me by stating " I have a sister of the same name as you."  This he
told me was Lady Marsh, widow of the late Sir Henry Marsh, Baronet
of Dublin.  This baronetcy I am sorry to say, is extinct, there being
no heir.  This is undoubtedly another of the Anglo-Irish Marshes.
I lived in Glasgow for 20 years and there was not during that time
one other person of the name, so far as known in that immense city.
There are no Scotch Marshes.  Hoping to have the circulars by
newspaper post,

I am, dear sir,

Yours respectfully,

J. PAUL MARSH.

REV. WILLIAM MARSH
of Beckenham, Eng.

*To face page xiii.*

When your historian was at Mosul on the Tigris, Lieut. Pengelly of the Indian navy was there during the Crimean war, making purchases of horses and mules for service in the English army before Sebastapool. He gave me the Life of Hedley Vicars, by Miss Marsh: and whoever has read that work and also her "English Hearts and English Hands," sees a solution of the labor question in her Christian treatment of English "Navvies" while they were building the Crystal Palace and when afterward, many of them went to the trenches in the Crimea. I have long had in my library the life of Rev. William Marsh and I take great pleasure in presenting to my American kinsmen from that work, his likeness, as a type of an all around English Marsh who united in his lineage, environment and soul-growth, much that is heroic from knightly descent, graceful in learned culture, refined in courtly associations, but above all Christian in due regard for all men, especially in most humble and constant service of the lowly. Happy for us could we all read his story, and put its splendid meaning into our lives.

I have not been able to make any extended and exhaustive study of the English Marshmen. As the years pass on, some other will do that work. So far as I have been able to carefully examine and to judge, there is as yet no proof, by exact dates and names, of the definite connection of any head of one of our Marsh tribes in America with his exact Marsh parent in the English family from which he came. Of course there has been in each case absolute connection, with some English Marsh parent and family which at some future day may be exactly traced.

On the side of our mothers we have several definite connections carefully traced. In this genealogy it may be noted that all the descendants of Gov. Joseph Marsh of Vermont and Judge Perez Marsh of Berkshire, Mass., can, through their mother's line, trace their descent from several kings of England. And when we remember that in thirty generations back (a thousand years) we each have probably had a hundred thousand ancestors, it would not be strange if every one of Marsh name in America were descended from an English king. And what of that! What if a ten thousandth or a millionth part of you be tinged with royal blood! We must ask, was the king noble, and is a drop of his blood worth having? If we knew its whole history might we not prefer to let that drop out?

Better be born of a noble yeoman than of an ignoble knight or king! As the case stands, so far as we know, we can highly honor our name for its martyrs, its printers, its prelates and princely men.

> " Down from the past has come,
> Mighty as the sun,
> Our father's name.
> As on a mountain's height;
> It shines a beacon light,
> To guide to paths of right
> And noble fame."
>
> —*S. D. Marsh, Paynesville, Ohio.*

---

Some may be pleased to know that *The Pedigrees* of Ye family of *Marsh* in England can be found in the following works :

Berries Kent Genealogies, page 460.
Visitation of Middlesex (Salisbury 1820 fol.), page 4.
Burke's St. James Magazine I, 243.
Burke's Landed Gentry (Snave Manor) 2, 3, 4, 5.
Burke's Landed Gentry (Gaynes Park) 2 supp. 3, 4, 5.
Burke's Landed Gentry (Springmount) 3, 4.
Burke's Landed Gentry (Ramridge) 4, 5.
Hunter's Deanery of Doncaster II, 370.
South Mimms by F. C. Cass, page 56.
Harleian Society, XIII, 10.

The above works can be found and referred to in the Boston Public Library and the Astor Library, New York.

The following is from Hottens "Original List of Emigrants from 1600 to 1700."

In ship "Plaine Joan" from London to Virginia May 15, 1635, John Marsh, age 26.

"He brought Attestacon of his Conformitie to ye orders and discipline of the Church of England."

From London to St. Christophers May 21, 1635 in ship " Mathew " William Marsh, age 26.

From London to Virginia July 27, 1635, in ship " Primrose " Francis Marsh, age 28 and Joseph Marsh age 33, both took oath of allegiance and supremicie, etc.

Monmouth Rebellion, Dec., 1685. From Dorchester jail to *Barbadoes* sold for ten years, political prisoner *Edward Marsh* in ship "Bettie" of London from ye port of Waymouth in Co. Dorset.

So we find that if many Marshes have been knighted, some have been martyred and at least one, for political offence, sold. And some became exiles in a new world.

In a church at Haverhill, Mass., where Marshmen of the Salem line settled, a bell "*in memory of the Marsh family*" has this inscription :

> "Peace to the past,
> Joy to the present,
> Welcome to the future."

That bell seems to ring out all unkind memories of the motherland, and to ring in pleasant recognition of American prosperity, and to peal out again, buoyant anticipation of still more favored Marshmen yet to be, wherever they may come in all the world.

In the homeland or new land we can all join :

> "Peace to the past,
> Joy to the present,
> Welcome to the future."

# THE MARSH FAMILY ASSOCIATION OF AMERICA.

Early in 1884 David C. Marsh of Montague, Mass., received a letter from Mrs. Pamelia Wellman (p. 123 and 464) of Parma, N. Y., dated Feb. 11, 1884, asking for records of the Marsh family, particularly of descendants of John Marsh of Hartford, Ct., of 1636; and stating that she was a descendant of Joseph Marsh who came to Lebanon, Ct., in 1700. This letter was shown to many members of the Marsh family in the vicinity and to J. Johnson of Greenfield, Mass., whose wife Climena was a daughter of Calvin Marsh of Montague, born Oct. 21, 1828. The matter of the ancestry of the family was frequently discussed whenever two or three of them were together until by mutual consent, David C. Marsh and wife, Sanford Marsh and wife and J. Johnson met at the home of Hannah R. and Elvira F. Marsh, sisters of Mrs. Johnson, on the afternoon of June 2, 1884 and effected a temporary organization by choice of David C. Marsh, chairman, J. Johnson, secretary and Sanford Marsh, treasurer. At an adjourned meeting, June 16, it was decided to hold a Marsh family gathering at Lake Pleasant, Montague, Mass., July 23, 1884.

"THESE SOUGHT THEIR REGISTER AMONG THOSE THAT WERE RECKONED BY GENEALOGY."

*—Ezra 2 : 62.*

The first regular meeting of the Marsh family association was held at Lake Pleasant in the town of Montague, Mass., in July, 1884, with a very good attendance. An organization was completed. D. W. Marsh of Amherst, Mass., was chosen president with several vice-presidents and J. Johnson, Esq., of Greenfield, secretary, which office he has held most acceptably to this day. E. B. Marsh, registrar of Amherst college was chosen treasurer.

The second meeting in 1885 was also held at Lake Pleasant. The attendance was estimated by the different reporters as 150 and 200. The following officers were elected : D. W. Marsh, president; Rev. Francis J. Marsh of Walpole, Luther R. Marsh of New York, John E. Marsh of Hartford, Horatio N. Marsh of Joliet, Ill., Prof. Charles D. Marsh of Ripon, Wis., William A. Marsh of Jamestown, N. Y., Riverius Marsh of New Brunswick, N. J., vice-presidents ; J. Johnson, secretary ; E. B. Marsh, treasurer.

For the genealogical committee the above officers were chosen with D. C. Marsh of Montague, Lucius Boltwood of New Haven, Zebina Marsh of Northfield, Mrs. Pamelia Wellman of Parma, N. Y., E. J. Marsh of Leominster, Mass., Dr. Edwin Stuart of New York, Geo. M. Carrington of Winsted, Ct., John W. Thompson of Five Islands, Nova Scotia, Charles Marsh of Springfield and Lucius B. Marsh of Boston.

Valuable addresses were given by Rev. Francis Marsh of Walpole and by Luther R. Marsh of New York. Parts of the following ode were sung as they have been at nearly every Marsh meeting since :

*Tune, America.*

1633—1887.

From England's sea-girt land
By God's high guiding hand,
Our fathers sailed.
They laughed at ocean's roar,
They found a broader shore,
And here forever more
They freedom hailed.

John Marsh was one of them,
Those ancient, stalwart men,
Their God, their King :
His Bible was his chart,
With wisest master-art,
He put it in his heart,
More light to bring.

And George of Hingham came,
And many a queenly dame,
And lovely bride :
And Marshes, as the leaves,
Or golden harvest sheaves,
Or drops that drip from eaves,
They multiplied.

B

The women toiled and spun,
A daily task was done
By girl and son.
The Marshes grew and spread,
The Marshes loved and wed,
The Marshes fought and bled,
And freedom won.

Now Marsh, be merriest man,
That ever walked or ran,
Or kissed a bride ;
Let Marshes none be queer,
And none be known to leer,
No Marsh must ever sneer,
Nor ever chide.

In truth we live and die
As others far and nigh,
For Marsh is man;
The Marshes come and go,
As come the rain and snow,
The Marshes ebb and flow,
*A little span.*

We boast no nobler name,
No bluer blood we claim,
Lest pride should fall;
Yet love we this our tree,
And come from land and sea
One gathering here to be,
And honor all.

Two hundred years have taught,
That every Marshman ought
To live for right,
To spend his little span
In doing what he can
To serve his God and Man
With all his might.
                —*D. W. Marsh, Amherst, Mass., July* 22, 1885.

The president gave the following address :

The Marsh family in the United States is composed of several
large branches. Two hundred and fifty years ago there were at least
six men of the Marsh name who had left the shores of old England
for this new world.

*Dwight W. Marsh*

*To face page xviii.*

According to Lunt's "New England Traits," the first of the six to come was John Marshe, who took oath March 24, 1633, and sailed a few days later in the ship Mary and John, Robert Sayres, master. This is the John Marsh who went to Salem. I have one account which says that a John Marsh took the freeman's oath at Quincy in 1634, and in 1635–6 went to Hartford, Ct. Savage says that John Marsh went to Hartford in 1636, but yet this first John was the one who went to Salem, 1633,—John Marsh our pioneer.

George Marsh of Hingham came very nearly as early; for he drew his home lot at Hingham, Mass., Sept. 18, 1635. Also in that year, 1635, four others came; for on May 15th, another John Marsh, age 26, having taken the oath of fidelity to the English King and crown, set sail on the Plain John, Richard Buckham, master, for Virginia, as all New England was then called. And in the same year, 1635, a week later than this second John Marsh, on May 21st, upon the Matthew of London, Goodlad, master, William Marsh, age 26, sailed for St. Christopher, and was possibly the William Marsh who came to Plainfield, Ct., in Cromwell's day, of whom an account says that he was at Boston in 1636. And on July 27, 1635, John or Jonathan Marsh, age 33, and Francis Marsh, age 28, came over on the Primrose, Captain Douglas, master. Thus in 1635 six of our name had sailed on five different vessels that year and one two years before. Samuel Marsh was at New Haven in 1647, Thomas Marsh came in 1648, Alexander Marsh of Braintree in 1654, and a John and Sarah Marsh had a son born in Boston in 1669. Others of our name followed.

And now after 252 years from the coming of the first John, 1633, we in 1885, are noting the great Marsh banyan tree that has spread over our land. We know the names of more than 5000 descendants of those early Marsh settlers. Men of our name are found in every part of our land, and the great family tree is grown so large that we cannot yet trace all the new trunks that drop, banyan-like, from the wide-spreading boughs and take root for a new life in new states and territories. One writes from New Orleans to know if he is a "twig of a branch" of this great tree.

The common name, Marsh, would indicate that most of the Marshes who came to this country from England between 1633 and the present time, must have had in England, a common origin, perhaps one or two centuries back from 1633. That origin may at some future time be traced out.

To-day we have to do with the new Marsh life in a new world; we mean to get acquainted with those enterprising men, most of them led by the strongest devotion to noblest principles, who braved the sea and the unknown to help plant a new nation.

We can see them beginning to land when Plymouth was thirteen years old, not content to rest on the new shore of the old mother ocean, whose waves, away back, washed Old England, but, forsaking their ships, and plunging with the foremost into the mysterious woods, wild with pathless tangles.

Soon they are found on the Connecticut river, among the first settlers of Hartford. Twenty-three years later they toil up the river, cutting paths through the woods, guided by blazed trees; men and youth on foot with their guns, mothers with their younger children on the pack saddle and pillion. Some with household goods struggle in boats against the current of the noble river, so much larger than the Thames, often poling and dragging against the current. Above the Holyoke gorge they come out upon the broad Indian meadows. They help found Hadley and Hatfield, and branching from Hadley, they and their descendants are pioneers eastward at Ware and Hardwick, northward at Sunderland, Montague and Northfield, westward at Whately, Conway and Hawley, at Worthington, and Pittsfield, and Dalton.

Branching out from Hartford, John Marsh[3], grandson of the original Hartford John, explores Litchfield, his brother Joseph is of the first settlers of Lebanon, Ct., and his brother Jonathan, with Nathaniel Stanley, founds New Hartford.

From Salem, some of that John Marsh's descendants go to Haverhill and "many to Maine." From all these early settlements mentioned in Massachusetts and Connecticut, Marsh men pass on as pioneers to many towns in Vermont and New York. And still later with the moving tide they push on, westward ho! to Detroit, Chicago, St. Louis, Wisconsin, Kansas, Colorado. They have long since been found in California and Oregon. At New Albany, Ind., Samuel Marsh built "The Volcano," the first steamer on the Ohio below the Louisville Falls, as we have written to us by one of his descendants in Florida.

By letters received during the past year we can trace the line of movement of many descendants of Alexander of Braintree, some going from Massachusetts to Nova Scotia, and from Nova Scotia through Ontario to the great west. Others of that line to East Haddam, Ct., and back to New Hampshire and circling to the neighborhood of Boston; others from East Haddam to Vermont and the great west. One of that family, Sylvester, after inventing wheat dryers that made his fortune in Chicago, came back East to build a railroad up Mt. Washington, upon a principle so admirable that it has been copied for climbing the Alps. Hon. Thomas Allen of St. Louis, whose father's first wife was a Marsh and the second a daughter of a Marsh, became president of the Iron Mt. railroad and a millionaire. The firm of Jordan & Marsh of Boston is well known. L. Milton Marsh of New York City is at the head of a very wide and benevolent Sabbath-school work. Rev. Theodore H. Marsh is Superintendent of Home Missions at Grand Rapids for the Synod of Michigan.

It is not too much to say that, wherever settled, Marshes have been among the leading men—captains, selectmen, doctors, ministers, merchants, representatives, judges. At Litchfield, Ct., Col. Ebenezer Marsh was judge for twenty-five years, and his daughter Mary was grandmother of Gov. Horatio Seymour. At Hartford, Vt., Col. Joseph Marsh was long a judge and for five years Dep. Governor of Vermont. At Pittsfield, Dr. Perez Marsh was long judge of Berkshire. The first meeting called for town purposes to organize Dalton was held at Judge Perez Marsh's house. His descendants passed from Berkshire largely to Hudson City and down the Hudson river to New York and Brooklyn.

Children of Samuel Marsh of New Haven founded Elizabeth, N. J. One letter from Detroit, another from Peoria, Ill., and a third from Plainfield in this state, give long lines from John of Medfield, Mass. (He was descended from John of Boston.)

The whole Marsh family, wherever found, have valued education. I know one graduate of Williams College and of Harvard law school who had three boys in college at once. His grandfather, Dr. Perez Marsh, was a graduate of Harvard, 1748. Two cousins Marsh at Hadley, grandsons of John of Hartford, one, son of Daniel, and one, of Jonathan, graduated at Harvard in the same class, 1705. The son of one of these Hadley-Harvard boys graduated at Harvard in 1728 and never married, but became for many years a noted teacher at Quincy, Mass. The celebrated Adams family of Quincy for early training probably owed much to him, John Quincy Adams being his pupil. The son of the other Hadley-Harvard boy graduated at. Yale in 1735. A grandson of Alexander of Braintree graduated at Harvard in 1726.

Charles Marsh, LL. D., of Vermont, graduated at Dartmouth college, 1786, and was long head of the Vermont bar, James Marsh, declining a professorship at Princeton, became professor at Hampden-Sidney college, Va., and soon after president of Vermont university at Burlington. He left his life-work in fragments, published by Prof. Torrey, but is considered by many the keenest metaphysician America has produced. George P. Marsh has written the history of the English language, and for his philological works ranks among the foremost all over the world. Time hardly allows me to speak of Prof. Leonard Marsh, who declined a professorship at Dartmouth, but went to Burlington, of President Sidney Marsh of Pacific University, Oregon, of Prof. O. C. Marsh of Yale, and of younger blood, lately passed into college work, in Prof. Charles Marsh of Ripon College, Wisconsin, and Edward B. Marsh, registrar and assistant librarian at Amherst and Prof. Arthur Marsh of Harvard College. Not far from here Dexter Marsh was first to call public attention to bird tracks. Amherst College owes very much to him. I have here a unique oration, delivered at Yale commencement in 1798, by Ebenezer Grant Marsh. It forms this little book, and is truly very learned, and was delivered when audiences were patient with sermons one or two hours long.

John Marsh, D. D., of Connecticut and Brooklyn, son of John Marsh, D. D., of Wethersfield, Ct., descended from George of Hingham, became very distinguished in the temperance cause.

William of Vermont, was active early and long in the anti slavery cause and proved that his principles were sincere by giving some $25,000 to the work.

Most of the Marshes have been too busy in making history to spend much time in writing it. But a few have deserved our highest gratitude for studying and recording something of the deeds and origin of others.

Rev. Frederick Marsh, when he died at Winchester, Ct., twelve years ago, aged 92, had done more genealogical work in our Marsh family than any other of his day. He was in correspondence with Charles Marsh, Esq., of Woodstock, Vt., and thus obtained from deeds and records most valuable facts as to the Lebanon Marshes and their connection with Hartford, Ct., and Hartford, Vt. He also had correspondence with Rev. Christopher Marsh of West Roxbury, Mass., as to the Alexander Marsh line. This venerable man, Rev. Frederick, of 92 years, living well on towards a century, was emphatically our pioneer in genealogy, and he left three manuscript volumes of valuable records. His grandson, George Marsh Carrington, graduate of Williams College, has given us most valuable aid with the utmost courtesy and good will.

Next comes E. J. Marsh, Esq., of Leominster, Mass. For twenty-five years, I think, he has given more or less attention to every part of the Marsh line, and as to the descendants of George Marsh of Hingham, no man living knows so much. He has a list of that line just about ready for publication. He has given aid of the utmost value in every part of our work.

I must mention next Mrs. Wellman of Parma, N. Y., a member of our genealogical committee, who has been very active for a number of years past, writing in all directions, getting valuable documents from the state capitals of Massachusetts and Connecticut, and leaving no stone unturned that she could lift alone or by getting help. She has had copied from the state archives of Connecticut a very interesting legal document signed in 1705 by six of John Marsh's children.

Some may ask, what has been done the past year? I hardly dare make our secretary blush by telling how much he has done, From a height to which none of the rest of us dare aspire, (6 foot 3, or more), he has been looking out all over our land and setting types in motion by newspaper courtesy in about every state in the Union, from the *Boston Journal* to the *New Orleans Picayune*. His work with the newspapers and by correspondence has borne much fruit.

Mrs. Sanford of Washington sends me from Claremont, N. H., most charming sketches of nearly all the descendants of Gov. Joseph Marsh of Vermont. These sketches would make a most interesting little volume if printed by themselves.

Frank B. Marsh of Springfield, Mass., a graduate of Amherst

college, has sent me a sketch, printed in the *Oil, Paint and Drug
Reporter* of New York City, very highly laudatory of his father, the late
Edward H. Marsh, one of the founders of the firm of Lazell, Marsh
& Gardiner, the third house in size of the drug stores in New York
City. He was a refined, Christian gentleman, and one of the most
successful business men who ever left old Hadley. He was a son of
Moses and grandson of Dr. Job, who was a son of a Moses and
grandson of Capt. Job of Hadley, who in turn was son of Daniel
and grandson of John of Hartford.

    **E.** A. Marsh, banker of Groton, N. Y., has been indefatigable in
tracing out all the descendants of Zimri Marsh, his grandfather, who
was a son of Ebenezer Marsh, 3d, of Montague.

    Joseph Marsh, bookseller of Northampton, has received and given
much light.

    Miss Northam of Phelps, N. Y., has sent much of value as to the
children of " Asa the aged." Who will find a father for that old
man ? Some who were like " Japhet in search of a father," last year,
have found out their line, and it made your committee glad to see their
joy. (From Boston records at Deerfield Memorial Hall I have found
that " Asa the aged was descended from John of Boston.")

    Riverius Marsh of New Brunswick, N. Y., manufacturer and mer-
chant, with a branch house at New York, has traced his ancestry by
a very careful search of Connecticut town records back to William
of Plainfield, Ct., who is said to have been in Boston in 1636. His
brother James, of Kent, England, is said to have been beheaded by
Cromwell, and his sisters took William from college and sent him for
safety to this country. Riverius has provided us with a very valuable
list of descendants of this college boy William.

    I would gladly give the work of many others, but in a list of over
three thousand names with which I have had personally to do, it is
simply impossible at this time in this short paper to even mention all.

    I must allude to highly valued letters from Joseph Marsh of Fire
Island, Nova Scotia, and from Miss E. E. Dana and Mrs. Edith
Longfellow Dana of Boston, and from Miss Brigham of Marlboro,
who has sent this bit of silk which came from London to Hadley 125
or more years ago. We have had help, too, from workers in other
family lines, especially from A. P. Pitkin, Esq., of Hartford, Ct.,
Martin Metcalf, Esq., of Battle Creek, Mich., Henry P. Andrews,

Esq., of Saratoga, N. Y., Hon. Lucius M. Boltwood of New Haven, and James M. Crafts, Esq., of Whately.

The officers of Amherst college library, Mr. Trumbull of Northampton city library and Mr. Hoadly, state librarian of Connecticut, have been very courteous in rendering aid.

Rev. Loring B. Marsh of Springfield has, years ago, done much work as to the Ware Marshes, and has valuable records and memoranda in his possession, which it is hoped will not be lost. The same is true of Dr. Stuart of New York as to the Montague Marshes. Our first president, D. C. Marsh of Montague, and also Sanford Marsh of that place, and the venerable Zebina Marsh of Northfield, have given valuable information, but we all wait for Dr. Stuart's more complete work on the Montague Marshes.

There are several young ladies of Marsh descent who have given very full records of their ancestry. Mrs. Mary Leeds Shepard of the city of Hudson, N. Y., has furnished all the descendants of her great grandmother, Lucretia Marsh Mellen.

Miss Florence E. Gill, of Greeley, Col., has given very completely the descendants of Irene Marsh of Hartford, Ct. Miss Bertha E. Adkins of Reynolds Bridge, Ct., has given all the descendants of Job Marsh, Jr., of New Hartford, Ct., for four generations. I was very glad to help her trace her ancestry back for five generations more.

O. L. Peck, Esq., of Toledo, Ohio, has given very complete record of the descendants of Sarah Marsh Peck, daughter of Dr. Perez Marsh.

E. Porter Belden of Sing Sing, N. Y., descended from Mary Marsh Porter of Wethersfield, Ct., who was daughter of Ebenezer Marsh of Hadley, writes a very interesting letter, and mentions that Col. Belden, one of Mary Marsh's descendants, was on Washington's staff. Mr. Marquand of Princeton college, has given information as to the Marsh descended Marquands.

Your committee have kept up active correspondence all the past year. Ten letters on Marsh genealogy have been taken from the the Amherst postoffice at once. They have come from New York City and Philadelphia, from Louisville and New Orleans, from Atlanta and Florida, from Detroit and Chicago.

Two very important mistakes have been corrected, one in the Hadley Book, the other in "Early Lebanon," a work which I found in Connecticut state library at Hartford, which has led the Boston Genealogical society astray.

We cannot begin to mention much of which we would be glad to speak. Do you wish to see a plot of the Hadley streets of earliest date and where Marshes have ever since been living at various places within a half mile of John Marsh's home lot in 1663? Ask Josiah D. Marsh of Hadley to show you.

In early times many boys were sent to college that they might become preachers. In colonial times ministers were not called Revs. but Mr. They did not perform marriage, but that honor belonged to the magistrate. The common people were not called Mr. even, but Goodman this or goodman that; the mother, Goodwife such an one. Perhaps for this reason military titles were the more sought.

John[2] Marsh's four grandsons at Hartford were Capt. John, Captain Jonathan, Captain Joseph and Lieut. Nathaniel. The title of ensign was put upon gravestones as well as that of captain or lieutenant. At East Hartford cemetery we have Captain Daniel and Ensign Daniel. We have Col. Joseph Marsh and Col. William and Col. Joel of Vermont about the time of the revolution. By order of Connecticut legislature troops from New Haven were sent to be under command of Capt. John Marsh in defending Litchfield from Indians. At Hadley we have Capt. Job, and his son, Dr. Perez, surgeon in Col. Williams' regiment, who had much work after the bloody battle near Lake George, where Col. Williams lost his life and the French general received his death wound. All our Hadley and Hatfield ancestors were for one generation familiar with the Indian war-whoop, and two of them, Jonathan and Daniel at Hadley, obtained wives whose husbands had been slain in battle by the Indians. I have found the names of some who died from prison horrors at New York by the English during the revolutionary war.

E. W. Marsh, a native of North Carolina, writes me from Atlanta, Ga., that his father was a captain in the revolutionary war, and died 104 years old, with fifteen children—eight sons, all of whom became merchants and were prosperous.

Speaking of age, Sarah Marsh Merrill of Hartford is said to have lived to be 106. We find a curious fact, that although some of our uncles lived to be old bachelors, most of our fathers preferred to marry, and most of them married outside our family name, and so connected us with a thousand families as good or better than ourselves. Now, of two brothers born in the old John Marsh place at Hadley, his grandsons, one lived and died there at the homestead, full of years, aged 92 and over. The other died aged 46 and a little over. One had three wives and the other died unmarried. Now, which had the wives? Alas! it was the youngster of 46, while the bachelor lived to be 92. Which shall we pity? Shall we say of the aged, "Poor man! to drag out 92 weary years with no wife or child?" Or shall we say of his brother, "Poor youth! hastened away by marrying too much?" I leave you to choose.

To return to the honor of military titles : my father was a lawyer, yet I remember as a boy over in Berkshire, hearing him called Captain Marsh far more frequently than "Squire." I have mentioned that the title of ensign was carved in stone, and even the least military title set a man and his family up. One good-wife when her goodman was made corporal, soon went to her neighbor's and said, "I am going to visit you just the same."

I have noticed this fondness for military rank, and this begrudging ordinary men the small honor of Sir and Mr., to call your attention to an important fact which appears to one who looks over the records of this and other families about the time of the revolutionary war. The college graduates of that day, the educated clergy, and especially prominent military men, were often loyal to what they deemed the only right way, to the King and law of England ; and not unfrequently the common people, the farmers and mechanics and less known men, had to depose their leaders, and to put in their places men who would be true to this our country and the rights of man. Honor, then, to the common brotherhood, the bone and sinew, the life and energy of the best principles, moral and religious, as well as civil. It might seem discourteous to this audience to mention Marsh names, but I may say that one of my ancestors, *not a Marsh*, although he had long been the foremost military man in Western Massachusetts, was put into Northampton jail as not sufficiently loyal to liberty as understood by George Washington and the American people. A clergyman not of our name had his church door closed against him by a military guard. But claiming to be minister of the town, he kept up preaching at his house till his death in 1779.

In Vermont, two military men of our name at the coming of Burgoyne had occasion to go to Canada, and in Connecticut one dropped a little from his high place in public esteem.

It is very hard for us, surrounded by all the inventions and appliances of modern life, to put ourselves back into the time of men, women and children as they lived 100, 200 and 250 years ago; 25 years ago, no telephone; 50 years ago, no telegraph; 60 years ago, no railroad; 100 years, no steamboat; 110 years ago, no Fourth of July; 150 years ago, no carriages in all the Connecticut Valley; 200 years ago, very few roads, and few towns to go to; 250 years ago, no towns at all and no bridle paths. The pioneers often began with log houses. Their first meeting-houses as buildings were cheap and in a few years gave place to better. Their houses, as one of our housebuilders informs me, for long years were of two rooms below and two chambers above, with a leanto behind. They had no brooms nor lamps, and pine knots, called candle-wood, were prized. Wives rode to church and brides to their new homes on a pillion. There were spinning wheels and looms but no factories. Early villages had no sidewalks. At Northampton, manure was put out of barns on to the principal street. At Hadley, geese waddled and quacked under the church. Ministers were not " settled on horse-back," but for life. Within sixty years, children at school, if the stage passed during recess have arranged themselves in a row and bowed and courtesied. To those children the minister was a very great and awful man. In very early days people were summoned to church by the sound of a trumpet or beat of a drum. On a wedding night brides were sometimes stolen, carried off, and not let go till the abductors were invited to share the festivities. Such were a few of the differences between our times and those of our Marsh fathers and mothers. On the whole, we may congratulate ourselves that they have provided for us better things than they had themselves, and we honor them for leaving so many comforts in England to endure much hardship for us. And what a change has been wrought in our land ! We have now far more comforts than they ever left behind in Old England. It must do us good to examine their useful lives. Our early fathers all of them feared God, and some of them honored the King.

This work of studying a noble history, and finding out whence we came, and tracing carefully our lines of descent, must go on. We

must ransack public libraries and town records, and records in the
old family Bibles and on gravestones, and hasten to gather what is
in the memory of the aged. We must compare notes. Different
members of a family line have partial records, which, put together,
give often great increase of light. Places of birth, and dates of
removal and places of ancestral residence, and full names, are of
utmost importance. Often a middle name hints a family connection.
Do not neglect this pleasant work, nor think your parentage of no
importance. Let us each be faithful to those who who have gone
before us, and honor our family name.

---

At the third Marsh meeting at Lake Pleasant in July, 1886,
addresses were delivered by Josiah D. Marsh, Esq., of Hadley, (of
which free use is made in this work pages six, seven and eight) and
by Col. Lucius B. Marsh of Boston. Both addresses were published
in the Marsh pamphlet of 1886 and the latter address was published
in the Genealogy of John Marsh of Salem in 1888.

The fourth annual reunion of the Marsh family was held at Unity
hall, Hartford, Ct., Aug. 3 and 4, 1887. The morning meeting was
called to order by the president of the association, the Rev. D. W.
Marsh, of Amherst, Mass. After an organ prelude the entire company sang :

> From Massachusetts mountains,
> From western prairies grand,
> From northern hillside fountains
> From southern pine-clad sand
> From many a rolling river
> And many a fertile plain,
> With love to all forever,
> We Marshes meet again.

The address of welcome was by Mr. Riverius Marsh of New
Brunswick, N. J., whose opening words were as follows :
"As we meet face to face in this beautiful city of Hartford, let our
watchword be 'Welcome!' We admire the refinement and culture
which clusters around this educational and commercial center. We
behold stately trees, abundant foliage, the carpet of the greensward,

lovely homes, while above us the old blue vault of heaven arches from sunrise to sunset, just the same as when our forefathers first beheld the primeval forests which bordered the banks of this romantic river.  We meet to cherish the memory of honored ancestors—because of that noble spirit of truth, born of experience, which will burn still brighter in future generations—as principle and truth become more deeply rooted.  We say welcome !"

After the transaction of routine business came an address by Mr. John E. Marsh of Hartford.  He began by telling of the early life of the pioneer in Braintree, Essex county, England, and spoke of his emigration to America in 1635, and of his arrival in Hartford the year following.  He owned thirty-six acres of land here, the homestead being located at the spot now marked by the junction of Temple and Front streets, neither of which, of course, were then in existence.  Following this came a detailed account of the controversy among the members of the old Center church, which led to his removing from Hartford in 1659 and going to Hadley, Mass.  Forty families in this city and twenty in Wethersfield moved away at the same time for the same reason.  The speaker then gave a rapid sketch of his life at Hadley, which was full of interest, coupled with some account of the marriage and place of settlement of each of his nine children.  The death of his wife, in 1662, was followed by his second marriage, two years later.  His own death occurred at Windsor, in 1688.  His son John, after marriage, lived in the old homestead in this city, and his sons were among the earliest settlers of Litchfield, Lebanon and New Hartford.

A speech of an informal nature was also made by Colonel Lucius B. Marsh of Boston, who spoke of the pleasure he had taken in making these researches, and said that during the past two years he had succeeded in acquiring considerable information regarding the family.  Colonel Marsh will be remembered as the officer who commanded the defences of New Orleans during the siege of Port Hudson.

At the close of the morning session the association proceeded in a body to view the site of the old homestead, after which they separated for dinner.  At 2 o'clock they reassembled at the hall, the session being opened with the singing of the Marsh ode, composed by the Rev. D. W. Marsh and set to the tune of " America."

The first event on the programme arranged for the afternoon was an address by Mr. George Marsh Carrington of Winsted, who spoke in relation to Jonathan Marsh, who went from here to New Hartford in 1736.

### CAPTAIN JONATHAN[3] MARSH.

*A pioneer settler of New Hartford. A paper read before the Marsh family reunion in Hartford, Aug. 3, 1887, by Judge George Marsh Carrington of Winsted.*

Of the twelve children of John[2] Marsh, Jr.; and Sarah Lyman his wife, of Hartford, five were boys. John, the eldest, was born in 1668 and Jonathan, the youngest, was born within the limits of this city 20 years after. Dispensing here with notice of the first eleven, I am to speak in a fragmentary way of Capt. Jonathan Marsh, the youngest of the twelve, and of his descendants. In the prime of his middle life the Captain found it necessary to seek a better location to win bread for himself and his family. No student of the early days of a community has failed to observe the truth of the saying of a political economist, " In a new country the spring of population uncoils itself with amazing velocity." The original " John of Hartford " was the father of nine children, John, Jr. by both wives, was the father of thirteen, while of his brothers and sisters, Samuel had 11, Jonathan and Lydia each had 8, Daniel and Hannah each had 7. Captain Jonathan himself had ten children. No wonder that in the early days, guiltless of commerce or manufactures, even this fertile valley, with the methods of cultivation and the limited markets of the time, could not support the swarms who poured from every family hive. Twenty miles northwest of where we are gathered today, was a tract of land, largely forest, which, to escape sequestration as colonial public land, had been hastily given by the General Assembly to the towns of Hartford and Windsor *in trust*. When the danger was passed and Sir Edmund Andros, the royal governor, was well away, the Commonwealth desired to repossess its lands, but found the towns not so ready to part with them. As the result of a compromise, to the share of Hartford fell four townships, and among them a tract of 35 to 40 square miles which, when erected into a township some years after, was called New Hartford. This new township fell to the share of 182 proprietors or land owners, of Hartford, in proportion to their property as rated on the list of 1720. In 1733 home lots were laid out and drawn by lot in what after inves-

tigation appeared the most eligible site in town, afterwards the out
lying lands were drawn, first one parcel, then another. Of all the
Hartford lands, only those in New Hartford were actually settled by
the sons of the proprietors, probably because, while none of the
others were valued at more than 10 shillings per acre, the New Hartford acre was considered worth 15 shillings. Every settler was
obligated in two years next ensuing his agreement with the committee,
"to build a tenantable house of 16 feet square on said land and
break up two or three acres of sod land, and in one year or more
after said two years are expired, personally inhabit by themselves or
family on said land and to be obliged to continue inhabiting said land
for the space of three years longer after the first three years are
expired." Among the earliest settlers, and so far as the enthusiastic
historian, Mrs. Sarah L. Jones, (without whose labors it would have
been impossible to prepare this paper,) has ascertained, the second
on the list was Jonathan Marsh. Like his brothers, a captain, he had
lived to see 48 years before he left his old for his new home. He
had married for his first wife the daughter of that impetuous man,
who, in the sudden darkness of a legislative session, laid hands on
the charter of Connecticut and made the oak immortal, Captain
Joseph Wadsworth. Compelled to surrender her to the grim destroyer,
his three children found a second mother in Elizabeth Loomis of
Windsor, and their number was increased to seven or eight before
emigration to the new settlement. The earliest settlers appear to
have spent two or three summers on the new lands clearing up the
forest, for every inch of land had to be made, and to have returned
to Hartford during the winters. The single handed battle with the
forces of nature began with the first arrival. Without comfortable
houses for themselves or their stock, without church or school house,
no roads, bridges, fences, wagons, carts, and largely even without
side saddles, without the means to buy or hire the efficient implements
to do the work imperatively necessary, their experience was most
trying and severe. We are without record of the particulars of those
early days. Neither the type nor the quill has left its marks for our
information. The first newspaper in Connecticut was not yet started.
Fifty years afterwards there were not a hundred post offices in the
United States. Other business than recording, claimed the pioneer's
imperative attention. We can surmise that the sheltering of them-

selves and their animals, the providing of food, water and wood, the erection of looms, the clearing up and burning of the forest trees would exercise the colonists' first and best efforts from the first ray of light in the morning till they could see no longer.  Little time did they have to build roads, bridges or other works for the common good when the struggle for existence was so severe that it taxed all their powers.  And yet it is not very strange to find that the public worship of Almighty God held a high place in their estimation, and that early efforts were made to provide a suitable place for such worship.  Here we come to matters of record.  In 1738 an agent was appointed to ask the General Assembly to fix a spot for a church building, which the next year was located by a committee from adjoining towns.  Preparations for building were commenced, " the length to be fifty foots and the bredth forty foots—" the length afterwards increased by " five foots."  After innumerable drawbacks and ten years of time, provision of rum and other liquors for raisings, etc., it was completed.  What would our western pioneers say to such an experience as that, and where would our church building societies be if all new settlements had the pluck of New Hartford ?  Truth it is, however, that not every new settlement is made of such stuff as the New Hartford settlement was, nor are their surroundings similar.  As in all other New England towns the town and the church were one at first.  The quaint and unique vote of the first town meeting is worthy of quotaion.

" *Voted*—That ye sd committee shall and are hereby empowered to make application to Mr. Baulden to come and settle in the town of New Hartford in the work of the ministry, and if the sd Mr. Baulden refuse to accept of their caul, then to Mr. Robords, and if ye sd Mr. Robords refuse, then to Mr. Marsh, sun to ye Rev. Mr. Marsh of Windsor, and if he refuse, then to Mr. Timo. Woodbridge."

The first two " refused to accept of their caul " and the lot fell upon another Jonathan Marsh, son of the first cousin of our pioneer. The difference between the two Jonathans is noted in the land records, the clergyman being called Jonathan Marsh, clerk.  For fifty-four or five years he was the faithful pastor of the church.  He raised a family of twelve children, none of whom permanently settled in New Hartford, but some were persons of more than usual prominence.  While speaking of him I will refer to an invaluable memorandum of bap-

C

tisms, marriages and deaths in the hand writing of the Rev. Jonathan
and covering the entire period of his ministry, rescued by Senator
Foster of Connecticut, from a Washington second hand book store
and now lodged in Eldridge Memorial hall in this city. And by
a curious coincidence with this gathering there was placed in
my hands three weeks ago a manuscript volume of sermons written
by the first pastor of the New Hartford church. It measures $6\frac{1}{4}$ x $3\frac{3}{4}$
inches, has 76 lines on first page, has eight pages and with a good
magnifier one is able to read the dates of preaching and the texts of
three sermons.

To return to our pioneer, Capt. Jonathan. The house he lived in
did good service till 1800, when its successor was built. He lived on
a hill whence he had a splendid view of a large range of hills and
valleys, an educator doubtless, though perhaps an unconscious one,
to his family of five sons and five daughters, the two youngest New
Hartford born. As his sturdy boys grew to manhood they proved
themselves like arrows in the hands of a mighty man. The tannery
of the place was on his farm, four vats still remain. Not till the
oldest was nearly 30 years of age did he multiply himself by two.
But that inevitable step in a family in due time found takers in nine
out of ten of these young Marshes. The sons found homes of their
own in town, the oldest and the unmarried one remaining at or near
the homestead, the other three pushing some little distance from the
original hive. Two of the daughters remained in town, three found
homes outside its limits. The heavy hills and the passage through
the town of the Farmington river and a large branch thereof, made
the construction of roads and bridges hard, long delayed and expen-
sive. The brutal barbed wire had not yet made fencing easy and to
avoid losing stock it was necessary to make some such provision as
this, from the records. "Marsh, Moses mark is as followeth; a
slanting crop the upper side the off ear.—Marsh, Job, mark is a crop
of the near ear and a half penny the under side each ear.—Marsh,
John, mark is a tennend in the near ear." The crops, the tennends
and the half pennies did not always avail to secure animals to their
owners. "Nov. ye 28, 1749." There is in the custody of Jonathan
Marsh a sorrel mare, white in the face, some white on the near hind
foot." One foot some white! Well that Jonathan was an honest
man or he would have kept that mare to her end.

An account book of one of the early Marshes is extant and supplies us with much valuable information. Entries as early as 1748, and thence onward, are made with a royal disregard of capitals and orthography. Other records that this man was a farmer and carpenter are here abundantly confirmed. One of the earliest records is, Thomas Wolton, " deter " to 35 pounds of beef, " old tenr." £2, 1s. Then follow charges for weaving tow cloth, 13 yards drouged (drugget), making a " wheall " and numerous charges for weaving showing that the women of the family bore their share of the common burden. (I find elsewhere a note that an unmarried male relative, partially insane, helped this family in weaving.) The *"reverant"* Jonathan Marsh is charged for sundry weaving, and mending of wheels and " spinning " a "run of shrew thread " and credited by " rates." These accounts, kept literally by single entry, with utter confusion of the prepositions " to " and " by," which are now used for debit and credit, headed by the names of the debtors and running from year to year, are balanced not by the equally footed columns and the double lines under them, but by these or similar words :—" October 14, then recken with Jeames Steel to balance accounts, there is due to mee £8, 10s, 4d," signed by the two. There are no ruled lines in the books but at the right hand of the page penciled lines are ruled, leaving three spaces, for £, s. and d., with each denomination always represented by two figures or a cipher and one figure. This family, farmers and carpenters out of doors and weavers in doors, appears to have had a more or less regular set of customers. The items of farm produce are butter, sugar, hops, honey, vinegar, cider, etc. Sledding wood, plowing two days, " my cattel to fetch bark, a well poll and well croch " are samples of other charging in the farm department. In the carpenter's department are charges for " framing, working on your barn, making a yoke for one ox, a betel, extring (axletree) a cart," and others. For indoor work the charges are mainly for weaving, occasionally one for " netin a pare of stockinis, makin a pare trouses," etc. The items of weaving are " plain cloth, fine cloth, part stripid, tow cloth, chect, checord, weaving eight yds and putting in short, hankerchief, lawn," a large variety of fabrics for, doubtless, a small number of looms. On page 54 is pinned a sample of cloth, of whose genuineness as a piece of what is there charged I would give something to know. But the miscella-

neous charges in this book fascinate. They lift a corner of the veil
woven by the years, and by hints of the things which entered into
their daily experience and a part of which they were, show us something of the lives of these sturdy men and women. Six shillings are
charged " for my oxen to Hartford," carting a barrel of shad from
Wethersfield cost three shillings. Jesse Goodwin pays 18s. for "the
hoss to farmingtown." Smith & Cadwell, the first partnership noticed,
pay £3, 15s. by carting a load of goods to the furnace and by bringing back a load of pigs to the forge, for " provisions that I found 4s.,
to keeping for the team 3s." Domestic help thus :—"for Susan's
work at your house a week 3s.;" Sylvester Ryder is charged " to
carrying a pig to Hartford and sold it, it waid 19 pound, one shilling
and sixpence," a most reasonable price ! The charge suggests
another item at the expense of the Rev. Jonathan. " By hunting
hogs one day and a half, one shilling," doubtless charged for the
principle of the thing, the amount being ridiculously small. This
was in 1770. The next difficulty with hogs in the ministerial line of
the Marsh family was many years after. A gentle, quiet man, who
had curbed his passions with an unsparing hand, in the later years of
a long life, one day read his paper sitting by the open window, occasionally, as was his custom, giving his family the benefit of what he
found, when he became much disturbed by the importunate cries of
a hungry pig in the pen some rods away. The care of the pig was
one of the duties he had assumed. The reader showed uneasiness,
remarked on the utter unreasonableness of the animal, whose appetite
just then was apparently quite keen, and when the noise would not
cease, he threw down his paper with the remark, nearest an objurga-
tion his family remembered hearing : " I hate to be ruled by a pig."

I notice that sundry " berrels " of " cyder " were produced after
some years by this Marsh man. After charging 18 " berrels " one
year to a certain man, the next season brings a charge of 18s. and
6d. for " 3 berrels of cyder, one was worked." Dr. Eldad Merrill
has 15 items in his account, of which seven were for " cyder." I
was startled to see the certificate of reckoning and balancing the
next spring was signed by the executors of the estate of Eldad Merrill, late of New Hartford deceased. In another account-book of
later date, but still in the last century, I find " Joseph Whitin Marsh "
(a grandson of Rev. Jonathan Marsh) in bold letters at the head of

half a page of items. Evidently he is now a young man, indeed the
records of baptism show him to be 23. He has "a horse to Bark-
hempsted meeting house, making a pare of trouses, a horse to Col.
petebones three times, a horse two nights, a horse to quilting one
night." What! does the young man go out sewing evenings? Ah!
here we have it! "To a horse to pettibones a Corting, two shillings," and the next item repeats the charge. Ah! Joseph, Joseph!
It is the old story! Nay, it is the young story! We of this later
and perhaps not altogether degenerate day, who ourselves had a
horse to " pettibones," or some other mans, can only say " All right,
my boy, go ahead." I would love to linger longer with these books,
whose rich yellow leaves hold other treasures, but I must only ask
your attention to the list of one of the family for taxation in 1790.

|  |  | £ | s. | d. |
|---|---|---|---|---|
| 1 horse, | - | - | 3 | |
| 2 oxen, | - | - | 6 | |
| 5 cows, | - | - | 10 | |
| 1 2-year-old, | - | - | 1 | |
| 1 house, 3 smoke, | - | | 10 | |
| 8 acres of low lands, | - | 4 | | |
| 84 " clear pas. | - | 13 | 12 | |
| 40 " bush grass, | - | 4 | | |
| 155 " woodland, | - | 3 | 17 | 6 |
| 1 head, | - | - | 18 | |
| 1 miner, | - | - | 9 | |

Smokes refer to fire places, a house being taxed according to the
number of these being called " smokes " for short. A " miner " is a
son between 16 and 21, who by the statute was assessed £9. You
observe that a farm of 287 acres was assessed at £25, 9s., 6d., the
value ranging from 10s. per acre for low land to 6d. per acre for
woodland. All the prices in the list were fixed by state law.
Evidently these toilers had not developed the idea that personal protection was worth nothing, for they taxed the head of the owner more
than two-thirds as heavily as they did his farm of nearly 300 acres.
The one invaluable thing on these pages is the autographs. Lament-
ing the absence of that of Capt. Jonathan we have those of all his
sons and most of his neighbors. In working at a genealogical record
one sometimes comes to feel as if the names that occur in such

frequency were about as mythical as those of the founders of that other country, once new,—Rome. But here you find yourself possessed of an interest you can hardly describe. You find that the very men of that seemingly far away time, once sat where you sit, handled the book you have before you, and wrote with their several hands the names that are under your eyes. If any of you who try it can escape without something of a feeling that you should put off your shoes from off your feet, you will have an experience different from mine. At first I was inclined to be amused over the queer spelling and quaint book-keeping, but I soon learned better. I found that the men had to work with all their strength from daylight to dark to subdue the demons of the wilderness, and provide for their rapidly increasing families in all the various particulars heretofore mentioned, necessary in a new country. The women, too, without a tithe of the modern facilities for doing work, had not only to provide the daily meals, but to milk the cows, make the soap, provide the lights, spin the yarn and weave and make up the fabrics for the family's need, but also to produce goods for the market and so help support the household. Everyone, great and small, had their energies taxed to the utmost in the struggle for existence. What time or facilities had they for education? It was 20 years after Captain Jonathan became a settler, before the first New Hartford school house was completed, all his children, except perhaps one, were then beyond school age. Not that educational fires were extinguished. They had, perforce, to smoulder, but they appeared whenever there was an opportunity. Some of the signatures to these balancing accounts are beautiful. Jos. Whiting Marsh, son of the pastor, was the first graduate of Yale college from New Hartford in 1763. No, instead of making merry over their defects, in a line which was not theirs at all, I stand with uncovered head before the men and women who, with heart and hand and brain, toiled year in and year out to lay the foundations upon which we have built, without which we could not be here, and which are so fruitful in blessings to us and those like us.

New Hartford had in 1756, 250 white inhabitants, in 1761, 674, in 1775 their number had increased to 1,001, and so it came about that in due course of time a second emigration set in, and from about 1780 there was a current that set strongly toward New York state and farther west. New Hartford, Oneida county, N. Y., was first settled and named by the sons of the Connecticut New Hartford, and among the four families who left in large numbers for the west, the historian places the name of Marsh.

I find in "Sketches of New Hartford" by Capt. H. R. Jones, an invaluable pamphlet to which I am greatly indebted, a statement that as late as 1776, forty years after Capt. Jonathan settled in New Hartford, the only two carts on Town Hill, the central part of the town, were owned by the son and grandson of our pioneer. Sleds were used for farming purposes. In that year 25 acres of land were offered by Daniel Marsh, a New Hartford farmer, son of the minister, for one of these carts and refused. By the way, this New Hartford family holds to the name Jonathan with great tenacity. Jonathan, Jr., was 21 years old when he went with his father from the town where we are, *his* son Jonathan made the carts just referred to before he was 20 years of age, *his* son Jonathan was town clerk for a time before his early death, his grandson Jonathan, deaf and dumb from his second year, is now 73 years old and is with us to-day, *his* son Jonathan died aged 15 at the Deaf and Dumb asylum in this city and lately I had the pleasure of taking by the hand his grand-nephew Jonathan, a young gentleman in his fifth year,—all bearing the surname Marsh. Longevity has characterized this family. Captain Jonathan was 95 years old when, after his many toils, he entered into rest. The average age of his ten children was $81\frac{3}{10}$ years. Think of it! How many parallels are there? His sister Sarah, who also settled in New Hartford, scored 106 years. Several of his descendants have passed 90. The family was represented in the wars of 1776, 1812 and 1861. One lady writes me that her grandfather was in the war of the revolution, her father in that of 1812 and her brother in the war of the rebellion.

The following is a sample of circulars with calls to our meetings :

### THE FIFTH ANNUAL GATHERING

#### OF THE

#### "MARSH FAMILY ASSOCIATION OF AMERICA,"

#### WILL BE HELD AT

#### BRIDGEPORT, CT.,

*Commencing Sept. 5th, 1888, at 10 o'clock A. M. and Closing Sept. 6th, at 1 P. M.*

---

The following are the officers chosen at Hartford, Ct., last year, 1887.

#### *President.*

COL. LUCIUS B. MARSH, of Boston, Mass.

#### *Vice-Presidents.*

WM. T. MARSH, of Litchfield, Ct.
RIVERIUS MARSH, of New Brunswick, N. J.
CHARLES E. MARSH, of New Milford, Ct.
JOHN E. MARSH, of Hartford, Ct.
SANFORD MARSH, of Montague, Mass.
HORATIO N. MARSH, of Joliet, Ill.
EPHRAIM GILMAN, of Chicago, Ill.
JAMES A. MARSH, of Cleveland, Ohio.
LUTHER R. MARSH, of New York.
EDWARD W. MARSH, of Bridgeport, Ct.

#### *Secretary.*

J. JOHNSON, of Greenfield, Mass.

#### *Treasurer.*

EDWARD B. MARSH, of Amherst, Mass.

#### *Historian.*

REV. D. W. MARSH, D. D., of Amherst, Mass.

## THE MARSH FAMILY.

This family have now held four annual gatherings. The last was held in the city of Hartford, Ct., Aug. 3d and 4th, 1887. The previous meetings were held at Lake Pleasant, in the town of Montague, Mass. These meetings have been attended by persons from the Canadian Dominion and various parts of the United States, and have elicited a very wide and growing interest. A very great amount of information as to persons of Marsh descent has been obtained, and still more is sought.

Mr. E. J. Marsh has published a volume of 200 pages, giving descendants of George Marsh, of Hingham, 1635. It is expected that Col. L. B. Marsh, of Boston, will publish an account of the descendants of John Marsh of Salem, 1633, this summer.

A pamphlet was published by the Association in 1886, giving an outline of the *descendants* for four generations, of six lines, viz., from John, of Salem, 1633; John, of Hartford, 1636; Samuel, of New Haven, 1646; Alexander, of Braintree, 1654; John, of Boston, 1669; William, of Plainfield, 1675. A few copies of this only are left. Price $1.00 each. (None are left now.) The design of the pamphlet was to give and draw out information, and the result has been excellent. We have now thousands of names of Marsh descent whose line we can exactly trace for a period of two and a half centuries, and through seven, eight or nine generations. We wish that all persons of Marsh descent into whose hands this leaflet may come, would give us all the dates they can of the marriage, birth, death, and also items as to residence and migrations, and employments of their ancestors or children, and send to Col. Lucius B. Marsh, No. 13 Tremont Temple, Boston, Mass.; Rev. Dr. D. W. Marsh, Amherst, Mass.; or to John E. Marsh, Esq., Hartford, Ct.

COL. LUCIUS B. MARSH, *President,*

13 Tremont Temple,

Boston, Mass.

J. JOHNSON, *Secretary,*
Greenfield, Mass.

## COME YE MARSHMEN.

1.

Each Marsh alive, of Eastern Shore
Or Middle West or Asia's door,
From Lake and Gulf, from mount and plain,
Up one and all ! We meet again.
Come, ye Marshmen.

2.

Come shadowy men of ages past,
On us your spell and shadow cast;
Your names we found in olden books,
Come show us here your old time looks.
Hail, ye Marshmen.

3.

Come tell the tales of lives ye led,
The girls you loved, the wives you wed,
Each child you had and fleeting dead,
Tell what you did and what you said.
Speak, ye Marshmen.

4.

And hail ! ye Marshmen yet to be,
To live and love when gone are we,
Bring all you can of fairer wives,
And better homes and grander lives.
Hail, ye Marshmen.
—*D. W. M., Amherst, Mass.*

*Lucius B. Marsh*

PRESIDENT MARSH FAMILY ASSOCIATION,
1887 to 1893.

*To face page xliii.*

The line of descent of Col. Lucius Bolles Marsh of 6 Columbus Square, Boston, is :

1. John[1] Marsh of Salem, the first Marsh so far as known to come to America, and Susannah Skelton, dau. of Rev. Samuel Skelton, pastor of the first Puritan church in America.

2. Zachary[2], bap. in Salem church, April 30, 1637, (first Marsh child born in America) m. Aug. 15, 1664, Mary Sillsbee, dau. of Henry of Lynn, Mass.

3. Ezekiel[3], b. 1676 at Danvers (Salem), m. July 1, 1702, Rebecca Gould.

4. Ensign Ezekiel[4], of Salem, bap. May 27, 1711, m. in 1732, Sarah Buffington.

5. Lieut. Ezekiel[5], b. at Danvers, Mass., Jan. 26, 1740, m. Abiah Hartshorne, dau. of Thomas.

6. Thomas Hartshorne[6], b. at Danvers, Mass., July 9, 1776, m. (2) Nov. 29, 1815, Sarah Curtis Bronsden.

7. Col. Lucius Bolles[7] Marsh, b. Danvers, April 18, 1818. (See his John Marsh of Salem 1633–1888.)

------

The fifth annual gathering of the Marsh Family association of America, held at Y. M. C. A. Hall, Bridgeport, Ct., Sept. 5th and 6th, 1888, was not as fully attended as could be desired'; but about 80 were present, mostly from Connecticut and Massachusetts, but some from New Jersey, New York, Rhode Island, Tennessee, Indiana and Long Island. In age they ranged from a few children of eight or ten years to the venerable Mansir W. Marsh of Belmont, now 88 years old.

Most of those present were on the shady side of life and their delight was to converse with each other on the subject of their genealogy. The chair was occupied by Col. Lucius B. Marsh of Boston, a fine looking man, with a clear voice, eye-glasses and iron-gray Burnsides. The secretary, J. Johnson of Greenfield, Mass., had a table at the president's right hand.

The first reunion was held at Lake Pleasant, in Massachusetts, July 23, 1884, the second and third were held at the same place, and the fourth at Hartford. The meeting this morning was opened with the singing of an original ode composed by Fanny Marsh of Binghamton, N. Y.

## ODE.

*Tune—Auld Lang Syne.*

We've gathered here from far and near,
  We Marshmen down to date,
To hold our council-fire in glee,
  And merry tales relate.
The promise God to Abram made,
  We bring to mind today—
Of *one* He's made a num'rous race,
  Like stars in bright array.

### CHORUS.

For Marshmen old, today, my friends,
  For Marshmen bold,
We bring a thought of kindness yet,
  For the Marsh of olden time.

We love to talk about the past,
  Our fathers old and gray,
Who braved the rough and stormy sea
  To leave oppression's sway.
They helped to found an empire grand,
  And Freedom's flag unfurled,
Beneath we stand on blood-bought land
  The dearest in the world.

### CHORUS.

For warriors old, the Marshmen bold
  Now dead and cold.
We bring a thought of kindness yet,
  For the Marsh of olden time.

And now a tribute soft we bring
  For all who've passed away,
The noble men and women too
  Who walked in wisdom's way.
How many left their mark on time,
  That long outlived their day:
  And *one* a song for every clime,
Brought " Martyn," come to stay.

CHORUS OMITTED FOR TUNE MARTYN.

*Composed by S. B. Marsh.*

" Jesus, lover of my soul,
    Let me to Thy bosom fly,
While the billows near me roll,
    While the tempest still is high.
Hide me, O, my Saviour hide,
    Till the storm of life is past;
Safe into the haven guide,
    Oh, receive my soul at last."

God bless the " Marshmen " as a clan,
    And give them strength each day,
To fight the " ups and downs " of life,
    And banish sin away.
And in that great and final day,
    When nations throng His bar,
May they be victors in the strife,
    The " Marshmen " near and far.

CHORUS.

For " Marshmen " old to-day my friends,
    For Marshmen bold.
We bring our song of kindness yet,
    For the Marsh of olden time.

Prayer was offered by Rev. Dwight W. Marsh of Amherst, Mass.,
and a ringing address of welcome was made by E. W. Marsh, Esq.,
of this city, in substance as follows : " We extend to you a cordial
welcome to the thriving and youthful city of Bridgeport. We hope
while you are with us you may find opportunity to see for yourselves
our busy city. We have three good sized parks which give us the
name Park City, also numerous manufacturing establishments, advan-
tageous railroad and water facilities for traffic of all kinds. We
have good public schools, a fine public library, and an institute near
Seaside Park for the special aid and improvement of women who are
employees of the extensive corset factory of the Warner Brothers, a
number of handsome private residences, and last, but not least, the
headquarters of the Greatest Show on Earth, including its original,
active, indefatigable and enterprising proprietor, P. T. Barnum, himself.

The Marsh family in Bridgeport now numbers some twenty families all of whom have become inhabitants of Bridgeport within a period of 33 years. Without boasting we may say that this portion of the family are an average at least of the goodly residents of our city. We claim to be honest, temperate, industrious, to pay our debts and take a part in the support of churches and the various public institutions of our city and we try to keep the name above reproach in the community. We have heretofore very little time or inclination to look after our ancestors and were we not here ourselves we might not be able to say that we ever had any. We shall be pleased to listen while some venerable Moses or commanding Joshua shall unroll the scroll of the past and exhibit to our vision a genealogical tree with the various branches thereto belonging, showing how the tribes that compose the Marsh family have spread over the land.

We shall be happy to know more than we do now about our forefathers. We rejoice that there are those who take great interest in these researches. We hope to hear from some of the tribe who visit us to-day and learn that we have an honorable ancestry; that they had a part and share in the formation of this free government."

President L. B. Marsh responded in a few well chosen remarks and reports of the secretary Mr. Johnson and the treasurer Edward B. Marsh of Amherst, were read.

Rev. D. W. Marsh of Amherst, the historian of the association, read an interesting paper on a " Lost Family."

The afternoon session was opened with singing "Come Ye Marshmen," an original ode by D. W. Marsh, music by Prof. John B. Marsh, of Elmira College, N. Y., and was followed by remarks by L. Milton Marsh of New York, secretary of the American S. S. Union, a descendant of John of Hartford, Ct., of 1636; William L. Marsh of Memphis, Tenn., a son of William of Goshen, Ct.; a letter from Alexander Marsh of Worcester, read by Riverius Marsh of New Brunswick, N. J.; a telegram from H. N. Marsh of Joliet, Ill.; "Absence enforced, but with you in spirit, Marshmen of the prairie to the tribes gathered at Bridgeport, send greeting and farewell;" and familiar talk by John E. Marsh of Hartford, with the story by the secretary of the origin and progress of the association ; the whole interspersed with singing, made up the exercises of the afternoon.

The evening was devoted to social talk and the election of officers

MANSIR W. MARSH.

To face page xlvii.

for the coming year as follows : President, Col. L. B. Marsh of Boston ; vice-presidents, Riverius Marsh of New Brunswick, N. J.; Charles E. Marsh, New Milford, Ct.; John E. Marsh of Hartford, Ct.; Horatio N. Marsh of Joliet, Ill.; Ephraim Gilmore of Chicago, Ill.; James A. Marsh of Cleveland, O.; Edward W. Marsh of Bridgeport, Ct.; Mansir W. Marsh of Belmont ; William L. Marsh of Memphis, Tenn.; John Edward Marsh of New York, N. Y., and Philip B. Stiness of Providence, R. I.; secretary, J. Johnson, Greenfield, Mass.; treasurer, Edward B. Marsh, Amherst, Mass.; historian, Rev. Dwight W. Marsh, Amherst, Mass. It was voted to hold the next meeting at Newark, N. J., about Sept. 1, 1889.

The meeting was opened the morning of Sept. 6th with singing of odes followed by pleasant remarks by those present, including Thomas Marsh of Easton, Ct., aged 78, and Mansir W. Marsh of Belmont, Mass., aged 88. After a photograph had been taken, the happy meeting ended with singing a closing song by S. D. Marsh, to the tune of " America."

The Line of Mansir Warren[6] Marsh is as follows :

1. John[1] Marsh and Sarah of Boston, 1669.

2. Joseph[2], b. at Boston, Feb. 3, 1671, m. March 2, 1692–3, Ann Thurogood.

3. Dea. John[3], b. at Boston, Aug. 2, 1696, m. in 1719, Martha Hartshorn of Dedham.

4. Lieut. Ebenezer[4] of Douglas, Mass., b. about 1731–35, m. Feb. 3, 1757, Acsah Stearns.

5. Ebenezer[5], b. Douglas, Mass., Sept. 3, 1766, m. in 1799, Sally Hunt of Dudley, Mass.

6. Mansir Warren[6] Marsh, b. in Wardsboro (New Dover), Vt., Aug. 7, 1800 and d. in Belmont, Mass., May 18, 1891, in his 91st year. Moved to Waltham, Mass., at the age of 21. Was married at the age of 31 and soon after moved to West Cambridge (now Arlington), onto a farm in the limits of what is now the town of Belmont. He conducted the same farm successfully for nearly 50 years. Was the father of 11 children all but one of whom lived to the age of man and womanhood. Was very prominent in town affairs being chairman of the board of selectmen of West Cambridge for many years. Was a member of the school committee and held

various other positions of trust and responsibility, besides representing his town in the legislature for one year. Upon the incorporation of the town of Belmont he became what might almost literally be termed the Town Father and held numerous positions being chairman of the selectmen for ten years. He was intensely patriotic and used his influence to the best of his ability at the time of the war of the rebellion, and sent two sons to the war both of whom lost their lives in the service of their country. In religion he was a Universalist and was a regular attendant on the church of that denomination in West Cambridge for many years, and was also superintendent of the Sunday school. He was always faithful and true to his trusts and a man of unswerving honesty and integrity. He was buried in the family lot at Arlington, "Camp Charles V. Marsh, Sons of Veterans," (named in honor of one of his sons) attending the funeral in a body.

The following "answer" was read at the Bridgeport meeting in 1888 and it was also sung at our last meeting in Hadley, Mass. Sept. 4, 1894:

### HAIL, MARSHMEN HAIL,

*Answer to*

### COME YE MARSHMEN.

" *Each Marsh alive*,"—so reads the call,
Is summoned to the chieftain's hall,
Some cannot there with clansmen stand,
But all send greeting to the band :—
      Hail, Marshmen, hail.

" *The shadowy men*,"—they dwell not here ;
Their names and deeds we each revere,
In memory dear, for us they live,
And would to all their greeting give :—
      Hail, Marshmen, Hail.

" *Our lives*,"—Not here can we rehearse,
Or tell their story now in verse,
But girls, and wives, and children dear,
Repeat with us the hearty cheer :—
      Hail, Marshmen, hail.

*John Edward Marsh*

To face page xlix.

"*When gone are we,*"—Yes, even then,
If now we quit ourselves like men,
A long and worthy line shall live,
The watchword still with joy to give:—
Hail, Marshmen, hail.
—*Charles A. J. Marsh, Minneapolis, Minn., Aug.* 9, 1888.

The Line of John Edward Marsh, of Rahway, N. J. and 51 Liberty St., New York, is as follows:

1. Samuel[1] Marsh, b. 1620, at New Haven, Ct., 1646, d. 1683; m. 1647? Comfort.

2. John[2], b. 1661, at New Haven; m. Elizabeth, dau. of Richard Clarke, about 1683?

3. Daniel[3], b. 1703? d. 1756; m. Mary Rolph, dau. of Margaret Connally and Henry Rolph.

4. John[4], b. 1727? m. Elizabeth Dunham.

5. Isaac[5].

6. Rolph[6].

7. John Edward[7].

The Line of Riverius Marsh is as follows:

1. William[1] Marsh of Plainfield, Ct., 1675; m. about 1682, Elizabeth Yeomans of Stonington, Ct.

2. Thomas[2], b. about 1687; m. Feb. 4, 1712, Eunice Parkhurst of Plainfield.

3. Elihu[3], b. July 12, 1717, of Mansfield and Fairfield, Ct.; m. Zeruiah Abbe, May 10, 1736.

4. John[4], b. Aug. 4, 1749; m. March 2, 1772, Abigail Wanzer of New Milford, Ct.

5. Elihu[5], m. Urania Stilson.

6. Riverius C[6]., b. at New Milford, Ct., May 28, 1802; m. Oct. 3, 1821, Eunice E. Camp.

7. Riverius[7] Marsh, b. Aug. 19, 1837, at Warren, Ct. Received a common school education including three terms at a boarding school. At the age of 16 he entered a store and post office at Litchfield, Ct., where he remained 15 years, succeeding to the business and held the position of postmaster some six years, besides serving as deputy U. S. collector. He then accepted a position as trav-

D

eling salesman for a large New York importing firm, then for a period
of nine years was secretary of the Ives Patent Lamp Company of
New York, during which time he visited Europe on business. He
was the inventor of library hanging lamps, later he started the New
Jersey Lamp and Bronze Works and took out some twenty-five patents.
Over two million of his patent faucets have already been sold, he
is now President of the Marsh Manufacturing Co. of New Brunswick,
N. J. and Manager of the Consolidated Gas Manufacturing Co. of New
Jersey. He is active in Christian work and has helped to establish
many Sunday schools through the talent system, for which he has furnished the necessary capital.

The sixth annual meeting was held at Newark, N. J. We have not
space for its report, nor to give farther notice of later meetings of the
association held at Amherst, Lake Pleasant and Hadley except the last.
The result has been gratifying. Riverius Marsh was chosen president
in 1893. In response to circulars and newspaper notices sent all over
the land much information has been gathered. Some 15,000 names
have been collected of the different tribes. In 1886 a pamphlet (now
out of print) was published by the association giving five generations of
six different families. In 1887, Mr. E. J. Marsh of Leominster, who
had begun his work years before this association came into existence,
published the descendants of George Marsh of Hingham, 1635. In
1888 Col. Lucius B. Marsh of Boston published the names of over
2,200 descendants of John Marsh of Salem, 1633.

And enough information has come in, in regard to descendants of
Samuel of New Haven, 1643, (almost entirely collected by John
Edward Marsh of Rahway, N. J.) Alexander of Braintree, 1654,
John of Boston, 1669 and William of Plainfield, 1675, to warrant the
publication of two or three more books of Marsh genealogy whenever members of these families will take hold of this work in earnest.
Indeed this rather extended notice of the association is published
here, including effort to give a representative photograph for each of
the tribes, to stimulate further honor of our Marsh ancestry.

The following extracts from the Springfield *Republican* will give a
glimpse of the ninth annual reunion at Hadley, Mass.:

*Riverius Marsh*

*To face page 1.*

ENTERTAINED ON GROUND OWNED BY MEMBERS OF THE FAMILY
ONE HUNDRED AND FIFTY YEARS AGO.

Hadley was just the place to hold such a meeting, for ever since 1660 the family has been represented there. The town hall is built on land formerly owned by one of the John Marsh family. Daniel Marsh owned and his son Job lived on this spot and sold the place in 1743. J. Dwight Marsh of Hadley, who has been one of the prime movers in working up the history of this family, presided at yesterday's meetings, which were held morning and afternoon, and dinner was served under the trees on his ample grounds. Of course Rev. Dr. D. W. Marsh, the untiring historian of the family, was present and added much to the interest of the occasion by bits of history which he interspersed during the day. Secretary Johnson of Greenfield was present too. As he is a well-known antiquarian and became a Marsh through marriage, he had something of interest to say when facts were to be submitted. In the name of the old town J. D. Marsh welcomed the family to Hadley in the following address of welcome :

Mr. President, ladies and gentlemen of the Marsh family association, kindred and friends of whatever name :—We have met here at our ninth annual meeting to cultivate a better acquaintance with each other and learn more of our ancestors. We have met before in the city and in the grove, each place more or less associated with the name of Marsh, and it is fitting that we meet here in Hadley, as here John Marsh of Hartford spent the last 28 years of his life and some of his descendants have made Hadley their home ever since ; and in their name we bid you a cordial welcome. As you look about our town we cannot point you to palatial buildings or large manufactories, as Hadley was settled largely by farmers, selecting this spot as one eminently fitted for that purpose. It may have changed somewhat, as in the list for 1771, 112 years after the settlement of the town, are 147 rateable polls, 88 dwelling houses and 25 tan houses, slaughter houses, etc. These have all disappeared and to-day Hadley ranks near the first of the towns in the state, in agricultural productions.

Did the minority in the church in Hartford, (seeking a place where they could be free from the dominion of Samuel Stone, and perhaps directed to this spot by their relatives in Northampton, who perhaps had some choice as to who their neighbors might be,) ascend Mt. Holyoke and look down on this beautiful valley, they saw not the view you see to-day of stately church spires, farm houses, broad streets lined with stately elm, meadows covered with their crops of varied hues, but even then it must have presented a picture of surpassing loveliness with the beautiful Connecticut river winding its serpentine way through these meadows, now hidden behind some knoll for a time, to come forth again still rolling on until, like a silver thread, it is lost in the hazy distance.

They laid out the town as one street 20 rods wide, with the river at each end, their plow land at the west, also enclosed by the river, disposing of every house-lot on the street. Such was Hadley for more than 50 years, when the children's children, wanting more room, began to build on the east side of the street we are now in, which was laid out like the first, 20 rods wide, and this corner lot on which now stands the town hall, meeting house and the old dwelling south of it, was granted to Daniel Marsh, and here his son Job lived, selling the place in 1743 to Josiah Pierce, and the old house stood until 1841 when it was removed to make room for this town hall. It is not my purpose to give you a history of this town, but I speak of this simply to show that this spot with others is associated with the name of Marsh and I will close by wishing that you all may derive both pleasure and profit from this meeting, and again we bid you a cordial welcome to this historic old town, the deeds of whose first settlers, though shrouded in mist and unwritten traditions, we will not let die. Some of you slept on the spot made memorable by the presence of the regicides who with their protectors, defied kingly power, and yet it was accounted unto them as a virtue. A spot called for more often by strangers than any other in town.

Dr. Marsh is preparing a history of the family, which will contain the names of 5,313 people. He has found much interesting data. An edition of 500 copies will be printed, and 120 of this edition has already been taken.

These officers were chosen at the afternoon session: President, Riverius Marsh of New Brunswick, N. J.; vice-presidents, J. Dwight Marsh, Charles E. Marsh of New Milford, Ct., Horatio N. Marsh of

Joliet, Ill., Ephraim Gilmore of Chicago, Ill., James A. Marsh of Cleveland, O., Edward W. Marsh and Sanford Marsh of Montague, John E. Marsh of Hartford, Ct.; secretary and treasurer, J. Johnson of Greenfield; historian, Rev. Dr. D. W. Marsh of Amherst; executive committee, Riverius Marsh of New Brunswick, N. J., Charles A. Marsh of New York. Those who attended the meeting registered their names from an inkstand which has been in the family since 1743, and it now belongs to J. D. Marsh. On the outside is cast these words : " A gift to the Rev. Mr. Marsh by Samuel Catlin, 1743." This was Rev. Elisha Marsh, who lived in Westminster, Mass., at the time, and was subsequently a judge in the New Hampshire courts. The oldest person to use the inkstand yesterday was Mrs. Lois Marsh of North Amherst, who is 82 years old. The following, among others, signed their names to the book of records : John E. Marsh of Hartford, Sanford Marsh of Montague, J. Dwight Marsh of Hadley, Vernet E. Cleveland of Hartford, Lucretia P. Marsh of this city, Julia M. Harrison of New Haven, Lucy R. Marsh of this city, Lois Marsh of North Amherst, Mrs. Austin B. Marsh of Amherst, Mrs. Mary L. Morgan of this city.

The line of James Richardson[8] Marsh of the Salem Branch is as follows :

1. John[1] Marshe took oath of allegiance in England, March 24, 1633-4, came to New England the same year, was allotted 30 acres of land in Salem, Mass., 20 in 1637 and 10 in 1638 ; m. in 1635 or 6, Susannah, dau. of Rev. Samuel Skelton, appointed by Gov. Endicott to organize at Salem, July 30, 1629 the first Puritan church in America. The church building was put up in 1636 or 7 and John Marshe's eleven children were baptized there. The name is always Marshe in Salem records.

2. Zachariah[2] of Salem, farmer, (called Zachary) the first of Marsh name born in America, bap. April 30, 1637 ; m. Aug. 15, 1664, Mary Sillsbee, dau. of Henry of Lynn.

3. Jonathan[3], b. at Danvers, Mass., April 14, 1672 ; wounded at the ferry, Haverhill, Mass., in the Indian fight 1708 ; m. (1) May 20, 1697, Mary Verry, b. 1668.

4. Jonathan[4], b. at Danvers, (then Salem) April 17, 1699 ; m. at Salem, April 26, 1726-7, Esther Osborne.

5. Samuel[5], b. probably at Sutton, Mass., in 1738 ; m. about 1762, Rebekah Wilder, b. 1744.

6. Jesse[6], b. at Barre, Mass., May 22, 1771 ; m. (2) Widow Lucy Dunbar, b. at Grantham, N. H., 1770.

7. Stillman Jackson[7], b. at Grantham, N. H., April 16, 1815 ; m. Jan. 12, 1838, Harriet Richardson, b. at Bethel, Vt. Feb. 1, 1817; they settled in Cavendish, Vt., where in a freshet he was drowned, April 23, 1847. His two brothers had been drowned, and later in 1864, a third brother was killed by a falling limb. The widow was robbed by her husband's partners and the robbers after that, "never had anything but misfortune and ruin." The widow was forced to resort to factory work and to pay quite a sum to settle the estate.

8. James Richardson[8] Marsh, b. at Cavendish, Vt., Feb. 1, 1839, had some bitter experience that at times comes to the fatherless. He lived with his mother's father in Sharon and West Woodstock, Vt., then in 1849–50 on a farm in North Bridgewater, Vt., then three years of hard life in a cigar manufactory at New Ipswich, N. H., "15 hours a day's work," with "board and a few clothes," then a year in the Empire hotel at Saratoga Springs. His mother, March 4, 1853 m. Samuel C. Patrick, tobacconist, of Lowell, Mass., and Oct. 16, 1854, J. R. Marsh "arrived home" and for 40 years since has lived with and been associated in business with Mr. Patrick. On Sept. 24, 1879, J. R. Marsh was made a Mason in William North lodge of Lowell, Mass. and Feb. 14, 1881, made a Royal Arch Mason in Mt. Horeb Chapter ; June 27, 1881, Ahasuerus Council ; and June 28, 1881, Pilgrim Commandery of Knights Templar ; and in Boston, April 28, 1882, Massachusetts Consistory of 32d Degree Scottish Rite Masons for the Northern Jurisdiction of the U. S. of America and Sept. 15, 1887 a Noble of Aleppo Temple of Boston, Mass. Residence No. 25, Prescott St., Lowell, Mass.

James R. Marsh

# HISTORY OF THIS BOOK.

When the Marsh family association was first formed we designed to put all of Marsh name into one work. But at our first meeting it appeared that Mr. E. J. Marsh of Leominster, Mass., had the descendants of George Marsh of Hingham 1635, all ready for the press and to be published in 1887. Also names multiplied upon us so fast that in a year or two we found that it would be entirely impracticable to compress the account of the six remaining tribes into one or two volumes; and that the association could not publish a volume for each separate tribe. Publication of each book must be left to members of that particular tribe. Accordingly Col. L. B. Marsh, who in 1888 was our President, published in that year the history of his tribe, John Marsh of Salem 1633 and his descendants.

Mainly by generous aid of Col. Marsh the descendants of Alexander of Braintree, 1654, John of Boston, 1669 and William of Plainfield, 1675, were put in readiness for publication by the historian. No one yet appears from those tribes ready to take the risk of publication.

Up to 1893 the state of this John of Hartford work was very much the same. Col. Marsh had very generously aided us up to the point of publication, although it was not in his line. And also entirely unsolicited, John Edward Marsh of N. Y. City and Rahway, N. J. (whose work is very largely upon his own line, Samuel of New Haven, 1646) offered to give $100 whenever the John of Hartford book should be published. The historian had tried to find some one of the Hartford line ready to go forward. He had written to a friend stating the case fully and offering to share half the expense, but met with no response. Finally in 1893, seeing no better way, he concluded to go forward himself and sent out the following circular, reproduced here with very slight additions and correction. The use of the name of the Marsh association was fully warranted by repeated votes of that body. How could men and women scattered all over America know whether your historian was trustworthy? Some guarantee was due. No doubt *some* of the following circulars went promptly to the waste basket. But others brought a fair response.

---

## THE MARSH FAMILY ASSOCIATION.

---

*Col. L. B. Marsh of Boston, President.*

---

To you, a descendant of John Marsh of Hartford 1636: a notice and a request.

By the long researches of John E. Marsh, Esq., of Hartford, Ct., p. 87, and J. Dwight Marsh, Esq., of Hadley, Mass., p. 373, (who in their family ancestry have represented John Marsh in the two places of his life residence, ever since 1636 and 1660) and by the very liberal aid of two gentlemen of Boston and New York of the Salem and the New Haven lines, the historian of the association has brought the genealogy of our Hartford branch to the point of publication, and now asks your help.

He is able to inform you that the names of several thousand descendants of our common ancestor John Marsh have been obtained, with very valuable information as to their residences, occupations and personal history. We can trace the main family currents as they have been flowing on for over 250 years. We note the inter-marriages with other most excellent families, bringing in and giving out valuable traits to enrich and enlarge family experience and outlook.

Among blood-descendants of John Marsh, one, Frances Appleton, p. 419, inspired Longfellow's Hyperion, and became his wife and the mother of his children. Another, Susan Marsh Lyman, p. 159, became the wife of Senator Edmunds. One, Mary Marsh, marrying Dr. Ezekiel Porter, p. 353, at his death, in 1775, asserted her woman's right to do what she could, took up his practice, rode his circuits, and became a noted physician. Her energy flowed on to her grandson, Capt. Belden, p. 354, who was for a time on Washington's staff. The son of Eunice Marsh, p. 424, became Maj. Gen. Larned, Paymaster U. S. Army.

Several have had to do with the making and shaping of states. Colonels Joseph, p. 132 and Joel Marsh, p. 184, were of the State Commissioners to name Vermont. Hon. Jonathan Marsh, p. 196, in 1818, was a member of the convention to form the present Constitution of Connecticut. Joseph Marsh, p. 132, for years a colonel of the revolutionary war, and judge, became the first Lieut. Governor of Vermont; and when the state gave an entire township, declined it, saying that the state had more need of it than he.

Col. Joseph Marsh led a regiment to Ticonderoga. Molly Marsh, dau. of Col. Ebenezer, p. 29, was mother of U. S. Senator Seymour of Vermont, and her grandson, Horatio Seymour, p. 33, became Governor of the State of New York, and his sister the wife of Sen. Conkling, p. 34.

Henry R. Selden, p. 355, Lieut. Governor of New York state, and his not less distinguished brother, Samuel Lee Selden, p. 355, both judges of the New York Court of Appeals, were descended from Hannah Marsh, p. 354. So was the wife of Maj.-Gen. Eaton, and her son Prof. Eaton, p. 356, of Yale. Hon. Richard Skinner, LL. D., p. 71, son of Susannah Marsh became Chief Justice and also Governor of Vermont.

Gen. Isaac Marsh, p. 322, of Stockbridge, Mass. bought a Vermont town of the Stockbridge Indians and named it Marshfield. George Marsh, p. 53, laid out and named Marshfield, Ohio.

B. L. Marsh, and Charles Marsh, p. 352, brothers of the firm of Jordan, Marsh & Co. of Boston, are well known as prominent among our largest merchants and most successful business men.

Our original John Marsh was a pioneer of Hartford, Ct. and Hadley, Mass. Some of his grandsons were pioneers of Litchfield, New Hartford and Lebanon, Ct., and of Ware, Sunderland, Montague, Mass., and some of the later generations became pioneers in Berkshire and in Vermont, New York and other states.

Other descendants of our Hartford John Marsh are U. S. Senator Samuel S. Phelps, p. 31, of Vermont, and his son Edward J. Phelps, p. 31, late minister of the United States to England, Charles Marsh, p. 153, of Vermont, M. C., LL. D., and a trustee of Dartmouth College for forty years: and his more distinguished son, George P. Marsh, p. 155, M. C., Minister to Constantinople and to Italy.

Joseph and Leonard Marsh, p. 151, were Professors in the University of Vermont ; C. Dwight Marsh, p. 374, is Professor at Ripon College, Wis.; Allan Marquand, p. 447, is Professor at Princeton ; Herbert Osborn, p. 270, is Professor at Ames, Iowa, and James Marsh, p. 149, was Professor at Hampden-Sidney College, Va., and President of the University of Vermont. Worthington Smith, p. 306, descended from Ann Marsh, was also President of the University of Vermont.

Dr. Jonathan, p. 356, and Dr. Perez Marsh, p. 403, were surgeons in the French war of 1755. We have also Gen. Isaac Marsh of Connecticut. Ebenezer, p. 29, and Perez Marsh, after his French war experience, were long judges in Litchfield County, Ct. and Berkshire County, Mass. A descendant of the latter was Thomas Allen, p. 445, M. C. of Missouri. One of his sisters married Judge Benjamin R. Curtis of Boston, p. 444, and another, Henry G. Marquand, p. 447, of New York.

Lieut. Col. C. W. Marsh, p. 457, was for some time on Gen. Schofield's staff at St. Louis. Henry Marsh, Williams College 1815, of Dalton and Pittsfield, Mass. p 448, for a time of Racine, Wis., Sandusky, O., and St. Louis, was the fourth person to graduate at Harvard Law School, was a lawyer, manufacturer and merchant, and had he not died of cholera at the age of 55, would have left deeper marks of his untiring energy.

Several of John Marsh's descendants have resided in foreign lands. Some are buried by the Tigris, p. 457, and one in South Africa, p. 250. Some live in England, p. 419, and many have gone West and South. In the distant state "where rolls the Oregan," Joseph Walker Marsh, p. 151, is Professor and Sidney Harper Marsh, p. 150, has been President of the Pacific University.

How can we help feeling some interest in this our broad-spread common family!

I have given mention of a few, not of Marsh name, into whose veins blood of John Marsh has been inflowing. I can give names of more than one hundred early colonial families some of whose life blood has been poured into our Marsh family. Pardon a few. From Hartford Colony, Webster, Wadsworth, Welles, Clarke, Hooker, Goodwin, Chester, Newberry, Buell, Pratt, Pitkin, Lewis, Trumbull, Bulkley, Spencer, Talcott, Merrill, Seymour, Loomis and many others ; from Plymouth Rock, Bradford, Carpenter, and LeBaron ; from the Bay State, Pynchon, Stoddard, Winthrop, Adams, Porter, Whitney, Dwight, Lawrence, Hawley, Williams, Holyoke, Edwards, Mattoon, Hoar, Gillett, Lyman, Montague, Smith, Barnard, Willard and many others.

The volume proposed will probably contain 600 or more pages, and several thousand names, and we propose, *if 150 copies are subscribed for at $5 a copy*, to publish within a few months. As to the style in which we mean to publish the work, the volume "John Marsh of Salem 1633—1888," (of which the New Englander and the New England Genealogical and Historical Register have written in high commendation) is a fair guarantee.

Please sign and return as promptly as convenient to Amherst, Mass., the accompanying slip, that we may know definitely whether you will take a copy or copies.

DWIGHT W. MARSH,

*Historian Marsh Family Association,*

AMHERST, MASS.

It took about a year to get 100 subscribers. As soon as that number was obtained, a circular with that list was sent out, which promptly brought additional subscriptions, due largely to the high character and example of the subscribers. We give the circular and also additional subscriptions.

Right here however, before giving the circular, the historian wishes to state most emphatically that, outside of his own family, in the compilation of this work, he has received more aid from John E. Marsh of Hartford, Ct., (p. 87) than from any other person, and we all owe him much gratitude for labor in our behalf continued for months and years.

And next, Josiah Dwight Marsh (p. 373) of Hadley, Mass., has been of inestimable service.

As the historian has been unable to use a pen freely for two years past, the aid received from his wife has alone enabled him to keep up a very extended correspondence and to correct proof and be ready for a hungry press.   None know better than he the kindness and value of such a helper.   Many others, only in less degree, deserve similar acknowledgements.

The histories of Hadley, Mass., and of Hartford County, and New Milford and Litchfield, Ct., have been carefully consulted and freely drawn upon, and also the pamphlet sketch of New Hartford and the pamphlet account of the famous Marsh and Buell gathering of over a thousand persons at Litchfield in 1844.   The Genealogical Library in Somerset St., Boston and libraries in New York, Hartford, Northampton, Amherst and Pittsfield have been visited persistently with scrutiny of every accessible genealogy and town history and study of all other available sources of information.   Letters without number have been written and many valuable replies received.   Please notice the many acknowledgements in the address printed on pages xiii to xxix.   Beside acknowledgements there given, thanks are particularly due to Miss Anna C. Marsh (p. 70) of Litchfield, now Mrs. Johnson ; and more recently to Miss Martha A. Peck of Pittsfield, Mass., (p. 414) to Mrs. Griffing of Franklin, Ct., (p. 364) and Mrs. Judge Curtis of New York, (p. 444) to G. S. Newman, Charlottesville, Va., and Mrs. C. B. Roe, N. Y. City; to Mrs. Senator Edmunds and Mrs. Talbot Rogers of Philadelphia, Mrs. Richardson of East Billerica, Mass., Miss Avery of Groton, Ct. and Mrs. Boardman of Newport, N. H.; and for growing interest and help to H. D. Marsh of Springfield (p. 85), Mary A. Marsh of Hartford and George S. Marsh of Whitewater, Wis.

The printers and their aids deserve and will please accept especial thanks for their interest and watchful care.

If notwithstanding the utmost care in proof reading a few slips have crept in (as on p. 94 in lines 9 and 16 this century for last, 18 for 17 and on p. 387 in line 8, a " her " for *he*) the intelligent reader will generally readily correct them.

The historian would gladly extend much farther his grateful recognition of aid received.   He has no complaints to make ; but on the contrary, wishes to emphasize his obligations to the very many who have cordially aided him.   His heart has been very warmly drawn out to his kindred for whom he has long been laboring with sincere goodwill.

## CIRCULAR.

JOHN MARSH OF HARTFORD, CT., 1636, AND HIS DESCENDANTS.

The following is a list of subscribers and subscriptions towards publication of the above work. It should be stated that Col. L. B. Marsh of Boston has paid over one hundred and twenty dollars to cover all past expenses, and that J. Edward Marsh of New York offers to pay $100 whenever the work is published.

| | | | |
|---|---|---|---|
| J. Edward Marsh, New York, p. xlix. | 4 | Copies, | $100 |
| George S. Marsh, Whitewater, Wis., p. 322, | 12 | " | 60 |
| Mary A. Marsh, Hartford, Ct., p. 80, | 8 | " | 40 |
| H. D. Marsh, Springfield, Mass., p. 85, | 5 | " | 25 |
| Col. L. B. Marsh, Boston, Mass., p. xliii, | 2 | " | 10 |
| John E. Marsh, Hartford, Ct., p. 87, | 2 | " | 10 |
| E. A. Marsh, Groton, N. Y., p. 298, | 2 | " | 10 |
| Mrs. A. L. Johnson, Winchester Center, Ct., p. 70, | 2 | " | 10 |
| Hon. H. N. Marsh, Joliet, Ill., p. 262, | 2 | " | 10 |
| J. Johnson, Greenfield, Mass., p. 266, | 2 | " | 10 |
| P. J. Marsh, Lansingburg, N. Y., p. 123, | 2 | " | 10 |
| A. B. Marsh, Mt. Vernon, N. Y., p. 226; | 2 | " | 10 |
| Hon. George M. Woodruff, Litchfield, Ct., | 2 | " | 10 |
| James R. Marsh, Lowell, Mass., p. liii. | 2 | " | 10 |
| Reg. E. B. Marsh, Amherst, Mass., p. 275, | 2 | " | 10 |
| Mrs. Susan Marsh Edmunds, Burlington, Vt., p. 159, | 2 | " | 10 |
| Mrs. E. S. Rogers, Philadelphia, Pa., p. 144, | 2 | " | 10 |
| Hon. Luther R. Marsh, Middletown, N. Y., p. 348, | 2 | " | 10 |

The following subscribed for one copy each at $5 a copy :

Prof. John B. Marsh, Elmira, N. Y., p. 386.

Judge G. M. Carrington, West Winsted, Ct., p. 214.

Joseph Marsh, Northampton, Mass., p. 256.

Josiah D. Marsh, Hadley, Mass,, p. 373.

Prof. Daniel C. Eaton, New Haven, Ct., p. 356.

Mrs. C. Marsh Eager, Racine, Wis., p. 459.

Sanford Marsh, Montague, Mass., p. 276.

Judge Charles P. Marsh, Woodstock, Vt., p. 177, d. Jan. 13, 1893.
Copy taken by his son J. W. Marsh, Chicago, Ill., p. 464.
Prof. C. Dwight Marsh, Ripon, Wis., p. 374.
William S. Marsh, Indianapolis, Ind., p. 171.
Mrs. James White, Williamstown, Mass., p. 453.
O. L. Peck, Esq., Toledo, O., p. 411.
Mrs. H. H. W. Clark, Thorndike, Mass., p. 400.
G. H. Griffing, Franklin, Ct., p. 364.
Henry W. Marsh, Manistee, Mich., p. 459.
Mrs. Maude Allen Atwater, Pittsfield, Mass., p. 446.
M. F. Dickinson, Esq., Boston, Mass., p. 377 and 467.
Mrs. Ira B. Johnson, Canaan, N. Y., p. 452, d. Aug. 15, 1893.
Prof. Herbert Osborn, Ames, Iowa, p. 270.
William C. Marsh, Bridgewater, N. Y., p. 204.
Nelson G. Hinckley, Esq., Hartford, Ct., p. 225.
Mrs. Harvey E. Rogers, Windsor, Ct., p. 205.
Mrs. John R. Smith, Spring Hill, Iowa, p. 206.
Charles Almeron Marsh, Needham, Mass., p. 187.
Prof. Joseph W. Marsh, Forest Grove, Or., p. 151.
Mrs. Mary B. Marsh, Judsonia, Ark., p. 274.
Margaret K. Rockwell, Manchester, Ct., p. 138.
Dr. E. Stewart, New York, p. 271.
Mrs. Mary C. Hart, Stamford, Ct., p. 43.
Daniel C. Marsh, Ware, Mass., p. 248.
Mrs. Clara C. Marsh, Racine, Wis., p. 454.
New York Historical Society, New York.
Wisconsin Historical Society, Madison, Wis.
Newberry Library, Chicago, Ill.
Mrs. Susan L. Jaques, Waterbury, Ct., p. 88.
W. A. Marsh, Jamestown, N. Y., son of Mansir, p. xlvii.
Mrs. Giles M. Johnson, Glastonbury, Ct., p. 104.
Lewis Marsh, Bristol, Ct., p. 61, d. Dec. 14, 1894.
George H. Marsh, Homer, Mich., p. 91.
J. W. Marsh, Purkinsville, Miss., 367.
Judge C. C. Baldwin, Cleveland, O.
B. D. Marsh, Plainfield, Vt., p. 86.
O. R. Marsh, Lockhart, Texas, p. 366.
Mrs. Maria Marsh Clark, Plainfield, N. J., p. 460.
H. C. Marsh, Chicago, Ill., p. 299.

Eleanor W. Allen, Boston, Mass., p. 446.

William C. Marsh, Springfield, Mass., p. 84.

Ira Rix Marsh, Chicago, Ill., p. 99.

Judge William Marsh, Quincy, Ill., p. 303, d. April 14, 1894.

Theodore D. Marsh, Alma, Mich., p. 284.

A. D. Schermerhorn, Omaha, Neb., p. 297.

Edward A. Marsh, West Newton, Mass.

Mrs. A. B. Laurie, West Newton, Mass., p. 88.

Elon A. Marsh, Battle Creek, Mich., p. 58.

George E. Marsh, Townville, Pa., p. 254.

Harriet A. Wood, Aurora, N. Y., p. 37.

Emmett W. Marsh, Amherst, Mass., p. 291.

Dr. E. H. Marsh, Mansfield Center, Ct., p. 261.

Morris W. Seymour, Bridgeport, Ct., p. 461.

Daniel Sheldon Marsh, New London, Ct., p. 320.

John W. Marsh, Jr., Hadley, Mass., p. 372.

Henry M. Marsh, Hadley, Mass., p. 391.

F. H. Richards, Hartford, Ct., see 221.

Charles H. Kellogg, Cincinnati, O.

Hon. Edward W. Marsh, Bridgeport, Ct.

Baxter Marsh, Amherst, Mass., p. 275.

Charles W. Marsh, New York, p. 394.

John W. Marsh, Warsaw, Ill., p. 176.

E. J. Marsh, Big Rapids, Mich., p. 268.

Mrs. A. S. Miles, Battle Creek, Mich., p. 57.

E. R. Marsh, Neenah, Wis., p. 203.

Here are a little over a hundred subscriptions and the amount (omitting one death) would be, if all paid in, $605. Nearly fifty more subscriptions are needed. Can you help to make up this number? Would it not be a pity to come so near success and then fail to publish, and this after several persons have given weeks, and one or two, months of gratuitous labor for the common good?

Can you not get some relative near you to subscribe?

We have over 5300 names in the work, and wills of John Marsh and a number of others, with other early documents. Such a work is of much more value than a monument.

Whatever you may decide, I am very truly your friend,

DWIGHT W. MARSH,
HISTORIAN MARSH FAMILY.

*Amherst, Mass., Aug. 10, 1894.*

## LATER SUBSCRIPTIONS.

Mrs. C. E. Richardson, East Billerica, Mass., p. 141, 3 Copies, $15

Mrs. J. M. Walker, Chicago, Ill.,                    2    "    10

W. C. Marsh, 621 Broadway, N. Y., p. 297,            2    "    10

The following subscribed for one copy each, at $5 a copy:

Mrs. C. B. Roe, 35 East 37th St., New York, p. 39.

Myron G. Marsh, Hartford, Ct., p. 216.

Frank A. Marsh, Chicago, Ill., p. 320.

Mrs. Millie Shultz, 29 Mary St., Battle Creek, Mich., p. 57.

Sibbie H. Marsh, Providence, R. I., p. 462.

Charles S. Marsh, Springfield, Mass., p. 241.

Mrs. William Willshire Riley, Cromwell, Ct., p. 380.

Frank M. Marsh, Springfield, Mass., p. 288.

J. Warner Marsh, Hadley, Mass., p. 372.

Horatio Marsh, Dwight, Mass.

Arthur Wetmore Marsh, Warsaw, Ill., p. 177.

Joseph F. Marsh, Winsted, Ct., p. 226.

Henry F. Marsh, Winchester, Ct., p. 217.

Norfolk, Ct. Library.

Frederick Bulkley Edwards, Hartford Ct., p. 384.

C. P. Marsh, Country Club, West Chester Co., N. Y., p. 303.

Mrs. F. Boardman, Newport, N. H., p. 147.

William F. J. Boardman, Hartford, Ct.

G. S. Newman, Charlottesville, Va., p. 42.

Mrs. E. W. Marsh, Hartford, Ct., p. 215.

Sherman W. Adams, Hartford, Ct.

Franklin L. Pope, Great Barrington, Mass., p. 377.

Edwin R. Marsh, New Haven, Ct., p. 181.

Eben Jones Marsh, p. 320.

Charles H. Leeds, Stamford, Ct., p. 436.

Before this entire number was made out, when Mr. George S. Marsh of Whitewater, Wis., added subscription for ten more copies to his previous call for two, the historian in October, 1894 ventured to commence printing. Much time and work have been given to this genealogy for the last ten years and may it prove of value to some now living and to others who come after us. Hail ye Marshmen yet to be!                                                    D. W. M.

In closing the introductory pages of this work I must not fail to express my indebtedness to the most expert genealogist whom I have personally known, Dr. D. Williams Patterson of Newark Valley, Tioga Co., N. Y.

In my three years' residence at Pittsfield, Mass., among numerous descendants of Dr. Perez Marsh and four years in St. Louis among others, and then two years in New York City where his descendants were still more numerous, by 1849 I had come to know many personally and to make out a list of some 400 descendants of my great-grandfather. But it was not till more than twenty years later when I met Dr. Patterson that I knew anything about my Marsh ancestry beyond Dr. Perez.

While at Owego, N. Y., 1871—76, one day in Newark Valley the wise Dr. took me into his *den*, and my eyes opened upon stacks of manuscript and the four walls crowded with more genealogical works than I have ever seen together, before or since, except in the Genealogical rooms at Boston. Out of the many volumes the Dr. took down the Hadley Book and introduced me to my great grandfather's great grandfather and all the Hadley line down to Perez. It was a new world. That revelation gave me my first strong genealogical impulse.

In later study I have found that the Hadley Book knows nothing of the return of John Marsh's oldest son to Hartford and gives none of his descendants, although names of this oldest branch fill nearly half of this volume.

In the last decade Dr. Patterson has written to me from his home and during his travels in Connecticut and once turned aside to visit me here in Amherst, giving me highly valuable information, advice and help.

E

# OUTLINE OF THIS WORK.

## I. JOHN[1] MARSH

of England, Hartford, Ct. and Hadley, Mass. and family, pp. 1–19.

## II. BRANCH 1.

John[2] Marsh and family of Hartford, Hadley and Hartford again pp. 20–25. His four sons and their descendants.

<table>
<tr><td>DIV. 1.</td><td>DIV. 2.</td><td>DIV. 3.</td></tr>
<tr><td>Capt. John[3]. The Litchfield Line and Hartford Continued, pp. 26–91.</td><td>Lieut. Nathaniel[3]. The Hartford and East Hartford Line, pp. 91–115.</td><td>Capt. Joseph[3]. The Lebanon Line and Vermont Marshes, pp. 115–188.</td></tr>
</table>

DIV. 4.

Capt. Jonathan[3]. The early New Hartford Line, pp. 189–227.

## III. BRANCH 2.

Samuel[2] Marsh of Hartford, Hadley and Hatfield, pp. 228–232. Descendants pp. 233–304.

<table>
<tr><td>DIV. 1.</td><td>DIV. 2.</td></tr>
<tr><td>Thomas[3] and Ware Marshes, pp. 233–251.</td><td>Ebenezer[3] and Montague Marshes, pp. 251–304.</td></tr>
</table>

## IV. BRANCH 3.

Jonathan[2] Marsh of Hadley, pp. 305–311. Descendants, pp. 311–325.
Rev. Jonathan[3], D. D. of Windsor, Ct., pp. 311–313.
Rev. Jonathan[4] of New Hartford, Ct., p. 313.
The Later New Hartford Line, pp. 313–325.

## V. BRANCH 4.

# LIST OF ILLUSTRATIONS.

*To face page* 1.

# John Marsh of Hartford and Hadley.

Born in England in 1618 he is believed to have come in 1635 when 17 years of age to Cambridge on Charles river by the bay, then laid out for the capital of Massachusetts, and called Newtown, and now included in the "greater Boston." According to Barber he was of the 100 men, women and children who in 1636 led by Hooker, Stone and Elder Goodwin took two weeks to make the journey with a herd of 160 cattle from Massachusetts Bay through a pathless wilderness to the beautiful shores of the Connecticut river. They emerged from the forest at the Indian town of Suckige, with much cleared land about it, now Hartford, the elegant capital of a noble and busy state. The cleared land was soon given to the "original proprietors." The name of John Marsh is found on the fine shaft erected at Hartford to the memory of these earliest settlers. This shaft stands in Hartford's oldest burial ground by the Central Church, "God's acre." His name is also on Hartford's earliest map of 1640, which gives with their names the home lots of the earliest settlers. Because he was a minor his home lot was *probably* not given him until he was 21, in 1639; for we read "Lands were recorded to John Marsh Feb., 1639–40 *part whereof* did belong to John Stone and were by him given to Samuel Stone and by said Stone to John Marsh of Hartford and now belongeth to him and his heirs." Also, "Thomas Beale had an allotment of lands sequestered for him, but he did not come to Hartford and they were given to John Marsh *before* Feb., 1639–40." One or both of these lots, 12 and 24 acres, making 36, made John Marsh's homelot. This lot was number 16 on the north side of the stream that now runs through Bushnell Park, and on the street then nearest the Connecticut river, where Temple and Front streets now cross. He not long after came to have 76⅞ths acres additional; in

.the distribution to "original proprietors" of common lands at the West end.  Later he had also 72 acres allotted to him, at now East Hartford, just across the river.

We naturally think of his life in three parts:

1. Up to his 18th year, 1618–1636, his English life of 17 years and then one year of sea and land before reaching Hartford.

2. Twenty-four years of Hartford life, from his 18th to 42d year, 1636 to 1660.

3. Twenty-eight years of Hadley life, from his 42d to his 70th year, 1660 to 1688.

His parting from England, the voyage across the Atlantic, the passing into Massachusetts Bay and Charles river, the stay at Cambridge and the plunge through pathless forests, must have stamped upon his young mind, life-long impression.

Of his English boyhood and of his parentage we know nothing. He doubtless came from Essex Co., Eng. for almost all Hartford's earliest settlers and their celebrated pastor Hooker came from Braintree, Essex Co., and John Marsh had a brother Joseph Marsh, clothier, of Braintree, and that Joseph Marsh had a "kinsman Joseph Marsh." He also had three sisters in England and the daughter of one of his sisters came, later on, to live in London.  John was no doubt familiar with the games and sports of English life and may possibly have seen London.  He had heard of Shakespeare who died, (1616) two years before he, John Marsh, was born.  During our ancestor's boyhood Hampden was stirring the English heart and Cromwell about to be.  Charles I. had moved many excellent men to leave England. John may have run away to the new world, or have been apprenticed to some one of the more important Hartford families, possibly to Webster's into which family he married after a few years.

"John Webster was a leading citizen of Hartford ; one of the 5 higher magistrates in 1639—holding office till 1655, when he became Deputy Governor, and after serving as Governor in 1656, resuming his office of High Magistrate and holding it till 1659," when he left Hartford.  (Memorial Hist. Hartford Co.)  Gov. Webster then led the great removal to Hadley, Massachusetts.

Our artist was not in Hartford when Hartford troops in 1637 under Col. Mason moved swiftly eastward and almost exterminated the Pequods with horrible fire and sword, but every Hartford boy and young man there and John Marsh among them, grew familiar with sights of friendly Indians under the forest trees and with wild stories of the tomahawk and scalping knife of hostile braves.

The ever-surviving story in genealogical study of " Three Brothers came over " does not willingly die in any family tradition, and it pops up, as to John Marsh, asking if he was not brother or son of some other Marsh who came over between 1633 and 1675. He might have been cousin but he could not have been brother or son of John of Salem, 1633, nor in any close relation to William of Plainfield, 1675, nor to John of Boston, 1669. He might have been a first or second cousin to Samuel of New Haven, 1643, or to George of Hingham, 1635, who was possibly uncle to Alexander of Braintree, 1654. But the terms of the will of his brother Joseph Marsh who died in Braintree, Eng. in 1676, seem to exclude by non-mention, the idea that Joseph had in America any brother but John of Hartford. So far as similar names would show he *might have been* related to the New Haven family. But so far as we *positively* know, John Marsh when he came had not a relative of Marsh name in America. We are not surprised that in less than five years, he took steps to have another assume his name and come to his side and these lines tell rather more of detail about it than we can absolutely affirm and they close with a question which we would be glad to have any one answer.

1635. *John Marsh, 17—Anne, a rosy girl of 14.*

From England's sea-girt land
Through God's high guiding hand
The Exmen sailed.
They laughed at Ocean's roar,
They sought a broader shore,
And here forevermore
They freedom hailed.

John Marsh sailed out with them,
Those dauntless Essex men.
Bold hearts and strong !
From home he dared to start,
From England chose to part,
A secret filled his heart,
And drew him on.

1640. *John*, 22—*Anne, abt.* 19.
By Hartford's river-flow,
You see them moving slow
    At even tide,
A start! with half surprise!
A smile, of listening skies!
A droop, of tell-tale eyes,
    A "yes," replied.

Did Hooker bid them stand,
Great "light of Western Land"
    And tie the knot?
Or Webster knit them one,
Then call her John "my son"?
Some how, this deed was done,
    And *how* forgot.

This was 252 years ago and our reporter not there.  John's twenty-four years of Hartford life, from his 19th to his 43d year must have been full of growth in that new environment of rich experiences and fresh clashings of wits and wills.  We know little of details.  He was on a Hartford jury 1649 and chimney viewer 1657.  He must have kept on contrasting two worlds of woods and waters; two Englands, old and new; two races, Anglo Saxon and Indian; and that in a focus of high thought, the capital of a colony.  Hooker was as profound a mind as ever came from England to our shores; held in high esteem by the foremost in England and almost idolized here as "the light of the western churches."  Since all were expected to attend religious services, John Marsh no doubt heard his Pastor Hooker's famous lecture, Thursday, May 1, 1638, whose principles lie at the foundation of our government.  The text was Deut. 1 : 13, "Take ye wise men" etc., the "Doctrine:"

1.  That the choice of public magistrates belongs unto the people by God's own allowance.

2.  The privilege of election, which belongs to the people, therefore must not be exercised according to their humors, but according to the blessed will and law of God.

3.  They who have power to appoint officers and magistrates, it is in their power also to set the bounds and limitations of the power and place to which they call them.

Reason 1.  Because the foundation of authority is laid firstly in the free consent of the people."

Hooker died July 7, 1647 "in epidemical sickness that prevailed throughout New England." John Marsh was therefore, 1636–1647, for eleven years under Hooker's pastorate and we think sometimes heard discussions and comments by such men as Winthrop, Elder Goodwin, Gov. Webster and Sec. Daniel Clarke. He saw by the great men "high magistrates" supposed witches tried; and heard one or two sentenced to death. The "Joseph Marsh" called to testify in one witch case in 1662 was *possibly* his third son and if so a lad of fifteen. But these dismal trials, like the early Pequod slaughter, were very exceptional. In general, life flowed on as placidly as the noble river by whose banks John Marsh's homestead lay. At that early home, all but one of his children were born. He had fair lands there at Hartford on each side of the Connecticut. His family grew and he prospered.

He signed as a "withdrawer" from the 1st church Hartford, July 11, 1656. The change from Hartford to Hadley, Mass., some 40 miles above on the same river, was brought about by two fundamental causes. One was, (when the Hartford hive became too crowded) the natural swarming tendency to "fresh fields and pastures new." The other, in the struggles of free thought, was the natural breaking away, even among warm friends, of the slightly more democratic from the slightly more aristocratic. The followers of Hooker, who was in advance of his age, tended to go with Gov. Webster and Elder Goodwin. John Marsh was of those who in their letter of March 12, 1656, refused longer to recognize Mr. Stone and called for an able and impartial mutual council. His name is attached to all the documents calling for greater freedom in removal from Hartford and in 1659–60 a large party moved up the river through the gorge between Holyoke and Tom, secured from Indians the broad river meadows and lands lying back and formed the new town of Hadley. At the time of this migration in 1660 John Marsh was 42, his wife Anne probably a little younger, their oldest son, John about 17, Samuel about 15, Joseph if living 13, (he probably died before marriage), Jonathan 11, Daniel 7, Hannah perhaps 9 or 5, and Grace perhaps 5 or 3.

The third period of John Marsh's life was almost entirely connected with Hadley, 28 years of fruitage and harvest time, 1660 to 1688, from his 42d to his 70th year. The names of John Webster

and John Marsh appear on the first town plot of Hadley as on that
of Hartford and also on Hadley's first town meeting records Oct. 8,
1660. By vote Hartford in 1660 gave the Jews who lived in John
Marsh's house liberty to stay seven months. He was no doubt in
Hadley. And yet he had rather mysterious connection with Northampton. He was one of the original members of the church there
at its organization June 18, 1661, and in a list in 1891 of over 4250
members of the Northampton church his name is second of all.
The following comes from J. Dwight Marsh's search of Hadley town
writings: "The first notice of John Marsh, which I find in the
Hadley records, is at the first town meeting held at Warner's house,
Oct. 8th, 1660, " Agreed that Jo Marsh hath his house lot with his
father, Mr. Webster, of Mr. Webster's, and he to have eight acres
allowed for it within the fence, and he to come up at spring next."
They had cast lots for their land in Feb. of 1660, and Mr. Webster
drew No. 19, and John Marsh No. 34. I think he came up in 1661,
as in December John Marsh and Will Webster engage for Robt.
Webster. He has his lands recorded the 19th of June, 1674, as
John Marsh, Sen. In 1675, John Marsh was one of the Selectmen.
This is the only time I find his name as a town officer, while the
names of his sons, Jonathan and Daniel, recorded first as Jonathan
and Daniel, and then as Lieut. Jonathan and Sergt. Daniel, and lastly
as Mr., which title they have on their tombstones, are on every page
of Hadley history from 1682 to 1715."

At the threshold of John Marsh's Hadley life he met with two
bitter experiences, one the death of his father-in-law, Gov. John
Webster, April 5, 1661; a great loss to his children and to Hadley.
Noah Webster of spelling book and dictionary fame, was Gov.
Webster's most distinguished descendant; but his two Hadley sons
were not thrifty and much needed a father's care, so that John Marsh
rather than they, came to represent their father. Indeed the widow
of one of Webster's sons had the gift of a lot from the town, and
suffered severely under charge of witchcraft.

The other trial, the following year, June 9, 1662, was the death of
his wife Anne (Webster) Marsh, who had been his delight for twenty-
two years, and yet now her sun went down at mid-day.

A flock of motherless children was about him, and after two years
he married, in 1664, Hepzibah (Ford) Lyman, daughter of Thomas

Ford and widow of Richard Lyman who had been from the first one of the most prominent men in Northampton. She had five Lyman children of ages not far from those of his own. The skies brightened for the two families, and two years later in 1666 his son John Marsh, aged about 23, married his new wife's daughter, Sarah Lyman. Soon after, the young couple moved to Hartford and lived in the old Marsh homestead all their lives of many years.

And as happy years passed on, John Marsh enjoyed the marriage and settlement of all but the youngest one of his adult children and the birth of 39 of his 55 grandchildren. His children settled at Hartford, Windsor, Northampton, Hadley and Hatfield; all upon the beautiful river along whose banks he had lived and traveled for 52 years. Of these 52 years 22 had been spent with his first wife and 19 with his second. Of Richard Lyman, Savage prints "He d. June 3, 1662 and his widow m. John Marsh of Hadley who thereupon removed to Northampton." He may have lived a year or two in Northampton; but of this there is yet no certainty. He was select-man of Hadley in 1675. That year was and is memorable in Hadley history and tradition. Also to John Marsh and many of his descend-ants that year and the following were memorable by the singular way in which wives were provided for two of his sons. The Indians did it. Aug. 5, 1675, Dorcas Dickinson lost her husband Azariah "slain in Swamp fight" and next year she married Jonathan Marsh. And Hannah (Lewis) Crow, lost her husband, Samuel Crow, "slain in Falls fight May 18, 1676" and your historian finds and makes note that she married his ancestor, Daniel Marsh, in less than six months, Nov. 5, 1676. Be not quick to condemn the haste of those wise widows. They knew the facts of battle where we have mingled fact and tradition. Do as you please about all mere tradition but read and accept all facts. Indians surely were very troublesome at Hadley in 1675 and Goffe after the accession of Charles II. was hid there, and tradition says that one Sunday he helped fight the Indians. You can believe or doubt it. Josiah Dwight Marsh, Esq., of Hadley whose entire ancestry and his own family from 1660 to 1894 have lived at, or within half a mile of John Marsh's Hadley home lot, in an address to the Marsh Family Association states the case fairly.

"In my house I have a picture representing Hadley attacked by the Indians in 1675, and the majestic figure of Goffe standing in the foreground rallying the panic stricken inhabitants. But, says the historian of to-day, "all tradition ; no Indians nearer Hadley than Deerfield that day." I have looked at the records of the town of that time and find that it was a time of great trouble for fear of the enemy, as they call them. Votes were passed that the fortifications be strengthened; brush be cut down in all home lots, so as not to be a hiding place for the enemy; that no less than 40, or more than 50 men should go outside the fortifications to gather the crops in the meadows, and they should dispose themselves in the best manner for protection ; and that all males over 16 go armed to church. A garrison was kept there in the winter of 1675 and summer of 1676. Had the Indians been successful, as at Deerfield, and Goffe been tomahawked, there would have been no need of secresy, but I notice that Goffe was on the winning side, in his public acts, whether as one of the judges of Charles I. or in a sword contest in Boston or New Haven, or fighting the Indians in Hadley; and to have published the story at that time would have been *death* to protectors as well as the protected. Now Peter Tilton, one of the protectors, was a very modest man, and would naturally object to that way of being taken off. I notice that in recording the list of Selectmen for the town, while giving every other man his full title as Capt., Lieut., Sergt., Cornet, etc., he would write his own name last, and simply as P. T., although entitled to more titles than any other man in town.

The Rev. Samuel Hopkins, writing in 1793 to President Stiles of New Haven, speaks of the tradition in the family of the Marshes; John Marsh being one of the Selectmen in 1674 would know the facts in the case, and thus very likely the tradition would be handed down in the family. And President Stiles speaks of meeting in Wethersfield a Mrs. Porter, a sensible and judicious woman, a daughter of Ebenezer Marsh, born next door to Peter Tilton's, and of her story in relation to the judges. Thus the Marshes are brought in for their share in these traditions." The historian of this family thinks rather approvingly of the undoubted fact that Hannah Lewis married Daniel Marsh and so became his foremother, because her first husband was slain by the Indians.

Hepzibah (Ford) (Lyman) Marsh died April 11, 1683. Her will made in 1677, was presented (to probate court, Northampton, Mass.) in March, 1684. It gives to her Lyman children, Richard, Thomas,

John, Hannah and Sarah (Lyman) Marsh, £10 each, and to her daughter Lydia Marsh £20. This was the daughter of John Marsh and Hepzibah (Lyman) Marsh born Oct. 9, 1667, making her age about ten when her mother's will was drawn, and less than 15½ at the time of her mother's death. Hepzibah Marsh's will proves that she lived in Hadley. It is found in the Probate court records at North-ampton and commences :

"I Hepzibah Lyman alias Marsh, of Hadley in ye county of Hampshire, being weak and crazy in body, yet through the blessing and good hand of God on me in perfect memory and sound understanding yet knowing not the day of my departure out of this troublesome world " etc.

"As for my soule, that I commit to God that gave it to me and to Jesus Christ wch I hope hath redeemed it and to ye holy spirit wch I hope through Grace hath sanctified it. As for my body that I commit to ye grave to be buried in a Comely and decent manner, there to rest till ye gen¹¹ Ressurrection wn though sown in corruption [it] shall I hope be raised in glory, and soule and body being united togeather shall immediately pass into glory."

After willing her property she gives motherly advice : "Giving to him and to ye rest of my children solemn and strict charges yt they walk in peace and unitie one with another but above all yt they walk in ye feare of the Lord attending diligently in ye way of all God's appointments for ye making sure and working out their own salvation with fear and trembling."

J. D. Marsh has copied for us John Marsh's will. He writes: "The next time I find John Marsh's name is in the Probate office at Northampton, March 3d, 1687–8.

## JOHN MARSH'S WILL.

" A true copy of the last will and testament of John Marsh of Hadley, who dyed at Windsor, presented at the Court at Northampton, the 4th of December, 1688.

I, John Marsh, of Hadley, in the county of Hampshire, in New England, being very sensible of mine own frailty and mortality, yet through the mercy of God, of sound mind and memory at present, doe make this my last will and Testament as follows ; I commit my selfe soule and body into the hands of the Almighty and Eternal God whose I am, and into the arms of my Dear Redeemer the Lord Jesus Christ, in whom I desire steadfastly to belong, and on whom do repose and rest alone for righteousness, life and salvation, leaving my body to be interred with a comely burial.

And for the outward estate the Lord hath blessed me withal, my will is, that after my just debts are paid, and funeral expenses discharged, that then I give to my son, John Marsh, ffive pounds.

I give to my son, Jonathan Marsh, all my Gold.

I give to my son, Daniel Marsh, my two Cob Irons.

I give to my daughter, Hannah Loomis, alias Marsh, thirty pounds, unless I pay a part of it before my decease, n'th, if so then so much shall be discounted from the Legacy.

I give to my son, Samuel Marsh all my lands within the township of Hadley.

I give to my daughter, Lydia Marsh, my green Rug.

I give to my grandson Baker, of Northampton, ffive pounds, when he shall attayne to the age of one and twenty years.

I give and bequeath to my daughter, Lydia Marsh, twenty pounds.

And all said Legacies, my will is, that my Executors see faithfully discharged. And I do constitute and appoint my loving sons, John Marsh and Samuel Marsh, to be Executors to this my will annulling and making voide all former wills at any time by me willed or bequeathed.

JOHN MARSH.

Sealed and subscribed in the presence of

THOMAS HOVEY,<br>THOMAS HEAD."

There can be no question that John Marsh in 1688 was "of Hadley" and not of Northampton or Hartford, and as to the place of his death, that it was Windsor, Conn. where his daughter Hannah (Marsh) Loomis then lived. Stiles in Hist. Windsor gives the date as "28, Sept. 1688, æ. 70." It is proper to add that our kinsman J. Dwight Marsh, Esq. of Hadley, who has taken great pains to get facts, thinks that his death at Windsor later than September was "probably in *November* 1688" and is inclined to this belief by the lateness of the following inventories, but that would make both the "28" and the "Sept." wrong.

"An Inventory of the estate of John Marsh, late of Hadley, deceased.

Windsor, Nov. 27, 1688.

Imp's—his wearing clothes, £02, 09s., 10d.

Priz's John Loomis, Joseph Loomis."

Hadley, Dec. 3, 1688.

|  | £ | s. | d. |
|---|---|---|---|
| due to the estate by bond, | 32 | 09 | 00 |

by wheat in the barn,                    2    10    00
by a young steer,                        2    00    00
by a Bedstead,                          00    06    00
        Prizers Nathaniel White, Sam'l Porter, Jr."

We note by his will and these inventories that his property was mainly given away before his death.

The following is the official record of his lands in Hadley.

## JOHN MARSH'S RECORD.

This Record beareing date this nineteenth daye of December Anno domini one thousand six hundred seaventy ffoure witnefseth that the towne of Hadley have given and granted unto John marsh sen᷒ an alottment or acommodation of lands acording to the value of one hundred pound Estate viz. one House-lott containing Eight Akars lyeing in two parcells one parcell containing ffive Akars one roode thirteene rod and one third of a rod as it lyes bounded by the land of Andrew werner north and Timothy Nash South Abutting on the Comon Streete East and the plane west. Allsoe in that tract of land called plane two Akars two roodes twenty six rod and two thirds of a rod which is in consideration of the remainder of his house lott as it lyes bounded.

Allsoe more in the plane two Akars one roode and ffifteene pole more or less bounded By the land Granted to robert boltwood west Abutting on a highway South and the adjoining ffurlong North.

Allsoe in the ffirst division of plowland in the Great meddow one parcell containing three Akars more or lefse bounded by the land Sometime Granted to Mr. John webster East and richard Churches land west Abutting on two highways North and South.

Allsoe in the meddow aforesaid one parcell more containing ffoure Akars more or lefse proportioned at one Hundred fortye and one rod to an Akar as it lyes bounded by the land of Timothye Nash East and Samuell Gardiner Sen᷒ west abutting on a high waye north and the adjoining ffurlong South in bredth eleven rod and one ffifth of a rod and a little better.

Allsoe in the ffort meddowe one parcell containing ffive Akars more or less proportioned at one Hundred and ninetye rod to an Akar as it lyes bounded by the land of Thomas dickinson South and Sam¹ moodies land and ye banke North abutting on the Great river west and the swampe East. Allsoe in the meddow called Hockanum one parcell containing ffoure Akars one roode and thirtye three pole more or lefse as it is proportioned at three roodes to an Akare bounded by the land Granted to Andrew bacon Nor'east and Jn° Crowe Sou'west abutting on the river Nor'west and the lotts running up the mountaine Southeast in bredth ffive rod and 4-10 of a rod : Allsoe over the river in Great pansett one parcell containing three Akars and one roode bounded by the land Granted to Mr. william westwood easterlye and Joseph baldwin westerlye. Abutting on the river Southerlye and a highwaye north-erlye in bredth ffive rod and 1-2.

Allsoe in litle pansett meddow one parcell two Akars and three roodes more or lefse proportioned at one Hundred and ffourtye rod to an Akar bounded by the land Granted to Joseph Fellong easterlye and Adam Nicholls Westerlye Abutting on the river Southerlye and the bank Northerlye In bredth ffoure rod.

All and every of which parcells of land lyeing and being within the bounds of the townshipp of Hadley with all the apurtenances and priviledges to all and every of whom belong the aforesaid towne of Hadley have ffreelye given to the said John marsh his heires executors and Afsigns fforever to have and to hould the same without any lett or molestation ffrom the s^d Towne or any other Claiming by ffrom or under them—

Copied from the original Proprietors Record of Peter Tillton.

CONN. RIVER

**HADLEY.**

*1663.*

Wm. Pixley.
John Gaylord.
John Ingram.

A. Nichols.

William Partrigg.

Thomas Coleman.

Samuel Smith.

Philip Smith.

Richard Montague.

John Dickinson.

Samuel Porter.

Thomas Wells.

John Hubbard.

Town Lot.

Mr. John Russell, Jr.

Samuel Gardner.

Chileab Smith.

Joseph Baldwin.

Robert Boltwood.

Francis Barnard.

John Hawks.

Richard Church.

Edward Church.

Meeting house.

*Highway.*

GREAT MEADOW.

Cemetery

N

*Middle highway to woods.*

Henry Clark.

Stephen Terry.

Andrew Warner.

John Marsh.

Timothy Nash.

John Webster.

William Goodwin.

John Crow.

Samuel Moody.

Nathaniel Ward.

William Markham.

Street 20 rods wide.

John Barnard.

Andrew Bacon.

Nathaniel Stanley.

Thomas Stanley.

John White.

Peter Tilton.

William Lewis.

Richard Goodman.

William Westwood.

Thomas Dickinson.

Nathaniel Dickinson.

*South highway to woods.*

John Russell, Sr.

Joseph Kellogg.

The John Marsh lot was occupied by John Marsh and his descendants from 1661 to 1821, one hundred and sixty years. The John Crow lot was occupied by Jonathan Marsh and his descendants, the Dickinsons, from 1673 to about 1840. The Wm. Lewis lot was occupied by Ebenezer Marsh and his descendants from 1710 to 1806. The Thomas Stanley lot was occupied by Capt. Job Marsh and his descendants from 1743 to 1820. The Nathaniel Stanley lot was occupied by Samuel Marsh and his descendants from 1745 to 1802. The Andrew Bacon lot was occupied by Capt. Moses Marsh from about 1740 to 1782.

The Samuel Porter lot was occupied by John Marsh[3] and his descendants from about 1722 to 1732.

# JOHN MARSH OF HARTFORD AND HIS DESCENDANTS.

*" Honor thy father and thy mother."*

## I. JOHN[1] MARSH,

Of England, Hartford, Ct. and Hadley, Mass., b. prob. 1618? in England, m. (1) abt. 1642, at Hartford, Ct., No. 2.

2. Anne, dau. Gov. John Webster. They had eight children, all born at Hartford. The family removed to Hadley in 1660, and, shortly after, Anne d. June 9, 1662, and he m. (2) Oct. 7, 1664, No. 3.

3. Hepzibah (Ford) Lyman, wid. Richard, dau. Thos. Ford of Hartford. She d. April 11, 1683, and John Marsh d. 28, Sept. 1688, æ. 70, at Windsor, Ct., prob. while on a visit to his daughter Hannah Loomis living there. Children, by first wife:

4. John, b. abt. 1643; m. Sarah Lyman, 45.
5. Samuel, b. abt. 1645; m. Mary Allison, 2821.
6. Joseph, bap. Jan. 24, 1647.
7. Isaac, bap. July 15, 1649; d. y.
8. Jonathan, b. Sept., 1649; m. Wid. Dorcas Dickinson, 3721.
9. Daniel, b. abt. 1653; m. Hannah Lewis, 3987.
10. Hannah, b. prob. 1655; m. Joseph Loomis, 14.
11. Grace, b. prob. 1657; m. Timothy Baker, 22.

By second wife :

12. Lydia, b. Oct. 9, 1667; m. David Loomis, 25.
John[1] Marsh had an adopted daughter,
13. Grace (Martin) Marsh; m. Nathaniel Phelps, 34. She was the daughter of his sister Lydia (Marsh) Martin. Tra-

ditional records say that "she had a false lover in England who married another. She came to Boston and was in danger of being sold for her passage." If so it is probable that her uncle rescued and adopted her as she is called his daughter in the document given later.

## 14 = 10.   HANNAH[2] MARSH

born prob.? 1655? (dau. John[1] and Anne) of Hadley; m. Jan. 28, 1775, No. 14.
    **14.** Joseph Loomis[3], of Windsor, Ct.,(John[2], Joseph[1]).  Children:
        15. Hannah, } b. Jan. 10, 1678.
        16. Ann,
        17. Joseph, b. Feb. 13, 1681.
        18. Joseph, b. Nov. 28, 1682.
        19. Grace, b. March 17, 1685.
        20. Lydia, b. April 15, 1686 ; d. æ. 16.
        21. Sarah, b. Jan. 8, 1693.

## 22 = 11.   GRACE[2] MARSH

b. prob.? 1657? (dau. John[1] and Anne) of Hadley, m. Jan. 26, 1673, Savage says Jan. 16, 1672, No. 22.
    **22.** Timothy Baker, son of Edward of Lynn and Northampton. She d. May 31, 1676.  They res. Northampton.  Children:
        23. Grace, b. 1673 ; d. Feb. 10, 1673.
        24. Timothy, b. 1675; d. y.; alive when will of John Marsh was made ; mentioned in the will of his grandfather who d. 1688.

## 25 = 12.   LYDIA[2] MARSH

b. Oct. 9, 1667 (dau. John[1] and Hepzibah) of Hadley; m. Dec. 8, 1692, No. 25.
    **25.** David Loomis of Windsor, Ct.  As youngest child she had £20, a double portion in her mother's will.  Children :
        26. Lydia, b. Oct. 21, 1693.
        27. David, b. Dec. 2, 1694.
        28. Aaron, b. Sept. 5, 1696.
        29. Hepzibah, b. Dec. 2, 1698.

30. Eliakim, b. July 27, 1701.
31. Elizabeth, b. Sept. 26, 1704.
32. Richard, b. Jan. 1, 1707.
33. Hannah, b. Aug. 2, 1709.


34 = 13.  GRACE MARTIN MARSH

adopted daughter of John[1] Marsh, b. 1656; d. Aug. 2, 1637, æ. 71;
m. Aug. 27, 1676, No. 34.

34.  Nathaniel[4] Phelps of Northampton, Mass., b. 1653; d. June
20, 1719, æ. 66 (Nathaniel[3], Timothy[2]. William[1]) and so gave a tinge
of Marsh blood to the Phelps and Huntington families of Hadley
including the Bishop.  Children :

35. Grace, b. Nov. 11, 1677?
36. Nathaniel, b. Nov. 1, 1678; d. May 1, 1690.
37. Samuel, b. Dec. 9, 1680; m. Dec. 12, 1706, Mary Edwards.
38. Lydia, b. Jan. 17, 1683; m. 1701, Mark Warner.
39. Grace, b. Nov 10, 1685; m. 1713, Samuel Marshall.
40. Elizabeth, b. Feb. 16, 1688; m. 1724, Jonathan Wright.
41. Abigail, b. Nov. 3, 1690; m. 1708, John Langton.
42. Nathaniel, b. Feb. 13, 1692; m. Abigail Burnham.
43. Sarah, b. May 8, 1695.
44. Timothy, b. 1697.


The following document from records in the office of the Secretary
of State of Conn. of date May 15, 1705, shows who were the then
living children of John Marsh and also gives light as to his sisters
and brother in England.

"John Marsh Heirs: Letters of attorney to Joseph Merrian and Mr. Allyn
Buckham in England.  To all people to whom these presents shall come:
We, John Marsh, Samuel Marsh, Jonathan Marsh, Daniel Marsh, Hannah
Marsh, Lydia Marsh and Grace Phelps, seven of the nephews and nieces of
Joseph Marsh the older of late of Braintree in the county of Essex, clothier,
deceased, residing in New England, Send greeting in our Lord God Ever-
lasting.

Whereas the said Joseph Marsh the older, the Testator, in and by his last
will and Testament, in writing bearing date on or about the two and twentieth day of May, Anno Domini one thousand six hundred seventy and six,
did (amongst other things) give, bequeath, demise and appoint in those words
or in words to the effect following (viz,) Item: I give and bequeath my freehold lands and tenements lying in Braintree, called by the name of Clay

Hills, or by any other name or names whatsoever, now in the occupation of
John Harris, unto my Sister Grace Tyres during the term of her natural life,
and after [her] decease my will is that my said Freehold Lands be sold by
my executors and trustees within one year after her decease and the money
arising thereof be equally divided among my sister Shorey's two sons and my
brother John Marsh's children, and my sister Martin's children, excepting
sixty pounds to the Executors and Possessors in trust for funeral expenses
and other charges, and as for my personal estate I give and bequeath to my
Executors and Executrix only my wearing apparel to John Shorey and forty
shillings to the poor in Braintree to be paid within three months after my
decease at the discretion of mine Executor or Executrix hereinafter named,
and I do hereby nominate [and] appoint my well beloved sister Grace Tyres
Executrix and my kinsman Joseph Marsh Executor of this my last will and
testament and I do request my loving friends Richard Thurlow of Cambridge,
Folmonger, Nathaniel Tyres, my brother-in-law, and William Ward of Taw-
ling, Possessors in trust and overseers, to see this my last will and testament performed as by the said will, relation being thereunto had, may appear.

And whereas the said Grace Tyres died about the fifteenth day of March
in the year of our Lord one thousand six hundred ninety and six, the said
Richard Thurlow, Nathaniel Tyres and Wm. Ward being also dead, and
whereas by a decretal order made in the court of Exchequer Chamber at
Westminister on Thursday the seven and twentieth day of June in the
twelfth year of the King, our late sovereighn Lord the King William the
third, in a cause therein impending wherein John Shorey the older of Braintree in the County of Essex [husband] of Mary Shorey who was sister of
Joseph Marsh the older of the same place, Clothier, John Shorey the younger
and Joseph Shorey, children of the said John Shorey the older, Robert
Exton of London, carmonger, and Mary his wife, one of the daughters of
Lydia Martin who was one of the other sisters of the said Joseph Marsh the
older, Lydia Kemphouse, widow, Sarah Conner, widow, Elizabeth, widow,
now the wife of Butcher, and Anna Porter, widow, daughters of the said
Lydia Martin, John Marsh, Samuel Marsh, Jonathan Marsh, Daniel Marsh,
Hannah Marsh and Lydia Marsh and Grace Phelps, all sons and daughters
of John Marsh who was brother of said Joseph Marsh the older, Plaintiffs
and the said Joseph Marsh Executor party to these presents Defendant: It
was among other things ordered and decreed that the said Estate of the said
Joseph Marsh, the Testator, should be forthwith sold to the best purchaser
and the money arising by sale thereof and what should remain over from the
defendants upon account therein mentioned, should be paid [and] divided
among the plaintiffs and the defendants as legatees and devisees in the will
of the said Joseph Marsh the Testator, pursuant to the direction thereof, and
that the amount coming due to such of the Plaintiffs as were not present,
should be paid to their order or assigns, and in default of such order or
assigns then to remain in the purchaser's hands for the use of such absent
persons, upon his giving security to answer and pay the same and that the
Plaintiffs' Defendants might procure one or more bid[d]er or bid[d]ers, pur-

chaser or purchasers for the said estate, and that the defendants should [each] convey all his [or her] right, title, interest, property, claim and demand whatsoever of and to the said Estate and premises, unto the person that should be the best bid[d]er, upon payment of such sums of money as should be agreed on for the sale of the premises; and whereas by an order of the same court, made and pronounced the fifth day of Dec. Anno Domini one thousand and seven hundred in the same (court) it is mentioned that the aforesaid Jonathan Boulder has bid more than any other person who offered to purchase the said premises, it was thereupon ordered, adjudged and decreed by the said court that the said Jonathan Boulder should be the purchaser of the same for the sum of one hundred and seventy one pounds, and that upon payment thereof the said defendants Marsh should convey the said premises unto the said Jonathan Boulder and his heirs and that the said defendants should deliver unto him the possession of the said premises and all deeds and writings conveying the same and that the said Jonathan Boulder should thereupon pay so much of the purchase money as would satisfy the said Defendant [This means the "Kinsman Joseph Marsh" the only living Executor or Possessor in trust] the aforesaid legacy of sixty pounds cash, deducting what was remaining in his hands for the rents and profits of said premises; and that he the said Jonathan Boulder should pay unto each of the nephews and nieces of the testator that were in England their several proportions of the said purchase money, and the residue thereof unto such of the said testators other nephews and nieces as were over broad sea, or their lawful Representatives empowered to see the same, when such person or persons or their Representatives should demand it and give proper discharges for the sums to them respectively due; and that the said Jonathan Boulder and his heirs should hold and enjoy the said premises and be quiet in the possession of the sums by the authority of this court against the complainants and defendants and all persons claiming by, from or under him, them or any of them or by, from or under the will of Joseph Marsh deceased, or in or and by the several orders remaining on record in the said court that, relation thereunto being had, may appear:

And whereas we, whose hands and seals are hereunto set and subscribed, are credibly informed that Jonathan Boulder of the parish of St. Mary Magdalene Bromondsay in the county of Surray Distiller hath actually purchased the said Estate pursuant to the said decree for the sum of one hundred and sentyone pounds of lawful money of England and hath paid to said executor and such of the said legatees and relatives of said Testator as do reside in old England their seven shares and proportion thereof, being six pounds two shillings eleven pence and one farthing apiece, as by a certain indenture of release bearing date the twenty third day of June Anno Domini one thousand seven hundred and one made between said Joseph Marsh the Executor of the first part, the said Jonathan Boulder of the second part and Thomas Tyres of the said Parish of St. Mary Magdalene Bromondsay in said county of Surry, Merchant and Thomas Danning of London, gent., of the third part, relation being had thereto and to a schedule indented thereunto may more fully and at large appear.

3

Now know that we the said John Marsh, Samuel Marsh, Jonathan Marsh, Daniel Marsh, Hannah Marsh, Lydia Marsh and Grace Phelps, Have, and every one of us hath, nominated, constituted, appointed and in our place put, and by these presents do, and every one of us doth, nominate, constitute, appoint and in our stead and place respectively put, our trusty friends Joseph Merrian, formerly of Boston in New England, gent., now residing in London and Allyn Buckham of the Parish of St. Johns, Wapping, Distiller, our two lawful and irrevocable attorneys, jointly or severally for us and every one of us, in our and in every one of our name or names, and for our and every one of our respective use, to ask, demand, receive and take of the said Jonathan Boulder, his heirs or assigns our several respective shares of the said purchase money and upon receipt thereof [to make] one or more release or releases of and for the same in our and everyone of our respective name or names, or in the name of himself for us, and every of our respective name, place and account and [to] execute and deliver and upon payment thereof or any part thereof to take such due course and use such lawful ways and means for us and in our name or names, and for our use and benefit respectively, as our said attorneys or either of them shall in our behalf think fit or be advised, giving hereby unto our said attorneys and to either of them our full and whole strength and authority in and about the premises, ratifying and confirming, and each and every one of us do hereby confirm and allow all and whatsoever our attorney shall lawfully do, or cause to be done in and about the same.

In witness whereof we and every one of us have hereunto set and subscribed our respective hands and seals this fifteenth day of May Anno Domini one thousand and seven hundred and five, in the fourth year of the Reign of our *late* Sovereign Lady Ann, by the grace of God [Queen] of England, Scotland, France and Ireland and *was* defender of the Faith.

JOHN MARSH,
SAMUEL MARSH,
JONATHAN MARSH,
DANIEL MARSH,
the mark [x] of Hannah Loomis,
DAVID LOOMIS in behalf of Lydia his wife,
NATHANIEL PHELPS in behalf of Grace his wife.

Rev. Christopher Marsh of W. Roxbury, Mass. reports as to John Marsh, " He was brother of Joseph Marsh of Braintree from which he certifies at Hartford 7 Nov., 1681, that he received money." This would imply that John was remembered directly by his brother. By the above document we learn that Joseph Marsh's will was made May 22, 1676; that under it Grace (Marsh) Tyres held the Clay Hills property until her death, March 15, 1696; that June 27, 1700 a decretal order was made in the Court at Westminster for the sale of this property to the highest bidder; that Dec. 5, 1700 the same court decreed that Jonathan Boulder be the purchaser for £171, and that the seven heirs in England having received about $30.75 apiece, release was given to him June 23, 1701, and that the seven heirs in America were now, May 15, 1705, seeking their share that would cost them more than their English cousins and if equal would only be £6, 2s. 11d. and one farthing apiece or some $215 in all. The lawyers and courts up to 1705, seem to have been nine years about it and to have taken over 20 per cent. of what they divided.

These are the names of the brothers and sisters in the order given in the will :

1. Joseph Marsh, will dated May 22, 1676.
2. Grace Marsh, m. Nathaniel Tyres and d. March 15, 1696.
3. Mary Marsh, m. John Shorey. Sons, John and Joseph.
4. John Marsh, b. 1618.
5. Lydia Marsh, m. —— Martin. Her children: 1, Mary; 2, Lydia; 3, Sarah; 4, Elizabeth; 5, Ann; 6, Grace, b. 1656, who came to her Uncle John Marsh in America and m. Nathaniel Phelps.

# BRANCH I.  THE HARTFORD BRANCH.

## 45 = 4.  JOHN[2] MARSH

Of Hartford, Hadley and Hartford, (John[1] and Anne [Webster]
Marsh of Hartford and Hadley) b. abt. 1643 ; m. (1) Nov. 28, 1666,
No. 45.

**45.** Sarah Lyman of Northampton, (dau. Richard and Hepzibah
[Ford] Lyman, who had become his father's second wife.) They
both had been born in Hartford, Conn., and after marriage returned
to Hartford and resided on the old Marsh homestead.  He was for
six years a selectman of Hartford 1677, '81, '87, time of Charter
Oak trouble, '88, '94, 1701.  In 1700 he was on a committee to build
a bridge over the Hockanum river in East Hartford.  His wife
received £10 by her mother's will.  She d. between 1688 and 1707,
and her late husband m. (2) Jan. 1, 1707-8, No. 46.

**46.** Susannah Butler, who d. Dec. 24, 1714.  Was she dau. of
Wm. Butler whose lot was next north?  His brother Daniel m. the
daughter of Wm. Lewis whose lot was next east.  He d. in 1727,
æ. 85.  Children by first wife :

47. John[3], b. 1668; m. Mabel Pratt, 91, and Elizabeth Pitkin, 92.
48. Nathaniel, } bap. March 5, 1671,  m. Elizabeth Spencer, 85a.
49. Joseph,    }                      m. Hannah, 1720.
50. Sarah, bap. Feb. 17, 1673 ; m. John Merrill, 59.
51. Elizabeth, bap. June 27, 1675 ; she or Lydia m. Joseph Pratt, 71.
52. Hannah, bap. Dec. 3, 1677 ; d. y.
53. Ebenezer, bap. Feb. 23, 1679; prob. d. y.
54. Hannah, bap. April 10, 1681 ; m. Dea. Olmsted, 72.
55. Lydia, bap. Jan. 13, 1684 ; she or Elizabeth m. Joseph Pratt, 71.
56. Hepzibah, bap. June 6, 1686 ; m. Jonathan Wadsworth, 84.

57. Jonathan, bap. Aug. 7, 1688; m. (1) Elizabeth Wadsworth,
    2400 ; m. (2) Elizabeth Loomis, 2401.
                    By second wife.
58. Susannah, b. Feb. 5, 1710-11.

A word here as to John Marsh's well.   At a meeting of the Marsh
Family Association in Hartford, Conn. in Aug., 1887, John E. Marsh,
Esq. of that city pointed out at the intersection of Temple and Front
streets the location of the old Marsh homestead and well of 1639.
Of the old well Mr. Allyn Stanley Kellogg, one of John Marsh's
descendants, writes pleasantly and truly.   Having written that Hannah[3] Marsh (John[2], John[1]) married Dea. Joseph Olmstead and that
in 1710 their daughter Hannah[4] married Caleb Stanley his ancestor,
he adds :  " I have observed that in former times matrimonial alliances
seemed often to result from *neighborly associations*.   The above named
Caleb Stanley was a son of Caleb Stanley, Jr., Secretary of the
Colony, who lived on a part of the original homelot of his grandfather Timothy Stanley ; the homelot adjoining that of John Marsh
and south of it.   As the second John Marsh succeeded to the occupancy of his father's homelot the young Caleb Stanley and Hannah
Olmstead would easily become acquainted while the latter was visiting
her grandfather.   They would drink water from the same well, in the
line between the two homelots, as appears by the agreement made for
using it in common by John Marsh and Capt. Caleb Stanley."
    It is asked did John[2] Marsh have a daughter Ruth?   His brother
Samuel had a daughter Ruth born 1685, also a daughter Elizabeth, b.
1683, who m. Oct. 27, 1714, Maynard Day of Hartford and this
probably came from the m. of Ruth Marsh to Wm. Cadwell of Hartford, Oct. 31, 1711.   We have at Hartford Second church the baptisms
seemingly of all of John's[2] children except John[3] the oldest whose
birth was probably at Northampton or Hadley.   This excludes Ruth.
    Did John Skinner marry a daughter of John[2] Marsh?   He is
called by John[3] repeatedly in accounts " Brother John Skinner,"
from 1709 to 1721.   He m. Rachel Pratt, Feb. 22, 1693 and she outlived him.   John[3] Marsh's first wife was Mabel Pratt, and John[3]
Marsh and Elizabeth (Pitkin) Marsh, his 2d wife, were witnesses
to John Skinner's will 1741.   As the two men married sisters, from
this probably came the strong friendship and brotherhood.   Lydia[3]
born 1684 could *not* have m. Skinner as early as 1693 and it was hardly

probable that Elizabeth³ b. 1675, m. before 1691 or 1692 when only 16 or 17. Either Elizabeth or Lydia seem to have married Joseph Pratt their father's "son-in-law" according to his will; and both seem to have died before their father's death in 1727. He makes no allusion to them in his will which we here give. John Skinner and Hezekiah Goodwin were on the inventory of his estate in 1727.

Hartford, Ct., Probate Records, 10 : 162, Aug. 1, 1727.

"The last will and Testament of John Marsh late of Hartford, deceasᵈ was now exhibited by [page broken] John Marsh, Nathaniel Marsh and Jonathan Marsh, Executors named in sᵈ Will," etc. Inventory also exhibited. 12 : 27, 28. Will of John Marsh, Senʳ. recorded.

Will copied from the original, on file, in perfect preservation. Endorsed, "Last Will, Serg't John Marsh, July, 1727."

The last will and Testament of John Marsh Senʳ, of Hartford in the county of Hartford in the colony of Connecticut in New England.

As god hath given the earth to the children of men dividing it to every one severally as he will, and doth Indulge to them the liberty of disposing their worldly Estates in a testamentary way to such as are to succeed them in the enjoyment thereof, and their doing this seasonably and in a just and prudent manner, Being a likely means to prevent after trouble and contention about it, therefore I who am old, and now languishing under those decays of Nature which forebode a speedy dissolution of it, do with submission to the will of God, make the following disposition of that part of the Earth which through his goodness is yet continued, In my possession.

- Impr : My will is that all my just debts and funeral expences be first paid without fraud or delay.

Item : I give to each of my daughters now living, besides what they have allready received, ten pounds, to be paid within a year after my decease, Either out of my lands att Inventory price, or in current pay of this colony, att the Election of my Executors, yet with this proviso that they bear their several proportions of the debts and charges before mentioned.

Item : I give to the children of my daughter lately deceased, ten pounds, over and above what she received In her life time, to be divided equally among them, and paid as the above said sums and upon the same condition.

Item : I Give to my son In law Joseph Pratt, five shillings.

Item : the rest of my Estate, that is to say all my lands not otherwise disposed of, whether divided or undivided I give to my sons to be equally divided between them. Excepting that I give forty shillings more to my Eldest son than to either of his brethren.

Lastly I do appoint and constitute my sons Executors of this my last will and testament.

And In confirmation of all that is above willed I have hereto set or caused

to beset my hand and seal this     day of     In the year of our lord one
thousand seven Hundred twenty six.

his<br>
JOHN [X] MARSH     [seal]<br>
mark.

In presence of us,
  SAMLL GREENE
  HEZEKIAH GOODWIN
  JOHN DAY.
           On the same paper, July 15, 1727,
  [Samuel Green made oath before Hez. Wyllys, Just. Pac⁵. that he saw John
Marsh sign his mark, and seal the above, etc. Aug. 1, 1727. Hez. Goodwin
made oath to the same effect.]

10 : 174.   Jan. 8, 172 7-8.

Capt. John Marsh Lt. Nathaniell Marsh Capt. Joseph Marsh and Jonathan
Marsh, sons heires and Executors of the Last Will and Testament of John
Marsh late of Hartford deceasᵈ, now exhibited an agreement under their
hands and seals for a settlement of sᵈ Estate to and amongst the heires, and
before this Court acknowledged the same to be their free act and deed, which
agreement is by this Court accepted and ordered to be recorded and kept on
file. [No reference to the record of this paper is *found by me*, in the Index.]

Paper on File, dated Jan. 6, 1727–8.

|            |                       |      |      |    |     |
|------------|-----------------------|------|------|----|-----|
| To John Marsh | (lands described, amt. | 75 | 00 | 00) |
| " Nathaniel | "                    | "  | "  | 73 | 00 | 00 |
| " Joseph | "                      | "  | "  | 72 | 00 | 00 |
| " Jonathan | "                    | "  | "  | 73 | 00 | 00 |

" And wee do further agree to pay what debts may be due from our father's
Estate in equal proportion. Also agreed that the remaining part of the
second Meadow Lott to the value of fifty shull shillings to be equally divided
between Joseph and Jonathan.

JOHN MARSH,<br>
NATHANIEL MARSH,<br>
JOSEPH MARSH,<br>
JONATHAN MARSH.

Mem. Bond, Dated Jan. 8, 1727–8.

A bond is filed with the above paper, signed by these four sons of John
Marsh, Decd :
  " The condition of the above written obligation is such ,that whereas John
Marsh late of Hartford, Deceased in and by his last Will and Testament
bequeath Legacies viz. To his daughter Sarah Ten pounds, To his daughter
Hannah Ten pounds, To his daughter Ann Ten pounds, and to the children
of his daughter Hepziba Deceased Ten pounds, To his son in law Joseph
Pratt five shillings " etc.

Copied by Allyn S. Kellogg, Hartford, Ct., Oct. 7, 1889.

## 59 = 50.   SARAH[3] MARSH

of Hartford, Conn., dau. John[2] and Sarah (Lyman) Marsh (John[1])
bap. Hartford Second church, Feb. 17, 1673; m. Sept. 29, 1694,
No. 59.

**59.** John[2] Merrill of Hartford (son of John[1] and Sarah [Watson]
Merrill) b. April 7, 1669; d. 1748. He gave to his wife Sarah one-
third moveable estate and use of one-half housing and lands.
Children:

60. John[4], b. Sept. 29, 1695; m. Lydia, res. W. Hartford until abt.
1734, then in New Hartford; d. 1762.

61. Sarah, b. Jan. 13, 1696-7; m. June 27, 1723, Stephen Olmsted
and d. before 1748. Their son Roger m. Eunice Marsh
of New Hartford.

62. Ebenezer, b. Dec. 18, 1698; m. prob. (2) wife April 9, 1730,
Mrs. Mary (Burnham) Webster, Wid. Capt. Stephen of
Hartford. Rem. from W. Hartford 1734-7 to New
Hartford and d. there 1789.

63. Elizabeth, bap. April 27, 1701.

64. Nathaniel, b. July 15, 1702; m. Nov. 16, 1729, Esther Warner, dau. Dr. Ephraim and Esther (Richards) Warner
of Waterbury, Ct. and d. there Oct. 28, 1772.

65. Anne, b. Nov. 16, 1704; m. Matthew Gillett, res. New
Hartford.

66. Caleb, b. July 14, 1707; m. Aug. 2, 1733, Mercy Sedgwick, dau. Sam'l and Mary (Hopkins) Sedgwick, b. Feb.
16, 1713; res. W. Hartford and d. Sept. 24, 1735, and
she m. (2) Ebenezer Mix and d. June 16, 1745. One
son Abijah and dau. Mercy.

67. Lydia, b. Nov. 24, 1709 in Hartford; unm. 1748.

68. Aaron, bap. May 6, 1711; m. April 9, 1640, Esther; res. W.
Hartford and d. 1747; Wid. d. there Nov. 29, 1798, æ. 85.

69. Cyprian, bap. Oct. 11, 1713; m. Elizabeth; res. W. Hartford
until after 1753, then in New Hartford; d. 1758.

70. Benjamin, mentioned only in his father's will.

## 71 = 51.   ELIZABETH[3] MARSH

of Hartford, Conn., dau. John[2] and Sarah (Lyman) Marsh, (John[1])
bap. June 27, 1675 was perhaps the daughter who m. "Joseph Pratt"
71, and made him "son-in-law" of her father.

## 72 = 54. HANNAH[3] MARSH

of Hartford, Conn., dau. of John[2] and Sarah (Lyman) Marsh (John[1])
bap. April 10, 1681 ; m. No. 72.

72. Dea. Joseph Olmsted of East Hartford, b. 1674. She d.
Aug. 22, 1760. He d. Feb. 25, 1762. Children :

73. Joseph[4], b. May 25, 1705 ; m. Martha White, Nov. 1, 1732,
Enfield.
74. Jonathan, b. Nov. 14, 1706 ; m. Dec. 28, 1738 Hannah Meaken.
He d. Dec. 9, 1770. She d. July 27, 1806.
75. William, b. Sept. 4, 1708 ; m. Elizabeth Pitkin.
76. Hannah, b. Aug. 6, 1810; m. Nov. 8, 1735, Caleb Stanley·
She d. Aug. 29, 1770. He d. June 28, 1789, Coventry.
77. Mabel, b. July 29, 1712 ; m. Jonathan Stanley. She d. June
17, 1774. He d. Aug. 20, 1788.
78. Asahel, b. Nov. 19, 1714 ; m. Hannah Pitkin. He d. Sept. 15,
1750. She d. March 26, 1783.
79. Sarah, b. Nov. 10, 1716 ; m. Feb. 5, 1742, Elisha Burnham.
He d. July 18, 1770. She d. Sept. 3, 1810.
80. Anna, b. Nov. 30, 1718 ; m. Jan. 14, 1741, Russel Woodbridge.
He d. Nov. 5, 1782. She d. 1808.
81. Naomi, b. March 1, 1721 ; m. (1) Capt. Gideon Wolcott, who
d. June 5, 1761 ; m. (2) Wm. Wolcott, Grad. Yale, 1734.
She d. Nov. 7, 1775, South Windsor.
82. Elihu, b. May 7, 1723 ; d. June 3, 1723.
83. Ashbel, b. Feb. 1, 1725-6; m. Nov. 3, 1757, Hannah Newberry. He d. May 17, 1791. She d. Feb. 5, 1806.

## 84 = 56. HEPZIBAH[3] MARSH

dau. John[2] and Sarah (Lyman) Marsh (John[1]) of Hartford, bap. June
6, 1686 ; m. Nov. 29, 1711, No. 84.

84. Jonathan Wadsworth of Hartford, son of Joseph Wadsworth
of Charter Oak fame, b. 1687 ; d. 1739. The Wadsworth family
has been a great blessing to Hartford ; and the Atheneum, as well as
the story of the Charter Oak, is a credit to their name and memory.
Hepzibah d. 1724. Children :

85. Hepzibah[4], b. Sept. 13, 1712 ; m. Hezekiah Collyer ; d. Nov.
20, 1770.
86. Hannah, b. July 8, 1714 ; m. Oct. 26, 1733, Daniel Bull.
87. Samuel, b. Oct. 25, 1716 ; m. Meliscent Cook of Harwinton
and d. Dec. 29, 1798.
88. Abigail, b. April 10, 1718.
89. Rebecca, b. Sept. 16, 1720 ; d. y.
90. Helena, b. June 2, 1724 ; d. Sept. 23, 1796.

By second wife Abigail Flagg, Mr. Wadsworth had four children.

# SKETCH OF THE FOUNDER OF LITCHFIELD.

## JOHN[3] MARSH

of Hartford, Litchfield and Hartford again was born in Hadley or Northampton, Mass. in 1668, the oldest son of John[2] and Sarah (Lyman) Marsh. All his children but one, the youngest, settled in Litchfield, Ct.

His boyhood and young manhood were spent at Hartford. Even in that focus of colonial authority and select thought he early attracted public attention. In 1704, at the age of 36 he became one of the selectmen as also in 1710 and 1714. He was then chosen by Hartford to explore its dimly known western lands; all Litchfield County except Waterbury on the south, being then unsettled. In 1715 he was the first Anglo-Saxon recorded to have trodden in that wilderness, and for 15 years his fortunes became connected with all the pioneer life of the County town, Litchfield, where later was the first ladies' seminary and for over 50 years the Gould Law School, then the most celebrated in America. The earliest record of the visit of any white man to that locality is as follows:

> " The Town of Hartford,
>
> Dr. to John Marsh
>
> May 1715, For 5 days, man and horse with expenses in viewing the
> Land at the New Plantation £2 0 0 "

He was commissioned by the Conn. Colony Lieut., May 17, 1717 and in May, 1722 Capt. and Justice of the Peace for Litchfield. The name John Marsh, for the first third of the History of Litchfield, occurs upon nearly every page, as the first explorer, one of the first selectmen, the first town clerk, an office he held for nine years, and at the beginning or end of nearly every public document in town transactions or acts of the Legislature. He is first of the list of proprietors. He drew second choice of village lots and chose next to Bantam river where he was appointed to erect a grist mill.

In 1724 Indians were hostile, the Legislature directed that mounts be built within the forts ; houses were fortified and a council of war was chosen in the record of whose acts John Marsh's name comes first. In 1726 thirty effective men were ordered by the Legislature to Litchfield, twenty from New Haven and ten from Wallingford, to be under the command of Capt. John Marsh for the defense of the town.

His name, as Lt. John Marsh of Hartford, and that of Dea. John Buell are the only ones recorded in the colonial patent for holding the Litchfield lands given to the settlers in the names of Kings Charles the II. and George.

That he did not relinquish hold upon Hartford appears in his being chosen selectman there in 1730, æ. 62, and again in 1735, æ. 67. The History of Litchfield thus sums up :

" The two most conspicuous and useful men among the original proprietors of the township were John Marsh and John Buell.

John Marsh had long been a prominent citizen of Hartford before he interested himself in the Western Lands; and from the time when he came out to 'view the new plantation,' in May, 1715, till about the year 1738, his name was intimately associated with the history of Litchfield. I need not recapitulate the many ways and times in which he was called upon by his fellow citizens to serve them in public employments, as detailed on the preceeding pages. He served this town in the various offices within her gift during the entire period of his residence here.

While an inhabitant of Hartford, he was often a Representative in the Legislature, a Justice of the Peace, an Associate Judge of the County Court, and a member of the Council of War. He returned to Hartford in his old age and died there. His remains lie interred in the old Burying Ground back of the Center Church. His children remained in this town, and his descendants here and elsewhere are very numerous."

After his return to Hartford he was ordered in 1732 by the Gen.
Court to build a church for the Second Society of Farmington. He
was appointed by Hartford to lay out two Conn. towns. The Conn.
Legislature met twice a year and I find record "Capt. John Marsh
rep'd Hartford 40 sessions." His oldest adult son represented
Litchfield 48 sessions. In 1744, the year of his death, John[3] Marsh
was on the war committee.

His will is in Hartford records and his great-great-grandson John[7]
E. Marsh, Esq., of Hartford is in possession of his very interesting
account book, which was also used by Hezekiah[4] Marsh the youngest
son of John[3] and Elizabeth (Pitkin) Marsh, the only one to return
with his father and keep up the family line at Hartford, all the others
settling at Litchfield.

In her will Elizabeth (Pitkin) Marsh leaves property "To my dau.
Elizabeth" and "To my sons Eben., Wm., Isaac, Geo., John, Tim.,
Hez."

---

## BRANCH I. DIVISION I. THE LITCHFIELD LINE.

---

### 91 = 47.   CAPT. JOHN[3] MARSH

b. 1668 [prob. at Hadley] of Hartford, Litchfield and Hartford, son
of John[2] and Sarah (Lyman) Marsh, (John[1]) res. Hartford and
pioneer Litchfield, Ct.; m. (1) Dec. 12, 1695, No. 91.

**91.** Mabel Pratt, who d. June 6, 1696. He m. (2) Jan. 6, 1698,
No. 92.

**92.** Elizabeth Pitkin. John[3] Marsh and Elizabeth his wife were
received to full communion March 15, 1712–13. He d. Oct. 1, 1744.
Elizabeth (Pitkin) Marsh, d. Hartford, Dec. 1, 1748, and their gravestones still stand by Centre Church. Children:

93. John[4], b. Jan. 31, bap. Feb. 4, 1699-1700; d. æ. 13.
94. Ebenezer, b. Nov. 3, bap. Nov. 11, 1701; m. Deborah Buell, 104.
95. Elizabeth, b. Nov. 20, bap. Nov. 23, 1703; m. John Bird, 102 and Wm. or Henry Cook, 103.
96. William, b. June, bap. July 1, 1706; m. Susanna Webster, 240.
97. George, b. Feb., bap. Feb. 29, 1708; m. Lydia Bird, 264.
98. Isaac, b. Nov. 8, bap. Nov. 27, 1709; m. Susanna Pratt, 558.
99. John, b. Oct. 20, bap. Nov. 2, 1712; m. Sarah Webster, 622.
100. Timothy, b. Oct. 1, 1714, bap. Sept.(?) 19, 1714; m. Sarah Nott, 680.
101. Hezekiah, b. April 26, bap. May 1, 1720; m. (1) Christian Edwards, 688.


## 102 = 95. ELIZABETH[4] MARSH

b. Hartford, Ct., Nov. 20, 1703, dau. of John[3] and Elizabeth (Pitkin) Marsh, (John[2], John[1]). See Litchfield *Enquirer* of Aug. 3, 1844, account of the Picnic, page 3; m. (1) No. 102.

**102.** John Bird; m. (2) No. 103.

**103.** Henry(?) Cook. Her father's accounts mention John Bird 1723-4 and 6, and Henry Cook a year or two later, and his will twice mentions "my daughter Elizabeth Cook" with a legacy of thirty pounds.


## 104 = 94. COL. EBENEZER[4] MARSH

of Litchfield, Ct., b. Hartford, Ct., Nov. 3, 1701, son of John[3] and Elizabeth (Pitkin) Marsh, (John[2], John[1]) Judge of Probate, Judge Co. Court, Rep. 48 sessions, Selectman from 1740, 13 years; m. abt. 1725, No. 104.

**104.** Deborah Buell, was the dau. of John and Mary (Loomis) Buell, b. Jan 24, 1708. He d. April, 1733, æ. 71 years and 5 months. She d. July, 1784, æ. 77. Children:

105. Deborah[5], b. Nov. 9, 1726; m. Archippus McCall, 117.
106. Elizabeth, b. Feb. 10, 1729-30; m. Nathaniel Goodwin, 120.
107. Lois, b. March 3, 1731; m. Mark Prindle, 129.
108. Hannah, b. March 24, 1733; m. (1) Edward Phelps, 130; m. (2) Mark Prindle.
109. Solomon, b. Feb. 10, 1735-6; m. Jerusha Marsh, 153.

110.   Ebenezer, b. March 4, 1737 ; d. May 12, 1737.
111.   Anna, b. May 25, 1738 ; m. John[5] Marsh, 630.
112.   Ebenezer, b. Oct. 7, 1740 ; m. (1) Lucy Phelps, 182.
113.   Ozias, b. April 5, 1743 ; d. 1760.
114.   Hepzibah, b. Aug. 29, 1745 ; m. Dr. Samuel Catlin, 140.
115.   John. b. Jan. 4, 1748 ; m. Rhoda McNiel, 229.
116.   Molly, b. Nov. 24, 1752 ; m. Moses Seymour, 141.


### 117 = 105.   DEBORAH[5] MARSH

of Litchfield, Ct., b. Nov. 9, 1726, dau. of Col. Ebenezer[4] and Deborah (Buell) Marsh (John[3], John[2], John[1]) ; m. No. 117.

**117.**   Archippus McCall of Goshen, Ct., spoken of as " prob. of Lebanon, had son Capt. Hobart McCall farmer at Lebanon, Ct." In the Litchfield *Enquirer's* account of " The Great Family Picnic of the Buells and Marshes " published Aug. 3, 1844, Deborah (Marsh) McCall is called " the mother of Mrs. Levi Coe and of a large family of McCalls of Lebanon." Children :

118.   Hobart, b. March 26, 1750; m. Sept. 30, 1773, Lucy Strong, four children, see Strong Genealogy.
119.   Mrs. Levi Coe.


### 120 = 106.   ELIZABETH[5] MARSH

of Litchfield, Ct., b. Feb. 10, 1729–30, dau. of Col. Ebenezer[4] and Deborah (Buell) Marsh (John[3], John[2], John[1]) ; m. No. 120.

**120,**   Nathaniel Goodwin, son of Abraham and Mary (Bird) Goodwin, b. Oct. 31, 1727 who d. May 18, 1777 of small pox. She d. Dec. 14, 1802. Children :

121.   Elizabeth[6], b. Aug. 2, 1752 ; d. Sept. 8, 1753.
122.   Solomon, b. April 26, 1755.
123.   James, b. April 18, 1757.
124.   Nathaniel, b. Feb. 4, 1760.
125.   Elizabeth, b. Jan 13, 1763. Elizabeth or Chloe m. Samuel Waugh.
126.   Chloe, b. Bible record, July 31, 1766, town, Aug. 14, 1766.
127.   Dorcas, b. Jan. 8, 1770, m. June 23, 1788 (?) Ozias Marsh, 637.
128.   Erastus, b. Dec. 19, 1772.
128.1   Lydia, b. Sept. 4, 1775 ; m. ——— Loveland.

## 129 = 107. LOIS⁵ MARSH

of Litchfield, Ct., b. March 3, 1731, dau. of Col. Ebenenzer⁴ and Deborah (Buell) Marsh (John³, John², John¹); m. No. 129.

**129.** Mark Prindle, who after her death m. her sister, the widow of Edward Phelps. Hon. Origen S. Seymour in his address in 1844 at the gathering at Bantam Lake, Litchfield, of not less than 1000 persons at the " Great Family Picnic of the Buells and Marshes " calls Mrs. Lois (Marsh) Prindle the mother of a family of that name now (1844) in Vermont.


## 130 = 108. HANNAH⁵ MARSH

of Litchfield, Ct., b. March 24, 1733, dau. of Col. Ebenezer⁴ and Deborah (Buell) Marsh (John³, John², John¹); m. (1) No. 130.

**130.** Edward Phelps of Litchfield and m. (2) as second wife, Mark Prindle. He d. May 28, 1804, æ. 70. Hon. O. S. Seymour gives her children :

    131. Capt. John Phelps⁶, father of No. 132.

      132. Samuel Shether⁷ Phelps, b.May 13, 1793 on Chestnut Hill, Litchfield; Yale college, 1811; Litchfield law school, settled in Middlebury, Vt.; paymaster, 1812 ; Col., Judge Vt. Supreme court; U. S. Senator, 1838-1850. " As a lawyer and statesman he ranked with Clay, Webster, Crittenden and Clayton. He d. in 1857. "Webster often saying that there was no man whom he felt to be so formidable in opposition before the Supreme court as " Sam. Phelps," and the Washington *Globe* that no man ever came to Washington who had so great an influence with the National administration. He was the father of Hon. Edward J. Phelps of Burlington, Vt.

   133. Mrs. David Pierpont. Had sons 134 and 135.

     134. Robert Pierpont, b. Litchfield, May 4, 1791; lawyer of Rutland, Vt.; Lieut. Governor and Judge of the Supreme Court of Vermont.

     135. John Pierpont, b. Litchfield, Sept. 10, 1805 ; grad. Litchfield law school and settled at Vergennes, Vt.; Judge Supreme Court of Vermont.

  136. Mrs. Eli Smith.

  137. Mrs. Aaron Seymour.

  138. Mrs. Grove Catlin. Grove Catlin had son 139.

139. Julius Catlin, b. in Harwinton, 1799; lived 20 years in Litchfield, clerk and merchant in Hartford, director U. S. bank Ct. branch, one of the committee to wind up its affairs after President Jackson's veto, Ct. Com. Gen. and Auditor, West Point visitor, Col. and Pres. Elector in 1856. In 1858 and on, Lieut. Gov. Ct.; m. in 1829 Mary Fisher of Wrentham, Mass.

### 140 = 114.　HEPZIBAH[5] MARSH

of Litchfield, Ct., b. Aug. 29, 1745, dau. Col. Ebenezer[4] and Deboran (Buell) Marsh (John[3], John[2], John[1]); m. No. 140.

140. Dr. Samuel Catlin b. Litchfield, Nov. 6, 1739. Geo. Catlin the famous illustrator of Indian life was of the Litchfield Catlins and educated there.

### 141 = 116.　MOLLY[5] MARSH

of Litchfield, b. Nov. 24, 1752, dau. of Col. Ebenezer[4] and Deborah (Buell) Marsh (John[3], John[2], John[1]); m. Nov. 7, 1771, No. 141.

141. Major Moses Seymour of Litchfield, son of Moses and Rachel (Goodwin) Seymour, b. Hartford, Ct., July 23, 1742, and lineal descendant of Richard Seymour, Hartford, 1636. In the Hist. of Litchfield, pages 157 to 160, there is an interesting sketch of Major Seymour. Born in Hartford he early came to Litchfield ; commissioned Capt. of a troop of horse in '76 he was made Capt. of a company in the 5th Reg. of cavalry and retained his connection with that Reg. during the war. In April, '77, at the Danbury alarm he moved his troops to help repel Gov. Tryon. At the capture of Burgoyne his troop did good service. At a dinner given English officers by American officers after the capitulation he heard Burgoyne give the toast " America and Great Britain against the world." He watched with a British officer the night after the battle.

For the rest of the war his services were mainly at Litchfield as Commissary of supplies, purchasing, storing, guarding and convoying. In 1781 by order of Gen. Wolcott with his dragoons he guarded a train of supplies from Litchfield to Fishkill for the French army.

In a polite official acknowledgement the French Commissary certifies to the protection of the " dragons."

At the peace of 1783 with rank of Major he retired to private life but in 1789 he was elected town clerk and re-elected annually all his life, *during 37 years*. From 1795 he was chosen Representative and continued for 16 sessions. He married Molly[5] Marsh, the youngest child of Col. Ebenezer[4] Marsh and they had one daughter and five sons whom the Litchfield historian calls " the most remarkable family of sons ever raised in Litchfield county." Mary (Marsh) Seymour d. July 17, 1826, æ. 73. Major Moses[5] (Moses[4] of W. Hartford, John[3], John[2], Richard[1] of Hartford 1636), d. Sept. 17, 1826, æ. 84. Children :

142. Clarissa[6], b. Aug. 3, 1772 ; m. Rev. Truman Marsh, 188.

143. Moses, b. June 30, 1774 ; m. Feb. 23, 1800, Mabel Strong, dau. of Gen. John and Agnes McCune, b. May 29, 1782. He was merchant, postmaster 25 years, High Sheriff from 1819 six years and introduced wool carding. See Strong Genealogy for nine children, ten grand-children and four great-grand-children.

144. Ozias, b. July 8, 1776; m. Selima Storrs. He was High Sheriff from 1825 nine years. They had :

145. Hon. Origen Storrs Seymour, b. Litchfield, Feb. 9, 1804 ; Yale college, 1824 ; LL. D., lawyer, Rep. and Speaker Ct. House, M. C. 1851–55 and eight years Judge Ct. Supreme Court.

146. Henrietta, m. Hon. Geo. Catlin Woodruff, b. Litchfield, Dec. 1, 1805 ; Yale college 1825, M. C. 1861–63 ; Judge Probate.

147. Selima, m. Judge D. C. Sanford.

148. Horatio, b. May 31, 1778 ; m. May, 1800 or 1802, Lucy Case of Addison, Vt.; Lawyer, Middlebury, Vt. ; U. S. Senator 1821–33, in '34 candidate for Gov. of Vt., Judge of Probate 1847–55, trustee Middlebury college 1810–55, LL. D. Yale '47 ; d. Nov. 21, 1857. Several children.

149. Henry, b. May 30, 1780; became wealthy merchant at Pompey, Onondaga Co., N. Y. Removed to Utica ; representative, senator, one of canal commissioners who constructed Erie canal, mayor, president of Farmers' Loan and Trust Co. Children :

150. Horatio, of Deerfield, b. 1810; LL. D., Governor New York, 1853–55, and 1862, and candidate for the presidency 1868. The widow of Senator Roscoe Conkling has just died Oct. 10, 1893, at Utica, N.

Y. She was a sister of the late Gov. Horatio Seymour, and a thoroughly educated woman of fine social qualities. She was charitably disposed, and assisted several young men and women to procure an education. Mrs. Conkling was one of the founders of the local chapter of the Daughters of the Revolution, in which she took an active interest. She leaves one daughter, Mrs. W. G. Oakman of New York city.

151. John of Utica; m. a daughter of Arthur Tappan.
152. Epaphroditus, b. July 8, 1783; president of the Brattleboro, Vt. bank; d. Brattleboro, 1853.

153 = 109.    CAPT. SOLOMON[5] MARSH

of Litchfield, Ct., b. Feb. 10, 1735-6, son of Col. Ebenezer[4] and Deborah (Buell) Marsh (John[3], John[2], John[1]); m. (1) his cousin, No. 153.

153. Jerusha[5] Marsh, No. 624, dau. Capt. John[4] and Sarah (Webster) Marsh (John[3], John[2], John[1]), b. Oct. 3, 1735. They had two children who both died young. He m. (2) No. 154.

154. Elizabeth[5] Webster b. Jan. 23, 1742, dau. of Ben[4]. and Elizabeth (Peck) Webster, (Jonathan[3], Robert[2], Gov. John[1] Webster) assessor 1763, Lieut. 1769, collector 1771. Capt. Solomon Marsh during the revolutionary war was appointed one with others to furnish clothing to Litchfield soldiers and to provide for their families. He was Rep. in Ct. Legislature in 1792. He gave an organ to the Episcopal church at a cost of $800. He d. May 30, 1804. His widow d. June 29, 1835. Children :

155. Deborah, d. y.
156. Jerusha, d. y.
157. James b. ——; m. May 10, 1785, Sarah McNiel, 165.1.
158. Solomon, b. Sept. 1, 1777; prob. the Capt. Solomon Marsh chosen by the legislature to present a sword to Major Wessells on his return from the Mexican war in 1849.
159. Betsey.
160. Olive, m. Levi Coe.
161. Lydia, m. March, 1792, Capt. Salmon Buell. She d. 1808.
162. David, b. Jan. 10, 1784; m. (1) Olive Osborne, 166.
163. Deborah, m. (1) Jabez McCall; (2) Geo. D. Kasson; (3) Abner Everitt.
164. Jerusha, m. 1809, Capt. Salmon Buell, b. 1767 and he d. 1868, æ. 100 years and 7 mos.
165. Huldah, m. Joshua Garritt.

165.1 = 157. JAMES[6] MARSH

of Litchfield, b. (?); son Capt. Solomon[5] (Col. Ebenezer[4], John[3], John[2], John[1]) ; m. May 10, 1785, No. 165.1.
165.1. Sarah McNiel. He was a selectman in Litchfield from 1799 for seven years. Children :

165.2    Elizabeth[7], b. March 10, 1786.
165.3    Jared, b. June 10, 1788.   Constable, 1818.
165.4    Orson, b. Nov. 23, 1790.
165.5    Archie, b. May 23, 1794.
165.6    Tracy, b. Oct. 27, 1796.   Constable, 1826.
165.7    Huldah, b. July 27, 1799.
.165.8   Kirby, b. Feb. 17, 1801.   Constable from 1829, seven years.
165.9    Sarah, b. Jan. 1, 1803.


166 = 162. MAJOR DAVID[6] MARSH

of Litchfield, b. Jan. 10, 1784, son of Capt. Solomon[5] and Elizabeth (Webster) Marsh, (Col. Ebenezer[4], John[3], John[2], John[1]) ; m. (1) No. 166.
166. Olive Osborne. He was Selectman in 1821 ; Rep. in Ct. legislature 1824 and 1825 and he or his son 1846 and 1847 ; d. Dec. 28, 1869; he m. (2) No. 167.
167. Lucina Allen. Children :
168.   Solomon[7], unm.
169.   David, m. Harriet Lewis, 172.
170.   William, unm.
171.   Olive, m. David C. Goodwin, 175.


172 = 169. DAVID[7] MARSH

of Litchfield, son of David[6] (Capt. Solomon[5], Col. Ebenezer[4], John[3], John[2], John[1]) ; m. No. 172.
172.   Harriet Lewis. Children :
173.   William F[8].
174.   Frederick B.

## 175 = 171.  OLIVE[7] MARSH

of Litchfield, dau. of David[6] ; m. No. 175.

**175.** David C. Goodwin.    Children :

176. Arthur W[8]., b. Sept. 21, 1851 ; m. Estelle Curtis.
177. Lillian E., b. Aug. 2, 1853.
178. Isabel R., b. Aug. 1, 1855; m. John Morse.
179. Lewis M., b. July, 1858.
180. Anna L., b. 1860.
181. David M., b. July, 1862.


## 182 = 112.  EBENEZER[5] MARSH

of Litchfield, Ct., son of Col. Ebenezer[4] and Deborah (Buell) Marsh, (John[3], John[2], John[1]), b. Oct. 7, 1740 ; m. (1) April 15, 1763, No. 182.
**182.** Lucy Phelps, who d. in 1772 ; and he m. (2) prob. abt. 1777, his cousin, No. 183.
**183.** Rhoda[5] Marsh dau. of Capt. John[4] (John[3], John[2], John[1]), No. 627 and he m. (3) No. 184.
**184.** Widow Hannah Peck.  He was Rep. in Ct. legislature, 1784–1788 and 1790.    Children :

185. Ebenezer[6], b. Jan. 17, 1764; m. Elizabeth Osborn, 192.
186. Samuel, b. June 17, 1765 ; Yale college, 1786; lawyer in Litchfield and in Norfolk, Va.  In 1809 he gave the lot on which St. Michael's church stands.
187. Ashbel, b. Nov. 12, 1766 ; m. Rachel Shether, 198.
188. Truman, b. Feb. 23, 1768; m. Clarissa Seymour, 202.
189. Kate, b. March 11, 1770; d. Dec. 10, 1770.
190. Katy, b. July 18, 1778; m. John Bissell, 201.7.
191. Lucy, b. Aug. 21, 1781 ; m. James Bloodgood.


## 192 = 185.  EBENEZER[6] MARSH

of Litchfield, b. Jan. 17, 1764, son of Ebenezer[5] and Lucy (Phelps) Marsh, (Col. Ebenezer[4], John[3], John[2], John[1]) ; m. No. 192.
**192.** Elizabeth Osborn.    Children :

193. Lucy[7].
194. Harry.
195. Samuel.
196. Sarah, became Mrs. Sally Smith.
197. Eliza, became Mrs. Phelps.

## 198 = 187. ASHBEL⁶ MARSH

of Litchfield, b. Nov. 12, 1766, son of Ebenezer⁵ and Lucy (Phelps) Marsh, (Col. Ebenezer⁴, John³, John², John¹); m. No. 198.

**198.** Rachel Shether. He was chosen in 1818 key keeper of Litchfield Borough. Children:

> 199. Ormond⁷, m. Ann Whistler, 201.1.
> 200. Sally, m. Thos. Trowbridge, Jr.
> 201. Polly, m. John Dewey.

## 201.1 = 199. ORMOND⁷ MARSH

b. Litchfield, Ct. about 1789 or '90, son of Ashbel⁶ and Rachel (Shether) Marsh, (Ebenezer⁵, Col. Ebenezer⁴, John³, John², John¹); m. in 1812 during the war, at Fort Gratiot, Detroit, No. 201.1.

**201.1.** Ann Whistler, dau. Capt. John Whistler, U. S. A. Children:

> 201.2 Harriet Anne⁸, b. 1818; m. W. R. Wood, 201.3.

## 201.3 = 201.2. HARRIET ANNE⁸ MARSH

b. Litchfield, Ct. in 1818 ; m. in 1844 at Detroit, Mich., No. 201.3.

**201.3.** William R. Wood, b. London, Eng. in 1810. Children:

> 201.4 William H⁹., b. 1844 at Sandwich, Canada West; m. in 1874, in Farmington, Minn., Frances C. Guiteau. They have: 1, Jane; 2, Wm. Robert; 3, Nannie; 4, Catherine.
> 201.5 Charles, b. 1846, Sandwich, C. W.; unm.
> 201.6 Annie Abbott, b. 1854, at Detroit, Mich.; is now, 1894, a teacher in Wells college, Aurora, Cayuga Lake, N. Y.

## 201.7 = 190. CATHERINE⁶ MARSH

b. Litchfield, Ct. July 18, 1778, dau. of Ebenezer⁵ and Lucy (Phelps) Marsh, (Col. Ebenezer⁴, John³, John², John¹); m. there in 1800, No. 201.7.

**201.7.** John Bissell, son of Zebulon. She d. in March, 1837. He d. March 22, 1855. Children:

201.8   Samuel Marsh[7], b. May, 1800; d. Nov. 14, 1837.
201.9   John, b. May, 1806; m. M. C. Holly, 201.31.
201.10  Edward, b. Nov. 27, 1808; m. V. D. de Paga, 201.16.
201.11  Lucy Ann, b. 1811; d. Aug. 16, 1822.
201.12  Katherine, b. 1816; m. Roswell Hoyt; d. Sept. 27, 1855.
201.13  Elizabeth C., b. Feb., 1818; m. J. B. Bogert, 201.25.
201.14  Mary Ellen, b. Oct. 7, 1820.
201.15  George Beckwith, b. Sept., 1824; was in U. S. brig Truxton, wrecked off the Mexican coast, and made prisoner of war. He joined the frigate Cumberland as sailing master and d. Sept. 10, 1848.

## 201.16 = 201.10.   EDWARD[7] BISSELL

b. Nov. 27, 1808, son of Catherine[6] (Marsh) and John Bissell; m. April 23, 1846, No. 201.16.
**201.16.**  Victorine Dubois de Paga, b. Nov. 18, 1825. He was for many years purser in the U. S. navy. He d. Jan. 24, 1876. Children :

201.17  Edward Manuel[8], b. Feb. 19, 1847; m. I. Haskins, 201.20.
201.18  Frederick Paul, b. Feb. 10, 1861; d. Jan. 23, 1879.
201.19  Ysabel Manuel, b. Jan. 20, 1863; m. Henry P. Eggleston. She d. May 3, 1892. Child: Sarah Jessup[9], d. Feb. 8, 1888.

## 201.20.=201.17.   EDWARD MANUEL[8] 'BISSELL

b. Feb. 19, 1847 ; m. No. 201.20.
**201.20.**  Isabella Haskins.  Children.
201.21  Victor Manuel[9], b. 1875.
201.22  Viola, b. 1877.
201.23  Leon Edward, b. 1879.
201.24  Herbert Harold, b. (?); d. 1882.

## 201.25 = 201.13.   ELIZABETH C[7]. BISSELL

b. Feb. 26, 1818, dau. of Edward and Catherine[6] (Marsh) Bissell; m. No. 201.25.

**201.25.** John Banta Bogert, b. Sept. 13, 1814. She d. May 9, 1872. Child:

> 201.26 Katherine Bissell⁸, b. Sept. 16, 1852; m. C. F. Roe, 201.27.

## 201.27 = 201.26. KATHERINE BISSELL⁸ BOGERT

b. Sept. 16, 1852, dau. of John Banta and Elizabeth⁷ (Bissell) Bogert, (Catherine⁶ [Marsh] Bissell, Ebenezer⁵ Marsh, Col. Ebenezer⁴, John³, John², John¹); m. July 29, 1874, No. 201.27.

**201.27.** Charles Francis Roe, b. May 1, 1848. He graduated at the U. S. military academy in June, 1868; served until 1888 in 1st U. S. cavalry and 2d U. S. cavalry and then resigned. He is now captain of "Troop A." National Guard of N. Y. state. Children:

> 201.28 Stephen Bogert⁹, b. Sept. 26, 1875.
> 201.29 Josephine Bissell, b. Aug. 1, 1877.
> 201.30 Charles, b. Feb. 22, 1880; d. Feb. 25, 1880.

## 201 = 201.9. JOHN⁷ BISSELL

b. Utica, N. Y., May 2, 1807; m. No. 201.31.

**201.31.** Martha C. Holly, d. May 20, 1875. He d. June 12, 1893. Children:

> 201.32 Katherine, b. Stamford, Ct., Aug. 26, 1831.
> 201.33 Marianna, b. in N. Y., July 11, 1836; d. Dec. 21, 1839.
> 201.34 Augustus Holly, b. Oct. 24, 1840; m. June 30, 1869, Sarah
>    M. Sterling, who d. Dec. 28, 1883. Children: 1, Mar-
>    garet Crawford⁹, b. Nov. 30, 1871; 2, John, b. Jan. 30,
>    1873; 3, Katherine Sterling, b. Sept. 11, 1874; 4, Charles
>    Sterling, b. Aug. 29, 1876; d. April 11, 1893.

## 202 = 188. REV. TRUMAN⁶ MARSH

of Litchfield, b. Feb. 23, 1768, son of Ebenezer⁵ and Lucy (Phelps) Marsh, (Col. Ebenezer⁴, John³, John², John¹); Yale college 1786, was rector of St. Michael's, Litchfield, 27 years. Before this from 1790 to 1799 he had been rector and resided at New Milford, Ct.,

being for the same nine years also rector of the Episcopal church at
New Preston with a salary there of 28 pounds " two-thirds produce
and one-third money." He m. at Litchfield, Oct. 27, 1791, his cousin,
No. 202.

**202.** Clarissa[6] Seymour, 142, dau. of Moses and Molly (Marsh)
Seymour, dau. of Col. Ebenezer[4] Marsh. "The wedding party left
Litchfield in the morning after the wedding services, and proceed-
ing toward New Milford, were met by a number of carriages and
escorted to the parsonage where the ladies had provided an introductory dinner and greeting. After dinner Mr. Marsh and Mr. Griswold "
(the Congregational minister) " being classmates, devoted the passing
hours to a review of earlier years and the company adjourned to the
rooms of the old town house, where, with appropriate music, the
party enjoyed the afternoon in dancing, —the two ministers' wives
having the honor of leading the company at the first dance." History New Milford. Returning 50 years after they left, Mrs. Marsh
" told one of the first-class citizens " still living 1882, that she had
never seen elsewhere such "harmony, union and good feeling,
between all churches and among all people."

At the celebration of the " Centennial of Litchfield," Aug. 13 and
14, 1851, two portraits were exhibited of Rev. Truman Marsh, one
painted 1789, the other 1842, one of his wife 1789 and one of her
mother Mary[5] (Marsh) Seymour, dau. of Col. Ebenezer[4] Marsh.
The rector d. March 28, 1851. His widow Mrs. Clarissa Marsh survived him more than 14 years, dying in her 94th year, Sept. 2, 1865.

Except the nine years at New Milford, nearly all their lives were
spent in Litchfield village. We learn from a notice of the aged
widow's death that St. Michael's church received substantial marks
of her liberality and that the Episcopal parsonage was her gift, that
she was the oldest inhabitant of the village and that if her husband
was pastor she was a noble mother in the church where he had long
been head and pioneer and had availed so much to give St. Michael's
its present commanding position in the diocese. Children :

    203.  Moses Seymour[7], b. Dec. 30, 1792 ; m. Flora Wheaton, 210.
    204.  Maria, b. Jan. 14, 1797 ; m. Geo. B. Webster, 216.1.
    205.  Truman, b. July 3, 1799; d. March 9, 1800.
    206.  Clarissa, b. April 29, 1802; m. Gerrett P. Welch, 217.
    207.  Delia, b. Dec. 23, 1804; d. July 30, 1807.
    208.  Catherine, b. March 20, 1807; m. Rev. Geo. Carrington.
    209.  Delia, b. Sept. 12, 1809; d. Oct. 21, 1875 ; m. Dr. J. Barnes,
          228.1.

210 = 203. MOSES SEYMOUR[7] MARSH

of New Milford and Litchfield, Ct. and Syracuse, N. Y., b. Dec. 30, 1792; d. Syracuse, Oct. 12, 1843. He m. at Pompey, N. Y., Aug. 19, 1820, No. 210.

**210.** Flora Wheaton, dau. of Augustus and Hannah Wheaton of New Milford, Ct., who was b. July 23, 1799 and d. Sept. 17, 1843. Children:

210.1    Henry Seymour[8], b. Pompey, N. Y., Jan. 19, 1822; d. New York City, Feb. 19, 1889. No children.

210.2    Truman Augustus, b. Pompey, Aug. 19, 1823; d. there Dec. 6, 1827.

211.    Clarissa Hannah, b. Pompey, Dec. 19, 1825; m. 212.

211.1    Richard Croyler, b. Pompey, Jan. 3, 1828; d. at Philadelphia, Pa., Dec. 24, 1888. No children.

211.2    Charles Epaphro, b. Syracuse, N. Y., Sept. 2, 1831; m. Cleveland, O., Feb. 1, 1854, Charlotte A. Bennett. He d. Cleveland, Nov. 21, 1877. They had only Flora, b. Cleveland, Nov. 15, 1855.

211.3    Catherine Mary, b. Syracuse, March 8, 1833, now (1891) resides in Brooklyn, N. Y. She m. Jan. 24, 1855, at Syracuse, Samuel Buell Woolworth, Jr. Children: 1, Catherine Marsh[9], b. May 27, 1857; m. and res. (1891) in Brooklyn; 2, Henry Seymour, b. April 21, 1858: d. ———; 3, Edward Dawson, b. March 14, 1861, res. (1891) in Brooklyn, as do 4, James and 5, Sophie.

211.4    George Webster, b. Syracuse, Sept. 29, 1835; d. there April, 1837.

211.5    George Webster, b. Syracuse, Jan. 29, 1839; d. Nov. 27, 1881. No children.


212 = 211. CLARISSA HANNAH[8] MARSH

of Pompey and Syracuse, N. Y., b. Dec. 19, 1825; m. at Pompey Hill, N. Y., Sept. 18, 1849, No. 212.

**212.** Edward Sebried Dawson, b. Nelson, N. Y., July 22, 1822. He was a merchant and they reside in Syracuse, N. Y. She was dau. Moses Seymour[7] and Flora (Wheaton) Marsh, (Rev. Truman[6], Ebenezer[5], Col. Ebenezer[4], John[3], John[2], John[1]). Children:

213.    Flora Marsh[9], b. June 3, 1850.

214.    Edward Seymour, b. Sept. 29, 1852; Grad. Coll. Pharmacy,

Philadelphia, March 12, 1874 and received alumni gold
medal for superior scholarship.

215. Homer Wheaton, b. March 6, 1856.
216. John Barker, b. Jan. 13, 1863.

## 216.1 = 204. MARIA[7] MARSH

of Litchfield, Ct., b. Jan. 14, 1797, dau. of Rev. Truman[6] and Clarissa
(Seymour) Marsh ; m. Sept. 26, 1819, No. 216.1.

**216.1.** George Buell Webster, b. Sept. 8, 1796. Mrs. Webster d.
Oct. 16, 1833, and he d. April 3, 1857. Children :

216.2 George Clerum[8], b. Dec. 28, 1822 ; m. Sarah E. Verplank,
dau. Judge Isaac Verplank. Children : 1, George
Clerum[9], m.; 2, Laura, and 3, Grace Seymour, both unm.

216.3 Julia Maria, b. May 12, 1828 ; m. Nov. 8, 1849, Geo. Lissant
Newman, of Charlottesville, Va.. b. Newerk, Eng.,
July 16, 1816, son of Wm. Henry and Jane (Cox) New-
man. They had one child :

216.4 Jane Ellen[9], b. March 21, 1851 ; m. H. L. Lyman, 216.5.


## 216.5 = 216.4. JANE ELLEN[9] NEWMAN

b. March 21, 1851 ; m. April 11, 1871, No. 216.5.

**216.5.** Henry Leslie Lyman, b. April 20, 1848, son of David
Russel Lyman, b. in Ct. but of Lynchburgh, Va., where he m. Elizabeth Hale Roberts of that place. Children now living :

216.6 Marianne Newman[10], b. Nov. 10, 1873.
216.7 David Russell, b. March 8, 1876.
216.8 Lilian Forbes, b. July 22, 1879.


## 217 = 206. CLARISSA[7] MARSH

of Litchfield, b. April 29, 1802, dau. Rev. Truman[6] and Clarissa[6]
(Seymour) Marsh, (Ebenezer[5], Col. Ebenezer[4], John[3], John[2], John[1]);
m. No. 217.

**217.** Gerrett P. Welch. Children :

218. Irene[8], d. y.
219. Caroline, d. y.

220. Delia, m. Wm. E. Dickinson. Their only child:
    221. Mary[9], m. Mr. Hart of Stamford, Ct. They have two children:
        222. Wm. D. Hart.[10]
        223. Irene Hart.
224. John, d. a few years before 1886.
225. Maria, d. y.
226. David T., m. Miss Bradley of Woodbury; res. W. Haven. No children.
227. Rosa P., m. Dr. Charles H. Vail. She is now a widow and resided with her mother in 1886 at Milton, Litchfield. Child:
    228. Walter.[9]

## 228.1. = 209. DELIA[7] MARSH

b. Litchfield, Ct., Sept. 12, 1809, youngest dau. of Rev. Truman and Clarissa (Seymour) Marsh; m. there May 22, 1831, No. 228.1.

**228.1.** Dr. Josiah Barnes, b. May 26, 1804, youngest son of Jonathan and Rachel (Steele) Barnes of Tolland, Ct. Dr. Barnes was a skillful and beloved physician. They removed in 1832 to Buffalo, N. Y. He d. there June 1, 1871, æ. 67. She d. Dec. 16, 1875. Children:

    228.2 Emily Catherine[8], b. Litchfield, March 5, 1832; d. Litchfield, July 17, 1837.
    228.3 Maria Catherine, b. March 5, 1836; m. R. R. Buck, 228.7.
    228.4 Edwin Randolph, b. Buffalo, Sept. 2, 1838; resides in Buffalo unm., an M. D.
    228.5 Wm. Josiah, b. Buffalo, Jan. 25, 1846; d. there Nov. 19, 1875.
    228.6 Laura Seymour, b. Feb. 14, 1850; m. F. M. Fisher, 228.11.

## 228.7 = 228.3. MARIA CATHERINE[8] BARNES

b. Buffalo, N. Y., March 5, 1836, dau. Delia[7] (Marsh) Barnes; m. Buffalo, N. Y., Nov. 8, 1866, No. 228.7.

**228.7,** Roswell Riley Buck, son of Winthrop and Eunice (Moseley) Buck of Wethersfield, Ct. Children:

    228.8 Harriet Moseley[9], b. Buffalo, Aug. 16, 1867.
    228.9 Winthrop Seymour, b. Buffalo, May 13, 1870; d. there May 24, 1878.
    228.10 George Sturges, b. Hyde Park, Chicago, Ill., Feb. 10, 1875.

### 228.11 = 228.6.   LAURA SEYMOUR[8] BARNES

b. Buffalo, N. Y., Feb. 14, 1850, dau. of Delia[7] (Marsh) Barnes ; m. there Oct. 11, 1876, No. 228.11.

**228.11,** Francis Marion Fisher.   Their children were all born at Buffalo.

228.12  Charles Edwin, b. June 18, 1877.
228.13  Marion Francis, b. Feb. 7, 1879.
228.14  Laura Barnes, b. Dec. 18, 1880.
228.15  Beverly Boyd, b. June 18, 1883.
228.16  George Roswell, b. Sept. 5, 1885.
228.17  Elsie Seymour, b. Aug. 4, 1888.
228.18  Francis Marion, 2d, b. July 3, 1893.


### 229 = 115.   JOHN[5] MARSH

of Litchfield, Ct., b. Jan. 4, 1748, son of Col. Ebenezer[4] and Deborah (Buell) Marsh, (John[3], John[2], John[1]); m. Sept. 14, 1769, No. 229.
**229.** Rhoda McNiel.   He d. Jan. 23, 1781.   Children :

230.  Rachel, b. Dec. 17, 1770; m. Horace Baldwin, 237.
231.  Charles, b. Dec. 23, 1771; m. Charlotte Roberts.  He was " drowned in the East mill pond."
232.  Deborah, b. July 18, 1773; m. Joseph Adams.  He was grand juror six years from 1802.  She d. July 27, 1857, æ. 84.
233.  Molly, b. Nov. 13, 1774; m. Isaac Tyler.
234.  Rhoda, b. June 24, 1777; m. Timothy Barber.
235.  Anna, b. April 14, 1799; m. Andrew Roland.
236.  John, b. Aug. 4, 1781; unm. d. Dec. 15, 1847.


### 237 = 230.   RACHEL[6] MARSH

of Litchfield, b. Dec. 17, 1770, dau. John[5] and Rhoda (McNiel) Marsh, (Col. Ebenezer[4], John[3], John[2], John[1]) ; m. June 24, 1791, No. 237.
**237.** Horace Baldwin, b. Litchfield, Ct., Sept. 27, 1765.  They had thirteen children :

237.1  Ann[7], b. April 8, 1792; m. Col. John Stone.
237.2  Clarissa M., b. May, 1793; m. Ezekiel Lovejoy.

237.3   Charles M., b. Feb. 27, 1794; d. Feb. 2, 1834; unm., (insane)..

237.4   Ashbel F., b. Sept. 30, 1796.

237.5   Horace, b. Feb. 9, 1798.

238.   Isaac, b. July 15, 1800.

238.1   William B., b. Jan. 7, 1803.

238.2   Samuel S., b. Aug. 29, 1804.

238.3   Rachel Buell, b. March 12, 1807; m. Nov. 5, 1829, Nath.. W. Winship. Had seven children.

238.4   Abigail, b. Dec. 10, 1808; m. Feb. 14, 1853, Gen. Elisha Pomeroy.

238.5   Mary, b. July, 1810; d. 1813.

238.6   John Marsh, b. July 2, 1813.

239.   Horatio Marsh, b. March 3, 1815; m. L. M. Strong. Child :.

239.1   Daniel[8], lived about two years.

## 240 = 96. CAPT. WILLIAM[4] MARSH

of Litchfield, Ct., b. Hartford, Ct., June, 1705; bap. Second Church;. Hartford, July 1, 1705, son of John[3] and Elizabeth (Pitkin) Marsh, (John[2], John[1]): m. Nov. 9, 1733, No. 240.

**240.** Susanna Webster. He was grand juror four years from 1735, selectman five years from 1747 and treasurer four years. from 1751. Children :

245.   Ann, b. June 23, 1735; m. Abner Baldwin, 249.

246.   Susannah, b. Jan. 16, 1737.

247.   Irene, b. Oct. 4, 1738; m. David Welch, 262.

248.   William, b. Sept. 14, 1740; m. Esther Roe. No children..

## 249 = 241. ANN[5] MARSH

of Litchfield, b. June 23, 1735, dau. of Capt. William[4] and Susanna. (Webster) Marsh, (John[3], John[2], John[1]); m. prob. (?) May 27, 1754, No. 249.

**249.** Abner Baldwin, b. in Durham, Ct., May 27, 1726, settled in. Litchfield ; d. April 26, 1781, æ. 55. Children :

250.   William[6], b. Feb. 28, 1755.

251.   Abner, b. March 16, 1756.

252.   James, b. Nov. 12, 1758.

253.   David, b. March 14, 1761 ; killed, 1771, by kick of a horse..

254.   John, b. Jan. 22, 1763 ; drowned June 3, 1764.

255.  John, b. June 3, 1764 ; m. Sally De Wolf and had son Elisha,
       and four daus.
256.  Charles, b. May 8, 1766.
257.  Susanna, b. Oct. 16, 1769 ; m. Asa Sanford, Litchfield.
258.  Anne, b. March 24, 1771 ; m. Thaddeus Landin.
259.  David, } b. July 30, 1773 ; d. 1773.
260.  Darius, }
261.  David, b. Feb. 20, 1776 ; d. Aug. 20, 1776.


262 = 247.   IRENE[5] MARSH

of Litchfield, b. Oct. 4, 1738, dau. Capt. William[4] and Susannah
(Webster) Marsh, (John[3], John[2], John[1]) ; m. No. 262.
   **262.**  Major David Welch.   Child :
       263.  Hon. John[6] Welch, b. Litchfield, Sept. 23, 1759.  Yale col-
              lege, 1778, merchant, justice peace, representative, sen-
              ator, member constitutional convention, judge and can-
              didate for congress.  Spent his life in Litchfield and d.
              Dec. 26, 1845, leaving a large estate.


264 = 97.   GEORGE[4] MARSH

of Litchfield, b. Hartford, Ct., Feb., 1708, bap. Second Church, Feb.
29, 1708, son of John[3] and Elizabeth (Pitkin) Marsh, (John[2], John[1]);
m. June 16, 1731, No. 264.
   **264.**  Lydia Bird.   He was lister from 1736 two years ; constable,
1737.  Children.
       265.  Ambrose[5], b. Feb. 27, 1732 ; m. Elizabeth Taylor, 279.
       266.  Roger, b. Oct. 31, 1733 ; m. Lucy Kilbourne, 335.
       267.  Adam, b. Aug. 4, 1735.
       268.  George, b. Sept. 25, 1736 ; m. Catherine Kilbourn, 470.
       269.  Elijah, b. perhaps, 1738 ; m. (?) 482.
       270.  Titus.
       271.  Lydia, b. (?) ; m. Joshua Garrett.   They had :
              272.  Daniel[6].
       273.  Sabra, b. (?) ; m. Mr. Camp.   They had :
              274.  Mrs. Isaac Ensign[6].
              275.  Mrs. Hezekiah Murray.
              276.  Mrs. Mansfield.
              277.  Mrs. Northrup.
              278.  Mrs. Abel Camp.

## 279 = 265. AMBROSE[5] MARSH

of Litchfield, Ct., b. Feb. 27, 1732, son of George[4] and Lydia (Bird) Marsh, (John[3], John[2], John[1]) ; m. Oct. 30, 1754, No. 279.

**279.** Elizabeth Taylor. This may have been a second marriage if the age of his oldest son at death is given correctly, which I doubt. Children :

- 280. Titus[6], b. prob. 1755 ; m. Eunice Peck, 286.
- 281. Thomas, m. Olive Peck, 306.
- 282. Lydia, b. March, 1761 ; m. Joseph Curtiss.
- 283. Nathaniel, m. Hannah Blakeslee, 312.
- 284. David, m. Roxanna Morse, 329.
- 285. Ambrose, m. Huldah Wilson, 333.

## 286 = 280. TITUS[6] MARSH

b. Litchfield, Ct., prob. (?) 1755, son of Ambrose[5] and Elizabeth (Taylor) Marsh, (George[4], John[3], John[2], John[1]) ; m. No. 286.

**286.** Eunice Peck, b. abt. 1757 or 8 ; d. 1840, æ. 70. Their children were all born in Litchfield. They removed to Pompey, Onondaga Co., N. Y. in 1806. He d. March 29, 1840, æ. 83 years, 8 months, which would give his birth abt. July, 1756. All the seven sons had died before 1886. Children :

- 287. Marovia[7], b. about 1784; d. Feb. 8, 1860, æ. 76 ; m. Betsey Newell, who d. March 30, 1848, æ. 70. They buried three sons and two grand-children are living, 1, James[9], in Iowa.
- 288, Daniel, b. about 1787 ; d. 1862, æ, 75 ; m. Ann O'Donaghey, b. about 1789 ; d. 1869, æ. 80. Children :
  - 288.1 Mary[8], m. Philo Newman. She d. leaving a dau. now m. and living in Racine, Wis.
  - 288.2 Betsey Ann, m. Victory J. Birdsey, 294.
  - 288.3 Jane, d. in 1882, leaving son Frank O'Donaghey[9].
- 289. Lynds, b. about 1791 ; d. in 1841, æ. 50 ; m. Harriet Peck and had six children all d. but Lambertus[8] living in Iowa. Of the others Homer[8], d. in Mich. and left sons Henry[9] and Charles, and Luther[8] d. in Ill. and left son Charles and dau. Mrs. Marshall, both living in Kansas.
- 290. Luman, m. (1) Maria Campbell, 295.
- 291. Canfield, b. March 9, 1792 ; m. S. Pettit, 297.

292. Harmon, m. Emily Newman, who d. in 1857. He d. in
        Indiana in 1875. They had: Harmon[8], and Henry who
        lives in Florida and has living there Harmon[9] m.; also
        Laura and Lucy.

293. Bird, d. " before he was three years old."

## 294 = 288.2   BETSEY ANN[8] MARSH

b. Pompey, N. Y.(?); m. No. 294.

**294.** Victory J. Birdsey of Pompey Hill, N. Y., and has had
nine children, seven living.  Children :

294.1  Col. Mortimer[9], lives at Fayetteville, N. Y.
294.2  Daniel, lives in Edmonds Co., Dak.
294.3  George of Cleveland, O.
294.4  Lucien lives in Iowa.
294.5  Victory J., of Syracuse, N. Y.  The two daus. live at home
        unmarried.

## 295 = 290.   LUMAN[7] MARSH

b. Litchfield, Ct.; m. (1) No. 295.

**295.** Maria Campbell, d. in 1816.  He m. (2) No. 296.

**296.** Julia Ann Remsen.  He d. in Kenosha Co., Wis. in 1861,
æ. 71.  His widow d. in 1884, æ. 87 and 10 months.  Children by
first wife :

296.1  Maria E.[8], unm., now of Kenosha, Wis.

        By second wife.

296.2  Marovia, d. in Wis. in 1875, left son Fred and dau. Hattie,
        m. Henry Barber of Waukegan, Ill.
296.3  Caroline, m. Milton Pettit of Kenosha, Wis.  She has
        living, Ossian[9], Elizabeth, m. Robert E. Mailer and
        Carrie, all living at Kenosha, Wis.
296.4  Daniel, lives in Lisbon, Dak. and has two sons living in
        Kenosha, Wis., Charles[9] and Henry.  Charles has two
        sons, Alvin[10] and Roy.
296.5  Remsen, lives in Lisbon, Dak., has Edwin[9] and Arthur and
        daus. Florence, m. to Frederick Bell living in Dak. and
        Julia at home.
296.6  Julia, m. Peter Wood; res. at Onowa, Ia. and has Kate
        Louise[9], m. Howard Van Wyck and lives in Milwaukee,
        Wis.

## 297 = 291. CANFIELD[7] MARSH

b. Litchfield, Ct., March 19, 1792, son of Titus[6] and Eunice (Peck)
Marsh, (Ambrose[5], George[4], John[3], John[2], John[1]); m. Oct. 4, 1818
at Delphi, N. Y., No. 297.

**297.** Sophronia Pettit, b. May 28, 1800; d. Dec. 8, 1855. He
d. Sept. 28, 1859. They lived at Pompey, N. Y. and had ten
children, the first four b. at Delphi and the last five at Cortlandville,
N. Y. Children :

297.1 Sophronia Eunice[8], b. Aug. 19, 1819; m. March, 1840,
Henry S. Candell. She d. March 18, 1872 or 3. Three
of her four children survived her. Her son d. a few
months since (1888). Margaret[9] Radway and Mary
Rice were in 1888 in Minn.

297.2 Canfield James, b. Dec. 30, 1820; m. June 27, 1842, N.
Maria Taylor and d. July, 1883, leaving Mrs. Emma[9]
Earle, Mrs. Alma Vickery and Mrs. Nora B. (Marsh)
— all living in Colo. and Theodore B., living at Anthony,
Kans.

298. Lucy Maria, b. June 28, 1822 ; m. Feb. 24, 1842, S. R. Kellogg,
b. 1815 and d. May 29, 1877. She survives, had five
daus. : Agnes Jane[9], m. in 1865, Jacob Gore and lives at
Crete, Wis., Helen Sophronia, b. Nov. 8, 1845 ; m. 1867,
Thompson McK. Wylie and d. March 4, 1869. Mary
Theresa[9], b. Sept. 10, 1848, m. Dec. 24, 1873, Wm. B.
Munson and with two children lives at Creston, Ia.;
Minerva Eleanor, b. May 5, 1851, m. April 13, 1868, Benj.
F. Parker and d. June 12, 1885 ; Lucy Ada, b. May 14,
1856, d. March 22, 1876.

299. Eleanor Mehitabel, b. Aug. 31, 1824; m. Dec. 19, 1844, Dr.
Andrew Durnford who d. Sept. 8, 1855. She lives and
has son Andrew[9], who lives at Auburn, N. Y. She res.
at Orlando, Florida.

300. John Stewart, b. June 29, 1827 ; m. 1849, Minerva L. Smith,
who d. Oct., 1876. They had one child, Blanch M[9].,
now Mrs. R. J. Ingram of Chicago.

301. Titus Albertus[6], b. Nov., 1829; d. Aug. 24, 1851.

302. William Henry, b. March 10, 1832 ; d. 1861.

303. Ann Venette, b. June 10, 1834; m. 1851, Dr. Everhard still
lives, had seven children, six living still.

304. Ambrose Augustus, b. Feb., 1837 ; m. 1859, Lucy A. Brain-
ard, had three children, Carrie Bell[9], Wm. Augustus and
Mary Eleanor. They live in Orlando, Orange Co.,
Florida.

305. George Gary, b. Sept. 9, 1838; d. Nov. 5, 1838.

5

## 306 = 281.  THOMAS[6] MARSH

b. Litchfield,, Ct., prob.(?) between 1755 and 1760, son of Ambrose[5] and Elizabeth (Taylor) Marsh, (George[4], John[3], John[2], John[1]) ; m. No. 306.

**306.** Olive Peck of Litchfield, sister of Eunice, wife of his brother Titus and prob. in 1806 removed with brothers and parents to Pompey, N. Y.    He was grand juror at Litchfield, 1804 and lister 1805.  Children:

307.  Milly[7], m. and had four children, (in 1886 a son lawyer in Chicago and another child living near Chicago.)
308.  Edward, had four children, a dau. in 1886 living in Wis. and grand-child in Manlius, N. Y.
308.1 Hiram.
308.2 Sally, had two children.
309.  Horatio, m. Phebe and d. in Chicago, 1881 ; left three sons :
310.  James[8].
311.  Charles V.
311.1 Edward.


## 312 = 283.  NATHANIEL[6] MARSH

of Litchfield, Ct., b. (?) son of Ambrose[5] and Elizabeth (Taylor) Marsh, (George[4], John[3], John[2], John[1]) ; m. (?) No. 312.

**312.** Hannah Blakeslee.  Children :

313.  Clara[7], b. 1783 ; d. 1800, æ. 17.
314.  Dennis, d. unm. in Sparta, Tenn.
315.  Levi, b. Feb. 8, 1795 ; m. Martha Boardman, 318.
316.  Riley, d. unm. in Winchester, Va.
317.  Miles, b. 1804 (?); no children; d. Thomaston, Ct., May 20, 1857, æ. 53.


## 318 = 315.  LEVI[7] MARSH

son of Nathaniel[6] and Hannah (Blakeslee) Marsh, (Ambrose[5], George[4], John[3], John[2], John[1]) b. Feb. 8, 1795 ; m. No. 318.

**318.** Martha Boardman, Rocky Hill, Ct., b. Feb. 21, 1792 ; d. July 29, 1867.  Children :

319. Adaline[8], b. Aug. 4, 1821; m. Noah A. Norton of Charleston, Mass. They had:

    320. Gertrude, b. May 1, 1846; unm.

321. Clarissa, b. Jan. 27, 1825; m. Edward Thomas, 325.

322. Henrietta, b. Sept. 14, 1827; d. Jan. 25, 1828.

323. Levi, b. March 24, 1832; d. April 21, 1832.

324. Riley, b. April 8, 1835; m. Ann Harrielson of Thomaston, Ct.


## 325 = 321. CLARISSA[8] MARSH

dau. Levi[7], (Nathaniel[6], Ambrose[5], George[4], John[3], John[2], John[1]) ; m. No. 325.

**325.** Edward Thomas of Thomaston, Ct. Children :

    326. Walter A[9]., b. Nov. 9, 1848; m. Sarah Woodward; d. May 9, 1888.

    327. Martha B., b. April 14, 1850; m. Frederick Canfield.

    328. Laura A., b. May 9, 1860; m. Newell Webster.


## 329 = 284. DAVID[6] MARSH

of Litchfield, son of Ambrose[5] and Elizabeth (Taylor) Marsh, (George[4], John[3], John[2], John[1]) ; m. No. 329.

**329.** Roxanna Morse. Children :

    330. Sheldon[7]. No children.

    331. Harry. Two children.

    332. Nisola. Two children.


## 333 = 285. AMBROSE[6] MARSH

of Litchfield, son of Ambrose[5], (George[4], John[3], John[2], John[1]) ; m. No. 333.

**333.** Huldah Wilson. Child :

    334. Huldah[7].


## 335 = 266. CAPT. ROGER[5] MARSH

of Litchfield, Ct., son of George[4] and Lydia (Bird) Marsh, (John[3], John[2], John[1]) b. Oct. 31, 1733; m. prob. about 1759, No. 335.

**335.** Lucy Kilbourn. He was made Captain in 1771. He was assessor, 1771 and 2; selectman, 1785 and 6. Children:

- 336. Honor[6], b. Aug. 12, 1760; m. Solomon Gibbs, 346.
- 337. James, b. Sept. 22, 1762; m. Ursula Hayden, 353.
- 338. Lucy, m. Bradham Valch Yale.
- 339. Susan, m. David Little, 363.
- 340. Roger, b. Dec. 9, 1768; m. Phebe Norton, 369.
- 341. Appleton, b. May 23, 1770; m. Elizabeth Hotchkiss, 374.
- 342. Horace, m. Eunice Morse, 419.
- 343. Abel.
- 344. Aaron, m. Martha Landon, 452.
- 345. Moses, b. Aug. 26, 1778; m. Dorcas Gillett, 458.

### 346 = 336.   HONOR[6] MARSH

of Litchfield, b. Aug. 12, 1760, dau. of Roger[5] and Lucy (Kilbourn) Marsh, (George[4], John[3], John[2], John[1]) ; m. No. 346.

**346.** Solomon Gibbs of Litchfield. Children:

- 347. Caroline, unm.
- 348. Elias, m.
- 349. Eli, m.
- 350. Idea, unm.
- 351. Frederick.
- 352. Aaron, m.

### 353 = 337.   JAMES[6] MARSH

of Litchfield, b. Sept. 22, 1762, son of Roger[5] and Lucy (Kilbourn) Marsh, (George[4], John[3], John[2], John[1]) ; m. Dec., 1890, No. 353.

**353.** Ursula Hayden of Windsor, Ct. He was lister three years from 1791 and grand juror four years from 1798. He d. May 25, 1857, æ. 95 years, 8 months, and 3 days. Children:

- 354. Laura Caroline[7], b. July 10, 1792; m. A. Osborn, 357.
- 355. George, b. Sept. 8, 1794; m. Caroline Gilbert, 358.
- 356. Lucy, b. Jan. 9, 1801; m. Noah Preston of Litchfield.

### 357 = 354.   LAURA CAROLINE[7] MARSH

of Litchfield, b. July 10, 1792, dau. James and Ursula (Hayden) Marsh; m. May 25, 1821, No. 357.

**357.** Amos Osborn, d. April 12, 1856, æ. 64. Children :

357.1 Ursula[8], b. May 16, 1824; m. Sept. 15, 1850, Homerus Washington Burnett.

357.2 Mary Amelia, b. Dec. 17, 1825 ; d. unm. 1840.

357.3 Sidney, b. Oct. 4, 1828; m. March 3, 1862, Phebe Preston.

357.4 Laura Caroline, b. Oct. 17, 1832 ; m. Sept., 1851, Erastus G. Fenn.

## 358 = 355. GEORGE[7] MARSH

of Litchfield, Ct., b. Sept. 8, 1794, son of James[6] and Ursula (Hayden) Marsh, (Roger[5], George[4], John[3], John[2], John[1]) ; m. Aug. 14, 1822, No. 358.

**358.** Caroline Gilbert, b. April 15, 1802. She was sister of Wm. L. Gilbert, the millionaire and philanthropist, famous as the Gilbert clock manufacturer of Winsted, Ct. As this connection helped materially to shape the lives of George Marsh and his children it is in order to mention here some of Mr. Gilbert's benefactions, viz. $100,000 to found and $400,000, to maintain the Gilbert home for the friendless at Winsted ; $40,000, to Gilbert school for colored girls at Winsted, La.; $500,000 for public school of high order in East Winsted, Ct.; $48,000, for tunneling the mountain for a better water supply of Winchester, (now Winsted) Ct.; $12,000 to Congregational and $3,000 to Episcopal churches of Northfield, Ct.; $19.000 ($1,000 each) to 19 nephews and nieces and divided stock in value $30,000, to James Woodruff and Ben. F. Marsh, nephews of Winsted, and his niece, Mrs. E. Whiting, of Canada.

George Marsh went to Ohio to sell clocks for the Gilberts. His family resided awhile at Athens, O. He traveled extensively over the state, entering government lands at $1.25 an acre and bought many acres in different counties. In 1834–5 he went to Van Wert Co. and was one of the four proprietors of Van Wert the county seat. In 1847–8 he moved his family from Athens to Van Wert, and purchased the St. Charles Hotel, now the De Puy House. At the first sale of lots he had a large tract of land carefully bounded, " to have all the lands except the commons for $150, but if Mr. Marsh will erect a sawmill within two years within one mile of Van Wert to pay only $100." He had large land transactions with James Watson

Riley whose father Capt. James (see Riley's Narrative and also sketch
under No. 4419) was Department Surveyor for North Western Ohio.
George Marsh also bought lands 50 miles east of St. Louis in
southern Illinois and had tenants and planted an orchard there.   He
accumulated much property although sometimes from taxes like
other large holders land-poor.

His name fills pages of history of North Western Ohio and of
Athens Co., on the Ohio river.   His wife Caroline (Gilbert) Marsh,
d. May 19, 1849.   After her death he returned to Athens where he
still had property and in course of time married a widow with several
children.   After his second marriage he laid out the town of Marshfield, O., a few miles west of Athens on the B. & O. S. W. R. R. Ohio
Division.   Marcus L. Griswold of Marshfield, O. writes, " George
Marsh died here." Mrs. Wm. Wiltshire Riley (see No. 4420) who
has supplied most of the above, writes, " Mr. Marsh was often at our
home in Columbus, O.   I saw them when he moved his family to
Van Wert.   I saw them in Athens in 1846."   She adds, " He went
back to Van Wert to his children and *I think there died.*   Peaceful be
his rest after his earthly toil, while others reap the harvest."   Children :

359.  James Gilbert⁸, b. March 3, 1824; d. Dec. 2, 1826.
359.1 Harriet Caroline, b. July 28, 1828; d. infancy.
359.2 Henrietta Caroline, b. March 22, 1830; m. Robert Gilliland
       and d. June 22, 1869.   They had: 1, Lenox⁹, b. July 4,
       1850, of Belmore, O.; 2, Katherine, d. in infancy.
359.3 James, d. y. in 1834.
359.4 George Hayden, b. Dec. 23, 1833; m. H. Vance, 361.
360.  Ben Frank, b. May 21, 1842 ; m. C. H. Doolittle, 362.


### 361 =359.4.  GEORGE HAYDEN⁸ MARSH

b. Dec. 23, 1833, son of George⁷, (James⁶, Roger⁵, George⁴, John³,
John², John¹); m. No. 361.

**361.**  Hilinda Vance.   In 1880 he resided on the Marsh farm
adjoining Van Wert on the east.   He is said to be " in some line of
manufacturing and quite wealthy, ' worth probably half a million.' "
Also " George H. Marsh of Van Wert is largely engaged in several
lines of business and in partnership with different individuals.   One
of his associates is the noted Senator Calvin S. Brice.   Child :

361.1  Katie⁹, b. Aug. 24, 1863; m. Arthur I. Clymer of Van
        Wert, Ohio.

## 362 = 360.  BENJAMIN F⁸. MARSH

of Athens and Van Wert, O. and of West Winsted, Ct., b. May 21, 1842, son of George⁷ and Caroline (Gilbert) Marsh, (James⁶, Roger⁵, George⁴, John³, John², John¹) ; m. Feb. 7, 1866, No. 362.

**362.** Catherine Hooker Doolittle, b. March 22, 1843. In the war of the rebellion he was in Co. E, 2d regiment infantry and lost an arm at Port Hudson. He was a member of the Connecticut legislature in 1886, and in 1892 was an assistant in the state treasury at Hartford. His mother's brother left him stock in the Gilbert Clock Co., valued at $10,000. He lives at West Winsted. Children :

    362.1  Katherine Harriet⁹, b. Dec. 14, 1870.
    362.2  George Hooker, b. March 20, 1872.
    362.3  Frank Gilbert, b. Aug. 24, 1886.

## 363 = 339.  SUSAN⁶ MARSH

of Litchfield, dau. of Roger⁵ and Lucy (Kilbourn) Marsh, (George⁴, John³, John², John¹) ; m. No. 363.

**363.** David Little. Children :

    364.  Julia⁷, b. Aug. 13 ; m. Rufus Thorpe. He d. 1886. No children.
    365.  Earle, b. Dec. 25 ; m. (1) Thankful Carrier; (2) Sally Judd.
    366.  Horace, b. 1811 ; unm.
    367.  Harriet, d. y.
    368.  Caroline, b. Jan. 19, 1813 ; unm.

## 399 = 340.  ROGER⁶ MARSH

of Litchfield, Ct., b. Dec. 9, 1768, son of Roger⁵ and Lucy (Kilbourn) Marsh, (George⁴, John³, John², John¹) ; m. No. 369.

**369.** Phebe Norton. He was lister at Litchfield, 1789 and grand juror, 1790. They removed to Manlius Square, N. Y. Children :

    370.  Nancy⁷, m. Lewis Johnson.
    371.  Emeline, m. William Scoville.
    372.  Burr.
    373.  Hamilton.

5*

### 374 = 341.   APPLETON[6] MARSH

of Litchfield, b. May 23, 1770, son of Roger[5] and Lucy (Kilbourn) Marsh, (George[4], John[3], John[2], John[1]); m. in 1794, No. 374.

**374.** Elizabeth Hotchkiss.   He went to Manlius Square, N. Y.; d. 1860, æ. 90.   Children :

>375. Linus[7], b. Dec., 1795; m. Phila Morse; four daus., two dead.
>376. Frederick, b. Sept., 1801 ; d. Jan., 1804.
>377. Morris, b. May, 1807 ; m. Jan., 1833.

### 377.1 = 377.   MORRIS[7] MARSH

of Litchfield, b. May 13, 1807, son of Appleton[6] and Elizabeth (Hotchkiss) Marsh, (Roger[5], George[4], John[3], John[2], John[1]); m. Jan., 1833, No. 377.1.

**377.1.** Alice Williams, b. April 8, 1815, d. May 11, 1889.   He d. Nov. 7, 1873.   Children :

>378. Elizabeth[8], b. Dec. 22, 1833 ; m. L. B. Nimbs, 389.
>379. Charles, b. Sept. 24, 1835 ; m. Miss Trumbull, 392.
>379.1 Amelia, b. April 24, 1837 ; d. Aug., 1838.
>380. Millie M., b. Aug. 9, 1839 ; m. John Shultz, 398.
>381. George W., b. Dec. 18, 1841 ; m. Matie King, 400.
>382. Uri J., b. May 6, 1844 ; m. March, 1870, Emma Trumbull.
>382.1 Eliza, b. April, 1847 ; d. June, 1849.
>383. Alice A., b. April 28, 1849 ; m. A. S. Miles, 403.
>384. William P., b. May 13, 1852 ; m. Lydia L. Pratt, 408.
>385. Elon A., b. April 24, 1854 ; m. Gertrude B. Huylor, 411.
>386. Frank A., b. Aug. 19, 1856; unm.
>387. Albert, b. Sept. 25, 1857 ; m. Etta Humphrey, 416.

### 389 = 378.   ELIZABETH[8] MARSH

of Litchfield, b. Dec. 22, 1833, dau. of Morris[7] Marsh, (Appleton[6], Roger[5], George[4], John[3], John[2], John[1]); m. April, 1862, No. 389.

**389.** L. Barnard Nimbs of Waterloo, N. Y.   Children :

>390. Cora[9], b. Feb., 1864.
>391. Edna, b. Feb., 1874.

### 392 = 379.   CHARLES[8] MARSH

of Litchfield, b. Sept., 1836, son of Morris[7] Marsh, (Appleton[6], Roger[5], George[4], John[3], John[2], John[1]); m. (1) in 1855, No. 392,

**392.** Jennie Trumbull. She d. 1859 and he m. (2) in 1867, her sister Mrs. Debbie Burnham. Children:

> 392.1 Lillian, b. 1857 ; d. y.
> 393. Charles[9], b. March, 1859; d. March, 1869.
>> By second wife.
> 394. Emma, b. March 17, 1870.
> 395. George M., b. 1872.
> 396. Minnie, b. Dec., 1874.
> 397. Albert, b. 1876.

### 398 = 380. MILLIE M[8]. MARSH

of Litchfield, b. Aug., 1838, dau. of Morris[7] Marsh, (Appleton[6] Roger[5], George[4], John[3], John[2], John[1]) ; m. Sept. 20, 1868, No. 398.

**398.** John Shultz of Battle Creek, Mich. Child:

> 399. Edith Iola[9], b. Nov. 25, 1872 ; m. April 18, 1892, Claude A. Banta. Child: Gertrude[10], b. March 6, 1894.

### 400 = 381. GEORGE W.[8] MARSH

of Litchfield, b. Dec. 18, 1841, son of Morris[7] Marsh, (Appleton[6], Roger[5], George[4], John[3], John[2], John[1]) ; m. Aug. 16, 1865, No. 400.

**400.** Matie King. Children:

> 401. George Ernest[9], b. Nov. 3, 1866.
> 402. Grace Emogene, b. May 5, 1870 ; m. Frederick Webber.

### 403 = 383. ALICE A[8]. MARSH

b. April 28, 1849, dau. of Morris[7] Marsh, (Appleton[6], Roger[5], George[4], John[3], John[2], John[1]) ; m. April 27, 1871, No. 403.

**403.** Amos S. Miles of Battle Creek, Mich. Children:

> 404. Clare Austin[9], b. Feb. 19, 1872 ; d. Feb. 1, 1880.
> 405. Bertie Louise, b. Aug. 13, 1874.
> 406. Bessie May, b. Dec. 26, 1878; d. Aug. 3, 1880.
> 407. Ray Victor, b. May 26, 1884 ; d. March 19, 1887.

### 408 = 384. WILLIAM P[8]. MARSH

of Litchfield, b. May 13, 1852, son of Morris[7] Marsh, (Appleton[6], Roger[5], George[4], John[3], John[2], John[1]) ; m. Aug. 6, 1876, No. 408,

**408.** Lydia L. Pratt.  Children :

409.  Harry L⁹., b. Feb. 13, 1879.
410.  Clayton C., b. May 13, 1883.


411 = 385.  ELON AUGUSTUS⁸ MARSH

b. April 24, 1854, son of Morris⁷ Marsh, (Appleton⁶, Roger⁵, George⁴, John³, John², John¹) ; m. May 11, 1876, No. 411. **411.** Gertrude Brokaw Huylor, b. July 27, 1858.  He is general manager Battle Creek, Mich. Machinery Co.  Children :

412.  Allon Huylor⁹, b. April 1, 1878.
413.  Montgomery M., b. May 2, 1880.
414.  J. Walter, b. June 26, 1882.
415.  Augustus Sharpe, b. April 2, 1884.
415.1  Clifford V., b. Feb. 8, 1887.


416 = 387.  ALBERT⁸ MARSH

son of Morris⁷ Marsh, (Appleton⁶, Roger⁵, George⁴, John³, John², John¹) b. Sept. 25, 1857 ; m. Oct. 8, 1879, No. 416. **416.** Etta Humphrey.  Children :

417.  Charles A⁹., b. Nov. 28, 1880.
418.  Louis F., b. July 14, 1883.
418.1  Clyde R., b. March 2, 1888.


419 = 342.  HORACE⁶ MARSH

of Litchfield, b. (?) son of Roger⁵ and Lucy (Kilbourn) Marsh, (George⁴, John³, John², John¹) ; m. in 1807, No. 419. **419.** Eunice Morse.  Children :

420.  Lucinda⁷, b. 1810; deaf mute, unm.
421.  Harriet, b. July 4, 1813; m. Henry D. Calkins, 429.
422.  Burritt, b. 1815 ; d. unm. about 1838.
423.  Bennett, b. 1817 ; prob. massacred by Indians as he started from California for Oregon and was not heard from afterwards.
424.  Clarissa, b. 1819; m. George Garritt, 435.
425.  Lucius, b. April 1, 1822; m. Phebe Curtiss, 439.
426.  Susan A., b. May 31, 1824 ; m. Richard Andrews, 443.
427.  Emeline, b. 1829; killed by lightning Aug. 27, 1887, æ. abt. 57.
428.  Andrew J., b. April 15, 1833; m. Caroline A. Waldron, 447.

## 429 = 421. HARRIET[7] MARSH

dau. of Horace[6] and Eunice (Morse) Marsh, (Roger[5], George[4], John[3], John[2], John[1]) b. July 4, 1813 ; m. Jan. 1, 1837, No. 429.

**429.** Henry D. Calkins, who d. May 14, 1884. Children :

    430. Arthur B[8]., b. Jan. 17, 1843; m. 1862, Emma R. Thompkins.
    431. Wilbur F., b. Dec. 15, 1844; m. Aug., 1863, Rowena M. Ball.
    432. Harriet I., b. Jan. 12, 1847 ; m. Dec. 25, 1874, Linus W. Kirk, Jr.
    433. Ward F., b. April 2, 1856 ; m. Aug. 16, 1877, Sarah Judson.


## 435 = 424. CLARISSA[7] MARSH

dau. of Horace[6] Marsh, (Roger[5], George[4], John[3], John[2], John[1]) b. 1819 ; m. No. 435.

**435.** George Garritt. Children :

    436. Burritt[8].
    437. Lewis.
    438. Dwight.


## 439 = 425. LUCIUS[7] MARSH

son of Horace[6] and Eunice (Morse) Marsh, (Roger[5], George[4], John[3], John[2], John[1]) b. April 1, 1822 ; m. April 1, 1845, No. 439.

**439.** Phebe Curtiss, d. Jan. 1, 1884. Children :

    440. Burritt[8], b. Jan., 1846; m. Sept. 3, 1885, Emeline A. Teeler. Child :
        441. Miles Lucius, b. Oct. 23, 1886.
    442. Lucy Phebe, b. Dec. 14, 1847 ; unm.


## 443 = 426. SUSAN A[7]. MARSH

dau. of Horace[6], (Roger[5], George[4], John[3], John[2], John[1]) b. May 31, 1824; m. Feb. 23, 1845, No. 443.

**443.** Richard Andrews of Wallingford, Ct. Children :

444. Susan E⁸., b. April 27, 1851.
445. Lillian, b. May 8, 1858.
446. William B., b. Jan. 25, 1861.

447 = 428. ANDREW J⁷. MARSH

son of Horace⁶, (Roger⁵, George⁴, John³, John², John¹) b. April 15, 1833 ; m. in 1864, No. 447.
**447.** Caroline A. Waldron. Children :

    448. Mary E⁸., b. May 12, 1865.
    449. George A., b. Aug. 25, 1866.
    450. Walter H., b. June 3, 1868.
    451. Burritt A., b. May 21, 1875.

452 = 344. AARON⁶ MARSH

of Litchfield, Ct., b. about 1774–6, son of Roger⁵ and Lucy (Kilbourn) Marsh, (George⁴, John³, John², John¹) ; m. in 1810, No. 452.
**452.** Martha Landon. He was assessor in Litchfield in 1811. Children :

    453. Child. Still born.
    454. Sylvia⁶, b. 1813 ; m. 1856, Joel Castle. She d. Nov. 11, 1887, æ. 74.
    455. James Erwin, b. 1818 ; m. 1842, Eveline Roper and d. 1842.
    456. Lucy A., b. July 4, 1820 ; m. March 29, 1858, Jerry B. Curtiss. Child :
        457. Eugene Marsh⁷, who m. Nov. 30, 1885, Fanny Coon.

458 = 345. MOSES⁶ MARSH

of Litchfield, son of Roger⁵ and Lucy (Kilbourn) Marsh, (George⁴, John³, John², John¹) b. Aug. 26, 1778 ; m. in 1818, No. 458.
**458.** Dorcas Little of Granby, Ct. He d. July 29, 1824, æ. 46. Children :

    459. Linus⁷, b. July 22, 1819 ; m. Frances G. Hall, 461.
    460. Lewis, b. Aug. 26, 1822 ; m. Eveline M. Stone, 465.

## 461 = 459. LINUS[7] MARSH

of Litchfield, b. July 22, 1819, son of Moses[6] and Dorcas (Little) Marsh, (Roger[5], George[4], John[3], John[2], John[1]); m. March 7, 1852, No. 461.

**461.** Frances G. Hall. He was grand juror five years from 1848. He was a veteran wagon maker of Westbrook, Ct. and d. Feb. 26, 1892. Children :

    462. Henry M[8]., b. Dec. 27, 1852; m. June 5, 1876. Child :
        463. Rose[9], b. July, 1886.
    464. Ellen C., b. Jan. 30, 1854.

## 465 = 460. LEWIS[7] MARSH

of Burlington, Ct., son of Moses[6] and Dorcas (Little) Marsh, (Roger[5], George[4], John[3], John[2], John[1]) b. Aug. 26, 1822 ; m. Sept. 21, 1848, No. 465.

**465.** Eveline M. Stone. Child :

    466. Mary E[8]., b. July 27, 1849; m. Edgar B. Bennett, 467.

## 467 = 466. MARY E[8]. MARSH

dau. of Lewis[7], (Moses[6], Roger[5], George[4], John[3], John[2], John[1]) b. July 27, 1849 ; m. April 9, 1865, No. 467.

**467.** Edgar B. Bennett. In the late war he was in Co. I. 1st regiment Ct. heavy artillery. Children :

    468. Minerva S[9]., b. July 9, 1867 ; m. 1888.
    469. Zola, b. Oct. 29, 1870.

## 470 = 268. GEORGE[5] MARSH

of Litchfield, b. Sept. 25, 1736, son of George[4] and Lydia (Bird) Marsh, (John[3], John[2], John[1]); m. in Litchfield, No. 470.

**470.** Catherine Kilbourn. Afterwards removed to Canada. Children :

471.  Rebecca[6].
472.  Elizabeth.
473.  George, m. Lydia Buell, b. 1767, sister Capt. Samuel.
474.  Jeremiah.
475.  Sylvia.
476.  Susan.
477.  Cyrus.
478.  Darius, (was he father of Mrs. Eof, wife of a banker in
       Boise City, Idaho?)
479.  Charles.
480.  Catherine.
481.  Harry.

## 482 = 269.  ELIJAH[5] MARSH

-of Litchfield, Ct., son of George[4] and Lydia (Bird) Marsh (John[3], John[2], John[1]) b. perhaps 1738; m. No. 482.

**482.** ——. Children:

483.  Anna[6], m. Asahel Peck.
484.  Nabby, m. Smith Pierpont.
485.  Elijah.
486.  Zebulon.
487.  Rhoda, m. Scoville.
488.  Ozias, b. Litchfield, Oct. 24, 1777 ; m. Parthenia Andrus, 490.
489.  Jesse, b. Dec. 25, 1780, in Litchfield; m.(1) Phebe Crofut, 523.

## 490 = 488.  OZIAS[6] MARSH

b. Litchfield, Ct., Oct. 24, 1777, son of Elijah[5], (George[4], John[3], John[2], John[1]); m. (1) Feb. 27, 1803, No. 490.

**490.** Parthenia Andrus, b. Sept. 20, 1784 ; d. July 30, 1816, and he m. (2) July 27, 1817, No. 491.

**491.** Phebe Noble, dau. of Nathan Noble, b. Feb. 27, 1792 ; d. March 21, 1869. He went to Illinois from near Binghamton, N. Y., in 1836. He d. Oct. 11, 1851. Children:

492.  Thomas D[7]., b. May 24, 1806 ; m. 499.
493.  Melicent A., b. July 20, 1810 ; d. Oct. 23, 1826.
494.  Noble T., b. Aug. 19, 1812.
495.  Harriet N., b. Jan. 1, 1815 ; m. Nathaniel Huggins.
496.  Gustavus A., b. April 11, 1818; m. Fidelia, 519.
497.  Ozias J., b. May 24, 1822.
498.  Phebe Sophronia, b. Oct. 17, 1827 ; m. Edson Huggins, 521.

## 499 = 492. THOMAS D[7]. MARSH

of Illinois, son of Ozias[6] and Parthenia (Andrus) Marsh (Elijah[5], George[4], John[3], John[2], John[1]) b. May 24, 1806, removed with his father's family from near Binghamton, N. Y. to Illinois in 1836. He m. No. 499.

**499.** ——. Children.

500. Sophia[8], m. (1) Amos W. Huggins, 505.
501. Benjamin Alden, d. at Cairo hospital in the war.
502. Noble Leroy, res. Galesburg, Ill.; owns largest feed and sale stable in the city and ships horses east. No. 43, North Cherry Street.
503. Hannah P., m. William W. Blair, who was in 83d Ill. Vol. in the war; is a carpenter and lives at Abingdon, Knox Co., Ill.
504. Ella F., m. Rev. J. L. Crawford, 508.

## 505 = 500. SOPHIA[8] MARSH

of Windsor, Mo., dau. of Thomas D[7]. Marsh, (Ozias[6], Elijah[5], George[4], John[3], John[2], John[1]) b. (?); m. (1) No. 505.

**505.** Amos W. Huggins, a missionary in Minnesota at the time of the Indian massacre in 1862. He was shot by the savages in his own yard. She was taken prisoner with her children and was a prisoner eight weeks when friendly Indians, dressed as savages bought her on pretence that they wanted to kill her. Three or four months after her escape she had another son. She m. (2) Mr. Hawthorne and is living in Windsor, Mo. Children :

506. Charles Loyal Huggins, San Francisco, Cal.
507. Amos Huggins, Berkley, Cal.

## 508 = 504. ELLA[8] MARSH

of Table Grove, Fulton Co., Ill., dau. of Thomas D[7]. Marsh, (Ozias[6], Elijah[5], George[4], John[3], John[2], John[1]) ; m. April 4, 1866, No. 508.

**508.** Rev. J. L. Crawford of the Cumberland Presbyterian church who was in the 83d Illinois Volunteers of the war. Children :

509.  Charles Alden[8], b. Jan. 7, 1867 ; d. Dec. 3, 1870.
510.  Sophronia Elizabeth, b. Oct. 3, 1868.
511.  Harriet Emma, b. June 12, 1870; m. Oct. 25, 1888, Moses C. Foster.
512.  Adna Biddle, b. June 2, 1872; d. Sept. 2, 1879.
513.  Leroy Wilson, b. Oct. 20, 1874.
514.  John DeWitt, b. May 27, 1877.
515.  Philena Bell, b. Nov. 2, 1879.
516.  Edith Eloise, b. Sept. 8, 1882.
517.  Agnes Josephine, b. Oct. 12, 1884.
518.  Alta May, b. June 10, 1887.

519 = 496.  CAPT. GUSTAVUS A[7]. MARSH

of Galesburg, Ill., b. April 11, 1818, son of Ozias[6] and Phebe (Noble) Marsh, (Elijah[5], George[4], John[3], John[2], John[1]) was Captain in the war of the rebellion.  He m. No. 519.

**519.**  Fidelia who still lives in Galesburg.  Child :

520.  Albert[8], res. in Galesburg.

521 = 498.  PHEBE SOPHRONIA[7] MARSH

dau. of Ozias[6] and Phebe (Noble) Marsh, b. Oct. 17, 1827 ; m. Sept. 11, 1844, No. 521.

**521.**  Edson Huggins.  She d. July 4, 1856.  Child :

522.  Eloise[8], m. John Stickney, principal of the high school, Knoxville, Ill.

523 = 489.  JESSE[6] MARSH

b. in Litchfield, Ct., Dec. 25, 1780, son of Elijah[5], (George[4], John[3], John[2], John[1]) removed to Broome Co., N. Y., about 1800.  He m. (1) July 19, 1803, No. 523.

**523.**  Phebe Crofut.  She d. in 1822.  He m. (2) Feb. 7, 1803, No. 524.

**524.**  Achsah Knowlton from Ashford, Ct.   Children :

525. Betsey[7], b. Dec. 23, 1805; m.
526. Levi, b. April 17, 1811; m. —— Keziah, 533.
527. Selinda, b. Oct. 29, 1817; m.
528. Sarah, b. May 6, 1820; m. Alonzo Dibble, 540.
529. Danforth K., b. June 30, 1826; m. Sarah Watrous, 544.
530. Miner P., b. Oct. 9, 1827; m. Catherine Farnham, 548.
531. Rev. John B., b. May 26, 1830; res, Catawba, N. C.; m. ——
      Rachel. No children.
532. Maurice Ozias, b. June 19, 1833; m. Rosetta.


### 533 = 526. LEVI[7] MARSH

b. Broome Co., N. Y., probably Harpursville, April 17, 1811, son of
Jesse[6] and Phebe (Crofut) Marsh, (Elijah[5], George[4], John[3], John[2],
John[1]) m. No. 533.

**533.** Keziah. Widow Keziah Marsh lived (1888)at Marshfield,
Pa. Children :

534. Walter E[8]., m. res. Pleasant Valley, Lincoln Co., Kansas and
      has children.
535. Thomas D., m. res. Tioga, Pa. and has children.
536. Phebe.
537. Mary.
538. Sarah.
539. James.


### 540 = 528. SARAH[7] MARSH

b. May 6, 1820, dau. of Jesse[6] and Phebe (Crofut) Marsh (Elijah[5],
George[4], John[3], John[2], John[1]); m. No. 540.

**540.** Alonzo Dibble and resides Harpursville, Broome Co., N. Y.
Children:

541. Jesse[8].
542. Charles.
543. Laura.


### 544 = 529. DANFORTH KNOWLTON[7] MARSH

b. Broome Co., N. Y., June 30, 1826, son of Jesse[6] and Achsah

6

(Knowlton) Marsh, (Elijah[5], George[4], John[3], John[2], John[1]), removed to Tioga Co., Pa., about 1846 ; m. June 30, 1852, No. 544.

**544.** Sarah Watrous.  Residence Marshfield, Pa.  Children :

    **545.** Howard Franklin[8], b. Jan. 5, 1854 ; m. Annie Brysen, 554.
    **546.** Emma Caroline, b. April 7, 1860 ; m. Feb., 1882, Samuel Champaign.
    **547.** Win Watrous, b. June 6, 1874.

## 548 = 530.  MINER PARKER[7] MARSH

b. probably Harpursville, Broome Co., N. Y., son of Jesse[6] and Achsah (Knowlton) Marsh (Elijah[5], George[4], John[3], John[2], John[1]), removed to Tioga Co., Pa., about 1850 ; m. 1858, No. 548.

**548.** Catherine Farnham.  Residence, Marshfield, Pa.  Children:

    **549.** Cora Sophia[8], b. 1860 ; m. about 1884, A. V. Wetmore.
    **550.** Annie, b. about 1863.
    **551.** Jesse, b. about 1865.
    **552.** Harry, b. about 1867.
    **553.** Hugh, b. about 1876.

## 554 = 545.  HOWARD FRANKLIN[8] MARSH

b. Tioga Co., Pa., Jan. 5, 1854, son of Danforth K[7]. and Sarah (Watrous) Marsh, (Jesse[6], Elijah[5], George[4], John[3], John[2], John[1]); m. June 19, 1882, No. 554.

**554.** Annie Brysen.  Residence, Wellsboro, Pa., is an attorney at law.

## 555 = 532.  MAURICE OZIAS[7] MARSH

b. June 19, 1833, in Broome Co., N. Y., son of Jesse[6] and Achsah (Knowlton) Marsh, (Elijah[5], George[4], John[3], John[2], John[1]); m. No. 555.

**555.** Rosetta.  Resides at Harpursville, Broome Co., N. Y. Children :

    **556.** Frederick.
    **557.** Fonda.

## 558 = 98.  QUARTERMASTER-GENERAL ISAAC[4] MARSH

of Litchfield, Ct., b. at Hartford, Ct., Nov. 8, 1709, bap. Nov. 27, son of John[3] and Elizabeth (Pitkin) Marsh, (John[2], John[1]); when a little over 11 years old, went with his father from Hartford in 1821, to Litchfield, Ct. He m. Dec. 23, 1735, No. 558.

**558.** Susannah Pratt of Hartford. His only living male descendant of Marsh name, Lewis Myron[8] Marsh, now 1892, living in Litchfield on land occupied by his Marsh ancestry from John[3] in 1721, has in his possession the original deed of his land given to John[3], and for six generations passed down from father to son ever since. He has also the original commission, given by Gov. Jonathan Law, commander in chief of his Majesty's troops in the colony of Connecticut, appointing Isaac[4] Marsh Quartermaster-General. Gen. Isaac Marsh and his wife Susannah lived to good old age and died within one month of each other in 1788; he on March 8, æ. 79 and she on April 6, æ. 76. His military associations account in part for the marriage of his daughter to Gen. Skinner. His own father was Captain John Marsh commissioned May, 1722; his oldest brother, Ebenezer, was Colonel, commissioned 1757, and his next younger brother, John[4], was Captain. Children:

> 559. Isaac[5], b. Sept. 11, 1736; m. Martha Lyman, 566.
> 560. Ruth, b. May 14, 1738; m. John Wadhams and they had:
> > 561. John Marsh[6] Wadham of Goshen, Ct.
> 562. Elizabeth, m. Roswell McNiel.
> 563. Elisha, b. Nov. 15, 1742; m. Honour Beckley, 576.
> 564. Sally, m. David King, grand juror 1780.
> 565. Susannah, b. Aug. 20, 1746; m. Gen. Timothy Skinner, 619.

### 566 = 559.  ISAAC[5] MARSH

b. Litchfield, Sept. 11, 1736, son of Gen. Isaac[4] and Susannah (Pratt) Marsh, (John[3], John[2], John[1]); m. Nov. 24, 1776, No. 566.

**566.** Martha Lyman. He d. Aug. 9, 1779, æ. 43. Child:

> 567. Isaac[6], b. Feb. 18, 1777.

### 568 = 567.  DR. ISAAC[6] MARSH

b. Litchfield, Feb. 18, 1777, only child of Isaac[5] and Martha (Lyman)

Marsh, (Gen. Isaac[4], John[3], John[2], John[1]); m. Oct. 2, 1803, his cousin, No. 568.

**568.** Mary[6] Marsh, 580, dau. of Elisha[5] and Honour (Beckley) Marsh, (Gen. Isaac[4], John[3], John[2], John[1]), b. Nov. 4, 1781. Dr. Isaac bought farm 1830 in Cornwall and gave up medicine. He d. at Cornwall, Ct., Sept. 1, 1829, æ. 53. His widow d. March 19, 1843. They had children all but one of whom d. unm. :

569.   Isaac[7], b. Dec. 15, 1803; clerk W. Cornwall Iron Co., town clerk, representative 1839-40 and 1851-2 ; lived 30 years at W. Cornwall; m. Nov. 29, 1843, Nancy Smith. He d. Jan. 29, 1879. No children.

570.   Anna, b. June 16, 1805; d. Nov. 18, 1829.

571.   Laura, b. May 1, 1807; d. Jan. 11, 1829.

572.   William, b. Dec. 4, 1808.

573.   Mary, b. Oct. 11, 1810; d. May 19, 1830.

574.   Almira, b. Dec. 9, 1812; d. April 11, 1837.

575.   Abigail, b. April 29, 1815 ; d. June 2, 1852.


## 576 = 563.   ELISHA[5] MARSH

of Litchfield, Ct., b. Nov. 15, 1742, son of Gen. Isaac[4] and Susannah (Pratt) Marsh, (John[3], John[2], John[1]) ; m. 1764, No. 576.

**576.** Honour Beckley. He d. Jan. 20, 1804. His widow d. in Sept., 1809. Children :

577.   Honour[6], b. July 23, 1766; m. Obed Buell, 581.

578.   Abigail, b. Nov. 15, 1769; m. Eliada Osborn, 597.

579.   Elisha, b. Aug. 27, 1772; m. Rhoda Kilbourn, 604.

580.   Mary, b. Nov. 4, 1781; m. Dr. Isaac Marsh, 568.


## 581 = 577.   HONOUR[6] MARSH

b. Litchfield, Ct., July 23, 1766, dau. Elisha[5] and Honour (Beckley) Marsh, (Gen. Isaac[4], John[3], John[2], John[1]); m. Dec. 25, 1788, No. 581.

**581.** Obed Buell. Children :

582.   Belinda[7].

583.   Elias.

584.   Elisha.

585.   L——.

586. Andrew.
587. Silas.
588. Melinda.
589. Honour.
590. Almira.
591. Obed A., m. ——, 594.
592. William E.
593. Charles H.


594 = 591. OBED A⁷. BUELL

m. No. 594.
594. ——. Children:
595. William A., and family are living on the old Buell homestead about three miles north of Litchfield village.
596. Lyman and family res. near Keokuk, Iowa,


597 = 578. ABIGAIL⁶ MARSH

b. Litchfield, Nov. 15, 1769, dau. Elisha⁵ and Honour (Beckley) Marsh, (Gen. Isaac⁴, John³, John², John¹); m. May 31, 1794 or 5, No. 597.
597. Eliada Osborn of Litchfield. Children:
598. Myron, b. Sept. 28, 1796.
599. John, b. Dec. 25, 1799.
600. Rebecca, b. April 28, 1801.
601. Elisha, b. May 4, 1804.
602. Nathan, b. July 27, 1807.
603. Dr. Eliada, b. Aug. 1, 1810.


604 = 579. ELISHA⁶ MARSH

b. Litchfield, Aug. 27, 1772, son of Elisha⁵ and Honour (Beckley) Marsh, (Gen. Isaac⁴, John³, John², John¹); m. 1802, No. 604.
604. Rhoda Kilbourn. He d. Dec. 16, 1841, and his widow d. March 5, 1850. Children:
605. Sally⁷, b. April 25, 1803; m. Oct. 6, 1852, Nathaniel Bissell, who d. June 15, 1872. She d.

606. Mary, b. Dec. 9, 1804; d. unm. Jan. 8, 1892, æ. 87.
607. Rhoda, b. Aug. 4, 1806; d. Feb. 12, 1882, æ. 75 years and six months.
608. Elisha, b. April 4, 1808; d. May 13, 1840.
609. Lewis, b. Nov. 28, 1810; d. April 24, 1865.
610. Elias, b. Sept. 18, 1812; d. July 20, 1820.
611. Myron, b. March 2, 1814; m. Clarissa A. Bradley 613.
612. George, b. Dec. 25, 1816; d. Dec. 17, 1817.

### 613 = 611. MYRON[7] MARSH

b. Litchfield, March 2, 1814, son of Elisha[6] and Rhoda (Kilburn) Marsh, (Elisha[5], Gen. Isaac[4], John[3], John[2], John[1]); m. Oct. 7, 1856, No. 613.
**613.** Clarissa A. Bradley. Children:

614. Anna Catlin[8], b. Aug. 23, 1857; m. Andrew L. Johnson, 616.
615. Lewis Myron, b. Dec. 29, 1861; m. Harriet Elizabeth Morse, 618.

### 616 = 614. ANNA CATLIN[8] MARSH

b. Litchfield, Aug. 23, 1857, dau. Myron[7] and Clarissa (Bradley) Marsh, (Elisha[6], Elisha[5], Gen. Isaac[4], John[3], John[2], John[1]); m. April 9, 1890, No. 616.
**616.** Andrew L. Johnson of Winchester Centre, Ct. She has done more than any other to give us the long list of Litchfield Marshes. Child:

617. Myron Marsh[9], b. March 24, 1891.

### 618 = 615. LEWIS MYRON[8] MARSH

b. Litchfield, Ct., Dec. 29, 1861, son of Myron[7] and Clarissa (Bradley) Marsh, (Elisha[6], Elisha[5], Gen. Isaac[4], John[3], John[2], John[1]); m. Feb. 25, 1885, No. 618.
**618.** Harriet Elizabeth Morse. "He is of the sixth generation of Marshes living on the same farm, one and one-half miles north of Litchfield Centre, that John[3] Marsh, explorer of Litchfield in 1715 and

pioneer 1721, bought; and he has the original deed given to John[3] Marsh in 1723, and all the other deeds down to the present day. He was before the birth of his sister's son, March 24, 1891, the only living male descendant of the first Elisha[6] Marsh.

## 619 = 565. SUSANNAH[5] MARSH

b. Litchfield, Ct., Aug. 20, 1746, dau. of Gen. Isaac[4] and Susannah (Pratt) Marsh, (John[3], John[2], John[1]); m. No. 619.

**619.** Gen. Timothy Skinner of Litchfield. Owing to youth Mr. Skinner did not become General till after the revolutionary war; but he was in 1780 and onwards, on various committees to collect money for the soldiers to purchase clothing and to inquire about army quotas. He was selectman in 1784 and town treasurer in 1790 and '91. Children :

620. Judge Roger[6], b. Litchfield, June 10, 1773; grand juror Litchfield 1797, lawyer, removed to Sandy Hill, N. Y. in 1806, representative N. Y. legislature 1810, 11 and 12, state senator 1818-21, U. S. attorney northern district N. Y. 1815-19 and judge U. S. district court till death. Res. Albany, N. Y. from 1819. He d. Aug. 19, 1825. Hon. Martin Van Buren afterwards president U. S. was his intimate friend and visited Litchfield with him in 1820. Van Buren wrote of him, " Being a widower myself and he a bachelor, we twice kept house together and did so at the period of his lamented death. I was with him through his last illness, held his hand when he died and mourned for him as for a sincere and affectionate friend."

621. Gov. Richard, LL. D., b. Litchfield, May 30, 1778; graduated Litchfield law school, settled in Manchester, Vt. 1800, became state attorney, speaker of Vt. house, judge of probate, member of congress, chief justice of Vt. and governor, was thrown from his carriage May 10, 1833 and d. in Middlebury, Vt. May 23, 1833, æ. 55. He m. Fannie Pierpont of Manchester. Their only son Mark Skinner lives in Chicago.

## 622 = 99. CAPT. JOHN[4] MARSH

b. Hartford, Ct., Oct. 20, 1712, son of John[3] and Elizabeth (Pitkin) Marsh, (John[2], John[1]), possibly in 1732 m. No. 622.

**622.** Sarah Webster. Although his father's record reads "John Marsh and Sarah Webster were married Aug. 20, 1733, by me, John Marsh, J. P." Capt. John[4] went to Litchfield with his father and family when a boy of nine, in 1821, and res. there most of his life. He was selectman ten years from 1755 and although Captain himself, had some spicy times in the revolution, as selectman in 1777 when his brother's son was suspected of toryism, as the young man's father Col. Ebenezer had been in 1763. (See History Litchfield, pages 83 and 107–9 and 114. Children :

    623.  John[5], b. Oct. 17, 1733, possibly '34 ; m. Anna Marsh, 630.
    624.  Jerusha, b. Oct. 23, 1735 ; m. Capt. Solomon Marsh, 153.
    625.  Elizabeth, m. Col Bezaleel Beebe, 654.
    626.  Rachel, m. Rev. Geo. Beckwith, 674.
    627.  Rhoda, m. Ebenezer Marsh, Jr., 183.
    628.  Mary, m. Benjamin Stone, Jr., 675.
    629.  Sarah, m. Dr. Seth Bird, 678.


## 630 = 623.   JOHN[5] MARSH

b. Litchfield, Oct. 17, 1733 or '34, son of Capt. John[4] and Sarah (Webster) Marsh, (Capt. John[3], John[2], John[1]) ; m. his cousin, No. 630.

**630.** Anna[5] Marsh, b. May 25, 1738, dau. Col. Ebenezer[4] and Deborah (Buell) Marsh (see No. 111.) He resided Morris, Ct., and d. there Dec. 3, 1806. Children :

    631.  Ozias[6], b. about 1764 ; m. Dorcas Goodwin, 637.
    632.  Sarah, b. Jan. 8, 1766 ; m. Dr. Clark Sanford, 645.
    633.  Anne Seymour, b. March 25, 1768 ; m. Dr. Clark Sanford, 645.
    634.  John, b. June 17, 1770 ; d. April 19, 1790.
    635.  Horace, b. July 10, 1772 ; m. Electa Beebe, 653.
    636.  Daniel, b. May 5, 1774.


## 637 = 631.   OZIAS[6] MARSH

of Litchfield, b. about 1764, son of John[5], (John[4], John[3], John[2], John[1]) ; m. June 23, 1788, No. 637.

**637.** Dorcas[6] Goodwin, dau. of Nathaniel Goodwin and Elizabeth[5] Marsh, (Col. Ebenezer[4], John[3], John[2], John[1]). Children :

638. Manorah.
639. Richard.
640. Susan.
641. Mary Ann.
642. Lydia.
643. William.
643.1 Horatio.


## 644 = 632. SARAH[6] MARSH

dau. John[5], (son of Capt. John[4]) and Anna[5] Marsh, (Col. Ebenezer[4], John[3], John[2], John[1]) ; m. No. 644.

**644.** Dr. Clark Sanford. She d. soon and Dr. Sanford m. her sister.


## 645 = 633. ANNE SEYMOUR[6] MARSH

dau. John[5] (son Capt. John[4], Capt. John[3], John[2], John[1]) and Anna[5] (Col. Ebenezer[4], Capt. John[3], John[2], John[1]) ; m. about 1785, No. 645.

**645.** Dr. Clark Sanford. They removed to Petersburg, Va., soon after marriage and most of their children were born in Virginia. Later Dr. Sanford resided in Greenwich, Ct. and was often called over 30 miles to New York City in dangerous cases. He d. at Greenwich, Sept. 5, 1819, in his 56th year. Mrs. Sanford " greatly beloved " d. June 20, 1847 in her 79th year. Children :

    646.• Josephus[7], b. 1786; M. D. a skillful surgeon and physician, sometime of Petersburg, Va.; d. of consumption in his 27th year at Prince Edward, Va.
    647. John C.
    648. Henry J.
    649. Pamela, m. Judge Brown of Rye, Ct. Had :
        650. Sanford C[8].
        651. Mary Pamela. (Mrs. Satterlee.)
        652. Anna Evelyn. (Mrs. Bissell.)


## 653 = 635. HORACE[6] MARSH

b. July 10, 1772, son John[5], (John[4], John[3], John[2], John[1]) and Anne[5]

(Marsh) Marsh, (Col. Ebenezer[4], John[3], John[2], John[1]) ; m. No. 653.
**653.** Electa Beebe of Canaan, Ct.


654 = 625.   ELIZABETH[5] MARSH

b. Litchfield, dau. Capt. John[4] and Sarah (Webster) Marsh, (John[3],
John[2], John[1]) ; m. July 11, 1764, No. 654.
**654.** Col. Bezaleel Beebe, b. Litchfield, April 27, 1841. There
is an interesting sketch of Col. Beebe in the History of Litchfield.
He was active in both the French and revolutionary wars, enlisting
when 17 ; was member of Major Rogers' celebrated rangers whose
exploits were published in London; was five years in the French
wars and from April, 1775 except when prisoner of war till 1781 in
the revolutionary war, rising to rank of Colonel and when Chief
Commander of the coast guard having the duties and pay of a Brig-
adier General.  He was representative 1781–83 and of the legislature 1792–3 and '95.  Several of his military letters are preserved in
the " Trumbull Papers."  He d. May 24, 1824, æ. 83 and Elizabeth
(Marsh) Beebe survived him about a year and d. in 1825.   Children :

655.  Harriet[6], d. unm.
656.  Elizabeth, m. Joshua Garrett.
657.  Rebecca, m. Reuben Rockwell and had :
    658.  Julius, b. 1805; member of congress and U. S. senator
        from Mass. 1854, and judge Mass. supreme court
        1859-71.  His wife dau. of Judge Walker and his
        son and dau. :
        659.  Francis W., member of congress from Pittsfield,
            Mass.
        660.  Cornelia, m. Nathan Bowditch of Boston, grandson
            of the astronomer.
    661.  Hon. Reuben Rockwell.
662.  Ebenezer, Major U. S. army; m. Catherine Fair Knox.
663.  James of Winchester, Ct.; m. Abi McEwen ; three times
        representative and twice senator in Ct. legislature, and
        of the corporation of Yale college.
664.  William, b. March 24, 1782 ; d. Nov. 18, 1861 ; seven times
        representative and in 1845 senator in Ct. legislature,
        president of Litchfield fire insurance company and also
        president Litchfield county foreign missionary society;
        m. Clarissa Sanford ; removed to Hartford, Ohio.

## 674 = 626. RACHEL[5] MARSH

b. Litchfield, dau. Capt. John[4] and Sarah (Webster) Marsh ; m. No. 674.

**674.** Rev. George Beckwith, graduated Yale college 1766, was pastor at South Farms, Litchfield. He is mentioned with honor among the revolutionary patriots in the History of Litchfield, page 114.

## 675 = 628. MARY[5] MARSH

b. Litchfield, dau. Capt. John[4] and Sarah (Webster) Marsh ; m. No. 675.

**675.** Benjamin Stone, Jr. Children :

676. Norman.
677. Harmon.

## 678 = 629. SARAH[5] MARSH

of Litchfield, dau. Capt. John[4] and Sarah (Webster) Marsh, (Capt. John[4], John[3], John[2], John[1]) ; m. No. 678.

**678.** Dr. Seth Bird, b. Jan. 4, 1733-4. He was selectman four years from 1770, grand juror 1786, a patriot on important committees preparatory to and during the revolutionary war. In Oct., 1776, Dr. Reuben Smith and Dr. Seth Bird were appointed by the Ct. legislature a committee to examine all persons offered as surgeons from Ct. in the continental army or navy, and to give certificates to those qualified. He was a son of John Bird and either his grandfather or his brother must have been the John Bird, No. 102, who was the first husband of Elizabeth Marsh. Dr. Seth d. 1804. We know of but one child of Dr. Seth and Sarah (Marsh) Bird. Child :

679. John[6], b. Litchfield, Nov. 22, 1768 ; Yale college 1786, lawyer in Litchfield; removed to Troy, N. Y. 1794, representative N. Y. assembly, member of congress ; d. at Troy, N. Y., 1806, æ. 38 ; m. (1) dau. Col. Joshua Porter of Salisbury; m. (2) Sally Buell of Troy. Had several children. Ex-Pres. Van Buren wrote " John Bird I did not know personally, but have always taken much

interest in his character and career.  He must, according to all accounts, have been one of the very ablest
men in the state, though a very eccentric one.   There
have been but few men among us, who have left behind
them so many racy anecdotes illustrative of their pecul-
iarities."

### 680 = 100.  TIMOTHY[4] MARSH

of Litchfield, Ct., b. at Hartford, Ct., Oct. 1, 1714, son of Capt.
John[3] and Elizabeth (Pitkin) Marsh, (John[2], John[1]); m. No. 680.
**680.** Sarah Nott.   Children:

> 681.  Timothy[5], b. 1736; m. Sarah Andrus, 684.
> 682.  Elizabeth, b. 1738; m. Joseph Kilbourn, 687.   Perhaps also
> 683.  Sarah, m. July 8, 1762, Thos. Norton.

### 684 = 681.  TIMOTHY[5] MARSH

son of Timothy[4] and Sarah (Nott) Marsh, (Capt. John[3], John[2], John[1])
b. 1736 ; m. (1) recorded at Farmington, Oct. 27, 1765, No. 684.
**684.**  Sarah Andrus.  He joined the Farmington church, Nov. 9,
1766 ; his child d. Nov. 28, and his wife Dec. 7, 1766.  He m. (2)
No. 685.

**685.**  Mary Coe.  He became at the age of 40 one of the martyrs
to British cruelty, for American liberty.   In May, 1776, he joined the
company of his uncle Capt. Beebe, (No. 654).   About Nov. 1, 1776,
Capt. Beebe and 36 picked men of this company were thrown into
Fort Washington by New York City to aid in its defence.   During
the siege the English lost about 1200, the Americans about 400.
The fort was surrendered on honorable terms, which as to the prisoners, were most cruelly and shamefully violated.   Crowded by
hundreds into the sugar house, 850 in one church, about 225 on
board the Glasgow,—for the first two days without food, dysentery and
small pox breaking out, very few survived.  Of Capt. Beebe's 36
stalwart picked men, on exchange of prisoners only eleven were able
to start homeward.   Only five failed to die on the way and of those
left behind only one lived.   But six of the thirty-six survived the
horrors of a short prison life.   We hardly wonder that the professed

infidel Ethan Allen, with clenched teeth, said to Capt. Beebe, "My creed is shaken. There ought to be a hell for that Lowrie." See History of Litchfield, pages 96–101. Timothy[5] Marsh was one of six out of eleven who died on the way home. He died for us. His widow married his sister Elizabeth's widower, No. 687. Child :

686. George, b. 1766 ; d. Nov. 28, 1766.

### 687 = 682. ELIZABETH[5] MARSH

dau. of Timothy[4] and Sarah (Nott) Marsh, (Capt. John[3], John[2], John[1]) b. 1738 ; m. Nov. 30, 1765, No. 687.

**687.** Joseph Kilbourn. She d. Oct. 15, 1777. He was a soldier in the revolutionary war and a prisoner in 1778. He m. (2) Mary (Coe) Marsh, widow of Timothy. He d. in Upper Canada after 1800, and his widow in Detroit, Mich., soon after.

---

### THE HARTFORD LINE CONTINUED.

---

### 688 = 101. CAPT. HEZEKIAH[4] MARSH

b. Hartford, Ct., April 26, 1720, son of Capt. John[3] (John[2], John[1]) and Elizabeth (Pitkin) Marsh. When an infant in 1721 he was taken with his father's family to Litchfield, Ct., where his sister and brothers settled. His father retained his interests in Hartford and returned there when Hezekiah was 11 or 12, about 1731. This youngest son settled in Hartford. He seems to have succeeded to his father's busi--

ness and influence and is mentioned in Hartford Co. Memorial History among the prominent men of Hartford. His father's large account book, with family records and hints of family occupations and business transactions, became Capt. Hezekiah's own account book and is a mine of information. It is now (1893) in the possession of his great-grandson, John E⁷ Marsh, Esq., 1190 Windsor Ave., Hartford. He m. (1) Dec. 1, 1744, No. 688.

**688.** Christian Edwards, dau. of John, who was b. 1727 and d. June 16, 1770. She was the mother of all his children. He m. (2) No. 689.

**689.** Elizabeth, widow of Levi Jones of Hartford. She d. Oct. 26, 1788, æ. 66. He m. No. 690.

**690.** Hannah Tiley, widow of Samuel, d. 1789. Capt. Hezekiah⁴ Marsh, d. 1791, æ. 71. By his will he gave his grand-daughter Christian⁶ Merrill, dau. Capt. Charles and Christian (Marsh) Merrill, " the sum of £30 when she shall arrive at eighteen years of age." He also manumitted his " negro girl, 'Phebe ' after she shall arrive at the age of 26 years, she being now 14." Children :

691.  Jerusha⁵, b. Aug. 28, 174-; m. Joseph Wadsworth, 699.
692.  John, b. Nov. 6, 1749; d. in infancy.
693.  Abigail, b. Nov. 29, 1750; m. Theodore Skinner. She d. 1808, æ. 57. Had five children.
694.  John, b. Oct. 4, 1753; m. Susan Bunce, 714.
695.  Christian, b. Aug. 8, 1755; m. Capt. Charles Merrill, 827.
696.  An unnamed son, b. and d. 1759.
697.  Anne, b. June 10, 1761; m. —— Bunce, 830.
698.  Hezekiah, b. March 2, 1763; m. Sarah Burnham, 833.


### 699 = 691.   JERUSHA⁵ MARSH

b. Hartford, Aug. 28, 174–, dau. of Capt. Hezekiah⁴ and Christian (Edwards) Marsh; m. Sept. 22, 1768, No. 699.

**699.** Capt. Joseph Wadsworth of Hartford, b. 1738, commander of a cavalry company in the revolutionary war and member of the Washington Life Guards. He left Hartford in 1802 and d. 1824, æ. 85 or 86. Children :

700.  Capt. Joseph⁶, b. 1769.
701.  Ambrose, b. 1773; m. Sarah Marsh, 708.
702.  Ira.

703. Hezekiah.
704. Jerusha.
705. Betsey, m. Josiah Capen.  They had:
    706. Eliza[7], m. James E[6] Marsh, 724.
707. Christie.


## 708 = 701.  AMBROSE[6] WADSWORTH

b. Hartford, 1773, son of Jerusha[5] (Marsh) and Capt. Joseph Wadsworth, Capt. Hezekiah[4] Marsh, (Capt. John[3], John[2], John[1]); m. No. 708.

**708.** Sarah[5] Marsh, who was probably dau. of John[4] Marsh of New Hartford, Ct., (Jonathan[3], John[2], John[1]), b. June 16, 1772. Children :

709. John[6] Marsh.
710. Horace.
711. Ambrose.
712. Sarah.
713. Elizabeth.


## 714 = 694.  JOHN[5] MARSH

of Hartford, Ct., b. Oct. 4, 1753, son of Capt. Hezekiah[4] and Christian (Edwards) Marsh, (Capt. John[3], John[2], John[1]); m. in 1783, No. 714.

**714.** Susan Bunce, b. 1765, dau. of Timothy of Hartford.  He d. 1817.  His widow d. 1827, æ. 62.  Children :

715. John[6], b. April 24, 1784, on the Marsh homestead " Up Neck " Hartford ; m. 1829, Chlora Mills; was a farmer ; d. Dec. 13, 1862, æ. 78.  No children.
716. Susan, b. Aug. 12, 1786 ; m. 1810, Samuel Beckwith, d. 1812. One son :
    717. Saul[7].
718. Edwards, b. June 15, 1788; m. (1) Mary Ann Eggleston, 725.
719. Michael, b. March 27, 1790; m. Catherine Allyn, 741.
720. Abigail, b. March 9, 1792; m. 1817, Palmer Clark.  She d. 1866.  Had children.
721. Frederick, b. Jan. 3, 1794; m. (1) Harriet Hills, 765.
722. Guy, C., b. Aug. 4, 1796; m. Lamira Way, 787.
723. Timothy B., b. Oct. 13, 1799; m. Abby Hubbard, 812.
724. James E., b. Dec. 25, 1801 ; m. Eliza Capen, 820.

725 = 718. EDWARDS[6] MARSH

b. Hartford, June 15, 1788, son of John[5] and Susan (Bunce) Marsh, (Hezekiah[4], John[3], John[2], John[1]); m. (1) in 1828, No. 725.

**725.** Mary Ann Eggleston, b. Feb. 24, 1798 ; d. Aug. 7, 1849. He m. (2) in 1853, No. 726.

**726.** Mary Stearns. He d. Jan. 22, 1860. Children:

   727. Seth Edwards[7], b. April 14, 1823; m. Mary Ann[7] Marsh, 730.
   728. George, b. Aug. 12, 1827 ; m. Kate M. Case, 734.
   729. Andrew, b. 1836 ; m. Julia A. Westland, 739.


730 = 727. MAJOR SETH EDWARDS[7] MARSH

b. Hartford, Ct., April 14, 1823, in the neighborhood known as " The Neck " near the Windsor line, son of Edwards[6] and Mary Ann (Eggleston) Marsh, (John[5], Hezekiah[4], John[3], John[2], John[1]). He m. Nov. 8, 1848, his second cousin, No. 730.

**730.** Mary Ann[7] Marsh, b. July 23, 1825, dau. of William[6] and Huldah Allyn (Wilson) Marsh of Windsor, (Hezekiah[5], Hezekiah[4], John[3], John[2], John[1]), see No. 837.

Major Marsh was a civil engineer by profession and was early engaged on the old Hartford & Providence R. R., now the New York & New England R. R., as division engineer in its construction before its opening in 1848. From this he went to the Ashuelot River road in New Hampshire, but in 1851 went to western New York as engineer in laying out the Rochester, Lockport & Niagara Falls R. R., and the Buffalo, Lockport & Niagara Falls R. R. In 1855 he returned to Hartford which was afterwards his home. The following year he was appointed city surveyor and was almost continuously thereafter in some public office, serving as councilman, alderman, city assessor, etc. For many years he was actively interested, as commissioner 1859–1864, and as chief engineer and superintendent, in the development of the water supply of Hartford. He built one of the largest of the city's reservoirs (1875) and had made the plans for and commenced work on the great storage reservoir in Farmington (capacity 6,000,000 gallons). " He did not live to see all his plans matured ; but his ideas have been adopted and incorporated in the general plan of construction now in course of execution." From 1874 to his

death he was president of the board of water commissioners and
under his management it became a great and paying corporation.
Mr. Marsh had many large railroad contracts, among them the building of the Hartford & Ct. Valley, and the Boston & New York Air
Line, with the great iron drawbridge across the Connecticut river at
Middletown. In 1868 he was chosen Major of the Putnam Phalanx,
a well known local military organization of two companies under a
major commandant and the usual company officers. He was long
connected with the Masonic fraternity, was past eminent commander
of Washington Commandery—the oldest organization of Knights
Templars in the United States and the only one that ever received
authority from the Grand Encampment of England—was at the time
of his death worshipful master of . St. John's lodge No. 4, scribe in
Pythagoras chap. No. 17, member of Wolcott council, No. 1, etc.
Mr. Marsh was a man of wide experience and sound judgment, whose
advice was often sought and richly valued, because of his great tech-
nical knowledge and illuminating common sense. He d. Sept. 25,
1878. His widow still lives in Hartford. Children :

731. Mary Ellen[8], b. Hartford, June 17, 1853; m. Nov. 26, 1874,
Horace Alonzo Bishop, b. July 2, 1849, son of Alfred
and Elizabeth (Jones) Bishop, of Andover, Ct. Mr.
Bishop is a rising merchant and manufacturer of Cleveland, Ohio, is president of the Western Grocers' Association, a prominent member of the Masonic fraternity
and other bodies. They have no children.

732. Carrie Louise, b. Dec. 10, 1859; d. Dec. 18, 1859.

733. Jennie Huldah, b. April 9, 1863; graduated Hartford female
seminary; m. Nov. 22, 1893, Frank Butler Gay of Hartford, who was b. (East) Granby, Ct., Nov. 15, 1856; s.
Alfred and Jane Skinner (Thrall) Gay. He is librarian
of the Watkinson library of reference, secretary of the
Ct. Historical society, registrar Ct. Society Sons of the
American Revolution, etc.

## 734 = 728. GEORGE[7] MARSH

b. Hartford, Aug. 12, 1827, son of Edwards[6] and Mary A. (Eggleston)
Marsh, (John[5], Hezekiah[4], John[3], John[2], John[1]); m. Jan. 1, 1857,
No. 734.

7

**734.**  Kate M. Case, b. Feb. 7, 1836; d. Malden, Mass., April 27, 1888, buried at Hartford.  He was a civil engineer.  He d. April 28, 1866.  Children :

> 735.  Alice⁶, b. Feb. 17, 1858; m. Sept. 21, 1881, Dwight Porter, a distinguished civil engineer.  Children :
>> 736.  Kate E⁹., b. July 9, 1882.
>> 737.  Annie A., b. Feb. 16, 1884.
>> 737.1  Helen.
>> 737.2  James.
>
> 738.  George Edward, b. Hartford, Dec. 8, 1865 ; m. Nov. 25, 1886, Irene T. Hathaway of Meriden, Ct.  At Cromwell, Ct., he occupies a responsible position with the N. Eng. Brown Stone Co.  They had two children :
> Harriet, b. Sept. 22, 1887, Malden, Mass.
> George Edward, Jr., b. Nov. 16, 1893, Cromwell, Ct.


### 739 = 729.  ANDREW⁷ MARSH

b. Hartford, 1836, son of Edwards⁶ and Mary A. (Eggleston) Marsh, (John⁵, Hezekiah⁴, John³, John², John¹) ; m. Oct. 27, 1862, No. 739.

**739.**  Julia A. Westland, b. July 16, 1843.  Children :

> 740.  Grace⁸ E., b. Feb. 24, 1864; m. Oct. 21, 1884, Leslie H. Wilson.
> Andrew Marsh d. in 1865.  His widow m. (2) Sept. 17, 1867, Geo. S. Charter and they had Addie E., b. Jan. 27, 1869 ; William W., b. Aug. 15, 1870; d. Dec. 27, 1877 and Oliver E., b. Jan. 8, 1873.


### 741 = 719.  MICHAEL⁶ MARSH

b. Hartford, March 27, 1790, son of John⁵ and Susan (Bunce) Marsh, (Capt. Hezekiah⁴, John³, John², John¹) ; m. about 1828, No. 741.

**741.**  Catherine Allyn.  They removed from Hartford to West Springfield, Mass., about 1840.  Children :

> 742.  Jane C⁷., b. Dec. 11, 1829; m. (1) Geo. W. Rice, 746.
> 743.  Charles, b. April 13, 1832 ; m. Helen Penniman, 752.
> 744.  Oliver, b. Feb. 27, 1835; m. Ella C. Ricker, 757.
> 745.  Daniel Jay, b. July 27, 1837 ; m. Harriet M. Gay, 762.

## 746 = 742. JANE C[7]. MARSH

b. Dec. 11, 1829, dau. Michael[6] and Catherine (Allyn) Marsh, (John[5], Hezekiah[4], John[3], John[2], John[1]); m. (1) April 11, 1849, No. 746.

**746.** George W. Rice, b. Nov. 7, 1824. He d. Aug. 4, 1856. She m. (2) Sept. 14, 1870, No. 747.

**747.** Rev. L. C. Eastman, b. June 11, 1822. (Children of Mrs. Rice:)

 748. Ada Jenny[8], b. Aug. 31, 1851; d. Oct. 6, 1852.
 749. George W., b. Dec. 20, 1853; m. June 21, 1881, Eva Bickmore, b. Sept. 20, 1859. They had:
  750. George W[9]., b. June 15, 1882.
 751. Katherine, b. July 12, 1856; m. April 12, 1882, R. W. Ellis, b. Dec. 26, 1856.

## 752 = 743. CHARLES[7] MARSH

banker at Springfield, Mass., b. April 13, 1832, son of Michael[6] and Catherine (Allyn) Marsh, (John[5], Hezekiah[4], John[3], John[2], John[1]) in Hartford, Ct.; graduated Williams college, valedictorian, 1855. He settled at Springfield, was treasurer of the savings bank 1857–9; secretary insurance company 1859–66; cashier Pynchon national bank 1866–89 and then president till his death Nov. 27, 1891. He had, beside Pynchon bank, other numberless financial responsibilities. His report as chairman of the finance committee of the American missionary association at its meeting in Northampton in 1890 was inspiring. He was treasurer Springfield and New London R. R., also of school for Christian workers, the Springfield hospital and the Springfield cemetery association. He was auditor of the corporation for the home of the friendless, trustee and vice-president of the institution for savings and president of the Springfield Clearing House. For some years he taught a large Bible class. He was an honor to Mark Hopkins, who taught young men how to think. See a much longer notice in Obituary Record of Williams college, 1891–92. He m. Oct. 22, 1857, No. 752.

**752.** Helen Penniman, who d. Nov. 20, 1894. The *Springfield Republican* of Nov. 21, says: " She was a woman of beautiful character, and the center of a lovely home life, who shared her husband's interest in good causes of all kinds. It was the best sort of a New England home, always open to those actively engaged in missionary and benevolent work." Children:

753. Lucy P$^8$., b. July 8, 1858 ; m. Nov. 14, 1883, William George Eckert, b. Aug. 11, 1849. Lives at Dorchester, Mass. Children :

    753.1 William George$^9$, b. Dec. 26, 1884.

    753.2 Charles Marsh, b. May 7, 1887.

    753.3 Raymond, b. March 29, 1891.

754. William Charles, b. Feb. 13, 1862. Treasurer Hampden Co., Mass.

755. Anna Bond, b. Nov. 26, 1865.

756. Edward Harding, b. Dec. 9, 1869 ; Williams college 1891 and now (1892) on staff Springfield *Republican*.


### 757 = 744. OLIVER$^7$ MARSH

b. Hartford, Ct., Feb. 27, 1835, son of Michael$^6$ and Catherine (Allyn) Marsh ; m. June 11, 1873, No. 757.

**757.** Ella C. Ricker, b. Oct. 17, 1855. Children :

    758. Jane C$^8$., b. July 27, 1874.

    759. Mary J., b. June 13, 1877.

    760. Allen R., b. Aug. 10, 1878.

    761. Robert P., b. Aug. 18, 1881.


### 762 = 745. DANIEL JAY$^7$ MARSH

b. Hartford, Ct., July 27, 1837, son of Michael$^6$ and Catherine (Allyn) Marsh, (John$^5$, Capt. Hezekiah$^4$, John$^3$, John$^2$, John$^1$) ; m. May 25, 1864, No. 762.

**762.** Harriet M. Gay, b. Oct. 15, 1840. " He removed to Springfield in 1850 where he was educated. In 1855 he went to St. Louis and in 1856 had charge of the first passenger train out of that city, on the Northern Missouri R. R. He returned to Springfield in 1858 and a year later was elected treasurer of the Springfield five cents savings bank which position he has held ever since. Mr. Marsh went to the war in 1862 as private in the 46th regiment M. V. M. He was promoted through the various ranks to lieutenant and served on detached duty as aid de camp on the staffs of Gen. Horace C. Lee, Gen. John A. Dix and Gen. John G. Foster. He acted as Adjutant General on the staff of Gen. Lee, and was mustered out in 1864. He served in the city government 1872 and has been president of the board of park commissioners ever since its organization in 1882." A prominent citizen of Hartford, Mr. Gay of the Watkin-

*Daniel F. Marsh*

*To face page 84.*

son Library, states to the historian that Springfield owes very much to Mr. Marsh for his untiring energy in promoting the interests of Forest Park, one of our best examples of what an American city of that size, can do for the out-door life and delight of its citizens. Children:

763. Henry Daniel[8], b. March 15, 1865. "He is secretary and corporation clerk of the Springfield five cents savings bank. Resides 42 Maple St., Springfield."

764. Oliver Allyn, b. Oct. 15, 1866; m. Nov. 16, 1893, Anna Rumrill Dwight. "He is manager of the New York branch of the Poland Water Co. Lives at 16 Columbus Place, New Rochelle, N. Y." Child: Elsie Dwight[9], b. Oct. 3, 1894.

## 765 = 721. CAPT. FREDERICK[6] MARSH

b. Hartford, Ct., "Up Neck," Jan. 3, 1794, son of John[5] and Susan (Bunce) Marsh, (Capt. Hezekiah[4], John[3], John[2], John[1]) ; m. (1) in 1815, No. 765.

765. Harriet Hills[7], of East Hartford. She was the dau. of Amos and Anne[6] (Marsh) Hills, (Capt. Daniel[5] Marsh, Daniel[4], Nathaniel[3], John[2], John[1]), who d. Jan. 22, 1839. He m. (2) No. 766.

766. Chloe W. Robbins of Rocky Hill, b. Jan., 1808. He was Captain of the Governor's Horse Guards. Was for years merchant tailor, firm Dimmock & Marsh. He had large clothing trade with the southern states. About 1834 he removed his family to Montpelier, Vt., and was farmer and hotel keeper. He d. 1868, æ. 74. Children:

767. Susan M[7]., b. June 11, 1816; m. Eliphalet W. Lyman.

768. Burrage D., b. March 14, 1818; d. Dec. 18, 1823.

769. Norman F., b. Oct. 28, 1819; d. Aug. 20, 1863. Had four children, one dead.

770. Sidney K., b. Sept. 12, 1822; m. A. L. Goodnow, 777.

771. Harriet H., b. March 12, 1825; m. 779.

772. Burrage D., b. April 26, 1827; m. 784.

773. Ann M., b. Feb. 18, 1829; m. —— Bulkley.

774. George S., b. April 7, 1831.

775. Eli F., b. June 10, 1834.

776. Infant daughter, d. 1841, æ. five days.

## 777 = 770.   SIDNEY K⁷. MARSH

b. Sept. 12, 1822, son of Capt. Frederick⁶ and Harriet (Hills) Marsh,
(John⁵, Capt. Hezekiah⁴, John³, John², John¹) ; m. No. 777.
**777.** Annette L. Goodnow. He d. of cholera in Sacramento,
Cal., Oct. 25, 1850. His widow m. Oliver M. Drake and d. Dec.
29, 1867, æ. 39. Child :

778. Frederick Grove, b. 1842 ; d. Feb. 18, 1863.


## 779 = 771.   HARRIET H⁷. MARSH

b. March 12, 1825, dau. Capt. Frederick⁶ and Harriet (Mills) Marsh,
(John⁵, Capt. Hezekiah⁴, John³, John², John¹) ; m. No. 779.
**779.** ——. Children :

780. Charles.
781. Hattie, d. æ. four years. ⎱ At the same time.
782. Nellie, d. æ. six months. ⎰
783. Katie.


## 784 = 772.   BURRAGE D⁷. MARSH

b. April 26, 1827, son of Capt. Frederick⁶ and Harriet (Hills) Marsh,
(John⁵, Capt. Hezekiah⁴, John³, John², John¹) ; m. No. 784.
**784.** ——. Lives in Plainfield, Vt., and had four children of
whom two are living. Children :

785. William D⁸., b. Oct. 18, 1857.
786. Hattie M., b. Nov. 22, 1859.


## 787 = 722.   GUY C⁶. MARSH

b. Hartford, Aug. 4, 1796, son of John⁵ and Susan (Bunce) Marsh,
(Capt. Hezekiah⁴, Capt. John³, John², John¹) ; m. in May, 1818,
No. 787.
**787.** Lamira May, b. April 27, 1802. Her grandmother's name
was Standish and she claimed descent from Captain Miles. He
resided in Hartford and d. Jan. 21, 1871, æ. 75. Of the widow her

*John E. Marsh*

To face page 87.

son writes "My mother died about 3 A. M. this Sunday morning, March 14, 1886, æ. about 84. My mother was for more than 60 years a sincere Christian woman and has no doubt entered the 'Everlasting Rest.'" Children :

788. John Edwards[7], b. April 3, 1819 ; m. Carrie M. Cook, 799.
789. Hattie H., b. Jan. 2, 1821 ; m. Oliver D. Seymour, 803.
790. Lemuel M., b. Feb. 1, 1823 ; d. July 29, 1827.
791. Henry C., b. June 21, 1824 ; d. July 19, 1827.
792. George W., b. Aug. 12, 1826 ; d. July 24, 1827.
793. Helen M., b. May 12, 1828 ; m. D. R. Cook. No children.
794. Susan L., b. July 2, 1830 ; m. Dr. John Jacques, 807.
795. George H., b. Aug. 11, 1833 ; Sergt. killed at battle of Antietam by first cannon shot, Sept. 17, 1862, in 8th Ct.
796. Alfred F., b. Sept. 2, 1835 ; m. Mary Eaton, 810.
797. Anne A., b. May 31, 1837 ; d. Oct. 7, 1837.
798. Allen S., b. Aug. 11, 1838 ; d. Dec. 1, 1841.

## 799 = 788. JOHN EDWARDS[7] MARSH

b. New Haven, Ct., April 3, 1819, son of Guy C[6]. and Lamira (May) Marsh, (John[5], Capt. Hezekiah[4], Capt. John[3], John[2], John[1]) all of Hartford, Ct.; m. Aug. 10, 1857, No. 799.

**799.** Caroline M. Cook of Monmouth Co., N. J. At the age of 11 he went to live with an uncle (John) who was a farmer and lived on the "Marsh place" in the north part of the town of Hartford, near the Windsor line, known as "Up Neck." He lived with this uncle about ten years, and afterwards engaged in teaching for 18 or 20 years. After the death of the uncle in 1862, he returned to the "Marsh place" and engaged in agricultural pursuits." Children :

800. John S[8]., b. Feb. 6, 1859 ; d. April 26, 1873.
801. Frank H., b. Feb. 26, 1861 ; d. April 26, 1862.
802. Lamira L., b. Oct. 5, 1866.

## 803 = 789. HARRIET H[7]. MARSH

b. Hartford, Jan. 2, 1821, dau. of Guy C[6]. and Lamira (May) Marsh, (John[5], Capt. Hezekiah[4], John[3], John[2], John[1]) ; m. in 1843, No. 803.

**803.** Oliver D. Seymour. Children :

804.  Oliver[8], b. 1844.
805.  Hattie.
806.  Nellie.


807 = 794.  SUSAN L[7]. MARSH

b. Hartford, July 2, 1830, dau. of Guy C[6]. and Lamira (May) Marsh, (John[5], Capt. Hezekiah[4], John[3], John[2], John[1]) ; m. about 1849, No. 807.

807.  Dr. John Jacques, who d. April 10, 1887.   Children :
    808.  Ferdinand, d.
    809.  Eugene, b. 1852.


810 = 796.  ALFRED F[7]. MARSH

b. Hartford, Sept. 2, 1835, son of Guy C[6]. and Lamira (May) Marsh, (John[5], Capt. Hezekiah[4], John[3], John[2], John[1]) ; m. in 1863, No. 810.

810.  Mary Eaton, b. May 7, 1841.   He d. March 23, 1888, æ. 53.  Child :
    811.  Mabelle[8], b. Oct. 25, 1867.


812 = 723.  TIMOTHY B[6]. MARSH

b. Hartford, Ct., Oct. 13, 1799, son of John[5] and Susan (Bunce) Marsh, (Capt. Hezekiah[4], Capt. John[3], John[2], John[1]) ; m. Dec. 27, 1836, No. 812.

812.  Abba Hubbard.   He d. 1860.   Children :
    813.  Julia H[7]., b. Nov. 24, 1836; m. in 1858, John B. Baldwin.
    814.  Timothy B., b. March 1, 1838; d. March 14, 1838.
    815.  Abbie B., b. Nov. 11, 1839; m. in 1859, Charles Laurie.
    816.  Ellen A., b. 1842; m. April 19, 1866, Geo. H. Ward.   She d. 1883.
    817.  Priscilla A., b. Jan. 21, 1845 ; d. Aug. 29, 1852.
    818.  Hubbard Z., b. Nov. 2, 1848 ; d. Dec. 15, 1856.
    819.  Priscilla A., b. Oct. 11, 1851.

## 820 = 724. JAMES E[6]. MARSH

b. Hartford, Dec. 25, 1801, son of John[5] and Susan (Bunce) Marsh, (Capt. Hezikiah[4], John[3], John[2], John[1]) ; m. Oct. 16, 1825, No. 820.

**820.** Eliza Capen[7], b. March 26, 1806, dau. Betsey[6] (Wadsworth) Capen, dau. Jerusha[5] (Marsh) Wadsworth, dau. Capt. Hezekiah[4] Marsh, see No. 706. He d. May 23, 1884, æ. 83. Children :

    821.   Eliza A[7]., b. July 31, 1827 ; m. March 14, 1847, Wm. A. Rogers, d. Feb. 3, 1892.

    822.   Elizabeth Adaline, b. April 7, 1832 ; m. April 22, 1867, Rev. Andrew S. Lovell, who d. Jan. 30, 1892. She d. Feb. 17, 1892.

    823.   Sarah A., b. June 12, 1834 ; d. Sept. 27, 1865, æ. 31.

    824.   James H., b. April 24, 1836 ; m. Anna E. Post, 825.


## 825 = 824. JAMES H[7]. MARSH

b. April 24, 1836, son of James E[6]. and Eliza[7] (Capen) Marsh, (John[5], Capt. Hezekiah[4], John[3], John[2], John[1]) ; m. Dec. 24, 1862, No. 825.

**825.** Anna E. Post.   Child :

    826.   Sarah Eliza[8], b. Oct. 6, 1868 ; m. Feb. 1, 1886, Louis T. Grant.


## 827 = 695. CHRISTIAN[5] MARSH

b. Hartford, Aug. 8, 1755, dau. Capt. Hezekiah[4], (Capt. John[3], John[2], John[1]) ; m. No. 827.

**827.** Capt. Charles Merrill, b. Sept. 1755, son of Hezekiah[4] and Sarah (Butler) Merrill. She d. Nov. 8, 1778, æ. 23 and he d. Jan. 3, 1805. Children :

    828.   Christian[6], b. July 3, 1777 ; m. May 15, 1798, John Root, Esq., of Granby, Ct.; a lawyer afterwards in Ohio. Her grandfather, Hezekiah[4] Marsh left her a legacy of £30. She d. July 25, 1825.

    829.   Sarah, b. Oct. 14, 1778 ; d. Dec. 8, 1778.


## 830 = 697. ANNE[5] MARSH

b. Hartford, June 10, 1761, dau. of Capt. Hezekiah[4], (Capt. John[3], John[2], John[1]) ; m. (1) No. 830.

**830.** Mr. Bunce. She m. (2) No. 831.
**831.** John Packwood, who d. Oct. 4, 1799. Child :
    832. John[6].

833 = 698.   HEZEKIAH[5] MARSH

b. Hartford, Ct., March 2, 1763, son of Capt. Hezekiah[4] and Christian (Edwards) Marsh ; m. in 1790, No. 833.
**833.** Sarah Burnham.   He d. in 1819 and Sarah d. Aug. 8, 1849, æ. 82.   Children :

    834. William[6], b. Jan. 24, 1790; m. Huldah A. Wilson, 836.
    835. Hezekiah, b. Jan. 13, 1792 ; m. Amanda Cook, 839.

836 = 834.   WILLIAM[6] MARSH

b. Hartford, Jan. 24, 1790, son of Hezekiah[5] and Sarah (Burnham) Marsh; m. May 9, 1822, No. 836.
**836.** Huldah Allyn Wilson, b. Oct. 4, 1795.   He d. Dec. 18, 1862, æ. 72.   She d. Sept, 4, 1882, æ. 87.   Children :

    837. Mary Ann[7], b. July 23, 1825 ; m. Seth E. Marsh, 730.
    838. William, b. Aug. 11, 1829; d. unm. May 27, 1862.

839 = 835.   HEZEKIAH[6] MARSH

b. Hartford, Jan. 13, 1792, son of Hezekiah[5] and Sarah (Burnham) Marsh, (Capt. Hezekiah[4], Capt. John[3], John[2], John[1]) ; m. in 1823, No. 839.
**839.** Amanda Cook.   She d. in 1839, he d. Aug. 27, 1880, æ. 82.   Children :

    840. Eliza[7], b. 1825; m. Jason G. Marble, 842.
    841. George H., b. Oct. 26, 1830; m. (1) J. E. Buell, 845.

842 = 840.   ELIZA[7] MARSH

b. Hartford in 1825, dau. Hezekiah[6]; m. in 1846, No. 842.
**842.** Jason G. Marble.   Children :

    843. Jane[8], m. William Shepherd.
    844. Adaline.

## 845 = 841. GEORGE H[7]. MARSH

b. Oct. 26, 1830, son of Hezekiah[6] Marsh, (Hezekiah[5], Capt. Hezekiah[4], Capt John[3], John[2], John[1]) : m. (1) Aug. 31, 1853, No. 845.

  **845.** J. E. Buell. She d. and he m. (2) June 23, 1869, No. 845.1.

  **845.1.** Carrie Redfield. Children :

    846. Ida J., b. Nov. 11, 1855 ; d. Jan. 10, 1856.
    847. May A., b. Aug. 6, 1856 ; m. Oct. 10, 1880.
    848. Lulu V., b. Dec. 7, 1874.
    849. Jennie L. V., b. Dec. 30, 1879.

---

## BRANCH I. DIVISION II.

## THE HARTFORD AND EAST HARTFORD LINE.

---

## 850 = 48. LIEUT. NATHANIEL[3] MARSH

baptized with his twin brother Joseph in the Second church at Hartford, Ct., March 5, 1671, son of John[2] and Sarah (Lyman) Marsh, (John[1]) ; m. about 1704, No. 850.

  **850.** Elizabeth Spencer. He was selectman in Hartford in 1723, while his older brother Capt. John[3] settled most of his children at Litchfield, settling only the youngest at Hartford, and his twin brother Joseph settled at Lebanon, Ct., and his youngest brother Capt. Jonathan settled at New Hartford, Ct., Lieut. Nathaniel remained at Hartford which then included East Hartford and Manchester, and his earlier descendants settled, some just across the Connecticut river at what is

now East Hartford, and others remained in Hartford city.   He was b.
1670 and d. 1848.   His children were all but Daniel, baptized in the
Second church, Hartford.   Lieut.  Nathaniel was admitted to full
communion, July 6, 1718, and his wife July 13, 1718.   Children:

> 851.  Nathaniel⁴, bap. Dec. 2, 1705; m. Thankful Goodwin, 856.
> 852.  Samuel, bap. July 20, 1707.
> 853.  Daniel, bap. 1809; m. Irene Bigelow, 877.
> 854.  Hannah, bap. Jan. 18, 1712–13.
> 855.  Lemuel, bap. March 9, 1718 ; m. Bathsheba Barrett, No. 1713.

## 856 = 851.  NATHANIEL⁴ MARSH

b. Hartford, and baptized Dec. 2, 1705, "wn" his father "owned ye
covenant," son of Lieut. Nathaniel³ and Elizabeth (Spencer) Marsh,
(John², John¹); m. about 1730, No. 856.

**856.** Thankful Goodwin, baptized Feb. 28, 1708–9, dau. Daniel
and Sarah (Easton) Goodwin.   He d. about 1734 or 5, and his widow
m. (2) May 21, 1736, Daniel Collyer.   Nathaniel's children :

> 857.  Samuel⁵, bap. May 9, 1731; m. Catherine Chenevard, 860.
> 858.  Thankful, b. about 1733; m. a Mr. Church ; in old age was
> left to the care of her brother's children.
> 859.  Nathaniel, b. about 1735.   His uncle Daniel Goodwin was
> made his guardian.

## 860 = 857.   CAPT. SAMUEL⁵ MARSH

b. Hartford, baptized Second church, May 9, 1731, son of Nathaniel⁴
and Thankful (Goodwin) Marsh, afterwards Mrs. Collyer.   He m.
Jan. 17, 1762, No. 860.

**860.** Catherine Chenevard, b. 1731 ; d. July 30, 1797, æ. 66.
Capt. Samuel was a leading merchant in the early days of Hartford
city, a member of the first board of aldermen after the city incorporation and largely engaged in the West Indian trade.   His estate
seems to have been very valuable.   He took his widowed sister Church
into his home and in his will provided for her care by his grand-
children.

His grave stone and those of his mother, wife and daughter are
still (1892) unremoved, side by side in the old graveyard of the

Center church, Hartford. They read :

"In memory of Mrs. Katherine Bull, wife of Mr. George Bull, and daughter of Capt. Samuel Marsh of Hartford who departed this life at *North Ampton* Sept. 20, A. D. 1800, aged 32 years."

"In memory of Mrs. Catherine Marsh, Consort of Capt. Samuel Marsh, who departed this life July 30, A. D. 1797, in the 67th year of her age."

"In memory of Mrs. Thankful Collyer, Relict of Mr. Daniel Collyer, who died Dec. 24, A. D. 1792, in ye 85 year of her age."

"In memory of Capt. Samuel Marsh who died Sept. 1st, 1802, in the 72d year of his age."

Children :

862. Child (stillborn), March 11, 1763.
862. Katy[6], bap. May 25, 1764; d. May 9, 1768, æ. 4.
863. Samuel, b. May 18, 1766; m. 868.
865. Katherine, b. June 19, 1768; m. George Bull, 876.
866. William (S.,?) b. July 1, 1770. Perhaps the Wm. S. Marsh who went from Hartford to Winchester, Ct. and m. (2) Sally, dau. of Richard Coit and published a book about Hartford.
867. Daughter, b. 1777 and d. Aug. 22, 1788, æ. 11.

## 868 = 863. SAMUEL[6] MARSH

b. Hartford, May 18, 1766, son of Capt. Samuel[5], (Nathaniel[4], Lieut. Nathaniel[3], John[2], John[1]), was a clerk of his father. He m. No. 868.

868. ———. John E. Marsh, Esq. of Hartford writes: "In my boyhood days there stood at the 'North End' where the Windsor road leaves the city, a rather pretentious gambrel-roofed house called the "Marsh House." This was once the property and residence of Samuel Marsh[6], and his family, consisting of wife, four sons and one daughter." These sons had willed to them from their grandfather the care of his aged sister widow Thankful Church. We do not know the name of their mother. He d. about 1830. He was a farmer in good circumstances. Children :

869. William Henry[7], d. a bachelor.
870. Charles.
871. Samuel I.
872. Edward, d. a bachelor.
873. Catherine Chenevard, b. 1801; m. Geo. Smith, 874.

## 874 = 873.   CATHERINE C⁷. MARSH

b. Hartford, 1801, dau. of Samuel⁶ Marsh ; m. about 1725, No. 874.
**874.** George Smith.   She d. Nov. 2, 1847, æ. 46.   Lies in North
·Cemetery.   Child :

> 875. Catherine⁸, b. June 26, 1826 ; m. Dec. 16, 1847, Jonathan
> Wells Babcock, b. Hartford, Ct., May 1, 1822, res.
> Richmond, Va.

## 876 = 865.   KATHERINE⁶ MARSH

b. Hartford, June 19, 1868, dau. Capt. Samuel⁵ and Catherine (Chen-
·evard) Marsh, (Nathaniel⁴, Lieut. Nathaniel³, John², John¹) ;   m.
No. 876.
**876.** George Bull.   She d. at Northampton, Mass., Sept. 20,
1800, and was buried at Hartford by the side of her mother.   See
No. 860.

## 877 = 853.   ENSIGN DANIEL⁴ MARSH

b. Hartford, perhaps in what is now East Hartford, in 1809, baptized
Oct. 30, 1709, son of Lieut. Nathaniel³ and Elizabeth (Spencer)
Marsh, (John², John¹) ;   m. about 1730, No. 877.
**877.** Irene Bigelow, b. 1711.   He resided in that part of Hartford which was then called the " Orford Soc.," and called later East
Hartford and Manchester.   A part of his property there may have
been the original 72 acres alloted to John¹ Marsh on that side of the
Connecticut river about 1666.   In the graveyard at Manchester are
these inscriptions :                         \
    " In memory of Mrs. Irene Marsh, wife of Ensign Daniel Marsh,
who departed this life March 27, 1790, in the 79th year of her age."
    " In memory of Ensign Daniel Marsh who departed this life Oct.
·6, A. D. 1793, in the 85 yr of his age."
    In his will he gives to " Grandson James " and to daughter Lucretia
·Wadsworth and " my other daughters!"   Children :

> 878. Daniel⁵, b. Feb. 6, 1732 ; m. (1) Ann Morrison, 903.
> 879. "Cate," perhaps b. 1734 ; d. 1759.

880. Jessee, b. 1736 or 7 ; m. Lucy, 1674.
881. Elizabeth, b. 1736 or 7 ; m. Joseph Olcott, 886.
882. Lucretia, m. —— Wadsworth.
883. James, b. 1746; m. Mary, 1680.
884. Irene, b. 1752 ; m. Lieut. Nathaniel Olcott, 900.
885. One of " my other daughters " for " Cate " and Irene died
before his will.


## 886 = 881.  ELIZABETH[5] MARSH

b. Hartford (East) 1736 or '37, dau. of Ensign Daniel[4] and Irene
(Bigelow) Marsh, (Lieut. Nathaniel[3], John[2], John[1]) ; m. in 1758,
No. 886.

**886.** Capt. Joseph Olcott. She d. March 9, 1823, æ. 87.
Children :

887. Jared[6], b. July 22, 1759.
888. Mabel, b. April 5, 1761.
889. Elizabeth, b. Jan., 1763.
890. Irena, b. Dec., 1764 ; m. David Wadsworth.
891. Catherine, b. Jan., 1767 ; m. Elias Clark.
892. Anna, b. Jan., 1769 ; m. Benj. Spencer.
893. Joseph, b. Dec., 1770 ; m. and settled in Egremont, Mass.
894. Rhoda, b. March 1773 ; m. John Brace.
895. Chloe, b. Aug., 1775 ; d. Aug., 1777.
896. Chloe, b. April, 1777 ; m. Giles Eggleston.
897. Gurdon, b. 1779 ; d. 1816.
898. Helen, b. Jan., 1782 ; m. Wm. Church.
899. Lucretia, b. Jan. 29, 1784 ; m. James Buell and had fourteen
children :


## 900 = 884.  IRENE[5] MARSH

b. Hartford (East) in 1752, dau. of Ensign Daniel[4] and Irene (Bigelow) Marsh ; m. about 1767, No. 900.

**900.** Lieut. Nathaniel Olcott. She d. " Oct. 25, 1776 in 24th
yr. of her age." And no wonder if married at 15. Children :

901. John[6], b. July 26, 1768 ; m. Betsey White, East Hartford and
had five children.
902. Elisha, b. May 10, 1770 ; m. Amelia Olmsted, East Hartford, and had five children.

## 903 = 878.  CAPT. DANIEL⁵ MARSH

b. East Hartford, Feb. 6, 1732, son of Ensign Daniel⁴ and Irene (Bigelow) Marsh, (Lieut. Nathaniel³, John², John¹) ; m. (1) in 1851, No. 903.

**903.** Anna Morrison, dau. of Dr. Normand, b. June 27, 1734, who d. March 30, 1770, æ. 36.  He m. (2) in 1771, No. 904.

**904.** Widow Hannah (Smith) Gleason, dau. of Gideon, who d. Oct. 9, 1778, æ. 44.  He m. (3) No. 905.

**905.** Widow Anna (Stanley) Pitkin, b. Jan. 17, 1740, dau. of William and Clemence (Olmsted) Stanley of East Hartford. She was the widow of Caleb Pitkin and brought an addition to Capt. Daniel's large family, and one of her sons Caleb Pitkin, Jr., after a few years married Hannah one of his daughters.  Her Pitkin sons settled at Marshfield, Vt.  Capt. Daniel came three times to visit his children and grandchildren and Jan. 7, 1797 she came too.  She d. May 14, 1797, æ. 57.  Capt. Daniel m. (4) in 1798, No. 906.

**906.** Margery Spencer, b. about 1749.  He was Sergeant in 1775 in a company of minute men commanded by Col. George Pitkin, who, on the news of the alarm at Lexington marched from Hartford to the relief of Boston.  He was also selectman for East Hartford in 1786 on for two years.  His house was in Spencer Lane, East Hartford.  The gravestones of Capt. Daniel and his four wives remain legible to this day in the old East Hartford burial ground.  The last two read " In memory of Capt. Daniel Marsh who died Sept. 28, 1818 in the 87 year of his age."  " In memory of Margery, relict of Capt. Daniel Marsh who died Dec. 4, 1822, aged 73."  Children :

> **907.** Susanna⁶, b. Oct. 9, 1752; probably " Child: Daniel Marsh, d. Dec." .Record First church Hartford, apparently before 1754.
> **908.** Anna, b. May 31, 1755; m. (1) Moses Pratt, 916.
> **909.** Allan, b. March 9, 1762; m. Mabel Case, 927.
> **910.** Irene, b. March 20, 1765; m. Joseph McKee, 1123.
>
> ### By second wife.
>
> **911.** Emily, b. Feb. 12, 1772; m. Timothy Kennedy, 1600.
> **912.** George, b. Jan. 6, 1773; d. Oct. 6, 1778 in sixth year. (Gravestone.)
> **913.** Mary, b. May 5, 1774; m. Dea. Spencer, 1669.
> **914.** Hannah, b. Aug. 7, 1775 ; m. Caleb Pitkin, 1670.
> **915.** Elizabeth, b. Feb. 28, 1777; m. —— King.

## 916 = 908. ANNE[6] MARSH

b. East Hartford, May 31, 1755, dau. of Capt. Daniel[5] and Anna (Morrison) Marsh, (Daniel[4], Lieut. Nathaniel[3], John[2], John[1]) ; m. (1) No. 916.

**916.** Moses Pratt. Children :

917. Hannah[7], m. Burrage Dimock.
918. Irene, m. David L. Isham.
919. Clarissa, m. Capt. James Pitkin.
920. Daughter, m. John Smith.
921. Samuel.

Anne[6] (Marsh) Pratt, m. (2) No. 922.

**922.** Amos Hills, Children :

923. Norman, m. Martha Beckwith.  Six children.
924. Harriet, m. Capt. Frederick[6] Marsh, 765.

Anne[6] (Marsh) Hills, m. (3) No. 925.

**925.** Peter Kibbee.  Child :

926. Sidney.


## 927 = 909. ALLAN[6] MARSH

b. East Hartford, March 9, 1762, son of Capt. Daniel[5] and Anna (Morrison) Marsh, (Daniel[4], Lieut. Nathaniel[3], John[2], John[1]) ; m. No. 927.

**927.** Mabel Case, b. 1769 ; d. May 27, 1849, æ. 80.  He d. Oct. 17, 1830, "age between 60 and 70," church records.  The order of birth of their twelve children we cannot tell exactly but have slight hint by dates of marriage and the four cases where birthtimes are given.  Children :

928. Daniel[7], b. Sept. 4, 1793; m. Esther Wells, 940.
929. ' Nancy, m. June 25, 1818, David Treat, who d. in 1823.  She d. Dec. 29, 1851.
930. Lucretia, m April 28, 1823, Chester McKee who d. Sept. 1, 1850.  Son :
   930.1. James H., d. Sept. 18, 1855.
931. Catherine, m. Oliver Bissell, 993.
932. Marion, b. 1800; d. Aug. 3, 1872, æ. 72.
933. Martha M., m. John Allen, 1022.
934. Mary, m. —— Gray, 1057.

8

935.  Emily, b. July 21, 1806; m. Alfred Griswold, 1070.
936.  Marcus, b. 1807–8; d. unm. Feb. 11, 1862, æ. 55.
937.  Rosanna, d. y. burned to death.
938.  George, m. ——. Probably the George Marsh m. to Sarah
      Gates of East Hartford, July 23, 1816, by Dr. Thomas
      Robbins.
939.  Timothy, unm.


940 = 928.  DANIEL[7] MARSH

b. East Hartford, Ct., Sept. 4, 1793, son of Allan[6] and Mabel (Case)
Marsh, (Capt. Daniel[5], Daniel[4], Lieut. Nathaniel[3], John[2], John[1]) ; m.
April 1, 1817, No. 940.
**940.** Esther Wells of East Hartford, dau. of Jonathan. He
removed in 1829 to Alexander, Genesee Co., N. Y.; about 1831 to
Sheldon, N. Y.; about 1833 to Bennington, Wyoming Co., N. Y.;
about 1837 to East China, about 1842 to Caneadea, 1846 to East
China, 1848 to Rochester, N. Y., 1853 to Felix, Grandy Co., Ill, 1858
to Oramel, N. Y., 1865 to Wilmington, Ill., where he d. Sept. 20,
1866.  His first six children were born at Manchester, Ct., the
seventh at East Hartford, the eighth and ninth at Alexander, N. Y.
and the tenth at Bennington, N. Y.   Children :

941.  Jane Lord[8], b. March 9, 1818; m. (1) Wyman Joslyn, 951.
942.  James Wells, b. Aug. 26, 1819; m. Laura Smith, 962.
943.  Ann Mariah, b. April 30, 1821; d. Oramel, N. Y., Oct. 12,
      1850.
944.  Seth Wells, b. March 30, 1823; m. Susan Ann Hanford, 967.
945.  Delia Stanly, b. May 1, 1825; m. Lawrence Tinslar, 978.
946.  Betsey Hall, b. March 13, 1827; d. Caneadea, N. Y., April
      13, 1846.
947.  Levi Chester, b. June 17, 1829; m. (1) Betsey B. Gowing, 982.
948.  Adelaide Jemima, b. Aug. 20, 1831; m. Milton H. Kil-
      burn, 989.
949.  Esther Wells, b. Feb. 24, 1834; d. Oramel, N. Y., Sept.
      5, 1851.
950.  Ellen Caroline, b. July 7, 1836; d. East China, N. Y., Nov.
      10, 1838.


951 = 941.  JANE LORD[8] MARSH

b. Manchester, Ct., March 9, 1818, dau. of Daniel[7], (Allen[6], Capt.

Daniel[5], Daniel[4], Lieut. Nathaniel[3], John[2], John[1]) ; m. (1) at East China, N. Y.. Oct. 1, 1836, No. 951.

**951.** Wyman Joslyn. She m. (2) at East China, Nov. 1, 1840, No. 952.

**952.** James Pierce Rounsville, son of Abiathar and Sophia (Pierce) Rounsville. She d. Oramel, N. Y., March 12, 1866. Children:

> 953. Esther Adelia[9], b. Nov. 6, 1841 ; m. Benj. N. Payne.
> 954. Welcom Ross, b. March, 1843; d. Oramel, N. Y., Feb. 18, 1863.

955 = 953. ESTHER ADELIA[9] ROUNSVILLE

b. Oramel, N. Y., Nov. 6, 1841, dau. Jane Lord[8] Marsh, (Daniel[7], Allan[6], Capt. Daniel[5], Daniel[4], Lieut. Nathaniel[3], John[2], John[1]) ; m. at Corning, N. Y., Oct. 9, 1867, No. 955.

**955.** Benjamin Nott Payne. Their children were all born at Corning. Children:

> 956. Stephen Henry[10], b. May 12, 1869.
> 957. Frederick Rounsville, b. Aug. 5, 1871.
> 958. Nathan Beers, b. Oct. 28, 1872.
> 959. Benjamin Wells, b. Dec. 28, 1874.
> 960. Esther Rounsville, b. June 18, 1876.
> 961. Willard Marsh, b. April 27, 1880.

962 = 942. JAMES WELLS[8] MARSH

b. Manchester, Ct., Aug. 26, 1819, son of Daniel[7] (Allan[6], Capt. Daniel[5], Daniel[4], Lieut. Nathaniel[3], John[2], John[1]) and Esther (Wells) Marsh ; m. Attica, N. Y., Sept. 22, 1842, No. 962.

**962.** Laura Smith, dau. Elisha and Amy (Burlingame) Smith of Attica. They resided at Alexander, N. Y. from marriage till his death, Oct. 9, 1844. Child :

> 963. Ira Rix, b. June 22, 1843; m. Rachel A. White, 964.

963 = 964. IRA RIX[9] MARSH

b. Attica, N. Y., June 22, 1843, son of James Wells[8] and Laura

(Smith) Marsh, (Daniel[7], Allan[6], Capt. Daniel,[5] Daniel[4], Lieut. Nathaniel[3], John[2], John[1]) ; m. at Wilmington, Ill., No. 964.

964. Rachel Ann White, dau. of Lewis Haines and Willamina (Watson) White of Wilmington. He resided in Alexander, N. Y., went to Batavia, N. Y., about 1846, to Gustavus, O., about 1850, to Fredonia, N. Y. about 1857, up to 1860, about one year in Buffalo, N. Y. in 1861, enlisted Aug. 12, 1862, in Co. B, 112th N. Y. Vols. and discharged June, 1865, removed Feb., 1866 to Braidwood, Will Co., Ill. and now resides in Chicago.  Children :

965.  Frederic Haines[10], b. Braidwood, Ill., June 9, 1877.
966.  Lydia Ruth, b. Braidwood, Ill., Feb. 17, 1885.


967 = 944.  SETH WELLS[8] MARSH


b. Manchester, Ct., March 30, 1823, son of Daniel[7] and Esther (Wells) Marsh, (Allan[6], Capt. Daniel[5], Daniel[4], Lieut. Nathaniel[3], John[2], John[1]) ; m. at Rochester, N. Y., Jan. 25, 1848, No. 967.

967.  Susan Ann Hanford, dau. of Comstock and Anna (Hayes) Hanford of Rochester.  Resided at Rochester, except was at Felix, Ill., 1854 to 1858.  All but one of their children were born at Rochester.  Children :

968.  Charles Wells[9], b. Nov. 15, 1848 ; m. Mazie McEwen, 974.
969.  May, b. May 7, 1851.
970.  Anna Esther, b. Feb. 1, 1854.
971.  Emma Jane, b. July 19, 1856, at Felix, Ill.  She m. at Rochester, July 19, 1882, Pomeroy Patrick Dickinson, son of Alfred and Martha ; res. Rochester, N. Y.
972.  Jesse Comstock, b. Aug. 29, 1866 ; d. March 9, 1868, at Rochester.
973.  Libby Brooks, b. July 5, 1870.


974 = 968.  CHARLES WELLS[9] MARSH


b. Rochester, N. Y., Nov. 15, 1848, son of Seth Wells[8] and Susan Ann (Hanford) Marsh, (Daniel[7], Allan[6], Capt. Daniel[5], Daniel[4], Lieut. Nathaniel[3], John[2], John[1]) ; m. at Pittsburg, Pa., Nov. 19, 1872, No. 974.

**974.** Mazie McEwen, dau. of James and Easter(?). Residence, Rochester, N. Y. and Pittsburgh, Pa. Children:

    975. Walter Aldridge, b. Pittsburgh, May 7, 1874.
    976. Charles Tennyson, b. Pittsburgh, Feb. 10, 1876.
    977. Virginia May, b. Pittsburgh, Aug. 22, 1878.

## 978 = 945. DELIA STANLY[8] MARSH

b. Manchester, Ct., May 1, 1825, dau. of Daniel[7] and Esther (Wells) Marsh, (Allan[6], Capt. Daniel[5], Daniel[4], Lieut. Nathaniel[3], John[2], John[1]); m. at Oramel, N. Y. about 1842, No. 978.

    **978.** Lawrence Tinslar, son of John and Nancy (Anthony) Tinslar of Nelson, N. Y. They resided at Angelica, Auburn and Rochester, N. Y. and removed about 1853 to Braceville, Ill. where she d. July 28, 1866. Children:

    979. Lucien Wells[9], b. Auburn, N. Y., Aug. 26, 1849; d. Braidwood, Ill., Oct. 3, 1871.
    980. Eva Alice, b. Braceville, Ill., July 23, 1856.
    981. Esther Adelaide, b. Braceville, Ill., May 13, 1866.

## 982 = 947. LEVI CHESTER[8] MARSH

b. East Hartford, Ct., June 17, 1829, son of Daniel[7] and Esther (Wells) Marsh, (Allan[6], Capt. Daniel[5], Daniel[4], Lieut. Nathaniel[3], John[2], John[1]); m. (1) at Oramel, N. Y., Feb. 22, 1857, No. 982.

    **982.** Betsey B. Gowing of Oramel. He m. (2) at Schenectady, N. Y., Sept. 21, 1865, No. 983.

    **983.** Carrie M. Meeker of Schenectady. He resided near Oramel, removed about 1853 to Felix, Ill., thence about 1869 to Carbondale, Ill. and a few years later to Watseka, Ill. his present residence. Children:

    984. Jennie Roancy[9], b. Dec. 11, 1857; m. M. F. Dunlap, 986.
    985. Fannie, b. Nov. 23, 1869 at Carbondale; d. there July 7, 1870.

## 986 = 984. JENNIE ROANCY[9] MARSH

b. Oramel, N. Y., Dec. 11, 1857, dau. of Levi Chester[8] and Betsey B. Gowing; m. May 21, 1879, at Watseka, Ill., No. 986.

**986.** Millard Filmore Dunlap of Jacksonville, Ill.  Children:
>    987.  Ralph Marsh[10], b. July 7, 1881, at Watseka, Ill.
>    988.  Clarence Ervin, b. July 27, 1883, at Jacksonville, Ill.


## 989 = 948.  ADELAIDE JEMIMA[8] MARSH

b. Alexander, Genesee Co., N. Y., Aug. 20, 1831, dau. Daniel[7] and Esther (Wells) Marsh, (Allan[6], Capt. Daniel[5], Daniel[4], Lieut. Nathaniel[3], John[2], John[1]); m. at Wilmington, Ill., Nov. 12, 1857, No. 989. **989.** Milton H. Kilburn.  They resided a few years at Wilmington, Ill., then a few at Ilion, N. Y., removed about 1872 to Watseka, Ill., after two or three years went to Danville, Ill., and about 1877 returned to Wilmington, where she d. July 31, 1880.  Children:
>    990.  Etta Elizabeth[9], b. Oct. 20, 1859, at Wilmington and d. there May 6, 1862.
>    991.  Milton Marsh, b. at Ilion, N. Y., Dec. 30, 1863; d. Watseka, Ill., Feb. 11, 1874.
>    992.  Cora Adelaide, b. July 12, 1868.


## 993 = 931.  CATHERINE[7] MARSH

b. East Hartford, Ct., dau. of Allan[6] and Mabel (Case) Marsh, (Capt. Daniel[5], Daniel[4], Lieut. Nathaniel[3], John[2],' John[1]); m. No. 993. **993.** Oliver Bissell.  Children:
>    994.  Celia[8], m. —— Gilman.
>    995.  Sarah F., b. Oct. 23, 1818; m. Thomas Moran, 1001.
>    996.  Elizabeth, m. —— Erving.
>    997.  Harriet, m. —— Hollister.
>    998.  Almira, b. Oct. 8, 1826; m. W. H. Wolcott, 1010.
>    999.  Mary, b. Dec. 13, 1832; m. Charles H. West, 1016.
>    1000.  Ann, m. —— Read; lives in Boston.


## 1001 = 995.  SARAH F[8]. BISSELL

b. Oct. 23, 1718, dau. of Catherine[7] (Marsh) Bissell, (Allan[6] Marsh, Capt. Daniel[5], Daniel[4], Lieut. Nathaniel[3], John[2], John[1]); m. April 3, 1838, No. 1001.

**1001.** Thomas Moran. Children :

    1002. John H[9]., b. Aug., 1839; d. Sept., 1839.

    1003. George E., b. July 1, 1842 ; m. July, 1861, Augusta Merriman.
      They had :

      1004-1008. 1, Mary[10]; 2, Jennie; 3, Ross ; 4, George ; 5, Millie.

    1009. Mary C., b. Aug. 26, 1849.


1010 = 998. ALMIRA[8] BISSELL

b. Oct. 8, 1826, dau. Catherine[7] (Marsh) Bissell, (Allan[6] Marsh, Capt. Daniel[5], Daniel[4], Lieut. Nathaniel[3], John[2], John[1]) ; m. Sept. 22, 1845, No. 1010.

    **1010.** W. H. Wolcott, of East Hartford. He d. Jan. 27, 1887, æ. 77. Children :

    1011. Ella[9], b. July 13, 1846; m. S. A. Kilbourn.

    1012. Fannie, b. April 9, 1850; m. F. B. Clark and had :

      1013-1015. 1, Elsie[10]; 2, Henry B.; 3, Frederick.


1016 = 999. MARY[8] BISSELL

b. Dec. 13, 1832, dau. of Catherine[7] (Marsh) Bissell, (Allan[6] Marsh, Capt. Daniel[5], Daniel[4], Lieut. Nathaniel[3], John[2], John[1]) ; m. March 27, 1852, No. 1016.

    **1016.** Charles H. West. Children :

    1017. Mary C[9]., b. Dec. 23, 1852 ; d. Nov. 17, 1853.

    1018. Catherine E., b. March 14, 1854 ; d. March 19, 1864.

    1019. Revilla A., b. April 23, 1856.

    1020. George Edward, b. April 25, 1858 ; d. March 27, 1864.

    1021. William W., b. Jan. 23, 1862.


1022 = 933. MARTHA M[7]. MARSH

b. East Hartford ? dau. of Allan[6] and Mabel (Case) Marsh, (Capt. Daniel[5], Daniel[4], Lieut. Nathaniel[3], John[2], John[1]) ; m. No. 1022.

    **1022.** John Allen. Children :

    1023. Martha Ann, b. Oct. 16, 1828; m. Geo. W. Clark, 1029.

    1024. Lucy, b. March 26, 1830 ; m. Charles W. Clark, 1034.

1025.  Emily, b. May 7, 1833 ; m. Giles M. Johnson, 1037.
1026.  Henry B.
1027.  Abby Jane, b. Feb. 17, 1836 ; m. (1) E. S. Chamberlain, Nov.
        26, 1855 ; m. (2) Lemuel Joslyn, Nov., 1876.
1028.  David T., b. Feb. 29, 1844 ; m. Alftina Wear, 1043.


1029 = 1023.  MARTHA ANN[8] ALLEN

b. Oct. 16, 1828, dau. Martha M[7]. (Marsh) Allen, (Allan[6] Marsh,
Capt. Daniel[5], Daniel[4], Lieut. Nathaniel[3], John[2], John[1]) ; m. Sept. 12,
1844, No. 1029.
  1029.  George W. Clark.  Children :
      1030.  William H[9]., b. July 1, 1849; m. (1) March 14, 1872, Eleanor
              M. Frink who d. Sept. 3, 1873; m. (2) Feb. 27, 1878,
              Mattie Griswold.
      1031.  Luella, b. Feb. 29, 1852 ; d. Aug. 27, 1852.
      1032.  Charles T., b. Feb. 13, 1856; m. May 19, 1881, Jennie
              Saunders.
      1033.  Alice D., b. June 17, 1863 ; d. Aug. 27, 1864.


1034 = 1024.  LUCY[8] ALLEN

b. March 26, 1830, dau. Martha M[7]. (Marsh) Allen, (Allan[6] Marsh,
Capt. Daniel[5], Daniel[4], Lieut. Nathaniel[3], John[2], John[1]) ; m. May 1,
1852, No. 1034.
  1034.  Charles W. Clark.  Children :
      1035.  Franklin[9], b. Aug. 15, 1853; m. Jan. 4, 1873, No. 1050.
      1036.  Charles, b. Nov. 16, 1856 ; d. Feb. 17, 1876, æ. 20.


1037 = 1025.  EMILY[8] ALLEN

b. May 7, 1833, dau. Martha M[7]. (Marsh) Allen, (Allan[6] Marsh,
Capt. Daniel[5], Daniel[4], Lieut. Nathaniel[3], John[2], John[1]); lives at Glastonbury, Ct.; m. Nov. 17, 1853, No. 1037.
  1037.  Giles M. Johnson.  Children :
      1038.  Mary Alice[9], b. Oct. 4, 1857 ; m. Oct. 24, 1876, F. C. South-
              mayd.  Child :

1039.  Irving Emerson, b. July 8, 1880.
1040.  Emily J., b. April 6, 1860.
1041.  Ellen A., b. June 26, 1862.
1042.  William E., b. March 10, 1867.

### 1043 = 1028.  DAVID T[8]. ALLEN

b. Feb. 29, 1844, son of John and Martha M[7]. (Marsh) Allen, (Allan[6] Marsh, Capt. Daniel[5], Daniel[4], Lieut. Nathaniel[3], John[2], John[1]) ; m. June 25, 1864, No. 1043.

**1043.**  Alftina Wear.  Children :
    1044.  John M[9]., b. June 5, 1865.
    1045.  Luella, b. Aug. 15, 1867.
    1046.  Frank, b. Aug. 3, 1869.
    1047.  Ida, b. Dec. 20, 1871.
    1048.  William, b. Dec. 27, 1873.
    1049.  Emma, b. Aug. 14, 1875.

### 1050 = 1035.  FRANKLIN[9] CLARK

b. Aug. 15, 1853, son of Lucy[8] (Allen) Clark, dau. of Martha M[7]. (Marsh) Allen, (Allan[6] Marsh, Capt. Daniel[5], Daniel[4], Lieut. Nathaniel[3], John[2], John[1]) ; m. Jan. 4, 1873, No. 1050.

**1050.**  ——.  Children :
    1051.  Arthur[10], b. Nov. 9, 1874.
    1052.  May, b. Oct. 27, 1875.
    1053.  Minnie, b. Oct. 6, 1876.
    1054.  Gertrude, b. Feb. 19, 1878.
    1055.  Frank, b. March 19, 1879; d. Aug. 5, 1879.
    1056.  Charles, b. March 26, 1880.

### 1057 = 934.  MARY[7] MARSH

b. East Hartford, dau. of Allan[6] and Mabel Case[6] Marsh, (Capt. Daniel[5], Daniel[4], Lieut. Nathaniel[3], John[2], John[1]) ; m. No. 1057.

**1057.**  —— Gray.  Children :
    1058.  Frederick[8], m. —— Frissell.  No children.
    1059.  Rosanna, b. Feb. 26, 1827 ; m. John Hibbert, 1060.

## 1060 = 1059. ROSANNA[8] GRAY

b. Feb. 26, 1827, dau. of Mary[7] (Marsh) Gray, (Allan[6] Marsh, Capt. Daniel[5], Daniel[4], Lieut. Nathaniel[3], John[2], John[1]); m. in 1851, No. 1060.

**1060.** John Hibbert.   Children:

    1061.  Alfred E[9]., b. April 1, 1852; d. Aug. 11, 1853.
    1062.  Mary E., b. April 8, 1854; m. John Del Hazen, 1067.
    1063.  Henry M., b. Feb. 14, 1857; d. July 19, 1857.
    1064.  Alice A., b. Nov. 25, 1859; m. Alfred M. Stager, Oct. 7, 1885.
    1065.  William J., b. April 5, 1861; d. Dec. 24, 1864.
    1066.  Frank A., b. Oct. 3, 1864; d. July 23, 1865.

## 1067 = 1062. MARY E[9]. HIBBERT

dau. Rosanna[8] (Gray) Hibbert, (Daniel[7] Marsh, Allan[6], Capt. Daniel[5], Daniel[4], Lieut. Nathaniel[3], John[2], John[1]) ; m. Oct. 15, 1879, No. 1067.
**1067.** John Del Hazen.   Children :

    1068.  Frederick W[10]., b. July 13, 1880; d. Oct., 1880.
    1069.  William H., b. Feb. 6, 1882.

## 1070 = 935. EMILY[7] MARSH

b. East Hartford, July 21, 1806, dau. of Allan[6] and Mabel (Case) Marsh, (Capt. Daniel[5], Daniel[4], Lieut. Nathaniel[3], John[2], John[1]); m. May 16, 1830, No. 1070.
**1070.** Alfred Griswold, who d. July 23, 1882.  She d. March 22, 1883.  Children :

    1071.  Marcus L[8]., b. Jan. 27, 1831 ; m. Louisa Davis, 1079.
    1072.  Rowena B., b. July 10, 1832 ; m. Asbury Creamer, 1092.
    1073.  Abigail H. b. Feb. 6, 1834 ; m. Velasco Taylor, 1111.
    1074.  A. Morgan, b. Nov. 25, 1835 ; killed in battle, Oct. 14, 1864.
    1075.  Emily J., b. June 1, 1838 ; m. May 30, 1875, Clinton Bennett.
    1076.  Mary M., b. Oct. 7, 1843; unm.
    1077.  Josephine M., b. Sept. 12, 1845 ; d. Sept. 8, 1872.
    1078.  Charles William, b. Dec. 29, 1848 ; m. Sarepta Harper.

## 1079 = 1071. MARCUS L[8]. GRISWOLD

b. Jan. 27, 1831, son of Emily[7] (Marsh) Griswold, (Allan[6], Capt. Daniel[5], Daniel[4], Lieut. Nathaniel[3], John[2], John[1]); m. June 21, 1853, No. 1079.

**1079.** Louisa Davis. Children:

    1080. Lewis A[9]., b. Oct. 14, 1854; m. Susan Conkey, 1083.
    1081. Martha E., b. Feb. 17, 1856; m. Wm. H. Clark, 1088.
    1082. Mary B., b. March 28, 1859.

## 1083 = 1080. LEWIS A[9]. GRISWOLD ·

b. Feb. 17, 1856, dau. Marcus L[8]. Griswold, (Daniel[7], Allan[6], Capt. Daniel[5], Daniel[4], Lieut. Nathaniel[3], John[2], John[1]); m. Feb. 27, 1878, No. 1083.

**1083.** Susan Conkey. Children:

    1084. Lilian E[10]., b. Oct. 11, 1877.
    1085. Harry C., b. Oct. 30, 1880.
    1086. Blanche B., b. May 7, 1883.
    1087. Cora E., b. March 6, 1885.

## 1088 = 1081. MARTHA E[9]. GRISWOLD

b. Feb. 17, 1856, dau. Marcus L[8]. Griswold, (Daniel[7], Allan[6], Capt. Daniel[5], Daniel[4], Lieut. Nathaniel[3], John[2], John[1]); m. Feb. 27, 1878, No. 1088.

**1088.** Wm. H. Clark. Children:

    1089. Elnorah[10], b. Dec. 14, 1878.
    1090. Ray H., b. June 11, 1881.
    1091. Mary M., b. Sept. 24, 1885.

## 1092 = 1072. ROWENA B[8]. GRISWOLD

b. July 10, 1832, dau. of Emily[7] (Marsh) Griswold, (Allan[6], Capt. Daniel[5], Daniel[4], Lieut. Nathaniel[3], John[2], John[1]); m. April 22, 1852, No. 1092.

**1092.**  Asbury Creamer.   Children :

    1093.  H. Alice[9], b. Oct. 29, 1853; m. Dr. A. K. Newman, 1100.
    1094.  Joseph Marsh, b. Nov. 16, 1855; d. Sept. 11, 1862.
    1095.  Carrie S., b. Nov. 29, 1858; m. L. A. Ruth, 1104.
    1096.  Jennie L., b. April 5, 1861 ; m. Reuben Wilson, 1108.
    1097.  Harry G., b. March 15, 1866.
    1098.  George M., b. Nov. 2, 1868.
    1099.  Robert A., b. March 2, 1875.


1100 = 1093.   H. ALICE[9] CREAMER

b. Oct. 29, 1853, dau. of Rowena B[8].. (Griswold) Creamer ; m. Sept. 11, 1878, No. 1100.

**1100.**  Dr. A. K. Newman.   Children :

    1101.  Grace[10], b. Oct. 30, 1879.
    1102.  Roland N., b. Aug. 31, 1881.
    1103.  Walter E., b. Dec. 21, 1883.


1104 = 1095.   CARRIE S[9].  CREAMER

b. Nov. 29, 1858, dau. of Rowena B[8]. (Griswold) Creamer ; m. Oct. 14, 1877, No. 1104.

**1104.**  L. A. Ruth.   Children :

    1105.  Minnie M[10]., b. Sept. 5, 1878.
    1106.  Clifford R., b. Oct. 4, 1881.
    1107.  Emmet M., b. Feb. 12, 1884.


1108 = 1096.   JENNIE L[9].  CREAMER

b. April 5, 1861, dau. Rowena B[8]. (Griswold) Creamer; m. April 5, 1881, No. 1108.

**1108.**  Reuben Wilson.   Children :

    1109.  Gertrude[10], b. Dec. 18, 1881.
    1110.  Daniel W., b. April 20, 1884.

## 1111 = 1073.  ABIGAIL H⁸. GRISWOLD

b. Feb. 6, 1834, dau. Emily⁷ (Marsh) Griswold ; m. June 24, 1856,. No. 1111.

**1111.** Velasco Taylor.  Children :

1112.  George H⁹., b. Nov. 2, 1851 ; m. Eliz. Dickinson, 1120.
1113.  Ella M., b. March 9, 1860 ; d. March 25, 1860.
1114.  Luella A., b. March 4, 1861.
1115.  Frank B., b. Sept. 30, 1863 ; d. Nov. 30, 1865.
1116.  Edward L., b. Aug. 17, 1865.
1117.  Lenora E., b. April 22, 1868.
1118.  Alfred V., b. Jan. 11, 1875.
1119.  Martha M., b. July 1, 1878.

## 1120 = 1112.  GEORGE H⁹. TAYLOR

b. Nov. 2, 1858, son of Abigail H⁸. (Griswold) Taylor ; m. Dec. 25,. 1878, No. 1120.

**1120.** Elizabeth Dickinson.  Children :

1121.  Isabella¹⁰, b. Sept. 28, 1879.
1122.  Henry D., b. Nov. 10, 1884.

## 1123 = 910.  IRENE⁶ MARSH

b. East Hartford, Ct., dau. Capt. Daniel⁵ and Irene (Bigelow) Marsh,. (Daniel⁴, Lieut. Nathaniel³, John², John¹) ; b. March 20, 1765 ; m.. Feb. 26, 1784, at Hartford, Ct., No. 1123.

**1123.** Joseph McKee.  They soon removed to Weybridge, Vt., and thence to Frankfort, N. Y., on the Mohawk, and in 1806 to· Ellisburgh, Jefferson Co., N. Y.  She had seven children who grew up, married and settled and had families in N. Y. state.  She d. Aug.. 25, 1828.  Joseph McKee, d. Nov. 20, 1829.  In 1885 three of her· children were living.  She had grandchildren in New York, Ohio, Indiana, Illinois, Michigan, Iowa, Colorado, New Mexico and Cali-- fornia.  Children :

1124.  Horace⁷, b. Dec. 4, 1784 ; m. Clarissa King.
1125.  Laura, b. May 8, 1787 ; m. (1) Avery Brown.
1126.  Mary, b. May 5, 1789 ; m. Abiah Jenkins.

1127.  Betsey, b. Nov. 1, 1792 ; m. William Woodward.
1128.  Almira, b. April 25, 1797 ; m. Zerah Todd.
1129.  Nancy, b. April 8, 1799; m. (1) Daniel Fraser.
1130.  Harriet Irene, b. April 18, 1806 ; m. Abram Ward.

----

It is with much regret that the compiler of this work, to save
space, feels obliged here to omit 526 names of grand-children and
later descendants of Irene[6] (Marsh) McKee and her sister Emily[6]
(Marsh) Kennedy.  They were mainly supplied by Miss Florence
Estelle[9] Gill of Greeley, Colo., dau. of Almira H[8]. (Otis) Gill, Laura[7]
(McKee) Otis, Irene[6] (Marsh) McKee, (Capt. Daniel[5] Marsh, Daniel[4],
Lieut. Nathaniel[3], John[2], John[1].)  With much care and labor the
compiler arranged these names for publication and now hopes to pre-
sent the manuscript as thus arranged, with a copy of this work to
Miss Gill in acknowledgement of the great interest she has taken.
     Her line of descent from Irene[6] (Marsh) McKee is :

1.   Laura[7] McKee, b. May 8, 1787; m. (2) July 11, 1813, John Otis,
       b. March 19, 1787.  He d. April 28, 1870 and she d. May
       24, 1873.
2.   Almira H[8]. Otis, b. April 4, 1824; m. Sept., 1847, Wm. Alden
       Gill, b. Oct. 9, 1807 ; d. Aug. 30, 1869.
3.   Florence Estelle Gill[9], b. July 23, 1849.

----

### 1600 = 911.   EMILY[6] MARSH

b. East Hartford, Ct., Feb. 12, 1772, dau. of Capt. Daniel[5] and
Hannah (Smith-Gleason) Marsh, (Daniel[4], Lieut. Nathaniel[3], John[2],
John[1]); m. about 1791, No. 1600.

**1600.**  Timothy Kennedy, b. Oct. 13, 1768 ; d. Aug. 1, 1844.
She d. April 14, 1851, æ. 79.   Children :

1601.  Emily[7], b. Aug. 23, 1792 ; m. Sidney Spencer.
1602.  Sally, b. Oct. 1, 1794 ; d. July 9, 1796.
1603.  Sally, b. Oct. 4, 1796 ; m. Benj. Howard.
1604.  Electa, b. Feb. 28, 1798 ; m. B. M. Colman.

1605. George S., b. June 4, 1801 ; m. May 5, 1828, Nancy Vibbert.
No children.
1606. Betsey, b. June 2, 1803 ; m. John Gangas.
1607. Hannah, b. Jan. 1, 1805 ; m. Daniel Charter.
1608. Irene, b. Jan. 1, 1808 ; m. Lehman Macknet.
1609. Rosanna, b. Aug. 22, 1810 ; d. Aug. 24, 1810.

## 1669 = 913. MARY⁶ MARSH

b. May 5, 1774, dau. of Capt. Daniel⁵, (Ensign Daniel⁴, Lieut. Nathaniel³, John², John¹) ; m. No. 1669.
1669. Dea. Gideon Spencer. " She d. æ. 86, he æ. 90."—*Vermont Gazette.* They settled in Marshfield, Vt. and their grandson Stephen Spencer lived where they did.

## 1670 = 914. HANNAH⁶ MARSH

b. East Hartford, Ct., Aug. 7, 1775, dau. of Capt. Daniel⁵, (Ensign Daniel⁴, Lieut. Nathaniel³, John², John¹) ; m. Dec. 12, 1793, No. 1670.
1670. Caleb Pitkin, Jr., b. Dec. 3, 1768. He was one of the first settlers of Marshfield, Vt., and is said to have named the town Marshfield after his wife's father and his own step-father Capt. Daniel Marsh who married, for the third of his four wives, Anna (Stanley) Pitkin, the mother of this Caleb and widow of Caleb Pitkin, his father, Feb. 26, 1794. The town is also said to have been named Marshfield from Gen. Isaac Marsh of Stockbridge, who bought it from the Stockbridge tribe of Indians. Caleb Pitkin, Jr., d. at Peacham, Vt., April 16, 1813 and Hannah (Marsh) Pitkin returned to son James and d. Dec. 24, 1823. Children :

1671. James⁷, b. Jan. 26, 1795 ; m. Bethia Parker ; lived on the
farm of his father at Marshfield.
1672. Susan, b. July 26, 1802 ; m. Charles Storrs ; resided at
Royalston, Vt.
1673. Asbel Stanley, b. June 4, 1807 ; m. May A. Washburn ; residence, Burlington, Vt.

## 1674 = 880.   JESSEE[5] MARSH

b. 1736 or '37, at Hartford, Ct., son of Ensign Daniel[4] and Irene (Bigelow) Marsh, (Lieut. Nathaniel[3], John[2], John[1]) ; m. No. 1674.
**1674.** Lucy.  He d. June 25, 1797, æ. 61.
Our record of the children of Jessee and Lucy Marsh is very imperfect.

> 1675.  Nathaniel[6].
> 1676.  Jerusha, bap. Feb. 21, 1763 ; m. Abel(?) Barber.
> 1677.  Roswell, bap. Aug. 4, 1766.
> 1678.  Child. (Child of Jessee Marsh, d. Dec. 24, 1771.)—Record First Church.
> 1679.  Son, b. 1766 or 7. (Son of Jessee Marsh, d. Oct. 17, 1776, æ. 10.)—Record First Church.

## 1680 = 883.   CAPT. JAMES[5] MARSH

b. Hartford, 1746, son of Ensign Daniel[4] and Irene (Bigelow) Marsh, (Lieut. Nathaniel[3], John[2], John[1]) ; m. No. 1680.
**1680.** Mary.  He resided at "Blue Hills" in Hartford and d. Feb. 24, 1788, æ. 42.  Children :

> 1681.  Child, b. 1774; (d. Nov. 7, 1778, æ. four years.)—Church Record.
> 1682.  Elizabeth[6], b. 1777; m. Kenyan; had dau. Elizabeth[7].
> 1683.  Polly, b. 1779; m. 1797, Capt. Ashbel Spencer.
> 1684.  Clarissa, b. 1781; m. either Hale or Collins.
> 1685.  Harriet, b. 1784; m. either Collins or Hale.
> 1686.  Child, d. June 25, 1784, æ. three months.—Church Record.
> 1687.  James, b. 1786; m. Chloe Elmore, 1688.

## 1688 = 1687.   CAPT. JAMES[6] MARSH

b. 1786 at "Blue Hills" Hartford, Ct., son of Capt. James[5] and Mary Marsh, (James[5], Ensign Daniel[4], Lieut. Nathaniel[3], John[2], John[1]) ; m. 1808, No. 1688.
**1688.** Chloe Elmore.  He received from his grandfather Ensign Daniel[4] Marsh his "upper lot in Hartford Long Meadow" also "about 13 acres" on "Pantry's Brook."  The property that James[5],

b. 1746, willed to this son James[6], b. 1786, was near Pantry's Brook and all not far from the present residence of John E. Marsh, Esq., 1190 Windsor Ave., Hartford.  Children:

    1689.  James E[7]. b., 1809; d. March 15, 1815, æ. 6.—Gravestone.
    1690.  Clarissa, b. Jan. 22, 1811; m. John G. Litchfield, 1694.
    1691.  Chloe, b. and d. 1814, æ. 5 months.—Gravestone.
    1692.  James, b. Dec. 14, 1819; m. Amanda Haskins, 1698.
    1693.  Chauncey, m. 1858, Sarah G. Tuttle, 1708.


## 1694 = 1690.  CLARISSA[7] MARSH

b. Jan. 22, 1811, dau. of Capt. James[6], (James[5], Ensign Daniel[4], Lieut. Nathaniel[3], John[2], John[1]) ; m. May 16, 1831, No. 1694.

  **1694.**  John G. Litchfield, b. June 1, 1802 and d. Aug. 21, 1869. Children :

    1695.  James H[8]., b. May 11, 1832.
    1696.  Clarissa Marsh, b. Jan. 10, 1840; m. Sept. 9, 1863, Major E. B. Preston.
    1697.  Lewis G., b. Feb. 16, 1842 ; d. Sept. 10, 1843.


## 1698 = 1692.  JAMES[7] MARSH

b. Dec, 14, 1819, son of Capt. James[6] and Chloe (Elmore) Marsh, (Capt. James[5], Ensign Daniel[4], Nathaniel[3], John[2], John[1]) ; m. 1842, No. 1698.

  **1698.**  Amanda Haskins.  He d. Aug. 19, 1868, æ. 49.

    1699.  Son, d. y.
    1700.  Roselle[8], b. Aug. 15, 1846 ; m. Edward Hills.


## 1701 = 1700.  ROSELLE[8] MARSH

b. Aug. 15, 1846, dau. James[7] and Amanda (Haskins) Marsh, (Capt. James[6], Capt. James[5], Ensign Daniel[4], Lieut. Nathaniel[3], John[2], John[1]) ; m. No. 1701.

  **1701.**  Edward Hills.  He resides in New Haven.  Employee, freight office, Consolidated R. R.  She d. Oct. 17, 1882, æ. 36.

Children :

    1702.  Lena Marsh[9].
    1703.  Harry Edward.
    1704.  Effie.
    1705.  George Herbert.
    1706.  Lottie.
    1707.  Louis.


## 1708 = 1693.   CHAUNCEY[7] MARSH

b. 18— son of Capt. James[6], (Capt. James[5], Ensign Daniel[4], Lieut. Nathaniel[3], John[2], John[1]) ; m. 1858, No. 1708. **1708.** Sarah G. Tuttle. He is a hack driver and resides in Hartford, Ct.   Children :

    1709.  Mary Grace[8], b. Sept. 15, 1859; m. June 1, 1882, George S.
            Bull and had :
       1710.  George Marsh[9].
    1711.  Clara Belle, b. July 7, 1862.          ⎫
    1712.  Clarence Birdsey, b. July 7, 1862 ;   ⎭ d. 1862, æ. seven weeks.


## 1713 = 855.   LEMUEL[4] MARSH

b. Hartford, Ct., bap. March 9, 1718, son Lieut. Nathaniel[3] and Elizabeth (Spencer) Marsh, (John[2], John[1]) ; m. about 1740–50, No. 1713. **1713.** Bathsheba Barrett of Hartford, b. 1718 and d. Feb. 24, 1796, æ. 78, (First Church Record) and their first child and only son died about the same time with his father, and his property was distributed at the same time to the four daughters, Mary probably not being then born. Lemuel[4] Marsh is mentioned in John[3] Marsh's account book in 1751, and "Widow Bathsheba" is also mentioned in 1751, so that he must have died in 1751, æ. 33. As he had five children before death he must have married about 1740–42. Bathsheba was the dau. of Jonathan Barrett of Hartford who "m. Rebecca Whapples, Nov. 12, 1714. He d. 1752, estate valued at £10,000. Children : viz.: James, Jonathan, Jerusha, Elizabeth, Bathsheba Marsh, Dorothy Warren, Sarah Farnsworth, Anna and

Mary Bennett." Bathsheba named one child after her mother and two after sisters. Children :

    1714. Nathaniel.
    1715. Rebecca, m. Hezekiah Latimer.
    1716. Rachel, m. Caleb Turner, Jr.
    1717. Anne.
    1718. Sabra, m. John Sheldon.
    1719. Mary, b. after father's d., b. prob. 1752; d. Jan. 13, 1754.

---

# BRANCH I. DIVISION III.

## THE LEBANON LINE.

---

### 1720 = 49. CAPT. JOSEPH[3] MARSH

b. Hartford, Ct., (see page 20), bap. March 5, 1671, son of John[2] and Sarah (Lyman) Marsh (John[1]), twin with Nathaniel, head of the East Hartford line, became himself head of the Lebanon line and its branches in Vermont and New York state. He m. (1) about 1696 at Hartford where his first and second children were baptized in the Second church, No. 1720.

**1720.** Hannah. Mrs. Hannah was baptized 1702 and admitted to full communion in 1725. In 1697 he became a proprietor at Lebanon, Ct., southeast from Hartford. It was like going to a new world. To start a town developed men; and Lebanon has been a notable town. He became selectman for successive years, as Mr.

Joseph Marsh in 1701, as Sergeant in 1710, as Lieutenant in 1718 and as Captain in 1730. He also represented the town in the general court of Connecticut in 1712, 1716, 1723, 1727 and 1731. He m. (2) Dec. 14, 1725, No. 1721.

**1721.** Sarah, widow of George Webster. Her will was dated 1759. (Letter Hon. Charles Marsh, Jan. 22, 1862.) Children:

> 1722. Elizabeth[4], bap. "Wn he owned ye covenant," Hartford Second Church, July 30, 1697.
> 1723. Joseph, b. Dec. 5, 1699, bap. in Second Church, Hartford, Dec. 10, 1699. He m. Mercy Bill, 1727.
> 1724. Hannah, b. Nov. 9, 1704; m. Feb. 24, 1732, Peleg Sprague.
> 1725. Pelatiah, b. Dec. 8, 1707, m. Mary Moore, 1735.
> 1726. Jonathan, b. Sept. 23, 1713, m. (1) Alice Newcomb, 1744.


## 1727 = 1723.   ENSIGN JOSEPH[4] MARSH

b. Hartford, Ct., Dec. 5, 1699, bap. Second church Dec. 10, 1699, son of Capt. Joseph[3] and Hannah Marsh, (John[2], John[1]), lived in Lebanon and d. there in 1753. He m. Sept. 25, 1723, No. 1727.

**1727.** Mercy Bill as some of his descendants record it or possibly Mercy Durkee as given in New England Geneological Register. His widow and four sons, in 1772, 3 or 4, as variously given, removed to Hartford, Vt. She d. in 1786. Children:

> 1728. Mercy[5], b. 1725, m. Israel Loomis, 1756.
> 1729. Joseph, b. Jan. 12, 1726-7; m. Dorothy Mason, 1926.
> 1730. Anna, b. 1729; m. Pelatiah[5] Marsh, 1737 and 1767.
> 1731. Abel b. 1735; m. Dorothy Udall, 2122.
> 1732. Elisha, b. 1738; m. —— Terry, 2205.
> 1733. Eliphalet.
> 1734. One account adds a Ruth and gives Mary for Mercy.


## 1735 = 1725.   PELATIAH[4] MARSH

b. Lebanon, Ct., Dec. 8, 1707, son of Capt. Joseph[3] and Hannah Marsh, (John[2], John[1]); m. May 10, 1731, No. 1735.

**1735.** Mary Moore of Southold. Probably the "mother of Jessee" d. at Hartford "æ. 88, Aug. 15, 1794." He removed to Sharon, Ct., in 1764 and d. there April 8, 1790, æ. 83. Children:

1737. Pelatiah[5], b. April 4, 1732; m. Anna[5] Marsh, 1730 and 1767.
1738. Mary, b. Dec. 22, 1733.
1739. Lucy, b. Feb. 14, 1736.
1740. Isaiah, b. Feb. 3 or 13, 1738.
1741. Silas, b. March 3, 1740; m. 1833.
1742. Jesse, b. Sept. 8, 1743; d. Oct. 25, 1822, æ. 79; m., and had son Elijah.
1743. Child, b. March 31, 1746.

## 1744 = 1726. JONATHAN[4] MARSH

b. Lebanon, Ct., Sept. 23, 1713, son of Capt. Joseph[3] and Hannah Marsh, (John[2], John[1]) ; m. (1) in 1733, No. 1744.

**1744.** Alice Newcomb. He resided at Lebanon. Alice d. June 17, 1752 and he m. (2) Dec. 4, 1752, No. 1745.

**1745.** Widow Keziah Phelps. Children:

1746. Elizabeth[5], b. July 26, 1735; m. William Metcalf, 1760.
1747. Hannah, b. Nov. 20, 1736; m. James Huntington, b. April 25, 1728. She d. at Norwich, Vt.
1748. John, b. March 10, 1739; m. 2276.
1749. Abraham, b. May 31, 1742; m. 2292.
1750. Joel, b. June 1, 1745; m. Ann, 2309.
1751. Zebulon, b. May 12, 1748, twin of Sarah.
1752. Sarah, b. May 12, 1748, bap. Aug. 5, 1753.
1753. Chloe, b. Nov. 12, 1750.
1754. Alice, b. Oct. 11, 1753; m. Daniel Wilcox.
1755. Submit, m. Thomas Huntington.

## 1756 = 1728. MERCY[5] MARSH

b. Lebanon, Ct., 1725, dau. of Ensign Joseph[4] and Mercy (Bill or Durkee) Marsh, (Capt. Joseph[3], John[2], John[1]) ; m. April 8, 1747, as third wife of No. 1756.

**1756.** Israel Loomis of Windsor, Ct. His children had been John, b. 1738 and d. 1739 ; Daniel, b. 1739 and Israel, b. 1742. She d. at Lebanon, Oct. 18, 1795. Children:

1757. Esther[6], b. Jan. 2, 1748.
1758. Mary, b. Aug. 19, 1749.
1759. John, b. Nov. 3, 1751. Revolutionary soldier, d. May 24, 1841, in his 90th year.

## 1760 = 1746. ELIZABETH⁵ MARSH

b. Lebanon, Ct., July 26, 1735, dau. of Jonathan⁴ and Alice (Newcomb) Marsh, (Capt. Joseph³, John², John¹); m. in 1754, No. 1760.

**1760.** Lieut. William Metcalf of Lebanon, b. March 26, 1726, son of Ebenezer and Thankful (Delano) Metcalf. She d. in 1775 and he m. (2) No. 1760.1.

**1760.1.** Joyce Phinehas who d. in 1784 and he m. (3) No. 1760.2.

**1760.2.** Widow of John Talcott, who d. April 16, 1809 and he d. also. Children :

1761. Theodore⁶, b. 1755 ; d. in Revolutionary army, æ. 22.
1762. Lovina, m. Rufus Lamb.
1763. Elizabeth, m. Jared Allen and settled in Cooperstown, N. Y.
1764. Ebenezer Delano, d. unm., æ. 60.
1765. Sarah, m. Sylvanus Haynes of Lebanon.
1766. Alice, m. George Roberts and settled at Utica, N. Y.


## 1767 = 1737. PELATIAH⁵ MARSH

b. Lebanon, Ct., April 4, 1732, son of Pelatiah⁴ and Mary (Moore) Marsh, (Capt. Joseph³, John², John¹); m. Dec. 28, 1752, his cousin, No 1767.

**1767.** Anna⁵ Marsh, dau. Ensign Joseph⁴ and Mercy (Bill) Marsh, (Capt. Joseph³, John², John¹), b. 1729. He d. "May 10, 1777, æ. 44." Anna d. "Oct. 20, 1802, æ. 72." They resided at Lebanon and all their children were born there. Children :

1768. Dan⁶, b. Sept. 24, 1754; m. Olive Warren, 1772.
1769. Amasa, b. Oct. 3, 1756. He d. Sept. 10, 1806, æ. 51.
1770. Ann, b. Oct. 13, 1758; d. April 10, 1825; m. James Webster, who d. April 24, 1829, æ. 77. Dau. Abigail, b. 1785, d. April 25, 1829, æ. 44.
1771. Pelatiah, b. Dec. 8, 1760; m. Elizabeth Witter, 1815.
1771.1 Earl, b. 1762, d. March 19, 1779, æ. 17.
1771.2 Parthena, b. 1766, d. Dec. 7, 1838, æ. 72.
1771.3 Mary, b. 1768; m. Cyrus Williams. He d. May 8, 1838, æ. 66. She d. May 28, 1842, æ. 74.

## 1772 = 1768. DAN⁶ MARSH

b. Lebanon, Ct., Sept. 24, 1754, son of Pelatiah⁵ and Anna⁵ (Marsh) Marsh, (Pelatiah⁴, Capt. Joseph³, John², John¹) ; resided in Colchester, Ct. He m. probably not far from 1780, No. 1772.

**1772.** Olive Warren. He d. July 26, 1828 and his widow March 2, 1848, æ. 90. Children :

    1773. Earle⁷, m. Ruby Abel, 1782.
    1774. Dan, b. Nov. 30, 1784 ; m. Eunice Downer, 1805.
    1775. Olive, m. Samuel Brown, and had
        1776. Newell S.
        1777. George C.
    1778. Lydia, m. Joseph Tully, and had
        1779. Ann.
        1780. Francis.
        1781. Sophia.

## 1782 = 1773. EARLE⁷ MARSH

b. Colchester, about 1782, son of Dan⁶ and Olive (Warren) Marsh, (Pelatiah⁵, Pelatiah⁴, Capt. Joseph³, John², John¹) ; m. about 1806, No. 1782.

**1782.** Ruby Abel. The inventory of his estate was about $1,000. Children :

    1783. Solomon⁸, b. 1808; m. Elizabeth Godden, 1786.
    1784. Maria, b. 1810; m. Elijah Kellogg, 1790.
    1785. Elizabeth, b. 1812 ; m. Eleazer Lacey, 1795.

## 1786 = 1783. SOLOMON⁸ MARSH

b. Colchester, Ct., 1708, son of Earle⁷ and Ruby (Abel) Marsh, (Dan⁶, Pelatiah⁵, Pelatiah⁴, Capt. Joseph³, John², John¹) ; m. No. 1786.

**1786.** Elizabeth Godden. Children :

    1787. Eliza Maria⁹, m. E. P. Burford of Richmond, Va., and had
        1788. Blanche.
        1789. A son who d. y.

## 1790 = 1784.  MARIA[8] MARSH

b. Colchester, 1810, dau. of Earle[7] and Ruby (Abel) Marsh, (Dan[6], Pelatiah[5], Pelatiah[4], Capt. Joseph[3], John[2], John[1]); m. No. 1790.

**1790.** Elijah Kellogg.  Children :

   1791.  Eliza Maria[9], who m. George Holmes, and had
      1792.  Nellie[10], who m. W. J. Humphries, and had
      1794.  Child.


## 1795 = 1785.  ELIZABETH[8] MARSH

b. Colchester, 1812, dau. of Earle[7] and Ruby (Abel) Marsh, (Dan[6], Pelatiah[5], Pelatiah[4], Capt. Joseph[3], John[2], John[1]); m. Sept. 24, 1834, No. 1795.

**1795.** Eleazer Lacey of Middletown, Ct.  She is living in Brooklyn, N. Y.  Children :

   1796.  Philip[9].
   1797.  Cornelia, m. Gustave Rudolph Ridyer, and had, 1, George, d., and 2, Lily, d.
   1798.  Emma Silliman, m. Silas Cook Force, and had, 1, Marguirette; 2, Attilie; 3, Emma; 4, Mabel.
   1799.  Eliza Marsh, m. Otto Heinze, 1804.
   1800.  Richard, m. Cornelia Lacey, and had, 1, Rosa Caroline; 2, Louise Elizabeth; 3, Richard Austen; 4, Frederick Otto.
   1801.  Helen Louise.
   1802.  Frank Bates.
   1803.  Henry Solomon.


## 1804 = 1799.  ELIZA MARSH[9] LACEY

dau. of Elizabeth (Marsh) Lacey, (Earle[7], Dan[6], Pelatiah[5], Pelatiah[4], Capt. Joseph[3], John[2], John[1]); m. No. 1804.

**1804.** Otto Heinze.  Children :

   1804.1  Alice[10], m. George Watsen, and had, 1, Christian Heinrich; 2, Arthur Otto; 3, Johann Karl.
   1804.2.  Arthur Philip.
   1804.3.  Otto Karl.
   1804.4.  Lida Marie, m. William Heitmann.

1804.5. Frederick Augustus.

1804.6. Herman.

1804.7. Edward.

1804.8. Paul, d. 1889.

1804.9. Adolf.


## 1805 = 1774. DAN⁷ MARSH

b. Colchester, Ct., Nov. 30, 1784, son of Dan⁶ and Ruby (Abel) Marsh, (Pelatiah⁵, Pelatiah⁴, Capt. Joseph³, John², John¹); m. about 1719, No. 1805.

**1805.** Eunice Downer, b. Bozrah, Ct., Oct. 17, 1791. He d. June 28, 1849, æ. 64. His widow d. April 6, 1873, æ. 82. July 5, 1849, Mrs. Eunice Marsh and Earle W. Marsh were appointed administrators on estate of Dan Marsh. The inventory was $7,053.82. The widow also Sept. 21, 1849 was made guardian of the estate and persons of her three minor children. Children :

1806. Caroline E⁸., b. Sept. 14, 1820; m. Feb. 3, 1847, H. Nelson Lee. They have one child :

1807. Helen M., b. April 19, 1857.

1808. Earle Warren, b. Oct. 15, 1822 ; d. March 21, 1887.

1809. Mary Hough, b. Dec. 26, 1824; d. April 8, 1847.

1810. Uriah, D., b. Nov. 24, 1826; d. Oct. 8, 1828.

1811. Edwin Downer, b. Oct. 18, 1831; m. Oct. 22, 1860, Lucretia Wasgatt. They had :

1812. Edwin Ralph, b. Jan., 1870; d. Jan., 1880.

1813. Henry Clay, b. Dec. 25, 1833; m. March 23, 1881, Helen M. Dunham.

1814. Eunice Swift, b. Sept. 13, 1836; m. Oct. 22, 1860, Oliver C. Ashton.


## 1815 = 1771. PELATIAH⁶ MARSH

b. Lebanon, Ct., Dec. 8, 1760, son of Pelatiah⁵ and Anna⁵ (Marsh) Marsh, (Pelatiah⁴, Capt. Joseph³, John², John¹), was m. at Montville, Ct., Jan. 20, 1785, by the Rev. Rozel Cook to No. 1815.

**1815.** Elizabeth Witter, b. March 3, 1759 at New London, Ct., dau. of Samuel and Eunice Witter. Their first child was born at Lebanon, Ct. and the others at Hebron, Ct. Their grandson P. J.

Marsh of Lansingburgh, N. Y. writes : "About the year 1800 my Grandfather Pelatiah Marsh removed with his family from Hebron, near Lebanon, Ct. to Williamstown, Mass., where they resided for three or four years and then removed to Grafton, Renssalaer Co., N. Y." There they died and were buried. Pelatiah[6] Marsh, d. at Grafton, Dec. 12, 1820, æ. 60 years. Elizabeth (Witter) Marsh, d. at Grafton, N. Y., Nov. 2, 1841, æ. 82. Children :

1816.   Anna[7], b. at Lebanon, Ct., March 26, 1786 Sabbath Day ; m. to Russell Clark, by the Rev. Seth Swift, at Williamstown, Mass., Dec. 25, 1806. Anna (Marsh) Clark d. at Alexandria, N. Y., April 9, 1863, æ. 77.

1817.   Elizabeth, b. Hebron, Ct., May 8, 1788, Tuesday ; d. Jan. 19, 1791, accidentally killed.

1818.   Eunice Way, b. Hebron, Jan. 2, 1791, Sabbath Day ; m. Nathan Barber, 1823.

1819.   Pelatiah, b. Hebron, July 31, 1793, Wednesday ; d. at Grafton, Aug. 31, 1810, æ. 18.

1820.   Amasa, b. Hebron, Feb. 10, 1799 ; d. Grafton, N. Y., Nov. 20, 1813, æ. 18.

1821.   Elizabeth, b. Hebron, Jan. 5, 1798, Tuesday ; m. to William Boansteel by Rev. John Younglove, Jan. 1, 1822. She d. at Hoosick Falls, N. Y., Jan. 13, 1841.

1822.   Prentiss Witter, b. Hebron, Ct., Oct. 16, 1800 ; m. Laura Tilley, 1825.


### 1823 = 1818.   EUNICE WAY[7] MARSH

b. Hebron, Ct., Jan. 2, 1791, (town record 1792) dau. of Pelatiah[6] and Elizabeth (Witter) Marsh, was m. by Rev. John Keeys, Dec. 12, 1811, to No. 1823.

**1823.** Nathan Barber. Her daughter writes : " I had one of the most noble mothers, Eunice Marsh, that ever graced this land. She was first in the early temperance cause, went on horseback to have people sign the pledge, had a talent to convey to others her own inspiration." The daughter certainly inherited her mother's earnestness and Christian devotion. Among other activities she was one of the very first to take an absorbing interest in the history of the Marsh family and she has written many letters to all parts of our land and collected most valuable information. She obtained for us the long document from the State Archives of Connecticut given in the early

Pelatiah J. Marsh

*To face page* 123.

part of this work, and has been indefatigable in doing what she could. We all ought to honor Mrs. Pamelia (Barber) Wellman, for by her deep love and honor of her mother " Eunice Marsh " she has been of great service to the entire Marsh family. Mrs. Barber d. at Sand Lake, N. Y., Sept. 3, 1846, æ. 55. Child;

1824. Pamelia[8], m. —— Wellman.

## 1825 = 1822. REV. PRENTISS WITTER[7] MARSH

b. Hebron, Ct., Oct. 16, 1800, son of Pelatiah[6] and Elizabeth (Witter) Marsh, was m. by Rev. Nathan Lewis, Jan. 9, 1823, to No. 1825.

**1825.** 'Laura Tilley of Petersburgh, N. Y., b. in 1802 in Connecticut. Mrs. Wellman, his niece, states that Rev. Prentiss W. Marsh, for advocating the freedom of the slaves, was to have been tarred and feathered at Syracuse, but he and his companions "escaped without any punishment, *with Christ in their hearts.*" He was one of the early champions of liberty for all. He d. at Lansingburgh, N. Y., Feb. 15, 1853, æ. 53. Laura (Tilly) Marsh d. at Lansingburgh, N. Y., Dec. 30, 1878, æ. 76. Children :

1826. Lucy Ann[8], b. Grafton, N. Y., June 13, 1824. She resides unm. at Lansingburgh, N. Y.
1827. Pelatiah James, b. Grafton, N. Y., Sept. 14, 1829. He m. Eliza A. Bailey, 1828.

## 1828 = 1827. PELATIAH JAMES[8] MARSH

of Lansingburgh and Albany, N. Y., b. Grafton, N. Y., Sept. 14, 1829, son of Rev. Prentiss[7] Witter and Laura (Tilley) Marsh, (Pelatiah[6], Pelatiah[5], Pelatiah[4], Capt. Joseph[3], John[2], John[1]); m. (1) Jan. 25, 1862, No. 1828.

**1828.** Eliza A. Bailey, Troy, N. Y., b. there Oct. 15, 1841. He m. (2) at Parma, N. Y., May 19, 1869, No. 1829.

**1829.** Lelia E. Tracy, b. at Parma, N. Y., Jan. 29, 1843. Mr. Marsh has been a large dealer in real estate with timber lands a specialty. His office is at 55 State St., Albany, N. Y. and his residence at Lansingburg, N. Y. He graduated at Union college 1853, and afterward had the degree of A. M. Children :

1830.  James Prentiss, b. Troy, N. Y., Oct. 25, 1862; graduated
       at Albany Medical college, 1884, practicing at Troy,
       N. Y.
                    By second wife.
1831.  Mary Ada, b. Lansingburgh, N. Y., Aug. 2, 1870.
1832.  George Tracy, b. Lansingburgh, N. Y., Aug. 9, 1874.  Now
       of Yale college, class of '98.


### 1833 = 1741.  SILAS[5] MARSH

b. Lebanon, Ct., March 3, 1740, son of Pelatiah[4] and Mary (Moore)
Marsh, (Capt. Joseph[3], John[2], John[1]); m. No. 1833.
1833. ——. He graduated at Yale college 1764 and the catalogue says d. in 1790. He became a lawyer and settled at Amenia,
Dutchess Co., N. Y., and there two of his sons certainly and probably all his children were born. He sent his oldest son to Yale.
After his death his widow was cared for at Lansing on Cayuga Lake
where all her children but Silas seem to have resided, with or near
her, till her death. Silas who was interested in soldiers' claims, gave
to his brother John and sister Elizabeth a farm in Lansing of 200
acres on condition that they care for their mother. Thomas had a
son born there and Fanny m. a Mr. Goodwin of Ludlowville in
that township of Lansing. We can seem to see that widow in serene
old age looking out upon many a sunset reflected in Cayuga lake,
but we are sad to think that none of her many descendants seem
able to tell the date of birth or marriage or death or even the maiden
name of the widow of one who was an A. M. of Yale in 1780, and
owes to Yale catalogues the preservation of the date of his
death in 1790. Children :

1834;  Silas[6], b. Amenia, N. Y., Jan. 28, 1766; m. Elizabeth,
       Beebe, 1839.
1835.  John, m. after his mother's death, possibly settled in Candor.
1836.  Elizabeth, m. after her mother's death.
1837.  Thomas, b. Amenia, July 26, 1776; m. Martha Campbell, 1900.
1838.  Fanny, m. —— Goodwin of Ludlowville, in Lansing, N. Y.


### 1839 = 1834.  SILAS[6] MARSH

b. Dutchess, Co., N. Y., Jan. 18, 1766, son of Silas[5], (Pelatiah[4],

Capt. Joseph[3], John[2], John[1]) ; graduated at Yale college, 1784 twenty years after his father, who seems to have taken his A. M. in 1780 when he put his boy in. Silas Jr. was a member of the P B K. His youngest son informs us, writing from New Brunswick, N. J., Aug. 5, 1888, in his 79th year : "My father Silas Marsh and my mother Elizabeth Beebe were neighbors in Dutchess Co., N. Y. They married and had 14 children, 10 of whom married and had children. My father studied law at Poughkeepsie, but his principal business was buying and selling soldiers' claims. They both died in the state of New York." His son Edward was born in Aurora, Cayuga Co., N. Y. and "probably others." His claim business explains his having the 200 acres on Cayuga lake to give for the care of his mother. He m. May 10, 1792, No. 1839.

**1839.** Elizabeth Beebe, b. April 6, 1774 ; d. about 1870. Children :

1840.  Elizabeth[7], b. May 5, 1793 ; m. —— Wright, 1855.
1841.  Julia, b. Oct. 29, 1795 ; m. —— Brown, 1860.
1842.  Charlotte A., b. Oct. 5, 1798 ; m. —— Beech.
1843.  Edward, b. March 26, 1800 ; m. No. 1865.
1844.  Oliver, b. June 22, 1801 ; m. ——. Children :
    1845.  Irving.
    1846.  Perry.
1847.  Olivia, (twin), b. June 22, 1801 ; m. —— St. John, 1872.
1848.  Caroline, b. March 20, 1803 ; m. —— McNaughton, 1879.
1849.  Adelia A., b. Aug. 11, 1804 ; m. —— Field ; d. Brockport, N. Y., Nov. 9, 1884.
1850.  Sophia, b. March 28, 1806 ; m. (1) Nathaniel Clark ; m. (2) —— Hargraves ; has resided in Rochester, N. Y. over 40 years.
1851.  Laura M., b. Jan. 2, 1808 ; m. —— Wallace, 1883.
1852.  Henry Beebe, b. Aug. 24, 1809 ; m. Frances H. Nelson, 1888.
1853.  Mary S., b. July 7, 1813.
1854.  Frederick A., b. Aug. 30, 1816.

## 1855 = 1840.  ELIZABETH[7] MARSH

b. May 5, 1793, dau. Silas[6] and Elizabeth (Beebe) Marsh, (Silas[5], Pelatiah[4], Capt. Joseph[3], John[2], John[1]) ; m. No. 1855.

**1855.** ——. Wright. Children all living in 1888 :
1856.  Martha Knowles[8], Rochester, N. Y.

1857.  Charlotte Hammond, Chicago, Ill.
1858.  Robert, resided at Bewdley, Canada.
1859.  Spencer, resided at Rock Island, Ill.


## 1860 = 1841.  JULIA[7] MARSH

b. Oct. 29, 1795, dau. of Silas[6] and Elizabeth (Beebe) Marsh, (Silas[5], Pelatiah[4], Capt. Joseph[3], John[2], John[1]) ; m. No. 1860.

**1860.** —— Brown. " Places of residence unknown, perhaps Toledo, O." Four children living in 1888 :

1861.  Sylvester[8].
1862.  Charles.
1863.  Augustus.
1864.  Julia, m. —— Rideout.


## 1865 = 1843.  EDWARD[7] MARSH

b. Aurora, Cayuga Co. N. Y., March 26, 1800, son of Silas[6] and Elizabeth (Beebe) Marsh, (Silas[5], Pelatiah[4], Capt. Joseph[3], John[2], John[1]) ; m. about 1822, No. 1865.

**1865.** ——. They had six children all born in East Bloomfield, Ontario Co., N. Y.:

1866.  James E[8]., b. May 10, about 1823; residence in 1885 in Walworth, N. Y.
1867.  Charles H., b. Oct. 13, 1825.  Last known was taken prisoner in the war of the rebellion.
1868.  Mary E., b. Dec. 14, 1833 ; m. Oct. 28, 1857, Warren B. Selby, a jeweler, in Farmington, Oakland Co., Mich., and resides there. House burned Oct. 9, 1872 and records were lost.
1869.  Alvah N., b. Oct. 1836, Caledonia Station, Mich.
1870.  Asa, d. y.
1871.  Ellen P., b. Feb. 9, 1841 ; m. Cogsdill; residence Charlotte, Mich.


## 1872 = 1847.  OLIVIA[7] MARSH

b. June 22, 1801, dau. of Silas[6] and Elizabeth (Beebe) Marsh, (Silas[5], Pelatiah[4], Capt. Joseph[3], John[2], John[1]) ; m. No. 1872.

**1872.** Mr. St. John.   Resides in Milford, Oakland Co., Mich.
and vicinity.   Children :

- 1873.   Martha[8].
- 1874.   Charlotte.
- 1875.   Eugenia.
- 1876.   Enos.
- 1877.   Oliver.
- 1878.   William.

## 1879 = 1848.   CAROLINE[7] MARSH

b. March 20, 1803, dau. of Silas[6] and Elizabeth (Beebe) Marsh,
(Silas[5], Pelatiah[4], Capt. Joseph[3], John[2], John[1]) ; m. No. 1879.

**1879.** Mr. McNaughton.   Children :

- 1880.   Henry[8], resides at Rochester, N. Y.
- 1881.   John, resides at Peru, Ind.
- 1882.   Maggie, resides at Sacramento, Cal.

## 1883 = 1851.   LAURA[7] MARSH

b. Jan. 2, 1808, dau. of Silas[6] and Elizabeth (Beebe) Marsh, (Silas[5]
Pelatiah[4], Capt. Joseph[3], John[2], John[1]) ; m. No. 1883.

**1883.** —— Wallace.   Children :

- 1884.   James[8], resides at Chicago, Ill.
- 1885.   William, resides at Chicago, Ill.
- 1886.   Julia, resides at Aurora, N. Y.
- 1887.   Gail, resides at Aurora, N. Y.

## 1888 = 1852.   HENRY BEEBE[7] MARSH

b. Aug. 24, 1809, son of Silas[6] and Elizabeth (Beebe) Marsh, (Silas[5],
Pelatiah[4], Capt. Joseph[3], John[2], John[1]) ; m. Sept. 22, 1843, No. 1888.

**1888.** Harriet Nelson.   They had seven children.   He has been
a jeweler and resides at New Brunswick, N. J.   He has given us most
of the information we have as to his father's descendants and writes
Aug. 5, 1888 when near his 79th birthday, " I was engaged in the
watch and jewelry business for most of my life, but old age and

weakness compelled me to give it up.  I am seventy-nine years old
Aug. 24, and have good health." Children :

1889.  Henry N[8]., b. June 6, 1844.
1890.  Edward B., b. Nov. 1, 1845 ; d. Oct. 11, 1850.
1891.  Mary Francès, b. Nov. 20, 1847 ; m. Joseph Fisher.  She d.
       March 17, 1877.  Child :
       1892.  Adelaide, b. April 5, 1874.
1893.  Edgar Jerome, b. July 26, 1851 ; m. Augusta Felter.  He d.
       May 18, 1883.  Child :
       1894.  Harriet A., b. July 9, 1872.
1895.  Eugene L., b. Feb. 2, 1860.
1896.  C. Arthur, b. Oct. 10, 1863 ; m. Minnetta C. Blue, 1898.
1897.  Leo, b. Nov. 24, 1866 ; d. Feb. 3, 1867.


1898 = 1896.  CHARLES ARTHUR[8] MARSH

b. Oct. 10, 1863, son of Henry Beebe[7] Marsh, (Silas[6], Silas[5], Pelatiah[4], Capt. Joseph[3], John[2], John[1]) ; m. Oct. 8, 1884, No. 1898.
1898.  Minnetta C. Blue.  Child :
       1899.  Edith I[9]., b. Sept. 25, 1885.


1900 = 1837.  THOMAS[6] MARSH

b. July 26, 1776 at Amenia, Dutchess Co., N. Y., near Sharon,
Litchfield Co., Ct., where his grandfather Pelatiah[4] removed from
Lebanon, Ct. and lived till his death in 1790 ; he was a hatter by
trade, son of Silas[5], (Pelatiah[4], Capt. Joseph[3], John[2], John[1]) ; m. at
Milton, N. Y., June 7, 1804, No. 1900.
1900.  Martha Campbell, dau. of Lieut. Spencer Campbell of the
revolutionary war.  He d. April 17, 1849.  They lived in Tompkins
Co. and moved to New Hudson, Allegany Co., N. Y.  Children :

1901.  Spencer[7], b. Lansing, N. Y. in 1807 ; m. No. 1907.
1902.  William, lived in Allegany Co., N. Y.
1903.  Betsey.
1904.  Maria.
1905.  Caroline Matilda, m. —— Trowbridge ; had son Col. Charles
       Egan Trowbridge of Greeley, Colo.
1906.  Fanny, m. —— Perry; residence at Mt. Tabor, Oregon.

1907 = 1901. SPENCER[7] MARSH

b. in 1807 at Lansing, N. Y., son of Thomas[6] and Martha (Campbell) Marsh, (Silas[5], Pelatiah[4], Capt. Joseph[3], John[2], John[1]); lived at Allegan, Mich.; m. No. 1907.

1907. ———. Children :

    1908. Frances[8].
    1909. Charles, m. No. 1919.
    1910. Kate, m. —— Clark,
    1911. Mary, m. —— and had :
        1912. Bessie, who is d.
        1913. May.
    1914. Henry, m. and has :
        1915. A daughter.
    1916. Edwin, d.
    1917. Edward, d.
    1918. Stella, d.


1919 = 1909. CHARLES[8] MARSH

son of Spencer[7] Marsh, (Thomas[6], Silas[5], Pelatiah[4], Joseph[3], John[2], John[1]); m. No. 1919.

1919. ———. He d. in 1881. Children :

    1920. Joseph.
    1921. Lulu, d. in 1880.
    1922. Frank.
    1923. Lee.
    1924. Neva.
    1925. Stanley.

## VERMONT MARSHES.

### Of the Lebanon Connecticut Line.

---

Not long before the revolution, seven grandsons of Capt. Joseph[3], Marsh, (John[2], John[1]) in the spirit of their grandfather, the Lebanon pioneer and proprietor of 1697, and of their grandfather's grandfather, pioneer and proprietor at Hartford 1636 and Hadley 1660, found their way to *New* Connecticut, now Vermont. Four were sons of Ensign Joseph[4] and three of his brother Jonathan[4]. Of these cousins, John[5], the oldest son of Jonathan[4], preceded the rest, as proved by birth of his son John[6] at Claremont, N. H. in 1759. His mother had d. in 1752. He is found a very little later across the river in Weathersfield, Vt. The two other sons of Jonathan[4] and the four sons of Ensign Joseph[4] with their widowed mother, in 1772 (Joseph's wife remaining a year at Lebanon) passed some 20 miles farther up the river and settled at the mouth of White river, calling their Green Mountain-Connecticut-Valley-town, Hartford, in memory of the colonial capital lower down. The French war, 1755-58, had brought all the Vermont region into larger notice and its termination had opened the way for a fresh northerly English migration. Where were fairer lands? The cousins acted wisely together and helped on new settlements. One-fourth of the first proprietors of Randolph, Vt., were these men of Marsh name. Yet the Revolution hindered that movement and· they all sold out and remained lower down the White river, at Woodstock, Hartland, Hartford, Quechee and eventually Bethel.

We have this important testimony from Hon. James Barrett, Judge ·of the Supreme Court of Vermont.

"Great Honor has been brought to the State by those who have borne the Illustrious name of *Marsh*, all vitalized by the same family blood."

## 1926 = 1729. GOV. JOSEPH[5] MARSH

b. Lebanon, Ct., Jan. 12, 1726–7, son of Ensign Joseph[4], (Capt. Joseph[3], John[2], John.[1]) His mother was Mercy Bill or Mercy Durkee, " In 1772 he came to Hartford in New Connecticut, and took up a large tract of land bounded north by White river, and south by the south bank of the Otta Quechee. And opposite where the Quechee broke into little islands, he built a very large house, of which the frame, windows and doors were brought on rafts from Connecticut. Early writers speak of the house as the " Baronial Mansion," and it is yet one of the finest places in Hartford or vicinity." The following extracts from a letter to D. W. Marsh have a fine flavor :

QUECHEE, VT., FEB. 13, 1893.

MR. MARSH—

*Dear Sir :* Your letter to our town clerk, Ex-Gov. Pingree of Hartford, Vt., is before me. He thought perhaps I might know something of the history of the Marsh family you mention. One volume of the town records of Hartford is lost, probably burned in some house where it had been borrowed, as was the habit in years past.

The reason Gov. Pingree referred to me for information is, that I live on the old Gov. Marsh place. He built the house which is a hundred years old this year. The rooms he lived in, have never been changed, even the cupboard where he had his rum, (a very temperate man too,) is just as it was a hundred years ago. This is a fine old place now, on the banks of the Quechee, surrounded by meadows, and the upland crowned with the forest " Primeval." Not an axe has been laid at the foot of a tree except those that have outlived their generation, or a pine that was not growing *better*, with time, and towering fifty feet above its *fellows*. Mr. Porter my husband, bought the Gov. Marsh place in 1846.

I have been looking over the Marsh " Deeds," and as I took up one after the other of these timeworn documents what Longfellow thought, and expressed, came to me.

"We have no title deeds to house or lands;
Owners and occupants of early date,
From graves forgotten stretch their dusty hands,
And hold in mortmain *still*, their old estates."

I loved many younger members of the Marsh family, but the grave has closed over them, and I am walking the same floors, and looking on the same landscape. The name of Elisha Marsh occurs often in the old deeds, and I think he, and Abel sleep in our little cemetery. When warm weather comes I will go there, and look over the old headstones. I will try and find out more about those brothers. There is one man in town that is older than myself. I will see him. You probably never received so long a letter from an old woman. (82)

Respectfully, Yours

JANE F. PORTER

Mrs. Porter has three quaint old chairs, that belonged to Gov. Joseph Marsh.

Judge Barrett says : "Having had much experience in business and public affairs he became at once active in the questions and controversies of the embryo state, and was soon called to stations of trust and responsibility."

In 1776 he was twice chosen a delegate for the County of Cumberland to the Provincial Congress of New York, but favored an independent state government, and under it was elected the first state governor.

The same year, 1776, he was commissioned Colonel of the northern or upper regiment of Cumberland county. What was then Cumberland county, forms now the counties of Windham, Windsor, Rutland and Bennington.

In 1777 he was a member of the convention that declared New Connecticut an independent state, changed its name to Vermont and pledged itself to resist by force of arms the fleets and armies of Great Britain. He was also member of the Convention that adopted the State Constitution, 3d and 4th of July, 1777.

At the call of Gen. Schuyler, the same year, he, with his oldest son, as one of his quota of men, marched to and had part in the battles of Bennington, White Hall, Fort Ann, Fort Edward, and Sandy Hill. A price of £40 was offered for his head.

He represented Hartford in the first general assembly under the State Constitution.

The same year ('78) he was elected Lieut. Governor, and re-elected '87, '88 and '89.   In the interim he represented Hartford in general assembly.   He was 12 years chief judge of Windsor county.   Was offered a township for his unpaid services, but refused to accept it. He was an active Christian, and liberal supporter of the religious and benevolent objects of his day and left a perpetual fund for the support of the church in Hartford.   He was tall, large and finely proportioned and of great muscular power.   Even at eighty he could lift weights his sons could not.   He was a bold and superior horseman ; wore small clothes and triangular hat to the last ; kept a chaise but preferred to ride on horseback.   Mrs. Sanford writes :   He was never irritable, rarely was, but could be, stern ; and had a close logical mind.   At eighty he showed no decay of mind or body, and people came from long distances to consult him.   But on the death of his wife, who left no Christian hope, he mourned himself to death. He would talk of nothing else for any long time, and would accept no diversion.

While Judge, his son Charles, then at the bar, was insulted by an opponent, and sprang up and struck him on the mouth.   His father gave Charles a most scathing rebuke.   Charles sprang to his feet, asked the forgiveness of the court, of his opponent, of his client whose cause he had jeopardized, and then of his father, as a father whose honored name he had disgraced.   Even strong men wiped their eyes, but the father sat calm and seemingly cold.

Deacon ——, a cabinet maker, made Joseph Marsh a chest of drawers that soon fell to pieces.   One winter day he came to the door and called my great-grandfather out.   " Gov. Mash !   Gov. Mash !   Our women !   Oh, our women—their frivolities will bring ruin on us !   Even dumb animals suffer !   Come out to my sleigh. I have got a pig with a crape cushion on its head !" with a long sigh.

My great-grandfather looked down from his six feet on him, " Never mind that, Deacon, but if one come with a *chest of drawers* on his head, I'll go and look at him."

He was very kind and gentle, but firm in all his family relations. My grandfather died when my mother was six months old.   At all the family gatherings, her grandfather held her on his knee and called himself her own father and was a father to her at all times.

He m. Jan. 10, 1750, No. 1926.

**1926.**  Dorothy Mason.  We can trace the descent of Mrs. Joseph[5] Marsh, Dorothy Mason, from Rev. Samuel Whiting born 1597 and his wife Elizabeth St. John, b. 1605, through Elizabeth Whiting, b. 1645 and her husband Rev. Jeremiah Hobart, b. 1630 and through Dorothy Hobart and her husband Daniel Mason, b. 1674 and on down to her own bright self.  We hardly know in which of these four names to feel the greater interest.  Major John Mason the first of his line in America was born in 1600, m. Anne Peck in 1639, came to Massachusetts as early as 1632 and to Windsor, Ct., in 1636. Thence in 1637 he led ninety men to the Pequot stronghold, smote them with cruel fire and sword and forever that same year broke up their tribal relations.  For this and other evidence of skill and force to lead, he was chosen deputy governor of Connecticut colony for eight years and also made major general and for six years sent commissioner to the New England congress.  He d. Jan. 30, 1672, æ. 72.

Edmund Hobart, great-grandfather of Dorothy (Hobart) Mason, wife of Daniel, grandson of Major John Mason, was of the family of the Earl of Buckinghamshire, and his descendant, Bishop Hobart of New York, when in England, was acknowledged as a relative, by the present earl.  He came from Hingham, England, to Charlestown, Mass. in 1633 and to Hingham in 1635.  Of deeper interest to us than any tinge of noble blood or royal descent, is the manliness of Edmund Hobart's son.  Rev. Peter Hobart, b. Hingham, England, 1604, of Magdalen college, Cambridge university 1625, became a preacher in England but "feeling oppressed by the impositions of the prelacy," emigrated to Hingham, Mass. in 1635 and became the first minister there.  His son Rev. Jeremiah b. 1630, graduated at Harvard 1650, was minister at Topsfield, Hampstead, L. I. and Haddam, Ct., in all 43 years.  His daughter Dorothy m. Daniel Mason.

Rev. Samuel Whiting was b. Nov. 20, 1597 in Boston, England, took degree of A. B., Cambridge university 1616, and A. M. 1620, came to Boston, Mass. 1636, was pastor at Lynn, Mass., 43 years. He had three sons, ministers, and his dau. Elizabeth b. 1645, m. Rev. Jeremiah Hobart.  His wife Elizabeth St. John, b. 1605, d. March 3, 1677, was the only dau. of the Rt. Hon. Sir Oliver St. John, Knt., Devonshire, England.  He was chief justice of England in the time of Oliver Cromwell, to whom he was nearly related by marriage.

Elizabeth St. John was of very noble lineage. In her was united the blood of ten of the sovereigns of Europe. Mrs. Sanford writes : " Mrs. Joseph Marsh, Dorothy Mason, was aunt of Jeremiah Mason the noted lawyer of Boston, sister of Mrs. Theodore Sedgwick and sister of Mrs. Senator Durfee of Connecticut. One of her ancestors was Elizabeth St. John, dau. of Baron St. John who was cousin of Queen Elizabeth, and descendant of Henry VII. She came in two lines from William the Conqueror, and direct from Alfred the Great, and by several royal marriages was allied to all the early royal powers of Europe.

Chancellor Walworth says, " hers is the finest genealogy in the United States." She was very beautiful and entertained the best society of Vermont and New England, with elegance. She had no handsome child, but many handsome grand-children. It was the custom in Hartford after service for the minister to walk out, then ' Gov. Mash,' all the people standing still." He d. Feb. 9, 1811.

The following is the Mason line of descent :

1.  Major John[1] Mason, b. in England, 1600 ; m. (2) July, 1639, Anne Peck, baptized in England, Nov. 18, 1619.
2.  Capt. Daniel[2] Mason, b. in Saybrook, Ct., April, 1652 ; m. (1) Margaret Denison, b. in Roxbury, Mass., Dec. 13, 1650, dau. of Edward and Elizabeth (Weld) Denison.
3.  Daniel[3] Mason, b. in Stonington, Ct., Nov. 26, 1674 ; m. April 19, 1704, Dorothy Hobart, third dau. of Rev. Jeremiah and Elizabeth (Whiting) Hobart.
4.  Jeremiah[4] Mason, b. in Stonington, Ct., March 4, 1705 ; d. Franklin, Ct., in 1779 ; m. May 24, 1727, Mary[3] Clark, b. in Haddam, Ct., about 1704, dau. of Thomas[2], William[1]; d. in Franklin, Ct., April 11, 1799.
5.  Dorothy[5] Mason, b. in Norwich, Ct., April 9, 1732 ; m. Joseph Marsh, Jan. 10, 1750. Children :

    1927. Lydia[6], b. Nov. 5, 1750; m. Josiah Rockwell, 1939.
    1928. Dorothy, b. April 23, 1752; m. Eliphalet Bill, 1974.
    1929. Rhoda, b. July 25, 1754; m. (1) Thomas W. Pitkin, 1984.
    1930. Joseph, b. Jan. 1, 1757; m. Serepta Wells, 1994.
    1931. Mary, b. Feb. 8, 1759; m. Elijah Mason, 2008.
    1932. Daniel, b. Jan. 2, 1761; m. Marion Harper, 2014.
    1933. Roswell, b. Lebanon, Ct., March 25, 1763; d. unm. June 30, 1784.
    1934. Charles, b. July 10, 1765 (bap. 21st); m. (1) Anne Collins, 2081.

10*  .

1935.  Roger, b. Aug. 17, 1767 (bap. 23d); m. Mary Chapman, 2100.
1936.  Parthena, b. Nov. 3, 1769, at Lebanon; m. Rev. E. Brainard,
2105.
1937.  William, b. Oct. 1, 1772, at Lebanon; m. Sarah Marshall,
2117.
1938.  Elizabeth, b. April 18, 1776, at Hartford, Vt.; m. Robert
Ham, 2118.

1939=1927.  LYDIA[6] MARSH

b. Lebanon, Ct., Nov. 5, 1750, dau. of Gov. Joseph[5] and Dorothy
(Mason) Marsh; m. June 18, 1768, No. 1939.
**1939.** Josiah Rockwell of Lebanon. They resided at Lebanon
and he d. there Nov. 22, 1812; his widow Nov. 14, 1814. Children:

1940.  Lathrop[7], b. at Lebanon, May 28, 1769; pastor Congregational
Church, Lyme, Ct.; m. (1) Olive Dutton of Lebanon,
Sept. 2, 1784; m. (2) Lucy Peck; d. at Lyme, March
14, 1828.
1941.  Azel, b. Oct. 14, 1771; d. at Charleston, S. C., unm., August,
1796.
1942.  Joseph, b. March 26, 1774; m. Sarah Huntington, 1949.
1943.  Lydia, b. March 25, 1777; d. unm. June 23, 1846.
1944.  Clarissa, b. May 4, 1780; m. Joseph Lyman; d. Jan. 6, 1855.
He d. Aug. 25, 1864.
1945.  Daniel, b. Oct. 4, 1782; m. Jan. 14, 1808, Prudence Wattles,
b. Lebanon, May 13, 1787; res. Manlius, N. Y., where
he d. Sept. 9, 1836, and she d. May 27, 1846.
1946.  Rhoda, b. June 5, 1785; m. John Champion, and d. Sept.,
1833.
1947.  Erastus, b. July 1, 1787; d. at Lebanon Jan. 6, 1856, unm.
1948.  Jabez, b. May 20, 1790; m. Eunice Bailey of Lebanon,
March 30, 1818, and d. at Norwich, Ct., Feb. 9, 1859.

1949 = 1942.  JOSEPH[7] ROCKWELL

b. March 26, 1774, son of Josiah and Lydia[6] (Marsh) Rockwell, (Gov.
Joseph[5] Marsh, Ensign Joseph[4], Capt. Joseph[3], John[2], John[1]); m.
April, 1800, No. 1949.
**1949.** Sarah Huntington, b. June 9, 1777, at Lebanon, dau. of
Andrew and Ruth (Hyde) Huntington. They resided at Lebanon
and she d. there Sept. 4, 1849 and he Sept. 29, 1849. Children:

1950.  Azel[8], b. May 5, 1801 ;  m. Laura Hill, 1958.
1951.  Philura, b. Nov. 26, 1802 ; d. May 26, 1817.
1952.  Emily, b. Nov. 6, 1804; d. unm., Dec. 14, 1859.
1953.  Eunice Huntington, b. June 21, 1807 ; d. unm., July, 1840.
1954.  Elijah Frink, b. Oct. 6, 1809; m. (1) Margaret K. McNeil, 1969.
1955.  Andrew Huntington, b. Nov.16,1811 ; m. Cor. R. Porter, 1973.
1956.  Ruth, b. March 6, 1814 ; d. May 5, 1814.
1957.  Sarah Ann, b. Oct. 16, 1816 ; d. Sept. 20, 1836.


1958 = 1950.  AZEL[8] ROCKWELL

son of Joseph[7] and Sarah (Huntington) Rockwell, (Lydia[6] Marsh,
Gov. Joseph[5], Ensign Joseph[4], Capt. Joseph[3], John[2], John[1]) ; m. Dec.
16, 1825, No. 1958.

1958.  Laura Hill.  Resided at Lebanon, where she d. April 8,
1861, and he d. Oct. 15, 1877.  Children :

 1959.  Ann Eliza[8], b. Sept. 28, 1827 ; m. Sept. 29, 1851, her mother's
         cousin, Charles Wesley Hill, b. Colebrook, Ct.; res.
         Mansfield, Ct., they have two children.
 1960.  Laura Lodisa, b. Feb. 14, 1831 ; m. Sept. 29, 1851, Hervey
         Nelson Powell of Burlington, Vt., settled in New Haven,
         Ct.  He d. 1881.  They had one child :
      1961.  Flora Alice, b. Sept., 1857 ; d. y.
 1962.  Hadassah Maria, b. Jan. 18, 1835 ; m. June, 1866, Henry A.
         Race of Farmington, res. Lebanon, have :
      1963.  Azel Rockwell.
      1964.  Frederick.
 1965.  Harriette Sophia, b. Nov. 14, 1839; m. May 25, 1857, Allison
         Norris Clark ; res. Plainville, Ct.  Have had five chil-
         dren, only one now living.
 1966.  Joseph Henry, b. Oct. 14, 1842; m. Jan. 22, 1868, Annice E.
         Brown of Providence, R. I.; res. at Warwick, R. I.
         Children :
      1967.  Howard Allison, b. Dec. 14, 1870 ; d. Sept. 10, 1876.
      1968.  Henry, b. Sept. 17, 1878.


1969 = 1954.  PROF. ELIJAH FRINK[8] ROCKWELL

son of Joseph[7] and Sarah (Huntington) Rockwell, (Lydia[6] Marsh,
Gov. Joseph[5], Ensign Joseph[4], Capt. Joseph[3], John[2], John[1]) b. Oct. 6,

1809 ; Yale college 1834, student at Princeton and at Columbia, S. C. Presbyterian minister, licensed 1839 ; m. (1) June 18, 1839, No. 1969.

**1969.** Margaret Kirtlandt McNiel, b. Aug. 13, 1817, at Fayetteville, N. C. He was pastor of the Presbyterian church, Slatersville, N. C. in 1841, and in 1850 professor in Davidson college, Mecklenburg Co., N. C. There his wife d. childless. He m. (2) Sept. 11, 1867, No. 1970.

**1970.** Elizabeth Homer Brown. He was professor at Davidson 18 years and returned to Slaterville as president of Concord Female college ; now resides at Cool Spring, Iredell Co., N. C. Children :

> 1971. Joseph Huntington, b. Oct. 27, 1868.
> 1972. Douglass, b. 1870 ; d. April 1, 1870.


1973 = 1955.   ANDREW HUNTINGTON[8] ROCKWELL

b. Nov. 16, 1811, son of Joseph[7] and Sarah (Huntington) Rockwell, Josiah and Lydia[6] (Marsh) Rockwell, (Gov. Joseph[5] Marsh, Ensign Joseph[4], Capt. Joseph[3], John[2], John[1]) ; m. Sept. 28, 1837, No. 1973.

**1973.** Caroline Ripley Porter of Columbia, Ct., settled at Lebanon and in 1841 removed to Columbia and in 1865 to Manchester, Ct., where he d. Dec. 31, 1884. His wife d. June 16, 1880. He belonged to the best type of New England character. He was for several years treasurer of the First Congregational society and in 1879 had charge of the funds for building the new church edifice. He took a deep interest in his kindred. Children :

> 1973.1. Calvin[9], b. Dec. 21, 1838, at Lebanon ; res. unm. at Manchester.
> 1973.2. Ferdinand, b. Nov. 18, 1840, at Lebanon ; m. Terisa Emogene Abby of Chester, Ct., and d. there March 4, 1874. Children :
> > 1973.3. James Huntington, b. Aug. 8, 1868.
> > 1973.4. Lucy Winifred, b. March 31, 1872.
> 1973.5. Margaret Kirtlandt, b. Dec. 12, 1843, at Columbia ; res. in Manchester, unm.


1974 = 1928.   DOROTHY[6] MARSH

b. at Lebanon, Ct., April 23, 1752, dau. of Gov. Joseph[5] and Dorothy

(Mason) Marsh, (Ensign Joseph[4], Capt. Joseph[3], John[2], John[1]) ; m. No. 1974.

**1974.** Eliphalet Bill.   Children :

    1975.  Benajah[7].
    1976.  Eliphalet.
    1977.  Mason, Dr., m. Rhoda Pitkin, his first cousin, 1987.
    1978.  Roswell.
    1979.  Noadiah.
    1980.  Mary, m. her first cousin, Thomas White Pitkin, 1986.
    1981.  Dorothy.
    1982.  Elizabeth.
    1983.  Almira.


## 1984 = 1929.  RHODA[6] MARSH

b. at Lebanon, Ct., July 25, 1754, dau. of Gov. Joseph[5] and Dorothy (Mason) Marsh, (Ensign Joseph[4], Capt. Joseph[3], John[2], John[1]) ; m. (1) No. 1984.

**1984.** Thomas White Pitkin.   Removed to Hartford, Vt. and was drowned there in 1785.   He was b. Sept. 25, 1749, son of Thomas and Elizabeth (White) Pitkin, and grandson of Rev. Thomas White, the first minister of Tolland, Ct.   She m. (2) No. 1985.

**1985.** Rev. Thomas Gross.   Children by first husband :

    1986.  Thomas W[7]., b. Dec. 5, 1772 ; m. his cousin Mary Bill, 1993.1.
    1987.  Rhoda, b. Oct. 26, 1774 ; m. her cousin, E. Mason Bill, and
           d. April 8, 1859.
    1988.  Samuel, b. Dec. 30, 1777 ; m. Elizabeth Hamblin, 1993.26.
    1989.  Ruth, b. 1780; never m.
    1990.  Rebecca, b. 1782.
    1991.  Lucy, b. Feb. 6, 1784; m. (1) Robert Ellis, Jr., of Saratoga
           Springs, N. Y., where he d.; she m. (2) Joseph Bishop
           Abrams.   She d. Feb. 20, 1856.   She had by first hus
           band Robert and Thomas Pitkin ;  by second husband,
        1991.1.  Lucy[8], b. March 15, 1826 ; m. James Sanford.   Mrs.
             Sanford had high literary attainment.
        1992.2.  Mary Pitkin, b. Feb. 28, 1828; m. J. C. P. Stevens.
             Dr. Stevens of Philadelphia, the noted author and
             scholar is descended from Mary Pitkin Stevens.
             See page 468.

            By second husband.

    1992.  Pitkin, a physician of Kingston, Canada.
    1993.  Horace, d. unm.

## 1993.1 = 1986. THOMAS WHITE⁷ PITKIN, JR.

b. Dec. 5, 1772, son of Rhoda⁶ Marsh and Thomas White Pitkin, (Gov. Joseph⁵ Marsh, Joseph⁴, Capt. Joseph³, John², John¹), was a farmer, living at Hartford, Vt. He m. Nov. 2, 1800, his cousin, No. 1993.1.

**1993.1.** Mary⁷ Bill, b. Nov. 8, 1777, dau. of Eliphalet M. and Dorothy⁶ (Marsh) Bill, (Gov. Joseph⁵ Marsh, Ensign Joseph⁴, Capt. Joseph³, John², John¹.) She d. May 9, 1835. He d. May 20, 1861. Children :

> 1993.2.  Lucia⁸, b. Jan. 19, 1802 ; d. Sept. 23, 1802.
> 1993.3.  Lucius, b. March 1, 1805 ; d. Sept. 3, 1806.
> 1993.4.  Thomas White, b. Feb. 23, 1807 ; d. unm. Aug. 21, 1880.
> 1993.5.  Mary, b. Jan. 23, 1809; m. Ora Wood, 1993.8.
> 1993.6.  Lucius, b. Oct. 4, 1812 ; m. Ellen F. Wood, 1993.22.
> 1993.7.  Eliza, b. Dec. 25, 1815 ; d. unm. Sept. 24, 1867.
> There were other children who d. y.

## 1993.8 = 1993.5. MARY⁸ PITKIN

b. Jan. 23, 1809, dau. of Thomas White⁷ and Mary⁷ (Bill) Pitkin, Rhoda⁶ (Marsh) Pitkin, (Gov. Joseph⁵ Marsh, Joseph⁴, Capt. Joseph³, John², John¹) ; m. June 1, 1836, No. 1993.8.

**1993.8.** Ora Wood, b. Oct. 22, 1802. He d. Aug. 7, 1882. She d. March 28, 1884. Children :

> 1993.9.   Edward⁹, b. March 26, 1837 : d. unm. May 28, 1884.
> 1993.10.  William H., b. Sept. 9, 1838, married.
> 1993.11.  Caroline E., b. June 23, 1840 ; m. A. R. Richardson, 1993.17.
> 1993.12.  Benjamin P., b. Feb. 22, 1842 ; m. March 22, 1871, Sarah J. Fellows.
> 1993.13.  Charles C., b. Feb. 23, 1844 ; d. May 20, 1846.
> 1993.14.  Mary Pitkin, b. March 1, 1846 ; m. Sept. 13, 1869, James G. Porter.
> 1993.15.  Emily Marsh, b. April 28, 1848 ; d. unm. May 10, 1867.
> 1993.16.  Charles C., b. May 23, 1850 ; m. Sept. 13, 1880, Emma Turner.

## 1993.17 = 1993.11. CAROLINE E⁹. WOOD

b. June 23, 1840, dau. of Mary⁸ (Pitkin) Wood, Thomas White⁷ and

Mary[7] (Bill) Pitkin, cousins and grandchildren (one by Rhoda[6] [Marsh] Pitkin, the other by Dorothy[6] [Marsh] Bill) of Gov. Joseph[5] Marsh, (Joseph[4], Capt. Joseph[3], John[2], John[1]). She m. Nov. 18, 1872, No. 1993.17.

**1993.17.** Albert R. Richardson of Billerica, Mass., b. Dec. 26, 1825. He d. Feb. 23, 1892. Mrs. Richardson writes "My mother and her brother Lucius Pitkin were the only children of my grandfather" (Pitkin) "who ever married, and Lucius married my half sister" (Ellen F. Wood) "so that all the descendants of my grandfather Pitkin are really of my father's family." Children :

> 1993.18. Alice M[10]., b. Oct. 23, 1875 ; d. May 24, 1884.
> 1993.19. Mary Wood, b. Aug. 29, 1877.
> 1993.20. Albert H., } b. Jan. 4, 1881.
> 1993.21. Alden B., }

## 1993.22 = 1993.6. LUCIUS[8] PITKIN

b. Oct. 4, 1812, son of Thomas White[7] and Mary[7] (Bill) Pitkin, he son of Rhoda[6] (Marsh), she dau. of Dorothy[6] (Marsh), (Gov. Joseph[5], Joseph[4], Capt. Joseph[3], John[2], John[1]) ; m. Aug. 26, 1854, No. 1993.22.

**1993.22.** Ellen Frances Wood, dau. of Ora Wood by his first wife, b. Dec. 22, 1832. He d. Oct. 12, 1867. Children :

> 1993.23. Ellen L[9]., b. Nov. 9, 1855 ; d. Jan. 6, 1866.
> 1993.24. Caroline Wood, b. Jan. 12, 1858.
> 1993.25. Lucius, b. March 12, 1860.

## 1993.26 = 1988. DR. SAMUEL[7] PITKIN

b. Hartford, Vt., Dec. 30, 1779, son of Thomas White and Rhoda[6] (Marsh) Pitkin, (Gov. Joseph[5] Marsh, Joseph[4], Capt. Joseph[3], John[2], John[1]) ; m. Aug. 23, 1807, No. 1993.26.

**1993.26.** Elizabeth Hamblin, b. Dutchess Co., N. Y., Nov. 16, 1782, dau. of Joshua and Pamelia (Bryant) Hamblin. She was of the same family as Vice-President Hamlin although spelling the name with a "b" as did early settlers. Dr. Samuel[7] Pitkin graduated from the medical department of Dartmouth college, and in the year 1806 removed to Ballston Springs where he entered upon the practice of medicine. He was very much in advance of his times, prescribing fresh air and water to his fever patients, when the general custom was to deny both. He used laughingly to say that only his reputation saved him from being incontinently turned from the house. During the war of 1812 he volunteered as surgeon. Three commissions were given him. In one he is appointed surgeon of a regiment of infantry in the county of Saratoga, whereof David Rogers is Lieut. Col. Commander dated, March 26, 1812. In another is appointed surgeon of a detachment of the militia of the state of New York, organized and called into the service of the United States by general orders, dated Aug. 29, 1814, etc. " In testimony whereof I have caused the seal of the state of New York for military commission to be hereunto affixed at the city of Albany the first day of September in the year of our Lord one thousand eight hundred and fourteen and in the 39th year of the independence of the United States." Both were signed by David D. Tompkins.

The third is an appointment as "assistant hospital surgeon of the 9th brigade of infantry of our said state," signed by De Witt Clinton.

He d. March 27, 1823. His widow d. June 25, 1829. Of these children, all born at Ballston Springs, N. Y., Mrs. Rogers the dau. of Caroline writes : " They were early left orphans, their home broken up and they scattered among relatives. They were all fine looking, my mother, (Caroline Pitkin) and her youngest sister Lucy remarkably beautiful, beautiful in spirit and character as well as in person. My uncle Samuel[8] was greatly beloved by all who knew him. When the cholera visited Saratoga he risked his life to save that of a friend; was the only one who went near him, or followed him to the grave. They all, but Pamelia, my father's second wife, died comparatively young." Children :

1993.27. Erasmus Darwin[8], b. June 24, 1808; m. F. Wilcox, 1993.33.
1993.28. Caroline Elizabeth, b. Nov. 3, 1810; m. J. Slocum, 1993.40.
1993.29. Pamelia Ellis, b. April 11, 1813; m. James Slocum, 2d wife.
1993.30. Elizabeth, b. April 24, 1815; d. unm. Oct. 28, 1836.
1993.31. Samuel, b. Oct. 5, 1817; d. unm. Feb. 15, 1854.
1993.32. Lucy, b. Feb. 8, 1823; d. unm. Feb. 5, 1840.

## 1993.33 = 1993.27.  ERASMUS DARWIN[8] PITKIN

b. Ballston Springs, N. Y., June 24, 1808, son of Dr. Samuel[7] and

Elizabeth (Hamblin) Pitkin, Thomas White and Rhoda[6] (Marsh) Pitkin, (Gov. Joseph[5] Marsh, Joseph[4], Capt. Joseph[3], John[2], John[1]); m. Oct. 9, 1838, No. 1993.33.

**1993.33.** Frances Wilcox of Saratoga, N. Y., who d. Jan. 29, 1877. Children all born at Saratoga Springs :

> 1993.34. George W[9]., b. Feb. 4, 1840; d. unm. Sept. 2, 1867.
> 1993.35. Caroline E., b. March 27, 1842 ; d. Aug. 8, 1843.
> 1993.36. Mary L., b. Jan. 20, 1844 ; d. unm. March, 1875.
> 1993.37. William Francis, b. April 13, 1847.
> 1993.38. J. Howard, b. Sept. 20, 1748 ; d. March 27, 1855.
> 1993.39. Samuel, b. March 19, 1852 ; d. March 25, 1855.

1993.40 = 1993.28.    CAROLINE E[8]. PITKIN

b Ballston Springs, Nov. 3, 1810, dau. of Dr. Samuel[7] and Elizabeth (Hamblin) Pitkin, Thomas White and Rhoda[6] (Marsh) Pitkin, (Gov. Joseph[5] Marsh, Joseph[4], Capt. Joseph[3], John[2], John[1]); m. Oct. 28, 1833, in Saratoga, N. Y., No. 1993.40.

**1993.40.** James Slocum, b. in Claverack, N. Y., Nov. 7, 1811. He was educated at Claverack academy, N. Y. His daughter Mrs. Talbot M. Rogers of Philadelphia writes : " My father, James Slocum, was a man of strong and noble character, a worthy descendant of Scotch Presbyterian and English Quaker ancestry. Firm in his convictions, resolute and courageous in upholding them. His intellect was vigorous and keen, his mind well-trained ; he had a great love of books, and was especially fond of the early history of our country. He never entered the arena of political life, although frequently urged to do so, but was always an enthusiastic supporter of the cause of liberty and right. From the year 1845 he acted with the anti-slavery party. In 1848, he was a delegate from the 21st congressional district of Pennsylvania to the Buffalo convention that nominated Martin Van Buren for president, and Charles Francis Adams for vice-president of the United States. He was the delegate to the free-soil convention at Pittsburg 1852, that nominated Hale and Julian. Brownsville was a ' station ' of the underground railroad between Virginia and Canada and his sympathy and influence were fully enlisted in favor of the slaves escaping from bondage. To a friend he wrote, ' I feel a great satis-

faction at my opposition to human slavery.   I have from early manhood continued firm in my belief that freedom should be national and
apply to all classes.'   To me he once said, 'I determined when I
started in life, never to lose my faith in God and man,' and to the
day of his death, he maintained a trust that no rude shock could
destroy."   He d. March 15, 1891, in Brownsville, Pa.   Children:

> 1993.41.   J. Elizabeth[9], b. Sept. 3, 1834;   m. T. M. Rogers, 1993.43.
> 1993.42.   Mary Eleanor, b. April 24, 1838;   d. unm. Sept. 11, 1869.


### 1993.43 = 1993.41.   J. ELIZABETH[9] SLOCUM

b. Keesville, N. Y., Sept. 3, 1834, dau. of James and Caroline E[8].
(Pitkin) Slocum, Dr. Samuel[7] Pitkin, Rhoda[6] (Marsh) Pitkin, (Gov.
Joseph[5] Marsh, Joseph[4], Capt. Joseph[3], John[2], John[1]);   m. Aug. 31,
1858, No. 1993.43.

**1993.43.**   Talbot Mercer Rogers of Philadelphia, Pa.   Educated
at Jefferson college but not a graduate.   Their home is at 3915 Spruce
St., Philadelphia.   Children:

> 1993.44.   Caroline Pitkin[10], b., Brownsville, Pa., Aug. 31, 1859;   m.
>        L. J. Papineau, 1993.48.
> 1993.45.   Eleanor S., b. Brownsville, May 21, 1865.
> 1993 46.   Mary Mercer, b., Philadelphia, Jan. 23, 1868.
> 1993 47.   James Slocum, b., Philadelphia, Nov. 21, 1871.   He grad-
>        uated in the preparatory school first in his class, passed
>        "exams." for Princeton without a condition.   His
>        mother, being devoted to New England, preferred Yale,
>        especially as so many of his ancestors had graduated
>        there, but threw responsibility of choice upon him.   To
>        please her he took examinations at New Haven, where
>        a gentleman said "Here is a little fellow in knicker-
>        bockers."   That "little fellow" passed without a "con-
>        dition";   but decided for Princeton because "there is
>        there more study and less foot-ball."   Then too he
>        liked the two literary societies, with their halls for
>        debating.   He graduated at Princeton 1893, and is now
>        studying law in the Law School of Penn. University,
>        and is also in the office of Wayne MacVeagh and Mr.
>        Bispham.

## 1993.48 = 1993.44.   CAROLINE PITKIN[10] ROGERS

b. Brownsville, Pa., Aug. 31, 1859, dau. of Talbot Mercer and Eliz-
abeth[9] (Slocum) Rogers, Caroline[8] (Pitkin) Slocum, Dr. Samuel[7]
Pitkin, Rhoda[6] (Marsh) Pitkin, (Gov. Joseph[5] Marsh, Joseph[4], Capt.
Joseph[3], John[2], John[1]) ; m. Aug. 24, 1880, No. 1993.48.

**1993.48.** Louis Joseph Papineau of Monte Bello in the Province
of Quebec, the grandson of one who is called "the greatest man
that French Canada ever produced." The Papineau estate fronts
fifteen miles on the Ottawa river and runs fifteen miles back. The
present head of the family and proprietor of the manor house and
magnificent park, Mr. Louis A. J. Papineau, son of the great Canadian leader, "married an American lady, Miss Westcott of Saratoga.
His only son, who resides with him, married Miss Rogers of Philadelphia, who is the mother of an interesting family of four sons,
the oldest of whom Louis Joseph[4], is twelve years old." The family
is American in its sympathies and English is the language of the
home.

"On a knoll in the wooded park, between the chateau and the
village, stands a small private chapel" which has become a veritable
Mt. Vernon of liberty-loving Canadians, for in its vault lie the bones
of the Patriot Louis Joseph Papineau, who in the assembly of 1834,
uttered this remarkable prophecy : "My honorable friend boasts of
his attachment to monarchy, and thinks that it can be perpetuated on
this continent. I will venture to say to him that instead of Europe
giving kings and kingdoms to America the day is not far distant
when America will give presidents and republics to Europe." Since
that prophecy Louis Napoleon has failed in his attempt to give a
king to Mexico, and France herself has become a republic.

## 1994 = 1930.   JOSEPH[6] MARSH

b. Lebanon, Ct., Jan. 1, 1757, son of Gov. Joseph[5] and Dorothy
(Mason) Marsh, (Ensign Joseph[4], Capt. Joseph[3], John[2], John[1]) ; m.
No. 1994.

**1994.** Serepta Wells, dau. of Judge Wells. "He was the oldest
son, and his father helped him build on the White river bank, three

11

miles from home a large house which is now owned by his grandson and remodeled and is a very fine old place.   It had a paneled partition between two large chambers that swung up and hooked into the back chamber ceiling, and the floor was of narrow boards running the full length, making a spring floor for dancing.   His bride brought the first carpet ever in Hartford.   She was very exclusive but very pleasant to family friends."—*Mrs. Lucy Ellis Sanford.*   He d. at Hartford, Vt., April 16, 1837 and his widow Sept. 5, 1843, æ. 83. Children :

> 1995.  Gratia[7], b. 1786; d. unm. April 23, 1858, see 1998.
> 1996.  Joseph Harry, b. about 1789; m. Sue M. Thayer, 2006.
> 1997.  Mary, b. April 22, 1793; m. lra Hazen, 1999.

## 1998.  GRATIA[7] MARSH

b. 1786, dau. of Joseph[6] and Serepta (Wells) Marsh, (Gov. Joseph[7], Ensign Joseph[4], Capt. Joseph[3], John[2], John[1]), lived in Hartford, Vt. and d. April 23, 1858.   " She was very much sought by gentlemen, was very pretty and very quiet; but, true to an early, broken attachment, she refused all others, and after her mother's death lived very quietly with an aged father and an adopted nephew and died unmarried.   In old age her early lover came to see her, more than a thousand miles.   They wept together over the unreturning past and parted with a kiss."—*L. E. S.*

## 1999 = 1997.  MARY[7] MARSH

b. Hartford, Vt., April 22, 1793, dau. of Joseph[6] and Serepta (Wells) Marsh, (Gov. Joseph[5], Ensign Joseph[4], Capt. Joseph[3], John[2], John[1]); m. No. 1999.

**1999.**  Ira Hazen of Hartford, Vt.   She d. June 6, 1861. Children :

> 2000.  Asa Hazen[8], b. April 22, 1821 ; m. Jan. 1, 1850, Clementine Porter.
> 2001.  Mary Louisa, b. Oct. 7, 1822 ; m. Aug. 26, 1850, John Paul, and d. April 19, 1854.

2002. Susan Josephine, b. Feb. 14, 1825; m. Nov. 27, 1849, Francis
Boardman of Newport, N. H. No children.

2003. Joseph Marsh, b. April 19, 1828. Entered Dartmouth College, was taken sick sophomore year and after seven
years confinement to the house d. Aug. 28, 1853.

2004. Ellen Serepta, b. July 7, 1830; d. Nov. 11, 1875.

2005. Walter Scott, b. May 14, 1833; m. Sept. 18, 1861, Caroline
Ann Fowler.

2005.1 Gratia Marsh, b. April 22, 1836; d. Aug. 16, 1837.

## 2006 = 1996. JOSEPH HARRY[7] MARSH

b. Hartford, Vt., about 1789, son of Joseph[6] and Serepta (Wells)
Marsh, (Gov. Joseph[5], Ensign Joseph[4], Capt. Joseph[3], John[2], John[1]);
m. in 1815, No. 2006.

**2006.** Sue M. Thayer, sister of Col. Sylvanus of Braintree, Mass.
Their son writing from Milton, Fla., Aug. 21, 1888, states "My
father, Joseph H. Marsh and his father Joseph Marsh were farmers
living in Hartford, Vt., when I first knew them. Our family moved
to Oberlin, Ohio about the year 1836, father and mother died at
Oberlin 25 years ago." L. E. S. states "Harry moved to Oberlin,
Ohio and never had any correspondence with his family or kins-
folk." Child:

2007. Joseph[8], b. Dec. 2, 1819. This Joseph Marsh writes: "I was
born in Hartford, Vt., Dec. 2, 1819." He mentions date
of his parents' marriage and proximate removal to
Oberlin, and adds, "the rest of our family of five died
unmarried, as also my father's sister Gratia or Gracia,
and mother's brother, Col. S. Thayer." A letter directed
to him later in 1892 was returned with postmark "Dead."

## 2008 = 1931. MARY[6] MARSH

b. Lebanon, Ct., Feb. 8, 1759, dau. of Gov. Joseph[5] and Dorothy
(Mason) Marsh, (Ensign Joseph[4], Capt. Joseph[3], John[2], John[1]); m.
her second cousin No. 2008.

**2008.** Elijah Mason, son of Peleg and Mary (Stanton) Mason.
James Mason[8] Cleveland and Gen. Hazen of the Civil Service Bureau

are her grandchildren.   After her death Mr. Mason m.   Miss Strong and moved to Ohio and Mrs.   President Garfield is his grandchild by second marriage.   Children :

    2009.   Clarissa[7].
    2010.   Mary.
    2011.   Roswell.
    2012.   Peleg.
    2013.   Miranda.


## 2014 = 1932.   DANIEL[6] MARSH


b. Lebanon, Ct., Jan. 2, 1761, son of Gov. Joseph[5] and Dorothy (Mason) Marsh, (Ensign Joseph[4], Capt. Joseph[3], John[2], John[1]) ; m. No. 2014.

**2014.** Marion Harper, b. May 14, 1769, dau. of Col. James of East Windsor, Ct. " He inherited the home on the Otta Quechee, Hartford, Vt. It was the seat of the most unlimited hospitality. He had eight children. Three of his sons were men of note, and two of his daughters were noted for beauty. " Aunt Marion " lived to a great age and was *very* fond of society, and was generous, hospitable and cordial. Her welcome was most hearty and her wit, even to the last, wonderful. We all loved to go and see her. Instead of sitting in the corner and holding my breath as at Uncle William's, we were told, " Run out of doors and make as much noise as you can."—*L. E. S.* Daniel[6] Marsh d. Dec. 11, 1829 ; Widow Marion March 18, 1851.   Children :

    2015.   Roswell[7], b. Jan. 26, 1793 ; m. (1) 2023.
    2016.   James, b. July 19, 1794 ; m. (1) Lucia Wheelock, 2024.
    2017.   Percy, b. June 19, 1796 ; d. unm. Jan. 18, 1844.   " She lost the use of her lower limbs by a severe sickness. I remember her rolling chair, her etherial form, sweet face, delicate hands, and gentle voice. She seemed a bit of an angel to me."—L. E. S.
    2018.   Leonard, b. June 29, 1799 ; } m. Anna L. Foote, 2049.
    2019.   Louisa, b. June 29, 1799 ; } m. George Udall, 2055.
    2020.   Arabella, b. Oct. 26, 1804 ; m. Chauncey Goodrich, 2061.
    2021.   Emily, b. Oct. 8, 1806 ; m. David Reed, 2064.
    2022.   Daniel, b. Jan. 19, 1809 ; m. Lucinda Hall, 2069.

## 2023 = 2016. ROSWELL[7] MARSH

b. Hartford, Vt. Jan. 26, 1793, son of Daniel[6] and Marion (Harper) Marsh, (Gov. Joseph[5], Ensign Joseph[4], Capt. Joseph[3], John[2], John[1]). "He lived in the house with his grandfather until he was 18 years old, when his grandfather died. When fitting for college he refused to take a leg of mutton to his boarding place for part payment as agreed. To humble him his father called James and told him he could go to college, and he took the mutton. But Roswell took offence and ran away. They tried in vain to trace him for some years. When James was at Andover theological seminary he rode 300 miles on horseback to Brownsville, Pa. to see him and reconciled him to his family. He moved to Steubenville, Ohio and became one of the most noted lawyers in the state. He had his mother's keen wit and boundless anecdote. I heard him when over 80, challenge any one to tell an anecdote he could not match. He had many offices and could have had higher, but so keenly felt his want of collegiate education he would not accept them. He m. No. 2023.

**2023.** ——. He was married twice, but left no children. "After the death of his second wife he came to Hartford, put a new gravestone for his uncle Roswell, as the old had cleft ; put a stone engraved for himself beside that of his grandfather, and asked Mrs. Porter to let him lie one night in the room in which he was born. He died in Steubenville, O. and was brought to Hartford, Vt. He was buried in flowers from the home of his birth, and the date, Aug. 16, 1875, carved on the otherwise finished stone. He was devoted to his mother and all his family."—*L. E. S.*

## 2024 = 2016. PRES. JAMES[7] MARSH, D. D.

b. July 19, 1794, at Hartford, Vt., son of Daniel[6] and Marion (Harper) Marsh, (Gov. Joseph[5], Ensign Joseph[4], Capt. Joseph[3], John[2], John[1]). He entered Dartmouth college in 1813. A college revival in 1815 changed his life and life-plans. He joined Hanover Congregational church Aug. 7, 1815 ; graduated valedictorian in 1817, and entered Andover. Was tutor at Dartmouth in 1818 and became engaged to Lucia Wheelock, dau. of John and niece of Pres.

Wheelock; in 1820 returned to Andover, lost health by over-study in extras, and went south in 1822 and returned to his father's farm. Was invited to Princeton in 1824, but accepted a professorship in Hampden-Sidney college, Va.; ordained Oct. 12, he was m. (1) to No. 2024, Oct. 14, 1824, and reached Hampden-Sidney college Oct. 30. He became President of the University of Vermont in 1826.

**2024.** Lucia Wheelock. His wife d. Aug. 18, 1828. In 1833 he resigned the presidency for a professorship and devoted the rest of his life to taking by reading and reflection " a comprehensive view of all parts of knowledge, as constituting an organic whole." He m. (2) his wife's sister, Jan. 1, 1835, No. 2025.

**2025.** Laura Wheelock. She d. Aug. 12, 1838. After his first sickness at Andover he was never strong and he d. July 3, 1842 in his 48th year. He left his great work in fragments which, with a memoir, were published by Prof. Torrey of Vermont university. Children :

> 2026. Sidney Harper[8], b. Aug. 29, 1825, at Harper's Ferry, Va.; m. E. Haskell, 2029.
> 2027. James Wheelock, b. June 27, 1827, Burlington, Vt. Grad. Vermont Univ., was Supt. of public instruction in the Sandwich Islands and d. there, unm., Jan. 26, 1860.
> 2028. Joseph Walker, b. March 22, 1836, Burlington, Vt.; m. M. M. Parmelee, 2038.

## 2029 = 2026.   PRES. SIDNEY HARPER[8] MARSH

b. Harper's Ferry, Va., Aug. 29, 1825, son of Pres. James[7] and Lucia (Wheelock) Marsh, (Daniel[6], Gov. Joseph[5], Ensign Joseph[4], Capt. Joseph[3], John[2], John[1]) ; m. No. 2029.

**2029.** Eliza Haskell of North Bloomfield, Ohio. He graduated at the University of Vermont and became president of the Pacific university at Forest Grove, Oregon, as early as 1860 and d. there Feb. 2, 1879. Children :

> 2030. James Wheelock[9], b. May 16, 1862.
> 2031. Mary Henrietta, b. Oct. 11, 1864 ; d. April 19, 1880.
> 2032. George Haskell, b. Sept. 9, 1866.
> 2033. Lucia, b. Oct. 13, 1868.
> 2034. Anna Lena, b. Dec. 20, 1870 ; d. Nov. 12, 1874.
> 2035. Leonard, b. April 2, 1873 ; d. Dec. 22, 1874.
> 2036. Emily, b. May 7, 1875 ; d. Dec. 11, 1876.
> 2037. Winifred, b. Sept. 18, 1877.

## 2038 = 2028. PROF. JOSEPH WALKER[8] MARSH

b. Burlington, Vt., March 22, 1836, son of Pres. James[7] and Laura (Wheelock) Marsh, (Daniel[6], Gov. Joseph[5], Ensign Joseph[4], Capt. Joseph[3], John[2], John[1]); m. at Waterloo, Province of Quebec, Aug. 26, 1862, No. 2038.

**2038.** Mary M. Parmelee, dau. of Rotus. He writes " I have been professor of Latin and Greek in Pacific university since I came here in 1867. Though baptized simply Joseph, I have called myself, since reaching manhood, Joseph Walker, out of respect and gratitude to Mrs. B. B. Walker, a lady who cared for me when a child." He lost his mother when two and father when four years old. Children, all but the first, born at Forest Grove, Ore.:

2039. James Rotus[9], b. Aug. 16, 1865, at Granby, Quebec.
2040. William Parmelee, } b. July 31, 1867
2041. Laura Wheelock, }
2042. Sidney Edward, b. Jan. 8, 1870.
2043. David Walker, b. Dec. 24, 1871.
2044. Joseph George, b. Feb. 22, 1874; d. Jan. 1, 1877.
2045. Frederick Leonard, b. May 2, 1876.
2046. John Daniel, } b. Nov. 27, 1877; d. Dec., 1877.
2047. Julia Mary, }
2048. Gertrude Emily, b. March 10, 1880.

## 2049 = 2018. PROF. LEONARD[7] MARSH

b. Hartford, Vt., July 29, 1799, son of Daniel[6] and Marion (Harper) Marsh, (Gov. Joseph[5], Ensign Joseph[4], Capt. Joseph[3], John[2], John[1]). Graduated at Dartmouth 1827, Medical college 1832 or 34. He studied and practiced with Dr. Mott of New York. L. E. S. writes : " Fell in love with my mother's sister-in-law, hadn't the courage to make proposal, and when she married gave up his New York practice and went home to the farm 'to die,' he said, but in fact to his mother's laugh at him. For several years however he would lie under the trees near the river and study. He refused a Dartmouth professorship, but after his brother Daniel's failure, went to Burlington and practiced medicine." He m. No. 2049.

**2049.** Anna L. Foote. He was made professor of Greek in Vermont university 1855-7 ; of Physiology 1857-70. He d. Aug.

16, 1870 and by his request his body was taken to Hartford, Vt."
Children :

2050.  Mary Moore[8], b. Aug. 28, 1848; d. Nov. 10, 1861.
2051.  William Foote, b. Feb. 19, 1850, res. Portland, Oregon.
2052.  George Foote, b. March 31, 1852; in 1885 res. Detroit, Mich.
2053.  Charles Leonard, b. Oct. 27, 1854; m. Sept. 11, 1877, Carrie
       Foote.  They have two girls.
2054.  Anne Louise, b. Aug. 19, 1859.


2055 = 2019.   LOUISA[7] MARSH

b. June 29, 1799, twin of Prof. Leonard, dau of Daniel[6] and Marion
(Harper) Marsh, (Gov. Joseph[5], Ensign Joseph[4], Capt. Joseph[3], John[2]
John[1]) ; m. No. 2055.
**2055.**  George Udall.  Children :
       2056.  George[8], d. y.
       2057.  George.
       2058.  Daniel.
       2059.  Franklin.
       2060.  Charles.


2061 = 2020.   ARABELLA[7] MARSH

b. Oct. 26, 1804, dau. of Daniel[6] and Marion (Harper) Marsh, (Gov.
Joseph[5], Ensign Joseph[4], Capt. Joseph[3], John[2], John[1]) ; m. in 1828,
No. 2061.
**2061.**  Chauncey Goodrich, Esq. of Burlington, Vt., b. in Hinsdale, Mass., 1698.  She d. in 1835.  He d. Sept. 11, 1858 in his
61st year.  Children :
       2062.  Marion[8], d. Dec. 4, 1858.
       2063.  Arabella.


2064 = 2021.   EMILY[7] MARSH

b. Oct. 8, 1806, dau. of Daniel[6] and Marion (Harper) Marsh, (Gov.
Joseph[5]; Ensign Joseph[4], Capt. Joseph[3], John[2], John[1]); m. No. 2064.

**2064.** David Reed. Children :
    2065. James[8].
    2066. Ogden.
    2067. Edward.
    2068. Hattie.


2069 = 2022. DANIEL[7] MARSH

b. Hartford, Vt., Jan. 19, 1809, son of Daniel[6] and Marion (Harper) Marsh, (Gov. Joseph[5], Ensign Joseph[4], Capt. Joseph[3], John[2], John[1]) ; m. Sept. 2, 1837, No. 2069.

    **2069.** Lucinda Hall. " He was lame. His father gave him the old home and farm." By business failure he lost it. In 1885 he was living at Holt, Taylor Co., Iowa and wrote " I think I am the last descendant of my grandfather Gov. Marsh, of my generation."
Children :
    2070. Roswell[8], b. Hartford, Vt., Dec. 15, 1838 ; d. Quiver, Ill., March 23, 1862.
    2071. Mary L. B., b. Hartford, Vt., Jan. 16, 1841 ; d. Cambridge, Mass., Sept. 14, 1858.
    2072. Daniel, b. Hartford, Vt., April 1, 1843 ; m. Sarah Cappel, had
    2073. Harry.
    2074. Charles H., b. Cambridge, Mass., Sept. 1, 1845 ; m. Mary A. Chapman. Children :
        2075. Roswell.
        2076. Mary Ellen.
        2077. Percy.
        2078. Ruth.
    2079. James, b. Taftsville, Vt., Oct. 22, 1847 ; m. Maggie Sarny, Child :
        2080. Frank.


2081 = 1934. HON. CHARLES[6] MARSH, LL. D.

b. Lebanon, Ct., July 10, 1765, son of Gov. Joseph[5] and Dorothy (Mason) Marsh, (Ensign Joseph[4], Capt. Joseph[3], John[2], John[1]) ; was a puny child and with his mother stayed at Lebanon with Mrs. Rockwell, his sister, for the first year that his father was at Hartford, Vt. He graduated at Dartmouth college in 1786, entered at once the

Litchfield, Connecticut law school; admitted to the Connecticut bar
in 1788; m. (1) 1789, No. 2081.

**2081.** Nancy Collins, b. Litchfield, May 17, 1768, dau. of John
and Lydia (Buell) Collins, grand-daughter of Rev. Timothy (first
minister in Litchfield) and Elizabeth Hyde. " On the north side of
the Quechee river, six miles from his father, at Woodstock, Vt., in
1789 he built his house and there he brought his bride. He rose rapidly
and President Washington appointed him state district attorney and he
soon, and for many years was accorded the first rank at the Vermont
bar. Judge Barrett says : " For breadth and profoundness of com-
prehension, for keenness and subtilty of discrimination, for rapidity
and justness of analysis, for clearness, strength and force of logical
argumentation, for effectiveness in advocacy, as well as for a thorough,
appreciative and practical familiarity with all the artificial technicalities
of the law he was long recognized by bench and bar as having no
superior, and, for all these qualities in combination, as having no
equal." He rarely spoke an hour. He talked quietly, to the court
and jury only, not heeding anybody outside, and with scarce a
gesticulation.

Yet he was most successful in winning cases apparently hopeless.
He was a member of the United States congress 1815–1817. Chief
Justice Williams said Mr. Marsh " wielded the most powerful weapon
of severity he ever knew." " He scarified, flayed and slaughtered
but with a polished weapon, and with the most quiet manner and
voice, and rigorous chasteness of language." His wit was keen and
ready. In politics he was a Federalist of the Washington school·
In theology he was a Calvinist of the Edwards school. He was one
of the founders and for many years president of the Vermont Bible
society, vice-president of the American Bible Society, and of the
American Education Society. Was forty years trustee of Dartmouth
college, president of trustees of Kimball Union academy. He gave
to his parish the site of the church and parsonage and contributed
liberally to them ; was constant in conference and prayer meeting.

Personally he was tall, well proportioned but spare, of fine sensi-
tive and nervous organization, with great self-control over a temper
that was quick and strong. He always wore black, but following the
cut of his early days, wore white cravat, turned-down collar and ruf-
fled shirt bosom to the last of his life. He was a model gentleman of

the old school and bore himself with great simplicity and courtliness and entertained the best society of New England and New York.

His first wife d. June 18, 1793, leaving two children. He m. (2) June 3, 1798, No. 2082.

2082.   Widow Susan (Perkins) Arnold, b. Oct. 9, 1776, dau. of Dr. Elisha and Sarah (Douglas) Perkins of Plainfield, Ct., and widow of Josias Lyndon Arnold, Esq. of St. Johnsbury, Vt.   " She was very elegant."   Hon. Charles[6] Marsh, d. at Woodstock, of acute inflammation of the lungs Jan. 11, 1849.   His mind had shown no symptom of decay and his judgment was sought until his last sickness.   His widow d. at Woodstock Jan. 3, 1853.   His portrait is at Darmouth college.   Children :

    2083.   Charles[7], b. 1790, at Woodstock; grad. Dartmouth College, 1813; m. Nov. 24, 1816, his second cousin, Mary Leonard b. Dec. 3, 1795, dau. of Timothy and Mary (Baldwin) Leonard of Lansingburgh, where he res., lawyer.   She d. Dec. 21, 1817.   He d. July 18,1818, near Louisville, Ky.

    2084.   Anna Collins, b. June 10, 1793; m. June 4, 1816, Dr. John Burwell of Woodstock, who d. 1846.   She d. Nov., 1855.

        Child :

        2085.   Mary Leonard[8], b. 1820; d. 1841, æ. 21, unm.

        By second wife.

    2086.   Lyndon Arnold, b. Feb. 26, 1799, at Woodstock; grad. Dartmouth College 1819, lawyer; m. Nov. 5, 1829, Lucy Gay Swan, res. Woodstock.   One child :

        2087.   Benjamin Swan, b. Sept. 1, 1830; grad. Dartmouth College, 1849.

    2088.   George Perkins, b. March 15, 1801 ; m. Harriet Buell, 2092.

    2089.   Joseph, b. April 16, 1807, at Woodstock ; grad. Dartmouth 1830, res. Burlington, Vt.   Prof. Theory and Practice of Medicine, Univ. of Vermont; d. unm. Nov. 7, 1841.

    2090.   Sarah Burrill, b. June 5, 1809; m. Wyllys Lyman, 2096.

    2091.   Charles, b. May 10, 1821 ; d. unm. April 13, 1873, at San Diego, Cal.   He was devoted to his parents, and gave up a liberal education because they needed him in their age.   He had a fine mind and the culture of travel and study.   He died while traveling for health, beloved and mourned by all the family circle.

2092 = 2088.   HON. GEORGE PERKINS[7] MARSH, LL. D.

" The statesman, diplomatist and author and in all departments of human learning accorded the first rank by the learned both of this country and of Europe." Born at Woodstock, Vt., March 15, 1801, son of Charles[6] and Susan (Perkins) Marsh, (Gov. Joseph[5] Ensign Joseph[4], Capt. Joseph[3], John[2], John[1]); graduated at Dartmouth college in 1820; lawyer; m. (1) April 10, 1828, No. 2092.

2092. Harriet Buell, dau. of Ozias of Burlington, Vt. Hon. George P. Marsh settled in Burlington, was elected to the Vermont supreme council in 1835 and to congress 1842–9. He was Minister Resident at Constantinople 1849–52. The writer of this genealogy starting for Turkey in 1849, took a letter of introduction to his namesake and kinsman from Gov. Fairbanks of Vermont; but going from Smyrna to the Tigris by the lower route through Syria, did not have an opportunity to present it in person at the oriental capital. As in case of other ministers of America, resident at the Sublime Porte, Mr. Marsh was of great service to his fellow countrymen, missionaries and travelers in that half-civilized and restless part of the world. He was a scholar and philologist, and by travel in northern Europe became an adept in the Scandinavian languages. He m. (2) No. 2093.

2093. Caroline Crane of Berkley, Mass., who became an author and a woman of note. In 1857 to 1859, Mr. Marsh was railroad commissioner for Vermont. In 1861 he was appointed U. S. minister to Italy and retained that high office until his death. He d. in Vallombrosa, Italy, where fall the many leaves, June 23, 1882 and was buried in the Protestant cemetery at Rome. His children were by his first wife. Children :

2094. Charles Buell[8], b. 1829; d. y.
2095. George Ozias, b. Aug. 24, 1832; a lawyer in N. Y. City, d. unm.

2096 = 2090. SARAH BURRILL[7] MARSH

b. at Woodstock, Vt., June 5, 1809, dau. of Charles[6] and Susan (Perkins) Marsh; m. Oct. 21, 1828, No. 2096.

2096. Wyllys Lyman of Hartford, Vt., b. at Burlington, Vt., May 5, 1797. He removed to Burlington and Mrs. Lyman d. there Sept. 1, 1841. He d. Dec. 1, 1862. Children :

2097.   Wyllys[8], b. Hartford, Vt., April 4, 1830; m. 2098.3.
2098.   Susan Marsh, b. Oct. 19, 1831 ; m. G. F. Edmunds, 2099.
2098.1  Joseph Marsh, d. y.
2098.2  Joseph Douglas, d. y.

## 2098.3 = 2097.   WYLLYS[8] LYMAN

b. at Hartford, Vt., April 4, 1830; m. in New York City in 1861,.
No. 2098.3.
   **2098.3.** Anna Bryan. He was a lawyer in New York City. The
following notice of him is from the *Daily Free Press* of Burlington,
Vt., Aug. 11, 1892 :

" Captain Wyllys Lyman, Fifth Infantry, was promoted on the
4th of July, 1892, to the rank of Major United States army, and
placed upon the retired list for disability from wounds received in
line of duty.

   Major Lyman is the only son of the late Wyllys Lyman of Burlington, Vt. He went to the front as adjutant of the Tenth Vermont
Volunteers, August, 1862. Except when absent wounded he was
present in all the battles of his regiment, viz.: At Kelly's Ford,
Va., Orange Grove, Wilderness, Spottsylvania, Tolopotomy, Cold
Harbor, Monocacy, Winchester, Fisher's Hill, Cedar Creek, Petersburg, April 2, 1865, and Sailor's Creek, April 6, 1865.

   At the battle of Cedar Creek on the 19th of October, 1864, when
the Tenth Vermont, under command of Col. William W. Henry led
in the charge, which resulted in the recapture of the guns of
McKnight's Regular Battery, from the enemy, Adjutant Lyman
while gallantly performing the duties of his position was severely
wounded in the thigh. The regiment lost that day nearly one-third
of the 297 officers and men who stood in line.

   In the final assault upon Petersburg April 2, 1865, the Tenth Vermont Regiment took a brilliant part and Major Lyman received the
following most complimentary notice in the reports of his commanding officer : " While I cannot speak in too high praise of the conduct.
of both officers and men, I desire to mention as deserving of special
consideration, Major Wyllys Lyman, who was among the first to
enter the rebel works with the color bearer, and performed most
efficient service during the day, using every exertion to keep the men.

together, and bring them forward to their duty." He was at this time promoted to be Lieutenant-Colonel of his regiment, and was mustered out of the United States service June 28, 1865. Lieut.-Col. Lyman was appointed Captain of the 40th U. S. Infantry, July 28, 1866; was transferred to the 25th Infantry April 20, 1869, and to the 5th Infantry Dec. 15, 1870. He was brevetted Major of the U. S. army March 2, 1867 for gallant and meritorious service in the battle of the Opequan, Va. In Major Powell's record of living officers of the United States army we find the following: Wyllys Lyman's services in the field with the army of the Potomac during the war of the rebellion from 1862 to 1865; engaged in the Indian campaign and battles under Gen. Miles in Texas and Montana from 1874–76; Deputy Governor Soldiers Home, District of Columbia, 1884–85; later on duty in the War Department, War Record office. Staff positions occupied: Adjutant Tenth Vermont Volunteers, Aug., 1862. Acting assistant Adjutant General of brigade 1862 to July, 1863. In addition to the battles mentioned above Col. Lyman participated in several engagements with the Indians in the campaign of Gen. Miles in 1874–76; brevetted Lieut.-Col. United States army for gallantry in the actions on the Washita river, Tex., Sept., 1874 against the Kiowa and Camanche Indians. Few Vermont soldiers have had a more brilliant record than this gallant officer, and he will receive the sincere congratulations of his many friends in Vermont upon his promotion." Child:

2098.4.   Charles George[9], b. New York City, Aug. 21, 1861; grad. at West Point in 1886, appointed July 1, 1886, 2d Lieut., U. S. Infantry; transferred Feb. 11, 1889, to the 2d Cavalry, and served in these regiments in Montana, Texas, Arizona and California. He is now, 1894, serving as Aide-de-Camp on the staff of Gen. T. H. Ruger, U. S. army. Of her brother, Wyllys[8] Lyman and his son Charles George[9] Lyman, Mrs. Senator Edmunds writes: "Philadelphia, Nov. 7, 1894. These two, with my nephew's infant son, are the only male descendants of our grandfather Charles Marsh of Woodstock, Vt., now living." Charles George m. June 25, 1890, Edith A. E. Clarke of San Francisco, b. in California, April 22, 1869. Child:

2098.5.   Edmunds[10], b. Sept. 19, 1891.

## 2099 = 2098.  SUSAN MARSH[5] LYMAN

b. Oct. 19, 1831, dau. of Wyllys and Sarah Burrill[7] (Marsh) Lyman, (Charles[6] Marsh, Gov. Joseph[5], Ensign Joseph[4], Capt. Joseph[3], John[2], John[1]); m. Aug. 11, 1852, No. 2099.

**2099.** George Franklin Edmunds was born in Richmond, Vt., Feb. 1, 1828. Admitted to the bar in March, 1849. Resided at Burlington, Vt. Elected to the legislature from Burlington, 1854– 1855 and 1857, 1858, 1859. Was speaker the last three years. Elected to the state senate from Chittenden Co., 1861, 1862. President *pro tem.* for these two years. Appointed to the U. S. senate in 1866, to succeed Senator Foot deceased, and continued a member 25 years until he resigned in 1891. Mrs. Edmunds writes from Newport, R. I., June 30, 1894: " It interests me very much to see that the Marshes and Lymans intermarried in two instances soon after their settlement in this country, and that their paths ran side by side for so long, and the Douglases, as well, and Perkins. I remember my grandmother's telling me that when she was journeying on horseback, to her new home in Vermont, with Dr. Arnold, they stopped at a blacksmith shop and a stage stopped there also and grandfather Marsh came into the shop and was introduced to her. He took a solid wrought iron flatiron stand from the anvil and presented it to her, saying that she must not say that he had not given her a wedding present. My grandmother gave it to me when I was married. I need not say that I have it now." [Dr. Arnold was her first husband].
Children :

2099.1.  Mary Mayhew[9], b. Burlington, May 11, 1854.
2099.2.  Julia Maynard, b. April 15, 1861, at Burlington ; d. July 15 1882.

## 2100 = 1935.  ROGER[6] MARSH

b. Aug. 17, 1767, at Lebanon, Ct., son of Gov. Joseph[5] and Dorothy (Mason) Marsh ; m. No. 2100.

**2100.** Mary Chapman of East Haddam, Ct., b. Oct. 5, 1773, dau. of Timothy and Sarah (Fuller) Chapman. He was a farmer in Hartford, Vt. His house was a large cottage and is still standing four miles from Dartmouth college. He was an esteemed Christian gentleman. Children ;

2101.  Levi[7] inherited the farm, went to Dubuque, Iowa, and d. unm.
2102.  Charles Chapman, grad. Dartmouth College, 1828; lawyer
       in New York. Left no children.
2103.  Edward Warren, grad. Univ. Vermont, 1836; lawyer N. Y.
       Inherited Franklin's property and never m.
2104.  Franklin, went clerk to N. Y. when 17, partner when 21, but
       lost largely; d. 1855, unm., with Warren his then only
       living brother.

2105 = 1936.  PARTHENIA[6] MARSH

b. at Lebanon, Ct., Nov. 3, 1769, dau. of Gov. Joseph[5] and Dorothy
(Mason) Marsh; m. No. 2105.

2105,  Rev. Elijah Brainard. " One of her four daus. was very
brilliant and thought it her duty to follow her kinsman, Brainard, to
the Indians. The chief was so determined to marry her, she was
forced to come home! She married an artist and moved to and died
in England."—*L. E. S.*  Children :

2106.  Nancy C[7]., d. 1847, unm.
2107.  Parthenia, m. Rev. Hart Talcott.
2108.  Lavinia.
2109.  Mary Marsh.
2110.  Susan L.
2111.  Henry Angus.
2112.  Elijah.
2113.  William S.
2114.  Carolus Columbus.
2115.  Joseph Marsh, d. three days old.
2116.  Joseph Marsh.

2117 = 1937.  WILLIAM[6] MARSH

b. Lebanon, Ct., (where his mother remained one year later than Gov
Joseph before going to Vermont) Oct. 1, 1772, son of Gov. Joseph
and Dorothy (Mason) Marsh, (Ensign Joseph[4], Capt. Joseph[3], John[2]
John[1]); m. No. 2117.

2117.  Sarah Marshall. They had no children. " He settled in
Pawlet, Vt. in 1816, but soon removed just across the state line to
Granville, N. Y., but late in life returned to Pawlet where he d. March

22, 1864, æ. over 91.   He was not a model young man, but after joining the Congregational church became a very active Christian.   History of Pawlet says: 'He was a pioneer in the anti-slavery cause, meeting its opponents in season and out of season, with firmness, and great ability.   He wrote articles in its advocacy and showed his sincerity by donating during his life over $25,000, to the furtherance of the cause.   He lived to see his principles triumph.'   He was noted for his liberality and private charity.   From his marriage to the death of his wife he never visited or was visited by his brothers.   When a mere child I went with my mother to his handsome house in Granville, I was sent to school during my *visit*!   The teacher questioned my right to be there, but on being told I was a niece of William Marsh, was very kind to me.   Uncle was very unused to noise and I scarcely dared breathe in the house.   After the war, July, 1864, he wrote a very nice and powerful letter to my sister urging her to bring her children up as friends and protectors of the new colored citizens!'"
—*L. E. S.*

## 2118 = 1938.   ELIZABETH[6] MARSH

b. at Hartford, Vt., April 18, 1776, dau. of Gov. Joseph[5] and Dorothy (Mason) Marsh, (Ensign Joseph[4], Capt. Joseph[3], John[2], John[1]); m. No. 2118.

**2118.**   Robert Ham.   Children:

    2119.   Ida[7].
    2120.   Sylvia, m. (1) James Snow of Hartford; he d. childless; m.
            (2) James Benson of South Royalston, Vt., left no child.
    2121.   Oral, d. unm.

## 2122 = 1731.   CAPT. ABEL[5] MARSH

b. at Lebanon, Ct., 1735, son of Ensign Joseph[4] and Mercy (Bill or Durkee) Marsh, (Capt. Joseph[3] John[2], John[1]); m. Dec. 26, 1754, No. 2122.

**2122.**   Dorothy Udall of Stonington, Ct.   So far as we know, the children were born at Lebanon, certainly the four we are able to give.   Capt. Abel was one of the early proprietors of Randolph, Vt., but owing to

12

the revolutionary war did not settle there but remained at Hartford,
Vt., where with mother and brothers he went in 1772. He received
$75 for acting as the agent of the Randolph proprietors in New
Jersey. During the revolutionary war he was sent by the New Connecticut commissioners to procure arms in Boston and in Connecticut and
Gov. Trumbull writing from Lebanon, Ct., to the committee of safety
at Boston mentions Capt. Abel Marsh and regrets that he cannot
supply the urgent need. Children:

> 2123. Olive⁶, b. Jan. 18, 1756.
> 2124. Abel, bap. Aug. 28, 1757; m. 2127.
> 2125. Samuel, bap. Feb. 12, 1764; m. 2135.
> 2126. Sarah, bap. May 20, 1764.
> 2126.1 (*Probably*) George, b. 1776; m. Hannah Carpenter, 2206.

### 2127 = 2124. ABEL⁶ MARSH

baptized Aug. 18, 1757, son of Capt. Abel⁵ and Dorothy (Udall)
Marsh, (Ensign Joseph⁴, Capt. Joseph³, John², John¹); m. (1) No.
2127.

**2127.** ——. Having removed with his father in 1772 to Hartford, Vt., he became a lumberman and had a sawmill opposite
Hartford in New Hampshire. He m. (2) No. 2128.

**2128.** Widow Miriam (Clawson) Chapman, b. in 1773. Becom-
ing involved, to avoid the barbarous custom of imprisonment for debt,
about the year 1808 he removed to New York state and d. in Syracuse soon after. In 1816 his widow, taking with her her sons Ziba
Wales Chapman, and Belorman Marsh, went to Elmira, N. Y. After
the marriage of her son Belorman Marsh she lived with him ten years
at Southport, near Elmira and then (till her death at Elmira in Jan.,
1846, æ. 83,) with her daughter Mrs. Lovisa (Chapman) Curtis who
had been brought up at Pawlet by William⁶ Marsh, the cousin of her
husband Abel⁶ Marsh. Children:

> 2129. Daughter.
> 2130. Daughter.
> 2131. Asahel⁷.
> 2132. Thena.
> 2133. Clark, drowned in Niagara river.
> By second wife.
> 2134. Belorman, b. Aug. 15, 1802; m. Mary Heller, 2140.

## 2135 = 2125. SAMUEL[6] MARSH

baptized at Lebanon, Ct., Feb. 12, 1764, son of Capt. Abel[5] and
Dorothy (Udall) Marsh, (Ensign Joseph[4], Capt. Joseph[3], John[2], John[1]);
came with his father in 1772 to Hartford, Vt.; m. No. 2135.

2135. Huldah ——. Settled in Hartland, Windsor Co., Vt.
Children :

2136. Otis[7], b. Nov. 6, 1789; m. Julia Ransom, 2303.
2137. Isaac.
2138. Serepta.
2139. Orpha. (Orpha Eliza Marsh [possibly a niece] m. March 31,
1835, Enos Woodmansir of Greensboro, Vt., b. April
16, 1816.)

## 2140 = 2134. BELORMAN[7] MARSH

b. at Hartford, Vt., Aug. 15, 1802, son of Abel[6] and Miriam (Clawson)
Marsh, (Capt. Abel[5], Ensign Joseph[4], Capt. Joseph[3], John[2], John[1]);
when seven or eight was taken with his father's family to Syracuse,
N. Y. where his father soon died ; when 14 years old in 1816 was
taken to Elmira, N. Y., "where he worked farms summers and taught
school winters" till he m. June 5, 1828, No. 2140.

2140. Mary Heller of Elmira. In the spring of 1833 he bought
a farm in Southport seven miles from Elmira in the wilderness and
there he lived until his death Dec. 30, 1862, æ. 60. Children :

2141. Emily[8], b. April 13, 1829, at Elmira ; teacher at Southport,
N. Y.
2142. Joseph Chapman, b. Dec. 14, 1830 ; m. (1) Harriet E. Rose,
2156.
2143. Guy, b. Sept. 25, 1832 ; d. Jan. 11, 1834.
2144. Clark Marsh, b. Dec. 26, 1833 ;     } m. Charlotte E. Kel-
                                          {     logg, 2160.
2145. Benjamin Franklin, b. Dec. 26, 1833 ; } m. Sarah Smith, 2168.
2146. Michael Heller, b. March 30, 1835 ; m. Cynthia Wattles, 2181.
2147. Albert, b. March 7, 1837 ; unm. works the home farm.
2148. John Wormley, b. Dec. 30, 1838 ; d. Dec. 12, 1864, in Nash-
ville hospital from wound at battle of Resaca.
2149. Mary Augusta, b. Feb. 27, 1840 ; d. at Southport, April
14, 1882.
2150. Fanny Eliza, b. May 15, 1842 ; d. at Southport, 1891.
2151. Julia Curtis, b. Dec. 3, 1843 ; m. A. J. Chapman, 2199.

2152.  Charles Heller, b. March 10, 1846; m. Jennie Tompkins, 2201.
2153.  Frank G., b. Nov. 5, 1848; m. L. E. Bailey, 2203.
2154. } twins, b. July, 1852 ; d. at birth.
2155. }


2156 = 2142.  JOSEPH CHAPMAN[8] MARSH

b. at Elmira, N. Y., Dec. 14, 1830, son of Belorman[7] and Mary (Heller) Marsh, (Abel[6], Capt. Abel[5], Ensign Joseph[4], Capt. Joseph[3], John[2], John[1]); m. (1) Dec. 5, 1859, No. 2156.
2156.  Harrietta Elizabeth Rose of Roseville, Pa. He m. (2) April 16, 1872, at Canton, N. Y., No. 2157.
2157.  Alice Isabell Hamlin.  By second wife no children ; resides in Pine City, N. Y.  Carpenter.  Children :

   2158.  Fanny Rose[9], b. Feb. 10, 1861 ; d. July, 1862. Southport, N.Y.
   2159.  Flora Belle, b. May 7, 1863; m. March 5, 1885, Jay Burton Rockwell, druggist, Elmira, N. Y.


2160 = 2144.  CLARK MARSH[8] MARSH

b. at Southport, N. Y., Dec. 26, 1833, son of Belorman[7] and Mary (Heller) Marsh, (Abel[6], Capt. Abel[5], Ensign Joseph[4], Capt. Joseph[3], John[2], John[1]) ; m. July 11, 1860, No. 2160.
2160.  Charlotte A. Kellogg of Canandaigua, N. Y.  He is a photographer.  Children :

   2161.  Jennie Estelle[9], b. May 15, 1862; m. her cousin, C. E. Marsh, 2170.
   2162.  Jessie Kate, b. July 10, 1864; m. March 18, 1884, Charles B. Bailey, Havana, N. Y.  Telegraph operator, Buffalo. They have :
       2163.  Hector Wilder, b. 1885.
   2164.  George Henry Dewitta, b. July 6, 1866, in Canandaigua, unm. Printer in Greeley, Colo.
   2165.  Artabella, b. Jan. 15, 1872, Havana, N. Y.  Schoolgirl, Greeley, Colo.
   2166.  Tiny May, b. Dec. 28, 1872, Havana. Schoolgirl, Greeley.
   2167.  Charles William, b. Dec.8,1874, Havana. Schoolboy,Greeley.

## 2168 = 2145.  BENJAMIN FRANKLIN[8] MARSH

b. at Southport, N. Y., Dec. 26, 1833, son of Belorman[7] and Mary (Heller) Marsh, (Abel[6], Capt. Abel[5], Ensign Joseph[4], Capt. Joseph[3], John[2], John[1]); m. Dec. 27, 1859, No. 2168.

**2168.** Sarah Smith. He is a photographer at Greeley, Colo. Children:

2169. Arthur Clark[9], b. April 21, 1861, Southport, unm.; on ranch, Greeley.

2170. Charles Edwin Marsh, b. Rochester, N. Y., May 16, 1862; m. his cousin, Jennie Estelle Marsh, 2161, Jan. 31, 1886, at Cheyenne, Wyo.  Barber at Pasadena, Cal.  Had dau. d. three weeks old.

2171. Cora Elouise, b. Feb. 15, 1864, Painesville, O.; m. Aug. 15, 1884, John C. Moshier, Bridgeport, Ct. Grocer, Greeley. Children:

2172. Paul[10], b. 1885.

2173. Jessie, b. 1886.

2174. Harry Benjamin, b. May 27, 1866, at Painesville, O.; d. Aug. 11, 1868.

2175. Tracy Colfax, b. Oct. 9, 1868, Painesville, O.; res. Greeley.

2176. Kitty Irene, b. Jan. 23, 1870, Painesville; grad. Greeley H. S., June, 1888.

2177. Hattie Roger, b. Oct. 13, 1871; d. Nov. 2, 1871.

2178. Frank Scott, b. Oct. 25, 1873, Greeley.

2179. Fred Earle, b. July 14, 1877, Greeley.

2180. Jay Lewis, b. June 20, 1881, Greeley.

## 2181 = 2146.  MICHAEL HELLER[8] MARSH

b. March 30, 1835 at Southport, N. Y., son of Belorman[7] and Mary (Heller) Marsh, (Abel[6], Capt. Abel[5], Ensign Joseph[4], Capt. Joseph[3], John[2], John[1]); m. in 1858, No. 2181.

**2181.** Cynthia Wattles, Binghamton, N. Y.  Resides at Wilmington, Del.  Machinist.  Children:

2182. Wyllis Joseph[9], b. Aug. 11, 1858; m. Miriam Francis, 2192.

2183. Fred Alfred, b. Aug. 4, 1859; m. Anna M. Poppins, 2195.

2184. Della May, b. Elmira, May 26, 1862; m. March 25, 1882, Verne Stage of Elmira, salesman, d. Nov. 2, 1882. Had:

2185. Henry V[10]., b. Sept. 13, 1882.

2186. Alida, b. March 10, 1864, Elmira, N. Y.; d. Feb. 4, 1880, of consumption.

2187.   Laura Agnes, b. Feb. 18, 1866; m. Jan. 12, 1866, Albert F.
    Kircher.   They have :
        2188.   Laura Agnes[10], b. Oct. 24, 1886, Elmira.
2189.   Fanny, b. 1873 ; d. y.
2190.   A son, b. 1876 ; d. y.
2191.   Mabel, b. March 20, 1880.


2192 = 2182.   WYLLIS JOSEPH[9] MARSH

b. Aug. 11, 1858, Elmira, N. Y., son of Michael Heller[8] and Cynthia
(Wattles) Marsh, (Belorman[7], Abel[6], Capt. Abel[5], Ensign Joseph[4],
Capt. Joseph[3], John[2], John[1]); m. Oct. 24, 1883, No. 2192.
    2192.   Miriam Francis.   Resides at Elmira.   Book-keeper Erie
R. R.   Children :
        2193.   Miriam Savannah[10], b. Sept. 25, 1885.
        2194.   Wyllis Walter, b. May 7, 1887, Elmira.


2195 = 2183.   FRED ALFRFD[9] MARSH

b. Aug. 4, 1859, Elmira, N. Y., son of Michael Heller[8] and Cynthia
(Wattles)Marsh, (Belorman[7], Abel[6], Capt. Abel[5], Ensign Joseph[4],
Capt. Joseph[3],John[2], John[1]) ; m. Nov. 18, 1880, No. 2195.
    2195.   Anna Mary Poppins.   He is car reporter for Erie R. R.
Children :
        2196.   Elmer[10], b. May 17, 1882 ; d. July 20, 1882, Elmira.
        2197.   Ralph, b. April 3, 1883, Elmira.
        2198.   Clayton Belorman, b. Oct. 21, 1886, Elmira.


2199 = 2151.   JULIA CURTIS[8] MARSH

b. at Southport, N. Y., Dec. 3, 1843, dau. of Belorman[7] and Mary
(Heller) Marsh, (Abel[6], Capt. Abel[5], Ensign Joseph[4], Capt. Joseph[3],
John[2], John[1]) ; m. Dec. 17, 1874, No. 2199.
    2199.   Andrew J. Chapman, of Minneapolis, Minn.   Lumberman.
He d. Sept. 13, 1777.   Child :
        2200.   Fannie Belle[9], b. Sept. 14, 1875, lives with grandmother.

## 2201 = 2152.  CHARLES HELLER[8] MARSH

b. at Southport, N. Y., March 10, 1846, son of Belorman[7] and Mary (Heller) Marsh, (Abel[6], Capt. Abel[5], Ensign Joseph[4], Capt. Joseph[3], John[2], John[1]); m. Jan., 1872, No. 2201.

**2201.**  Jennie Tompkins, Canandaigua.  He d. Feb. 16, 1874. He was a photographer at Oswego, N. Y.  Child:

2202.  Maud Elizabeth[9], b. Jan., 1873.

## 2203 = 2153.  FRANK G[8]. MARSH

b. at Southport, N. Y., Nov. 5, 1846, son of Belorman[7] and Mary (Heller) Marsh, (Abel[6], Capt. Abel[5], Ensign Joseph[4], Capt. Joseph[3], John[2], John[1]); m. Jan. 23, 1871, No. 2203.

**2203.**  Lamoria Eugenia Bailey.  Resides at Binghamton.  He was a machinist.  Child:

2204.  Minta[9], b. Nov. 25, 1874, Elmira.      .

## 2205 = 1732.  ELISHA[5] MARSH

b. 1738 at Lebanon, Ct., son of Ensign Joseph[4], (Capt. Joseph[3], John[2], John[1]); m. No. 2205.

**2205.**  —— Terry.  He removed from Lebanon with his brothers Gov. Joseph[5], Capt. Abel[5] and Eliphalet[5] and his mother Mercy to Hartford, Vt., in 1772.  They were possibly parents of George[6], the husband of Hannah Carpenter, 2206, who was propably the son of Capt. Abel, but may have been a son of Eliphalet or Elisha.  Perhaps grandparents of:

2205.1.  Joseph[7], b. Jan. 6, 1792; m. Philana Yates, 2224.
2205.2.  Nelson, of Hinsdale, N. Y.; m. 2273.

## 2206 = 2126.1.  GEORGE[6] MARSH

b. in 1776, grandson of Ensign Joseph[4], (Capt. Joseph[3], John[2], John[1]), son may be of Capt. Abel[5], and if not, then must be of Elisha[5] or Eliphalet[5]; m. No. 2206.

**2206.** Hannah Carpenter, b. Nov. 16, 1775. "He came into this town" (Sardinia, Erie Co., N. Y.) "in Nov., 1825 from Woodstock, Windsor Co., Vt.," with his one son and five daughters. Mrs. Lucy E. Hopkins a grand-daughter writes: "They were nearly four weeks on the way, and the oldest daughter stopped at Black river and there met her husband. I have often heard my grandfather tell how very tired they all were on reaching this stopping place where grandmother had a brother, Arba Carpenter. Stopping awhile they concluded to make a home here." He d. March 8, 1848. His widow d. Dec. 30, 1862 in Sardinia. Children:

2207. Armida[7], m. Calvin Collins. Both are dead. Their children live near Rochester, N. Y.:
    2207.1. George[8], m. and has children.
    2207.2. Minerva, m. Thomas Creathers and has children.
    2207.3. Alphonso, m. A. A. Eldridge, no children.
    2207.4. Darwin.
    2207.5. Susan, m. and d.
2208. Susan, m. Charles Goss, moved about 45 years ago to Wisconsin, and she d. 20 years ago in Missouri.
2209. Polly, b. 1809; m. Stowell Collins, brother of Calvin. She d. in Sardinia in 1837. They had two children who went to Sunrise, Minn.:
    2209.1. Ermina[8], m. Geo. Guyun now dead, and had one child.
    2209.2. Adeline, m. John Masuen, and she d. many years ago and he later of consumption. Two children one living.
2210. George, b. March 1, 1810; m. Eliza Howard, 2213.
2211. Orpha, b. Woodstock, Vt., 1815; m. in Sardinia, N. Y., in 1837, J. H. Watson who d. Topeka, Kan., Nov., 1890, and she d. June, 1860. They had:
    2211.1. Emily A[8]., b. about 1841; m. about 1867, Tyler Stearns and settled at once in Kansas. Of three children, one dau. is living.
    2211.2. Alice R., d. æ. about 22.
2212. Emily, b. Woodstock, Vt., d. unm., between 1870 and 80.

## 2213 = 2210. GEORGE[7] MARSH

b. at Woodstock, Vt., March 1, 1810, son of George[6] and Hannah (Carpenter) Marsh, (either Abel[5], Elisha[5] or Eliphalet[5], Joseph[4],

Capt. Joseph³, John², John¹) ; m. in Sardinia, N. Y., Jan. 7, 1836, No. 2213.

**2213.** Eliza Howard, b. at Alstead or Langdon, N. H., April 13, 1813. George Marsh d. March 23, 1888, æ. 78. His widow was living in 1893. Children :

> 2214. Chloe E⁸., b. Feb. 18, 1837 ; m. Nov. 16, 1856, B. S. Pierce. She d. Nov. 15, 1872. They had two children:
>
> > 2215. F. W⁹., b. Oct. 14, 1857 ; m. and lives in Texas with one child.
> > 2216. Clara D., b. May 5, 1866 ; m. Sept. 10, 1885, P. C. Goodermote, lives in Sardinia with one child.
>
> 2217. Charles, b. Oct. 15, 1840 ; d. Feb. 26, 1843.
> 2218. Lucy E., b. Jan. 7, 1844 ; m. E. C. Hopkins, 2221.
> 2219. Alice D., b. Aug. 6, 1846 ; m. March 8, 1876, Hiram Emerson. They have one child :
>
> > 2220. Sumner E⁹., b. Jan. 8, 1881.

### 2221 = 2218. LUCY E⁸. MARSH

b. Sardinia, N. Y., Jan. 7, 1844, dau. of George⁷ and Eliza (Howard) Marsh, (George⁶, perhaps Elisha⁵, Joseph⁴ Capt. Joseph³, John², John¹) ; m. Oct. 3, 1867, No. 2221.

**2221.** Emory C. Hopkins. Children :

> 2222. Georgie⁸, b. Oct. 1, 1870 ; d. Dec. 9, 1871.
> 2223. Arthur, b. July 8, 1878.

### 2224 = 2205.1. JOSEPH⁷ MARSH

b. at Woodstock, Vt., Jan. 6, 1792, possibly son of Samuel⁶, Capt. Abel⁵ or else grandson of Elisha⁵ or Eliphalet⁵ who were brothers of Capt. Abel. His son William S. Marsh writes from Indianapolis that his father was brought up " at Woodstock, Vt., and was cousin to Prof. George Marsh." He was no doubt second cousin to the Hon. George P. Marsh who was not a professor. He might have been second cousin by being descended from either of the three brothers of Gov. Joseph⁵, Capt. Abel⁵, Elisha⁵ or Eliphalet⁵, sons of Ensign Joseph⁴, Capt. Joseph³, John², John¹. His son writes, " Joseph was in the war of 1812 under Gen. Harrison and Maj. Croghan." Soon after returning, he m. No. 2224.

**2224.** Miss Philena Yates, b. April 22, 1793. Emigrated to Cattaraugus Co., N. Y., about 1818, probably to Hinsdale, where his brother "Nelson" settled. About 1820, Joseph and two brothers of his wife, with their families, passed down the Allegheny and the Ohio in "family boats" and landed opposite Cincinnati in Kentucky. He followed boating wood and stone into Cincinnati, took violent cold and lung fever and d. Oct. 16, 1821. His widow m. in 1824, Luther Hopkins, a New Hampshire man, and in 1824 moved across the river into Ohio, leased a farm from William S. Hatch of Cincinnati, and d. there Feb. 13, 1836. Children :

> 2225. Joseph Wales[8], b. at Woodstock, Jan. 23, 1816; m. M. A. Roll, 2229.
> 2226. Royal F., b. Aug. 28, 1817; scalded and d. May 27, 1820.
> 2227. Parmelia, b. at Hinsdale, N. Y., April 17, 1819; m. William Wasson, 2242.
> 2228. William Smith, b. in Kentucky, Feb. 28, 1821; m. Sarah A. Hays, 2250.

### 2229 = 2225.   JOSEPH WALES[8] MARSH

b. at Woodstock, Vt., Jan. 23, 1816, son of Joseph[7] and Philena (Yates) Marsh; m. in 1841, No. 2229.

**2229.** Martha Ann Roll. He learned the saddle and harness business in Cincinnati, O. and made it his life work. In 1852 moved to Indianapolis. Had 11 children of whom four died in infancy, seven are living of whom two are boys. Children :

> 2230. William[9], b. at Cincinnati, April 17, 1842; m. Mary E. Jenkins, 2232.
> 2231. Joseph, m. and has family. Resides in the state of Washington.

### 2232 = 2230.   WILLIAM[9] MARSH

b. at Cincinnati, O., April 17, 1842, son of Joseph Wales[8] and Mary Ann Marsh ; m. Nov. 13, 1864 at Brownsburg, Ind., No. 2232.

**2232.** Mary E. Jenkins. He is at Osawatomie, Kansas in the bridge and building department Missouri Pacific railroad. Children :

2233. Miles E[10]., b. Brownsburg, Aug. 18, 1865; m. L. J. Gibson, 2240.
2234. Walter D., b. at Brownsburg, Oct. 8, 1867.
2235. Luther E., b. at Curtisville, Ind., March 3, 1872.
2236. Fanny Z., b. at Tipton, Ind., March 30, 1874; d. at Holden, Mo., Oct. 23, 1878.
2237. Ona A., b. at Holden, Mo., Dec. 29, 1879.
2238. Daisy D., b. at Holden, Mo., Aug. 24, 1881.
2239. Will Bert, b. at Holden, Mo., April 7, 1885.

## 2240 = 2233. MILES E[10]. MARSH

b. at Brownsburg, Ind., Aug. 18, 1865, son of William[9] and Mary Ann (Jenkins) Marsh ; m. at Holden, Mo., Jan. 29, 1890, No. 2240.

**2240.** Electa J. Gibson. Child :

2241. Walter Frank[11], b. Aug. 13, 1891, at Paoli, Kansas.

## 2242 = 2227. PARMELIA[8] MARSH

b. at Hinsdale, N. Y., April 17, 1819, dau. of Joseph[7] and Philena (Yates) Marsh; after going with her parents to Kentucky and Ohio returned to her birthplace when 17 years old and soon m. to No. 2242.

**2242.** Elihu Murray Wasson. He was a merchant and lumberman of Hinsdale. Children :

2243. William[9], now d.
2244. Thomas J., now of Detroit, Mich.
2245. Francis, now of Rochester, N. Y.
2246. Wales, now of Buffalo, N. Y.
2247. Lewis, now of Indianapolis, Ind.
2248. Thornton, now of Indianapolis, Ind.
2249. Sarah, now of Olean, N. Y.

## 2250 = 2228. WILLIAM SMITH[8] MARSH

b. in Kentucky opposite Cincinnati Feb. 28, 1821, "and this proved a sad year for the family as the husband and father died Oct. 16, 1821, æ. 29 years, 8 months and 10 days," son of Joseph[7] and Philena (Yates) Marsh. When 15 years old he commenced the saddle and harness trade and is yet in the business; m. in 1846, No. 2250.

**2250.** Sarah Ann Hays, who d. in 1880. They moved to Indiana in 1863 and to Indianapolis in 1864. He m. (2) in 1886, Widow Jane V. (Cochran) Hamlin. Children:

2251. Pamelia[6], b. June 14, 1847; m. Elon E. Case, manufacturer of bed springs and carpet stretchers. Children:
2252, Ervin; 2253, Clarence; 2254, Frank; 2255, Minnie; 2256, Mabel; 2257, Ella.

2258. Elizabeth, b. Oct. 30, 1848; m. John B. McNeley, R. R. agent, had: 2259, Harry Bond; 2260, Bert Stanley, both R. R. clerks.

2261. Alice, b. Sept. 13, 1850; m. Edwin Wolver of Frankfort, Ind., express agent. Moved to St. Paul, Minn. Child:
2262. Maud[10].

2263. Royal Wales, d. y.
2264. William Smith, d. y.
2265. Arvilla, b. Jan. 16, 1857; m. Thos. Rodibaugh, printer. Children:
2266, Ida Sarah; 2267, Harold; 2268, Phoebe.

2269. Walter Scott, b. Jan. 28, 1861; m. Mary Raisener. Child:
2270. Ralph Raisener[10].

2271. Hugh, b. Feb. 4, 1863; m. Lulu Donavant. He is assistant foreman in R. R. car works, Madison, Ill.

2272. Harry Lincoln, d. y.


### 2273 = 2205.2.  NELSON[7] MARSH

b. at Woodstock, Vt., in 1790 or 1794; removed to Hinsdale, Cattaraugus Co., N. Y., about 1818, was probably grandson of Elisha[5], and had at Hinsdale brother Joseph No. 2234 and sisters, Mrs. Emery Wood, Mrs. Banfield, Mrs. Sherman and the first Mrs. Henry Smith and the second Mrs. Henry Smith. He d. not long after his m. to No. 2273.

**2273.** ——. Children:

2274. Nelson H[8]., living at Hinsdale.
2275. A daughter, living at Hinsdale.


### 2276 = 1748.  JOHN[5] MARSH

b. at Lebanon, Ct., March 10, 1739, son of Jonathan[4] and Alice (Newcomb) Marsh, (Capt. Joseph[3], John[2], John[1]); m. No. 2276.

2276. ——. We think there is no doubt that he went to Claremont, N. H., on the Connecticut river and to Weathersfield, Vt., opposite shortly after. 1. He disappears from Connecticut. 2. His father Jonathan is one of three incorporators of Hartford, Vt. 3. His sister Hannah marries James Huntington and goes to Norwich, Vt., adjoining Hartford, Vt. 4. His brothers Abraham and Joel go to Hartford, Vt. 5. The John who appears at Claremont and Weathersfield can be traced to no other source. 6. The grandson of this Claremont and Weathersfield John Marsh, Judge Charles P. Marsh of Woodstock, Vt., writes that Hon. Charles Marsh of Woodstock and his father, John second, born at Claremont, claimed to be cousins. They would be second cousins by the identity of John[5], son of Jonathan[4] with the John who had son John born at Claremont and in no other way. The Historical collections of Vermont tell us that at Weathersfield, Vt., John Marsh and his sons Joseph and John, Jr., in 1777, refused to subscribe with the sons of liberty. The only thing that looks at all doubtful is the having a son born when the father was only 20 years, 6 months and 9 days old. Yet marriages at 19 are not at all unknown although uncommon. The children and descendants we now give are of John Marsh of Claremont, almost certainly identical with John[5] of Lebanon. Children :

2277. John[6], b. Sept. 19, 1759; m. (1) Martha Grout, 2283.
2278. Joseph, probably lived awhile at Clarendon, Rutland Co., Vermont.
2279. Daniel or Samuel, b. perhaps 1777 or 1778 ; went to Pomfret, N. Y. and had a farm on the Lake Erie shore. Child:
2280. Peter[7]. Judge Charles P. Marsh visited his uncle and cousin there about 1868 and thinks his uncle was then 90 or 91 and that their names were as given above, Peter had a son and dau.
2281. Son[8], b. about 1838.
2282. Daughter.

## 2283 = 2277. JOHN[6] MARSH

b. at Claremont, N. H., Sept. 19, 1759, son of John[5], who soon removed to Weathersfield, Vt. and then eventually the son. He m. (1) No. 2283.

2283. Martha Grout, b. Sept. 25, 1753 of Weathersfield, who d. there Nov. 22, 1813. He m. (2) Nov., 1814, No. 2284.

**2284.**  Anstis Williams of Weathersfield.  In this John's boyhood parties of Indians from Canada frequently passed up and down the country and usually spent a night each way in his father's log cabin which was of comfortable size.  "They used to play with him and hold him in their laps and he lost all fear, but his father and mother were glad to have them go, yet sure, for good reason, to treat them as well as they could."  Letter from Judge Charles P. Marsh.  This John[6] d. at Perkinsville in the town of Weathersfield, Vt., Jan. 10, 1845.  Children :

2284.1    John[7], b. April 6, 1786 ; d. May 18, 1786.
2284.2    Sophia, b. Dec. 22, 1788 ; d. May, 1790.
2284.3    Sophia, b. Feb. 4, 1791 ; m. John S. Potwin, 2286.1.
2285.     Benjamin F., b. Dec. 4, 1792 ; m. Ruth Wetmore, 2287.
2285.1    John, b. Nov. 3, 1796 ; d. March 22, 1814, æ. 17.
2285.2    Bridgman, b. Jan. 30, 1799 ; d. N. Y. City, unm. about 1841.
          By second wife.
2286.     Charles Phelps, b. Jan. 7, 1816 ; m. Mary E. Wright, 2290.

## 2286.1 = 2284.3.    SOPHIA[7] MARSH

b. Feb. 4, 1791, dau. of John[6] and Martha (Grout) Marsh ; m. about 1814, No. 2286.1.

**2286.1**  John S. Potwin of Weathersfield, Vt.  Both died many years ago.  Children :

2286.2.    Abigail[8], m. George Pomeroy, both dead.
2286.3.    Martha, m. Benjamin Buckingham, he is dead, she is in Chicago.
2286.4.    Mary, m. and lives in N. Y. City.
2286.5.    Charles W., m. Sarah Sturgis and d. several years ago in Zanesville, O.

## 2287 = 2285.    BENJAMIN F[7]. MARSH

b. Dec. 4, 1792, son of John[6] and Martha (Grout) Marsh, (John[5], Jonathan[4], Capt. Joseph[3], John[2], John[1]) ; m. Sept. 15, 1813, in New Brunswick Province, Dominion of Canada, No. 2287.

**2287.**  Ruth Wetmore.  Their son John W. writes from Warsaw, Ill., Dec. 30, 1892 : " My father when a young man in 1810 went to New

Brunswick shortly before the war of 1812, and the war coming on, could not get home, and did not hear from home till after the close of the war, and the first letter received by him from home informed him of the death of his mother and his brother John and the marriage of his father to Anstis Williams and also the marriage of his sister Sophia. He remained in New Brunswick at St. John till 1832, engaged in commerce. In the fall of 1832, during the Black Hawk war, he emigrated to St. Louis, Mo. and in April, 1833, settled in Hancock county, Ill. At that time Warsaw had not been laid out, and the only families here were those of Mark Aldrich, John R. Wilcox and Isham Cochran. Mr. Marsh's family remained at F. Edwards until Christmas, 1833, when having completed the house now standing on his farm, four miles east of Warsaw, he removed them thither. On this farm he continued to reside until the spring of 1863, when, on account of his son Arthur having joined the army, he took up his abode with his son John W. Marsh, Esq. of Warsaw, where he remained up to the time of his death. His wife d. in 1838.

Two of Mr. Marsh's sons have been officers in the army. His son, B. F. Marsh, Jr., volunteered at the opening of the war, in the 16th Illinois infantry. Subsequently he joined the 2d Illinois cavalry as captain, and in Dec., 1864, held the position of lieutenant colonel, commanding that regiment. On several occasions he distinguished himself on the battle field. Arthur W. Marsh raised company C, 118th Illinois volunteers, and served with distinction until 1863, when he was killed in a skirmish with the rebels in Louisana.

Mr. Marsh was a man of polished manner, urbane and courteous. Physically, but few finer specimens of man could anywhere be found. He loved his country and hated a rebel and a rebel sympathizer. Never neutral upon any subject, whatever cause he espoused, he supported with all the zeal in his nature. Hence he had warm friends, and in his active days, bitter enemies. Tenacious of his own rights he never invaded the rights of others.

About 1854 he met with an accident on a railroad car, which rendered him a cripple, and which no doubt shortened his days. Being from this cause unfitted for business, he retired from contact with the world. Thus the asperities of former days were softened, and at the time of death he enjoyed the respect and esteem of the entire community. He was one of the most prominent men of Hancock

county and one of its earliest settlers.   Judge Charles Phelps Marsh,
his half brother, writes : " One of his last acts was to vote for Abraham Lincoln.   He had been sick and feeble for some days and daily
prayed that his life might be spared so that he might vote for Lincoln
—and it was."   He d. Nov. 23, 1864, æ. 71 years, 11 months and 19
days.   Children :

2287.1.   Charles Carroll[8], b. 1814; d. 1838, in Texas.
2287.2.   John Wellington, b. 1815; m. E. B. Baldwin, 2288.
2287.3.   Martha Sophia, m. Cyrus Felt, 2288.6.
2287.4.   Elizabeth Ruth, m. C. Richmond.
2287.5.   Deborah Charlotte, m. James Lazaddu; d. 1860.
2287.6.   Caroline Amelia, m. E. Richmond.
2287.7.   Benjamin F., b. Nov. 19, 1835; m. J. E. Miller, 2289.
2287.8.   Arthur W., b. 1837 ; Captain and d. in war, 1863.


## 2288 = 2287.2.   JOHN WELLINGTON[8] MARSH

b. in 1815, son of Benjamin F[7]. and Ruth (Wetmore) Marsh, (John[6],
John[5], Jonathan[4], Capt. Joseph[3], John[2], John[1]) ; m. Nov. 27, 1849,
No. 2288.
   2288.   Eudocia B. Baldwin.   He is a lawyer residing at Warsaw,
Hancock Co., Ill.   Living children :

2288.1.   Mary E[9]., b. Nov. 1, 1854.
2288.2.   Helen S., b. Feb. 19, 1858; m. Jan., 1891, Rev. William
          Barden.
2288.3.   Carrie Potwin, b. Feb. 9, 1866.
2288.4.   Adde Rose, b. Oct. 20, 1868.
2288.5.   John Wetmore, b. July 23, 1872.


## 2288.6 = 2287.3.   MARTHA SOPHIA[8] MARSH

dau. of Benjamin Franklin and Ruth (Wetmore) Marsh ; m. in 1836,
No. 2288.6.
   2288.6.   Cyrus Felt.   She d. in Jan., 1852.   Child :

2288.7.   Martha Elizabeth[9], b. Jan. 20, 1852 ; m. Jan. 20, 1870, Mar-
          vin T. Brown.   Child :
     2288.8.   Helen[10], b. Dec. 13, 1871.

Charles P. Marsh.

To face page 177.

2289 = 2287.7.   COL. BENJAMIN F⁸. MARSH, M. C.

b. Nov. 19, 1835, son of Benjamin F⁷. and Ruth (Wetmore) Marsh, (John⁶, John⁵, Jonathan⁴, Capt. Joseph³, John², John¹); m. (1) in 1860, No. 2289.

**2289.**  Josephine E. Miller.  They resided in Warsaw, Hancock Co., Ill., where he was a lawyer.  She died July 31, 1872.  He m. (2) Jan. 1, 1881, No. 2289.1.

**2289.1.**  Jane E. Coolbaugh.  He has been a member of congress for several years.  See his excellent war record in the sketch of his father.  Children:

    2289.2.  Arthur Wetmore⁹, b. Oct. 25, 1865.
    2289.3.  Bertha J., b. Nov. 5, 1867.
    2289.4.  Charles Carroll, b. Sept. 20, 1871.
             By second wife.
    2289.5.  William Coolbaugh, b. Nov. 30, 1881.
    2289.6.  Richard Oglesby, b. March 27, 1883.
    2289.7.  Benjamin Franklin, b. Nov. 6, 1884.

2290 = 2286.   JUDGE CHARLES PHELPS⁷ MARSH

b. Weathersfield, Vt., Jan. 7, 1816, son of John⁶ and Austis (Williams) Marsh, (John⁵, Jonathan⁴, Capt. Joseph³, John², John¹); m. (1) in Woodstock, Vt., July 2, 1844, No. 2290.

**2290.**  Mary Elizabeth Wright, dau. of Rev. Worthington Wright, the pastor of the Congregational church in Woodstock.  She was the mother of all his children.  She d. July 3, 1854.  He m. (2) July 20, 1859, No. 2291.

**2291.**  Helen Amelia Brayton of Swanton, Vt.  Mr. Marsh graduated from the University of Vermont at Burlington in August, 1839; was admitted to the bar in 1843, commenced practice in Woodstock, was a member of the law firm Washburn & Marsh for 25 years a union only terminated by the death of Gov. Washburn in Feb., 1870. He acquired a handsome competence, yet was simple and unostentatious with an easy dignity that belongs to a natural and unassumed dignity of character.

Mr. Marsh was state's attorney for Windsor county for four years from 1861 to 1865, a member of the constitutional convention in

13

1870, a member of the house of representatives of Vermont in 1886 and in 1888, and chairman of the judiciary committee of the house during his second term, and was appointed one of the assistant judges of Windsor county court in May, 1887. This office of judge came to him entirely unsought.

Judge Marsh died of acute pneumonia during a term of the court Jan. 13, 1893. Messages of sympathy came to the home.

" I have lost one of my earliest and most valued benefactors, and the village and state have lost one of their most worthy citizens," writes Judge Adams of St. Louis.

"I mourn the loss of a most valued friend," writes Mr. Norman Williams from Chicago.

" He was one of the warmest friends the University has had," says President Buckham, " and his interest in the institution led him into a kindly friendship for its president, which to me was very delightful."

Gov. Fuller, in a most kindly note of condolence, alludes to Judge Marsh's "many excellent and rare qualities of mind and manner," and to the great loss to his family and to the community. " I knew him so well (and only recently received a letter from him) that the blow has been peculiar to me."

A message from Hon. Justin S. Morrill at Washington speaks of Mr. Marsh as " my old and excellent friend."

Mr. Marsh in his political opinions might be emphatically styled "thorough." He began life an ardent Whig. Endorsing the nomination of General Harrison for president in 1840, he entered heartily into the stirring scenes of that brilliant campaign. In 1844 he conducted with great ability a campaign paper, advocating the election of Henry Clay as president. Others might change in their political opinions, but there was no change in him, and while the slavery agitation, the free soil slide and the temperance movement drew many away from old party ties, he remained loyal to the Whig cause, till the party dissolved in 1853. After that he became a Republican and to the new party remained through life as strict and uncompromising in his attachments as he had been to the old. In this connection it is proper to allude to one peculiar characteristic of Mr. Marsh. In discussing political questions, especially those of a local nature, or in talk upon the social topics of the day he would often exhibit a grim humor that was perfectly irresistible. In these displays of caustic wit, which began early in life and continued late, it may be he was not always particular in what direction the shafts flew; yet from bitterness of spirit towards others he was entirely free, as they will allow who knew him well and knew him long.

He gave of his means to aid many a young man whom he found worthy and ambitious to secure an education. His acts of unselfish and not stinted, though always studiously reticent, liberality are acknowledged in private by men now in professional life whom Mr. Marsh has befriended. It is known to some of Judge Marsh's older friends that in his own young days, when the facilities of school and college were much less easy of access, Mr. Marsh himself felt compelled to relinquish his studies at the university, from lack of means, and was befriended and aided to go on by Consul Jarvis of Weathersfield, who afterwards refused to accept any interest upon his repaid investment in the early education of the graduate and attorney. This may give a reason why more than one young man has warmly recognized Mr. Marsh as a friend and benefactor.

For quite a number of years Mr. Marsh had been accustomed to provide for three annual prizes of $25.00 each, to be awarded to the most successful student in each of the three departments of Latin, Greek and Mathematics, at the university.

By the provisions of his will, after making liberal provision for his widow and his surving son and family, Mr. Marsh makes the following public bequests :

To the University of Vermont, five scholarships, of one thousand dollars each ($5,000) to be designated as the C. P. Marsh scholarships, for the benefit, first, of needy and worthy young men and women from Windsor county. Also one thousand dollars ($1,000) to endow a scholarship in memory of Charles Munson Marsh, for the benefit, first, of students from Woodstock.

A scholarship endowed some twenty years ago by Mr. Marsh in memory of his son who was drowned in the lake while a student in the university, was known as the Edwin Wright Marsh scholarship.

To St. James' Episcopal church, Woodstock, $500.

To the Congregational church, Woodstock, $500.

To the Riverside cemetery association of Woodstock, in trust, $1,000.

Mr. Marsh was instrumental in procuring the organization and incorporation of the new cemetery association, in securing and laying out the grounds so beautifully located by the picturesque winding banks of the Otta Quechee. To that resting place by the riverside he has now been borne. The mound and the memorial, the gateway and hedge and winding path will long commemorate the honored citizen who is buried there. Mrs. Marsh is still living. Children :

2291.1  John Worthington[8], b. Aug. 31, 1845 ; a lawyer and lives in Chicago.
2291.2  Charles Munson, b. May 31, 1847 ; d. Feb. 26, 1887.
2291.3  Edwin Wright, b. March 25, 1849 ; d. Sept. 19, 1868 while a freshman in the University of Vermont.
2291.4  George M., b. Sept. 27, 1853 ; d. Dec. 16, 1854.


## 2292 = 1749.  ABRAHAM[5] MARSH

b. at Lebanon, Ct., May 31, 1742, son of Jonathan[4] and Alice (Newcomb) Marsh, (Capt. Joseph[3], John[2], John[1]) ; m. No. 2292.

**2292.** ——. He removed to Hartford, Vt., of which town his father was one of three incorporators. At the age of 22 he had a son baptized at Lebanon, Ct. Child :

2293.  Abraham[6], bap. Sept. 23, 1764 ; m. Mary D., 2294.


## 2294 = 2293.  ABRAHAM[6] MARSH

b. at Lebanon, Ct., baptized Sept. 23, 1764, son of Abraham[5] Marsh, (Jonathan[4], Capt. Joseph[3], John[2], John[1]) ; m. No. 2294.

**2294.** Mary D. Resided at Hartford, Vt. Children :

2295.  Abram[7], b. June 15, 1802 ; m. Rhoda Short.
2296.  Alice Ann. Spinster, d. in Vermont.
2297.  Hammond. Went west.


## 2298 = 2295.  REV. ABRAM[7] MARSH

b. June 15, 1802, at Hartford, Vt., son of Abraham[6] and Mary D. Marsh, (Abraham[5], Jonathan[4], Capt. Joseph[3], John[2], John[1]) ; graduated

REV. ABRAM MARSH.

*To face page* 180.

at Dartmouth college in 1825, studed theology at Andover; m. (1)
No. 2298.

**2298.** Rhoda Short. He was ordained June 23, 1829, installed
at Tolland, Ct., Nov. 30, 1831. His wife d. when his son was "about
twelve or thirteen" and he m. (2) April 6, 1842, No. 2299.

**2299.** Mary Hall Cooley of Norwich, Ct. He was dismissed
from the Tolland church in 1869 after 38 years of pastoral life there.
He d. Sept. 2, 1877, being over 75 years of age. His widow survived
him but a few years. Children:

　　2300. Siloam Short[8], b. Oct. 30, 1831; m. F. J. Buck, 2301.
　　2300.1 Daughter, d. y.
　　2300.2 James Parmelee, b. Oct. 11, 1838; m. Julia A. Sprague, 2302.


### 2301 = 2300. SILOAM SHORT[8] MARSH

b. at Tolland, Ct., Oct. 30, 1831, son of Abram[7] and Rhoda (Short)
Marsh, (Abraham[6], Abraham[5], Jonathan[4], Capt. Joseph[3], John[2],
John[1]), m. April 17, 1854, No. 2301.

**2301.** Frances Johnson Buck, b. Nov. 2, 1828. He d. May 11,
1857. She d. April 1, 1892. Child:

　　2301.1. Edwin Rice[9], b. Jan. 27, 1857; m. Anna G. Clarke, 2301.2.


### 2301.2 = 2301.1. EDWIN RICE[9] MARSH

b. in New Haven, Ct., Jan. 27, 1857, son of Siloam Short[8] and Frances
Johnson (Buck) Marsh, (Rev. Abram[7], Abraham[6], Abraham[5], Jonathan[4], Capt. Joseph[3], John[2], John[1]); m. June 2, 1887, No. 2301.2.

**2301.2.** Anna Gooch Clarke, b. at Bridgeport, Ct., Nov. 6, 1863.
Children:

　　2301.3. LeRoy Wadsworth[10], b. New Haven, Ct., Aug. 26, 1889;
　　　　　　d. Dec. 4, 1889.
　　2301.4. Carlton Lewis, b. New Haven, Ct., Sept. 10, 1891.


### 2302 = 2300.2. JAMES PARMELEE[8] MARSH

b. at Tolland, Ct., Oct. 11, 1838, son of Rev. Abram[7] Marsh, (Abra-

ham⁶, Abraham⁵, Jonathan⁴, Capt. Joseph³, John², John¹); m. April
15, 1865, No. 2302.

2302.    Julia A. Sprague.    Children:

    2302.1.    James Buckingham⁹, b. March 28, 1866; m. March 29, 1893,
        Laura Beatrice Corbusier.  Child:
        2302.2.    Charlotte Corbusier, b. May 7, 1894.
    2302.3.    Walter Everett, b. Dec. 12, 1870.

2303 = 2136.  OTIS⁷ MARSH

b. at Hartland, Vt., Nov. 6, 1789, son of Samuel⁶ and Huldah Marsh,
(Capt. Abel⁵, Joseph⁴, Capt. Joseph³, John², John¹); m. Feb. 9, 1815,
No. 2303.

2303.  Julia Ransom, b. Woodstock, Vt., Sept. 30, 1794, sister
of Truman Bishop Ransom, who was killed in the Mexican war at
the storming of Chapultepec.  Her line of descent from Joseph¹
Ransom, Lyme, Ct., was Matthew² of Lyme, b. Aug. 23, 1711; m.
Sarah Way, d. 1760, serving in the French and Indian war; his widow
moved to Woodstock, Vt., about 1781 and d. in 1799, æ. 84.  Her
son George³, m. in Lyme in 1768, Annie Tiffany.  Amasa⁴, b. Jan.
31, 1769, went with his father to Woodstock, Vt., and m. there Abigail
Root, their daughter was Julia⁵ Ransom.  Of Otis Marsh his son
Benjamin F., writes from Helena, Montana, July 22, 1887 : " My
father was second cousin to Charles Marsh of Woodstock, Vt." He
also states that his birthplace was in what is now known as Taftsville
on the Quechee river, three miles from Woodstock.  He had many
relatives in Woodstock and Hartland.  They moved to Jeffersonville,
Ind., where Otis⁷ Marsh d. March 25, 1855, and Julia (Ransom)
Marsh d. there Dec. 20, 1871.  Children:

    2303.1.    Benjamin F⁸., b. Nov. 7, 1815; m. M. D. Blish, 2304.
    2303.2.    Abigail R., b. Feb. 11, 1817; m. Jan. 11, 1836, Joseph P.
        Wyatt. Two sons, 1,F.O⁹.; 2, George. She d. Jan.19,1890.
    2303.3.    Samuel, b. March 11, 1817; m. May 5, 1846, Hannah S.
        Ayres.  He d. in July, 1862.
    2303.4.    Otis Mason, b. April 13, 1821; m. March 30, 1847, Mary
        Jane Stevens. He d. at Lake Charles, La., Dec. 26, 1892.
    2303.5.    Orpha G., b. Nov. 29, 1822; m. June 25, 1850, William E.
        Thomas.  Lives at Richview, Ill.
    2303.6.    Truman R., b. Aug. 20, 1824 ; d. Jan. 20, 1825.

2303.7.  Julia, b. Dec. 8, 1825 ; d. Oct. 30, 1834.
2303.8.  Amanda A., b. April 24, 1828; m. July 15, 1852, William
         Dixon.
2303.9.  Amasa R., b. April 6, 1830; m. A. E. Heiskell, 2305.
2303.10. Jane M., b. June 24, 1832 ; d. March 16, 1854.
2303.11. Jacob W., b. Aug. 20, 1834; d. Aug. 16, 1835.
2303.12. Hulda C., b. Aug. 29, 1836; m. Dec. 25, 1855, Nathan S.
         Hawkins.

2304 = 2303.1.   BENJAMIN F$^8$. MARSH

b. at Taftsville, Vt., Nov. 7, 1815, son of Otis$^7$ and Julia (Ransom)
Marsh, (Samuel$^6$, Capt. Abel$^5$, Joseph$^4$, Capt. Joseph$^3$, John$^2$, John$^1$) ;
m. in Woodstock, Vt., Aug. 21, 1845, No. 2304.

**2304.** Mary D. Blish.  Their son George writes from Butte City,
Mont., that his father was a railroad engineer in Texas at the outbreak
of the civil war and was imprisoned for his union sympathy.  In 1893
he was living at Helena, Mont.  Children :

2304.1.  George$^9$, b. at Rutland, Vt., in 1847.
2304.2.  Emma D., now Mrs. Woodman, Helena, Mont.
2304.3.  Flora A., now Mrs. Davis, Helena, Mont.

2305 = 2303.9.   AMASA RANSOM$^8$ MARSH

b. April 6, 1830, son of Otis$^7$ and Julia (Ransom) Marsh, (Samuel$^6$,
Capt. Abel$^5$, Joseph$^4$, Capt. Joseph$^3$, John$^2$, John$^1$) ; m. June 5, 1856,
No. 2305.

**2305.** Ann E. Heiskell, b. Sept. 29, 1837.  He d. at Inland,
Iowa, where his family remained, Feb. 10, 1892.  Children :

2305.1.  Jennie$^9$, b. Feb. 12, 1857.
2306.    Otis Robert, b. Feb. 20, 1859; m. A. F. Willey, 2308.
2307.    Mary Frances, b. Oct. 11, 1861 ; m. June 30, 1892, Robert
         C. Weston.
2307.1.  Thomas Rawson, b. Aug. 27, 1864.
2307.2.  Margaret Julia, b. Feb. 6, 1866 ; d. April 18, 1867.

2308 = 2306.   OTIS ROBERT$^9$ MARSH

b. Feb. 20, 1859, son of Amasa Ransom$^8$ and Ann E. (Heiskell)

Marsh, (Otis[7], Samuel[6], Capt. Abel[5], Joseph[4], Capt. Joseph[3], John[2], . John[1]); m. Oct. 14, 1886, No. 2308.

**2308.** Addie F. Willey.    Children:
    2308.1.  Walter Gay[10], b. Sept. 8, 1887.
    2308.2.  Rena Pearl, b. July 7, 1889.
    2308.3.  Willey Ransom, b. Oct. 2, 1891.

2309 = 1750.  COL. JOEL[5] MARSH

b. at Lebanon, Ct., June 1, 1745, son of Jonathan[4] and Alice (Newcomb) Marsh, (Capt. Joseph[3], John[2], John[1]); m. Jan. 25, 1770, No. 2309.

**2309.** Ann, b. Nov. 18, 1743.  Their first child was born at Lebanon, Ct., April 15, 1771.  Then we have record of four b. at Hartford, Vt., from 1775 to 1781, and then two b. at Bethel, Vt., Oct., 1783 to May, 1786.  These show where the mother was and probably the home.  Col. Joel Marsh figured largely in the early history of New Connecticut not yet Vermont.  With his cousins, Col. Joseph, Capt. Abel and Elisha Marsh he was an early proprietor of Randolph and also of Bethel, Vt.  The embryo state had a southern regiment with Joseph Marsh as colonel and a northern in which Joel was captain and major and apparently colonel, early in the revolution.  He was a member of the convention to adopt the constitution of Vermont.

The proprietors of Bethel, Vt.  "Voted," "Dec. 13, 1779," "that Col. Joel Marsh be an additional proprietor," "and the said Marsh do accept of the Mill Lot which contains 450 acres" also that he "do build a good sawmill by the first day of September next and a good gristmill by the first day of November following upon the forfeiture of five thousand pounds, extraordinary Providence excepted." He drove an ox team up the bed of the White river, built a log house and commenced on the mill as supposed in 1780, but Indians, "extraordinary Providences," burned Royalton in October and settlers hurried away.  He finished the mill in 1781 which was for several years the only one in that region and Col. Joel Marsh was known as the miller.  He soon built the first frame house which 100 years later was in good preservation.  Col. Joel d. March 11, 1807.  His widow d. May 6, 1813.  Children:

2310.  Jonathan[6], b. April 15, 1771 ; m. Irene Ainsworth, 2317.
2311.  Peleg Sanford, b. Oct. 18, 1775 ; m. Mary Mills, 2350.
2312.  Mary, b. March 26, 1778 ; unm. and d. at Peleg S. Marsh's,
       æ. over 70.
2313.  John, b. April 25, 1779 ; m. and had family and resided at
       Stockbridge, Rochester and Bethel, Vt.
2314.  Ann, b. Dec. 30, 1781.
2315.  Joel, b. at Bethel, Oct. 28, 1783 ; m. and had one son and two
       daus. (unm.) went to Maryland.
2316.  Mason, b. at Bethel, May 1, 1786.

## 2317 = 2310.  JONATHAN[6] MARSH

b. at Lebanon, Ct., April 15, 1771, son of Col. Joel[5] and Ann Marsh,
(Jonathan[4], Capt. Joseph[3], John[2], John[1]) ; m. Jan. 8, 1806, No. 2317.
2317.  Irene Ainsworth, b. Oct. 20, 1786.  He was town clerk for
25 years, justice of the peace for many years and a member of the
legislature.  He d. in 1850, æ. 79.  Irene (Ainsworth) Marsh d.
May 28, 1861.  Children :

2318.  Mary[7], b. Nov. 18, 1806; m. Aug. 6, 1832, Rollin Richmond ;
       d. Oct. 29, 1842.  Children :
2319.  George Nelson[8].
2320.  Rollin M.
2321.  Irene, b. July 17, 1808; m. Wm. Adams, 2327.
2322.  Albert G., b. June 12, 1810; m. Sept. 27, 1841, Ellen E.
       Ainsworth.  No children.  She d. Feb. 27, 1893 in
       Bethel, Vt.  He was town clerk for many years and
       held many other offices.  Represented the town in the
       legislature.
2323.  Almeron, b. May 13, 1813 ; m. Susan Pearson, 2345.
2324.  Augusta C., b. Nov. 19, 1820 ; m. George Townsend.  Child :
2325.  Augusta[8].
2326.  Anna A., b. April 27, 1827, d. Sept. 12, 1842.

## 2327 = 2321.  IRENE[7] MARSH

b. at Bethel, Vt., July 17, 1808, dau. of Jonathan[6] and Irene (Ainsworth) Marsh, (Jonathan[4], Capt. Joseph[3], John[2], John[1]) ; m. April
28, 1834, No. 2327.
2327.  William Adams.  She d. April 21, 1872.  Children :

2328.  William Rayborn[8], b. Jan. 26, 1835; m. E. A. Davis, 2331.
2329.  Ellen Augusta, d. 1842.
2330.  Rush Mason, b. June 2, 1845.


## 2331 = 2328.  WILLIAM R[8].  ADAMS

b. at Bethel, Vt., Jan. 26, 1835, son of Irene[6] (Marsh) Adams, (Jonathan[6], Col. Joel[5], Jonathan[4], Capt. Joseph[3], John[2], John[1]) ; m. in 1856, No. 2331.

**2331.**  Eudora Adelaide Davis, dau. of Rev. S. A. Davis.  He is now town clerk of Bethel and has held the office for over 25 years and justice of the peace for about 25 years.  He is a bookseller. Children :

2332.  Leslie Ray[9], b. March 11, 1857 ; m. Sept. 14, 1892, Clara I. Latimer and resides at St. Albans, Vt.
2333.  Rollin Marsh, b. May 24, 1858; m. Sept., 1886, Cora E. Parker, and resides at Boston.
2334.  Mary Ellen, b. Jan. 3, 1860; resides at Bethel.
2335.  Minnie Josephine, b. July 29, 1861 ; d. 1864.
2336.  Elmer Davis, b. April 19, 1863 ; d. 1864.
2337.  Florence Isadore, b. Jan. 25, 1865 ; residence at Northampton, Mass.
2338.  Gilbert Lincoln, b. Aug. 3, 1866; residence at Hanford, Cal.
2339.  Bennie William, b. April 30, 1868 ; d. 1869.
2340.  Percy Rush, b. Aug. 29, 1869; residence at Boston.
2341.  William Davis, b. Oct. 9, 1870; residence at Middlebury, Vt.
2342.  Harry Elmer, b. Jan. 4, 1873.
2343.  Stella Eudora, b. Feb. 16, 1877.
2344.  Arthur Armin, b. June 13, 1878.


## 2345 = 2323.  ALMERON[7] MARSH

b. at Bethel, Vt., May 13, 1813, son of Jonathan[6] and Irene (Ainsworth) Marsh, (Col. Joel[5], Jonathan[4], Capt. Joseph[3], John[2], John[1]) ; m. Jan., 1842, No. 2345.

**2345.**  Susan Pearson.  He was drowned in Nov., 1844 and his widow m. and removed to Iowa.  Child :

2346.  Charles Almeron[8], b. Aug. 10, 1844; m. (1) A. Townsend, 2347.

## 2347 = 2346. CHARLES ALMERON[8] MARSH

b. at Bethel, Vt., Aug. 10, 1844, son of Almeron[7] and Susan (Pearson) Marsh, (Jonathan[6], Col. Joel[5], Jonathan[4], Joseph[3], John[2], John[1]); m. (1) in summer of 1866, No. 2347.

**2347.** Augusta Townsend of Bethel. She d. Oct. 8, 1867, æ. 22. He m. (2) April 4, 1872, No. 2348.

**2348.** Clara, b. Liverpool, Nova Scotia, Jan. 11, 1850. Charles A. Marsh from boyhood was separated from his mother and in later life resided away from relatives. He now lives at Needham, Mass. His father died when he was but three months old, his only child d. when two months old and his first wife d. six weeks later. Child:

   2349. Frankie C[9]., d. Aug. 29, 1867, æ. two months.

## 2350 = 2311. PELEG SANFORD[6] MARSH

b. at Hartford, Vt., Oct. 18, 1775, son of Col. Joel[5] and Ann Marsh, (Jonathan[4], Capt. Joseph[3], John[2], John[1]); m. by Rev. Thomas Robbins, D. D., Feb. 9, 1813, at East Windsor, Ct. to No. 2350.

**2350.** Mary Mills. Children:

   2351. Harriet[7], b. Nov. 12, 1813; m. Solon Cummings. Both d. Children:
      2352. Jane[8].
      2353. Mary.
      2354. Solomon C.
   2355. Jane C., b. Jan. 29, 1815; m. Luke Hemmingway, both d. Children:
      2356. Fred[8].
      2357. Ellen.
   2358. Mary Ann, b. Aug. 28, 1816; m. Jacob Smith. Children:
      2359. Edward[8], d.
      2360. Sarah, m. Frank Wight, and resides in East Bethel.
   2361. Joel, b. Jan. 29, 1818; m. Maria Jones, both d. No children.
   2362. Augustine M., b. Jan. 30, 1820; m. Rosette Meserve, 2371.
   2363. Charles P., b. April 7, 1822; m. Elizabeth Farley, 2374.
   2364. Sarah, b. Jan. 16, 1824; m. John Morse. Children:
      2365. Fannie[8].
      2366. Nellie.
   2367. Ellen S., b. Nov. 15, 1826; unm.; d.
   2368. Laura, m. Leonard Saunders. Children:
      2369. Clara[8].
      2370. Mary.

## 2371 = 2362.  AUGUSTINE M.[7] MARSH

b. at Bethel, Vt., Jan. 30, 1820, son of Peleg Sanford[6] and Mary (Mills) Marsh, (Col. Joel[5], Jonathan[4], Capt. Joseph[3], John[2], John[1]) : m. No. 2371.

**2371.** Rosette Meserve.  He has represented Bethel in the legislature and held many town offices.  He and wife (1892) are living in Bethel.  Children :

> 2372.  Fred A[8].
> 2373.  George A.


## 2374 = 2363.  CHARLES P[7]. MARSH

b. at Bethel, Vt., April 7, 1822, son of Peleg Sanford[6] and Mary (Mills) Marsh, (Col. Joel[5], Jonathan[4], Capt. Joseph[3], John[2], John[1]) ; m. No. 2374.

**2374.** Elizabeth Farley, who is d.  He resides at Bethel. Children :

> 2375.  Ellen[8], m. Nathaniel Whittier.  Three children.  Resides at Barre, Vt.
> 2376.  Lizzie, d.
> 2377.  James P., b. Jan. 5, 1858; m. Lucy Williams.  Resides at Bethel.  Child :
>> 2378.  ———.

## BRANCH I.  DIVISION IV.

## THE ELDER NEW HARTFORD LINE.

*(To be carefully distinguished from the younger New Hartford Line which comes under Branch 3d.)*

---

## 2400 = 57.  CAPT. JONATHAN³ MARSH

b. Aug. 7, 1688, at Hartford, Ct., son of John² and Sarah (Lyman) Marsh.  His mother was dau. of Richard Lyman of Hartford and Northampton.  His father was son of John¹ Marsh and Anna Webster, dau. of Gov. Webster, all of Hartford, Ct., and Hadley, Mass.  He m. probably in 1714, No. 2400.

**2400.**  Elizabeth Wadsworth of Hartford, dau. of Capt. Joseph of Charter Oak fame, who left in his will £30, £10 each, to her three children.  Her brother Jonathan Wadsworth, No. 84, had already m. in 1711 Hepzibah³ Marsh, sister of Capt. Jonathan³ and from this Hepzibah³ (Marsh) Wadsworth through Samuel⁴ b. 1716, Gurdon⁵ b. 1748 came Gurdon's grandson, Gurdon Wadsworth⁷ Russell, M. D., who wrote " Up Neck," Hartford, vividly describing a part of Hartford where many of Marsh and Wadsworth name have resided. After the death of his first wife Capt. Jonathan Marsh m. (2) probably in 1723, No. 2401.

**2401.**  Elizabeth Loomis of Windsor.  Was she not Elizabeth³ Loomis, b. Sept. 26, 1704, No. 31, dau. of David and Lydia² (Marsh) Loomis of Windsor?  After her husband d. in 1783 she went to Hartford and lived 12 years with her dau. Hannah, Mrs. Thomas Wadsworth in the " Up Neck," Hartford and d. in " 1795," said to be æ. " 98," but *if the dau. of Lydia (Marsh) Loomis*, she was only 91.  Capt. Jonathan³ Marsh was to New Hartford largely what his brother Capt. John³ Marsh, 20 years older, was to Litchfield, an explorer, one of the first three selectmen, and the second on the list of earliest settlers. He explored in 1733 and removed with his family in 1736. " He lived on a hill where he had a splendid view of hills and valleys." His children were mainly born at Hartford. Born 1688 this Patriarch of the New Hartford line d. 1783, æ. 95. Children :

2402.  Jonathan⁴, bap. May 1, 1715; m. Theodocia Kellogg, 2412.
2403.  Joseph, b. Jan. 18, bap. Jan. 19, 1717; unm., see No. 2422.
2404.  Elizabeth, bap. Feb. 12, 1720–21; m. Joseph Marsh, 3819.
     By second wife.
2405.  Sarai, bap. June 28, 1724; m. Abraham Kellogg, 2423.
2406.  John, bap. July 2, 1727; m. Lucina Seymour, 2435.
2407.  Job, bap. March 8, 1729–30; m. (1) Lydia Church, 2445.
2408.  Moses, b. 1731; m. Sarah Merrill, 2454.
2409.  Eunice, b. 1736; m. Roger Olmsted, 2466.
2410.  Lois, bap. Oct. 28, 1742; m. (1) Rev. E. Davenport, 2467.
2411.  Hannah, bap. Oct. 16, 1746; m. Thomas Wadsworth, 2478.


2412 = 2402.   JONATHAN⁴ MARSH

b. at Hartford, Ct., baptized May 1, 1715, son of Jonathan³ and Elizabeth (Wadsworth) Marsh, (John², John¹) ; removed when 21 with his father to New Hartford, Ct., was a farmer, wheelwright and carpenter and had the experience of a pioneer. He lived three-fourths of a mile north of the church on the east side of the highway. He m. April 4, 1745, No. 2412.

2412.  Theodocia Kellogg, dau. of Isaac, one of the early settlers. They lived long in patriarchal simplicity. Theodocia's chief employment for many years was weaving. This carpenter was not unlike Joseph of old. His grandson Rev. Frederick, who lived to be 92, describes a picture almost oriental, as he saw and remembered his grandfather with prayers about sunset, thanksgiving for all descendants, white locks and an attitude reverent, standing before God. The aged wife d. March 5, 1795 after 60 years of married life. Seven years later the husband followed, Jan. 12, 1802, æ. 87. Children :

2413.  Theodocia⁵, b. July 13, 1747; m. (1) John Gilbert, 2480.
2414.  Ruth, b. July 14, 1749; d. unm. March 7, 1813.

2415. Chloe, b. Nov.12, 1750,(?) bap. Nov. 18,1751; m. Elijah Flower, Jr., a captain in the revolutionary war; removed to New Hartford, N. Y., about 1791. No children.

2416. Mary, b. July 22, 1754; m. Elijah Seymour, 2488.

2417. Jonathan, b. March 1, 1757; m. Damaris Pitkin, 2497.

2418. Elizabeth, b. Oct. 13, 1759; m. Roger Sheldon, 2507.

2419. Ashbel, b. July 11, 1762; m. Abigail Ward, 2519.

2420. Cynthia, b. April 13, 1765; m. Rufus Northway, 2528.

2421. Esther, b. Aug. 8, 1768; d. Aug. 18, 1769.

## 2422 see 2403. JOSEPH⁴ MARSH

b. at Hartford, Ct., Jan. 18, baptized Jan. 19, 1717–8, son of Jonathan³ and Elizabeth (Wadsworth) Marsh, (John², John¹); never married. Judge George Marsh Carrington, as to Joseph's birth gives me this : "I have, Joseph b. at Hartford, Jan. 18, 1719 (from an old account book of Ashbel Marsh, Sr., in whose family he lived and died)." This Ashbel. 2419, son of Jonathan² lived at the homestead of his grandfather the original proprietor. Joseph and Ashbel in 1776 had each a cart made by Ashbel's brother the third Jonathan, the only carts on Town Hill, in constant demand by borrowing neighbors, who otherwise must use ox sleds for all farm work. About 1776 Ashbel was offered and refused 25 acres of land for his cart. Joseph gave his farm to the maker of his cart. He "d. Dec. 21, 1812, æ. nearly 94." If the Hartford baptism is correct it was nearly 95.

## 2423 = 2405. SARAH⁴ MARSH

b. at Hartford, Ct., baptized June 28, 1724, dau. of Capt. Jonathan³ and Elizabeth (Loomis) Marsh, (John², John¹); m. June 17, 1747, No. 2423.

2423. Abraham Kellogg, son of Isaac, b. 1720, of New Hartford. She d. about 1796, æ. about 72. He d. Jan. 13, 1805. Children :

2424. Esther⁵, b. March 24, 1748; m. Col. Aaron Austin, one of the ablest men ever born in New Hartford, eminent as soldier, civil officer and citizen; d. 1829, æ. 84. She d. 1826, æ. 78.

2425.  Abraham, b. Jan. 27, 1750; m. Sarah Seymour dau. of John
       Seymour.  One of his descendants is Col. Abraham G.
       Kellogg of Winsted, Ct.
2426.  Solomon, b. Dec. 10, 1751; removed to and founded New
       Hartford, N. Y.
2427.  Moses, b. Feb. 23, 1754, twin of Elias; m. Mabel Merrill;
       was father of Col. Norman Kellogg.
2428.  Elias, b. Feb. 23, 1754; captain and father of Capt. Charles
       D. Kellogg.
2429.  Phinehas, b. June 7, 1756; helped Solomon found New
       Hartford, N. Y., in 1785-9.
2430.  Martin, b. July 16, 1758; m. Lucy Seymour, and removed to
       Oneida Co., N. Y.; d. about 1832.
2431.  Frederick Webster, b. Jan. 31, 1761; m. —— Merrill.
2432.  Sarah, b. June 3, 1763; m. Martin Smith, father of Col.
       Seth Smith distinguished in the revolution.  They
       removed to Ashtabula, O.
2433.  Truman, b. Jan. 3, 1766; m. Hannah Merrill.
2434.  Elizabeth, b. June 17, 1768; m. Dr. Josiah Hatch and removed
       to Granville, Mass.


2435 = 2406.  JOHN[4] MARSH

b. at Hartford, Ct., June 30, 1727 and baptized in the Second church
July 2, 1727, son of Jonathan[3] and Elizabeth (Loomis) Marsh, (John[2],
John[1]); resided at New Hartford, Ct.; m. (1) Feb. 2, 1858, No. 2435.
**2435.**  Lucina Seymour, who d. May 14, 1762.  He m. (2) June
17, 1763, No. 2436.
**2436.**  Sarah Nash, b. West Hartford, April 26, 1738, dau. of
Moses and Rebecca (Graves) Nash, d. July 17, 1775, æ. 37.  He m.
(3) Nov. 27, 1777, No. 2437.
**2437.**  Mrs. Miriam Sedgwick, widow of William Sedgwick, b.
about 1729.  She was dau. of Capt. Daniel Webster, great-grandson
of Gov. John Webster.  She m. (1) Elias Haskins, (2) William
Sedgwick, (3) John[4] Marsh.  Her five children were all born before
her third marriage.  Before 1800 he removed with James[5] his son to
Bridgewater, N. Y., and d. at Paris, N. Y., Nov. 10, 1805, æ. 78 years,
4 months and 10 days.  The widow d. at West Hartford, Ct., Sept.
17, 1819, æ. 90.  Children :

2438.  John[5], b. Nov. 25, 1758; m. Anna Cale, 2544.
2439.  Nathaniel, b. July 12, 1761; m. and d. Jan. 31, 1791.

2440. Lucina, b. June 15, 1764; m. Timothy Dawson.
2441. James, b. June 1, 1767; m. Elizabeth Case, 2548.
2442. Sarah, b. Dec. 16, 1769; d. Aug. 2, 1771.
2443. Sarah, b. June 16, 1772; probably m. Ambrose Wadsworth, 701.
2444. Abigail, b. May 30, 1775; d. Sept. 21, 1775.

### 2445 = 2407. JOB[4] MARSH

b. at Hartford, Ct., baptized Marsh 8, 1729–30, son of Jonathan[3] and Elizabeth (Loomis) Marsh, (John[2], John[1]); was a resident of New Hartford from his boyhood in 1736. He married (1) in 1745, No. 2445.

**2445.** Lydia Church. He m. (2) No. 2446.

**2446.** Jemima, who was b. in 1728. He lived about a quarter of a mile from Lake Wonksunkmunk where he built a house. His grand-daughter Mrs. Anna Merrill, dau. of his son Roswell, was b. in this house and after living mainly there 93 years d. in it Oct. 30, 1882. The old cider mill of her grandfather still stands where unfortunately her only brother was drowned in a tub of apple juice, when very young. Near this lake was the house of John Marsh, older brother of Job, and also of Job's sons, Amos and Job, Jr., as well as Roswell's, the old place. John's house was torn down in 1849. Mrs. Jemima Marsh d. Jan. 15, 1810, æ. 82. Job Marsh, Sr., d. in his own house New Hartford, Sept. 12, 1822, æ. 93. Children :

2447. Job[5], b. May 12, 1755; m. Salome Beach, 2585.
2448. Amos, bap. Feb. 6, 1759; probably m. July 21, 1785, Lydia Benham.
2449. Elijah, bap. April 8, 1759; in the navy during the revolutionary war, captured and paroled at St. Christophers, Caribbee Islands by the Governor General and returned home and d. unm.
2450. Roswell, bap. July 15, 1761; m. Anna Crow, 2670.
2451. Lucretia, bap. March 18, 1764; m. Solomon Churchill, 2676.
2452. Peletiah, bap. Feb. 22, 1767.
2453. Elisha, bap. Dec. 25, 1774.

### 2454 = 2408. MOSES[4] MARSH

b. about 1731,(?) son of Jonathan[3] and Elizabeth (Loomis) Marsh, (John[2], John[1]); m. May, 1757, No. 2454.

14

**2454.** Sarah Merrill. Resided at New Hartford, Ct. Was a shoemaker. He d. at New Hartford, about 1790, æ. 60. Children:

2455. Sarah[5], bap. Feb. 5, 1758; m. David Covil and went west.
2456. Moses, bap. Sept. 19, 1759; d. y.
2457. Moses, bap. Jan. 8, 1761; d. y.
2458. Anna, bap. April 18, 1762; m. Allyn Goodwin, 2691.
2459. Amy, b. April 20, bap. April 21, 1765; m. Eli Seymour, 2698.
2460. Lucy, b. April 20, bap. April 21, 1765; m. Theodore Lee.
2461. Mina or Mica, b. and bap. Nov. 15, 1767; d. y.
2462. Moses, bap. March 25, 1770, of Hartford, "d. Sept. 27, 1794, æ. 24 or 5."
2463. Lois, bap. April 11, 1773; m. John Seymour, 2704.
2464. Hannah, b. Nov. 26, 1775, bap. Feb. 26, 1776.
2465. Elizabeth, bap. July 26, 1778.

## 2466 = 2409.   EUNICE[4] MARSH

b. 1736, dau. of Jonathan[3] and Elizabeth (Loomis) Marsh, (John[2], John[1]); m. at New Hartford, Feb. 9, 1758, No. 2466.
**2466.** Roger Olmstead, b. June 9, 1728, who d. June 6, 1800 in his 72d year. She d. May 24, 1807 in her 71st year. Children:

2466.1. Gamaliel[5], bap. June 17, 1759; m. 1786, Esther Goodwin.
2466.2. Jesse, bap. June 6, 1762.
2466.3. Roger, bap. Aug. 26, 1764.
2466.4. Eunice, bap. July 12, 1767, probably d. y.
2466.5. Michael, b. 1771; m. Abigail Hopkins.
2466.6. Sarah, bap. Oct. 10, 1773.
2466.7. Elizabeth, bap. June 16, 1776.
2466.8. "Eunice, dau. of Roger Olmsted, bap. Sept. 27, 1778."
2466.9. Elijah, b. 1782.
2466.10. Philo, b. 1784.

## 2467 = 2410.   LOIS[4] MARSH

b. at New Hartford, baptized Oct. 28, 1742, dau. of Jonathan[3] and Elizabeth (Loomis) Marsh, (John[2], John[1]); m. (1) Nov. 30, 1769, No. 2467.
**2467.** Rev. Ebenezer Davenport of Greenwich, Ct. She m. (2), No. 2468.
**2468.** Judge Hugh White, b. Feb. 15, 1733, of Whitesborough, N. Y. They left Middletown, Ct., in 1784. Children:

2469. Daniel C⁵.
2470. Joseph.
2471. Hugh.
2472. Ansel, living in 1851 on Long Island.
2473. Philo, b. 1767, as he "d April 12, 1849, æ. 82."
2474. Rachel.
2475. Aurelia.
2476. Polly.

## 2478 = 2412. HANNAH⁴ MARSH

b. at New Hartford, Ct., baptized Oct. 16, 1746, dau. of Jonathan³ and Elizabeth (Loomis) Marsh, (John², John¹); m. No. 2478.
**2478.** Thomas Wadsworth of "Up Neck," Hartford, Ct. They lived two miles Up Neck. After Jonathan³ Marsh's death in 1783, Elizabeth (Loomis) Marsh went to Hartford and lived, until her death in 1795, 12 years with this daughter Hannah. When Thomas Wadsworth died his widow Hannah removed to Whitesborough, N. Y. and lived with her sister Lois (Marsh) White until her, Mrs. Judge White's, death in 1829, and then lived with her nephew, Dea. James Marsh of Bridgewater, N. Y. and d. there Feb. 19, 1840, æ. 93. Child :

2479. A daughter⁵, who d. æ. 17.

## 2480 = 2413. THEODOCIA⁵ MARSH

b. at New Hartford, Ct., July 13, 1747, dau. of Jonathan⁴ and Theodocia (Kellogg) Marsh, (Jonathan³, John², John¹); m. (1) Aug. 9, 1767, No. 2480.
**2480.** John Gilbert. Removed to Herkimer, N. Y. She m. (2) in 1795, Capt. Cook and resided many years in Sullivan, N. Y. and d. in Cazenovia. The children were all born at New Hartford. Children :

2481. Theodocia⁶, b. Jan. 25, 1768; m. (1) Feb. 14, 1778, Wm. Cook, 2535.
2482. Esther, b. 1770; m. Josiah Shepherd; res. Canajoharie, N.Y.
2483. Elizabeth, m. Mr. Thomas; removed to the Genesee, N. Y.
2484. Giles, resided at Deerfield, Rome and Cazenovia, N. Y.
2485. Chloe, b. about 1777 and d. at New Hartford, about 1790, æ. 13.

2486.  John, removed with parents to Herkimer, N. Y., returned to New Hartford and removed about 1800 to Clinton, N. Y.

2487.  Hiram, removed with parents to Herkimer, with stepfather to Sullivan and then to Pompey, N. Y.


2488 = 2416.  MARY[5] MARSH

b. at New Hartford, Ct., July 22, 1754, dau. of Jonathan[4] and Theodocia (Kellogg) Marsh, (Capt. Jonathan[3], John[2], John[1]); m. July 3, 1777, No. 2488.

2488.  Elijah Seymour, son of John Seymour.  Removed in 1791 or 2 to New Hartford, N. Y. thence to Marcellus and Skeneateles where he d. in 1806 and she d. in 1839, æ. 84 years, 10 months and 27 days.  The children were all born at New Hartford.  Children :

2489.  Nathaniel[6], b. March 21, 1777.

2490.  Polly, b. Sept. 23, 1778.

2491.  Elijah, b. Nov. 4, 1779.

2492.  Abigail, b. June 22, 1783.

2493.  Catherine, b. April 13, 1785.

2494.  Laura, b. May 20, 1787.

2495.  Orlando, b. April 26, 1789.

2496.  Miles, b. Feb. 4, 1793.


2497 = 2417.  JONATHAN[5] MARSH

b. at New Hartford, Ct., March 1, 1757, son of Jonathan[4] and Theodocia (Kellogg) Marsh, (Capt. Johnathan[3], John[2], John[1]) ; m. about 1779, No. 2497.

2497.  Damaris Pitkin, b. Oct. 12, 1756, dau. of Caleb and Damaris (Porter) Pitkin, and resided at New Hartford.  He was a farmer, carpenter (made the oxcarts) selectman and often representative and member of the convention in 1818 which formed the present constitution of Connecticut.  Mrs. Marsh d. Aug. 12, 1830, æ. 74. He d. at New Hartford Jan. 27, 1838, æ. 80.  Children :

2498.  Frederick[6], b. Sept. 18, 1780; m. Parnal Merrill, 2710.

2499.  Wyllys, b. Sept. 23, 1782 ; m. Rhoda Goodwin, 2716.

2500.  Lucy, b. Nov. 20, 1784; m. Chas. Bush Richards, 2724.

2501.  Electa, b. Feb. 18, 1787 ; d. July 7, 1789.

2502.  Electa, b. March 1, 1789; m. Randall Warner, 2739.

2503.  Cynthia, b. Oct. 16. 1791; resided at New Hartford and d. unm. April, 1875.

2504.  Lois, b. Oct. 28, 1792.

2505.  Jonathan, b. Oct. 18, 1795; d. Feb. 18, 1796.

2506.  Jonathan Pitkin, b. Feb. 13, 1798; m. Temperance Cleveland, 2741.

## 2507 = 2418.  ELIZABETH[5] MARSH

b. at New Hartford, Ct., Oct. 13, 1759, dau. of Jonathan[4] and Theodocia (Kellogg) Marsh, (Capt. Jonathan[3], John[2], John[1]); m. May 6, 1778, No. 2507.

**2507.**  Roger Sheldon, b. at Windsor, Ct., March, 1756. Resided at New Hartford and Pine Meadow, Ct., and removed in 1809 to Huron, Wayne Co., N. Y. She was insane in late years, but recovered and d. Sept. 25, 1845. The children were all born in New Hartford.

Children :

2508.  Amanda[6], b. July 22, 1779; m. 1798, Gen. Chauncey Humphrey of Simsbury and removed to Albany, N. Y.

2509.  Norman, b. Sept. 19, 1781; m. Mrs. Roxana (Stone) Adams, removed in 1809 to Huron, N. Y.

2510.  Wareham, b. Jan. 13, 1784; m. about 1805, (1) Honor Deming, mother of his ten children.

2511.  George, b. Sept. 12, 1786; m. Polly Cowles, had eleven children.

2512.  Grove, b. Sept. 12, 1786; d. in summer of 1800.

2513.  Elizabeth, b. April 16, 1788; m. George Roberts and had three children.

2514.  Maria, b. Feb. 22, 1780(?); m. Jonathan West.

2515.  Aralzamon, b. Feb. 4, 1793; m. Susan Parker.

2516.  Ralph, b. Oct. 25, 1795; m. Margaret Upson, had six children.

2517.  Florilla, b. April 12, 1798; m. Wm. Mudge and had two children.

2518.  Harriet, b. Dec. 6, 1801; m. John Wood and had seven children.

## 2519 = 2419.  ASHBEL[5] MARSH

b. at New Hartford, Ct., July 11, 1762, son of Jonathan[4] and Theodocia (Kellogg) Marsh, (Capt. Jonathan[3], John[2], John[1]); m. at Somers, Ct., Nov. 27, 1788, No. 2519.

**2519.** Abigail Ward, b. 1767. He built a house in 1800 on the old place, the homestead of Capt. Jonathan, the proprietor, and shaded his grounds with beautiful maples, some 24, of which most were drawn from East Mountain in a bundle tied to the yoke of his cattle. He refused 25 acres of land offered by Daniel Marsh for his oxcart. He owned two solid silver spoons made in New Hartford. He bought Daniel's place when he moved west and used the cellar stones to build the wall in front of his own grounds. He resided where he was born till he d. Nov. 19, 1815. His widow d. at New Hartford, Aug. 10, 1816. Children :

> 2520. Abigail⁶, b. Aug. 23, 1790; d. March 31, 1795.
> 2521. Esther, b. March 17, 1792 ; m. Luther Loomis, 2745.
> 2522. Chloe, b. Sept. 21, 1793; m. Samuel Hotchkiss, 2751.
> 2523. Minerva, b. March 19, 1795 ; m. Chandler Rossiter, 2769.
> 2524. Ashbel, b. Oct. 28, 1796; m. (1) Huldah Rossiter, 2770.
> 2525. George, b. April 27, 1799; m. Clarinda Barnum, 2774.
> 2526. Grove Sheldon, b. Aug. 17, 1804; m. Olive M. Perkins, 2789.
> 2527. James Ward, b. Sept. 17, 1806; alive and unm. in 1885.

## 2528 = 2420.   CYNTHIA⁵ MARSH

b. at New Hartford, Ct., April 13, 1765, dau. of Jonathan⁴ and Theodocia (Kellogg) Marsh, (Capt. Jonathan³, John², John¹) ; m. Feb. 13, 1791, No. 2528.

**2528.** Rufus Northway. Resided at New Hartford and Trenton, N. Y., and from about 1835 with her daughter, Mrs. Whiton, at Ithaca, N. Y. Mr. Northway d. there Feb. 10, and Mrs. Northway, March 3, 1840. Children :

> 2529. Aralzamon⁶, b. Oct. 7, 1793; d. Oct. 24, 1799.
> 2530. Erastus, b. May 4, 1796; d. June 1, 1800.
> 2531. Cynthia, b. at New Hartford, N. Y., Aug., 1798; m. (1) Henry K. Stockton who d. Upper Alton, Ill., in 1838. She was a matron at Monticello Seminary, Godfrey, Ill.; m. (2) John Mason of Godfrey, Ill.
> 2532. Harriet, b. at New Hartford, N. Y., Jan. 16, 1801; m. Jan. 16, 1849, Martin Lyon of Genoa, N. Y.
> 2533. Rufus, b. at Paris, N. Y., Nov. 18, 1803 ; publisher, Utica, N. Y.; m. in 1826 Elizabeth Scram, had six children.
> 2534. Sylvia, b. at Trenton, N. Y., March 9, 1807 ; m. Geo. Whiton and resided in 1887 in Ithaca, N. Y., and had five children.

## 2535 = 2481. THEODOCIA[6] GILBERT

b. at New Hartford, Ct., Jan. 25, 1768, dau. of Theodocia[5] (Marsh) Gilbert, (Jonathan[4] Marsh, Capt. Jonathan[3], John[2], John[1]); m. in 1788, No. 2535.

**2535.** Capt. William Cook. He came from Harwinton in 1786 to New Hartford, was a prominent man, representative in Connecticut legislature 1813–1818, built for its day the finest house on Town Hill, was a blacksmith and forged every nail used in building his house which he sold to New Hartford's second minister, Dr. Edward Dorr Griffin, afterwards president of Williams college. Children:

2536. Laura[7], b. July 23, 1789; m. (1) about 1810, Henry H. Newell; m. (2) Mr. Hotchkiss and d. at St. Louis, Mo., Sept. 28, 1838.

2537. Theodocia, b. Nov. 14, 1791; m. Harlow Spencer and removed to St. Louis; she was a teacher; d. at St. Louis, March 11, 1878. Children:

    2538. Sherman[8].

    2539. Julius, graduated at Amherst college in 1854.

2538. Delia, b. March 29, 1794: went as missionary to Mackinaw in 1825, afterwards as teacher to St. Louis.

2539. William, b. April 15, 1797; d. at New Hartford, Ct., Dec. 13, 1871.

2540. Chloe Gilbert, b. July 19, 1799.

2541. Calvin, b. Jan. 3, 1803; d. March 5, 1804.

2542. Calvin, b. Feb. 18, 1805; a physician; d. Sept. 26, 1841.

2543. Richard, b. Jan. 25, 1808(?); a lawyer of marked ability; d. at Toledo, O., Nov. 13, 1839.


## 2544 = 2438. DEA. JOHN[5] MARSH

b. at New Hartford, Ct., Nov. 25, 1758, son of John[4] and Lucina (Seymour) Marsh, (Capt. Jonathan[3], John[2], John[1]); m. Aug. 18, 1791, No. 2544.

**2544.** Widow Annah (Gaylord) Cale of Middletown, whose first husband was John Cale. John[5] Marsh was a soldier in the revolution, a farmer and a deacon in the Congregational church. His wife and two children were baptized June 8, 1794. They removed to Barkhamsted, Ct. and remained there till his death, Sept. 18, 1843. Children:

2544.1.   Harriet[6], b. Aug. 4, 1792; m. John George, and settled in
N. Y. State, d. childless.

2544.2.   Fanny, b. probably Aug. 4, 1792, as she and Harriet were
bap. June 8, 1794.

2544.3.   Nathaniel, b. Sept. 4, 1794; m. Mary Baldwin, 2545.

2544.4.   John Cale, b. March 14, 1796; by typhus fever was made
insane for years, and d. Aug. 9, 1838.


2545 = 2544.3.   NATHANIEL[6] MARSH


b. at New Hartford, Sept. 4, 1794, son of John[5] and Annah (Gaylord)
(Cale) Marsh, (John[4], Capt. Jonathan[3], John[2], John[1]) ; m. Nov. 8,
1829, No. 2545.

2545.   " Polly " Baldwin of Barkhamsted.   Nathaniel had moved
with his father from New Hartford to Barkhamsted.   In the war of
1812 he enlisted in a company of State troops called out for the
defence of New London.   He was a farmer, inclined to be reticent,
and of retiring manners, but very intelligent and of excellent character.   His wife d. Aug. 17, 1865.   He was a consistent member of
the First Congregational church in Winsted, Ct. to which place he
moved a short time before his death, June 28, 1870.   Children :

2545.1.   Gaylord[7], b. Sept. 12, 1830; m. S. A. Paine, 2546.

2545.2.   Mary Ann, b. May 17,1832; d. of consumption May 18, 1858.

2545.3.   James Truman, b. Jan. 12, 1834; d. of consumption in
Hartford retreat, May 17, 1865.

2545.4.   Susan Martha, b. July 19, 1835; has spent her life in very
successful teaching.   Several years in Ct., several in
Mass., and now in South Carolina.

2545.5.   Julina, twin, b. Aug. 20,1839; m. Nov. 24, 1859, Warren A.
Doolittle, and d. of consumption July 28, 1866, leaving
young children : 1, Winthrop[8]; 2, Agnes, adopted by her
aunt Susan ; 3, Charles, adopted by Robert Holcomb.

2545.6.   Twin, b. and d. Aug. 20, 1839.

2545.7.   Emily, b. March 21, 1841; lives in East Northfield.

2545.8.   Ellen, b. Dec. 15, 1842; lives in Winsted.


2546 = 2545.1.   GAYLORD[7] MARSH


b. at New Hartford, Ct., Sept. 12, 1830, son of Nathaniel[6] and Polly
(Baldwin) Marsh, (John[5], John[4], Capt. Jonathan[3], John[2], John[1]) ; a

piano-tuner and violin-maker of considerable repute; m. May 14, 1862, No. 2546.

**2546.** Susan Amanda Paine. In 1863 Gaylord enlisted in the 19th regiment of Connecticut volunteers; but he was sent home as unfit for military duty. In 1864 he enlisted in the 3d U. S. regiment artillery band and served three years. He has resided for the greater part of his married life in Winsted, Ct. Children:

2546.1. Winona Louise[8], b. Feb. 8, 1869.
2547. Gaylord Allen, b. June 8, 1882.


2548 = 2441. DEA. JAMES[5] MARSH

b. at New Hartford, Ct., June 1, 1767, son of John[4] and Sarah (Nash) Marsh, (Capt. Jonathan[3], John[2], John[1]); m. about 1794, No. 2548.

**2548.** Elizabeth Case. Removed with his father before 1800 to Bridgewater, N. Y., where he d. 1854. Children:

2549. Hiram[6], b. Jan. 15, 1795; m. Laura S. Stanley, 2560.
2550. Sylvester, b. Oct. 16, 1796; d. in childhood.
2551. Harlow, b. June 25, 1798; d. about 1850; no children.
2552. James, b. March 14, 1801; m. Eliza Allen, 2572.
2553. Eliza, b. April 16, 1803; d. 1826. No children.
2554. John Lindley, b. Oct. 2, 1805; m. Caroline Benham; he d. in 1885. Child:
 2555. Henry L[7]., resides at Fairburg, Ill.
2556. Lucia, b. Nov. 8, 1808; m. Jeremiah Knight, 2576.
2557. Luke E., b. Oct. 20, 1810; m. Sophia Turner, 2582.
2558. Sarah, b. July 28, 1812; m. E. S. Payne, had three children, all d. y. Resides at Brooklyn, N. Y.
2559. Lois W., b. June 30, 1815; d. unm.


2560 = 2549. REV. HIRAM[6] MARSH

b. probably at New Hartford, Ct., Jan. 15, 1795, son of Dea. James[5] and Elizabeth (Case) Marsh, (John[4], Capt. Jonathan[3], John[2], John[1]); m. No. 2560.

**2560.** Laura S. Stanley. He was a merchant in Cassville, N. Y., removed in 1837 to Galesburg, Ill., became Principal of Primary Department of Knox college, when about 45 was ordained and served the American Home Missionary society in Wisconsin about 20 years, was very successful, having a revival in each of the seven or eight churches where he labored.   A few years before death he said to his oldest son, " I believe my personal labors as a layman were blessed in the conversion of as many souls as were my more extended opportunities in the ministry."   He d. in 1874.   Children:

2561.  L. Milton[7], b. May 8, 1820; m. Julia E. Fairchild, 2565.
2562.  Hiram Stanley, b. Aug., 1825; deacon of the church at Fond du Lac, Wis.
2563.  James Dwight, b. Aug., 1827 : d. March 19, 1854, æ. 26 years, 6 months and 28 days.
2564.  Edward Payson, b. Aug. 17, 1833 ; m. Mary Parker, 2568.


2565 = 2561.   SECRETARY L. MILTON[7] MARSH

b. at Oneida Co., N. Y., May 8, 1820, and the family removed to Galesburg, Ill. in 1837.   He was son of Rev. Hiram[6] and Laura (Stanley) Marsh, (Dea. James[5], John[4], Capt. Jonathan[3], John[2], John[1]) ; m. at Mineral Point, Wis., Feb. 10, 1849, No. 2565.

**2565.**  Julia E. Fairchild, b. at Pitcher, N. Y., Sept. 6, 1831, dau. of Lemuel and Celia (Thatcher) Fairchild.   He was in business in Wisconsin until nearly 40, then entered upon the missionary work of the American Sunday School Union in 1859.   He labored seven years in Wisconsin, then in Massachusetts, Wisconsin, Iowa and Kansas, organizing between 400 and 500 schools and gathering nearly 20,000 members.   He visited New England annually for 25 years, securing for the American Sunday School Union tens of thousands of dollars.   He was for a time acting secretary of missions in Philadelphia and in May, 1883 was made secretary in New York, remaining in that important position until his death April 4, 1892, æ. 71 years, 10 months and 26 days.   Children:

2566.  Julia E[8]., b. at Sheboygan Falls, Wis., June 6, 1850; m. Edward Payson Atkinson at St. Louis, Oct. 31, 1876. Children:
2566.1.  Julia Pearl[9], b. Nov. 15, 1877.
2566.2.  Daisy, b. Jan. 4, 1880.
2567.  Charles L., b. at Milwaukee, Wis., June 25, 1862 ; m. June 25, 1891, Mary Trumbull Harwood of New Haven, Ct., who d. March 21, 1892.

## 2568 = 2564. EDWARD PAYSON⁷ MARSH

son of Rev. Hiram⁶ and Laura (Stanley) Marsh, (James⁵, John⁴, Capt. Jonathan³, John², John¹); m. at Vinland, Wis., April 9, 1857, No. 2568.

**2568.** Mary Parker, b. at Thurman, N. Y., July 27, 1834. In business in Neenah, Wis. Active in church and Sunday school work. The children were all born in Neenah. Children:

2568.1. Carrie Helen⁸, b. Jan. 2, 1859; d. Sept. 27, 1865.
2569. Mary Helen, b. July 17, 1866; m. Sept. 7, 1892, William Bristol Shaw, b. at Ripon, Wis., Aug. 4, 1863 and resides at 24 Elk St., Albany, N. Y. Address New York State Library.
2570. Henry Edward, b. Feb. 12, 1871.
2571. Charles Neal, b. Oct. 15, 1874.


## 2572 = 2552. JAMES⁶ MARSH

b. March 14, 1801, son of Dea. James⁵ and Elizabeth (Case) Marsh, (John⁴, Capt. Jonathan³, John², John¹); m. No. 2572.

**2572.** Eliza Allen. They had several children. Children:

2573. ——.
2574. ——.
2575. Rev. Charles E⁷., pastor at Lawn Ridge, Ill.


## 2576 = 2556. LUCIA⁶ MARSH

b. Nov. 8, 1808, dau. of Dea. James⁵ and Elizabeth (Case) Marsh, (John⁴, Capt. Jonathan³, John², John¹); m. No. 2576.

**2576.** Jeremiah Knight. Children:

2577. Arthur⁷, physician, Sauquoit, Oneida Co., N. Y.
2578. Robert, resides at Carbondale, Kansas.
2579. A daughter, m. —— Miller, a Methodist Episcopal clergy-man, Kansas.
2580. Mary, m. —— Thatcher. Teacher in N. Y. state.
2581. Fanny, m. Charles Thomas, Cassville, N. Y.

## 2582 = 2557. LUKE E⁶. MARSH

b. Oct. 20, 1810, son of Dea. James⁵ and Elizabeth (Case) Marsh,
(John⁴, Capt. Jonathan³, John², John¹); m. in 1839, No. 2582.
**2582.** Sophia C. Turner, b. in 1817. Children:

2583. Albert S⁷., b. Dec. 22, 1845; d. Jan. 2, 1857.
2584. William C., b. Dec. 11, 1853; resides at Bridgewater, N. Y.


### 2585 = 2447. JOB⁵ MARSH

b. at New Hartford, Ct., May 12, 1755, son of Job⁴ and either
Lydia (Church) Marsh or Jemima Marsh, (Capt. Jonathan³, John²,
John¹); was a soldier in the revolutionary war and m. in 1781,
No. 2585.
**2585.** Salome Beach of Goshen, b. June 16, 1763. They lived
at the south of Lake Wonksunkmunk, "off in the lots." He d.
April 20, 1835, æ. 80, nearly. His widow d. Jan. 7, 1842, æ. nearly
79. Children:

2586. Patty⁶, b. Sept. 21, 1783; d. May 13, 1835.
2587. Candace, b. Oct. 4, 1787; m. Elizur Bissell, 2594.
2588. Miles, b. April 23, 1791; m. Lydia Scovill, 2601.
2589. Ebenezer, b. June 4, 1794; m. Clarissa Spencer, 2611.
2590. Elisha, b. March 21, 1798; m. Ruth Allen, 2650.
2591. Eliza, b. July 30, 1800; unm. and lived for over 50 years in
    the family of Erastus L. De Forest at Watertown, Ct.
    Accumulated some $8,000 or $10,000. She d. Nov.
    23, 1888.
2592. Hiram, b. Nov. 13, 1803; ⎰ m. Rachel Brown, 2656.
2593. Hila, b. Nov. 13, 1803; ⎱ m. Jesse Hotchkiss, 2659.


### 2594 = 2587.   CANDACE⁶ MARSH

b. at New Hartford, Ct., Oct. 4, 1787, dau. of Job⁵ and Salome
(Beach) Marsh, (Job⁴, Capt. Jonathan³, John², John¹); m. May 25,
1806, No. 2594.
**2594.** Elizur Bissell, who d. March 31, 1838. Children:

2594.1. Marcus⁷, b. June 13, 1807; d. June, 1859.
2595. Fidelia, b. March 28, 1812.

2596. Lucius, b. Jan. 17, 1815; d. Aug. 10, 1817.
2597. Sophia, b. Aug. 12, 1818; d. March 8, 1862.
2598. Frederick, b. June 24, 1821.
2599. Byron, b. June 19, 1824.
2600. Ellen, b. 1827.

## 2601 = 2588.  MILES[6] MARSH

b. at New Hartford, Ct., April 23, 1791, son of Job[5] and Salome (Beach) Marsh, (Job[4], Capt. Jonathan[3], John[2], John[1]); m. (1) Jan. 18, 1820, No. 2601.

**2601.** Lydia Scovill, b. Sept. 10, 1799, who d. Sept. 1, 1825. He m. (2) April 3, 1827, No. 2602.

**2602.** Esther A. Watson, b. March 29, 1796. He d. March 7, 1863 and she d. March 30, 1874. Children:

2603. Julia Ann[7], b. Sept. 12, 1822; m. Fred. Woodruff, 2618.
2604. Lydia Scovill, b. June 16, 1825; m. April 8, 1875, Harvey G. Rogers, and resides in Windsor, Ct.
By second wife.
2605. Fannie Eliza, b. Oct. 31, 1830; m. John R. Smith, 2625.
2606. Emeline Florilla, b. Sept. 16, 1832; m. Charles Adkins, 2627.
2607. Miles Watson, b. Sept. 28, 1834; d. Jan. 27, 1863.
2608. Elvira Esther, b. Nov. 23, 1836; m. Thomas T. Wilsdon, 2635.
2609. Fidelia Beach, b. Dec. 19, 1838; m. Giles A. Messenger, 2639.
2610. Ansel Cornelius, b. Dec. 19, 1841; d. Sept. 24, 1848.

## 2611 = 2589.  EBENEZER[6] MARSH

b. at New Hartford, Ct., June 4, 1794, son of Job[5] Marsh, (Job[4], Capt. Jonathan[3], John[2], John[1]); m. in 1814, No. 2611.

**2611.** Clarissa Spencer, b. Nov., 1784. He d. Jan. 17, 1839. She d. Nov. 26, 1875. Children:

2612. Sabrina[7], b. April 30, 1816; d. Sept. 19, 1845.
2613. Henry, b. April 18, 1818; resides at New Hartford, Ct.
2614. Adeline C., b. Oct. 9, 1821; m. Frederick Woodruff, 2618.
2615. Eunice, b. Aug. 11, 1824; m. Allyn Goodwin. She d. July 29, 1841. Child:
2616. Stanley[8], b. July 14, 1841; d. Jan. 25, 1842.
2617. Maria, b. March 31, 1828; d. Sept., 1829.

## 2618 = 2614. ADELINE C[7]. MARSH

b. Oct. 9, 1821, dau. of Ebenezer[6] and Clarissa (Spencer) Marsh, (Job[5], Job[4], Capt. Jonathan[3], John[2], John[1]); m. No. 2618. **2618.** Frederick Woodruff. She d. April, 1852 and he m. (2) March 23, 1853, Julia Ann[7] Marsh, No. 2603, b. Sept. 12, 1822, dau. of Miles[6] Marsh, son of Job[5], Job[4], Capt. Jonathan[3], John[2], John[1]. Children :

2619. Emerson[8], d. y.
2620. John Frederick, b. July 9, 1842; m. Jan. 7, 1877, Mary D. Roraback, b. March 7, 1847.
2621. Stanley Riley, b. April 13, 1845 ; m. Emilie Manning, b. Sept. 21, 1851.
2622. Alfred Henry, b. May 5, 1847 ; m. Feb. 16, 1873, Mary A. Hine, b. Feb. 16, 1849. Child :
2623. Frederick Alfred[9], b. March 7, 1876.
2624. Lena Adeline, b. Nov. 7, 1863.


## 2625 = 2605. FANNIE ELIZA[7] MARSH

b. Oct. 31, 1830, dau. of Miles[6] and Esther (Watson) Marsh, (Job[5], Job[4], Capt. Jonathan[3], John[2], John[1]); m. Jan. 31, 1869, No. 2625. **2625.** John R. Smith. Resides at Spring Hill, Iowa. Child :

2626. Marshal W[8]., b. Feb. 9, 1872.


## 2627 = 2606. EMELINE FLORILLA[7] MARSH

b. Sept. 16, 1832, dau. of Miles[6] and Esther (Watson) Marsh, (Job[5], Job[4], Capt. Jonathan[3], John[2], John[1]); m. June 6, 1854, No. 2627. **2627.** Charles Adkins, b. July 31, 1818, who d. Jan. 18, 1882. Resided at Reynolds Bridge, Ct. Children :

2628. Eliza Jane[8], b. Oct. 4, 1855 ; d. Jan. 17, 1882.
2629. Bertha Emeline, b. Feb. 13, 1861 ; resides at Reynolds Bridge. Of invaluable aid in this genealogy.
2630. Alice Marsh, b. Feb. 20, 1863 ; } resides at Reynolds Bridge.
2631. Agnes Weed, b. Feb. 20, 1863 ; } d. July 26, 1864.
2632. Henry Miles, b. May 7, 1865 ; resides at Reynolds Bridge.
2633. Frederick Mason, b. Feb. 6, 1867. }
2634. Fanny Amanda, b. Feb. 6, 1867; } d. July 10, 1868.

2635 = 2608. ELVIRA ESTHER[7] MARSH

b. Nov. 23, 1836, dau. of Miles and Esther (Watson) Marsh, (Job[5], Job[4], Capt. Jonathan[3], John[2], John[1]); m. June 15, 1857, No. 2635.
  **2635.** Thomas T. Wilsdon, b. Nov., 1834. She d. March 27, 1858. He resides in Bristol, Ct. Child:

  2636. Elvira Marsh[8], b. March 9, 1858; m. Matthew Peebles; resides at Winnipeg, Manitoba. Children:
    2637. Talbot F[9].
    2838. Arthur W.


2639 = 2609. FIDELIA BEACH[7] MARSH

b. Dec. 19, 1838, dau. of Miles[6] and Esther (Watson) Marsh, (Job[5], Job[4], Capt. Jonathan[3], John[2], John[1]); m. June 15, 1857, No. 2639.
  **2639.** Giles A. Messenger, b. Jan. 14, 1835. Resides at Bakersville, Ct. Children:

  2640. Gilbert Lothrop[8], b. Sept. 17, 1858.
  2641. Arthur Williston, b. Dec. 3, 1860.
  2642. Lilla Annie, b. Feb. 27, 1864. }
  2643. Lizzie Emeline, b. Feb. 27, 1864; } d. April, 1864.
  2644. Carrie Fidelia, b. Sept. 2, 1865.
  2645. Mary Esther, b. April 8, 1869.
  2646. Jennie Adeline, b. Aug. 24, 1871.
  2647. Ida Louisa, b. July 22, 1875; d. Nov., 1875.
  2648. Julia Isabelle, b. Oct. 20, 1878.
  2649. Stella Elvira, b. Aug. 18, 1883; d. Oct. 15, 1883.


2650 = 2590. ELISHA[6] MARSH

b. at New Hartford, Ct., March 21, 1798, son of Job[5] Marsh, (Job[4], Capt. Jonathan[3], John[2], John[1]); m. 1823, No. 2650.
  **2650.** Ruth Allen, b. Nov. 29, 1796. He d. Aug. 15, 1874. She resided at Burrsville and d. Aug. 23, 1889. Children:

  2651. Hila J[7]., b. July 6, 1825; d. March 5, 1873.
  2652. Bradley L., b. March 12, 1832; m. Sarah Ellen Roberts who d. Aug. 10.
  2653. Maria L., b. Dec. 13, 1833; resides at Burrville, Ct.
  2654. Levi B., b. May 2, 1836; resides at Burrville, Ct.
  2655. Elisha A., b. June 29, 1839; m. and resides at Bakersville, Ct.

## 2656 = 2592.  HIRAM[6] MARSH

b. at New Haven, Ct., Nov. 13, 1803, son of Job[5] and Salome (Beach) Marsh, (Job[4], Capt. Jonathan[3], John[2], John[1]); m. 1836, No. 2656.

**2656.** Rachel Brown, b. Feb. 10, 1814. He d. Dec. 27, 1890, and she d. Jan. 8, 1891, both in Ohio.  Children :

2657. Louisa[6], b. Dec. 23, 1837.
2658. Almira, b. Aug. 10, 1840.

## 2659 = 2593.  HILA[6] MARSH

b. New Hartford, Ct., Nov. 13, 1803, dau. of Job[5] and Salome (Beach) Marsh, (Job[4], Capt. Jonathan[3], John[2], John[1]); m. Oct. 9, 1828, No. 2659.

**2659.** Jesse Hotchkiss, b. Oct. 5, 1804.  She d. June 30, 1884, and he Jan. 13, 1885.  Children :

2660. Candace S[7]., b. May 18, 1829; m. and resides at Harwinton, Ct.
2661. Martha L., b. Feb. 6, 1831 ; m. and resides at Harwinton, Ct.
2662. Eliza M., b. Jan. 9, 1833; m. and resides at Harwinton, Ct.
2663. Albert J., b. Nov. 30, 1834; m. and resides at Middletown, Ct.
2664. Hila A., b. March 25, 1837 ; d. Sept. 15, 1858.
2665. Harriet E., b. March 3, 1840; m and resides in Michigan.
2666. Ruth E., b. Aug. 29, 1842 ; resides at Harwinton.
2667. Elmer J., b. March 26, 1845; m. and resides in Harwinton.
2668. Mary J., b. March 11, 1847 ; m. and resides in Kansas.
2669. Ermina C., b. Dec. 24, 1851 ; resides at Harwinton.

## 2670 = 2450.  ROSWELL[5] MARSH

b. at New Hartford, Ct., baptized July 15, 1761, son of Job[4] Marsh, (Capt. Jonathan[3], John[2], John[1]); resided at New Hartford in the house where he was born, built by his father; m. Jan. 18, 1789, No. 2670.

**2670.** Anna Crow, b. about 1768, as she d. Jan. 6, 1828, æ. 59. His home was near the fine sheet of water in the northwestern part of New Hartford, a mile and a half long and a half mile wide whose thick groves "are the most pleasant resort imaginable." An old cider mill stood near the house and there, his only son, when very young, was drowned in a tub of apple juice. Roswell Marsh d. Sept. 26, 1843, said to be 83. Children :

2671. Anna⁶, b. Aug. 28, 1789, "d. Oct. 30, 1882, æ. 93;" m. Norman Merrill, 2679.
2672. Pelatiah, b. Oct., 1793, drowned Nov., 1797.
2673. Maria, b. Nov. 18, 1798; m. Ira Seymour, son of Chauncey Seymour.
2674. Fannie, b. May 1, 1801 ; m. Truman Kellogg of New Hartford, Ct.
2675. Sabrina, b. Nov., 1806; m. James Franklin Henderson. She d. Aug., 1849.


2676 = 2451.   LUCRETIA⁵ MARSH

b. at New Hartford, Ct., baptized March 18, 1764, dau. of Job⁴ Marsh, (Capt. Jonathan³, John², John¹) ; m. No. 2676.

2676. Solomon Churchill. Went to Newington, Hartford Co. Children :

2677. Nancy⁶, b. 1795; m. Leonard C. Hubbard and "July 20, 1887, in Berlin, Ct., living, 92 years of age " therefore b. 1795. She died in 1892 æ. 97.
2678. Jemima, b. 1806 ; living in Berlin, 1887, æ. 81, therefore b. 1806, unm. Jemima is now, Sept. 3, 1894, living, 89 years of age.


2679 = 2671.   ANNA⁶ MARSH

b. at New Hartford, Ct., Aug. 28, 1789, dau. of Roswell⁵ and Anna (Crow) Marsh, (Job⁴, Capt. Jonathan³, John², John¹) ; m. No. 2679.

2679. Capt. Norman Merrill, who was long a selectman and held other town offices of New Hartford, commanded a company of horse and served several years in the legislature. He built a "fine looking farmhouse" about 1815 where they lived until May, 1846 and nine of their eleven children were born there. He then exchanged with his son Roswell Marsh Merrill for the house which had been built by

Job[4] Marsh his wife's grandfather, where his wife and her father Roswell[5] had been born. He made much money by contracting to build roads and dams and bridges. He d. May 4, 1861. His widow d. Oct. 30, 1882, æ. 93, in the house where she was born near Lake Wonksunkmunk. Children:

2680.  R. Marsh[7], m. Frances Turner. Children: 1, Oliver[8]; 2, Horace F.; 3, Belle.
2681.  Fayette, m. Emily Atwood of New Hartford; d. y.
2682.  Frederick, m. Elizabeth Holcomb; son d. y.
2683.  Norman B., m. Elizabeth Jerome, dau. of Rev. Amasa Jerome. Children: 1, Frank[8]; 2, Mary; 3, Edward; 4, Charles.
2684.  Augustus, m. Adeline Wooding. Children: 1, Addie[8]; 2, Grace.
2685.  Josiah, d. unm. in railroad accident.
2686.  Henry J., m. —— Tucker, dau. of Nelson Tucker; had six children, three died of diphtheria in Jan., 1876.
2687.  Candace, m. Gordon W. Henderson. Their only son William G. d. in the war.
2688.  Frank, d. unm.
2689.  Anna, m. Shubael Henderson; d. April 27, 1882, æ. 63.
2690.  Catharine, b. 1834; unm.


### 2691 = 2458.   ANNA[5] MARSH

b. at New Hartford, Ct., baptized April 18, 1762, dau. of Moses[4] and Sarah (Merrill) Marsh, (Càpt. Jonathan[3], John[2], John[1]); m. July 11, 1782, No. 2691.

**2691.**  Allyn Goodwin of Hartford, Ct., b. Dec. 26, 1756, son of William and Margaret (Cook) Goodwin, who was born and always resided in Hartford. He d. May 21 or 25, 1825 and she d. Dec. 30, 1826. Children:

2692.  Elizabeth[6], b. Feb. 16, 1783; d. Sept. 15, 1784.
2693.  Anna, b. Aug. 28, 1784.
2694.  Horace, b. Sept. 11, 1787; silversmith; Major 1858–1862, of the famous Putnam Phalanx. He was over six feet tall, very erect, of commanding presence and a highly esteemed citizen.
2695.  Elizabeth, b. Nov. 2, 1792.
2696.  Allyn, b. Aug. 5, 1797.
2697.  Nabby, b. June 2, 1802; d. Feb. 5, 1803.

*Frederick Marsh*

## 2698 = 2459. AMY[5] MARSH

b. at New Hartford. Ct., April 20, and baptized April 21, 1765, dau. of Moses[4] and Sarah (Merrill) Marsh, (Capt. Jonathan[3], John[2], John[1]); m. Nov. 27, 1788, No. 2698.

**2698.** Eli Seymour of West Hartford, b. Nov. 1, 2761, son of Elisha and Abigail (Sedgwick) Seymour. He served in Col. Wyllis' regiment from 1780 to the end of the war. Was of guard on the trial of Maj. Andre and guarded him to the place of execution. A Quaker in later years. Amy d. in Jan., 1805. He m, (2) Widow Salome Sexton and she had three children. Children of Amy (Marsh) Seymour :

2699. Elisha[6], b. Nov. 14, 1790; d. at West Hartford, Dec. 5, 1790.
2700. Abigail, b. Jan. 27, 1792 ; m. ——— Wilson; d. March 26, 1882, Palmyra, N. Y.
2701. Elisha, b. April 27, 1794; d. in Aug., 1805.
2702. George, b. June 5, 1796; d. Jan. 3, 1871 ; resided at Milford, Mich.
2703. Isaac, b. Dec. 26, 1798; m. Lydia and had one son. Killed by the fall of a house in a whirlwind, Gloversville, N. Y., June 5, 1828.

## 2704 = 2463. LOIS[5] MARSH

baptized April 11, 1773 at New Hartford, Ct., dau. of Moses[4] and Sarah (Merrill) Marsh, (Capt. Jonathan[3], John[2], John[1]) ; m. 2704.

**2704.** John Seymour, b. at West Hartford, Ct., Jan. 29, 1774, son of John and Lydia (Wadsworth) Seymour. Their children were all born in West Hartford and all baptized there Sept. 20, 1805. They removed to Black River, Turin, N. Y. in 1817. Children :

2705. Jeremiah[6].
2706. Orsamus, d. in Wethersfield in Nov., 1815, æ. 18.
2707. John Jason, resides in Adrian, Mich.
2708. Horace Colton, d. at Turin, N. Y., Jan., 1824, æ. 22.
2709. Lois, m. ——— Reade.

## 2710 = 2498. REV. FREDERICK[6] MARSH

b. at New Hartford, Ct., Sept. 18, 1780, son of Jonathan[5] and Damaris (Pitkin) Marsh, (Jonathan[4], Capt. Jonathan[3], John[2], John[1]) ; after "the great revival in Yale college" in 1801 he joined the college church in 1802 and graduated in 1805. He studied in the Theological school of Rev. Asahel Hooker of Goshen, settled in 1809 over the church in Winchester, Ct. and remained their pastor 42 years, he owned the homestead 64 years. He m. at New Hartford, May 22, 1809, No. 2710.

**2710.** Parnal Merrill, b. New Hartford, Aug. 7, 1782, dau. of Josiah and Lydia (Flower) Merrill. She d. æ. 77, March 11, 1860. Rev. Frederick[6] Marsh was trustee of East Windsor and Hartford Theological seminary for 30 years, 1836–66. He d. Feb. 6, 1873, æ. 92 years, 4 months and 19 days.

This venerable and holy man became deeply interested in the history and genealogy of the families of his town and region. More than 40 years ago, at his request, the present historian of our family sent to the Rev. Frederick Marsh a list of 270 descendants of Judge Perez Marsh of Berkshire Co., Mass. In an address by Judge George Marsh Carrington before the Marsh family association upon the New Hartford branch, Aug. 3, 1887, in his own words "to lift a corner of the veil woven by the years" the Judge closes with this well deserved tribute :

" These notes would be seriously lacking if they contained no reference to one, great grandson to Capt. Jonathan, who, as he approached 70 years and laid aside active duties, spent much time and effort in preserving the statistics and history of his own family and other New Hartford matters, subjects of his early recollections. Few men of any name leave behind them three good sized manuscript volumes of family and local history. The idea was largely new forty years ago, but he grasped the importance of it. One is struck with the deep religious tone pervading these records. To him " the one thing needful " was no myth. He measured men by the importance in which they held it. No man had a better right. For 64 years he went in and out before his people, in sickness and health, in sunshine and in shadow, a sympathetic, true minister of the gospel of Jesus Christ. He did not chafe at the righteous requirements of God, he did not belittle his profession or himself by unbecoming conduct therein nor did he try to let down the high standard of the King of Kings. He did have an intense longing for the salvation of every one he knew, for he knew that without personal faith in Jesus Christ they were *lost*. He had a keen and lively interest in current events, all of which he referred to the hand of God working among men for the best and highest good of all. He was profoundly conscious that he was an imperfect man, but when his friend of 40 years, the senior Fellow of the corporation of Yale college, stood over his body the best words he could find were " Behold an Israelite indeed in whom there is no guile." With small experience but with some observation of what riches, position and honor can do for a man, beyond any and all of them do I prize the inheritance, though poorly developed, which I derive from the character and the simple goodness of my revered grandfather, Frederick Marsh." Children :

2710.1.  Louisa Merrill[7], b. May 16, 1810, at Winchester, Ct.; a teacher and d. there May 9, 1831.

2710.2.  Catherine, b. April 3, 1812 ; m. Rev. George Carrington, 2711.

2710.3.  Jonathan Pitkin, b. April 26, 1814 ; m. Paulina Bowditch, 2712.

2710.4.  Frederick Edward, b. Dec. 30, 1816; m. Matilda G. Marsh, 2713.

2710.5.  Sarah Ann, b. Dec. 29, 1819, at Winchester, Ct.; d. Sept. 26, 1823, at New Hartford, Ct.

2710.6.  Joseph Merrill, b. Sept. 15, 1823; m. C. G. Eggleston, 2714.

2710.7.  Howard Pitkin, b. April 12, 1826 ; m. H. E. Hotchkiss, 2715.

2710.8.  Henry Flower, b. April 12, 1826; m. E. S. Frissell, 2715.2.


2711 = 2710.2.  CATHERINE[7] MARSH

b. at Winchester, Ct., April 13, 1812, dau. of Rev. Frederick[6] and Parnal (Merrill) Marsh, (Jonathan[5], Jonathan[4], Capt. Jonathan[3], John[2], John[1]) ; m. at Winchester, Ct., June 17, 1835, No. 2711.

2711.  Rev. George Carrington, b. at North Canaan, Ct., June 28, 1796, son of James and Huldah (Ford) Carrington. He graduated at Yale college in 1822, New Haven Theological seminary in 1825, was ordained and installed pastor of North Goshen, Ct., Congregational church, Aug. 27, 1829, dismissed Sept. 24, 1833, installed junior pastor, Hadlyme Congregational church, Feb. 25, 1835, dismissed Feb. 22, 1842, and removed to Illinois April, 1843, and d. at Rushville, Schuyler Co., Ill., Oct. 31, 1843. Catherine (Marsh) Carrington returned home to her father in Winchester and resided there for 30 years and then from 1874 lived with her eldest son at West Winsted, Ct., until her death Feb. 10, 1883. Children :

2711.1.  George Marsh[8], b. at Hadlyme, Ct., April 11, 1836. He
has become Judge George Marsh Carrington, having
lived in Colebrook, Ct., from 1845-1853, fitted for college
at East Windsor Hill, Ct., and graduated at Williams
college in 1861; there health failed and after various
experiments he settled at West Winsted, Ct., 1870, as
local insurance agent. He m. at West Hartford, Ct.,
April 26, 1865, Julia Purple Mitchell, b. at Chatham, Ct.,
March 21, 1837, dau. of Levi and Sally Chamberlain
(Johnson) Mitchell, who graduated at Mt. Holyoke
seminary in 1861. He was appointed in 1886 by the
Ct. legislsture member for the 4th congressional district
of the state board of education. He was elected judge
of probate for the district of Winchester from April,
1887 to 1895. Adopted child, William George, b. at
Hartford, Ct., Aug. 2, 1879.

2711.2.  Edward Frederick, b. at Hadlyme, Dec. 25, 1837; enlisted
private, 19th Connecticut volunteers, 1862, became Regiment Quartermaster Sergeant, discharged 1865 in July,
after 1867 mainly in clock business in New York and
Chicago; m. at Lewiston, Ill., Aug. 4, 1873, Mrs. Martha
Jane (Grier) Goodman. No children.

2711.3.  Louisa Merrill, b. at Hadlyme, June 30, 1840, lived with
her mother in Winchester till 1874, then in West Winsted, Ct. Librarian of Beardsley library.


2712 = 2710.3.   JONATHAN PITKIN[7] MARSH

b. at Winchester, Ct., April 26, 1814, son of Rev. Frederick[6] and
Parnal (Merrill) Marsh, (Jonathan[5], Jonathan[4], Capt. Jonathan[3], John[2],
John[1]); became (at 23 months) deaf and dumb, was educated at the
Hartford asylum and left in 1832; m. at Douglas, Mass., Jan. 24,
1840, No. 2712.

2712.  Pauline Bowdish, b. at Douglas, March 24, 1817, deaf and
dumb from birth, dau. of Nathaniel and Paulina (Buffam) Bowdish.
He is a cabinet maker and has resided in Hartford, New York, Willimantic and Boston and in Thomaston and Bristol, Ct. He has
been a public religious teacher of the deaf and dumb.   Children :

2712.1.  Catherine Bowdish[8], b. at Willimantic, Ct., Aug. 14, 1842;
graduated at the American asylum for deaf and dumb;
m. Boston, Mass., March 26, 1867, Adam Acheson,
deaf and dumb son of George and Elizabeth (Bella)

Acheson, b. at Slane, Ireland, Meath Co., Dec. 13, 1832. Children all mutes :

  1. Pauline Marsh[9], b. at Boston, Oct. 31, 1867.
  2. Eugene Adam, b. at Chicago, Aug. 12, 1869.
  3. Julia Grace, b. at Roslindale, Mass., Oct. 13, 1872 ; d. there Feb. 21, 1873.
  4. Washington Dutee, b. at Roslindale, Feb. 22, 1874.
  5. Kate Louise, b. at Roslindale, Jan. 8, 1876.
  6. Gertrude Annie, b. at Roslindale, Oct. 2, 1883.

2712.2. Pauline Merrill, b. at Willimantic, May 21, 1845 ; graduated at the American asylum for mutes; m. at Boston, Aug. 9, 1866, Edwin Nathans Bowes, mute, b. at Pottsville, Pa., March 19, 1836, son of John Rodolph and Sophia Louise (Nathans) Bowes. Children all can hear :

  1. Edwin Jonathan[9], b. at Boston, Aug. 14, 1867 ; m.
  2. John Rodolph, b. at Chicago, Feb. 4, 1870; m.
  3. Frederick Marsh, b. at Roslindale, Jan. 16, 1873.
  4. Louise Edith, b. at Roslindale, Aug. 25, 1877.

2712.3. Jonathan Frederick, b. at Willimantic, Ct., May 15, 1849 ; d. a pupil at the American asylum, July 3, 1864.


## 2713 = 2710.4. FREDERICK EDWARD[7] MARSH

b. at Winchester, Ct., Dec. 30, 1816, son of Rev. Frederick[6] and Parnal (Merrill) Marsh, (Jonathan[5], Jonathan[4], Capt. Jonathan[3], John[2], John[1]) ; m. (1) at Brooklyn, L. I., Jan. 2, 1844, his first cousin, No. 2713.

**2713.** Matilda (Goodwin[7]) Marsh, b. at North Hartford, May 10, 1820, No. 2721, dau. of Wyllis[6] and Rhoda (Goodwin) Marsh, (Jonathan[5], Jonathan[4], Capt. Jonathan[3], John[2], John[1]). She d. at New Harford, Jan. 5, 1860. He m. (2) at New Hartford, May 8, 1862, Mrs. Eliza Ann (Loomis) Spencer, widow of John Spencer and dau. of Abijah and Margaret (Barrett) Loomis, b. at New Hartford, Dec. 24, 1815. He lives in New Hartford. Farmer. Children :

2713.1. Edward Wolcott[8], b. at New Hartford June 17, 1845 ; resides at Hartford, a plumber; m. at Hartford, Nov. 7, 1872, Addie, b. Oct. 31, 1845, at Hartford, dau. of Alexander and Amanda (Crane) Thompson. Children :

  1. Frank Thompson[9], b. at Hartford, Jan. 6, 1874.
  2. Mary Ida, b. at Hartford, May 3, 1875.
  3. Edena Louisa, b. at Hartford, Feb. 26, 1877.

2713.2.  Myron Goodwin[8], b. at New Hartford, Ct., May 26, 1847 ; m.
at Windsor, Ct., April 25, 1877, Carrie Burt Clapp, dau.
of Spencer and Drusilla M. (Thrall) Clapp, b. at Windsor, Sept. 10, 1856.  He is clerk in Hartford and resides
in Windsor.  Children :

 1.  Arthur Myron[9], b. at Hartford, Feb. 8, 1880.
 2.  Anna Edwards, b. at Windsor, Nov. 14, 1883.
 3.  Ethel Emma, b. at Windsor, Aug. 29, 1888.

2713.3.  Frederick Wyllys, b. at New Hartford, Nov. 3, 1853 ; m.
at West Winsted, Ct., April 24, 1878, Rebecca Elizabeth,
dau. of Charles Wilmot and Mary Ann (Cole) Richards,
b. at Birmingham, Eng., Sept. 3, 1854.  He resides at
Winsted, a plumber.  Superintendent of the Baptist
Sunday school.  Children:

 1.  Howard Frederic[9], b. at Windsor, June 15, 1879 ;
  d. there April 12, 1884.
 2.  Clifford Loomis, b. at Winsted, Oct. 19, 1880.
 3.  Elizabeth Matilda, b. at Winsted, March 16, 1885.

2714 = 2710.6.  JOSEPH MERRILL[7] MARSH

b. at Winchester, Ct., Sept. 15, 1823, son of Rev. Frederick[6] and
Parnal (Merrill) Marsh, (Jonathan[5], Jonathan[4], Capt. Jonathan[3], John[2],
John[1]) ; m. at Winchester, May 5, 1848, No. 2714.

2714.  Candace Gilbert Eggleston, b. at Winchester, May 5, 1827,
dau. of Benjamin and Sophia (Atkins) Eggleston of Torrington, Ct.
He enlisted Aug. 7, 1862, private Co. F, 19 Connecticut volunteers,
dismissed for disability Feb. 16, 1863.  Farmer in New Hartford and
Winchester, representative in Connecticut general assembly 1871,
was on collation committee at centennial of the town about 1871 ;
removed May, 1878 to Neosho, Mo., and d. there Jan. 27, 1879.
Buried at Winchester.  Children :

 2714.1.  Joseph Frederick[8], b. at New Hartford, Ct., Feb. 7, 1852 ;
  m. (1) at Winchester, Nov. 26, 1874, Cornelia F. Johnson,
  b. at Morris, Ct., July 9, 1851, dau. of William and Cornelia Ann (Loomis) Johnson.  She d. at Washington,
  Ct., Dec. 31, 1882.  He m. (2) at Winchester, Aug. 12,
  1885, her sister Martha Johnson.  Children:

   1.  Grace Parnal[9], b. at Winchester, Sept., 1877.
   2.  Jonathan, b. at Washington, Ct., Dec. 26, 1882.
   3.  Cornelia Elizabeth, b. Colebrook, Ct., July
    26, 1887.

4. Katherine Candace, b. at Colebrook, Ct., April 9, 1889.

2714.2. Henry Floyd, b. at New Hartford, Dec. 11, 1853; m. Colebrook, Ct., Oct. 14, 1880, Eunice Elizabeth Sage, dau. of Hiram and Lucy (Judd) Sage, b. at Colebrook, 1851. Children :

    1. Bessie Eunice[9], b. at Winchester, June 27, 1881.

    2. Howard Sage, b. Sept. 8, 1885.

2714.3. Ellen Candace, b. at New Hartford, March 2, 1856; m. at Hartford, June 2, 1879, Lemuel Hurlbut, b. Baltimore, Md., Dec. 1, 1850, son of Samuel and Elizabeth (Goddard) Hurlbut. He d. Winchester, Aug. 10, 1888. Children :

    1. Lemuel[9], b. at Hartford, Ct., April 11, 1882; d. at Washington, Ct., Aug. 4, 1883.

    2. Ruth, b. at Winchester, Feb. 4, 1886.

2714.4. Parnal Sophia, b. at New Hartford, Aug. 8, 1858; d. there Feb. 14, 1859.

2714.5. Sylvia Jane, b. at New Hartford, June 18, 1860; graduated at the Connecticut normal school, New Britain, Ct.; m. at Winchester, Nov. 9, 1892, Leonard S. Whitcomb of Cornwall, Ct., b. Aug. 7, 1825.

2714.6. Mary Louisa, b. at Winchester 1868; graduated at the Hartford hospital for trained nurses, 1892; resides at Hartford, Ct.


## 2715 = 2710.7. HOWARD PITKIN[7] MARSH

b. at Winchester, Ct., April 12, 1826, twin, son of Rev. Frederick[6] and Parnal (Merrill) Marsh, (Jonathan[5], Jonathan[4], Capt. Jonathan[3], John[2], John[1]) ; m. at New Haven, Ct., June 10, 1856, No. 2715.

**2715.** Harriette E. Hotchkiss, b. New Haven, May 18, 1828, dau. of John B. and Harriet (Stevens) Hotchkiss. He was manufacturer's agent and merchant; d. at New Hartford, Feb. 4, 1864, buried in Winchester. Child :

    2715.1. Harriette Parnal[8], b. at New Hartford, Feb. 13, 1861; teacher in New Haven public schools.


## 2715.2. =2710.8. HENRY FLOWER[7] MARSH

b. at Winchester, Ct., April 12, 1826, twin, son of Rev. Frederick and Parnal (Merrill) Marsh ; m. at South Amenia, N. Y., June 11, 1855, No. 2715.2.

**2715.2.** Elizabeth Sarah Frissell, b. at Peru, Mass., Dec. 10, 1826, youngest dau. of Amasa and Zeviah (Pierce) Frissell of Peru. She d. in New York, Aug. 24, 1870 and he d. in that city, Aug. 17, 1888. Both were buried in South Amenia, N. Y. He was a mechanic and for many years an officer in the 13th St. Presbyterian church. No children.

### 2716 = 2499.  WYLLYS[e] MARSH

b. at New Hartford, Sept. 23, 1782, son of Jonathan[5] and Damaris (Pitkin) Marsh, (Jonathan[4], Capt. Jonathan[3], John[2], John[1]); m. (1) Dec. 23, 1807, No. 2716.

**2716.** Rhoda Goodwin, baptized Aug. 18, 1782, dau. of Jonathan and Esther (Benham) Goodwin, all of New Hartford, and lived on his place there for many years. His wife d. June 26, 1823. He married (2) Harriet (Gilbert) Munson and d. March 26, 1867, æ. 84. Children:

2717.  Archibald[7], b. at New Hartford, Sept. 24, 1808; m. at Canton, Ct., Nov. 18, 1834, Lydia Ann Church, b. at Montville, Ct., Sept. 6, 1815, dau. of Prentice and Prudence Church of Montville. She d. at Salisbury, Ct., Aug. 8, 1851, and he m. (2) at Plainville, Ct., May 6, 1853, Delia Richards, b. at New Haven, Ct., May 13, 1821, dau. of Russell and Sarah (Olmsted) Richards of Plainville, Ct. He d. at Plymouth, Ct., Feb. 17, 1870, childless and she d. some ten or more years afterward.

2718.  Wolcott, b. June 5, 1810; m. Mary G. Munson, 2723.1.

2719.  Wyllys Goodwin, b. at New Hartford, Jan. 19, 1814; m. Oct., 1837, Eunice Banning. He d. March 22, 1838. No child.

2720.  Henry, b. March 4, 1817; d. at New Hartford, unm., June 5, 1843.

2721.  Matilda Goodwin, b. at New Hartford, May 10, 1820; m. F. E. Marsh, 2713.

By second wife.

2722.  Rhoda, b. at New Hartford, Oct. 28, 1824; m. James D. Lyman, 2723.10.

2723.  Nelson Gilbert, b. at New Hartford; m. Oct. 23, 1828, Louisa M. Strong, 2723.12.

## 2723.1 = 2719. WOLCOTT[7] MARSH

b. at New Hartford, Ct., June 5, 1810, son of Wyllys[6] and Rhoda (Goodwin) Marsh, (Jonathan[5], Jonathan[4], Capt. Jonathan[3], John[2], John[1]); graduated at Amherst college in 1835 ; m. at New Hartford, Aug. 13, 1837, No. 2723.1.

**2723.1.** Mary Gilbert Munson, b. at Barkhamsted, Ct., dau. of Horace Dwight and Harriet (Gilbert) Munson. Mrs. Munson became the second wife of Wolcott Marsh's father. He taught school in New Brunswick, N. J. and Brooklyn, N. Y. She d. at Brooklyn, Sept., 1839 and he m. (2) at the house of his uncle F. Marsh, at Winchester, Ct., May 5, 1843, No. 2723.2.

**2723.2.** Sylvia Sadd, b. at New Hartford, Feb. 28, 1814, dau. of Harvey and Lydia (Merrill) Sadd, then of North Hartford, and niece of Mrs. F. Marsh. He d. at New Hartford, Oct. 9, 1845 and she m. (2) June, 1855, Calvin R. Strong of Kankakee, Ill., and afterwards (3) Abner Bates of Syracuse, N. Y. where she died. Children :

2723.3. Wolcott Pascal[8], b. at Brooklyn, N. Y., March 15, 1839; m. Anna C. Thompson, 2723.5.

By second wife.

2723.4. Mary Louise, b. at Brooklyn; d. at Oberlin, Ohio, June 11, 1858, æ. 13, and was buried at Austinburg.

## 2723.5 = 2723.3. WOLCOTT P[8]. MARSH

b. at Brooklyn, N. Y., March 15, 1839, son of Wolcott[7] and Mary Gilbert (Munson) Marsh, (Wyllys[6], Jonathan[5], Jonathan[4], Capt. Jonathan[3], John[2], John[1]); enlisted April 17, 1861, Co. A, 1st Connecticut Infantry Vols., three months; m. May 7, 1861, No. 2723.5.

**2723.5.** Anna Cecelia Thompson, dau. of Alexander and Amanda (Crane) Thompson of Hartford, b. at Hartford, Dec. 19, 1841 ; he participated in Bull Run battle ; appointed Oct., 1861, 2d Lieut. Co. A, 8th Connecticut volunteers, whence he was promoted to 1st Lieut. and Capt. Co. F, participating in the attacks on Roanoke Island and New Berne, N. C. and in battles of South Mountain, Antietam and Fredericksburg. He resigned Dec. 19, 1862 on account of ill health, became a farmer in Simsbury and Bloomfield, Ct., a clerk in Hartford, a boot and shoe dealer in Springfield, Mass.; removed to Ontario,

Cal., about 1890, where he resided on a farm and d. in the summer of 1894. Children :

2723.6.   Wolcott H[9]., b. at Simsbury, Ct., Sept. 19, 1863.
2723.7.   Annie Matilda, b. at Bloomfield, Ct., July 27, 1865; m. at Hartford,Ct., Oct. 19, 1887, Leslie Upson McClure, b. at Hartford, Nov., 1862, son of David and Lucy (Upson) McClure. Child: 1. Marion[10], b. at Hartford, Aug. 15, 1888.
2723.8.   Mary Munson, b. at Hartford, Ct., Oct. 31, 1866; m. Sept. 17, 1890, George Britton Harding, clerk, son of Daniel and Charlotte (Matthews) Harding, b. Aug. 8, 1863. Child : 1. Helen[10], b. at Ontario, Cal., June 12, 1891.
2723.9.   Frank Thompson, b. Sept. 10, 1868; d. March 5, 1870.


2723.10 = 2722.   RHODA[7] MARSH

b. at New Hartford, Ct., Oct. 28, 1824, dau. of Wyllys[6] and Harriet Gilbert (Munson) Marsh, (Jonathan[5], Jonathan[4], Capt. Jonathan[3], John[2], John[1]); m. at New Hartford, Nov. 24, 1853, No. 2723.10.
2723.10.   James Daniel Lyman, b. at New Hartford, Oct. 23, 1823, youngest son of Daniel and Jerusha (Merrill) Lyman of New Hartford. She d. there Dec. 16, 1856 and he m. (2) Eliza Stone of Cornwall. Children :

2723.11.   Henry Marsh[8], b. at New Hartford, Aug. 17, 1855; m. there March 29, 1882, Anna E. Crowley, b. at Tolland, Mass., June 24, 1856, dau. of Cornelius and Mary (Reardon) Crowley. He lives in Avon, Ct., a farmer. Children :
   1.  Alice Rhoda[9], b. at New Hartford, July 17, 1883.
   2.  Clarence H., b. at Hartford, Jan. 4, 1887.
   3.  Raymond H., b. at Simsbury, Ct., May 5, 1891.


2723.12 = 2723.   NELSON GILBERT[7] MARSH

b. at New Hartford, Ct., Oct. 23, 1828, son of Wyllys[6] and Harriet Gilbert (Munson) Marsh, (Jonathan[5], Jonathan[4], Capt. Jonathan[3], John[2], John[1]); m. at New Hartford, Oct. 28, 1850, No. 2723.12.
2723.12.   Louisa M. Strong, dau. of Thomas and Harriet (Geer) Strong of New Hartford. She d. there April 11, 1858 and he m. (2) at New Hartford, Nov. 19, 1858, No. 2723.13.

**2723.13.** Mary Cratty, b. at New Britain, Ct., May 3, 1837.
Both are dead. He d. at New Hartford, March 20, 1867. Children :·

2723.14. Frank[8], b. at New Hartford, Jan. 1, 1853, d. y.

By second wife.

2723.15. Walter John, b. at New Hartford, Aug. 3, 1860; m. at New Haven, Ct., Sept. 19, 1886, Lillia Mabel Babcock, b. at New Haven, March 5, 1861, dau. of Albert Lewis and Mary Ann (Fullerton) Babcock. Children :

1. Vera[9], b. at New Haven, June 20, 1889.
2. George Albert, b. at Santa Maria, Cal. Aug. 21, 1892.

2723.16. George Edward, b. at New Hartford, July 11, 1862; m. at New Haven, Ct., Sept. 5, 1889, Frances Palmer Wooster, b. at Goshen, Ct., Oct. 7, 1869, dau. of Henry Sterling and Anna Elizabeth (Palmer) Wooster. No· children.

## 2724 = 2500. LUCY[6] MARSH

b. at New Hartford, Ct., Nov. 20, 1784, dau. of Jonathan[5] and Damaris (Pitkin) Marsh, (Jonathan[4], Capt. Jonathan[3], John[2], John[1]) ; united with the church in 1805 ; m. Feb. 23, 1807, No. 2724.

**2724.** Dea. Charles Buck Richards son of Aaron and Lydia Richards, b. Feb. 6, 1780. Charles B. Richards and his wife, Lucy M., settled about half a mile south of his father's homestead, on a portion of his father's extensive tract of land, and afterward built a brick house on the corner of the road leading to North Canton. He united with the First Congregational church in 1802. They changed their relation to the Second or North church, Dec. 25, 1808, of which church he was deacon for several years. The First church was situated on Town Hill, the Second at New Hartford, north village, much nearer their home. Lucy Marsh Richards died Aug, 19, 1857. Deacon Charles B. Richards died at New Hartford in 1869. They were the parents of ten children, who were " all members of the church." Children :

2725. Cornelia[7], b. April 25, 1808.
2726. Lucy Adams, b. May 2, 1810; m. Wilson B. Sprague, 2735.
2727. Frederick, b. June 16, 1812 ; m. (1) Jane A. Hills; (2) Sarah J. Pettee.
2728. James, b. Jan. 26, 1815 ; d. Jan. 5, 1816.

2729.  Electa, b. Dec. 6, 1817; m. Sanford Olmsted; resides at Georgetown, O.
2730.  James Marsh, b. May 11, 1819; m. (1) Elizabeth; (2) N. S. Olcott of Sandisfield, Mass.
2731.  John, b. July 5, 1822; m. Kate L. Cady, 2738.1.
2732.  Mary Elizabeth, b. Aug. 14, 1825; m. Rev. Isaac Devoe, Mechanicsville, N. Y.
2733.  Selah, b. Feb. 9, 1827; d. March 20, 1827.
2734.  Julia, b. May 2, 1830; m. Aug., 1871, Horace Knight.


2735 = 2726.   LUCY ADAMS⁷ RICHARDS

b. at New Hartford, Ct., May 2, 1810, dau. of Lucy⁶ (Marsh) Richards, (Jonathan⁵ Marsh, Jonathan⁴, Capt. Jonathan³, John², John¹); m. Oct. 19, 1831, No. 2735.
   2735.  Wilson B. Sprague or Spring.   Children:
      2736.  Frederick C⁸., b. Sept. 7, 1836.
      2737.  Jane E., b. Oct. 1, 1838.
      2738.  Mary A., b. June 3, 1845; d. June, 1848.


2738.1 = 2731.   DEA. JOHN⁷ RICHARDS

b. at New Hartford, July 5, 1822, was the third and youngest son of Deacon Charles B. Richards and his wife Lucy Marsh, (Jonathan⁵, Jonathan⁴, Capt. Jonathan³, John², John¹), representing two of the old and promint families of the town since its early days.   He was a graduate of Williams college and was educated for the ministry, but was never settled over a parish, returning after leaving college to his paternal farm, which was his life-long home.   He was for many years one of the school visitors of the town.   He represented New Hartford in the general assembly of 1878, and was an influential member of the Congregational church, of which he was deacon at the time of his death, which occurred Jan. 3, 1892 ; his age was 69 years. He was universally respected as a man of strict integrity and unassuming Christian worth.   John Richards m. Dec. 23, 1863, No. 2738.1.
   2738.1.  Catherine Cady.   She is still living in 1894.   They had no children.

### 2739 = 2502. ELECTA[6] MARSH

b. at New Hartford, Ct., March 1, 1789, dau. of Jonathan[5] and Damaris (Pitkin) Marsh, (Jonathan[4], Capt. Jonathan[3], John[2], John[1]) ; m. No. 2739.

**2739.** Randall Warner, b. at Plymouth, Ct., Sept. 20, 1781, son of John and Anna (Sutliff) Warner. He d. at Plymouth, Nov. 25, 1853 and she d. Feb. 13, 1865. Child:

> 2740. ——.

### 2741 = 2506. JONATHAN PITKIN[6] MARSH

b. Feb. 13, 1798 at New Hartford, Ct., son of Jonathan[5] and Damaris (Pitkin) Marsh, (Jonathan[4] Capt. Johnathan[3], John[2], John[1]) ; m. at Canton, Ct., Nov. 14, 1832, No. 2741.

**2741.** Temperance Cleveland, b. June 2, 1802, dau. of Johnson and Sylvia Cleveland. "He was town clerk, a prominent man, well remembered by many now (1883) living." He d. Dec. 4, 1837 and she May 4, 1862. His widow Temperance Marsh in 1850 built a new house and used the old house for a barn. Child:

> 2742. Elizabeth[7], m. R. Gaylord Steele and d. Feb. 28, 1865. She was "an accomplished woman." Children :
>> 2743. Arthur G[8].
>> 2744. Vara E.

### 2745 = 2521. ESTHER[6] MARSH

b. at New Hartford, Ct., March 17, 1792, dau. of Ashbel[5] and Abigail (Ward) Marsh, (Jonathan[4], Capt. Jonathan[3], John[2], John[1]) ; m. No. 2745.

**2745.** Luther Loomis. He bought in 1820 of Roswell Marsh a house nearly opposite the church on Town Hill, but in 1844 built the house, since his death occupied by his wife's brother Grove S. Marsh. Mr. Loomis d. Oct. 26, 1867. His wife resided at New Britain, Ct. and d. March 28, 1883, in her 92d year. Children :

> 2746. Eliza[7], m. Cornelius D. Loomis.
> 2747. Mary Ann, m. Elizur Brown.

2748.  Caroline, m. Harvey Loomis, brother of C. D. Loomis.
2749.  Esther, m. Dea. Jason C. Keach.
2750.  Sarah, after her sister's death m. C. D. Loomis.


2751 = 2522.   CHLOE[6] MARSH

b. at New Hartford, Sept. 21, 1793, dau. of Ashbel[5] and Abigail
(Ward) Marsh, (Jonathan[4], Capt. Jonathan[3], John[2], John[1]) ; m. May
29, 1814, No. 2751.
**2751.**  Samuel Hotchkiss of Burlington, Ct.   He d. at New Hartford, Ct., Jan. 6, 1859.   She d. at Collinsville, Ct., Jan. 15, 1886, æ.
92 years and 3 months.   Children :

2752.  Eliza Ann[7], b. April 19, 1815 ; d. June 14, 1817.
2753.  Abigail, b. Nov. 2, 1816 ; m. March 15, 1842, Selden Millard
        of West Hartford, Ct.; removed to Eureka, Cal.   He
        d. at Arcata, Cal., May 16, 1883.
2754.  Willard, b. Aug. 15, 1818 ; m. July 23, 1843, Sarah Cromack.
        2761.1.
2755.  Wolcott, b. July 17, 1820 ; d. Dec. 7, 1839.
2756.  Correll Upson, b. July 16, 1822 ; m. April 14, 1850, Laura M.
        Boyden, who d. at New Hartford, May 20, 1858.
2757.  Eliza Ann, b. May 29, 1824 ; m. May 27, 1846, Francis N.
        Holley of Torrington.   She d. May 15, 1866.   He d.
        1878, both at Torrington.
2758.  Minerva Rossiter, b. June 3, 1826 ; m. Nelson G. Hinckley,
        2763.
2759.  Robert, b. June 9, 1828 ; d. Oct. 29, 1848, at New Hartford.
2760.  Harriet Maria, b. May 28, 1830 ; d. at Collinsville, Ct., Jan.
        24, 1874.
2761.  George, b. Feb. 26, 1833 ; removed to Arcata, Cal.
2762.  Eugene, b. June 1, 1839 ; d. Sept. 21, 1845.


2762.1 = 2754.   WILLARD[7] HOTCHKISS

b. at New Hartford, Ct., Aug. 15, 1818, son of Samuel and Chloe[6]
(Marsh) Hotchkiss, (Ashbel[5], Jonathan[4], Capt. Jonathan[3], John[2],
John[1]) ; m. July 23, 1843, No. 2762.1.
**2762.1.**  Sarah Cromack.   He d. May 19, 1868, at Pine Meadow,
Ct.   Children :

2762.2. Mary[8], m. Bentley Frazier and had a dau[9]. who m. Geo. Wilcox of New Hartford and they had son Frazier Bentley[10].

2762.3. Isabella Alice, m. W. Scott Gould, and had sons:
    1. Harry Hotchkiss[9], d.
    2. Willard Joseph of Plantsville.

2762.4. Alfred, m. Ellen Thayer of Collinsville. Children:
    1. Nellie W[9].
    2. Edward.

2762.5. Minerva, m. Wm. Robinson of Collinsville.

2762.6. Jennie L., m. Goodsell Codaire of Collinsville. Children:
    1. Bessie H[9].
    2. Minnie.
    3. Alfred.
    4. George, who d.

2762.7. Willard E., m. Belle Willson, resided at Burlington, Ct.; Children:
    1. Willard[9].
    2. Harry.

## 2763 = 2758. MINERVA ROSSITER[7] HOTCHKISS

b. at New Hartford, June 3, 1826, dau. of Chloe[6] (Marsh) Hotchkiss, (Jonathan[5], Jonathan[4], Capt. Jonathan[3], John[2], John[1]); m. Sept. 19, 1849, No. 2763.

**2763.** Nelson G. Hinckley of Hartford, Ct. Children:
    2764. Howard Nelson[8], b. at Hartford, Ct., Sept. 28, 1850 and m. Nov. 2, 1871, Belle Eliza Slate. Children:
        2765. Hattie Rossiter[9], b. at Hartford, May 19, 1874.
        2766. Clara Belle, b. at Hartford, Sept. 17, 1879.
        2767. Robert Horace, b. at Chicago, March 28, 1882.
        2768. Lena Howard, b. at Hartford, Dec. 29, 1885.
        2768.1. Samuel Dwight, b. at Hartford, May 13, 1888; d. Jan. 23, 1891.

## 2769 = 2523. MINERVA[6] MARSH

b. at New Hartford, Ct., March 19, 1795, dau. of Ashbel[5] and Abigail (Ward) Marsh, (Jonathan[4], Capt. Jonathan[3], John[2], John[1]); m. No. 2769.

**2769.** Chandler Rossiter. She d. Oct. 14, 1825, æ. 30.

16

### 2770 = 2524.  ASHBEL[6] MARSH

b. at New Hartford, Ct., Oct. 28, 1796, son of Ashbel[5] and Abigail
(Ward) Marsh, (Jonathan[4], Capt. Jonathan[3], John[2], John[1]) ; m. (1)
No, 2770.

**2770.** Huldah Rossiter, and m. (2) No. 2771.
**2771.** Laura Kellogg.  He d. in 1884, æ. 88.  Children :

    2772.  Lucius[7], m. ——.  Children:
      2772.1.  Allen Bradley, veterinary surgeon; residence at Mt.
           Vernon, N. Y.
      2772.2.  James.
      2772.3.  Henry.
      2772.4.  Charles.
      2772.5.  Lucius.
      2772.6.  John.
    2773.  Allen.

### 2774 = 2525.  GEORGE[6] MARSH

b. at New Hartford, Ct., April 27, 1799, son of Ashbel[5] and Abigail
(Ward) Marsh, (Jonathan[4], Capt. Jonathan[3], John[2], John[1]) ; resided
at New Hartford and Killingworth, Ct.; m. in 1837, No. 2774.

**2774.** Clarinda M. Barnum, b. 1813 ; d. 1882, æ. 69.  He d. in
Killingworth, Dec. 20, 1879, æ. 80.  Children :

    2775.  Helen M[7]., b. 1838; d. in 1869.
    2776.  George B., b. 1840; d. in the army 1863.
    2777.  Anna E., b. 1842 ; m. Alfred A. Williams, 2781.
    2778.  Henry C., b. 1844 ; m. Sarah E. Stevens, 2785.
    2779.  Joseph J., b. 1848; m. Emma E. Metcalf, 2786.
    2780.  Frankendell E., b. 1852 ; d. 1871.

### 2781 = 2777.  ANNA E[7].  MARSH

b. in 1842, dau. of George[6] and Clarinda (Barnum) Marsh, (Jonathan[5],
Jonathan[4], Capt. Jonathan[3], John[2], John[1]) ; m. in 1883, No. 2781.

**2781,** Alfred A. Williams, b. 1833 and d. May, 1889 ?  Children :

    2782.  Clara E[8]., b. 1874 ; d. 1875.
    2783.  Charles F., b. 1878.
    2784.  Herbert A., b. 1880.

## 2785 = 2778. HENRY C[7]. MARSH

b. in 1844, son of George[6] and Clarinda (Barnum) Marsh, (Ashbel[5], Jonathan[4], Capt. Jonathan[3], John[2], John[1]) ; m. No. 2785.

**2785.** Sarah E. Stevens, b. 1851. He enlisted in 1861 and served through the war ; is now postmaster at Killingworth, Ct.

## 2786 = 2779. JOSEPH J[7]. MARSH

b. in 1848, son of George[6] and Clarinda (Barnum) Marsh, (Ashbel[5], Jonathan[4], Capt. Jonathan[3], John[2], John[1]) ; m. in 1878, No. 2786.
**2786.** Emma E. Metcalf, b. 1861. Children':

2787. Norah J[8]., b. 1880 ; d. 1881.
2788. Ira P., b. 1883.

## 2789 = 2526. GROVE SHELDON[6] MARSH

b. at New Hartford, Ct., Aug. 17, 1803, son of Ashbel[5] and Abigail (Ward) Marsh, (Jonathan[4], Capt. Jonathan[3], John[2], John[1]) ; m. Sept. 25, 1836, No. 2789.
**2789.** Olive M. Perkins, b. at Becket, Mass., Feb. 16, 1804, dau. of Asa Perkins. He appears to have been an enterprising man, buying and building. One purchase was a " Sabbath Day House" which he devoted to the manufacture of leather. He built a sawmill on East Brook in 1842. He d. May 18, 1885, æ. nearly 81. Children :

2790. Edward P[7]., b. Sept. 20, 1837 ; d. 1845.
2791. Angeline Clarissa, b. June 4, 1840; living in New Hartford.
2791.1. Laura Minerva, b. Oct. 11, 1843 ; m. April 30, 1867, James H. Ryder ; she d. March 13, 1872.

# BRANCH II. THE HATFIELD BRANCH.

### DESCENDANTS OF SAMUEL[2] MARSH THE SECOND SON.

### 2821 = 5.   SAMUEL[2] MARSH

b. at Hartford, Ct., about 1645, son of John[1] Marsh and Anne (Webster) Marsh, dau. of Gov. and Agnes Webster, when 15 or 16 removed in 1660 to Hadley, Mass., with his parents. His mother died in June, 1662 and his father m. Widow Lyman in Oct., 1664, his older brother John[2] m. Sarah Lyman in 1666 and removed soon to Hartford. Samuel[2], m. May 6, 1667, No. 2821.

**2821.** Mary Allison. He made his home just across the Connecticut river, north, in what was then Hadley but soon became Hatfield. He was a weaver. A loom made by him of wood cut in Hatfield, kept in care of Ebenezer[3], Ephraim[4], Samuel[5], extorts this confession from Zebina[6]: "This loom, although I am sorry to say it, I cut up for fire wood in the town of Montague, Mass., about one and one-half or two miles west of Lake Pleasant." Became freeman in 1690, was selectman 1695, 1697, 1700, and 1705 ; and in 1706 was made representative to Massachusetts legislature ; was also in 1706 selectman and made deacon and was selectman 1708, 1709, 1711 and 1713. Mary (Allison) Marsh d. Oct. 13, 1726, æ. 78. The deacon followed her Sept. 7, 1728, æ. 83. Children :

2822.   Mary[3], b. Feb. 27, 1668 ; d. y.
2823.   Samuel, b. Feb. 11, 1670 ; m. 2834.
2824.   John, b. Nov. 6, 1672 ; m. prob. ? Mary, 2837.
2825.   Rachel, b. Oct. 15, 1674 ; m. John Wells, 2839.
2826.   Grace, b. Jan. 7, 1677 ; m. Thomas Goodman, 2848.

2827. Mary, b. May 24, 1678; m. Joseph Morton, 2856.·
2828. Thomas, b. Jan. 10, 1680; m. Mary Trumbull, 2865.
2829. Hannah, b. Sept. 18, 1681; m. Richard Billings, 2875.
2830. Elizabeth, b. July 31, 1683; m. Oct. 27, 1714, Maynard Day of Hartford, Ct. No children.
2831. Ruth, b. June 16, 1685; prob.? the Ruth Marsh who m. Wm. Cadwell of Hartford, Ct., Oct. 31, 1711.
2832. Ebenezer, b. May 1, 1687; m. Elizabeth Gillett, 2880.
2833. Sarah, mentioned in her father's will on record at Northampton, Mass.

2834 = 2823.  SAMUEL³ MARSH

b. Feb. 11, 1670, probably in Hadley, perhaps in Hatfield, son of Samuel² and Mary (Allison) Marsh, (John¹); resided at Hatfield, Mass., and m. No. 2834.

2834. ——. He was selectman in 1704 and 1705. Did he have?

2835. William, who m. 1720, Rebecca Nash b. at Hatfield, April 20, 1699; d. May 12, 1768, æ. 69.
2836. Who was Col. Seth Marsh of Hatfield, 1783?

2837 = 2824.  JOHN³ MARSH

b. at Hatfield, Mass., Nov. 6, 1672, son of Samuel² and Mary (Allison) Marsh, (John¹); m. No. 2837.

2837. Mary ——. He resided doubtless in Sunderland, originally a part of (first Hadley and then) Hatfield, and is, we think, the one referred to in Sheldon's address, 212th anniversary of the Indian attack on Hatfield. We read thus : " A petition to the General Court gives the name of John Marsh as one of the band of fighters on the meadows. By another official list we find ' John Marsh and Sarah Dickinson, two Hatfield persons,' named among the captives." He adds, " I have looked for some romantic sequel to this unfortunate visit to Deerfield and Canada."

He is in all probability " John Marsh of Sunderland 1721," and as in Springfield court records, " John Marsh of Sunderland, 1732," who conveyed his homestead to the town in 1741 and d. Jan. 11, 1744, leaving his widow Mary Marsh.

2838 ?   Was Susannah Marsh who m. Benjamin Barrett in Sunderland, 1731, member of Sunderland church in 1738 and
dismissed as " separatist " 1753, his daughter?


2839 = 2825.  RACHEL[3] MARSH

b. at Hatfield, Mass., Oct. 15, 1674, dau. of Samuel[2] and Mary
(Allison) Marsh, (John[1]): m. about 1699, No. 2839.

**2839.**  John Wells of Hatfield, b. Sept. 15, 1670.   Children :

2840.   John[4], b. March 12, 1700; resided at Amherst and Hardwick,
Mass.; d. 1746.
2841.   Joseph, b. March 4, 1702 ; resided at Amherst and Sunderland, Mass.
2842.   Samuel, b. Nov. 19, 1704; resided at Hatfield.
2843.   Aaron, b. Sept. 2, 1707 ; d. Aug. 9, 1778, æ. 71.
2844.   Sarah, b. Jan. 21, 1710.
2845.   Jonathan, b. April 4, 1713 ; resided at Shutesbury.
2846.   Noah, b. Jan. 18, 1719 ; resided at Whately.
2847.   Abigail.  For 137 descendants of John[1] Marsh, through
Samuel[2], Rachel[3] and Noah[4] Wells, see History of
Whately, Mass.


2848 = 2826.  GRACE[3] MARSH

b. at Hatfield, Mass., Jan. 7, 1677, dau. of Samuel[2], and Mary
(Allison) Marsh, (John[1]) ; m. about 1698 ? No. 2848.

**2848.**   Thomas Goodman of Hatfield, b. Sept. 16, 1673 ; d. Oct.
5, 1748.   She d. May 28 or 29, 1756.   Children :

2849.   Mary[4], b. Nov. 15, 1699; d. unm. Jan. 3, 1769.
2850.   Thomas, b. Dec. 15, 1701.
2851.   Samuel, b. March 10, 1704; captive at Fort Massachusetts
in 1746 and d. in Canada.
2852.   Rachel, b. Oct. 1, 1706 ; m. Daniel Dickinson, June 14, 1750.
2853.   Abigail, b. July 3, 1709 ; d. unm. Jan. 24, 1795.
2854.   Elazar, b. Sept. 4, 1711.
2855.   Nathan, b. Dec. 29, 1713.


2856 = 2827.  MARY[3] MARSH

b. at Hatfield, May 24, 1678, dau. of Samuel[2] and Mary (Allison)
Marsh, (John[1]); m. about 1699?, No. 2856.

**2856.** Joseph Morton, son of Richard and Ruth Morton, b. April, 1672; d. Sept. 28, 1730; resided at Hatfield, Mass.  Children:

2857. Ruth[4], b. Dec. 15, 1699; d. Oct. 30, 1730.
2858. Elizabeth, b. April 4, 1704; m. Samuel Warner of Hatfield.
2859. Abigail, b. July 18, 1707, d. y.
2860. John.
2861. Thankful, b. May 21, 1713; m. Ephraim Allen of Hatfield.
2862. Joseph, b. Oct. 24, 1715; d. prob. about 1744, left no family.
2863. Abigail, b. Oct. 18, 1720.
2864. Mary, d. April 10, 1723.

## 2865 = 2828.  THOMAS[3] MARSH

b. at Hatfield, Mass., Jan. 10, 1680, son of Samuel[2] and Mary (Allison) Marsh, (John[1]); resided at Hatfield and Ware, Mass.  He m. 1702, No. 2865.

**2865.** Mary Trumbull of Suffield, Ct.  The family removed to Ware about 1730.  He d. 1759.  His widow, Mary Marsh of Congregational church records, d. June 27, 1765.  Children all born at Hatfield:

2866. Thomas[4], b. May 1, 1703; d. unm. 1728.
2867. Mary, b. Oct. 27, 1704; m. Moses Smith, 2892.
2868. Samuel, b. 1706; m. Zeruiah Thomas, 2895.
2869. Rachel, b. 1708.
2870. Ruth, b. Feb. 15, 1710; m. Jacob Cummings.
2871. Judah, b. July 25, 1712; m. Hannah Olmstead, 2905.
2872. Joseph, b. April 14, 1714; m. Abigail Simmons, 2917.
2873. Ephraim, b. Jan. 5, 1717; m. Sarah Olmstead, 2924.
2873.1. Daniel, b. June 12, 1719; insane.
2874. Martha, b. April 12, 1721; m. Ebenezer Marsh, 3094.

## 2875 = 2829.  HANNAH[3] MARSH

b. Sept. 18, 1681, at Hatfield, dau. of Samuel[2] and Mary (Allison) Marsh, (John[1]); m. March 18, 1703, No. 2875.

**2875.** Richard Billings of Hatfield, b. April 7, 1672.  Children:

2876. Sarah[4], b. Jan. 9, 1704; m. April 8, 1730, Samuel Gillett.

28**. Hannah, b. July 14, 1706; m. Nathan Wait, son of Jeremiah
Wait, and grandson of the hero Benjamin Waite who
rescued 19 Canada captives, see History of Hadley, pp.
184–187.
2878. Richard, b. Sept. 14, 1709; d. unm. May 26, 1780.
2879. Damaris, b. Nov. 26, 1712; m. Samuel Church.
Those who wish can find in the History of Whately, additional, 137 Wells, 118 Waits and 62 Mortons, making 317
more descendants of John[1] and Anne (Webster) Marsh
through Samuel[2] and Mary (Allison) Marsh.

## 2880 = 2832.    EBENEZER[3] MARSH

b. at Hatfield, Mass., May 1, 1687, son of Samuel[2] and Mary (Allison)
Marsh, (John[1]); m. 1707, No. 2880.
2880.    Elizabeth Gillett, probably dau. of Joseph Gillett, and b.
1689. (Joseph was b. Nov. 2, 1664 and settled in Hatfield, son of
Joseph Gillett of Simsbury, Ct. Joseph, Jr., m. (1) Nov. 3, 1687,
Esther Gull. He removed to West Hartford, Ct.) Ebenezer[3] Marsh
was one of the first settlers of Sunderland about 1714. Settled on
lot nine, after a few years sold to Dea. Isaac Hubbard. Probably
removed to Montague. He d. Sept. 9, 1747, æ. 60. Children:

2881. Elizabeth[4], b. June 4, 1710; } m. 1749, Jonathan Burt.
2882. Ebenezer, b. June 4, 1710; } d. y.
2883. Ephraim, b. June 12, 1712; d. Aug. 1, 1714.
2884. Esther, b. July 15, 1714; m. 1738, Jeduthan Sawyer; removed
to Lebanon, Ct.
2885. Ebenezer, b. about 1716; m. Martha[4] Marsh, 3094.
2886. Ephraim, b. 1718; m. Sarah Mattoon, 3193.
2887. Enos, b. Dec. 11, 1721; m. (1) Judith Hawks, 3208.
2888. Dorothy, b. 1723; m. Nathaniel Gunn, Jr.
2889. Mary, b. 1725; d. 1747, æ. 22.
2890. Thankful, b. 1728; member of Sunderland church, 1748; m·
Asahel Gunn.
2891. Hannah, b. 1733; m. Joseph Merchants.

## HATFIELD BRANCH. THE WARE LINE.

DESCENDANTS OF SAMUEL[2] AND THOMAS[3].

### 2892 = 2867.  MARY[4] MARSH

b. at Hatfield, Mass., Oct. 27, 1704, dau. of Thomas[3] and Mary (Trumbull) Marsh, (Samuel[2], John[1]); m. Nov., 1726, No. 2892.

**2892.** Moses Smith, son of Jonathan Smith, of Hatfield, b. Sept. 8, 1702. He removed to Ware and d. probably 1849, administration on his estate granted July 4, 1749. The son of Widow Mary Smith was b. in Sterling but baptised in Hardwick. Children :

2893.  Mary[5], bap. Jan. 1, 1737.
2894.  Moses? bap. April 28, 1751.  .

### 2895 = 2868.  SAMUEL[4] MARSH

b. at Hatfield, Mass., 1706, son of Thomas[3] and Mary (Trumbull) Marsh, (Samuel[2], John[1]); removed to Ware, about 1730; m. Jan. 18, 1731–2, No. 2895.

**2895.** Zeruiah Thomas, dau. of William Thomas. He d. about 1745. His widow m. (2) March 2, 1746–7, Isaac Pratt, son of John Pratt. She d. April 18, 1798. Children :

2896.  Eunice[5], b. Jan. 15, 1733; d. y.
2897.  Amos, b. Nov. 15, 1733; m. Beulah Leonard, 2932.
2898.  Mary, b. June 13, 1735; m. Jan. 31, 1754, Solomon Emmons of Quobbin. (Enfield.)
2899.  Eunice, b. Nov. 20, 1737.

2900. Patience, b. July 20, 1740 ; m. April 5, 1754, Henry Gilbert
of Brookfield.
2901. Thankful, b. Feb. 1, 1741-2. ∤
2902. Submit, b. Feb. 1, 1741-2. ∫
2903. Miriam, b. Jan. 18, 1743.
2904. Samuel, b. Feb. 18, 1744-5.

### 2905 = 2871. JUDAH⁴ MARSH

b. at Hatfield, Mass., July 25, 1712, son of Thomas³ and Mary
(Trumbull) Marsh, (Samuel², John¹) of Ware from 1730 ; m. Nov. 4,
1736, No. 2905.

**2905.** Hannah Olmstead, dau. of Capt. Jabez, who was Captain
of 10th Company 4th regiment in expedition against Louisburg
under Gen. Pepperell in 1744. He bought 500 acres in and about
Ware village. Hannah was b. April 22, 1718 and d. Oct. 20, 1793.
Judah Marsh d. May 7, 1801. He and his father's family were of
the very earliest settlers in Ware, at " Marsh Mills." Children :

2906. Elijah⁵, b. Nov. 10, 1737 ; m. March 4, 1759, Elizabeth
Demond, dau. of Dr. Edward Demond of Ware and d.
Nov. 1, 1765.
2907. Joel, b. March 31, 1739, baptized April 5 and d. y.
2908. Thomas, b. Aug. 14, 1741 ; m. Mary Thomas, 2935.
2909. Rachel, b. at Ware, July 20, 1743 ; m. (1) Silas Adams of
Brookfield ; m. (2) James Gilmore of Ware ; d. March
18, 1832.
2910. Hannah, b. March 13, 1746 ; m. (1) May 28, 1766, Joseph
Luce ; m. (2) July 4, 1769, Moses Brown, and d. Jan. 28,
1816.
2911. Thankful, b. Aug. 9, 1748 ; m. Wm. Breckenridge, 2948.
2912. Dorothy, b. May 29, 1750, bap. April 28, 1751 ; m. Dec. 22,
1768, Thomas Winslow, Jr. of Hardwick ; resided at
Ware ; d. Feb. 15, 1829, æ. 79.
2913. Jonathan, b. May 7, 1752 ; m. Anna Pepper, 2951.
2914. Mary, bap. July 7, 1754 : prob. d. y.
2915. Judah, b. May 22, 1757 ; m. Elizabeth Smith, 2953.
2916. Joel, b. July 7, 1759 ; m. Annis Smith, 2957.

### 2917 = 2872. JOSEPH⁴ MARSH

b. at Hatfield, Mass., April 14, 1714, son of Thomas³ and Mary

(Trumbull) Marsh, (Samuel², John¹) ; resided and d. at Ware, Mass.;
m. May 17, 1750, No. 2917.

2917. Abigail Simmons, dau. of Joseph Simmons and only own
sister of Col. Benjamin Simmons of Williamstown, Mass., and Bennington, Vt., Name spelt Simons and Simonds. Children :

2918. Samuel⁵, b. Jan. 22, prob. 1751, perhaps 1752; d. Feb. 20,.
1790.

2919. Joseph, b. July 10, 1753; m. Mary Wheeler, 2979.

2920. Ebenezer, b. Dec. 24, 1755; m. dau. of Mather Gray of
Warren, worked for him a whitesmith, prob. murdered..

2921. Sarah, b. June 8, 1758; m. a Pratt of Belchertown and he
murdered her.

2922. John, b. Sept. 21, 1760, brought up by Capt. John Raymond
of Hardwick ; removed to Butternut, N. Y. His name
is among the first settlers. *N. Y. Gazetteer.* Soldier
" 1780, July," described " John Marsh, æ. 19, height 5.
feet, 6 inches, fresh complexion."

2923. Benjamin, b. Dec. 27, 1764 ; removed to Genesee River, N. Y..


## 2924 = 2873. EPHRAIM⁴ MARSH

b. at Hatfield, Mass., Jan. 5, 1717, son of Thomas³ and Mary (Trum--
bull) Marsh, (Samuel², John¹) of Ware, Mass.; m. Oct. 8, 1741,
No. 2924.

2924. Sarah Olmstead, b. May 21, 1726, dau. of Capt. Jabez
Olmstead, of 10th company Massachusetts regiment, expedition
against Louisburg, 1744. Children :

2925. Noah⁵, b. Feb. 2, 1742-3, bap. April 17.
2926. Elisha, b. Dec. 19, 1743.
2927. Huldah, bap. Sept. 14, 1746.
2928. Sarah, bap. April 28, 1751.
2929. Mary, bap. Oct. 5, 1755; d. y.
2930. Mary, bap. July 8, 1759. ⎱
2931. Miriam, bap. July 8, 1759. ⎰


## 2932 = 2897. AMOS⁵ MARSH

b. at Ware, Mass., Nov. 15, 1733, son of Samuel⁴ and Zeruiah·
(Thomas) Marsh, (Thomas³, Samuel², John¹) ; m. No. 2932, published.
July 16, 1757.

2932.   Beulah Leonard of Rutland.   Children :

2933.   Samuel⁶, bap. Sept. 24, 1758.

2934.   Mercy, bap. Oct. 5, 1760.


2935 = 2908.   THOMAS⁵ MARSH


b. at Ware, Mass., Aug. 14, 1741, son of Judah⁴ and Hannah (Olmstead) Marsh, (Thomas³, Samuel², John¹) ; m. (1) June 26, 1766, No. 2935.

2935.   Mary Thomas, dau. of Widow Mary Thomas of Ware, d. about 1777–8 ; m. (2) No. 2936.

2936.   Widow Lois Thayer, Widow of Micah ; resided at Ware and Greenwich, Mass. and d. June 14, 1813.   Children:

2937.   Elijah⁶, b. April 22, 1767. }
2938.   Sarah, b. April 22, 1767 ; } m. pub. May 14, 1789, Elijah Cleveland, 2947.1.

2939.   Ephraim, b. March 19, 1771 ; m. (1) Hannah Simons, 2987.

2940.   Mary, b. March 7, 1773; m. pub. July 14, 1793, John Oaks ; resided at Hawley, Mass. and in Pennsylvania.

2941.   Lydia, b. March 10, 1775 ; m. Asa Joy of Plainfield and resided at Hawley, Mass. and Palmyra, N. Y.

2942.   Prudence, b. Feb. 19, 1777 ; m. Joseph Barnard, 3075.

By second wife.

2943.   Lois, b. June 24, 1779; m. John Gardiner of Ware.

2944.   Abigail, b. June 6, 1781 ; m. Feb. 26, 1802, Amos Hunter of Enfield.

2945.   Thomas, b. Oct. 24, 1784; m. Aug. 18, 1805, Damaris Baker of Newfane, (Vt.?) ; resided at Penfield, N. Y.

2946.   Roxana, b. Sept. 10, 1786; resided at Hawley, Mass.

2947.   Thayer, b. Jan. 24, 1791 ; m. March 29, 1812, Lucina Joslyn, dau. of Abraham Joslyn.


2947.1 = 2938.   SARAH⁶ MARSH


b. April 22, 1767, dau. of Thomas⁵ and Mary (Thomas) Marsh ; m. No. 2947.1, published May 14, 1789.

2947.1.   Elijah Cleveland of Hardwick, Mass., b. June 1, 1754. They lived at Hardwick.   He d. July 15, 1812.   She d. April 2, 1842.   Children :

2947.2.   Elijah[7], b. Oct. 17, 1790; d. Oct. 22, 1856.
2947.3.   Royal, b. March 25, 1793; d. Feb. 26, 1875.
2947.4.   Sally, b. 1795.
2947.5.   Polly, b. May 12, 1797; d. May 1, 1854.
2947.6.   Joseph, b. Aug. 17, 1800; d. May 15, 1894.
2947.7.   Calvin, b. Oct. 2, 1803; d. June 4, 1878.
2947.8.   Alvin, b. Aug. 3, 1807.
2947.9.*  Cutler, b. 1811; d. 1812.


## 2948 = 2911. THANKFUL[5] MARSH

b. at Ware, Mass., Aug. 9, 1748, dau. of Judah[4] and Hannah (Olmstead) Marsh, (Thomas[3], Samuel[2], John[1]); m. No. 2948.

**2948.** William Breckenridge, b. Sept. 19, 1723, son of William and Agnes (Sinclair) Breckenridge of Ware. Children:

    2949.   William Sinclair[6].
    2950.   Judah Marsh.


## 2951 = 2913. JONATHAN[5] MARSH

b. at Ware, Mass., May 7, 1752, son of Judah[4] and Hannah (Olmstead) Marsh, (Thomas[3] Samuel[2], John[1]); m. (1) No. 2951.

**2951.** Anna Pepper, dau. of Jacob Pepper of New Braintree, Mass. He resided at Ware; m. (2) Dec. 1, 1824, Mary (Aiken) Paige, widow of Moses Paige and b. Jan. 17, 1769. Jonathan[5] Marsh, d. Sept. 16, 1838, æ. 86. He was selectman 1796, 1797 and 1799 in Ware. Children:

    2951.1.   Jacob[6], b. about 1789; m. Abigal Howard, 3082.
    2951.2.   Jonathan.
    2951.3.   Sewell.
    2951.4.   Eunice, Mrs. James Cargill.
    2951.5.   Foster, m. Lucy Thomson, 3085.
    2952.   Sophia, Mrs. Harvey Van Tassel.


## 2953 = 2915. JUDAH[5] MARSH

b. at Ware, Mass., at " Marsh Mills," May 22, 1757, son of Judah[4] and Hannah (Olmstead) Marsh, (Thomas[3], Samuel[2], John[1]); m. (1) No. 2953.

**2953.** Elizabeth Smith, dau. of Dea. Maverick.   He m. (2) Feb. 20, 1800, No. 2954.

**2954.** Jerusha Collins, dau. of Gamaliel Collins.   He resided at Ware and was selectman there in 1795.  He d. Feb. 10, 1817. Children :

    2955.   Zenas[6], b. about 1793; m. Fanny Clifford, 3059.
    2956.   James Sullivan, b. March 1, 1807 ; m. S. E. Harwood, 2956.1.


## 2956.1. = 2956.   JAMES SULLIVAN[6] MARSH

b. at Ware, Mass., March 1, 1807, son of Judah[5] and Jerusha (Collins) Marsh, (Judah[4], Thomas[3], Samuel[2], John[1]); m. Jan. 19, 1841, No. 2956.1.

**2956.1.** Sarah E. Harwood, b. at Barre in 1819.   She d. Feb. 28, 1873.   He d. Feb. 25, 1884.   Children :

    2956.2.   George S[7]., b. at Ware, July 23, 1742 ; m. N. M. Cole, 2956.4.
    2956.3.   Nelson E., b. at Ware, Feb. 4, 1854; d. May 10, 1858.


## 2956.4 = 2956.2.   GEORGE S[7]. MARSH

b. at Ware, July 23, 1842, son of James Sullivan[6] and Sarah E. (Harwood) Marsh, (Judah[5], Judah[4], Thomas[3], Samuel[2], John[1]) ; m. Dec. 7, 1871, No. 2956.4.

**2956.4.** Nellie M. Cole, b. at Cornwall, Ct., Aug. 18, 1849.   He is a cotton carder.   Children :

    2956.5.   Hattie A[8]., b. Sept. 13, 1871.
    2956.6.   Morton L., b. Sept. 2, 1875; d. Jan. 10, 1881.
    2956.7.   Carlton D., b. June 19, 1884.


## 2957 = 2916.   JOEL[5] MARSH

b. at Ware, Mass., July 7, 1759, son of Judah[4] and Hannah (Olmstead) Marsh, (Thomas[3], Samuel[2], John[1]); m. Sept. 20, 1785, No. 2957.

**2957.** Annis Smith, b. Nov. 11, 1765, dau. of Hugh or Elihu Smith of Palmer, Mass. He resided at Ware and removed to Hardwick, about 1800 and d. April 12, 1804. Widow Annis Marsh m. (2) Oct. 18, 1807, Jonathan Warner and d. May 17, 1859, æ. nearly 94. Children:

    2958. Phila[6], b. Feb. 17, 1788; m. Martin Mandell, 2962.
    2959. Delphia, b. June 12, 1790; d. unm. of spotted fever, March 25, 1810.
    2960. Dwight, b. Aug. 19, 1793; m. Mary C. Holt, 2970.
    2961. Joel Smith, b. Oct. 21, 1803; m. Abigail D. Gleason, 2972.

## 2962 = 2958. PHILA[6] MARSH

b. at Ware, Mass., Feb. 17, 1788, dau. of Joel[5] and Annis (Smith,) Marsh, (Judah[4], Thomas[3], Samuel[2], John[1]); m. Sept. 18, 1808, No. 2962.

**2962.** Martin Mandell of Hardwick and d. Feb. 14, 1879, æ. 91. Children:

    2963. Delphia[7], b. Feb. 25, 1810; d. unm. May 19, 1832.
    2964. Elbridge, b. April 8, 1812; m. June 18, 1844, Lucy R. Paige. See History of Hardwick for five children.
    2965. Henry, b. Jan. 12, 1814; removed to Ohio.
    2966. Charles, b. Jan, 7, 1816; m. Martha Stone, for five children see History of Hardwick.
    2967. Harriet, b. Oct. 24, 1818; d. Feb. 27, 1821.
    2968. Joel Dwight, b. Nov. 6, 1820; m. (1) Mary E. Dean. See History of Hardwick for (2) wife and 6 children.
    2969. Phila, b. April 5, 1824; m. April 17, 1850, Dr. J. B. Thomas of Palmer.

## 2970 = 2960. DWIGHT[6] MARSH

b. at Ware, Mass., Aug. 19, 1793, son of Joel[5] and Annis (Smith) Marsh, (Judah[4], Thomas[3], Samuel[2], John[1]); m. Nov. 4, 1817, No. 2970.

**2970.** Mary C. Holt, dau. of Rev. Thomas Holt, and he d. Jan. 25, 1823. He had a farm on the road from Ware to Gilbertville. His widow d. April 20, 1866, æ. 68. Child:

    2971. Mary Ann[7], b. March 1, 1819; m. April 25, 1845, Joel W. Fletcher of Leominster and d. April 25, 1850.

## 2972 = 2961.   JOEL SMITH[6] MARSH

b. at Ware, Mass., Oct. 21, 1803, son of Joel[5] and Annis (Smith) Marsh, (Judah[4], Thomas[3], Samuel[2], John[1]) ; had a store on Hardwick common and is now a grocer in Springfield, Mass.; m. June 6, 1837, No. 2972.

**2972.** Abigail Drury Gleason, dau. of Josiah Gleason of New Braintree, Mass. He was the youngest of four children, all of whom are dead. His father died when he was but six months old, and with the assistance of his mother, he was educated in the public schools of Hardwick and later was sent to Leicester and Amherst, where he fitted himself for a teacher. On finishing his studies he bought a farm in his native town, and for several years taught the Hardwick schools in winter and worked on his farm during the summer. He carried on this double occupation for about nine years, when ill health caused him to change, and he entered upon a mercantile life. In 1832 he purchased a general store and carried on business there until 1852, when he sold his store and removed to Springfield, Mass., and entered into a partnership with Theodore Stearns in a store near the corner of Main and Howard streets, but a year later the firm was dissolved, Mr. Marsh carrying on the business. In 1861 he bought out the store of O. W. Sage and with the assistance of his sons, George and Charles S., conducted the two stores. On the death of his younger son, George, in 1866, the two stores were consolidated and the store removed to Sturtevant's block. The name of the firm was changed to J. S. Marsh & Co., Mr. Marsh having general oversight of the business. In 1876 the firm name was changed to J. S. Marsh & Son, and the company removed to its present quarters in Barnes block. Mr. Marsh finally gave up the active management of his business to his son. He was the father of six children, all of whom are dead, with the exception of Charles S. Marsh. He was a member of the First Congregational church, and was also a faithful worker for the success of the republican party. Mrs. Abigail Marsh d. in 1885. He d. æ. almost 90, Aug. 31, 1893 and two days later the *Springfield Graphic* published a fine likeness and said : "Joel S. Marsh, the venerable business man who died Thursday morning, has been for 90 years following a path in life that has brought him the faith and friendship of the many to whom he has catered in his forty years of merchant life in this city. He has always been a conspicuous figure in his place of business, the grocery store of J. S. Marsh & Son, until the weight of years and toil caused him to retire recently, leaving the business in the care of his son, Charles S. Marsh." Children:

2973. Joel Dwight[7], b. May 10, 1838; d. April 18, 1845.
2974. Josiah Gleason, b. June 1, 1839; d. Feb. 5, 1844.
2975. Charles Smith, b. May 15, 1842; partner with father at Springfield.
2976. Abby Maria, b. Dec. 4, 1843; d. Dec. 9, 1863.
2977. Henry Mandell, b. Sept. 15, 1845; d. June 24, 1847.
2978. George Parsons, b. Jan. 16, 1848; d. April 13, 1866.

### 2979 = 2919. JOSEPH[5] MARSH

b. at Ware, Mass., July 10, 1753, son of Joseph[4] and Abigail (Simmons) Marsh, (Thomas[3], Samuel[2], John[1]); m. No. 2979.

**2979.** Mary Wheeler, dau. of George Wheeler; resided at Concord and Greenwich and d. at New Salem, April 7, 1829. Children:

2980. Reuben[6]. b.—— 20, 1784; m. Else Howard, dau. of Barzillai Howard of Brookfield and Delia Mead of Hardwick.
2981. Sarah, b. July 8, 1787; m. May 7, 1815, Joel Hyde son of Othniel.
2982. Joseph, m. Olive Packard, N. H.
2983. William, m. Parnel Lawrence, dau. of Josiah Lawrence of Brookfield; resided at Greensborough.
2984. Moses, m. Lois Wakefield, resided at Webster.
2985. Ephraim, m. Rhoda, dau. of John Brown of Sterling and Betsey Reed of Shutesbury.
2986. Mary, d. unm. at Sterling.

### 2987 = 2939. EPHRAIM[6] MARSH

b. at Ware, Mass., March 19, 1771, son of Thomas[5] and Mary (Thomas) Marsh, (Judah[4], Thomas[3], Samuel[2], John[1]); m. (1) Aug. 2, 1795, No. 2987.

**2987.** Hannah Simons, dau. of Jotham Simons of Ware. He resided at Greenwich and Hawley. He m. (2) Widow Susannah (Towne) Leonard. He d. 1861 at the age of 90. Children:

17

2988. Proctor[7], b. 1796; d. Sept. 10, 1767, æ. 70 years and 11 months. He m. Elizabeth Polley, dau. of Asa Polley of Savoy, b. 1802, and d. Hawley, Mass., Oct. 8, 1867, æ. 67. No children.

2989. Mercy, m. Alvin Thayer, son of Asa Thayer of Plainfield; removed to Chatham, O.

2990. Ephraim, b. 1801; d. April 17, 1843, æ. 42; m. Charlotte Loomis of Springfield.

2991. Wilder, b. March 20, 1804; m. Rachel Chamberlain, dau. of Aaron of Hawley; resided at Cicero, N. Y. Child:

2992. Welcome[8], b. about 1825, went to California.

2993. Hannah, b. March 16, 1806; m. Solomon Howe, Jr., of Enfield; resided at Ware. Son:

2994. Charles[8].

By second wife.

2995. Leonard, b. May 15, 1811; m. Lois Parker, 3002.

2996. Mary, b. Feb. 14, 1813; m. Amos Crosby, 3012.

2997. Emily, b. July 12, 1814; m. Amasa Walter, 3017.

2998. Abner, b. Jan. 10, 1816; m. Loa Rice, 3021.

2999. Theodore, b. March 30, 1818; d. Oct., 1837, æ. 19 years and 6 months.

3000. Susannah, b. in Nov.; m. Mark Stacy, and resided in Belchertown. Child:

3001. Ida Julia[8], b. Aug. 31, 1849.


3002 = 2995.   LEONARD[7] MARSH

b. at Hawley, Mass., May 15, 1811, baptized at Hawley, July 28, 1811, son of Ephraim[6] and Susannah (Towne) (Leonard) Marsh, (Thomas[5], Judah[4], Thomas[3], Samuel[2], John[1]); m. Nov. 27, 1834, **3002.** Lois Parker, b. Aug. 14, 1812, dau. of Abraham Parker of Hawley, Mass., and resided at Hawley and North Amherst, Mass., d. Nov. 16, 1888, æ. 77 years, 6 months. Children:

3003. Jane Augusta[8], b. Sept. 28, 1835; m. Lorin Ball, 3026.

3004. Theodore Chapman, b. March 31, 1838; m. Ann E. Smith, 3036.

3005. Albert Engenius, b. Dec. 20, 1840; m. Ann E. Ayres, 3038.

3006. Lucretia, b. June 12, 1843; unm. resides at Amherst.

3007. Joel Wentworth, b. Jan. 20, 1845; d. Aug. 31, 1849.

3008. Monroe Proctor, b. Feb. 17, 1849; m. Gertrude E. Field, 3042.

3009. William Ingram, b. Jan. 26, 1852; m. Flora Willis, 3044.

3010. Twin son, b. Jan. 26, 1852; d. Jan. 29.

3011. Achsah, b. Feb. 17, 1855; d. April 17, 1859.

## 3012 = 2996. MARY[7] MARSH

b. at Hawley, Feb. 14, 1813, baptized at Hawley, April 18, 1813, dau. of Ephraim[6] and Susannah Marsh, (Thomas[5], Judah[4], Thomas[3], Samuel[2], John[1]); m. No. 3012.

    **3012.** Amos Crosby. Resided at Springfield, Mass. Children:

        3013. Martha[8].
        3014. Ellen.
        3015. Mary Susan.
        3016. Emma Jane.

## 3017 = 2997. EMILY[7] MARSH

b. July 12, 1814, dau. of Ephraim[6] and Susannah Marsh, (Thomas[5], Judah[4], Thomas[3], Samuel[2], John[1]); m. No. 3017.

    **3017.** Amasa Walter. Resided at Nassau, N. Y. Children:

        3018. Mary[8].
        3019. Agnes.
        3020. Amasa B.

## 3021 = 2998. ABNER[7] MARSH

b. at Hawley, Mass., Jan. 10, 1816, baptized May 25, 1816 at Hawley, son of Ephraim and Susannah Marsh, (Thomas[5], Judah[4], Thomas[3], Samuel[2], John[1]); m. No. 3021.

    **3021.** Loe Rice, dau. of Capt. Luther of Hawley, Mass.; removed from Plainfield, Mass., to Milo, Mille Lacs Co., Minn., in June, 1861. Children:

        3022. George Towne[8], b. Nov., 1843; m. Rosa, 3045.
        3023. A son, d. y.
        3024. Juliet, b. June, 1848; m. Henry Edwards, 3052.
        3025. Henry Wilson, unm.

## 3026 = 3003. JANE AUGUSTA[8] MARSH

b. Sept. 28, 1835, dau. of Leonard[7] and Lois (Parker) Marsh,

(Ephraim[6], Thomas[5], Judah[4], Thomas[3], Samuel[2], John[1]) ; m. Oct. 31, 1856, No. 3026.

**3026.** Lorin Ball of East Street, Amherst, Mass.  Children :

> 3027. Isabel Augusta[9], m. Oscar Barron.
> 3028. Nettie Addie.
> 3029. Minnie Lucretia.
> 3030. Ella Jerusha.
> 3031. John Henry.
> 3032. Leonard La Fontain.
> 3033. William Monroe.
> 3034. Allen St. Clair.
> 3035. Bertha Lois.

3036 = 3004.  THEODORE CHAPMAN[8] MARSH

b. March 31, 1838, son of Leonard[7] and Lois (Parker) Marsh, (Ephraim[6], Thomas[5], Judah[4], Thomas[3], Samuel[2], John[1]) ; m. Jan. 1, 1860, No. 3036.

**3036.** Ann Eliza Smith.  Children :

> 3037. Consider Smith[9].

3038 = 3005.  ALBERT EUGENIUS[8] MARSH

b. Dec. 10, 1840, son of Leonard[7] and Lois (Parker) Marsh, (Ephraim[6], Thomas[5], Judah[4], Thomas[3], Samuel[2], John[1]) ; m. Feb. 27, 1870, No. 3038.

**3038.** Ann Eliza Ayres of Hadley.  Children :

> 3039. Lilla[9].
> 3040. Myrtie Adella.
> 3041. Herbert Cary.

3042 = 3008.=MONROE PROCTOR[8] MARSH

b. Feb. 17, 1849, son of Leonard[7] and Lois (Parker) Marsh, (Ephraim[6], Thomas[5], Judah[4], Thomas[3], Samuel[2], John[1]) ; m. May 8, 1878, No. 3042.

**3042.** Gertrude Elizabeth Field, b. May 8, 1855, and resides at North Amherst, Mass. Child:

3043. Mary Warren[9], b. April 11, 1881.

## 3044 = 3009. WILLIAM INGRAM[8] MARSH

b. Jan. 26, 1852, son of Leonard[7] and Lois (Parker) Marsh, (Ephraim[6], Thomas[5], Judah[4], Thomas[3], Samuel[2], John[1]); m. June 30, 1882, No. 3044.

**3044.** Flora Willis of North Amherst. Resides at North Amherst.

## 3045 = 3022. GEORGE TOWNE[8] MARSH

b. Nov., 1843, son of Abner[7] and Loe (Rice) Marsh, (Ephraim[6], Thomas[5], Judah[4], Thomas[3], Samuel[2], John[1]); m. May 8, 1878, No. 3045.

**3045.** Rosa ———, b. June, 1851. Children:

3046. Silvy E[9]., b. Sept., 1870.
3047. Flora E., b. Jan., 1873.
3048. Emerelt I., b. March, 1875.
3049. George E., b. June, 1877.
3050. Rosella, b. Jan., 1880.
3051. Julia May, b. May, 1883.

## 3052 = 3024. JULIET[8] MARSH

b. June, 1848, dau. of Abner[7] and Loe (Rice) Marsh, (Ephraim[6], Thomas[5], Judah[4], Thomas[3], Samuel[2], John[1]); m. No. 3052.

**3052.** Henry Edwards, b. March, 1843. Resides in Minnesota. Children:

3052.1. Charles B[9]., b. Jan., 1868.
3052.2. Etta M., b. Aug., 1870.
3052.3. Simie R., b. Oct., 1872.
3052.4. L. Alberta, b. July, 1878.
3052.5. Abner H., b. Sept., 1880.
3052.6. R. Mabel, b. April, 1883.

## 3053 = 2956.   ZENAS[6] MARSH

b. at Ware, about 1793, son of Judah[5] and Elizabeth (Smith) Marsh, (Judah[4], Thomas[3], Samuel[2], John[1]) m. about 1815, No. 3053.

**3053.** Fanny Clifford.   They lived in Hardwick and had nine sons.   He d. July 2, 1834, æ. 41.   Children :

3053.1.   Samuel Clifford[7], b. Nov. 26, 1816; m. Abbie S. Wright, 3054.
3053.2.   Zenas, b. Dec. 10, 1818; m. in 1846, Marcia A. Blood.
3053.3.   Gamaliel, b. Sept. 5, 1820; m. (1) L. P. Chandler, 3055.
3053.4.   William C., b. Sept. 10, 1822 ; m. (1) E. Foster, 3065.
3053.5.   Pliny C., b. March 8, 1824; m. in 1847 or 8, Sarah A. Parsons.   He d. 1886.
3053.6.   Wyatt C., b. Feb. 5, 1826; m. Dec., 1844, Olive Anderson.   He d. May 16, 1892.
3053.7.   Daniel C., b. Dec. 5, 1827; m. (1) Mary Wood, 3069.
3053.8.   Eli C., b. May 24, 1829; m. Sarah D., 3072.
3053.9.   George H., b. Sept. 27, 1831 ; d. Feb. 20, 1832.
3053.10.  Fanny Ann, b. April 22, 1834; m. Jan., 1851, Calvin Kimball and d. Feb., 1852.

## 3054 = 3053.1.   SAMUEL CLIFFORD[7] MARSH

b. at Hardwick, Mass., Nov. 26, 1816, son of Zenas[6] and Fanny (Clifford) Marsh, (Judah[5], Judah[4], Thomas[3], Samuel[2], John[1]) ; m. June 30, 1846, No. 3054.

**3054.** Abbie S. Wright of Spencer, Mass.   He resided in Ware, Hardwick and Spencer and d. Aug. 15, 1877.   Child :

3054.1.   George Henry[8], b. March 26, 1848 ; m. June 25, 1873, Carrie Beaumont Olmstead.   He lives in Spencer and deals in general hardware, stoves and plumbing.   Child :
3054.2.   Ray Beaumont[9], b. Aug. 18, 1874.

## 3055 = 3053.3.   GAMALIEL[7] MARSH

b. at Hardwick, Mass., Sept. 5, 1820, son of Zenas[6] and Fanny (Clifford) Marsh, (Judah[5], Judah[4], Thomas[3], Samuel[2], John[1]) ; m. (1) (published April 23, 1842,) May 11, 1842, No. 3055.

**3055.** Laura P. Chandler, b. June 9, 1822.   They resided at Worcester, Chicopee and Ware, Mass.   She d. Oct. 16, 1860, æ. 38. He m. (2) Oct. 20, 1863, No. 3056.

**3056.** Vashti Stebbins Hitchcock, b. Dec. 8, 1828. Children:

3057. George W[8]., b. June 18, 1843; a candy maker at Chicago, Ill.; d. Aug. 29, 1894.

3058. Lucy Helen, b. June 9, 1845 ; d. Aug. 24, 1851, æ. 6.

3059. Charles H., b. at Worcester, May 29, 1851 ; d. Nov. 13, 1852.

3060. Edwin S., b. Jan. 29, 1854, was in Texas and in 1894 was a plumber in Chicago, unm.

3061. Laura E., b. April 11, 1856 ; d. Oct. 6, 1860.

3062. Clara, b. July 10, 1858 ; d. Nov. 9, 1858.

By second wife.

3063. Nellie E., b. Aug. 3, 1868.

3064. Abner Helcheveh, b. Sept. 2, 1870 ; m. March 4, 1891, Rose Mary Louise Fisher of London, England. Occupation, clerk.


3065 = 3053.4.  WILLIAM C[7]. MARSH

b. in Hardwick, Mass., Sept. 10, 1822, son of Zenas[6] and Fanny (Clifford) Marsh, (Judah[5], Judah[4], Thomas[3], Samuel[2], John[1]) ; m. (1) in June, 1844, No. 3065.

**3065.** Eunice Foster, b. in Barnard, Vt., Oct. 23, 1823. She d. March 17, 1847 and he m. (2) Nov. 23, 1847, No. 3066.

**3066.** Delia B. Converse, b. in Ware, Mass. Sept. 27, 1827. Children all by second wife :

3066.1. Edwin[8], b. Dec. 16, 1848 ; d. Oct. 1, 1849.

3066.2. William K., b. April 24, 1852 ; m. I. M. Clisby, 3067.

3066.3. Frederick E., b. Sept. 18, 1856 ; m. K. A. Thompson, 3068.

3066.4. Clara A., b. Dec. 23, 1858; d. May 13, 1884.

3066.5. Dwight G., b. May 26, 1864.

3066.6. Worthington C., b. May 19, 1867 ; m. Lilla Jacobs.


3067 = 3066.2.  WILLIAM KIMBALL[5] MARSH

b. April 24, 1852, son of William C[7]. and Delia B. (Converse) Marsh, (Zenas[6], Judah[5], Judah[4], Thomas[3], Samuel[2], John[1]) ; a tinsmith ; m. May 23, 1877, No. 3067.

**3067.** Ida M. Clisby. Child :

3067.1. Gertrude M[9]., b. May 13, 1878.

3068 = 3066.3.    FREDERICK E[8]. MARSH

b. Sept. 18, 1856, son of William C[7]., and Delia B. (Converse) Marsh,
(Zenas[6], Judah[5], Judah[4], Thomas[3], Samuel[2], John[1]) ; electro plater ;
m. May 20, 1879, No. 3068.

**3068.** Katie Amelia Thompson.    They live at Ware, Mass.
Children :

    3068.1.    Carrie Luella[9], b. Nov. 15, 1881.
    3068.2.    Alton Thompson, b. Dec. 4, 1883.
    3068.3.    Edith Amelia, b. Oct. 16, 1892.


3069 = 3053.7.    DANIEL C[7]. MARSH

b. at Hardwick, Mass., Dec. 5, 1827, son of Zenas[6] and Fanny
(Clifford) Marsh, (Judah[5], Judah[4], Thomas[3], Samuel[2], John[1]) ; is a
tinsmith ; m. (1) Dec. 5, 1849, No. 3069.

**3069.** Mary Wood, b. at Fairlee, Vt., Oct. 14, 1828. She d.
Sept. 27, 1880 and he m. (2) April 6, 1881, No. 3070.

**3070.** Martha Elizabeth Aldrich, b. Jan. 5, 1846.    Children :

    3070.1.    Mary Eva[8], b. Feb. 5, 1855 ; d. April 16, 1855.
    3070.2.    Marietta, b. Nov. 10, 1860 ; m. J. W. Shewbrooks, 3071.
    3070.3.    Samuel Henry, b. Nov. 15, 1860; d. Nov. 19, 1860.


3071 = 3070.2.    MARIETTA[8] MARSH

b. Nov. 10, 1860, dau. of Daniel C[7]. and Mary (Wood) Marsh,
(Zenas[6], Judah[5], Judah[4], Thomas[3], Samuel[2], John[1]) ; m. Feb. 14, 1881,
No. 3071.

**3071.** John W. Shewbrooks, b. at Northampton, Mass., June 6,
1859.    He is a carpenter.    Children :

    3071.1.    Nellie Mina[9], b. Jan. 13, 1882.
    3071.2.    John Augustus, b. Sept. 2, 1883.
    3071.3.    Daniel Marsh, b. Feb. 12, 1885.
    3071.4.    James Clough, b. Jan. 2, 1889 ; d. Aug. 8, 1889.
    3071.5.    Elizabeth Adele, b. Nov. 23, 1890.
    3071.6.    Junietta Works, b. June 13, 1892.
    3071.7.    Mary Eva, b. Nov. 20, 1893.

## 3072 = 3053.8. ELI C[7]. MARSH

b. at Hardwick, Mass., May 24, 1829, son of Zenas[6] and Fanny (Clifford) Marsh, (Judah[5], Judah[4], Thomas[3], Samuel[2], John[1]) ; m. Dec. 1, 1853, No. 3072.

3072. Sarah D., b. Dec. 13, 1832. They live in Boston. Children :

3072.1.  Ida Forestine[8], b. Feb. 1, 1860; d. Aug. 24, 1860.
3073.  Mary Abbie, b. Aug. 24, 1861 ; m. Feb. 5, 1878, Wm. P. Ryder, 3074.


## 3074 = 3073. MARY ABBIE[8] MARSH

b. Aug. 24, 1861, dau. of Eli C[7]. and Sarah D. Marsh, (Zenas[6], Judah[5], Judah[4], Thomas[3], Samuel[2], John[1]) ; m. Feb. 5, 1878, No. 3074.

3074. William P. Ryder of Boston, Mass. Teamster and forwarding agent for the Baltimore Steamship Company, following his father for forty years. Children :

3074.1.  William P[9]., b. Aug. 10, 1879.
3074.2.  Mabel C., b. Sept. 1, 1883.


## 3075 = 2942. PRUDENCE[6] MARSH

b. at Ware or Greenwich, Mass., Feb. 9, 1777, dau. of Thomas[5] and Mary (Thomas) Marsh, (Judah[4], Thomas[3], Samuel[2], John[1]) ; m. published Nov. 28, 1796, No. 3075.

3075. Joseph Barnard. Children :

3076.  Benjamin[7].
3077.  Edward.
3078.  William.
3079.  Henry.
3080.  Sarah.
3081.  Anna.


## 3082 = 2951.1. JACOB[6] MARSH

b. at Ware, about 1789, son of Jonathan[5] and Anna (Pepper) Marsh, (Judah[4], Thomas[3], Samuel[2], John[1]) ; m. about 1805, No. 3082.

**3082.** Abigail Howard.  He d. Sept. 13, 1850, æ. 71.  Children :

3082.1.  John P[7]., b. about 1806 of Ware ; m. Ruth Terry, 3083.
3082.2.  Abigail P., Mrs. Chester Pierce.
3082.3.  Jacob.
3082.4.  Dorcas, m. Lyman Alden.
3082.5.  Benjamin H.


3083 = 3082.1.  JOHN P[7]. MARSH

b. about 1806, son of Jacob[6] and Abigail (Howard) Marsh, (Jonathan[5], Judah[4], Thomas[3], Samuel[2], John[1]) ; m. No. 3083.

**3083.**  Ruth Terry.  He d. Jan. 4, 1883, æ. 77.  Child :

3083.1.  John L[8]., m. Annie R. Bacon.  He served in the war of
the rebellion.  Child :
3084.  Ruth M.[9]


3085 = 2951.5.  FOSTER[6] MARSH

b. about 1797 ? son of Jonathan[5] and Anna (Pepper) Marsh, (Judah[4], Thomas[3], Samuel[2], John[1]) ; m. No. 3085.

**3085.**  Lucy Thomson.  Resided at Ware.  Selectman, 1821, 1822, 1825 and 1834.  Children :

3086.  Loring Bradlee[7], b. Feb. 12, 1816 ; Yale college 1840 ; m. (1) C. S. Fish, 3090.
3087.  Dwight Foster.
3088.  S. J., 32 Rutland St., Boston.
3089.  Samuel Dexter, Yale college 1844 ; d. 1853.  He was a missionary of the American Board in South Africa.


3090 = 3086.  REV. LORING BRADLEE[7] MARSH

b. at Ware, Mass., Feb. 12, 1816, son of Foster[6] and Lucy (Thomson) Marsh, (Jonathan[5], Judah[4], Thomas[3], Samuel[2], John[1]) ; Yale college, 1840 ; Yale theological seminary, 1843 ; m. June 17, 1846, No. 3090.

**3090.**  Catherine S. Fish.  He was acting pastor in Iowa, a teacher in Berlin, Mass.  Ordained and pastor at North Scituate, R. I., 1858

–1861, at Wading River, N. Y., 1862–1865, where he m. (2) May 3, 1865, No. 3091.

**3091.** Emily Tuthill Skidmore, dau. of Albert and Charity (Tuthill) Skidmore of Wading River. He preached at various places in New York, Connecticut and Massachusetts till 1883, when he retired to Springfield, Mass. and d. June 22, 1891, æ. 75 years, 4 months and 10 days. He had one son and three daus. of whom one or two were at Mt. Holyoke college and they live in Springfield, Mass. Children :

        3092.   ———.
        3093.   ———.
        3093.1. ———.
        3093.2. ———.

---

# HATFIELD BRANCH. THE MONTAGUE LINE.

---

DESCENDANTS OF SAMUEL[2] AND EBENEZER[3].

Ebenezer[3] Marsh passed from Hatfield to Sunderland and Montague, Mass.

---

3094 = 2885.   EBENEZER[4] MARSH

b. at Sunderland, Mass., about 1716, son of Ebenezer[3] and Elizabeth (Gillett) Marsh, (Samuel[2], Jonn[1]) ; probably m. Nov. 17, 1741, his cousin, No. 3094.

**3094.**  Martha[4] Marsh, No. 2874, b. April 12, 1721, dau. of Thomas[3], (Samuel[2], John[1].) He removed from Sunderland to Montague,"Hunting Hills," and d. May 6, 1800, æ. 83 or 84. Children :

- 3095.  Joseph[5], b. at Montague, Mass., 1742 ; m. Rebecca, 3103.
- 3096.  Israel, b. at Montague, Mass., 1744 ; prob. m. 3176.
- 3097.  Lydia, b. 1746, at Montague.
- 3098.  Mary, b. 1748, at Montague.
- ·3099.  Ebenezer, b. 1750, at Montague; m. Eunice Sprague, 3184.
- 3100.  Martha, b. 1752, at Montague.
- 3101.  Eunice, b. Aug. 3, 1757.
- 3102.  Editha, b. Oct. 2, 1762.

### 3103 = 3095.  JOSEPH[5] MARSH

b. at Montague, Mass., in 1742, son of Ebenezer[4] and Martha[4] (Marsh) Marsh, (Ebenezer[3], Samuel[2], John[1]) ; m. No. 3103.

**3103.**  Rebecca, whether in Montague or Conway, to which place he removed, is not apparent. All his children of whom we know, were baptized at Conway, Mass.; the first two on the same day, by Rev. Mr. Ashley. In some of the towns in those days there was much jealousy as to allowing newcomers to get land and foothold and at Conway " Joseph Marsh yeoman and Joseph Marsh, Jr., laborer with wives and children and all dependants " were warned away on 15 days notice. Children :

- 3104.  Joseph[6], b. prob. 1766, bap. Oct. 23, 1768 ; n▶ see 3110.
- 3105.  Asenath, bap. Oct. 23, 1768 ; Conway records give " Intention of m. between Moses Merchants of Montague and Asenath Marsh of. Conway, Nov. 2, 1787."
- 3106.  Martha, bap. Aug. 5, 1770. " Moses Hawley of Montag⬤ and Martha Marsh of Conway intend marriage, March 22, 1794.
- 3107.  Abigail, bap. Nov. 8, 1772.
- 3108.  Elijah, bap. April 28, 1776 ; m. (1) Tamzin Howes, 3116.
- 3109.  Rebecca, bap. Sept. 5, 1779 ; m. " Feb. 6, 1806, Mr. David Bascom of Halifax, Vt. to Miss Rebecca Marsh of Hawley."

### 3110 = 3104.  JOSEPH[6] MARSH

b. possibly at Montague, probably at Conway, Mass., son of Joseph[5] and Rebecca Marsh, (Ebenezer[4], Ebenezer[3], Samuel[2], John[1]), baptized with sister Oct. 23, 1768, mentioned in Conway records, "Joseph Marsh, Jr. and Patty Lyon (**3110**.) intend marriage, July 14, 1792." We have also in Hawley records among marriages, " Mr. Joseph Marsh, Jr., to Miss Betsey Taylor, (**3111**.) Oct. 17, 1809." He resided in Hawley. Children :

3112. Apollos[7], b. at Conway?; resides at Springfield, Mass. Had "several daughters." **f,**

3113. Ebenezer, b. at Conway?; resides at Springfield, and had several daus. and

3114. Ebenezer[8].

3115. Asenath.


3116 = 3108. ELIJAH[6] MARSH

b. at Conway, baptized April 28, 1776, family records say b. "Feb. 8, 1777 ?" son of Joseph[5] and Rebecca Marsh, (Ebenezer[4], Ebenezer[3], Samuel[2], John[1]); m. (1) May 27, 1800, No. 3116.

**3116.** Tamzin Howes, who was baptized with her dau., "Oct. 18, 1812, Tamzin daughter and Tamzin wife of Elijah Marsh." (Hawley baptisms.) He resided in Hawley, Mass. His wife Tamzin d. May, 1814. He m. (2) Sept. 8, 1814, No. 3117.

**3117.** Elizabeth Alden, dau. of Barnabas, b. at Ashfield, Feb. 7, 1787. He d. Aug. 25, 1830. His widow d. Dec. 9, 1855. Children :

3118. Emily[7], b. Aug. 5, 1801, bap. at Hawley, Oct. 20, 1805; d. May, 1810.

3119. Loron, b. Nov. 9, 1803, bap. at Hawley, Oct. 20, 1805; m. Julia Rice, 3131.

3120. Sylvanus, b. March 16, 1805 ; d. Aug. 19, 1844.

3121. Luther, b. May 30, 1809 ; m. Susan Breed, 3134.

3122. Tamzin H., b. June 28, 1812 ; m. Philander Miller, 3143.

By second wife.

3123. Martha Alden, b. May 31, 1815 ; d. June 10, 1837.

3124. Elijah, b. April 23, 1817 ; d. April 27, 1834.

3125. A son, b. May 27; d. May 28, 1819.

3126. Emily, b. April 20, 1820 ; d. Feb. 14, 1844.

3127. Joseph, b. May 26, 1822 ; m. (1) Mary E. Jenny, 3166.

3128. Jonathan Alden, b. July 27, 1824; m. (1) Harriet L. Miller, 3168.

3129. A son, b. Aug. 28, 1826 ; d. same day.

3130. A son, b. July, 1827 ; d. same day.

3131 = 3119. LORON[7] MARSH

b. at Hawley, Mass., Nov. 9, 1803, "baptized *Loring*, Oct. 20, 1805," son of Elijah[6] and Tamzin (Howes) Marsh, (Joseph[5], Ebenezer[4], Ebenezer[3], Samuel[2], John[1]) ; m. Feb. 2, 1835, No. 3131.

**3131.** Juliann Rice. Now (1885) resides in Riceville, Pa. Children :

3132. A son[8], b. July 17, 1837 ; d. Aug. 28, 1839.
3133. Tamzin V., b. Aug. 1, 1840; d. Aug. 4, 1869; m. May 29, 1859, Oscar Trantim. Child :
3134. Lillian[9], b. Oct. 29, 1860; d. April 15, 1873.


3134 = 3121. LUTHER[7] MARSH

b. at Hawley, Mass., May 30, 1809, son of Elijah[6] and Tamzin (Howes) Marsh, (Joseph[5], Ebenezer[4], Ebenezer[3], Samuel[2], John[1]) ; m. (1) Aug. 22, 1832, No. 3134.

**3134.** Susan Breed, b. Sept. 18, 1808, and d. April 13, 1845. He resided at Townville, Pa. He m. (2) Sept. 4, 1845, No. 3135.

**3135.** Elizabeth Thompson, b. Oct. 7, 1811. She d. Dec. 22, 1890. Children :

3136. Henry L[8]., b. June 29, 1833 ; d. Oct. 21, 1856.
3137. A dau., b. June 13, 1836 ; d. June 13, 1836.
3138. Emily M., b. July 2, 1840; d. Oct. 6, 1846.
3139. Susan S., b. Jan. 15, 1845 ; d. Nov. 28, 1884.
          By second wife.
3140. Joseph E., b. Nov. 12, 1848; d. March 6, 1866.
3141. George E., b. June 5, 1851 ; m. Sept. 6, 1879, Adele Baker, b. March 13, 1858. Child :
3142. Ruby[9], b. March 11, 1883.


3143 = 3122. TAMZIN H[7]. MARSH

b. at Hawley, Mass., June 28, 1812, dau. of Elijah[6] and Tamzin (Howes) Marsh, removed to Wayne, Pa., and m. Jan. 8, 1835, No. 3143.

**3143.** Philander Miller, b. Sept. 17, 1807, and d. Feb. 28, 1877. Children :

3144. Susan A⁸., b. Sept. 30, 1836 ; m. (1) Joseph E. Alden, 3156.
3145. Eliza J⁸., b. June 1, 1839 ; m. Oct. 29, 1861, Richard Hannah
    of Fairburg, Ill. She d. Sept. 18, 1865. Children :
    3146. Lester V⁹., b. Oct. 29, 1862.
    3147. Jessee F., b. Aug. 4, 1865 ; d. Sept. 28.
3148. Rufus S., b. Nov. 13, 1840; d. Jan. 13, 1855.
3149. Lauretta T., b. Oct. 15, 1842 ; d. March 8, 1846.
3150. Elijah M., b. May 11, 1845.
3151. Lewis C., b. July 2, 1847. (
3152. Luther C., b. July 2, 1847. )
3153. Florette T., b. Jan. 13, 1849; m. Sept. 18, 1872, Orson Follet.
    Children :
    3154. Virgil O⁹., b. July 6, 1876; d. June 15, 1877. .
    3155. Zoe O.. b. Sept. 12, 1882.

## 3156 = 3144. SUSAN A⁸. MILLER

b. in Wayne, Pa., Sept. 30, 1836, dau. of Philander and Tamzin H⁷.
(Marsh) Miller, (Elijah⁶, Joseph⁵, Ebenezer⁴, Ebenezer³, Samuel²,
John¹) ; m. (1) Dec. 31, 1856, No. 3156.
    **3156.** Joseph E. Alden, who d. Sept. 18, 1864. She m. (2) Dec..
26, 1873, No. 3157.
    **3157.** Clark Howard. Children :
    3158. Tamie E⁹., b. April 20, 1858 ; m. E. G. Martin, 3162.
    3159. Ina M., b. April 14, 1862 ; m. Lyle Sutlif, 3164.
    3160. Vernia C., b. Nov. 6, 1867.
        By second husband.
    3161. Cecil D., b. March 11, 1884.

## 3162 = 3158. TAMIE E⁹. ALDEN

b. April 20, 1858, dau. of Joseph E. and Susannah A⁸. (Miller)
Alden, (Tamzin H⁷. Marsh, Elijah⁶, Joseph⁵, Ebenezer⁴, Ebenezer³,
Samuel², John¹) ; m. Oct. 1, 1881, No. 3162.
    **3162.** Edwin G. Martin of Elgin. Child:
    3163. Gary E¹⁰., b. Dec. 8, 1882.

## 3164 = 3159. INA M⁹. ALDEN

b. April 14, 1862, dau. of Joseph E. and Susannah A⁸. (Miller)

Alden, (Tamzin H[7]. Marsh, Elijah[6], Joseph[5], Ebenezer[4], Ebenezer[3], Samuel[2], John[1]); m. July 4, 1879, No. 3164.

**3164.** Lyle Sutlif of Columbus.   Child :

3165.  Vernia L[10]., b. May 20, 1880.

3166 = 3127.   JOSEPH[7] MARSH

b. at Hawley, Mass., May 26, 1822, son of Elijah[6] and Elizabeth (Alden) Marsh, (Joseph[5], Ebenezer[4], Ebenezer[3], Samuel[2], John[1]); removed to Whately, Mass., where he m. (1) July 20, 1848, No. 3166. **3166.** Mary E. Jenny, dau. of Reuben Jenny.   She d. Nov. 28, 1848.   He m. (2) June 6, 1860, No. 3167. **3167.** Mary C. Parsons, b. March 17, 1837, dau. of Josiah.   They reside in Northampton, Mass., where he is a bookseller.

3168 = 3128.   JONATHAN ALDEN MARSH

b. at Hawley, Mass,, July 27, 1824, son of Elijah[6] and Elizabeth (Alden) Marsh, (Joseph[5], Ebenezer[4], Ebenezer[3], Samuel[2], John[1]); now (1885) residing in Corry, Pa.; m. (1) in 1854, No. 3168. **3168.** Harriet L. Miller of Scott, Cortland Co., N. Y.   She d. in 1858.   He m. (2) in 1859, No. 3169. **3169.** Delana Edson, b. Sept. 6, 1832.   Children :

3170.  Hattie[8], b. April 6, 1858; m. in 1877, Matthew Brunday.
        Children :
        3171.  Josephine[9].
        3172.  Benjamin.
                By second wife.
3173.  Linda A., b. Jan. 6, 1861.
3174.  Bertha Z., b. June 6, 1865.
3175.  Levern A., b. June 30, 1882.

3176 = 3096.   ISRAEL[5] MARSH

b. at Montague, Mass., 1744, son of Ebenezer[4], Ebenezer[3], Samuel[2], John[1] and Martha[4], Thomas[3], Samuel[2], John[1] ; m. No. 3176.

**3176.** ————. He resided at Montague, where in 1766 he did "two days moing," (old account book) and in Conway, Mass. and later "near Schoharie Bridge, N. Y." "Israel raised a large family of boys." Perhaps of the number were (?) as we find from Conway baptisms. Children :

    3177.  Israel[6], m. Lucy. Children :
        3178.  Lucy[7], bap. May 30, 1783.
        3179.  James. bap. April 7, 1785.
        3180.  Israel, bap. Nov. 1, 1787.
    3181.  Elijah, b. when?; m. Betsey. Children :
        3182.  Mary B[7]., bap. May 26, 1827.
    3183.  Francis W., bap. Jan. 28, 1829.

## 3184 = 3099.  CAPT. EBENEZER[5] MARSH

b. at Montague, Mass., 1750, son of Ebenezer[4], (Ebenezer[3], Samuel[2], John[1] and Martha[4], Thomas[3], Samuel[2], John[1]); m. Dec. 13, 1777, No. 3184.

**3184.** Eunice Sprague, b. about 1733 or 1734, dau. of Ebenezer and Eunice (Montague) Sprague. Her mother, Eunice Montague, d. April 28, 1774, æ. 67. Capt. Ebenezer Marsh resided in Montague. He was a "minute man" April 22, 1775. He probably had daus. and the order of birth of his sons is not certain. Children :

    3185.  Ebenezer[6], b. prob. 1778–1780; m. Clarissa Bardwell, 3189.
    3186.  Zenas, b. perhaps 1780–1782 ; m. and resided in N. Y. state. Had one dau.:
        3186.1.  Elvira[8], b. (?) ; m. ——— Vanderlip; resided awhile in Ill.; d. and left one son :
        3186.2.  Guy[9] Vanderlip, b. about 1850.
    3187.  Martin, b. perhaps 1782–1783 ; reported to have gone to sea and not heard from. Zebina Marsh remembers him.
·    3188.  Zimri, b. June 8, 1785; m. Creusa Hubbard, 3604.

## 3189 = 3185.  EBENEZER[6] MARSH

b. at Montague, Mass., perhaps in 1778, son of Ebenezer[5] and Eunice (Sprague) Marsh, (Ebenezer[4], Ebenezer[3], Samuel[2], John[1]) ; m. about 1800–1801, No. 3189.

18

**3189.**  Clarissa Bardwell, dau. of Reuben Bardwell.   She d. Nov. 6, 1806.  Children :

    3190.  Lucy B[7]., b. perhaps 1802 ; m. Hilkiah Hawks of Deerfield.
    3191.  Lyndon A., b. Feb. 6, 1804 in Canada.   Lived in Shelburne, Mass.
    3192.  Rolla, b. April 6, 1806; m. in Rochester, N. Y., Betsey Ward. Lived in Mohekanville, N. Y.


3193 = 2886.  EPHRAIM[4] MARSH

b. at Montague, Mass., in 1718, son of Ebenezer[3] and Elizabeth (Gillett) Marsh, (Samuel[2], John[1]) ; resided at Montague ; m. March 27, 1746, No. 3193.

**3193.**  Sarah Mattoon of Northfield, b. Feb. 21, 1723, dau. of Eleazar Mattoon.   She " Consort " d. April 9, 1797, æ. 74.   He d. June 27, 1805, æ. 89.   Children :

    3194.  Elizabeth[5], b. May 25, 1747.
    3195.  Eliezer, b. March 28, 1749; m. Bethesda Houghton, 3205.
    3196.  Sarah, b. Dec. 7, 1750.
    3197.  Ephraim, b. Nov. 13, 1752; m. No. 3216.
    3198.  Rebekah, b. March 20, 1755; d. Feb. 1, 1835.
    3199.  Mercy, b. May 27, 1757 ; m. Enos[5] Marsh, 3291.
    3200.  Thankful, b. May 27, 1757, twin of Mercy.
    3201.  Philip, b. Dec. 1759 ; d. June 4, 1761.
    3202.  Philip, b. June 2, 1761 ; d. Jan. 18, 1772.
    3203.  Samuel, b. Jan. 19, 1763 ; m. Martha Edwards, 3225.
    3204.  Esther, b. Aug. 21, 1765 ; d. May 18, 1766.


3205 = 3195.  ELIEZER[5] MARSH

b. at Montague, Mass., March 28, 1749, son of Ephraim[4] and Sarah (Mattoon) Marsh, (Ebenezer[3], Samuel[2], John[1]) ; m. No. 3205.

**3205.**  Bethesda Houghton, b. about 1757.   They resided in Montague.   He d. Aug. 31, 1822 and she d. Feb. 14, 1846, æ. 88. Children :

    3206.  Eliezer[6], b. June 7, 1800; m. (1) Nancy Coon, 3236.
    3207.  Elijah, b. Dec. 18, 1801 ; m. Sarah Harmenia Marsh, 3241.

## 3208 = 2887. ENOS[4] MARSH

b. at Sunderland, Mass., Dec. 11, 1721, son of Ebenezer[3] and Elizabeth (Gillett) Marsh, (Samuel[2], John[1]); member of Sunderland church, 1749; m. (1) in 1751, No. 3208.

**3208.** Judith Hawkes, the mother of his six children. He resided in Montague. His wife d. June 9, 1776. He m. (2) in 1778, her sister, No. 3209.

**3209.** Widow Mary (Hawkes) Smeed, who d. March 27, 1803. He was a revolutionary soldier, "in appearance tall, dignified and venerable." He d. in Montague, Feb. 16, 1810, in his 89th year.
Children :

3210.  Enos[5], b. May 9, 1755 ; d. y. }
3211.  Judith, b. May 9, 1755; d. y. }
3212.  Jonathan, b. Aug. 17, 1756 ; m. Freedom Taylor, 3245.
3213.  Judith, b. Aug. 11, 1758 ; d. unm. Sept. 21, 1778.
3214.  Enos, b. March 18, 1760; m. Mercy[5] Marsh, 3291.
3215.  Joshua, b. Aug. 8, 1765 ; m. (1) Mindwell Crosbee, 3340.

## 3216 = 3197. EPHRAIM[5] MARSH

b. at Montague, Mass., Nov. 13, 1752, son of Ephraim[4] and Sarah (Mattoon) Marsh, (Ebenezer[3], Samuel[2], John[1]) ; m. No. 3216.

**3216.** Probably Esther, as the dau. of Philander is said to have been "named after her grandmother." They resided in Montague.
Children :

3217.  Sylvester[6], b. July 14, 1777 ; d. July 26, 1808.
3218.  Philander, b. April 16, 1779; m. Marah Paulk, 3454.
3219.  Ephraim, b. June 3, 1782; m. Eleanor Day, 3478.
3220.  Nathan, b. Sept. 2, 1784.
3221.  Philip, b. March 2, 1788; m. Jan. 26, 1809, Clarissa Hawley, and removed to N. Y.
3222.  Eliphaz, b. Sept. 6, 1790.
3223.  Abel, b. May 2, 1793 ; d. 1876 ; m. No. 3482.
3224.  Apollos, b. Oct. 19, 1795 ; d. Sept. 3, 1798.

## 3225 = 3203. SAMUEL[5] MARSH

b. at Montague, Mass., Jan. 19, 1763, son of Ephraim[4] and Sarah

(Mattoon) Marsh, (Ebenezer[3], Samuel[2], John[1]); m. March 5, 1793, No. 3225.

3225.   Martha Edwards, b. April 10, 1767, " bap. April 17, 1768," dau. of Jonathan and Rebecca (Smith) Edwards of Amherst and grand-daughter of Nathaniel Edwards of Northampton.   Mr. Samuel[5] Marsh d. Nov. 4, 1836, æ. 73 years, 8 months and 15 days.   (Copied from old record of Samuel Marsh in account book kept from 1754 before his birth, and in 1887 still in possession of his son Zebina Marsh after his father's death.)   Children :

3226.   Asa[6], b. April 5, 1794 ;  medical student Yale college ; d. April 1, 1816, at New Haven, Ct.
3227.   Justin b. March 14, 1796 ; m. (1) Jane Deming, 3485.
3228.   Sarah, b. Jan. 30, 1798 ; d. April 2, 1800.
3229.   Samuel, b. Dec. 2, 1799 ; drowned July 10, 1832.
3230.   Solomon, b. Dec. 2, 1799 ; m. March 5, 1828, Luetta Arnold ; d. in Iowa.
3231.   Martha, b. July 25, 1801 ; m. Joseph Fiske, 3501.
3232.   Fanny, b. April 30, 1803 ; m. Hovey Moody, 3507.
3233.   Mary, b. May 30, 1805 ; d. June 3, 1805.
3234.   Zebina, b. June 28, 1806 ; m. (1) Permelia B. Slater, 3515.
3235.   Rufus, b. Nov. 11, 1809 ; d. Oct. 16, 1810.

## 3236 = 3206.   ELIEZER[6] MARSH

b. at Montague, Mass., June 7, 1800. son of Eliezer[5] and Bethesda (Houghton) Marsh, (Ephraim[4], Ebenezer[3], Samuel[2], John[1]) ; m. (1) June 22, 1823, No. 3236.

3236.   Nancy Coon, who d. Dec. 7, 1825 ; m. (2) Jan. 15, 1827, No. 3236.1.

3236.1.   Jemima Clark.   The first wife had one son.   There was a large family and they lived in Montague.   Children :

3236.2.   Warren[7], b. May 17, 1824 ; m. No. 3546.
            By second wife.
3237.   Nancy, b. Dec. 10, 1827 ; m. (1) Albert Wright, 3549.
3237.1.   William E., b. March 31, 1829 ; m. Lucia E. Temple, 3555.
3237.2.   Philo, b. April 16, 1831 ; m. Mercy L. Temple, 3571.
3237.3.   Stephen D., b. Oct. 31, 1832 ; m. Sarah A. Anthony, 3573.
3238.   David C., b. Oct. 19, 1834 ; m. Mary Woodward, 3580.
3239.   Ucerbia C., b. Nov. 27, 1836 ; m. Willard H. Baker, 3588.
3240.   Austin B., b. Nov. 7, 1838 ; m. Minerva Lamb, 3593.

3240.1.  Mary C., b. Oct. 7, 1840; d. Oct. 12, 1845.
3240.2.  Harriet S., b. March 18, 1842; m. John Woodward, 3599.
3240.3.  Edward N., b. Aug. 19, 1844; m. Jan., 1868, Emily Hubbard.
3240.4.  Elliot H., b. Nov. 6, 1846; m. Aug. 15, 1884, Eunice
Anthony, 3240.5.

## 3240.5 = 3240.4.  DR. ELLIOT H[7]. MARSH

of Mansfield Centre, Ct.; m. Aug. 15, 1884, No. 3240.5.

**3240.5.** Eunice Anthony.  Children :

3240.6.  Elsie Gray[8], b. Feb. 3, 1887.
3240.7.  Elliot Clark, b. Aug. 3, 1888; d. Dec. 26, 1893.

## 3241 = 3207.  ELIJAH[6] MARSH

b. at Montague, Dec. 18, 1801, son of Eliezer[5] and Bethesda
(Houghton) Marsh, (Ephraim[4], Ebenezer[3], Samuel[2], John[1]); m.
No. 3241.

**3241.**  Sarah Harmenia[7] Marsh, b. 1804, (see No. 3457), dau. of
Philander[6] Marsh, (Ephraim[5], Ephraim[4], Ebenezer[3], Samuel[2], John[1].)
Children :

3242.  Elijah[7].
3243.  Levi.
3244.  James.

## 3245 = 3212.  JONATHAN[5] MARSH

b. at Montague, Aug. 17, 1756, son of Enos[4] and Judith (Hawkes)
Marsh, (Ebenezer[3], Samuel[2], John[1]); m. about 1779, No. 3245.

**3245.**  Freedom Taylor.  Children :

3246.  Judith[6], b. March 9, 1780; m. Aug. 8, 1808, Amos C. Willis,
b. Dec. 24, 1776.
3247.  Quartus, b. Aug. 26, 1782; m. Sally Holt, 3251.
3248.  Luther, b. Feb. 2, 1785; m. (1) Velina Taylor, 3261.
3249.  Calvin, b. Aug. 6, 1787; m. Roxy Smith, 3278.
3250.  Charlotte, b. June 12, 1792; m. Elijah Hinckley.

## 3251 = 3247.   QUARTUS[6] MARSH

b. at Montague? Aug. 26, 1782, son of Jonathan[5] and Freedom
(Taylor) Marsh, (Enos[4], Ebenezer[3], Samuel[2], John[1]); m. in 1809,
No. 3251.

**3251.** Sally Holt, b. 1780. They settled in Crete Township near
Joliet, Ill., in 1835. She d. April, 1853. He d. Dec. 24, 1854.
Children :

    3252.  Mary Ann[7], b. 1810; d. unm. about 1837.
    3253.  Horatio Nelson, b. Nov. 15, 1812; m. (1) Mary Kile, 3258.
    3254.  Jonathan, b. Dec. 21, 1815; m. Abia Brown and d. Dec. 11,
           1877.
    3255.  Edwin, b. March 13, 1818.
    3256.  Henry, b. June 25, 1820.
    3257.  Francis, b. Sept. 24, 1822.


## 3258 = 3253.   HORATIO NELSON[7] MARSH

b. Nov. 15, 1812, son of Quartus[6] and Sally (Holt) Marsh, (Jonathan[5], Enos[4], Ebenezer[3], Samuel[2], John[1]); m. (1) Oct. 4, 1835,
No. 3258.

**3258.** Mary Kile, who was b. Dec. 17, 1812 and d. Dec. 19,
1840. He m. (2) April 29, 1844, No. 3258.1.

**3258.1.** Levina M. Pond, b. May 18, 1818, who d. Oct. 13, 1868,
and he m. (3) Feb. 9, 1870, No. 3258.2.

**3258.2.** Jennie R. Foster, b. Oct. 3, 1831.

The following is from a notice of his 80th birthday, Nov. 15, 1892,
in the *West Side Presbyterian* of Joliet, Ill.: "About 1828 his parents
emigrated to Western New York, and lived there until 1835, in which
year they came to Will county, and settled in what is now known as
Crete township,—Mr. Marsh coming to Joliet.   Here he continued
his business of cabinet making until 1847, when he purchased the
*True Democrat*, which he continued to publish until 1852.   In 1852
he took charge of the affairs of the C. R. I. & P. railroad in Joliet,
and remained in charge for a number of years, with the exception of
an interval of three years, from 1864 to 1867, during which time he
was postmaster of Joliet.   Mr. Marsh also served for several terms
as a member of the city council.   He is at present the senior member
of the real estate firm of H. N. Marsh & Co.

Mr. Marsh has lived a life of great usefulness to his fellowmen. He has been actively engaged in all the great reform movements of his time. He was one of the earliest advocates and friends of the temperance movement, and continues to give it his hearty support. He was one of the most faithful adherents of the abolition cause, and has been, and is, a friend to every movement that has for its object the enlightment and moral advancement of men. He has a mind well-stored with the best thoughts of literature, history and ethics, and, though modest to the point of diffidence in the presence of an audience, he has rare faculties of entertainment when comfortably situated by his own fireside.

Mr. Marsh has been for many years an intelligent, conscientious, consistent and devoted supporter of the christian religion. He was one of the charter members of our church, and is the only male member who remains with us, of those who laid the foundations of our loved organization. He continues to be the senior ruling elder, and one of the most zealous workers in the church, regularly attending both of the Sunday services, and the mid-week prayer meeting; by his conduct, giving an example of fidelity to younger servants of the Master. At eighty, Mr. Marsh is a splendid example to the young men of our congregation, of a life rooted and grounded in the eternal principles of right, as they are set forth in the gospel of Christ. Temperance, integrity, uprightness of heart, make the man.

We heartily congratulate Mr. Marsh on attaining his four score years, and sincerely trust that he may be spared many more years, to give his aid and counsel to the conduct of our church." Children :

3258.3.  William Henry[8], b. Aug. 15, 1840; d. Nov. 30, 1865, from the effect of wounds received at the first attack on Vicksburg in Jan., 1862.

By second wife.

3258.4.  Clarissa C., b. Dec. 21, 1846; d. March 18, 1848.
3258.5.  Frank E., b. June 27, 1849; m. (1) K. Richmond, 3259.

## 3259 = 3258.5. FRANK E[8]. MARSH

b. June 27, 1849, baptized " Francis Egbert," but known socially, officially and in business as Frank E., son of Horatio Nelson[7] and Levina (Pond) (Marsh, Quartus[6], Jonathan[5], Enos[4], Ebenezer[3], Samuel[2], John[1]); m. (1) Feb. 4, 1873, No. 3259.

**3259.**  Kate Richmond, b. Aug. 18, 1851.   She d. May 16, 1879.
He m. (2) Nov. 7, 1882, No. 3259.1.

**3259.1.**  Ida Pierce, b. Feb. 16, 1856.   She d. Jan. 13, 1891 and
he m. (3) June 27, 1892, No. 3259.2.

**3259.2.**  Jessie Gaskell, b. Feb. 26, 1862.   Children:

> 3259.3.  Horatio Richmond[9], b. Feb. 13, 1874, student at Illinois
> state university, nearly through his college course and
> preparing to be a medical missionary.
> 3259.4.  Loren W., b. Aug. 6, 1877; student at the Illinois state
> university.

> By second wife.

> 3260.  Ralph, b. April 16, 1889.

### 3261 = 3248.  LUTHER[6] MARSH

b. at Montague, Feb. 2, 1785, son of Jonathan[5] and Freedom (Taylor)
Marsh, (Enos[4], Ebenezer[3], Samuel[2], John[1]) ; m. (1) Oct. 19, 1808,
No. 3261.

**3261.**  Velina Taylor, b. Oct. 21, 1787 ; d. Sept. 12, 1817.   After
the death of his first wife he left Montague and settled first at Parma,
N. Y. and in 1851 at Swanton, O.   He m. (2) June 12, 1831,
No. 3262.

**3262.**  Esther Beach, who d. Nov. 26, 1832.   He m. (3) June 20,
1833, No. 3263.

**3263.**  Sarah Shelden, b. Aug. 16, 1815, who d. Sept. 22, 1851.
He d. May 24, 1871.   Children:

> By first wife.

> 3264.  Richard[7], b. Sept. 13, 1810; m. Sarah Barnes and had eight
> children.   He d. Nov. 20, 1880.   Widow and three chil-
> dren living in 1885.
> 3265.  Herrick, b. Feb. 15, 1813; m. Sarah Green, 3269.
> 3266.  George T., b. Sept. 5, 1817; d. Sept. 25, 1838, æ. 21.

> By second wife.

> 3267.  Irena, b. June 12, 1831 ; d. Nov. 12, 1833.

> By third wife two children who d. y. and then:

> 3268.  George H. L., b. Oct. 15, 1843; m. (1) Margaret Mattoon,
> 3272.

### 3269 = 3265.  HERRICK[7] MARSH

b. at Montague, Mass., Feb. 15, 1813, son of Luther[6] and Velina

(Taylor) Marsh, (Jonathan⁵, Enos⁴, Ebenezer³, Samuel², John¹) ; m. No. 3269.

**3269.** Sarah Green.  Children :

    3270. Mary⁸, m. George Frent, and resides at Genoa, O. and has four children.

    3271. Rena, m. Elijah B. Hauseman resides at Swanton, O., and has three children.

### 3272 = 3268.  GEORGE H. L⁷. MARSH

b. at Parma, Monroe Co., N. Y., Oct. 15, 1843, son of Luther⁶ and Sarah (Shelden) Marsh, (Jonathan⁵, Enos⁴, Ebenezer³, Samuel², John¹) ; his father took him when 8 years old to Swanton, Fulton Co., Ohio. His mother d. Sept. 22, 1851.  He m. (1) in 1866, No. 3272.

**3272.** Margaret Mattoon, b. Jan. 1, 1850.  She d. Feb. 22, 1870. He m. (2) June, 1870, No. 3273.

**3273.** ——.  She d. April 4, 1871.  He m. (3) Feb. 19, 1879, No. 3274.

**3274.** Esther Ann Hewitt, b. March 31, 1843.  Children :

    3275. Luther Ryal⁸, b. Aug. 3, 1867.

    3276. William Henry, b. Dec. 27, 1869.

                By second wife.

    3277. Mary Eliza, b. April 3, 1871, (mother d. April 4) ; d. March, 1872.

### 3278 = 3249.  CALVIN⁶ MARSH

b. at Montague, Aug. 6, 1787, son of Jonathan⁵ and Freedom (Taylor) Marsh, (Enos⁴, Ebenezer³, Samuel², John¹) ; m. Feb. 23, 1814, No. 3278.

**3278.** Roxy Smith, b. 1787, dau. of Samuel C. Smith.  He lived in Montague, last in Federal street ; d. May 26, 1844.  She d. June 4, 1858.  Children :

    3279. Clarissa⁷, b. Nov. 26, 1814 ; d. Nov. 21, 1839.

    3280. Electa S., b. March 18, 1817 ; d. July 10, 1843.

    3281. Julia A., b. Aug. 26, 1819 ; d. Oct. 31, 1839.

    3282. Hannah R., b. Oct. 7, 1822.

    3283. Elvira F., b. Sept. 18, 1825 ; d. Oct. 25, 1884.

3284.  Climena, b. Oct. 21, 1828; m. Jonathan Johnson, 3286.
3285.  Charlotte, b. May 5, 1831 ; d. Nov. 28, 1839.

### 3286 = 3284.  CLIMENA[7] MARSH

b. at Montague, Oct. 21, 1828, dau, of Calvin[6] and Roxy (Smith) Marsh, (Jonathan[2], Enos[4], Ebenezer[3], Samuel[2], John[1] ); m. Dec. 26, 1854, No. 3286.

**3286.** Jonathan Johnson, Esq., of Greenfield, Mass., b. Oct. 1, 1825. Secretary and treasurer of the Marsh Family Association. Children :

3287.  Calvin Henry[8], b. Oct. 18, 1855; m. Nov. 17, 1886, Hattie E. Marriott.
3288.  James Clement, b. Aug. 3, 1857 ; m. Sept. 20, 1886, Cora C. Morse.
3289.  Julia Isabel, b. July 20, 1859.
3290.  Darwin Marsh, b. Jan. 28, 1861 : m. Oct. 6, 1885, Nettie B. Boyden.

### 3291 = 3214.  ENOS[5] MARSH

b. at Montague, Mass., March 18, 1760, son of Enos[4] and Judith (Hawkes) Marsh, (Ebenezer[3], Samuel[2], John[1]) ; m. about 1785, his cousin No. 3291.

**3291.** Mercy[5] Marsh, b. May 27, 1757, dau. of Ephraim[4], (Ebenezer[3], Samuel[2], John[1]), see 3199 ; resided at Montague.   Enos d. Feb. 28, 1842, æ. 82.   Mercy d. Aug. 4, 1842, æ. 85.   Children :

3292.  Lucius[6], b. July 29, 1786; m. (1) Rachel Hawley, 3298.
3293.  Perhaps an Enos?
3294.  Mercy, b. 1790; d. Aug. 31, 1815, æ. 25.
3295.  Lorinda, m. David Edwards of Amherst, Mass.
3296.  ———; m. Asa Edwards, and removed to Morristown, Vt.
3297.  Enos, b. Feb. 6, 1799; m. Rebecca Hawley, 3318.

### 3298 = 3292.  DEA. LUCIUS[6] MARSH

b. at Montague, Mass., July 29, 1786, son of Enos[5] and Mercy[5] Marsh, (Enos[4], Ebenezer[3], Samuel[2], John[1]) ; m. (1) May 12, 1808, by Dr. Parsons, No. 3298.

**3298.** Rachel Hawley of Amherst, Mass. They resided at Montague. She d. June 16, 1832, æ. 54? (Zebina Marsh, copy from headstones of old cemetery Montague.) It makes her seven or eight years older than her husband. He m. (2) No. 2398.1.

**2398.1.** Hannah Taylor of Montague, who d. Nov. 20, 1840, æ. 42. He m. (3) No. 2398.2.

**2398.2.** Parmelia R., who d. March 10, 1873, æ. 79. Dea. Lucius Marsh d. Dec. 5, 1870, æ. 84. Children:

> 3299. Zechariah Hawley[7], b. March 1809; d. Dec. 17, 1810, æ. 1 year and 10 months.
> 3300. Zechariah Hawley, b. in 1811; m. Luthera Johnson, 3302.
> 3301. Elvira, b. Dec. 26, 1814; m. Samuel W. Ross, 3315.

**3302 = 3300. ZECHARIAH HAWLEY[7] MARSH, M. D.**

b. at Montague, 1811, son of Dea. Lucius[6] and Rachel (Hawley) Marsh, (Enos[5], Enos[4], Ebenezer[3], Samuel[2], John[1]); m. Jan. 10, 1842? No. 3302.

**3302.** Luthera Johnson, b. Nov. 17, 1822. He practiced at Dana and Howell, Mich. Children:

> 3303. Helen L[8]., b. March 17, 1845; m. Geo. B. Lake, 3306.
> 3304. Frank H., b. July 12, 1847; m. Elizabeth M. Archer, 3308.
> 3305. Edwin J., b. May 29, 1849; m. Alma L. Burr, 3313.

**3306 = 3303. HELEN L. MARSH**

b. March 17, 1845, dau. of Zechariah Hawley[7] and Luthera (Johnson) Marsh, (Lucius[6], Enos[5], Enos[4], Ebenezer[3], Samuel[2], John[1]); m. Dec. 25, 1878, No. 3306.

**3306.** George B. Lake, who d. at Topeka, Kansas, April 27, 1884. He was at his death chief engineer of the Topeka, Atchison & Santa Fe railway, having been 13 years in service and rising to charge of the entire system. He received high honor from the Kansas and Michigan papers. He graduated in 1869 in the engineering class of Michigan university and was only 38 when he died. Children:

> 3307. George E[9]., b. at Topeka, Kansas, Nov. 26, 1880.
> 3307.1. Mary Helen, b. at Howell, Mich., Sept. 22, 1882.

## 3308 = 3304.  FRANK H[s]. MARSH

b. July 12, 1847, son of Zechariah Hawley[7] and Luthera (Johnson) Marsh, (Dea. Lucius[6], Enos[5], Enos[4], Ebenezer[3], Samuel[2], John[1]) ; m. about 1870, No. 3308.

**3308.** Elizabeth M. Archer.  He d. Nov. 10, 1878.  Children :

    3309.  Lucius H[9]., b. Dec. 20, 1871 ; d. Aug. 14, 1872.
    3310.  Albert J., b. Feb. 11, 1873.
    3311.  Ella B., b. Nov. 29, 1874.
    3312.  Charles F., b. Sept. 11, 1876.


## 3313 = 3305.  EDWIN J[s]. MARSH

b. May 29, 1849, son of Zechariah Hawley[7] and Luthera (Johnson) Marsh, (Dea. Lucius[6], Enos[5], Enos[4], Ebenezer[3], Samuel[2], John[1]) ; m. No. 3313.

**3313.** Alma L. Burr.  He is attorney at law at Big Rapids, Mich. Child :

    3314.  Frank B[9]., b. March 4, 1880.


## 3315 = 3301,  ELVIRA[7] MARSH

b. at Montague, Mass., Dec. 26, 1814, dau. of Dea. Lucius[6] and Rachel (Hawley) Marsh, (Enos[5], Enos[4], Ebenezer[3], Samuel[2], John[1]) ; m. No. 3315.

**3315.** Samuel W. Ross of Deerfield, Mass.  Widow resided at Amherst.  Children :

    3316.  Francis[8], b. 1835 ; d. March 26, 1836, æ. 10 months.
    3317.  ———.  Mrs. Ross had a grand-daughter Mrs. Frank Bolter who resided in South Amherst.


## 3318 = 3297.  ENOS[6] MARSH

b. at Montague, Mass., Feb. 6, 1799, son of Enos[5] and Mercy[5] (Marsh) Marsh, (Enos[4], Ebenezer[3], Samuel[2], John[1]) ; m. April 20, 1820, No. 3318.

**3318.** Rebekkah Hawley, dau. of Chester Hawley of Hadley. He resided in Montague. He probably d. soon after 1830 as with no later children, we have mention that after her father's death his dau. Augusta went to reside with her grandfather Chester Hawley until she went to Wisconsin and married in 1846.   Children :

    3319.  Harriet Newell[7], b. Aug. 28, 1823 ; m. Chas. P. Osborn, 3322..
    3320.  Augusta Hawley, b. April 16, 182- ; m. Wm. Montague
           Whitney, 3335.
    3321.  Nancy Maria, b. June 12, 1830.


## 3322 = 3319.   HARRIET NEWELL[7] MARSH

b. at Montague, Mass., Aug. 28, 1823, dau. of Enos[6] and Rebecca (Hawley) Marsh, (Enos[5], Enos[4], Ebenezer[3], Samuel[2], John[1]) ; m. at Lafayette, Wis., May 1, 1844, No. 3322.

**3322.** Charles Paine Osborn, b. at Hadley, Mass., Nov. 22, 1817. Since 1863 resided at Fairfax, Linn Co., Iowa.   Children all b. at Lafayette, Wis.:

    3323.  Dwight Pomeroy[8], b. April 17, 1845 ; d. June 9, 1858.
    3324.  Charles Hunt, b. Dec. 16, 1848 ; m. Lucie M. Evans.
    3325.  Harriet, b. Nov. 8, 1853 ; d. Oct., 1887.
    3326.  Herbert, b. March 19, 1856 ; m. Alice I. Sayles, 3332.
    3327.  George McClellan, b. April 8, 1862.


## 3328 = 3324.   CHARLES HUNT[8] OSBORN

b. at Lafayette, Wis., Dec. 16, 1848, son of Harriet N[7]. (Marsh) Osborn, (Enos[6], Enos[5], Enos[4], Ebenezer[3], Samuel[2], John[1]) ; m. at Western, Neb., Nov. 24, 1879, No. 3328.

**3328.** Lucie Maria Evans.   Children :

    3329.  Dwight Evans[9], b. at Northampton, Rooks Co., Kan., Nov..
          27, 1880.
    3330.  Fannie Harriet, b. at Northampton, Rooks Co., Kan., July·
          18, 1883.
    3331.  Nannettie, b. at Logan, Ottawa Co., Kan., Nov. 20, 1885.

2332 = 3326.  PROF. HERBERT[8] OSBORN

b. at Lafayette, Wis., March 19, 1856, son of Harriet Newell[7] (Marsh) Osborn, (Enos[6], Enos[5], Énos[4], Ebenezer[3], Samuel[2], John[1]); m. at Manchester, Iowa, Jan. 19, 1883, No. 3332.

3332. Alice Isadore Sayles. He is professor in the Agricultural college at Ames, Iowa. Children:

    3333. Morse Foster[9], b. at Ames, Iowa, Jan. 7, 1887.
    3334. Herbert Tirrill, b. at Ames, Iowa, Dec. 6, 1887.


3335 = 3320.  AUGUSTA HAWLEY[7] MARSH

b. at Montague, Mass., April 16, 1827, dau. of Enos[6] and Rebecca (Hawley) Marsh, (Enos[5], Enos[4], Ebenezer[3], Samuel[2], John[1]), after her father's death lived for a time with her grandfather Chester Hawley of Plainville, Hadley, Mass., then went to Wisconsin and m. May 6, 1846, No. 3335.

3335. William Montague Whitney, son of Isaac Whitney, b. Aug. 28, 1819. Resided in 1884 in Fairfax, Iowa. He went west to Rockport, Ill., about 1836 when 17 with his uncle Richard Montague. He d. April 24, 1893. His widow has two children, nine grand-children and five great-grand-children. Children:

    3336. Harriet Love[8], b. Feb. 18, 1847.
    3337. Laura Augusta, b. Dec. 16, 1849; d. March 10, 1850.
    3338. Frank William, b. April 17, 1855.
    3339. Isaac Eugene, b. May 25, 1858; d. Feb. 9, 1876.


3340 = 3215.  JOSHUA[5] MARSH

b. Aug. 8, 1765, at Montague, Mass., son of Enos[4] and Judith (Hawkes) Marsh, (Ebenezer[3], Samuel[2], John[1]); m. (1) Dec. 30, 1793, No. 3340.

3340. Mindwell Crosbee, b. Oct. 25, 1769; d. Aug. 25, 1808, æ. 38 years and 10 months. She was dau. of John and Mindwell (Houghton) Crosbee of Wendell, Mass. He m. (2) Jan. 25, 1809, No. 3341.

3341. Abigail Clary of Leverett, Mass., b. Sept. 20, 1769; d.

May 9, 1848, æ. 78 years, 7 months and 19 days. Except in Leverett from 1812 ,to 1816 he lived in Montague and d. Feb. 1, 1855, æ. 89 years, 5 months and 23 days. Children :

    3342. Mindwell[6], b. June 14, 1795 ; m. James Stewart, 3349.
    3343. Joshua, b. April 25, 1797 ; m. Mary Hawley, 3357.
    3344. Eliza, b. Sept. 24, 1798 ; d. Feb. 5, 1800, æ. 1 year, 4 months and 11 days.
    3345. John Crosbee, b. July 9, 1800 ; m. Elcipha Marsh, 3408.
    3346. Cynthia, b. March 26, 1802 ; d. unm. at Bethel, Vt., May 5, 1881, at the home of her nephew Anson J. Marsh, buried at Randolph, Vt., æ. 79 years, 1 month and 9 days.
    3347. Orsamus, b. Aug. 21, 1804 ; m. Lucinda Hawley, 3532.
    3348. Dexter, b. Aug. 22, 1806 ; m. (1) Rebecca Slate, 3542.

## 3349 = 3342. MINDWELL[6] MARSH

b. at Montague, Mass., June 14, 1795, dau. of Joshua[5] and Mindwell (Crosbee) Marsh, (Enos[4], Ebenezer[3], Samuel[2], John[1]) ; m. March 5, 1818, No. 3349.

**3349.** James Stewart, Jr., of Montague. From May 1, 1816 to March 7, 1841, she kept a journal made of great use by her son Dr. Edwin Stewart of New York City in preparing her lineage. She d. in Amherst, Mass., March 2, 1870, æ. 74 years, 8 months and 18 days. Children :

    3350. Eliza[7], b. at Montague, Jan. 26, 1819 ; m. Sept. 17, 1845, Harvey Douglas Felt of Amherst, who d. there in 1853. She d. April 22, 1852, æ. 33 years, 2 months and 26 days. Child :
    3351. Mary Abigail[8], b. March 15, 1847 ; m. July 1, 1869, Granville S. Patterson of New York. Children:
        3351.1. George Walter[9], b. Aug., 1870 ; d. July 2, 1872.
        3351.2. Justin, b. and d. April 16, 1872.
    3352. Edwin, b. at Amherst, Feb. 7, 1823 ; m. Mary E. Flagg, 3354.
    3353. Abigail, b. at Montague, May 14, 1825 ; d. at Amherst, Oct. 3, 1839, æ. 14 years, 4 months and 19 days.

## 3354 = 3352. DR. EDWIN[7] STEWART

b. at Amherst, Mass., Feb. 7, 1823, son of Mindwell[6] (Marsh) Stewart, (Joshua[5] Marsh, Enos[4], Ebenezer[3], Samuel[2], John[1]) ; m. April 1, 1849, No. 3354.

**3354.** Mary Elizabeth Flagg, b. Sept. 17, 1818, dau. of Dea. Abijah and Mary (Longley) of Boylston, Mass.   Dr. Stewart is a physician in New York City and deserves the thanks of the Marsh family for the great pains he has taken to collect and put in most admirable order his Marsh record.   Better than some, he cherishes his mother's memory.   Children :

3354.1.   Edwin Abijah[8], b. Dec. 9, 1849 in Oakham, Mass.; d. Aug. 30, 1853, in New York, æ. 3 years, 8 months and 21 days.
3354.2.   Frederick James, b. Nov. 19, 1851, in Oakham ; d. March 18, 1856, in New York, æ. 4 years, 3 months and 29 days.
3354.3.   Frank Herbert, b. March 12, 1854, in New York ; d. May 3, 1861, in New York, æ. 7 years, 1 month and 21 days.
3354.4.   Jessie Fremont, b. Dec. 27, 1855, in New York ; m. there May 24, 1882.   Richard Palmer Vail of New York, b. 1852 or 3.
3354.5.   Merritt Lugar, b. Feb. 25, 1860; m. Mary M. Flagg, 3355.

3355 = 3354.5.   MERRITT LUGAR[8] STEWART

b. at New York City, Feb. 25, 1860, son of Dr. Edwin[7] and Mary Elizabeth (Flagg) Stewart, (Mindwell[6] [Marsh] Stewart, Joshua[5] Marsh, Enos[4], Ebenezer[3], Samuel[2], John[1]) ; m. Sept. 11, 1883, in Boylston, Mass., No. 3355.

**3355.** Mary Martha Flagg, b. Dec. 11, 1860, dau. of Hon. Levi Lincoln and Caroline Elizabeth (Barnes) Flagg of Boylston, Mass. Children :

3355.1.   Marion Evangeline[9], b. Aug. 16, 1884 in Ridgewood, N. J.; d. in New York, Feb. 21, 1892, æ. 7 years, 6 months and 5 days.
3355.2.   Merritt Gordon; b. Jan. 10, 1886, in Ridgewood.
3355.3.   Howard Stanley, b. April 10, 1888 in New York ; d. there Oct. 20, 1891, æ. 3 years, 6 months and 10 days.
3355.4.   Jennie Flagg, b. Jan. 18, 1890 in New York.
3356.   Florence Marion, b. Feb. 17, 1893 in New York.
3356.1.   Stanley Clifford, b. Aug. 26, 1894 in New York.

3357 = 3343.   JOSHUA[6] MARSH

b. at Montague, Mass., April 25, 1797, son of Joshua[5] and Mindwell (Crosbee) Marsh, (Enos[4], Ebenezer[3], Samuel[2], John[1]) ; m. April 26, 1821, in Hadley, Mass., No. 3357.

**3357.** Mary Hawley of Plainville, Hadley, b. April 24, 1803, dau. of Chester Hawley. She d. March 3, 1881, æ. 77 years, 10 months and 9 days. He d. May 28, 1882, æ. 85 years, 1 month and 3 days. He spent his entire life in Montague and there all their children were born. Children:

 3358. Chester[7], b. March 17, 1822; m. (1) Catherine M. Severance, 3370.
 3359. Charles, b. March 4, 1824; m. Mary B. Edwards, 3374.
 3360. Baxter, b, April 22, 1826; m. Jane H. Ware, 3388.
 3361. Sanford, b. June 5, 1828; d. May 12, 1833.
 3362. Levi, b. June 30, 1830; m. Martha A. Easton, 3395.
 3363. Alanson, b. June 15, 1832; m. April 12, 1855, at Fox Lake, Wis., Mary Almeda Thompson, 3364, b. at Nunda, N. Y., Feb. 26, 1836. He d. July 10, 1859. They had two adopted children.
 3365. Mary Amelia, b. July 21, 1834; d. July 10, 1859.
 3366. Alfred, b. Jan. 26, 1837; m. Martha L. Rawson, 3399.
 3367. Susan Fidelia, b. Feb. 23, 1839; d. Aug. 5, 1842.
 3368. Sanford, b. Dec. 13, 1841; m. Mary E. Blodgett, 3405.
 3369. Cyrus, b. Jan. 12, 1843; of Co. F. 34th Reg. Mass. Vols.; d. in Montague, March 8, 1863 of army disease.

## 3370 = 3358.  CHESTER[7] MARSH

b. at Montague, Mass., March 17, 1822, son of Joshua[6] and Mary (Hawley) Marsh, (Joshua[5], Enos[4], Ebenezer[3], Samuel[2], John[1]); m. May 31, 1848, No. 3370.

 **3370.** Catherine M. Severance, b. April 13, 1827. She d. June 10, 1861 and he m. (2) Dec. 18, 1861, No. 3370.1.

 **3370.1.** Mary Philips, b. March 28, 1840. He d. at Hartford, Ct., Jan. 19, 1890. Children:

 3371. Ada Louise[8], b. May 2, 1851; unm.
 3372. Fred Horace, b. May 15, 1860; d. Jan. 1, 1861.
      By second wife.
 3373. Edna Winifred, b. April 7, 1870.

## 3374 = 3359.  CHARLES[7] MARSH

b. at Montague, Mass., March 4, 1824, son of Joshua[6] and Mary

19

(Hawley) Marsh, (Joshua[5], Enos[4], Ebenezer[3], Samuel[2], John[1]) ; m. in Beaver Dam, Wis., Oct. 1, 1848, No. 3374.

**3374.** Mary B[7]. Edwards, b. at Hadley, Mass., June 18, 1828, dau. of Lorinda[6] (Marsh) Edwards, No. 3295 and grand-dau. of Enos[5], Enos[4], Ebenezer[3], Samuel[2], John[1]. They lived in various places as the birthplaces of their children show and he d. in Judsonia, Ark., Jan. 1, 1888, where his widow resided in 1893. Children :

3375. Charles Carroll[8], b. at Beaver Dam, Wis., Oct. 8, 1849 ; m. M. Browning, 3381.
3376. Mary Ella, b. at Beaver Dam, May 5, 1852 ; m. J. H. Browning.
3377. Erving Edwards, b. at Westfield, Mass., April 2, 1855 ; d. June 2, 1856.
3378. Harry Willis, b. at Waterloo, Iowa, Nov. 13, 1858 ; d. unm. Dec. 17, 1879.
3379. Alice Isabel, b. at Waterloo, Iowa, Aug. 25, 1861 ; m. in Judsonia, April 15, 1884, Dr. J. W. Burns of Little Rock, Ark. Child :
3380. Alice Imogene, b. Oct. 22, 1887.


3381 = 3375. CHARLES CARROLL[8] MARSH

b. at Beaver Dam, Wis., Oct. 8, 1849, son of Charles[7] and Mary B[7]. (Edwards) Marsh, (Joshua[6], Joshua[5], Enos[4], Ebenezer[3], Samuel[2], John[1]) ; m. in Judsonia, Ark., July 11, 1874, No. 3381.

**3381.** Margaret Elizabeth Browning of Judsonia, b. March 23, 1851. He d. there Oct. 19, 1876. Child :

3382. Minnie Ada[9], b. July 15, 1875, in Judsonia.


3383 = 3376. MARY ELLA[8] MARSH

b. at Beaver Dam, Wis., May 5, 1852, dau. of Charles[7] and Mary B[7]. (Edwards) Marsh, (Joshua[6], Joshua[5], Enos[4], Ebenezer[3], Samuel[2], John[1]) ; m. at Judsonia, Ark., March 3, 1875, No. 3383.

**3383.** Judson Hincley Browning. Children all b. at Judsonia :

3384. Lulu Viola[9], b. Sept. 11, 1878.
3385. LeRoy Judson, b. Oct. 31, 1880.
3386. Alice M., b. Jan. 3, 1884.
3387. Charles Carroll, b. Aug. 1, 1888.

## 3388 = 3360. BAXTER[7] MARSH

b. at Montague, Mass., April 22, 1826, son of Joshua[6] and Mary (Hawley) Marsh, (Joshua[5], Enos[4], Ebenezer[3], Samuel[2], John[1]); m. April 27, 1852, No. 3388.

**3388.** Jane H. Ware, b. at Somerset, Vt., May 13, 1829. He resided in Greenfield, Mass., and of late years in Amherst, Mass. Children:

    3389.  Edward Baxter[8], b. at Greenfield, March 22, 1853; m. E. R. Wiggin, 3392.

    3390.  Clarence Hawley, b. at Greenfield, Nov. 11, 1856; d. Nov. 2, 1858.

    3391.  Carrie Amelia, b. at Greenfield, Sept. 24, 1859; resides at Amherst.

## 3392 = 3389. EDWARD BAXTER[8] MARSH, M. A.

b. at Greenfield, Mass., March 22, 1853, son of Baxter[7] and Jane H. (Ware) Marsh, (Joshua[6], Joshua[5], Enos[4], Ebenezer[3], Samuel[2], John[1]); m. Aug. 10, 1882, at Exeter, N. H., No. 3392.

**3392.** Emma Rumrill Wiggin, dau. of Ammi Ruhamah and Zilpha (Brigham) Wiggin, b. April 23, 1853. He graduated at Amherst college in 1876 and was principal of Amherst high school and now Registrar of Amherst college. Children:

    3393.  Clarence Edward[9], b. at Amherst, June 27, 1883.

    3394.  Arthur Brigham, b. at Amherst, June 15, 1885.

## 3395 = 3362. LEVI[7] MARSH

b. at Montague, Mass., June 30, 1830, son of Joshua[6] and Mary (Hawley) Marsh, (Joshua[6], Enos[4], Ebenezer[3], Samuel[2], John[1]); m. June 4, 1857, No. 3395.

**3395.** Martha Abigail Easton of Jacksonville, Vt., b. Aug. 5, 1835, dau. of Pliny and Sylvia (Russell) Easton. Children:

    3396.  Clarence Elbert[8], b. Dec. 2, 1858; d. July 8, 1859.

    3397.  Clara Elberta, b. April 5, 1860; unm.

    3398.  Mary Fidelia, b. March 15, 1862; m. Dec. 27, 1882, Jacob Edwin Yerkes of Cecil Co., Md., b. July 31, 1856.

## 3399 = 3366.  ALFRED[7] MARSH

b. at Montague, Mass., Jan. 26, 1837, son of Joshua[6] and Mary (Hawley) Marsh, (Joshua[5], Enos[4], Ebenezer[3], Samuel[2], John[1]); m. Aug. 7, 1867, No. 3399.

**3399.** Martha Louise Rawson of Alstead, N. H., b. Nov. 5, 1845. Children :

    3400.  Frank Chester[8], b. Jan. 5, 1869; d. in Rochester, N. H., Aug. 7, 1869.
    3401.  Roland Hill, b. May 8, 1870.
    3402.  Walter Kimball, b. April 17, 1872.
    3403.  Bertha Louise, b. Oct. 15, 1875.
    3404.  Annie Grace, b. Jan. 6, 1884.

## 3405 = 3368.  SANFORD[7] MARSH

b. at Montague, Mass.. Dec. 13, 1841, son of Joshua[6] and Mary (Hawley) Marsh, (Joshua[5], Enos[4], Ebenezer[3], Samuel[2], John[1]); m. in South Deerfield, Mass., Nov. 28, 1867, No. 3405.

**3405.** Mary Ellen Blodgett, b. in South Deerfield, March 27, 1843, dau. of Simeon and Elizabeth (Everett) Blodgett. They reside at Montague. Children :

    3406.  William Sanford[8], b. Dec. 4, 1868; m. Aug. 2, 1892, Julia E. Gates of Halifax, Vt.
    3407.  Burton Everett. b. May 13, 1872.

## 3408 = 3345.  JOHN CROSBEE[6] MARSH

b. at Montague, Mass., July 9, 1800, son of Joshua[5] and Mindwell (Crosbee) Marsh, (Enos[4], Ebenezer[3], Samuel[2], John[1]); m. (1) April 8, 1823, No. 3408.

**3408.** Elcipha[7] Marsh of Westhampton, No. 3456, b. Feb. 6, 1802, dau. of Philander[6] and Marah (Paulk) Marsh, (Ephraim[5], Ephraim[4], Ebenezer[3], Samuel[2], John[1]), they resided in Leverett, Mass., where Elcipha d. Feb. 5, 1859, æ. 57.  He m. (2) Oct. 18, 1859, No. 3409.

**3409.** Hannah Reed who d. Sept. 8, 1870, æ. 67.  He d. at the home of his son-in-law in Westfield, Mass., Dec. 23, 1870, æ. 70. Their graves are side by side in Leverett cemetery.  Children :

3410. Lebbeus Eaton[7], b. April 11, 1824 ; m. (1) Sarah Gibbs, 3416.
3411. Marah Augusta, b. Aug. 12, 1826; m. (1) Hammond Doane, 3422.
3412. Anson J., b. April 28, 1829; m. (1) Laura P. Cummings, 3429.
3413. Henry Allen, b. May 1, 1834 ; d. May 6, 1834.
3414. Julia E., b. July 14, 1835 ; m. George W. Sibley, 3439.
3415. Austin C., b. Oct. 10, 1838 ; m. Elizabeth Jane Miner of New York City; went in 1875 to Texas and d. there July 31, 1876. No children.

### 3416 = 3410. LEBBEUS EATON[7] MARSH, M. D.

b. at Leverett, Mass., April 11, 1824, son of John Crosbee[6] and Elcipha[7] (Marsh) Marsh, (Joshua[5], Enos[4], Ebenezer[3], Samuel[2], John[1]) ; m. May 23, 1848, No. 3416.

**3416.** Sarah Gibbs, dau. of Solomon and Mary (Cutler) Gibbs of Prescott, Mass., d. June 9, 1877, in Central City and is buried in Greeley. He m. (2) in Denver, No. 3416.1.

**3416.1.** Anna Elizabeth Portia, M. D., b. Sept. 6, 1837, dau. of Rev. George and Hannah (Hunt) Eastman of Farmington, Mich. and Denver, Col. Resided at Dana, Granby, and Wales, Mass., and Greeley, Col. Children :

3417. George Westell[8], b. Aug, 5, 1850 ; unm. and "lives out west."
3418. Charles Eaton, b. Sept. 14, 1852 ; d. Aug. 5, 1867.
3419. Hattie J., b. May 30, 1855 ; m. Frank E. Johnson. He d. in Belleville, O., Dec. 31, 1883. No children.
3420. Julius Emerson, b. March 11, 1858; d. March 14, 1858. ⎰
3421. Julian Estelle, b. March 11, 1858; d. March 10, 1859. ⎱

### 3422 = 3411. MARAH A[7]. MARSH

b. at Leverett, Aug. 12, 1826, named for her mother's mother, Marah (Paulk) Marsh, dau. of John Crosbee[6] and Elcipha (Marsh) Marsh, (Joshua[5], Enos[4], Ebenezer[3], Samuel[2], John[1]) ; m. (1) No. 3422.

**3422.** Hammond Doane of Dana, Mass., b. March 30, 1827, who d. March 7, 1855. After his death she m. (2) Jan. 1, 1859, No. 3423.

**3423.** George F. Lawton. They resided at Troy, N. Y. Children :

3424. Julia Elmyra[8], b. July 15, 1851 ; m. Dec. 14, 1876, Frederick Whiting Barnum of Troy, N. Y., b. July 3, 1849.

Children :

3424.1.   Wallace Doane, b. April 29, 1878.
3424.2.   Florence, b. Aug. 29, 1880.
          By second husband.
3425.   William Marsh, b. Nov. 12, 1859; m. 1886, Millie Woodward.
3426.   Edward Parker, b. Nov. 25, 1863; unm. in 1886.
3427.   Mary Elizabeth, b. Dec. 11, 1865; unm. in 1886.
3428.   Eva Florence, b. March 16, 1869; d. April 12, 1869.


3429 = 3412.   ANSON J[7]. MARSH

b. at Leverett, Mass., April 28, 1829, son of John Crosbee[6] and
Elcipha (Marsh) Marsh, (Joshua[5], Enos[4], Ebenezer[3], Samuel[2], John[1]);
m. (1) March 25, 1850, No. 3429.
3429.   Laura P. Cummings of Amherst, Mass,   They removed to
Bethel, Vt.   His wife died Feb. 23, 1856.   He m. (2) Oct. 13, 1857,
No. 3430.
3430.   Abbie M. Trask of Braintree, Vt., who d. July 12, 1859.
He m. (3) April 15, 1860, No. 3431.
3431.   Nancy J. Lewis of Bethel, Vt.   He has been of very great
service in preserving a record made by his father more than 50 years
ago, and added to by the son, giving more fully the long line to his
own grand-children from John Marsh of Hartford 1636 down, than
is often found anywhere.   Children :

3432.   Laura A[8]., b. Dec. 27, 1852; m. Theodore J. Williams, 3443.
3433.   Charles Anson, d. Nov. 12, 1855; d. Feb. 20, 1856.
          By second wife.
3434.   Abbie Ella, b. July 22, 1858; m. Siloan Flint, 3446.
          By third wife.
3435.   Addie N., b. July 21, 1862; m. Henry H. Lane, 3450.
3436.   May E., b. Aug. 22, 1867.
3437.   Fred A., b. April 1, 1873.
3438.   Austin F., b. April 11, 1875.


3439 = 3413.   JULIA E[7]. MARSH

b. at Leverett, Mass., July 14, 1835, dau. of John Crosbee[6] and
Elcipha (Marsh) Marsh, (Joshua[5], Enos[4], Ebenezer[3], Samuel[2], John[1]);
m. May 6, 1854, No. 3439.

**3439.** George W. Sibley of Westfield, Mass. He d. March 23, 1869. They had seven children of whom four d. in infancy. Children :

    3439.1.  George Hammond[8], b. March 27, 1855 ; d. April 16, 1858 ; was born in North Dana.

    3440.  Julia Ella, b. March 11, 1858.

    3441.  Frank Ellsworth, b. June 22, 1861.

    3442.  Charles Austin, b. Dec. 9, 1863.

    3442.1.  Carrie A., b. Jan. 22, 1867 ; d. Aug. 2, 1867.

    3442.2.  Edith Marsh, b. March 22, and d. Aug. 17, 1869.

    3442.3.  Minnie Porter, b. March 22, and d. March 26, 1869.

### 3443 = 3432. LAURA A[8]. MARSH

b. Dec. 27, 1852, dau. of Anson J[7]. and Laura P. (Cummings) Marsh, (John Crosbee[6], Joshua[5], Enos[4], Ebenezer[3], Samuel[2], John[1]) ; m. Aug. 7, 1869, No. 3443.

    **3443.** Theodore J. Williams of Braintree, Vt. Children :

    3444.  Charles Anson[9], b. Aug. 25, 1870 ; resides at Braintree.

    3445.  Jehiel Francis, b. Jan. 26, 1873.

### 3446 = 3434. ABBIE ELLA[8] MARSH

b. July 22, 1858, dau. of Anson J[7]. and Abbie M. (Trask) Marsh, (John Crosbee[6], Joshua[5], Enos[4], Ebenezer[3], Samuel[2], John[1]) ; m. Sept. 1, 1872, No. 3446.

    **3446.** Siloan Flint. Lives in Strafford, Vt. Children :

    3447.  Lutie Lucinda[9], b. Sept. 18, 1875.

    3448.  Minnie Laura, b. July 14, 1878.

    3449.  Rufus Siloan, b. July 4, 1884.

### 3450 = 3435. ADDIE N[8]. MARSH

b. at Bethel, Vt., July 21, 1862, dau. of Anson J. and Nancy J. (Lewis) Marsh, (John Crosbee[6], Joshua[5], Enos[4], Ebenezer[3], Samuel[2], John[1]) ; m. Feb. 11, 1880, No. 3450.

**3450.** Henry H. Lane. Resides at Braintree, Vt. Children:

    3451. Bertha Evelyn[9], b. March 4, 1881.
    3452. Everett Harrison, b. Dec. 29, 1883.
    3453. Ernest Henry, b. Oct, 1, 1885.

3454 = 3218.    PHILANDER[6] MARSH

b. at Montague, Mass., April 16, 1779, son of Ephraim[5] Marsh, (Ephraim[4], Ebenezer[3], Samuel[2], John[1]) ; m. (1) No. 3454. **3454.** Marah Paulk. He resided at Westhampton, Mass. a number of years. He m. (2) No. 3454.1.

  **3454.1.** Irene Pomeroy of Southampton. No children:

    3455. Lorenzo[7], b. 1800.
    3456. Elcipha, b. Feb. 6, 1802; m. April 8, 1823, John Crosbee Marsh, 3408.
    3457. Sarah Harmenia, b. 1804 ; m. Elijah[6] Marsh, 3241.
    3458. Hollister F., b. July 10, 1806; m. No. 3463.
    3459. Esther, b. 1808; "named for her grandmother"; m. Orin Barton.
    3460. Philander S., b. 1810; m. Sylvia Montague, 3466.
    3461. Julius, b. 1812 ; m. Marion Hull of Westfield, Mass.
    3462. Almond, b. 1814 ; supposed to be killed by a railroad accident near Philadelphia, Pa.

3463 = 3458.    HOLLISTER F[7]. MARSH

b. July 10, 1806, probably at Montague, perhaps at Westhampton, son of Philander[6] and Marah (Paulk) Marsh, (Ephraim[5], Ephraim[4], Ebenezer[3], Samuel[2], John[1]) ; m. No. 3463. **3463.** ——. Removed to Fennville, Allegan Co., Mich. He wrote when nearly 80, May 24, 1886, giving considerable account of his ancestry but very little of his own family. He d. Sept. 1886. Children :

    3464. Hollister F[8]., m. and resided at Allegan, Allegan Co., Mich.
      Child :
    3465. Arthur.

## 3466 = 3460. PHILANDER S⁷. MARSH

b. probably at Montague, 1810, son of Philander⁶ and Marah (Paulk) Marsh, (Ephraim⁵, Ephraim⁴, Ebenezer³, Samuel², John¹); m. May 8, 1835, No. 3466.

**3466.** Sylvia Montague, b. March 2, 1816, at Westhampton, Mass., dau. of David Montague. He resided at Chicopee Falls, where his wife d. Nov. 2, 1850, and later at Lenox, Mass. Children:

> 3467. Francis Myron⁸, b. Feb. 18, 1837; m. Emma L. Keith, 3471.
> 3468. Charles Smith, b. Oct. 13, 1840; m. Harriet E. Parsons, 3475.
> 3469. Enos Montague, b. Aug. 5, 1844; d. Aug. 11, 1849.
> 3470. Sylvia Montague, b. Oct. 21, 1850; adopted by grandfather David Montague; m. March 1, 1871, Amos Drury Rice; resides at Westhampton. No children.

## 3471 = 3467. FRANCIS MYRON⁸ MARSH

b. Feb. 18, 1837, perhaps Chicopee Falls, son of Philander S⁷. and Sylvia (Montague) Marsh, (Philander⁶, Ephraim⁵, Ephraim⁴, Ebenezer³, Samuel², John¹); m. Oct. 26, 1858, at Lenox, Mass., No. 3471.

**3471.** Emma Louisa Keith. He resides at Springfield, Mass. Children:

> 3472. Marion Emily⁹, b. June 9, 1866, at Pittsfield, Mass.
> 3473. Louretta Alice, b. Jan. 3, 1872, at Pittsfield, Mass.
> 3474. Montague Root, b. Jan. 19, 1876, at Springfield, Mass.

## 3475 = 3468. CHARLES SMITH⁸ MARSH

b. Oct. 13, 1840, probably at Chicopee Falls, son of Philander S⁷. and Sylvia (Montague) Marsh, (Philander⁶, Ephraim⁵, Ephraim⁴, Ebenezer³, Samuel², John¹); lived early at Chicopee Falls and Lenox, Mass.; in the civil war was clerk in Provost Marshal's office, Baton Rouge, La., 1862-3; is merchant 25 High Street, Boston and resides at Newton, Mass. He m. Dec. 29, 1864, No. 3475.

**3475.** Harriet Emeline Parsons of Easthampton, Mass., dau. of Edward Parsons. Children:

> 3476. Edmond Parsons⁹, b. Dec. 17, 1867, at Easthampton.
> 3477. Enos Montague, b. Feb. 2, 1876, at Newton, Mass.

3478 = 3219.  EPHRAIM[6] MARSH

b. at Montague, Mass., June 3, 1782, son of Ephraim[5] and Esther Marsh, (Ephraim[4], Ebenezer[3], Samuel[2], John[1]); m. (1) in 1809, No. 3478. **3478.** Eleanor Day. He left Hadley to engage in the carriage business at Springfield. Miss Nina M. Marsh of Bridgewater, Mass., writes Oct. 8, 1894 : "My grandfather fought in the war of 1812, was an aid on Gen. Ripley's staff at the battle of Lundy's Lane." He m. (2) at Clyde, N. Y., No. 3479. **3479.** Miss Fuller. "He d. in 1858." Children :

    3479.1.  Frances Augusta[7], b. April 5, 1812.
    3479.2.  Harriet, b. June 23, 1814. }
    3479.3.  Pamela, b. June 23, 1814. }
              By second wife.
    3479.4.  William F., b. April 8, 1840; m. M. J. Williams, 3480.


3480 = 3479.4.  WILLIAM F[7]. MARSH

b. at Clyde, Wayne Co., N. Y., April 8, 1840, son of Ephraim[6] and —— (Fuller) Marsh, (Ephraim[5], Ephraim[4], Ebenezer[3], Samuel[2], John[1]); m. Jan. 8, 1868, No. 3480. **3480.** Mary J. Williams, b. at Clyde, N. Y., Jan. 8, 1853. "He was with the first Michigan infantry through the four years of the civil war." Child :

    3481.  Nina M., b. at Westfield, Mass., May 29, 1872.


3482 = 3223.  ABEL[6] MARSH

b. at Montague, Mass., May 2, 1793, son of Ephraim[5] and Esther Marsh, (Ephraim[4], Ebenezer[3], Samuel[2], John[1]); m. No. 3482. **3482.** ——. Resided in Coldwater, Mich. and d. in 1876. Children :

    3483.  Alanson[7], resided at Coldwater ; a physician.
    3484.  Angie F., at Quincy, Mich., "fine people."

3485 = 3227. REV. JUSTIN[6] MARSH

b. at Montague, Mass., March 14, 1796, son of Samuel[5] and Martha (Edwards) Marsh, (Ephraim[4], Ebenezer[3], Samuel[2], John[1]); m. (1) Sept. 14, 1830 No. 3485.

**3485.** Jane Elizabeth Deming, dau. of Dr. Fenn Deming, b. at Westfield, N. Y., May 9, 1810; d. at Tekonsha, Mich., Oct. 6, 1848. He m. (2) Feb. 17, 1852, No. 3486.

**3486.** Mrs. Roxana S. Dwight of Delhi, Mich., who d. May 12, 1894. Rev. Justin Marsh lived upon his father's farm, until he was nineteen years of age. While a student at the Amherst academy he united with the First Congregational church of Amherst, Mass., April 25, 1819. He entered Yale college in Aug., 1820. After one year at Yale he removed to Amherst college when it was first opened and graduated Aug. 25, 1824. He spent one year in teaching in Caldwell, N. J. He studied theology with Rev. Allen McLean of Simsbury, Ct. He was licensed to preach at Manchester, Ct., by the Hartford North Association, Feb. 6, 1827, and was ordained in the church of Dr. Noah Porter at Farmington, Ct., Oct. 14, 1828, and became the pastor of a colony from Farmington that had gone to Mina, Chautauqua Co., N. Y. He united with the Presbytery of Buffalo in 1829. Other fields of labor in New York, were West Aurora in Erie Co., Napoli, Cattaraugus Co., and Orangeville in Genesee now Wyoming Co.

In 1837 he was a member of the Synod of Genesee, which was " exscinded " by the General Assembly of that year. Early in 1838 he removed to Battle Creek, Mich., and united with the Presbytery of Marshall. He was the first Commissioner from that Presbytery to the General Assembly of the Presbyterian church and was present on the third Thursday of May, 1838 at the opening of the Assembly in the Seventh Presbyterian church in Philadelphia. And when the " New School Commissioners, after organizing the General Assembly, adjourned to the First Presbyterian church of that city, he went with them. He remained a minister of the New School Presbyterian church, until that distinction was abolished by the ' Reunion ' in 1869."

His fields of labor in Michigan were Battle-Creek, Leoni, Stony-Creek, Tekonsha, Lodi, Concord, Franklin and Somerset. He also acted at different times as Presbyterian missionary in Detroit and

Monroe Presbyteries, exploring the field and organizing churches.
He was an able and faithful preacher of the gospel. He retired
from active ministerial work in 1864 and lived with his oldest son.
He d. at Portland, Mich., Jan. 19, 1872. Children:

    3487. Florella D[7]., b. at Westfield, N. Y., Oct. 7, 1831; m. May 14,
        1875, Isaac Bougham, and d. at Portland, Mich., May
        3, 1883 without issue.
    3488. Augustus, b. June 1, 1834; m. Martha S. Hewitt, 3490.
    3489. Theodore D., b. July 22, 1837; m. Sarah Lamb, 3498.


3490 = 3488.   REV. AUGUSTUS[7] MARSH

b. at Aurora, Erie Co., N. Y., June 1, 1834, son of Rev. Justin[6] and
Jane (Deming) Marsh, (Samuel[5], Ephraim[4], Ebenezer[3], Samuel[2],
John[1]); graduated at Michigan University 1855, Auburn Theological
Seminary 1860, ordained at Blissfield, Mich. Nov. 14, 1860; m. Sept.
10, 1863 No. 3490.

3490. Martha S. Hewitt, b. Jan. 1, 1841. His places of preach-
ing were all in Michigan. At Brooklyn, May, 1860–Nov., 1862;
Grand Rapids, First Presbyterian church, Nov., 1862–Nov., 1865;
Portland, Dec., 1865–May, 1875; Cadillac, June, 1875–June, 1883;
Mackinaw City, June, 1883–Nov., 1887; Hesperia, Nov., 1887–May
1891.—At Birmingham, Dec., 1891, where he now resides in 1894.
Children :

    3491. Jane Deming[8], b. Grand Rapids, Mich., Aug. 20, 1864.
    3492. Theodore Walter, b. Portland, Mich., April 12, 1867.
    3493. Stewart Augustus, b. Portland, Mich., June 24, 1870.
    3494. Esther Hewitt, b. Portland, Mich., Aug. 16, 1871.
    3495. Edward Clark, b. Portland, Mich., Feb. 19, 1875.
    3496. Alice Rebekkah, b. Clam Lake, Mich., April 20, 1876.
    3497. Harry Widdicomb, b. Grand Rapids, Mich., Sept. 22, 1887.


3498 = 3489.   REV. THEODORE D[7]. MARSH, D. D.

b. at Orangeville, N. Y., July 22, 1837, son of Rev. Justin[6] and Jane
Elizabeth (Deming) Marsh, (Samuel[5], Ephraim[4], Ebenezer[3], Samuel[2],
John[1]); graduated at Michigan University in 1857, taught four years,

graduated at Auburn Theological Seminary in 1864 ; m. May 5, 1864,. No. 3498.

**3498.** Sarah Lamb of Branchport, N. Y. Theodore D. Marsh was ordained by the Presbytery of Marshall at Tekonsha, Mich., April, 1864, and after marriage May 5, 1864, went with his wife to Colorado, then a new territory, where he spent four years as pastor of the churches of Central City and Black Hawk, returned to Michigan in 1868, and was pastor six and a half years at Hastings, five years at Paw Paw, and then for nine years superintendent of home missions of the Synod of Michigan ; residing at Grand Rapids ; then pastor three and a half years at Ludington, then, after nearly a year's intermission recruiting his health, pastor at Richland, Mich., his present residence in 1894. He was active in the establishment of Alma college, at Alma, Mich., has been a trustee of the college from its beginning and received from the college the degree of D. D. in June, 1894. Children :

 3499. Flora Louise[8], b. Central City, Col., March 10, 1865; grad. at Michigan female seminary, June, 1886; m. Dec. 29, 1892, Wm. T. Welch and they live at Paw Paw, Mich.

 3500. Frank Lee, b. Hastings, Mich., June 14, 1871 ; grad. at Alma college, 1894.

## 3501 = 3231. MARTHA[6] MARSH

b. at Montague, Mass., July 25, 1801, dau. of Samuel[5] and Martha (Edwards) Marsh, (Ephraim[4], Ebenezer[3], Samuel[2], John[1]) ; m. May 16, 1826, No. 3501.

**3501.** Joseph Fisk, 2d, of Wendell, Mass., b. April 17, 1800. Martha (Marsh) Fisk, d. Dec. 24, 1842 at Wendell, æ. 41. Children born at Wendell :

 3502. Asa S[7]., b. April 2,1827 ; d. Jan. 19, 1829, æ. 2.

 3503. Martha A., b. Nov. 2, 1828; m. May 31, 1848, Willard H. Fleming. Child :

  3504. Inez[8], m. 1878, Frank Holton.

 3505. Electa T. Fisk, b. Feb. 9, 1834 ; m. Feb. 26, 1861, George Hall. Child :

  3506. George[8], b. 1868.

## 3507 = 3232. FANNY[6] MARSH

b. at Montague, Mass., April 30, 1803, dau. of Samuel[5] and Martha
(Edwards) Marsh, (Ephraim[4], Ebenezer[3], Samuel[2], John[1]); m. Jan.
9, 1834, No. 3507.
**3507.** Hovey Moody, 2d, of Granby, Mass. Beside the children
given below there were two who d. in South Hadley, Mass. Children :

    3508. Austin[7], b. at South Hadley, June 30, 1836.
    3509. Charles, b. at South Hadley, Oct. 5, 1838;; m. Mary L.
        More, 3511.
    3510. Jane, b. at Granby, Feb. 24, 1841 ; m. at South Hadley, Jan.
        1, 1867, S. K. Jackson. No children. Resided in 1885
        at Shoshone, Idaho.

## 3511 = 3509. CHARLES[7] MOODY

b. at South Hadley, Mass., Oct. 5, 1838, son of Fanny (Marsh)
Moody, (Samuel[5] Marsh, Ephraim[4], Ebenezer[3], Samuel[2], John[1]) ; m.
at Rockingham, Vt., Nov. 16, 1868, No. 3511.
**3511.** Mary L. More. Children :

    3512. Eva[8], b. at South Hadley, April 9, 1870 ; d. July 30, 1870.
    3513. Victor Hovey, b. June 6, 1872.
    3514. Bertha L., b. Jan. 29, 1882.

## 3515 = 3234. ZEBINA[6] MARSH

b. June 28, 1806, in Montague, Mass., son of Samuel[5] and Martha
(Edwards) Marsh, (Ephraim[4], Ebenezer[3], Samuel[2], John[1]) ; " Homo
sui generis," living to great age, daring to think and original in his
thought, very familiar with his Bible, removed from his church as a
" separatist " i. e. forced to " separate " because holding to immersion,
very literal in interpretation and therefore finding abundant proof of
the present utter unconsciousness of all the dead until the constantly
expected second advent and last trump. He was much interested in
Marsh genealogy, a venerable attendant at several of our annual
meetings, remembering very many who passed to distant states or
other worlds long ago, a veritable Yankee " Old Mortality " with

quiet persistence visiting many old graveyards and recording for our use forgotten dates and names. He treasured his grandfather's old, huge account book, begun in 1754 and gave us to copy its valuable dates and names. He m. (1) June 4, 1834, in Gill, Mass., (by S. S. Howland, Esq.,) No. 3515.

**3515.** Permelia Bathsheba Slate, dau. of Samuel and Bathsheba Slate of Gill. She d. in South Hadley, Mass., Aug. 25, 1846. He was m. (2) Sept. 21, 1857, by Obed Slate, Esq., to No. 3516.

**3516.** Sarah Abesconder Holton, b. in Northfield, Mass., Jan. 11, 1812 and d. there April 2, 1865. He m. (3) by Henry Marsh, Esq., in Amherst, Mass., Jan. 7, 1866, No. 3517.

**3517.** Widow Amy (Cook) Gibson, b. Dec., 1806. His various places of residence appear in the birthplaces of his children. In his old age his home was mainly at Northfield, Mass. He d. there Jan. 7, 1893, æ. 86 years and 6 months. Children :

    3518. A dau[7]., b. April 28, 1835 ; d. same day.
    3519. Harriet Lovina, b. Dec. 21, 1837 ; m. Austin M. Stevens, 3522.,
    3520. Julia Parthenia, b. June 4, 1840 ; m. Michael Malley, 3523.
    3521. Charles Addison, b. South Hadley, Aug. 10, 1846 : d. there
        Sept. 8, 1846.

### 3522 = 3519. HARRIET L[7]. MARSH

b. at Montague, Mass., Dec. 21, 1837, dau. of Zebina[6] and Permelia B. (Slate) Marsh, (Samuel[5], Ephraim[4], Ebenezer[3], Samuel[2], John[1]) : m. in Northfield, Mass., by Simeon A. Field, Dec. 4, 1872, No. 3522.

**3522.** Austin M. Stevens, b. at Montague, Aug. 26, 1842.

### 3523 = 3520. JULIA PARTHENIA[7] MARSH

b. at Bombay, N. Y., June 4, 1840, dau. of Zebina[6] and Permelia B. (Slate) Marsh, (Samuel[5], Ephraim[4], Ebenezer[3], Samuel[2], John[1]) ; m. in Hinsdale, N. Y., by Caleb Todd, Esq., Sept. 19, 1858, No. 3523.

**3523.** Michael Malley, b. in Ireland, Aug. 22, 1831. Children :

    3524. Hattie Maria[8], b. at Hartford, Ct., June 25, 1859 ; d. Sept.
        10, 1859.
    3525. William Luther, b. at Montague, Jan. 9, 1861.

3526.  Lucina, b. at Chicago, Ill., Dec. 21, 1862 ; d. there Dec. 22, 1862.

3527.  Mary P., b. at Earlville, Ill., Jan. 11. 1864.

3528.  Martha Esther, b. Aurora, Ill., Oct. 12, 1870.

3529.  John Edward, b. at Northfield, Mass., Jan. 22, 1875 ; d. there Sept. 7, 1875.

3530.  Charles Addison, b. at Northfield, Jan. 22, 1876.

3531.  Julia Beulah, b. at Northfield, May 6, 1877 ; d. same day.

## 3532 = 3347.  ORSAMUS[6] MARSH

b. at Montague, Mass., Aug. 21, 1804, son of Joshua[5] and Mindwell (Crosbee) Marsh, (Enos[4], Ebenezer[3], Samuel[2], John[1]) ; m. Nov. 9, 1826, No. 3532.

**3532.** Lucinda[5] Hawley, b. at Hadley, Mass., Oct. 9, 1807, dau. of Chester[4] Hawley, (Zechariah[3], Samuel[2], John[1]). He removed near the end of 1835 to Bowen's Corners, Granby, Oswego Co., N. Y. and after living there more than 50 years he d. there Nov. 30, 1880, æ. 76 years, 3 months and 9 days. His widow d. there April 15, 1888, æ. 80 years, 6 months and 6 days. Children :

3532.1.  Isaac Warner[7], b. Sept. 25, 1827 ; m. Mary E. Signor, 3533.

3532.2.  Edward Crosbee, b. July 9, 1829 ; m. Martha Preston, 3535.

## 3533 = 3532.1.  ISAAC WARNER[7] MARSH

b. in Plainville, Hadley, Mass., Sept. 25, 1827, son of Orsamus[6] and Lucinda (Hawley) Marsh of Hadley and Greenfield, Mass., and Granby, Oswego Co., N. Y., (Joshua[5], Enos[4], Ebenezer[3], Samuel[2], John[1]) ; m. March 15, 1849, No. 3533.

**3533.** Mary Etta Signor, b. in Eldridge, N. Y., dau. of Peter and —— (Corwin) Signor. He d. in Granby, Oct. 12, 1880, æ. 53 years and 27 days. Children all b. in Granby :

3533.1.  Edgar Jay[8], b. Dec. 29, 1849 ; m. Margaret Chapman 3534.

3533.2.  Charles Frederick[8], b. Jan. 6, 1854 ; m. Jan. 6, 1874, Eliza Etta Fort, b. at Granby, Jan. 6, 1858, dau. of James J. and Catherine Fort. Adopted dau.: Millie A., b. July 1, 1878.

3533.3.  Isaac Earnest, b. Aug. 28, 1858 ; m. Oct. 18, 1880, Louise Fort of Granby, sister of his brother's wife. Child :

3533.4.  Catherine Etta[9], b. at Granby, July, 1881.

## 3534 = 3533.1. EDGAR JAY⁸ MARSH

b. at Granby, Oswego Co., N. Y., Dec. 29, 1849, son of Isaac Warner[7] and Mary Etta (Signor) Marsh, (Orsamus[6], Joshua[5], Enos[4], Ebenezer[3], Samuel[2], John[1]); m. at Granby, Feb. 1, 1871, No. 3534.

**3534.** Margaret Chapman, b. at Granby, July 28, 1851, dau. of Asa and Phebe (Carpenter) Chapman, of Granby. Children:

3534.1. Minnie Belle[9], b. at Hastings, Oswego Co., N. Y., Dec. 16, 1871.

3534.2. Milton Jay, b. in South West, Oswego Co., N. Y. Sept. 14, 1875.

## 3535 = 3532.2. EDWARD CROSBEE⁷ MARSH

b. at Greenfield, Mass., July 9, 1829, son of Orsamus[6] and Lucinda (Hawley) Marsh, (Joshua[5], Enos[4], Ebenezer[3], Samuel[2], John[1]); m. March 25, 1851, in Ira, Cayuga Co., N. Y., No. 3535.

**3535.** Martha Ann Preston, b. May 15, 1835, in Clay, Onondaga Co., N. Y., dau. of Benjamin and Mary Ann (Belote) Clay. Children all b. in Granby:

3535.1. Mary Olivia[8], b. Feb. 3, 1855; unm. in 1891.

3535.2. Victor Eugene, b. Dec. 16, 1856; m. Alice I. Hudgin, 3536.

3535.3. Edward Frank, b. Nov. 14, 1858; m. Elma T. Randall, 3539.

3535.4. Homer Preston, b. June 17, 1867; a physican; graduated at the University Medical college in New York in the spring of 1891.

3535.5. Willis Baxter, b. May 12, 1871; d. Oct. 15, 1882, æ. 11 years, 5 months and 3 days.

## 3536 = 3535.2. VICTOR EUGENE⁸ MARSH

b. at Granby, N. Y., Dec. 16, 1856, son of Edward Crosbee[7] and Martha Ann (Preston) Marsh of Granby and later of Fulton, N. Y., (Orsamus[6], Joshua[5], Enos[4], Ebenezer[3], Samuel[2], John[1]); m. July 4, 1877, No. 3536.

**3536.** Alice Isabel Hudgin, b. at Pictou, Canada, April 25, 1855, dau. of Alfred and Mary (Wilmer) of Volney, N. Y. Children:

20

3536.1.   Amy Eugenia[9], b. at Volney, July 10, 1878.

3537.     Harry John, b. April 8, 1880, Oswego Falls, N. Y.

3538.     Judson Prosser, b. at Granby, March 18, 1883.

3539 = 3535.3.   EDWARD FRANK[8] MARSH, M. D.

b. at Granby, Oswego Co., N. Y., Nov. 14, 1858, son of Edward Crosbee[7] and Martha Ann (Preston) Marsh, (Orsamus[6], Joshua[5], Enos[4], Ebenezer[3], Samuel[3], John[1]), of Granby and Fulton, N. Y.; m. Nov. 19, 1879, No. 3539.

**3539.**   Elma Theresa Randall, b. at Hannibal, Oswego Co., N. Y., May 25, 1855, dau. of Harvey and Catherine (McBride) Randall, of Hannibal.   Children:

3540.   Mabel Randall[9], b. at Oswego Falls, May 5, 1883.
3541.   Edward Harvey, b. at Oswego Falls, Sept. 7, 1886.

3542 = 3348.   DEXTER[6] MARSH

b. at Montague, Mass., Aug. 22, 1806, son of Joshua[5] and Mindwell (Crosbee) Marsh, (Enos[4], Ebenezer[3], Samuel[2], John[1]) ; m. (1) No. 3542.

**3542.**   Rebecca Slate of Bernardston, Mass., b. Aug. 10, 1810, dau. of Z. and Rebecca (Warden) Slate who d. in Greenfield, Mass., May 15, 1838.   He m. (2) Nov. 25, 1839, No. 3543.

**3543.**   Eunice Moselle Everett, b. Dec. 10, 1815.   He d. at Greenfield, Mass., April 2, 1853, æ. 46 years, 7 months and 10 days. He had a short life but left well known "footprints."   Dr. Stewart of New York adds : " He became widely known to the scientific men of both this country and Europe by his discovery of fossil footprints in the New Red Sandstone of the Connecticut River Valley.   After his decease, specimens from his geological and mineralogical cabinet, were eagerly sought by the leading cabinets of the world.   For an extended notice of him and his work see ' The American Republic ' for July 22, 1855, published in Greenfield, Mass."   See also any leading encyclopedia.   Children :

3544.   Arabella[7], b. Dec. 3, 1835, in Greenfield ; unm. in 1884.
3545.   Frank Slate, b. Dec. 29, 1837 ; m. (1) Mary Jane Abernathy, 3558.1.

By second wife.

3545.1. George Everett, b. Dec. 4, 1840; m. Fannie E. Crosby, 3558.5.

3545.2. Ella May, b. May 21, 1849; d. Feb. 10, 1876, æ. 26 in Greenfield.

3545.3. Emogene Dexter, b. Jan. 16, 1853; m. Jerome V. Allen, 3558.7.


## 3546 = 3236.2. WARREN[7] MARSH

b. at Montague, Mass., May 17, 1824, son of Eliezer[6] and Nancy (Coon) Marsh, (Eliezer[5], Ephraim[4], Ebenezer[3], Samuel[2], John[1]) ; m. No. 3546.

**3546.** Nancy Coon. She d. Jan. 29, 1869. He d. March 16, 1886. Children :

3547. Emmett W., b. Jan. 28, 1850; m. July 19, 1894, Almy L. Sylvester.

3548. Melvin E.


## 3549 = 3237. NANCY[7] MARSH

b. at Montague, Mass., Dec. 10, 1827, dau. of Eliezer[6] and Jemima (Clark) Marsh, (Eliezer[5], Ephraim[4], Ebenezer[3], Samuel[2], John[1]) ; m. (1) March 31, 1848, No. 3549.

**3549.** Albert Wright. She m. (2) Nov., 1871, No. 3549.1.

**3549.1.** Deacon William Guild. Children :

3550. Flora E[s]., b. Feb. 26, 1852 ; m. Daniel Mason. Child :
    3551. Adella[9], b. Aug., 1872.

3552. Nellie, b. June 3, 1855; m. Frank Wetherbee.

3553. Arthur, b. Oct., 1861.

3554. Lillie, b. Feb. 28, 1863.


## 3555 = 3237.1. WILLIAM C[7]. MARSH

b. at Montague, Mass., March 31, 1829, son of Eliezer[6] and Jemima (Clark) Marsh, (Eliezer[5], Ephraim[4], Ebenezer[3], Samuel[2], John[1]) ; m. Jan. 18, 1854, No. 3555.

**3555.** Lucia E. Temple. Resided at Woodstock, Vt. Children :

3556.  George W⁸., b. Dec. 24, 1854; m. Hattie Churchill, 3559.
3557.  Mercy Jane, b. April 15, 1857; m. Clarence Carlisle, 3561.
3558.  Edward P., b. Sept. 23, 1860; m. Fannie Liberty, 3565.


### 3558.1 = 3545.  FRANK SLATE⁷ MARSH

b. at Greenfield, Mass., Dec. 29, 1837, son of Dexter⁶ and Rebecca
(Slate) Marsh, (Joshua⁵, Enos⁴, Ebenezer³, Samuel², John¹); m. (1)
in Altona, Knox Co., Ill., No. 3558.1.
   **3558.1.** Mary Jane Abernethy, b. at Cornwall, Vt., dau. of Abram
F. Abernethy, later of Altona.  She d. Oct. 8, 1872, æ. 28.  He m.
(2) Oct. 23, 1873, in Grinnell, Iowa, No. 3558.2.
   **3558.2.** Mrs. Celestia (Eaton) Wood, b. at Palmer, Mass., Feb. 13,
1836, dau. of Eli Eaton of Somers, Ct. and widow of Edwin P.
Wood, whom she had m. July 5, 1853.  Residence Plum Creek,
Neb.  Children :

   3558.3.  Charles D⁸., b. at Altona, Jan. 30, 1866.
   3558.4.  Hattie A., b. at Altona, March 12, 1868.


### 3558.5 = 3545.1.  GEORGE EVERETT⁷ MARSH

b. at Greenfield, Mass., Dec. 4, 1840, son of Dexter⁶ and Eunice
Moselle (Everett) Marsh, (Joshua⁵, Enos⁴, Ebenezer³, Samuel², John¹);
m. June 29, 1876, No. 3558.5.
   **3558.5.** Fannie Eunice Crosby, b. at Decatur, O., Nov. 20, 1853.
Child :

   3558.6,  George Everett⁸, b. May 6, 1877.


### 3558.7 = 3545.3.  EMOGENE DEXTER⁷ MARSH

b. at Greenfield, Mass., Jan. 16, 1853, dau. of Dexter⁶ and Eunice
Moselle (Everett) Marsh, (Joshua⁵, Enos⁴, Ebenezer³, Samuel², John¹);
m. Aug. 22, 1881, No. 3558.7.
   **3558.7.** Jerome Varney, b. Nov. 15, 1851, son of Fay and Angeline (Ford) Varney of Hoosick, N. Y. and later of North Adams,
Mass.

## 3559 = 3556.  GEORGE W{marsh}. MARSH

b. Dec. 24, 1854, son of William C[7]. and Lucia E. (Temple) Marsh, of Woodstock, Vt., (Eliezer[6], Eliezer[5], Ephraim[4], Ephraim[3], Samuel[2], John[1]); m. June 24, 1884, No. 3559.

**3559.** Hattie Churchill.  Child:

3560.  Ruth[9], b. Sept. 6, 1885.

## 3561 = 3557.  MERCY JANE[5] MARSH

b. April 15, 1857, dau. of William C[7]. and Lucia E. (Temple) Marsh, (Eliezer[6], Eliezer[5], Ephraim[4], Ebenezer[3], Samuel[2], John[1]); m. Feb. 13, 1877, No. 3561.

**3561.** Clarence Carlisle.  Children:

3562.  Lillian Edith[9], b. Nov. 5, 1879.
3563.  Walter Marsh, b. Dec. 2, 1883.
3564.  Eusebia Marcia, b. May 25, 1890.

## 3565 = 3558.  EDWARD P[5]. MARSH

b. Sept. 23, 1860, son of William C[7]. and Lucia E. (Temple) Marsh, of Woodstock, Vt., (Eliezer[6], Eliezer[5], Ephraim[4], Ebenezer[3], Samuel[2], John[1]); m. April 20, 1884, No. 3565.

**3565.** Fannie Liberty.  Children:

3566.  Lucia Helen[9], b. Jan. 17, 1885.
3567.  Nellie Georgiana, b. Aug. 17, 1886.
3568.  Allain Louis, b. Feb. 3, 1888.
3569.  Elizabeth Frances, b. Dec. 5, 1889.
3570.  William Edward, b. Nov. 21, 1891.

## 3571 = 3237.2.  PHILO[7] MARSH

b. at Montague, Mass., April 16, 1831, son of Eliezer[6] and Jemima (Clark) Marsh, (Eliezer[5], Eliezer[4], Ebenezer[3], Samuel[2], John[1]); m. Nov. 29, 1855, No. 3571.

**3571.** Mercy Temple.  Child:

3572.  Walter[8], b. Nov., 1857.

3573 = 3237.3.  STEPHEN D[7]. MARSH

b. at Montague, Mass., Oct. 31, 1832, son of Eliezer[6] and Jemima (Clark) Marsh, (Eliezer[5], Ephraim[4], Ebenezer[3], Samuel[2], John[1]); m. Jan. 9, 1856, No. 3573.

**3573.** Sarah A. Anthony.  Child :

    3574.  Francis S[8]., b. Aug., 1857.
    3575.  Lillian J., b. March, 1860.
    3576.  Carrie.
    3577.  Eva, d.
    3578.  George.
    3579.  Ola.

3580 = 3238.  DAVID C[7]. MARSH

b. at Montague, Mass., Oct. 19, 1834, son of Eliezer[6] and Jemima (Clark) Marsh, (Eliezer[5], Ephraim[4], Ebenezer[3], Samuel[2], John[1]); m. Jan. 6, 1858, No. 3580.

**3580.** Mary Woodward.  He had the honor in 1884 of being the first president of the Marsh Family Association.  He resides at Montague.  Children :

    3581.  Charles D[8]., b. Sept. 1, 1860; M. D.; m. Dec. 10, 1886, Sarah
        M. Rugg.  Child :
        3581.1.  Robert Deane[9], b. Sept. 24, 1890.
    3582.  Mary Elizabeth, b. May 18, 1863 ; m. Austin Washburn, 3584.
    3583.  Edna G., b. April 4, 1872.

3584 = 3582.  MARY ELIZABETH[8] MARSH

b. at Montague, May 18, 1863, dau. of David C.[7] and Mary (Woodward) Marsh, (Eliezer[6], Eliezer[5], Ephraim[4], Ebenezer[3], Samuel[2], John[1]); m. June 22, 1881, No. 3584.

**3584.** Austin Washburn.  Children :

    3585.  Una Maud[9], b. April 6, 1882.
    3586.  Ralph Austin, b. Aug. 21, 1889, d. June 29, 1894.
    3587.  Mildred A., b. Feb. 13, 1891.

## 3588 = 3239.  UCERBIA[7] MARSH

b. at Montague, Nov. 27, 1836, dau. of Eliezer[6] and Jemima (Clark) Marsh, (Eliezer[5], Ephraim[4], Ebenezer[3], Samuel[2], John[1]); m. Oct., 1852, No. 3588.

**3588.** Willard H. Baker.  Children:

  3589. Hiram Eugene[8], b. Dec. 12, 1854.
  3590. Ida N., b. Nov. 20, 1855; m. Charles Leader.
  3591. Willard Byron, b. Dec. 24, 1857, d. Aug., 1861.
  3592. Mary M., b. Sept. 1, 1860; m. Forest Baker, Feb., 1881.

## 3593 = 3240.  AUSTIN B[7]. MARSH

b. at Montague, Nov. 7, 1838, son of Eliezer[6] and Jemima (Clark) Marsh, (Eliezer[5], Ephraim[4], Ebenezer[3], Samuel[2], John[1]); m. Feb. 21, 1861, No. 3593.

**3593.** Minerva Lamb.  He d. May 26, 1872.  Children:

  3594. Ada M[8]., b. Aug. 6, 1865; m. Wallace D. Murray, March 23, 1885.  Children:
    3595. Clifton Wallace[9], b. Jan. 24, 1887.
    3596. Edith Ada, b. April 9, 1890.
  3597. Willie A., b. June 14, 1869, d. Oct. 10, 1869.
  3598. Freddie B., b. Dec. 9, 1870, d. July 1, 1871.

## 3599 = 3240.2.  HARRIET S[7]. MARSH

b. at Montague, March 18, 1842, dau. of Eliezer[6] and Jemima (Clark) Marsh, (Eliezer[5], Ephraim[4], Ebenezer[3], Samuel[2], John[1]); m. Oct. 5, 1860, No. 3599.

**3599.** John Woodward.  Children:

  3600. Franklin J[8]., m. Lillian Eva Maxam, Dec. 2, 1891.
  3601. Minnie H., m. Feb. 18, 1890, Geo. E. Raymond.  Child:
    3602. Lillian Eva[9], b. June 5, 1891.
  3603. Arthur, b. April 13, 1883.

## 3604 = 3188.  ZIMRI[6] MARSH

b. at Montague, Mass., June 8, 1785, son of Ebenezer[5] and Eunice

(Sprague) Marsh, (Ebenezer[4], Ebenezer[3], Samuel[2], John[1]) ; m. in 1806, No. 3604.

**3604.** Creusa Hubbard, b. Jan. 18, 1787, dau. of Caleb and Tryphena (Montague) Hubbard. They removed to New York state after a few years, residing in Schenectady and Skaneateles and Moravia and went to Groton, N. Y. about 1822. He d. there June 6, 1843. His widow removed, as did several of her children, to Quincy, Ill. and d. there Sept. 9, 1864. Children :

> 3605. Augustus Clark[7], b. Oct. 26, 1806; m. Lydia Finney, 3612.
> 3606. Lucius Hubbard, b. May 25, 1809; m. Huldah Finney, 3633.
> 3607. Ebenezer Sprague, b. March 25, 1813; m. Lavinia Barstow, 3655.
> 3608. Abigail Smith, b. Nov. 20, 1815; m. Wm. Crawford, 3658.
> 3609. Emily, b. Sept. 13, 1818; d. Groton, May 19, 1825.
> 3610. William, b. May 11, 1822 ; m. Cornelia M. Woods, 3669.
> 3611. Caleb Phineas, b. Aug. 24, 1824 ; m. Laura S. Baldridge, 3677.

### 3612 = 3605.  AUGUSTUS CLARK[7] MARSH

b. at Montague, Mass., Oct. 26, 1806, son of Zimri[6] and Creusa (Hubbard) Marsh, (Capt. Ebenezer[5], Ebenezer[4], Ebenezer[3], Samuel[2], John[1]). He m. Dec. 24, 1828, No. 3612.

**3612.** Lydia Finney. They lived at Groton, N. Y. until the year 1845. Soon after the death of his wife at Groton, June 28, 1844 he removed to Cincinnati, O., where he m. Aug. 26, 1846, No. 3613.

**3613.** Hannah Alvord. About the year 1850 they removed to Quincy, Ill., spending there the remainder of his life. He was a prominent Odd Fellow, held the office of alderman of the city several years and was president of the Quincy savings bank and of the first national bank, holding the latter position at the time of his death at the age of 57, April 6, 1864. His widow d. in 1871. Children :

> 3614. Ashley Kellogg[8], b. Groton, Aug. 31, 1834 ; d. there Feb. 13, 1838.
> 3615. Mary Emily, b. Nov. 7, 1838; m. F. D. Schermerhorn, 3618.
>    By second wife.
> 3616. Wilbur Clark, b. Aug. 23, 1852; m. Kate E. Sedgwick, 3625.
> 3617. Frank Alvord, b. Sept. 14, 1856; m. Martha J. Ward, 3631.

### 3618 = 3615.  MARY EMILY[8] MARSH

b. at Groton, N. Y., Nov. 7, 1838, dau. of Augustus C[7]. and Lydia

(Finney) Marsh, (Zimri[6], Ebenezer[5], Ebenezer[4], Ebenezer[3], Samuel[2], John[1]); m. at Quincy, Ill., Feb. 8, 1859, No. 3618.

**3618.** Francis Dwight Schermerhorn. She d. there Oct. 1, 1865. Children:

    3619. Augustus Dwight[9], b. Jan. 12, 1860; m. Mary E. Sharp, 3622.

    3620. Mary Emily, b. Quincy, Ill., Aug. 22, 1861; d. there Feb. 12, 1875.

    3621. Lydia, b. Quincy, March 3, 1863; m. at Buffalo, N. Y., June 26, 1894, L. Adelbert Barber.

**3622 = 3619. AUGUSTUS DWIGHT[9] SCHERMERHORN**

b. at Quincy, Ill., Jan. 12, 1860, son of Francis Dwight and Mary Emily[8] (Marsh) Schermerhorn, (Augustus C[7]. Marsh, Zimri[6], Capt. Ebenezer[5], Ebenezer[4], Ebenezer[3], Samuel[2], John[1]); m. at Omaha, Neb., Sept. 1, 1885, No. 3622.

**3622.** Mary Eliza Sharp. Having attended public schools from 1869 to 1877, he entered the employ of the Union Pacific railway in 1879 with a surveying party in Idaho, and continued survey of new lines in Oregon and Montana until in 1881 was assigned position of assistant engineer at Omaha, Neb. In 1884 appointed division engineer of the Nebraska Division Union Pacific Railway headquarters at Omaha where he now resides. Children:

    3623. Mary[10], b. Omaha, July 19, 1886.

    3624. Gertrude, b. Omaha, Oct. 29, 1888.

**3625 = 3616. WILBUR CLARK[8] MARSH**

b. at Quincy, Ill., Aug. 23, 1852, son of Augustus Clark[7] and Hannah (Alvord) Marsh, (Zimri[6], Capt. Ebenezer[5], Ebenezer[4], Ebenezer[3], Samuel[2], John[1]); m. at Chicago, Ill., Nov. 20, 1873, No. 3625.

**3625.** Kate E. Sedgwick. He removed to Minneapolis, Minn., in 1882 where he engaged in the manufacturing business. In 1890 removed to New York City assuming the duties of the office of secretary of the New York National Building and Loan Association which position he now holds. Children:

    3626. Wilbur Theodore[9], b. La Prairie, Ill., Oct. 28, 1874.

    3627. Arthur Clark, b. Quincy, Ill., May 10, 1881.

3628.  Freddy C., b. Minneapolis, Minn., July 29, 1883; d. there
       April 30, 1884.
3629.  Florence, b. Minneapolis, Aug. 11, 1886.
3630.  Katherine E., b. N. Y. City, Oct. 28, 1892.


3631 = 3617.   FRANK ALVORD⁸ MARSH, M. D.

b. at Quincy, Ill., Sept. 14, 1856, son of Augustus Clark[7] and Hannah (Alvord) Marsh, (Zimri[6], Capt. Ebenezer[5], Ebenezer[4], Ebenezer[3],
Samuel[2], John[1]); m. Dec. 25, 1877, at La Prairie, Ill., No. 3631.
**3631.** Martha J. Ward.  He removed in 1883 to Malvern, Iowa.
He is a graduate of the Iowa State Medical college.  In 1891 he
removed to Seward, Neb., where he is at present located as a prac-
tising physician.  Child :

3632.  Mabel Alvord[9], b. Nauvoo, Ill., April 30, 1881.


3633 = 3606.   LUCIUS HUBBARD[7] MARSH

b. at Schenectady, N. Y., May 25, 1809, son of Zimri[6] and Creusa
(Hubbard) Marsh, (Capt. Ebenezer[5], Ebenezer[4], Ebenezer[3], Samuel[2],
John[1]); m. at Groton, N. Y., March 3, 1833, No. 3633.
**3633.**  Huldah Finney, sister of the wife of his brother Augustus
C.  Engaged there in the milling and mercantile business many years
—building a fine brick store on the site of the one occupied by his
father half a century before.  He d. at Groton, Sept. 5, 1885, at the
age of 76, his wife having d. there four years previously, Oct. 3,
1881.  Children :

3634.  Eugene Augustus[8], b. Aug. 3, 1834 ;  m. Minnie M. Davies,
       3638.
3635.  Hiram Clark, b. May 12, 1836 ; m. Sarah Bedell, 3643.
3636.  Dexter Hubbard, b. Aug. 16, 1840 ; m. W. M. Backus, 3648.
3637.  Creusa, b. March 30, 1845 ;  m. L. A. Barber, 3653.


3638 = 3634.   EUGENE AUGUSTUS⁸ MARSH

b. at Groton, N. Y., Aug. 3, 1834, son of Lucius Hubbard[7] and

Huldah (Finney) Marsh, (Zimri[6], Capt. Ebenezer[5], Ebenezer[4], Ebenezer[3], Samuel[2], John[1]); m. at Athens, Pa., Oct. 21, 1869. No. 3638.

**3638.** Minnie M. Davies, who d. at Groton, Nov. 3, 1894. Most of his life has been passed in Groton although he lived in Illinois from the year 1859 to 1861 and after marriage resided in Ithaca six years in the position of deputy county clerk. He enlisted in 1861 serving as 1st Lieut. Co. K, 137th Regt. N. Y. Vols. He has been connected with the Groton carriage company as accountant and book-keeper for several years and now in addition is holding the office of postmaster at Groton. Children :

   3639. Adelbert Davies[9], b. Groton, Jan. 6, 1871.
   3640. Millard Caleb, b. Groton, Dec. 23, 1872.
   3641. Mabel, b. at Groton, June 16, 1876.
   3642. Dexter Hubbard, b. Ithaca, Jan. 6, 1881.

### 3643 = 3635. HIRAM CLARK[8] MARSH

b. at Groton, N. Y., May 12, 1836, son of Lucius Hubbard[7] and Huldah (Finney) Marsh, (Zimri[6], Capt. Ebenezer[5], Ebenezer[4], Ebenezer[3], Samuel[2], John[1]); m. at Grand Island, N. Y., Oct. 5, 1859, No. 3643.

**3643.** Sarah Bedell. He commenced work in a printing office at Havana, N. Y. in the year 1849, attended school afterwards at Groton academy, married in 1859, worked as a printer at Saratoga Spings, Ithaca, Syracuse and Buffalo, was the founder and publisher of the *Groton Journal* in 1866, in 1872 removed to Davenport, Iowa, where he became part owner and publisher of the *Davenport Gazette* until 1882 when he removed to Chicago, Ill., where he with his son Ossian, are still engaged in the job printing business under the firm name of H. C. Marsh & Son. Children :

   3644. Ossian Bedell[9], b. May 28, 1860; m. J. A. Houghton, 3646.
   3645. Frances Emily, b. Saratoga Springs, N. Y., Nov. 7, 1861.

### 3646 = 3644. OSSIAN BEDELL[9] MARSH

b. at Saratoga Springs, N. Y., May 28, 1860, son of Hiram Clark[8] and Sarah (Bedell) Marsh, (Lucius Hubbard[7], Zimri[6], Capt. Ebenezer[5],

Ebenezer[4], Ebenezer[3], Samuel[2], John[1]); in railroad business at Davenport several years, removed to Chicago in 1882, is partner with his father; m. at Davenport, Iowa, Sept. 28, 1886, No. 3646.

**3646.** Jennie Adele Houghton. Child:

3647. Fannie Edith[10], b. Davenport, July 1, 1888.

## 3648 = 3636.   DEXTER HUBBARD[8] MARSH

b. at Groton, N. Y., Aug. 16, 1840, son of Lucius Hubbard[7] and Huldah (Finney) Marsh, (Zimri[6], Capt. Ebenezer[5], Ebenezer[4], Ebenezer[3], Samuel[2], John[1]); m. at Groton, Dec. 3, 1862, No. 3648.

**3648.** Wealthea M. Backus. He went to school at Groton academy, succeeded to the mercantile business of his father when 18 years of age and followed it until the year 1865 when he organized the first national bank of Groton, holding the position of cashier until 1890, when he was elected president, which position he now holds. He is also largely interested in, and president of the Groton carriage company, Crandall machine company, secretary and treasurer of the Dwight farm and land company of Dwight, North Dakota, director in the Groton bridge and manufacturing company, etc. He has always resided at Groton. Children:

3649. Florence Lillian[9], b. Oct. 9, 1864; m. Frank Tanner, 3651.
3650. Carrie Sophia, b. Groton, March 14, 1868.

## 3651 = 3649.   FLORENCE LILLIAN[9] MARSH

b. at Groton, N. Y., Oct. 9, 1864, dau. of Dexter Hubbard[8] and Welthea M. (Backus) Marsh, (Lucius Hubbard[7], Zimri[6], Capt. Ebenezer[5], Ebenezer[4], Ebenezer[3], Samuel[2], John[1]); m. at Groton, Oct. 14, 1891, No. 3651.

**3651.** Frank Tanner. Child:

3652. Mary Creusa[10], b. Groton, Jan. 17, 1893.

## 3653 = 3637.   CREUSA[8] MARSH

b. at Groton, N. Y., March 30, 1845, dau. of Lucius Hubbard[7] and

Huldah (Finney) Marsh, (Zimri⁶, Capt. Ebenezer⁵, Ebenezer⁴, Ebenezer³, Samuel², John¹); m. at Groton, June 21, 1873, No. 3653.

   **3653.** L. Adelbert Barber. She d. at Auburn, N. Y., March 30, 1883. Child:

      3654. Marsh⁹, b. Auburn, N. Y., Feb. 25, 1879.


## 3655 = 3607. EBENEZER SPRAGUE⁷ MARSH

b. at Moravia, N. Y., March 25, 1813, son of Zimri⁶, and Creusa (Hubbard) Marsh, (Capt. Ebenezer⁵, Ebenezer⁴, Ebenezer³, Samuel², John¹); m. at Groton, N. Y., Dec. 29, 1842, No. 3655.

   **3655.** Lavinia Barstow. He spent the early years of his life in Groton, was a justice of the peace there many years, represented the county of Tompkins in the legislature. From 1868 to 1872 held a position in the comptroller's office at Albany, was inspector of state arsenals under Gov. Seymour, holding a position in the custom house, N. Y. City for a time. He was an ardent democrat, scrupulously exact in all matters of business or duty. He resided also at Waverly, N. Y. and Elmira. He died at Elmira, N. Y., May 11, 1874, leaving a wife and two children, a son and daughter, Charles B., and Florence M., who followed him in the years 1878 and 1875. His widow is now living at Groton, N. Y. Children:

      3656. Charles Barstow⁸, b. Groton, N. Y., July 1, 1844; d. New York City, June 14, 1878.

      3637. Florence May, b. Groton, July 14, 1850; d. Elmira, April 19, 1875.


## 3658 = 3608. ABIGAIL SMITH⁷ MARSH

b. Nov. 20, 1815, probably at Moravia, N. Y., where her next older and next younger brothers were born, dau. of Zimri⁶ and Creusa (Hubbard) Marsh, (Capt. Ebenezer⁵, Ebenezer⁴, Ebenezer³, Samuel², John¹); m. Jan. 25, 1837, No. 3658.

   **3658.** William Crawford. Soon after they removed to Geneva, N. Y., where they remained until 1858, when the family removed to La Prairie, Ill., from which place after a residence of ten years they removed to and settled in Quincy, Ill. She died there May 2, 1878, leaving her husband and four children who still survive her in that city. Children :

> 3659. Carrie Phebe[8], b. March 24, 1838 ; m. Harry H. Cober, at La Prairie, Ill., and resides at Quincy.
> 3660. George B., b. Nov. 14, 1839; m. E. Carroll, 3663.
> 3661. William Henry, b. July 16, 1842 ; m. K. E. Crandall, 3665.
> 3662. Mary Ann, b. Oct. 6. 1844 ; m. John H. Cober, 3666.

### 3663 = 3660.  GEORGE B[x].  CRAWFORD

b. at Geneva, N. Y., Nov. 14, 1839, son of Abigail[7] (Marsh) Crawford, (Zimri[6] Marsh, Capt. Ebenezer[5], Ebenezer[4], Ebenezer[3], Samuel[2], John[1]) ; m. at Geneva, March 15. 1864, No. 3663.

> 3663. Emma Carroll.  They have resided at Hannibal. Mo. and Quincy, Ill.  Child :
>> 3664. Edward L[9]., b. Hannibal, May, 1866 : m. in 1891, Jennie McBrotney.

### 3665 = 3661.  WILLIAM HENRY[x]  CRAWFORD

b. at Geneva, N. Y., July 16, 1842, son of Abigail[7] (Marsh) Crawford, (Zimri[6] Marsh, Capt. Ebenezer[5], Ebenezer[4], Ebenezer[3], Samuel[2], John[1]) ; m. there Oct. 25, 1865, No. 3665.

> 3665. Kittie E. Crandall.  He was a railroad conductor at Quincy. Ill., but from ill health obliged to resign some years since.

### 3666 = 3662.  MARY ANN[x]  CRAWFORD

b. at Geneva, N. Y., Oct. 6, 1844, dau. of Abigail[7] (Marsh) Crawford, (Zimri[6] Marsh, Capt. Ebenezer[5], Ebenezer[4], Ebenezer[3], Samuel[2], John[1]) ; m. at La Prairie, Ill., Nov. 7, 1866, No. 3666.

> 3666. John H. Cober.  He d. June 15, 1874.  Children :
>> 3667. William C[9]., b. Quincy, Ill., March 15, 1868 ; m. there Nov. 26, 1890, Mary Annette Cowley.  Child :
>>> 3667.1.  Marian Ivah[10], b. 1891.
>> 3668. Carrie M., b. Quincy, Feb. 19, 1872.

## 3669 = 3610.   JUDGE WILLIAM[7] MARSH

b. at Moravia, N. Y., May 11, 1822, son of Zimri[6] and Creusa
(Hubbard) Marsh, (Capt. Ebenezer[5], Ebenezer[4], Ebenezer[3], Samuel[2],
John[1]) ; m. at Lockport, N. Y., Aug. 29, 1848, No. 3669.

**3669.** Cornelia M. Woods.  "He was graduated at Union college,
New York, in July, 1842.  He was admitted as attorney-at-law, by
the supreme court of New York in July, 1845, and commenced practice at Ithaca, N, Y., in 1846, entering into partnership with Hon.
Alfred Wells.  He was elected district attorney of Tompkins county
in 1850 and moved to Quincy, Ill., May, 1854, where he was in active
practice until June, 1885, when he was elected circuit judge, without
opposition, which office he held with honor and credit, alike to the
bench and himself, until June, 1891, when he resumed law practice
and (as for nearly 40 years) is still June 21, 1893, one of Quincy's
most valuable citizens."  He d. at Quincy, April 14, 1894.  Children :

> 3670.  Mary Murray[8], b. Aug. 10, 1849 ; m. Don A. Sweet. 3674.
> 3671.  Cornelia Woods, b. Ithaca, N. Y., March 20, 1851 : m. at
>          Quincy, Ill., Dec. 31, 1885, Chester A. Babcock.
> 3672.  William Augustus, b. Quincy, Ill., Nov. 24, 1854 ; d. there
>          June 27, 1857.
> 3673.  Lawrence Woods, b. Quincy, May 28, 1863 ; in business there.

## 3674 = 3670.   MARY MURRAY[8] MARSH

b. at Lockport, N. Y., Aug. 10, 1849, dau. of Judge William[7] and
Cornelia M. (Woods) Marsh, (Zimri[6], Capt. Ebenezer[5], Ebenezer[4],
Ebenezer[3], Samuel[2], John[1]) ; m. at Quincy, Ill., May 7, 1872,
No. 3674.

**3674.**  Don A. Sweet.  Children :

> 3675.  William Marsh[9], b. Quincy, May 7, 1873, d. there July 12, 1885.
> 3676.  Cornelia Martha, b. Quincy, Nov. 14, 1878.

## 3677 = 3611.   CALEB PHINEAS[7] MARSH

b. in Groton, N. Y., Aug. 24, 1824, son of Zimri[6] and Creusa
(Hubbard) Marsh, (Capt. Ebenezer[5], Ebenezer[4], Ebenezer[3], Samuel[2],
John[1]) ; m. at Cincinnati, O., Jan. 1, 1852. No. 3677.

**3677.** Laura S. Baldridge. He passed the early years of his life in Groton and vicinity. At 21 years of age went to Cincinnati, O., and was employed as bookkeeper in the wholesale hardware house of Tyler, Davidson & Co., in which he subsequently became a partner, retiring therefrom in 1865 and removed to New York City where he has since resided, making with his wife several trips abroad. Has been connected with several large enterprises, was one of the firm of Herter Bros. for a time. Afterwards president of the Tucker and Carter Cordage Co., and secretary of the National Cordage Co., on its organization, from which position he resigned Sept., 1892 and started soon after with his wife for a two years trip around the world. They have no children. He returned in 1894.

# BRANCH III. THE HADLEY—WINDSOR—NEW HARTFORD BRANCH.

---

### 3721 = 8. JONATHAN[2] MARSH

b. at Hartford, Ct., Sept., 1649, son of John[1] and Anne Webster, dau. of Gov. Webster, removed with his father's family to Hadley, Mass., in 1660 and there spent his life. He was freeman 1690 and representative to the Massachusetts general court in 1701, in which year he placed his only son living, in Harvard college to graduate in 1705. Gov. Hopkins seven times governor of Hartford colony, dying in 1657, left property which eventually helped New Haven and Hartford schools and Harvard college and Cambridge grammar school, and was also the foundation of Hopkins academy at Hadley in 1666 and 7. There Jonathan Marsh had his son fit for Harvard and saw him after graduating in 1705, return to be the academy teacher 1706–7. Who can tell the wide influence of that academy as Gov. Hopkins expressed it, "breeding up hopeful youths at grammar school and college for the public service of the country in future times?" Jonathan[2] Marsh m. July 12, 1676, No. 3721.

**3721.** Dorcas, widow of Azariah Dickinson, slain in the swamp fight Aug. 5, 1675. She d. Aug. 15, 1723, æ. 69, (then b. about 1654.) He d. July 3, 1730, æ. 80 years and 10 months. Children :.

> 3722. Dorcas[3], b. Dec. 29, 1677 ; m. Ichabod Porter, 3730.
> 3723. Ann, b. Sept. 13, 1680 ; m. Samuel Cook, 3738.
> 3724. Mary, b. Feb. 9, 1683 ; m. Wm. Dickinson, 3748.
> 3725. Jonathan, b. Aug. 7, 1685 ; m. Margaret Whiting, 3811.
> 3726. Sarah, b. Dec. 4, 1687 ; m. Noah Cook, 3755.
> 3727. Hannah, b. Feb. 12, 1690 ; m. Samuel Dickinson, 3769,
> 3728. Daughter, b. July 27, 1692 ; d. æ 2 days.
> 3729. Son, b. Sept. 14, 1698 ; d. Sept., 1698.

21

## 3730 = 3722.  DORCAS³ MARSH

b. at Hadley, Mass., Dec. 29, 1677, dau. of Jonathan² and Dorcas Marsh, (John¹) ; m. July 4, 1700, No. 3730.

**3730.** Ichabod³ Porter of Hadley, b. June 17, 1678, son of Samuel² and Hannah (Stanley) Porter, John¹ of Windsor, Ct. Children :

3731.  Dorcas⁴, b. 1703.
3732.  Mehitable, b. July 20, 1706.
3733.  Son, b. and d. April 28, 1707.
3734.  Hannah, b. July 21, 1708.
3735.  Mary, b. April 24, 1711.
3736.  James, b. Sept. 19, 1714 ; m. Eunice Belden.
3737.  Sarah, b. Feb. 2, 1718.
        In the Dwight Book, p. 335 and on, are given the names of 283 descendants of Dorcas³ Marsh and so of her grandfather John¹ Marsh of Hartford.

## 3738 = 3723.  ANN³ MARSH

b. at Hadley, Mass., Sept. 13, 1680, dau. of Jonathan² and Dorcas Marsh, (John¹) ; m. June 21, 1698, No. 3738.

**3738.** Lieut. Samuel³ Cook, b. Nov. 16, 1672, son of Capt. Aaron² Cook of Hadley, Aaron¹ Cook of Northampton ; d. Sept. 16, 1746, æ. 73.  She d. March 30, 1758, æ. 77.  Children :

3739.  Ann⁴, b. June 6, 1700 ; m. Feb. 26, 1725, Aaron Cook, and d. Dec. 27, 1776.
3740.  Sarah, b. June 7, 1703 ; m. Dec. 7, 1726, Timothy Eastman, Jr.
3741.  Hannah, b. April 22, 1706 ; m. March 20, 1730, Wm. Dickinson, Jr.
3742.  Samuel, b. Jan. 10, 1709; H. C., 1735, ordained pastor 2d Ch., Cambridge, 1739; m. 1740, Sarah Porter.  Min. 44 years ; had 12 children, 11 by 2d wife, Anna Cotton, of whom Sarah m. Rev. Jonathan Burr, and eight grandchildren, of whom the last surviving, Miss Anne Bradlaw d. Nov. 30, 1869, in the old parsonage at Arlington, æ 84.
3743.  Mehitable, b. Nov. 10, 1711 ; m. Jan. 31, 1734, Jonathan Smith.  Worthington Smith, her grandson, was Pres. of Univ. of Vermont.
3744.  Jonathan, b. March 28, 1714; d. April 12, 1714.
3745.  Joanna, b. May 10, 1715 ; d. June 13, 1715.

3746.   Miriam, b. Oct. 14, 1716; m. Nov. 17, 1743, Josiah Pierce, a
remarkable man, H. C. 1735: town clerk, Hadley,
teacher and sometimes preacher although not ordained,
Rep. to Gen. Court four times and twice delegate to the
Provincial Congress in 1774 at Concord, 1775 Cambridge.
3747.   Jonathan b. Jan. 17, 1722.


## 3748 =3724.   MARY³ MARSH

b. at Hadley, Mass., Feb. 9, 1683, dau. of Jonathan² and Dorcas
Marsh, (John¹); m. about 1703, No. 3748.

**3748.**   Sergt. William³ Dickinson of Hadley, b. May 18, 1675,
son of Nehemiah² and Nathaniel¹. He was often selectman and
rose to rank of ensign. He d. June 24, 1742. Children:

3749.   Mary⁴, b. Feb. 23, 1704; m. April 6, 1727, John Smith, son
of Ebenezer.
3750.   William, b. April 26, 1706; m. Hannah Cook.
3751.   Dorcas, b. March 21, 1709; m. Hezekiah Smith.
3752.   John, b. Nov. 27, 1715; m. Martha Cook.
3753.   Josiah, b. Aug. 8, 1724; m. Sybil Partridge.
3754.   Elisha, b. May 18, 1829.


## 3755 = 3726.   SARAH³ MARSH

b. Dec. 4, 1687, at Hadley, Mass., dau. of Jonathan² and Dorcas
Marsh, (John¹); m. Nov., 1716, No. 3755.

**3755.**   Noah³ Cook, son of Westwood² and Sarah (Coleman)
Cook, Capt. Aaron¹ and Sarah² (Westwood) Cook, William¹ Westwood. Noah³ Cook was b. at Hadley, April 5, 1694 and d. June 17,
1760. Sarah³ (Marsh) Cook d. Sept. 4 or 5, 1746. Children:

3756.   Sarah⁴, b. Nov. 8, 1717; m. Sept. 8, 1743, Elisha Cook, 3762.
3757.   Noah, b. Feb. 4, 1720; d. May 17, 1725, æ 5.
3758.   Coleman, b. June 12, 1722; d. Aug. 20, 1746, æ 24.
3759.   Joseph, b. Nov. 24, 1724.
3760.   Dorcas, b. March 28, 1727; m. Aaron Goodrich.
3761.   Noah, b. Feb. 12, 1730.

## 3762 = 3756. SARAH⁴ COOK

b. Nov. 8, 1717, dau. of Sarah³ (Marsh) Cook, (Jonathan² Marsh, John¹) ; m. Sept. 8. 1743, her father's cousin, No. 3762.

**3762.** Elisha Cook.    Children :

    3763.  Coleman⁵, b. Aug. 3, 1747; m. Jan. 31, 1771, Hannah Smith. Children :

    3764.  James⁶, b. Sept,, 1777.

        m. (2) June 1, 1801, Ruhamah Deane.    Children :

    3765.  Enos Foster⁷ Cook, banker at Amherst, Mass., b. Oct. 29, 1816 ; m. April 22, 1840, Sarah Jane White, dau. of Daniel.    Children :

        3766.  William Foster⁸, b. July 1, 1855.
        3767.  Frederick Louis, b. Feb. 18, 1858.
        3768.  Mary Maria, b. Feb. 1, 1861.

        For more full account of these families descended from Jonathan² Marsh, John¹, see Hadley Book.


## 3769 = 3727.  HANNAH³ MARSH

b. at Hadley, Mass., Feb. 12, 1690, dau. of Jonathan² and Dorcas Marsh, (John¹) ; m. Oct. 17, 1711, No. 3769.

**3769.**  Samuel² Dickinson, son of Nehemiah² Dickinson, (Nathaniel¹), brother of William, who m. her sister Mary.    He was b. at Hadley, Aug. 16, 1682.    They removed to Shutesbury, Mass.    She d. June 10, 1729 and he d. about 1747.    Children :

    3770.  Samuel⁴, b. Oct. 16, 1712; m. Esther White, dau. Nathaniel.
    3771.  Jonathan, b. Jan. 16, 1715; m. Sept. 26, 1745, Dorothy Stoughton, dau. of John of Windsor, Conn.    Of their children :

        3772.  Lucy⁵, b. Nov. 9, 1746; m. Zaccheus Crocker of Sunderland.    Of their descendants are Daniel B. and Stoughton and their children of the " Plum Trees," Sunderland.

    3773.  Azariah, b. July 10, 1717 ; m. Sept. 16, 1747, Eunice Stoughton, dau. John, res. Shutesbury and Amherst.    Children:

        3774.  Eunice⁵, b. April 10, 1749; m. Joseph Eastman.
        3775.  Hannah, b. Dec. 24, 1750; m. Eleazer Cowles.
        3776.  Azariah, b. April 13, 1753 ; m. Mary Eastman, 3781.

3777. Oliver, b. March 27, 1757; m. (1) Hannah Strickland, and (2) Dorothy Whiting. He d. May 12, 1842, childless, æ 86. He built and endowed North Amherst church.

3778. Nathaniel, b. Sept. 3, 1721; m. (1) Thankful, who d. March 9, 1783, æ. 60. He m. (2) Jan. 18, 1787, widow Jemima Wales. He had nine children, all by first wife, and d. July 10, 1806.

3779. Hannah, b. March 6, 1723.

3780. Nehemiah, b. June 15, 1726; m. Nov. 14, 1749, Amy, dau. of John Stoughton of Windsor. They had three children. He d. Jan. 23, 1779, she d. Jan. 27, 1784. They res. in Shutesbury and Amherst.


## 3781 = 3776. AZARIAH[5] DICKINSON

b. April 13, 1753, son of Azariah[4] Dickinson, Hannah[3] (Marsh) Dickinson, (Jonathan[2] Marsh, John[1] of Hartford); m. Dec. 22, 1785, No. 3781.

3781. Mary Eastman, dau. of Joseph Eastman of Amherst; resided at Amherst; d. Aug. 31, 1813. Children:

3782. Sarah L[6]., b. June 17, 1787; d. Sept. 1, 1788.

3783. Ransom, b. May 8, 1789; m. Betsey Dickinson, dau. of Aaron Dickinson; resided at Sunderland and was liberal to North Amherst church.

3784. Austin, b. Feb. 15, 1791; graduated at Dartmouth college in 1813, clergyman; m. in 1836, Laura W. Camp and d. Aug. 15, 1849.

3785. Daniel, b. June 18, 1793; m. (1) Louisa Adams, 3788.

3786. Baxter, b. April 14, 1795; Yale college 1817, clergyman, D. D.; m. June 4, 1823, Martha Bush.

3787. Hannah, b. June 3, 1797; m. Austin Loomis of Amherst.


## 3788 = 3785. DANIEL[6] DICKINSON

b. at Amherst, Mass., June 18, 1793, son of Azariah[5], Azariah[4], Hannah[3] (Marsh) Dickinson, (Jonathan[2], John[1]); m. (1) Feb. 17, 1819, No. 3789.

3789. Louisa Adams, d. March 6, 1828, æ. 30. He m. (2) June 25, 1829, No. 3790.

**3790.** Tammy Eastman. They resided at Amherst. He d. Dec. 25, 1874, æ. 81. His widow d. Oct. 15, 1887, æ. 86. Through the influence of Mr. Daniel Dickinson, who was very prominent in North Amherst affairs, his uncle, "Land'ord Oliver," after some years agreed to the removal of the condition that he, "being sole owner and proprietor of the meeting house lately erected," had inserted in all the original pew deeds "which forfeited the sale of the pew in case any negro or mulatto was admitted to the possession or occupancy of it." The meeting house was dedicated Nov. 15, 1826 and the exclusive condition remained until the interior was remodeled. Daniel[6] Dickinson was captain of a cavalry company enrolled for the war of 1812, justice of the peace 40 years and several times represented Amherst in the general court. "A *pillar* in the church!" Children :

> 3791. Mary Adams.
> 3792. Daniel Austin, b. April 1, 1822.
> > By second wife.
> 3793. Louisa, b. July 14, 1830; grad. at Mt. Holyoke, 1857 ; m. Sept. 30, 1857, Rev. John M. Green, D. D.; resided at Hatfield and Lowell, Mass. Six children.
> 3794. William Eastman, b: June 11, 1832, Rev., Grad. A. C. 1855, M. A. 1858, pastor at Chicopee for years, resides at Amherst, Mass.; m. Sept. 6, 1860, Eliza Hobart, b. Oct. 6, 1832. Child :
> > 3795. Edward Baxter[8], b. March 3, 1863; m. Sept. 6, 1892, Caroline R. Bemis of Chicopee. He is a dentist at Amherst.
> 3796. Sarah Tamson, b. May 19, 1834; m. April 19, 1865, Rev. Frederic B. Phelps. Children :
> > 3797. Frederic William[8], b. April 13, 1866; Amherst college, 1885 ; Prof. at Washburn college, Topeka, Kansas, then Prof. Pac. Theo. Sem., Oakland, Cal.; d. lamented at Tucson, Arizona, Feb. 27, 1893, æ. 26 years and 10 months.
> > 3798. Charles Dickinson, b. Nov. 29, 1868 ; Amherst college, 1889.
> > 3799. Edith Sophia. b. June 14, 1871 ; d. Sept. 17, 1884.
> > 3800. Myron Austin, b. Aug. 2, 1873; d. Nov. 3, 1894.
> > 3801. Julia Eastman, b. March 15, 1875.
> > 3802. Florence Dell, b. May 14, 1876.
> > 3803. Isabelle Maud, b. July 25, 1877.
> 3804. George, b. 1836; d. y.

3805.   Charles Read, b. Oct. 16, 1837; m. Aug. 16, 1865, Ardelia
Harris, dau. of Edwin Harris of Hatfield.   Resides at
Amherst.   Children :

3806.   Edwin Harris[8], b. March 22, 1868; m. Nellie Cowles,
4392.

3807.   Louisa, b. Sept. 24, 1869; grad. at Mt. Holyoke college.

3808.   Laura Austin, b. Nov. 15, 1870; grad. at Mt. Holyoke
college.

3809.   Raymond Daniel, b. Dec. 7, 1878.

3810.   Edward Baxter, b. May 5, 1840; d. 1866.

In History of Hadley, among descendants of the above four
daus. of Jonathan[2] Marsh of Hadley of whom two mar-
married Cookes and two Dickinsons, these descendants
largely remaining near Hadley and Amherst, I have 515
names, and adding from the Dwight book 283 descendants of the daughter Dorcas who m. Ichabod Porter of
Hatfield we have from Jonathan Marsh's five daughters
798 persons retaining his blood but not his name.   To
perpetuate that name he had but one son, Rev. Jonathan[3]
Marsh of Windsor, Ct., and but one *grandson with
children*, Rev. Jonathan[4] Marsh of New Hartford, Ct.

# THE WINDSOR, CT. FAMILY.

## 3811 = 3725.   REV. JONATHAN[3] MARSH, D. D.

b. at Hadley, Mass., Aug. 7, 1685, son of Jonathan[2] and Dorcas
Marsh, (John[1]); graduated at Harvard college, 1705, teacher at
Hadley Hopkins academy, 1706–7, salary £30 ; settled at Windsor,
Ct., June, 1710 ; m. July 13, 1710, No. 3811.

3811.   Margaret Whiting, b. Jan. 5, 1690, dau. of Joseph and
Anna (Allyn) Whiting.   Her father m. (1) Oct. 6, 1671, Mary Pynchon, b. Oct. 28, 1650, and (2) in 1676, Anna Allyn, both grand-
daughters of William Pynchon the founder of Springfield, Mass.
Rev. Jonathan[3] Marsh, at first settled as colleague of Rev. Mr.

Mather, remained pastor there at Windsor 37 years by the beautiful
river of all his days, until his death æ. 62.  He published "election
sermons," delivered before the general court, in 1721 and 1737.
His success is thus alluded to in the "History of the First church of
Hartford:"  "Meantime, only so far away as Windsor, a very remarkable revival had taken place under the ministry of Rev. Jonathan
Marsh."  Yet like many of the strong men of his day he was wary
of new measures.  In 1741 he was of the council that disapproved
of "faintings and convulsions" as necessary for conviction of sin,
and of visions for the bodily eye.  At one time he was honored with
a military guard to escort him.  He d. Sept. 8, 1747.  Margaret
(Whiting) Marsh, d. Dec. 8, 1747.  She made a nuncupative (oral)
will very near the hour of her death, having intended to send for her
brother Whiting the next day, and in the custom of the time, mentions
her son in precedence of his older sister.  (Hartford Records.)
Children:

3812.  Margaret⁴, b. June 10, 1711; m. Rev. Nathaniel Roberts of
      Torrington, Ct., and d. Oct. 18, 1747, æ. 36.
3813.  Jonathan, b. Jan. 1, 1714; m. (1) Elizabeth Sheldon, 3820.
3814.  Mary, b. July 19, 1716; m. Rev. Stephen Heaton of Goshen,
      Ct., who d. suddenly Dec. 29, 1788, leaving his widow
      and one child, perhaps the "Isaac, son of Mary Marsh
      baptized June 29, 1777."
3815.  Dorcas, b. Aug. 31, 1718; m. Jabez Bissell of Windsor, Ct.
3816.  Hannah, b. May 28, 1723.
3817.  Joseph, b. Nov. 10, 1727; m. Elizabeth Marsh, 3819.
3818.  Ann, b. Jan. 28, 1730.  Did she m. about 1748, Capt. Isaac
      Sheldon?

## 3819 = 3817.   JOSEPH⁴ MARSH

b. at Windsor, Ct., Nov. 10, 1727, son of Rev. Jonathan³ of Windsor
and Margaret (Whiting) Marsh, (Jonathan², John¹); m. about 1747
or later, No. 3819.

3819.  Elizabeth⁴ Marsh, No. 2404, dau. of Capt. Jonathan³ and
Elizabeth (Wadsworth) Marsh, (John², John¹).  She was baptized at
Hartford, Ct., Feb. 12, 1721, and her grandfather Capt. Joseph Wadsworth of Charter Oak fame left her £10 in his will.  Joseph⁴ Marsh
of Windsor entered the service of his country in stirring times.  He

made his will and d. at Meriden, Ct., on his way home from camp in New York, Aug. 15, 1776. He gave all his property to his widow for her natural life and then to the North society " for the support of the Gospel Ministry or schooling as they judge best." Elizabeth m. (2) April 7, 1779, Samuel Cole, probably of Norwalk, Ct., and d. a widow April 25, 1800, æ. about 80. She left no children.

## THE YOUNGER NEW HARTFORD LINE.

### 3820 = 3813.  REV. JONATHAN⁴ MARSH

b. at Windsor, Ct., Jan. 1, 1714, son of Rev. Jonathan³ and Margaret (Whiting) Marsh, (Jonathan², John¹); graduated at Yale college, 1735, ordained and settled Oct., 1739, at New Hartford, Ct., where he remained pastor between 54 and 55 years until death. The family of Rev. Jonathan⁴ and his descendants need to be carefully distinguished from those of his father's cousin Capt. Jonathan³ son of John², John¹. Both were of New Hartford, the Capt. one of the very first settlers, the parson the first minister settled there. When his house was built, about 1740, Rev. Mr. Marsh told the men present that they must cut away the white birches between there and Mr. Israel Loomis' house before they could have anything to eat or drink as he wanted to see his nearest neighbor's house. They fell to, cut the way clear and had the refreshments including a good supply of rum. He had a slave who did his house and farm work. This negro, named Moses, set out an orchard of some fifty apple trees which was always called " Moses' orchard." Father Marsh as was customary in those days, considered a little stimulant essential to health of farm laborers, especially in haying. Yet he was a thoughtful man and knew that these stimulants sometimes bite like an adder. One day he gave Moses a bottle containing a moderate quantity of cider brandy and to divert his attention from the quantity to the quality told him that it was very old. Moses took the bottle, held it up to the light and with a disappointed wink replied, " Yes, Massa, but berry small of his age." He told Mr. Tucker one day " It would be no sin to worship your drag for it is ' like nothing in the heavens above or the earth beneath. ' " Rev. Jonathan[4] Marsh was twice married. He had a little book in which he thus records his two marriages :

3820. " Jonathan Marsh nuptus fuit cum Elizabeth Sheldon, Hartfordia, Feb. 26, 1740, per D. Whitman."

3821. " Jonathan Marsh nuptus fuit cum Mariana (Lawrence) Kieth, Hartfordia, May 27, 1751, per D. Dorr." This little book now more than 150 years old, in which he kept some or all his church records, has a curious history. John E. Marsh, Esq., of Hartford, 1893, thus describes it : " Some one came across it in Washington, D. C. and sent it to Hon. Origen S. Seymour, connected with the Marsh family, see No. 145. He presented it to the corporation of Memorial Hall, Hartford, where I found it. It is bound in leather, is about six by four inches in size and less than an inch in thickness. The cover is off and the leaves all loose. The work is finely and closely written. How it got to Washington is a mystery." Of his first wife who had six children the following record is significant. " Her child, Elizabeth, was born May 10, baptized 15. She d. of a Sab. morning May 20, 1749, æ. about 30 years." He had twelve children, of whom seven were daughters and five sons, and all but one son grew up, and ten were married. His second wife Marianna Keith was a young widow with two daughters one of whom m. William Ellery, a prominent merchant of Hartford, and became grandmother of Thomas H. Seymour, governor of Connecticut and minister to Russia. The following records were written by Jonathan Marsh 125 years ago : " Mem. Susanna Ellery d. at my house June 22, 1868, æ. 28. She was eldest daughter of my wife." " Wm. Chas. Hulett m. Mary Ann Keith, Mrs. Marsh's second daughter Nov. 29, 1761." Widow Keith was sister of John Lawrence, treasurer of the colony; a lady of many accomplishments, whose friends opposed her burying her graces in the wilderness of New Hartford, actually over twenty miles from the capital. The following pen portrait is by Rev. Frederick Marsh, who lived to be 92. No. 2710. " Mr. Marsh was above the medium height and size of men, well proportioned, grave and venerable in appearance, of a social turn of mind, and accustomed to wear a large wig. He was settled on the halfway plan; was Arminian in his theological views. In his preaching, as I remember him, when about fourteen years old, was not animated, and as it seemed to me, never earnest and rousing. I remember to have been seriously affected on seeing and hearing him address the people on funeral occasions." A fac simile of his signature is found in the History of Hartford county, vol. 2, p. 540. His salary was £100 to be increased £10 a year till it became £150. He was given choice of pews. Indians were allowed in the church only on towns pleasure. There was "suitable preparation of liquer" for meeting house "raising." During 55 years of ministry he never attended the Hartford North Consociation. As did most of the Connecticut ministers in 1741 and 1744, he opposed Whitfield. He d. 1794, æ. 80. His widow Marianna was always called "Madame Marsh" by his parishoners. After his death she resided in Somers, Ct., with her daughter Mrs. Cooley and was buried there. Children :

> 3822. Ann⁵. "b. and bap. Feb. 22, 1741, at Hartford;" m. Zebulon Seymour, 3834.
> 3823. Joseph Whiting, "b. Feb. 6, 1742-3, bap. on ye 13 day;" "d. at Granada, W. Ind., March 21, or April 26, 1764, æ. 21." "My oldest son." He grad. at Yale college 1763, the first college graduate from New Hartford. He went as soldier under Gen. Lyman in the expedition against Havana.
> 3824. Jerusha, b. Aug. 20, 1744, at Hartford and bap. by Mr. Whitman; m. Sept. 21, 1765, Joseph King of Middletown, Ct.
> 3825. Daniel, "b. Feb. 4, 1746, bap. Feb. 9, 1746"; m. Jerusha Treat, 3853.
> 3826. Isaac, "b. Oct. 18, bap. 25, 1747"; m. Lucy Smith, 3861.
> 3827. Elizabeth, b. May 10, 1749; m. Aug. 10, 1780, Jerijah Merrill of New Hartford and d. Aug., 1786.
>
> By second wife.
>
> 3828. Margaret, "b. and bap. ye Sept. 8, 1752"; m. Luke Cooley, 3841.
> 3829. "Jona. Marsh, my son, b. Jan. 10, 1754, at night, and was bap. ye 13, and d. Oct. 4, 1757."
> 3830. Fanny, b. Jan. 23, 1756? m. July 25, 1788, John Collins.
> 3831. Mary, b. about 1757? m. June 27, 1775, Abner Beach, 3847.
> 3832. John Lawrence, "my son was b. and bap. July 22, 1759"; he m. in 1796, Lucy (Smith) Marsh, widow of his brother Gen. Isaac Marsh. She d. Dec. 19, 1840, æ. 85.
> 3833. Hannah, "my dau. b. March 18, 1761, and bap. March 22, 1761 ;" m. (1) Caleb Watson, 3849.

## 3834 = 3822. ANN⁵ MARSH

b. at Hartford, Ct., Feb. 22, 1741, dau. of Rev. Jonathan⁴ and Elizabeth (Sheldon) Marsh, (Rev. Jonathan³, Jonathan², John¹); m. Sept. 25, 1759, No. 3834.

**3834.** Capt. Zebulon Seymour, of Hartford, Ct., b. Sept. 12, 1736, son of Zebulon and Keziah (Bull) Seymour. He held several town offices and was a prominent citizen of Hartford; d. July 27, 1807, æ. 70. Mrs. Ann (Marsh) Seymour d. in Nov., 1812. Children, several d. y.:

3835. Mary Ann, bap. at New Hartford, Jan. 21, 1760; d. Mr. Marsh's record April 19, 1767, grave stone April 10, 1766, æ. 6.
3836. Joseph Whiting, b. 1763; m. (1) Lovisa, dau. of Eli Warner. She d. at Hartford, July 31, 1798. He m. (2) Lucy Sharp, Dec. 22, 1799, widow of Jacob Baldwin and d. at Hartford Sept. 7, 1815, in 53d year. Had 11 children, widow d. at Richmond, Va., July, 1842.
3837, Epaphras, b. 1767; m. April 27, 1791, Lucy Bliss of West Springfield; d. at Hartford, Sept., 1796, æ. 29. Widow d. at Springfield, Mass., Dec. 4, 1797, æ. 27. Three children.
3838. Fanny, d. y.
3839. Jerusha, prob. d. y.
3840. Harriet, b. Jan. 3, 1782; m. Nathaniel Webb, long principal of Stone school, Hartford, who d. Aug. 8, 1841. She d. at Hartford, Sept. 19, 1866, had eight children.


## 3841 = 3828. MARGARET⁵ MARSH

b. Sept. 8, 1752, dau. of Rev. Jonathan⁴ and Marianna (Lawrence) Marsh of New Hartford, (Rev. Jonathan³ of Windsor, Jonathan² of Hadley, John¹ of Hartford); m. Sept. 12, 1786, No. 3841.

**3841.** Luke Cooley of Somers, Ct. After the death of her father in 1794, her mother resided with her at Somers. " The old armchair, several articles of furniture and some brought from the home of Rev. Jonathan⁴ Marsh of New Hartford are now (1885) in possession of his great-grand-daughter, Mrs. Margaret Marsh⁷ (Cooley) Warren of Boston, Mass. Children:

3842.  Luke[6], d. unm.
3843.  Jonathan Marsh, m. Naomi Hills of Longmeadow, Mass.,.
         and had 12 children all of whom lived to be married.
         The third dau.:
     3844.  Margaret Marsh[7], m. Franklin C. Warren of Boston,
              Mass., and had four children :
         3845.  May C[8].
     3846.  Harriet, m. John Wright Warren of Lincoln, Mass. and had
              ten children, two sons and eight daus.


### 3847 $=$ 3831.  MARY[5] MARSH

b. about 1757, dau. of Rev. Jonathan[4] and Marianna (Lawrence–
Keith) Marsh, (Rev. Jonathan[3] of Windsor, Jonathan[2] of Hadley,
John[1] of Hartford) ; m. June 27, 1775, No. 3847.

**3847.**  Abner Beach of Goshen, Ct.   Child :
     3848.  " Isaac[6], son of Mary Marsh, bap. June 29, 1777."


### 3849 $=$ 3833.  HANNAH[5] MARSH

b. at New Hartford, Ct. March 18, 1761, dau. of Rev. Jonathan[4] and
" Mary Anna " (Lawrence–Keith) Marsh, (Rev. Jonathan[3] of Windsor,
Jonathan[2] of Hadley, John[1] of Hartford) ; m. (1) Nov. 15, 1779,
No. 3849.

**3849.**  Caleb Watson of New Hartford.   She was separated from
him and after his death she m. (2) a prominent merchant of Hartford,
who was postmaster under Benjamin Franklin, No. 3850.

**3850.**  William Ellery, b. about 1740.   He m. (1) Nov. 26, 1761,
Susanna Keith, dau. of Mrs. Rev. Jonathan[4] Marsh, b. about 1740.
She d. in Rev. Jonathan Marsh's house June 22, 1768, æ. 28.   He
m. (2) Experience Ledyard.   He m. (3) Hannah (Marsh) Watson,
widow of Caleb Watson.   He d. Aug. 27, 1812, æ. 72.   She d. Jan.
15, 1838, æ. 76.   His third child dau. of Susanna Keith.
     3851.  Jane[6], b. April 24, 1766; m. Maj. Henry Seymour, son of
              Thomas and Mary (Ledyard) Seymour and their son :
         3852.  Thomas H[7]., b. 1808; d. 1868, was Gov. of Connecticut
                  and U. S. Min. to Russia.  See N. E. Gen. Reg.
              1889, p. 315.

## 3853 = 3825.  DANIEL[5] MARSH

b. at New Hartford, Ct., Feb. 4, 1746, son of Rev. Jonathan[4] and
Elizabeth (Sheldon) Marsh of New Hartford, (Rev. Jonathan[3], D. D.,
of Windsor, Ct., Jonathan[2] of Hadley, Mass., John[1] of Hartford);
m. about 1771-2, No. 3853.

**3853.** Jerusha Treat. He resided first at New Hartford where,
as we find in Rev. Jonathan[4] Marsh's little record book, seven of his
children were baptized up to Dec. 3, 1783. Two of his children
Patty and Wolcott were probably born in Paris, N. Y., (Sauquoit
Valley,) to which place he removed among the early settlers, for their
names do not appear in the little book. This "invaluable memorandum of baptisms, marriages and deaths in the handwriting of the
Rev. Jonathan, and covering the entire period of his ministry," was
" rescued by Senator Foster of Ct., from a Washington second hand
bookstore." John E. Marsh, Esq. of Hartford, No. 799, writes that
Senator Foster "sent it to Hon. Origen S. Seymour, No. 145, who
presented it to the corporation of ' Memorial Hall ' in Hartford."
There he found it and copied for us its Marsh statistics. He describes
it as "bound in leather, about six by four inches and less than an
inch in thickness, the cover off and the leaves all loose, in manuscript
finely and closely written. How it got to Washington is a mystery."
It seems probable that Daniel[5] removed to Paris, N. Y. in 1784 or
1785. Children, (seven were born at New Hartford, Ct.):

3853.1. Jerusha[6], bap. Dec. 27, 1772 ; m. Spencer Briggs. She
had a grand-dau. Mrs. Esther Ann Briggs.
3853.2. Josiah Whiting, bap. April 30, 1775.
3853.3. Daniel, bap. Feb. 13, 1777 ; d. y.
3853.4. A son, bap. Nov. 10, 1777 ; "d. soon."
3853.5. Daniel Sheldon, bap. May 30, 1779; m. L. Gilbert, 3854.
3853.6. George, bap. June 10, 1781.
3853.7. Samuel Treat, bap. Dec. 3, 1783.
3853.8. Patty, m. Timothy Gridley. Her dau. is Mrs. William S.
Pierce of Central Square, N. Y.
3853.9. Wolcott, b. March 1, 1788 ; m. Lucy Hart, 3858.


## 3854 = 3853.5.  DANIEL SHELDON[6] MARSH

b. at New Hartford, Ct., baptized May 30, 1779, son of Daniel[5] and

Jerusha (Treat) Marsh, (Rev. Jonathan[4], Dr. Jonathan[3], Jonathan[2], John[1]) ; m. No. 3854.

**3854.** Lydia Gilbert, b. July 18, 1783, dau. of Theodore and Hannah (Chapin) Gilbert. The Gilberts and Chapins were from Connecticut and among the early settlers of Paris and Sauquoit Valley, N. Y. Daniel Sheldon[6] Marsh and wife settled in Sauquoit. He d. June 10, 1853 in his 75th year. She d. March 29, 1860, in her 77th year. Children :

 3854.1. Daniel Sheldon[7], b. 1813; m. H. S. Peck, 3855.
 3854.2. Almira.


3855 = 3854.1. DANIEL SHELDON[7] MARSH

b. 1813, probably at Sauquoit, N. Y., son of Daniel Sheldon[6] and Lydia (Gilbert) Marsh, (Daniel[5], Jonathan[4], Jonathan[3], Jonathan[2], John[1]) ; m. Nov. 14, 1842, No. 3855.

**3855.** Henrietta Sophia Peck, b. Nov. 6, 1818, dau. of Virgil and Mary (Phillips) Peck of New York state. Mr. Peck was an English-man, b, May 11, 1793, a cotton merchant of Mobile, Ala., who d. of yellow fever, Nov. 22, 1828. Mary Phillips was the dau. of Col. Pearly and Alice (Howe) Phillips of New York state. Mrs. H. S. (Peck) Marsh, d. Aug. 11, 1893. She was considered very beautiful and as possessing much refinement and strength of character and gifted with rare conversational powers. For her social and sympa-thetic nature she was greatly admired by all who knew her. Daniel S[7]. Marsh was a prominent citizen of Penn Yan, N. Y. and on his death Oct. 16, 1848, the merchants there passed the following resolu-tions :

" *Resolved*, that this community in common with ourselves, who have so long transacted business around him, will learn with heartfelt sorrow the sudden removal of one from our midst, who was all that is upright as a merchant, amiable as a man, devoted as a Christian, and endearing as a husband and father."

" *Resolved*, that we mingle our unaffected sympathies and condo-lence with the afflicted family of the deceased. But with the calm composure that could only arise from the firm conviction that their present severe trial is only ' As the small dust of the balance, com-pared with the far more exceeding and eternal weight of glory now in full possession by the departed."

" *Resolved*, that we cordially recommend all classes of our fellow citizens to attend with us the funeral of Mr. Marsh from his late residence on Wednesday morning at 10 o'clock, and that during the solemn services all the stores be closed." — *Penn Yan Paper.* Children :

    3855.1.  Daniel Sheldon[8], b. Dec. 15, 1844 ; m. A. Smith, 3856.
    3855.2.  Frank Allen, b. at Penn Yan, Feb. 20, 1846 and resides in Chicago, unm. in 1894.
    3855.3.  Eben Jones, b. May 5, 1848 ; m. Ella Sherman, 3857.


## 3856 = 3855.1.  DANIEL SHELDON[8] MARSH

b. at Penn Yan, N. Y., Dec. 15, 1844, son of Daniel Sheldon[7] and Henrietta Sophia (Peck) Marsh, (Daniel Sheldon[6], Daniel[5], Rev. Jonathan[4], Dr. Jonathan[3], Jonathan[2], John[1]) ; m. July 28, 1871, No. 3856.

**3856.**  Adriana Smith, b. June 27, 1844, dau. of Nathan Denison and Mary Abby (Morgan) Smith.  Nathan D. Smith was a prominent citizen of New London, Ct., and they both were descendants of colonial settlers, of Norwich, Ct. and New London, Rev. Nehemiah Smith and James Morgan, the latter b. in Wales in 1607 and a captain in the Indian wars of the colonial period.  Mr. and Mrs. D. S. Marsh reside in New London.  Children :

    3856.1.  Cora Adriana[9], b. at Chicago, Ill., June 18, 1872.
    3856.2.  Daniel Sheldon, b. at New London, Sept. 28, 1876.


## 3857 = 3855.3.  EBEN JONES[8] MARSH

b. at Penn Yan, N. Y., May 5, 1848, son of Daniel Sheldon[7] and Henrietta Sophia (Peck) Marsh, (Daniel Sheldon[6], Daniel[5], Rev. Jonathan[4], Rev. Dr. Jonathan[3], Jonathan[2], John[1]) ; m. in Chicago, Sept. 12, 1875, No. 3857.

**3857.**  Ella Sherman, b. June 22, 1852, dau. of Brig. Gen. Vol. Frank T. and Eleanor Norton (Vedder) Sherman of Chicago.  Miss Vedder was of Holland Dutch descent.  They reside at Chicago. Children :

    3857.1.  Roger Sherman[9], b. at Chicago ; d. in infancy.
    3857.2.  Eben Jones, b. Sept. 29, 1880 ; d. Feb., 1881.
    3857.3.  Margaret, b. June 4, 1887.

## 3858 = 3853.9. WOLCOTT[6] MARSH

b. March 1, 1788, probably near Utica, N. Y., son of Daniel[5] and Jerusha (Treat) Marsh, (Rev. Jonathan[4] of New Hartford, Ct., Rev. Dr. Jonathan[3] of Windsor, Ct., Jonathan[2] of Hadley, Mass., John[1] of Hartford); m. Jan. 20, 1811, No. 3858.

**3858.** Lucy Hart, b. July 12, 1790. His father's family removed from New Hartford, Ct., to Oneida Co., N. Y., probably before his birth. Wolcott removed to Alexander, N. Y. He d. May 8, 1849 and his widow in May, 1875. Children :

3858.1. Elmina[7], b. Jan. 7, 1812; d. unm. Oct. 17, 1837.

3858.2. Evaline, b. April 12, 1813; m. July 1, 1840, Samuel Goff. She d. Nov. 11, 1856. Children :

  1. Alice E[8]., b. Jan. 12, 1843; m. Wm. Moraan (living in 1894).

  2. James R., b. April, 1846; m. —— Ross, (living in 1894).

3858.3. Sanger, b. Aug. 27, 1815; m. (1) Harriet Horton, 3859.

3858.4. Almina, b. Oct. 14, 1817 ; m. Horace Sumner and d. March 29, 1889.

3858.5. Patty, b. Sept. 30, 1819; m. Jan. 26, 1841, C. W. Van De Bogart. Children : 1, Wolcott[8]; 2, Lucy; 3, Charles; all these are married. The mother is living (1894).

3858.6. Mary, b. Nov. 13, 1821; living (1894) unm.

3858.7. Wolcott, b. Dec. 24, 1824; d. June 27, 1835.

3858.8. Lucia, b. Feb. 1, 1828; m. Jan. 14, 1850, F. F. Farnham. Children:

  1. Ella A[8]., b. July 6, 1853; m. Nov. 26, 1874, Carlos L. Waldo.

  2. Katie, b. May 10, 1856; m. —— Baker.

3858.9. Adeline, b. April 3, 1830; m. Oct. 13, 1853, James F. Allen. Child : Jennie F[8]., b. Sept. 19, 1854; m. Dec. 17, 1874, Alfred C. Parkinson, (living in 1894).

## 3859 = 3858.3. SANGER[7] MARSH

b. Aug. 27, 1815, son of Wolcott[6] and Jerusha (Treat) Marsh, (Daniel[5], Rev. Jonathan[4], Rev. Dr. Jonathan[3], Jonathan[2], John[1]); m. (1) Dec. 27, 1841, No. 3859.

**3859.** Harriet Horton. After her death he m. (2) Jan. 30, 1849, No. 3859.1.

**3859.1.** Chelvea Pratt. He d. Oct. 29, 1872. Children :

3859.2. George Sanger[8], b. Jan. 17, 1843; m. (1) H. A. Blackman, 3860.

22

By second wife.

3859.3.  Inez, b. July 9, 1851 ; m. B. C. Waul.

3859.4.  Hattie, b. May 23, 1858; m. J. E. Webster.

3859.5.  May, b. Aug. 8, 1861 ; m. June 3, 1886, A. F. Buck.

### 3860 = 3859.2.  GEORGE SANGER⁶ MARSH

b. Jan. 17, 1843, son of Sanger⁷ and Harriet (Horton) Marsh, (Wolcott⁶, Daniel⁵, Rev. Jonathan⁴ of New Hartford, Ct., Rev. Dr. Jonathan³ of Windsor, Ct., Jonathan² of Hadley, Mass, John¹ of Hartford) ; m. (1) June 6, 1865, No. 3860.

**3860.**  Hattie A. Blackman.  After her death he m. (2) May 20, 1874, No. 3860.1.

**3860.1.**  Rebecca Jane Wight.  He is president of the Citizen's State Bank of Whitewater, Wis.  Children:

3860.2.  Fred Blackman⁹, b. Oct. 1, 1866, Monday ; d. at White-water of typhoid fever, Oct. 15, 1879, æ. 13.

3860.3.  Henry Horton, b. Dec. 14, 1870, Wednesday, at White-water ; d. at Elwyn, Pa., of pneumonia, æ. 11.

By second wife.

3860.4.  Alice Rebecca, b. at Whitewater, Feb. 25, 1877, Sunday, 3 P. M.

3860.5.  Fitch George, b. at Whitewater, Oct. 25, 1879, Saturday, 6.30 A. M.

### 3861 = 3826.  GEN. ISAAC⁵ MARSH

b. at New Hartford, Oct. 18, 1747, baptized Oct. 25, 1747, son of Rev. Jonathan⁴ and Elizabeth (Sheldon) Marsh of New Hartford, (Rev. Dr. Jonathan³ of Windsor, Ct., Jonathan² of Hadley, Mass., John¹ of Hartford, Ct.) ; m. (son's Bible, 1775) probably 1774, No. 3861.

**3861.**  Lucy Smith, (Bible) b. 1756, dau. of Dea. Martin Smith. The records of the little book of the father of Gen. Isaac and the copy of the Bible records of the General's son do not agree.  Sometimes the baptism dates earlier than the birth, and then of course one of the two is wrong : i. e. Son's record gives Elizabeth b. July 4, 1780 and her father's little book, gives baptized " Elizabeth Sheldon,

To face page 322.

dau. of Isaac Marsh Nov. 7, 1779." Gen. Isaac Marsh is called "Capt. Isaac Marsh of Stockbridge" in his father's little book from 1778 to 1784 and "Col. Isaac Marsh of Stockbridge, June 29, 1792," altho Gen. Isaac d. at Tyringham, near Stockbridge, Mass., Aug. 27, 1792, æ. 44, apparently away from home. His residence at Stockbridge led to his familiarity with the Stockbridge Indians and to his purchasing from them, for £140, the township in Vermont which had been granted to them in 1782. They deeded the township to Gen. Isaac Marsh July 29, 1789. The deed was signed by 18 Indians then residents of New Stockbridge, Montgomery Co., N. Y., now Stockbridge, Madison Co. The Vermont township was called Marshfield in honor of Gen. Isaac Marsh, whom the Vermont *Gazeteer* confuses with Capt. Daniel[5] Marsh, No. 903, who m. widow Anna (Stanley) Pitkin, whose sons were of the first settlers of Marshfield. Capt. Daniel's dau. Hannah m. Caleb Pitkin, his wife's son, and the parents visited their children there several times even up to the very year of Mrs. Marsh's death. None of Gen. Isaac's children went that way. After his death his widow m. his brother John Lawrence Marsh and d. Dec. 19, 1840, æ. 85. Children:

3862. Isaac[6], bap. "July 16, 1775;" d. "æ. about 88 years;" m. No. 3872.

3863. "Lucy, dau. of Capt. Isaac of Stockbridge," bap. "Jan. 25, 1778;" m. —— Hulbert, 3873.

3864. "Elizabeth Sheldon," bap. "Nov. 7, 1779; m. —— Dwyer; d. 1849, æ. 69."

3865. "Normand, son of Capt. Isaac Marsh of Stockbridge," bap. "March 3, 1782," probably d. y.

3866. Nancy, b. Sept., 1782; m. —— Couch; d. Oct., 1852, æ. 70.

3867. "Mary Ann, dau. of Capt. Isaac of Stockbridge," bap. "Feb. 22, 1784;" she m. Josiah Spencer, 3881.

3868. Erastus, b. Dec., 1784, possibly 1785; d. Jan. 4, 1831, æ. 47; m. and had a child: prob. son Erastus S., graduated at Yale college 1829; d. a physician in 1849.

3869. William S., b. June 15, 1788; m. No. 3875.

3870. Joseph Whiting, b. Aug. 16, 1791, bap. June 29, 1792; m. (1) Hannah Stow, 3877.

3871. Havilah, bap. "son of Isaac Marsh (died) Sept. 4, 1793."

3872 = 3862. ISAAC[6] MARSH

b. probably at New Hartford, Ct., baptized July 16, 1775, son of

Gen. Isaac[5] and Lucy (Smith) Marsh, (Rev. Jonathan[4], Rev. Dr. Jonathan[3], Jonathan[2], John[1]).


### 3873 = 3863.  LUCY[6] MARSH

b. probably at Stockbridge, Mass., baptized " dau. Capt. Isaac[5] Marsh of Stockbridge, Jan. 25, 1778," m. No. 3873.

**3873.** —— Hulbert.  She d. April 27, 1861.  Child :

    3874.  Eliza[7], m. —— Rodgers.


### 3875 = 3869.  WILLIAM S[6]. MARSH

b. probably at Stockbridge, Mass., June 15, 1788, son of Gen. Isaac[5] and Lucy (Smith) Marsh, (Rev. Jonathan[4] of New Hartford, Ct., Rev. Jonathan[3] of Windsor, Ct., Jonathan[2] of Hadley, Mass., John[1] of Hartford); m. No. 3875.

**3875.** ——.  Did he publish book ? see 866.  A William S. Marsh Justice of the Peace, 1833–38.  He d. Aug. 19, 1867, æ. 79.  Child :

    3876.  Sarah[7], m. —— Rodgers.


### 3877 = 3870.  JOSEPH WHITING[6] MARSH

b. probably at Stockbridge, Mass., Aug. 16, 1791 and baptized by his grandfather a year later, June 29, 1792, son of Gen. Isaac[5] and Lucy (Smith) Marsh of Stockbridge, (Rev. Jonathan[4] of New Hartford, Ct., Rev. Jonathan[3] of Windsor, Ct., Jonathan[2] of Hadley, Mass., John[1] of Hartford) ; m. (1) Oct. 4, 1815, No. 3877.

**3877.** Hannah Stow, b. about 1795, dau. of Zebulon Stow in Stockbridge.  She d. Sept. 12, 1843, æ. 48.  He m. (2) Oct. 31, 1845, No. 3878.

**3878.** Widow Sarah (Cowdrey) Paine, b. Dec. 15, 1794, dau. of Ambrose Cowdrey of East Hartland.  She gave $1000 to the church in East Hartland.  She d. Aug. 9, 1869.  He d. Feb. 8, 1882, æ. 90. Children :

    3879.  Zebulon Stow, b. March 6, 1823 ; d. July 16, 1824, æ. 1 year
        and 4 months.

    3880.  Zebulon Whiting, b. June 12, 1825 ; d. July 30, 1845, æ. 20.

## 3881 = 3867. MARY ANN[6] MARSH

b. probably at Stockbridge, Mass., 1783, and baptized by her grandfather "Mary Ann, dau. of Capt. Isaac " " of Stockbridge, Feb. 22, 1784," dau. of Gen. Isaac[5] and Lucy (Smith) Marsh, (Rev. Jonathan[4] Rev. Jonathan[3], Jonathan[2], John[1]) ; m. Jan. 3, 1803, No. 3881.

**3881.** Josiah Spencer of Springfield, Ohio.   She d. June 4, 1841, æ. 59, (in 59th year?).   Children :

3882.   Wolcott M., b. Feb. 16, 1804 ; m. Cornelia Jones, of Stockbridge, Mass.

3883.   Richard S., b. Jan. 23, 1806.

3884.   Josiah F., b. May 6, 1808.

3885.   Isaac W., b. Jan. 26, 1813.

3886.   Charles, b. Oct. 31, 1816.

3887.   Mariana, b. Sept., 1822.

# BRANCH IV.  THE HADLEY LINE.

The outlines of Hadley street as given on several pages following are taken from the arrangement of the names of tax payers as given in the Hadley book for the years indicated.  The ages given are for the time of the tax.

The places where John[1] Marsh, Daniel[2] Marsh and a number of Daniel's descendants lived for more than 160 years can be readily traced on these pages.  The street is just about a mile long, running north and south.  The river at the north end running west towards Northampton, taking five miles to come around to the south end of the street where it runs east.

The plan of the burial plat of Daniel[2] Marsh as it exists in the old Hadley cemetery in 1894 is worthy of notice.

Samuel Gardner. |20

*North way to meadow.*

**1663.**

Chileab Smith. |19

*From Hist. Hadley.*
*page 32.*

Joseph Baldwin. |18

Robert Boltwood. |17

Francis Barnard. |16

☐

John Hawks. |15   Meeting house.

Richard Church. |14

Edward Church. |13

*Midway to meadow.*

Henry Clark. |12

Stephen Terry. |11

Andrew Warner. |10

*Northampton road, opened 1832.*

John¹ Marsh. ae abt. 45. |9

Timothy Nash. |8

John Webster, d. 1661. |7

Wm. Goodwin. |6

John Crow. |5

Samuel Moody. |4

Nathaniel Ward. |3

William Markham. |2

*South way to meadow.*

Joseph Kellogg. |1

*Aquavitae meadow.*

1| William Partrigg.

2| Thomas Coleman.

3| Samuel Smith.

4| Phil. Smith.

5| Richard Montague.

6| John Dickinson

7| Sam. Porter, æ. abt. 28.

8| Thomas Wells.

9| John Hubbard, æ. abt. 36.

10| Town Lot.

11| Mr. John Russell, Jr.

*Mid-highway to woods.*

12| John Barnard.

13| Andrew Bacon.

14| Nath'l Stanley, æ. abt. 49.

15| Thos. Stanley, æ. abt. 24.

16| John White.

17| Peter Tilton.

18| Wm. Lewis, æ. abt. 43.

19| Richard Goodman.

20| Wm. Westwood, æ. abt. 57.

21| Thomas Dickinson.

22| Nathaniel Dickinson.

*South way to woods.*

23| John Russell. Sr.

N

Ferry

Conn. River

**HADLEY.**

*1681.*

*From Hist. Hadley, page 211.*

20

19

18

17

16

15    Meeting house.

14

13

12

11

10

John¹ Marsh, ae abt. 63.    9

8

7

6

Jonathan² Marsh, abt. 31    5
Daniel² Marsh, abt. 28.

4

3

2

1

N

1

2

3

4

5

6

7    { Samuel Porter, abt. 56, m. abt. 1659, Hannah Stanley.

8

9    John Hubbard, abt. 55.

10

11    { Russell house where regicides were hid.

12

13

14

15

16

17    { Peter Tilton, regicides at times here.

18    " Lewis land."

19    Widow Goodman.

20    { Capt. Aaron Cooke, ae. 41, m. 1661, Sarah Westwood, ae. 37.

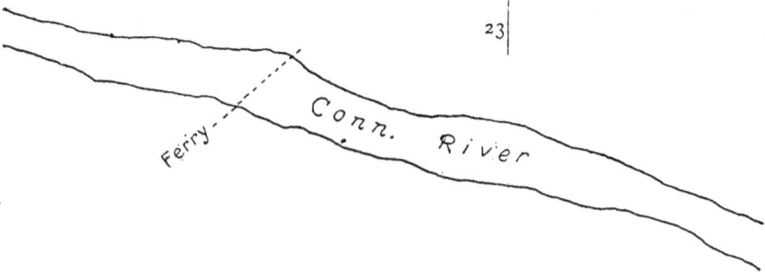

21

22

23

Ferry

*Conn. River*

## HADLEY.

## 1687.

*From Hist. Hadley,*
*page 212.*

20 |
19 |
18 |
17 |
16 |
15 | Meeting house.
14 |
13 |

12 |
11 |
10 |

John¹ Marsh, abt. 69,
d. 1688.

9 |
8 |
7 |

Jonathan² Marsh, abt.
37, Daniel² Marsh abt.
34, m. 1676, Hannah
(Lewis) Crow.

6 |
5 |
4 |
3 |
2 |

1 |

N

1 |
2 |
3 |
4 |
5 | Samuel Porter, abt. 61
6 | and Hannah Stanley.
7 |
8 |
9 |
10 |
11 |

12 |
13 |
14 |
15 | Samuel Porter, Jr., 27,
16 | m. 1683, Joanna Cooke,
    | 22, dau. Capt. Aaron.
17 |
18 | "Lewis land."
19 |
20 | Capt. Aaron Cooke, 47
21 | Sarah Westwood.
22 |

23 |

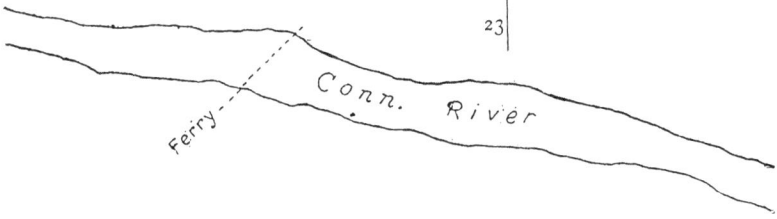

*Conn. River*

*Ferry*

# *HADLEY.*

## **1720.**

*From Hist. Hvdley,*
*page 286.*

Meeting house.

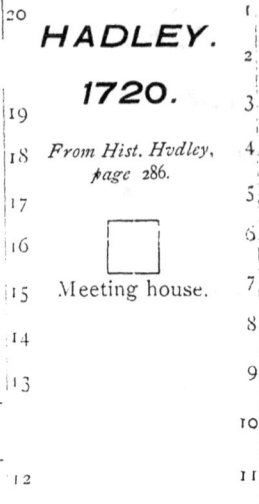

N

20
19
18
17
16
15
14
13
12
11

1
2
3
4
5
6
7
8
9
10
11

10
9
8
7
6
5
4
3
2
1

"Mr. Dan.² Marsh,"
abt. 67, and Hannah
(Lewis) Marsh.

Mr. Jonathan² Marsh,
abt. 70, & Sergt. Wm.
Dickinson who m.
Mary³ Marsh, dau.
Jonathan.

12
13
14
15
16
17
18
19
20
21
22
23

Corp. Sam. Dickinson
and Hannah³ Marsh,
dau. Jonathan².

Mr.Sam.Porter². Esq.,
ae. 60, wife d. 1713,
ae. 49.

Sergt. John³ Marsh,43,
Ebenezer³ Marsh, 32,
sons of Daniel².

Lt. Sam. Cooke, 48, m.
1698, Ann³ Marsh, 40,
dau. Jonathan².

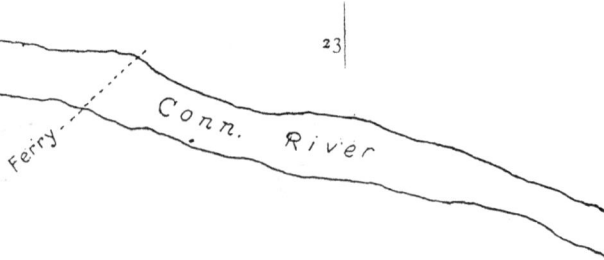

Ferry

Conn. River

## 1731.

*From Hist. Hadley.*
*page* 291.

Meeting house.

N

20
19
18
17
16
15
14
13
12
11
10
9
8
7
6
5
4
3
2
1

Heirs of Wm.³ Marsh,
d. 1727, ae. 30, and
Dan.³ Marsh, Jr., their
father, Dan.², d. 1725,
ae. 72, Dan.³ d. 1770,
ae. 92.

Ensign Wm. Dickin-
son, and Mary³ Marsh
Dickinson.

1
2
3
4 { Heirs of John³ Marsh,
5 } and Wid. Sarah (Wil-
   ( liams) Marsh.
6 Samuel Porter.
7
8
9
10
11
12
13 { Dea. Sam. Dickinson,
   } Hannah³ Marsh, d.
   ( June 10, 1729, ae. 29.
14 ( Capt. Job³ Marsh, son
   | of Dan.² ae. 41, m. 1713
15 { Mehitable Porter, ae.
16 ( 37, d. 1739, ae. 44.
17 Joseph Eastman.
   ( Ebenezer³ Marsh, son
18 } of Dan.² ae. 43, and
   ( Sarah Eastman.
19 ( Lt. Sam. Cooke, ae. 59.
20 } Ann³ (Marsh) Cooke,
   ( ae. 51.
21
22
23

Conn. River

Ferry

HADLEY.

1770.

*From Hist. Hadley.*
page 431.

Meeting house.

20
19
18
17
16
15
14
13
12
11
10
9
8
7
6
5
4
3
2
1

Ebenezer[4] Marsh, Jr.,
49, and "his aged fath-
er," Ebenezer[3], Sr., 82,
d. 1772, ae. 84.

N

1
2
3
4
5
6
7
8
9
10
11
12
13
14
15
16
17
18
19
20
21
22

Capt. Moses[4] Marsh,
Phoebe, wid.Sam.[4]
and son Sam.[5]
Daniel[4] Marsh.

Sons of Job[3]

Lt. Jonathan Cooke,
Ruth Goodman, gr'nd
dau. Grace Marsh.

23

Ferry

Conn. River

# DANIEL² MARSH, SON OF JOHN¹, BURIAL LOT HADLEY CEMETERY.

Mrs. Miriam³, 1765.
+

Mr. Ebenezer⁴, 1795.
+
Mrs. Sarah, 1794.                    Mrs. Mary³, 1759.
+                                    +
                                     Hannah⁵, 1753.
                                     +
                                     Job⁵, 1754.
                                     +
                     Ebenezer⁵, 1761.    Timothy⁵, 1751.
                     +                   +
                                     Daniel⁵, 1751.
                                     +

Mr. Daniel³, 1770.
+
                              Job, 1726.
                              +
                              Judith⁴, 1725.
                              +
                              Sargt. John³, 1725.
                              +

              Mr. Samuel⁴, 1760.
              +
                       William⁴, 1726.
                       +

     Hannah⁵, 1746.                    Mr. Daniel², 1725.
     +                                 +
     Moses⁵, 1746.
     +
     Moses⁵, 1757.
     +
                                  Capt. Job³, 1746.
                                  +
     Dr. Job⁵, 1797.              Mr. William³, 1727.
     +                            +
     Mrs. Elizabeth, 1823.
     +

Mehitable, wife of Capt. Job³, in Porter lot.
+
                              Drawn by J. D. Marsh.

## 3987 = 9.  DANIEL[2] MARSH

b. at Hartford, Ct., about 1653, son of John[1] Marsh of Hartford and Hadley, and Anne Webster, dau. of Gov. John Webster of Connecticut, came with his father and family when seven years of age to Hadley, Mass. He must have remembered all his life the breaking up at Hartford below and the journey up the beautiful river and the founding of the new town, Norwottock, in the broad valley where red men had wandered for ages in sight of Mt. Holyoke and Mt. Tom, and the higher Green mountain ranges east and west. He must have always remembered the death of his mother's father, Gov. Webster, whose home was with them, coming as that blow did to the new colony within a year of the settlement; and his burial April 5, 1661, he could not forget, nor the death of his mother June 6, 1662. In 1675 and 1676 there was serious trouble with the Indians and his brother and he were led to marry young widows whose first husbands had been not long slain. He m. Nov. 5, 1676, No. 3987.

3987. Widow Hannah (Lewis) Crow, whose husband Samuel "was slain at Fallsfight, May 18, 1676," less than six months before. Hannah[3] Lewis was dau. of William[2] and Mary (Hopkins) Lewis, who lived and died at Farmington, Ct. William[2] was son of William[1] and Felix Lewis who came to America in 1632. This earliest William Lewis was a resident of Braintree and Cambridge, Mass., then of Hartford's first settlers in 1636 and in 1660 a founder of Hadley. He represented Hadley in 1662 and Northampton in 1664. He removed to Farmington, Ct. before Nov. 29, 1677. The Lewis home lot in Hadley was bought by Daniel Marsh and occupied later by two of Daniel's sons. But Daniel himself never resided there. Shortly after marriage we find him and his brother Jonathan at the lot which had belonged to John Crow. John Crow removed to Hartford and Jonathan and Daniel Marsh bought his lot. On or before the death of his father, Daniel removed to the home lot and remained there for life. In 1669 we first find his name signed to a public document. He became one of the principal landowners in the town, in 1701 standing second as to quantity and in 1720, fourth in valuation. In 1699 he was assigned a lot on Pine Plain 16 rods by 80, eight acres, which included the tract where now stand the town house and meeting house and his son Capt. Job Marsh lived for a while at that

corner of Middle street.  For 13 different years between his 29th
and 62d year, 1682 and 1715, he was chosen one of the selectmen.
He was sent representative to Boston in 1692 and often afterward.
In 1689 he was on an important committee as to the grammar
school.  He sent his third son to Harvard college 1701–1705.  He
d. Feb. 24, 1725, æ. 72.  After 168 years his gravestone may be
seen with those of 22 of his children and their descendants, in his
burial lot in Hadley graveyard.

Children :

3988.   Daniel³, b. Oct. 29, 1677 ; d. unm. Feb. 15, 1770, æ. 92.  He
        lived on the original John¹ Marsh place where his
        father had lived before him and where his brother Ebe-
        nezer³ and Ebenezer⁴, Jr., succeeded him.
3989.   John, b. March 9, 1679; m. (1) Joanna Porter, 3996.
3990.   Joseph, b. Jan. 16, 1685 ; m. Anne Fiske, 4026.
3991.   Ebenezer, b. April 22, 1688; m. (1) Mary Parsons, 4041.
3992.   Job, b. June 11, 1690; m. (1) Mehitable Porter, 4049.
3993.   A daughter, b. and d. 1692.
3994.   Hannah, b. May 17, 1694 ; m. Daniel? Kent, 4057.
3995.   William, b. Jan. 3, 1697 ; m. Hannah Porter, 4059.
        Hannah Lewis had eleven children.  The three young Crows,
        born before her marriage to Daniel Marsh, were of
        course brought into his family and brought up with his
        children.  They married well.  See History of Hadley.


3996 = 3989.   SERGT. JOHN³ MARSH

b. at Hadley, Mass., March 9, 1679, son of Daniel² and Hannah
(Lewis) Marsh, (John¹), was in an Indian fight in 1704.  His mother
had no doubt told him how her first husband was killed by red men
and the husband of his Aunt Dorcas Marsh too in 1675 and 1676.
Five Hampshire towns had been given up for a year or two.  Then
in his boyhood came the " second Indian war 1688 to 1698 " and then
" 1702 to 1713 " the "third Indian war."  Feb. 29, 1704 was a day
to be remembered by him.  French and Indians fell upon Deerfield,
set the town on fire, murdered and scalped, slew 38 in the palisaded
village, and took 112 captive.  John³ Marsh of Hadley and John³ Marsh
his cousin of Hatfield were of the soldiers from Hadley and Hatfield
who 57 in number hurried to burning Deerfield ; they drove the Indians
out, fought them in Deerfield meadow, followed them a mile and

more and had to retreat leaving nine of their number dead.   In all, of the 112 captives, two escaped, 22 were slain or perished on the way to Canada, 28 remained in Canada and 60 returned.   The famous antiquarian, George Sheldon of Deerfield, states that he is in doubt which John Marsh is the one numbered among the captives in the official list : but as it reads " John Marsh and Sarah Dickinson two Hatfield persons " see No. 2837, we must conclude that it was not Sergt. John Marsh of Hadley, although Hadley History, p. 273, mentions him as in the fight.   " Hadley had five men slain."   He had hardly time to go to Canada and back for he m. June 27, 1704, No. 3996.

3996.  Joanna[4] Porter of Hadley, b. Dec. 24, 1687, dau. of Hon. Samuel[3] and Joanna (Cook) Porter, William[2] Porter of Hadley, John[1] Porter of Windsor, Ct.   Joanna Cooke was dau. of Capt. Aaron Cooke.   Joanna (Porter) Marsh died and he m. (2) Feb. 2, 1715, No. 3997.

3997.  Hannah Barnard, b. June 8, 1684, dau. of Capt. Samuel and Mary (Colton) Barnard.   She d. Sept. 31, 1716, æ. 32.   He m. (3) Oct. 19, 1718, No. 3998.

3998.  Sarah[3] Williams, b. Oct. 2, 1688, dau. of Isaac[2] and Judith (Cooper) Williams, (Robert[1] Williams.)   She was sister of Rev. William Williams of Hatfield, settled there in 1685 and of Ephraim Williams who removed from Hatfield to Stockbridge.   John[3] Marsh had a lot of three acres in Northampton deeded to him by Jonathan Rust, May 29, 1716 " with housing thereon."   He d. Sept. 2, 1725.   His widow probably m. (2) July 28, 1732, James Grey and d. June 1, 1759.   Children :

3999.   John[4], b. Aug. 25, 1710; d. y.
4000.   Abigail, b. prob. 1716; m. Waitstill Hastings, 4005.
4001.   Martha, b. prob. 1720; m. Moses Graves, 4011.
4002.   Anna, b. prob. 1721 or 22; m. Elisha Allis, 4018.
4003.   John, b. 1723; d. July 3, 1826, æ. 3.
4004.   Judith, b. 1725; d. Nov. 1, 1725, æ. 8 months.


4005 = 4000.   ABIGAIL[4] MARSH

b. at Hadley, Mass., probably 1716, (because probably dau. of Hannah Barnard) dau. of Sergt. John[3] Marsh, (Daniel[2], John[1]) ;   m. (1) Oct. 1, 1736, No. 4005.

**4005.** Dr. Waitstill[3] Hastings, b. at Hatfield, Jan. 3, 1714, son of Dr. Thomas[2] and Mary (Field) Hastings, (Thomas[1] Hastings) all of Hatfield. Her name Abigail belonging to an aunt of Hannah Barnard was a favorite name in the Barnard family, and her age compared with that of her husband, and the name Hannah Barnard given to her child, seem strong indications that she was Hannah (Barnard) Marsh's daughter. She m. (2) No. 4005.1.

**4005.1.** Col. Bulkley of Colchester, Ct. She m. (3), No. 4005.2.

**4005.2.** Rev. Mr. Little of Colchester. Dr. Waitstill Hastings d. April 22, 1748 and Mrs. Abigail[4] (Marsh) (Hastings-Bulkley) Little, "d. as early as 1758." Children (of Dr. Waitstill Hastings):

4006. John[5], b. Jan. 10, 1738; Hon. Magistrate 36 years. Either senator or councilor of Massachusetts 28 years; d. Dec. 6, 1811; m. about 1764, Content Little, who d. April 9, 1829 in her 89th year. See History of Hadley for nine children and for grandchildren.

4007. Abigail, b. Feb. 28, 1739: m. Solomon Woolcott of Williamstown.

4008. Hannah Barnard, b. March 16, 1742; m. Nathaniel Kellogg of Dalton; was with Dr. Perez Marsh, No. 4680, one of the earliest settlers of Dalton.

4009. Mary, b. Jan. 10, 1744.

4010. Samuel, b. March 14, 1747; d. Feb. 28, 1748.


4011 = 4001. MARTHA[4] MARSH

b. at Hadley, Mass., probably 1719 or 1720, as reported History of Hadley, "d. Feb. 3, 1755, æ. 35," dau. of Sergt. John[3] and Sarah (Williams) Marsh, (Daniel[2], John[1]); m. Feb. 24, 1743, No. 4011.

**4011.** Moses[4] Graves of Hatfield, b. Feb. 1, 1700, son of Jonathan[3] and Mary (Parsons) Graves, (Isaac[2] and Thomas[1] of Hartford, 1645 and Hatfield). Children:

4012. Judith[5], b. Dec. 4, 1743; killed by lightning. June 19, 1754.

4013. Elijah, b. Nov. 14, 1745.

4014. Moses, b. Feb. 3, 1748.

4015. John, b. Jan. 13, 1750; d. Aug. 6, 1751.

4016. John, b. March 13, 1752.

4017. Martha, b. April 6, 1754.

23

4018 = 4002.   ANNE[4] MARSH

b. at Hadley, Mass., probably in 1721 or 1722, dau. of Sergt. John[3] and Sarah (Williams) Marsh, (Daniel[2], John[1]) ; m. Dec. 20, 1744, No. 4018.

**4018.**   Elisha[4] Allis, b. Dec. 3, 1716, son of Ichabod[3] and Mary (Belding) Allis, (John[2], William[1]), freeman Braintree, 1640, removed to Hatfield about 1661.   They resided in Hatfield, Mass.   Children :

4019.   Elisha[5], b. 174-; m. (1) Jan. 27, 1774, Mary[5] Dickinson, dau. of Obadiah[4] and Martha Dickinson, (Nathaniel[3], Joseph[2], Nathaniel[1]); m. (2) Mary[5] Ingram, dau. of Samuel[4] and Mary (Boltwood) Ingram, (John[3], John[2], John[1]); removed to Brookfield,Vt. and was long known as "Old Squire Allis."

4020.   Anna, m. Dr. Josiah Pomeroy and rem. to Kinderhook, N. Y.

4021.   Electa, d. soon.

4022.   Josiah, b. 1754; Col. of Northampton, was prominent there,

4023.   John, b. Jan. 18, 1756 ; a wealthy farmer of Hatfield; m. Sept. 30, 1779, Esther[6] Partridge of Hatfield, b. March 26, 1761, dau. of Lieut. Samuel[5] and Abigail (Dwight) Partridge, Cotton[4], Samuel[3] and Mary (Cotton) Partridge, Col. Samuel[2] Partridge, "after the death of Col. Pynchon (1703) the most important man in all the western part of the province " of Mass., William[1] Partridge of Hartford and Hadley.   See Dwight book, pp. 761-764.

4024.   Abel, m. (1) Baker ; (2) Mansfield of Derby, Ct.: resided at Whately and Conway, Mass.

4025.   William, m. Sophia Smith of Springfield.


4026 = 3990.   REV. JOSEPH[3] MARSH

b. at Hadley, Mass., Jan. 6, 1685, son of Daniel[2] and Hannah Marsh, (John[1]) ; graduated at Harvard college in 1705 called "Mr." in catalogue ; admitted to Cambridge church as "student " Nov. 28, 1703, ordained 1709 and settled May 18, 1709, pastor of the first church of Braintree, now Quincy, Mass.; m. June 30, 1709, No. 4026.

**4026.**   Ann Fiske, dau. of his predecessor, Rev. Moses Fiske. He had previously preached at Tiverton, R. I. then belonging to Massachusetts, having been sent by order of the general court, as that town had neglected to provide themselves as required by law. He procured a substitute at Tiverton, and remained at Braintree first church 17 years until his death, March 8, 1725-6, æ. 41.   More than 150 years ago he was spoken of there as one "whose memory is precious to you." His widow lived in Quincy to great age. Children :

> 4027.  Joseph[4], b. Dec., 1710; grad. at Harvard, 1728, is believed never to have married, was long a teacher in Quincy, fitting many eminent men for college. Among his pupils were Gen. Cobb and many of the Quincy and Adams families, including at least one of the presidents of the United States, John Quincy Adams. He kept school in the house that had been occupied by his father and his mother and her unmarried children afterwards. It was on the westerly side of Franklin street and about 20 rods from School street. As late as 1858 it was occupied by William P. Hardwich.
>
> 4028.  Daniel, b. July 27, 1712.
> 4029.  Hannah, b. July 10, 1716 ; adm. to full com. first church in 1729.
> 4030.  Mary, bap. Feb. 2, 1718 ; m. Rev. J. Adams, 4033.
> 4031.  Anne, b. or bap. April 19, 1722 ; d. soon.
> 4032.  Anne, b. Oct. 23, 1723 ; m. Col. Josiah Quincy, 4039.

## 4033 = 4030.   MARY[4] MARSH

b. at Braintree, now Quincy, Mass., baptised Feb. 2, 1718, dau. of Rev. Joseph[3] and Ann (Fiske) Marsh, (Daniel[2], John[1]); m. May 19, 1746, No. 4033.

**4033.**  Rev. Jedediah Adams, b. Jan. 21, 1711, son of Dea. Peter Adams, graduated at Harvard college. 1733 ; ordained first minister at Stoughton, Feb. 19, 1746 ; d. Feb. 25, 1799, æ. 88, in 53d year of his ministry.   Children :

> 4034.  Peter[5], b. April 9, 1747 ; d. y.
> 4035.  Mary, b. 1750.
> 4036.  Hannah, b. April 4, 1753.
> 4037.  Jedediah, b. Dec. 29, 1755.
> 4038.  Peter, b. June 3, 1756 ; grad. at Harvard college. 1778 ; d. in 1832.

## 4039 = 4032.   ANNE[4] MARSH

b. at Quincy, Mass., Oct. 23, 1723, dau. of Rev. Joseph[3] and Ann

(Fiske) Marsh, (Daniel[2], John[1]) ; m. as his third wife, July 11, 1762, No. 4039.

4039. Col. Josiah Quincy of Quincy; graduated at Harvard college, 1728. He d. 1784 and Widow Anne (Marsh) Quincy in 1803. Child:

  4040. Nancy, b. Nov. 12, 1763; m. July 17, 1783, Rev. Asa Packard of Marlborough; Harvard college, 1783; ordained 1785; d. 1843. She d. a few years later.


4041 = 3991.   CORNET EBENEZER[3] MARSH

b. at Hadley, Mass., April 22, 1688, son of Daniel[2] and Hannah (Lewis) Marsh, (John[1] of Hartford and Hadley); his title showing that he bore the flag in a troop of horse; m. (1) in 1710, No. 4041.

4041. Mary Parsons, b. about 1690, dau. of Jonathan Parsons. They resided in Hadley upon the William Lewis lot which had been bought by his father, Daniel[2]. He was chosen by the town, 1717, constable, 1720 on committee to build bridge over Bachelor's river. On May 4, 1721 Jonathan Graves, Jonathan Coles. Ebenezer Wells grant him their rights to land south of Mt. Holyoke designed by the proprietors and partly laid out for a village. This started South Hadley. He was chosen 1723, 1725 and 1731, fence viewer; 1735 selectman and assessor. In 1735 also his dau. Mary m. Dr. Ezekiel Porter and removed to Wethersfield, Ct., where also his sons Jonathan and John not long after follow. Elisha was in Harvard college and graduated 1738. That year he was juryman at Springfield, and Hadley voted to raise and give Mr. Hezekiah Porter of Farmington, Ct., bonesetter, £62 if he settle in Hadley and £52 if in Hatfield or Northampton. April 14, 1739, Ebenezer Marsh sold to Hezekiah Porter the north half of his homelot with house, barn and fencing and May 24, 1741 bought it back. In J. Pierce's diary we read, "May 6, 1744, Cornet Marsh admonished in church; he withdraws. March 5, 1746, I went this day at Cornet Marsh's desire with him to Rev. Mr. Williams, to desire him to move to have his confession red. March 16, church voted Mr. Marsh's confession red next Sabbath. Jan. 23, 1747, Indian soldier dies at Cornet Marsh's about 50 years of age." Mary (Parsons) Marsh, d. July 2, 1759, in her 69th year. Cornet Marsh m. (2) Feb., 1760, No. 4042.

**4042.** Miriam ——, who d. July 30, 1765 in her 63d year. In his will dated April 14, 1764, he gives to his son Ebenezer five acres on the south side of his home lot with orcharding and buildings thereon and to son John five acres on the north side (which Dr. Ezekiel Porter sold to Benjamin Colt, Nov. 5, 1761, though not recorded until Oct. 30, 1765) also to Dr. Ezekiel Porter a lot of land "for doctoring my former wife." He removed with his son Ebenezer[4] to the original John[1] Marsh place in his later years and there in 1770 his brother Daniel[3] d. unm Feb. 15, 1770, æ. 92 and there we find record that Ebenezer[4] the son was assessed in 1770 on valuation £150, 7s. of which "for his aged father" £34. And there Cornet Ebenezer Marsh, d. in 1672, æ. 84. Children:

4043. Elisha[4], b. March 27, 1713; m. (1) Widow Lathrop, 4062.
4044. Mary, b. March 3, 1715; m. Dr. Ezk. Porter, 4095.
4045. Jonathan, b. 1720; m. Sarah Hart, 4133.
4046. Ebenezer, b. 1723; m. Sarah Eastman, 4287.
4047. Hannah, b. prob. 1724?; m. Samuel Ely, 4098.
4048. John, b. 1726; m. Abigail Bulkley, 4395.

### 4049 = 3992. CAPT. JOB[3] MARSH

b. at Hadley, Mass., June 11, 1690, son of Daniel[2] and Hannah (Lewis) Marsh, (John[1]); m. (1) Sept. 24, 1713, No. 4049.

**4049.** Mehitable[4] Porter, b. Sept. 12, 1694, dau. of Hon. Samuel[3] and Joanna (Cooke) Porter, (Samuel[2], John[1]) of Windsor, Ct, He built a house, in 1715 as tradition says, on the south east corner of Pine Plain street and the middle highway to the woods where the town hall and First church now (1895) stand. That land, eight acres, 80 by 16 rods, was given to Daniel[2] Marsh, April 5, 1699, in a division by the town. At the same time a similar lot immediately south was allotted to Experience[3] Porter whose dau. Hannah m. 1722, William[3] Marsh and lived there next to Capt. Job[3] his brother. Town records mention Capt. Job[3] Marsh, first 1719, fence viewer, 1724, committee on cutting staddles (the town made persistent efforts to save young trees) 1725 fence viewer, 1727 till death in 1746, 19 years, town clerk, also both town clerk and treasurer, except one year, from 1738 till death, and in 1738 also selectman and assessor, 1744 committee on highway to Pelham, 1745 to prosecute trespassers.

Pierce's diary calls him Capt. and also his monument gives him that title. Hon. Samuel Porter, importer, representative, judge and county sheriff, d. July 29, 1722, leaving to his family an estate of over £10,000, £196 in goods were on way from London; 1642 acres of land in Brookfield were to be equally divided among his seven children. He left in his will £700 to his dau. Mehitable Marsh. He had lived on the Stanley lot which came into possession of Capt. Job Marsh; just when does not appear nor how soon he moved there from Pine Plain street, where he was recorded in 1720. (History Hadley, p. 286.) In 1731 he is recorded at the Stanley lot. (See History Hadley, p. 291.) June 9, 1733 he bought of Joseph[3] Smith a home lot of five acres with its buildings next north from his own Stanley lot for £190 in bills of credit. He evidently sold the lot where the town hall and First church now (1895) stand in 1742. The deed says " 3d Nov., 1742, Job Marsh of Hadley sells to Josiah Pierce, Gentleman a certain Homelot containing eight acres more or less bounded north on a highway, south William Marsh deceased or his heir William Marsh a minor, west on the Pine Plain street and east on Isaac Selden, with a Dwelling House, Well, Barn, Hovelling, Orcharding, Fencing, etc." And J. Pierce's diary reads, " Feb. 28, 1743, This day I receive deed of homelot of Mr. Marsh at 330 pounds." "May 17, 1743, Mr. Marsh moves out of my house." These two extracts will interest descendants of Judge Perez[4] Marsh of Berkshire Co., son of Capt. Job[3]. " Sept. 9, 1741. Received of Mr. Job Marsh £1, 4s, in or for buying several books." " Aug. 15, 1744. Go to Cambridge and offer Perez Marsh to college. (Accepted.)" Mr. Job Marsh must have had tenants in one or more of his houses. Mehitable (Porter) Marsh d. July 13, 1739, æ. 44. He m. (2) Sept. 19, 1742, No. 4050.

4050. Rebecca Pratt of Hartford, Ct. He d. Aug. 29, 1746. His will, dated Aug. 15, 1746, gives to his beloved wife Rebecca " one hundred pounds old tenor out of my personal estate and my negro man Robin to be at her own disposal forever, and the improvement of the third part of my real estate during the time of her remaining my widow." After special gifts to Moses, Perez and Joseph he adds, " To my sons Samuel and Daniel the remainder of my Real and Personal estate." In the division Samuel had the five acre home lot and buildings north side and Daniel the five acre lot and buildings south. Before 1770 Capt. Moses[4], son of Job[3] had the five acre home lot next north (the original Andrew Bacon lot) and the families of these three brothers were side by side. Mrs. Rebecca Marsh soon removed to Hartford, Ct. and was buried there in the old church yard Sept. 29, 1768. Children:

4051. A daughter[4], b. and d. Oct. 18, 1714.
4052. Moses, b. March 20, 1718; m. Hannah Cook, 4501.
4053. Samuel, b. April 19, 1721; m. Phebe Porter, 4565.
4054. Daniel. b. Jan. 28, 1725; m. Hannah Parsons, 4594.
4055. Perez, b. Oct. 25, 1729; m. Sarah Williams, 4680.
By second wife.
4056. Joseph, b. Nov. 6, 1743; d. Sept. 22, 1746.

## 4057 = 3994. HANNAH[3] MARSH

b. at Hadley, Mass., May 17, 1694, dau. of Daniel[2] and Hannah (Lewis) Marsh, (John[1]); m. Dec. 1, 1731, No. 4057.

**4057.** Capt. "*John* Kent," said by Goodwin "b. 1687-8 of Suffield, Ct.; m. (2) Dec. 1, 1732, Hannah Marsh of Hadley, Mass.; d. 1737." Child:

4058. Hannah[4], b. Aug. 11, 1735; d. Dec. 4, 1735.

## 4059 = 3995. WILLIAM[3] MARSH

b. at Hadley, Mass., Jan. 3, 1697, son of Daniel[2] and Hannah (Lewis) Marsh, (John[1]); m. Feb. 28, 1722, No. 4059.

**4059.** Hannah[4] Porter, b. March 25, 1701, dau. of Experience[3], Samuel[2], John[1] of Windsor. Her father about this time sold his place to John[3] Marsh, Daniel[2], John[1], brother of William[3] and the daughter went soon to the lot which Experience Porter had received on Pine Plain street, next south of Daniel Marsh's in the division of 1669. (See History Hadley, p. 199.) This is the lot next south of the first church in Hadley. Experience Porter removed to Mansfield, Ct. Mr. William Marsh d. Nov. 3, 1727. He was owner of half the original John[1] Marsh lot, and in 1743 his minor son William[4] owned the Pine Plain lot. The inventory of William[3] Marsh's estate included " guns, horns, powder, pistols, holster, etc. Homestead £90. Total, £547, 10s., 6d." Widow Hannah Marsh removed to

Mansfield, Ct., and m. (2) in May, 1735, Major Joseph Storrs of
Mansfield, and d. Aug. 28, 1741.   Children:

    4060.  William⁴, b. 1724; d. Aug. 17, 1726, æ. 2.
    4061.  William, b. 1727; d. unm. in Mansfield.

## THE NEW HAMPSHIRE LINE.

### 4062 = 4043.   REV. AND JUDGE ELISHA⁴ MARSH

b. at Hadley, Mass., March 27, 1713, son of Cornet Ebenezer³ and
Mary (Parsons) Marsh, (Daniel², John¹); graduated at Harvard college 1738 and settled at Westminster, Mass., then "Narraganset No.
2," Oct. 20, 1742, on the day of incorporation of the town; salary
£150 a year in addition to land.   He m. (1) No. 4062.

    **4062.**  Widow Deborah (Lorin) Lathrop of Boston, a skillful
painter, a lady of wealth who set her table with china and silver and
brought her own servants from Boston.   She d. Nov. 21, 1756, æ. 39.
They had "'tis said" worthless continental money enough to paper
a house.   He m. (2) July 25, 1757, No. 4063.

    **4063.**  Susannah (Wilder) Willard, whose first husband, Col.
Samuel Willard, b. at Lancaster, Nov. 12, 1718, had m. this Susanna
of Lancaster in 1743 and resided at Petersham.   He d. ill in camp,
Oct. 25, 1755 in command of his regiment of 800 men.

    Rev. Elisha was in Westminster about 28 years, leaving in 1770,
though dismissed from his pastorate in 1758.   He then removed to
Walpole, Cheshire Co., N. H. and lived 14 years more and became
Judge of Court of Common Pleas.   He d. in 1784, in Lancaster at
the house of his wife's brother from effects of a fall from his horse
in Roxbury, Mass.

His well-known great-grandson, Luther R. Marsh, Esq. of New York, once a partner of Webster, long a commissioner of Central Park, who is retired at Middletown, N. Y., after a practice of 53 years, describes his ancestor as "sprightly and original," says well, "he found it impossible to contain himself within ministerial conventionalities. He was constantly violating the puritan tone of that day. His wit bubbled over the pulpit enclosure." Tradition said that he once stepped down from the pulpit and in the sanctuary engaged his farm help for the next day; that he was so positive that one member of the church with himself made a majority. The centennial orator of Westminster records that the houses and church were protected against Indians by stockades and muscular Christians took muskets to meeting and charge was brought against the minister for "stumping one of his church members on the Sabbath, to swop powder horn-strings with him." A county sheriff had occasion to serve process upon the town of Westminster and could legally do it by serving the writ on any townsman. He first met the parson, as he rode in; took off his hat, handed him the writ and said, "The Grace of God, Mr. Marsh," and Rev. Elisha gave instant retort, "Yes, by the hands of the devil."

He was put on trial for saying "That obedience is the condition of salvation;" also for saying, "that if all that was required of a man was to believe, then the condition of salvation was easy and pleasant to fools;" also "that he would as soon worship the devil, as worship such a being as required more of his creatures than they are able to perform, and that he did not worship such a being."

After 125 years from his settlement the historical discourse of Parson Rich sums up fairly, "The originality of his language and the keen force of his logic, so wittily and boldly expressed, showed that he possessed no ordinary mind, and, if not much devotion, yet a good deal of common sense and of eminently practical faith."

His name is evidently permanently written upon the town and his thought helped mark its history. We cannot help agreeing with his not less unique and witty great-grandson, Luther R. that his characteristics fitted him better for the law than the ministry. We do not wonder that this great-grandson visiting Westminster a few years since sought out the old meeting house that had moved about, became a store and then a barn, and knocked out from one of the massive timbers an oak pin that had seasoned for 140 years and had listened for 15 years to sermons of the Rev. Elisha.   Children :

4064.   Elisha⁵, b. March 28, 1750-51 ; m. No. 4066.
4065.   Sarah, b. 1752-56; m. Thomas Brigden, Esq. and d. in 1774, with no children.
By second wife.
4065.1.   Benjamin, b. 1758-68; m. Hannah Graves and settled. at Chesterfield, N. H.   Child :
    4065.2.   Reuben⁶, m. Mary Wetherbee, 4080.
4065.3.   A " Daniel Marsh," b. 1765 or 6, " d. 1857, æ. 92, at Walpole, N. H." Was he possibly son of Rev. Elisha? "Jane Adams of Londonderry, b. Jan. 2, 1767 ; m. Dec. 31, 1794, Daniel Marsh." N. E. Register.


### 4066 = 4064.   CAPT. ELISHA⁵ MARSH

b. March 28, 1750-1, at Walpole, N. H., son of Rev. Elisha⁴ and Deborah (Lathrop) Marsh, (Cornet Ebenezer³, Daniel², John¹) ; m. No. 4066.

4066,   ——. He lived at Walpole. The historian has made many efforts in vain to get anything but the names of these children. Men's marriages average at 24 and births average two years interval. This guess work would give dates as follows.   Children :

4067.   Elisha⁶, b. 1776? at Walpole, moved to Onondaga Co., N. Y., had dau. Mrs. Pierce.
4068.   Josiah, b. 1778 ? at Walpole.
4069.   Lorin, b. 1780? at Walpole.
4070.   Susan, b. 1782 ? m. Dr. J. P. Hopkins, 4072.
.071.   Luther, b. 1784; m. Emma Rawson, 4075.


### 4072 = 4070.   SUSAN⁶ MARSH

b. at Walpole, N. H., possibly about 1782, dau. of Capt. Elisha⁵ Marsh, (Rev. Elisha⁴, Cornet Ebenezer³, Daniel², John¹) ; m. No. 4072.

4072.   Dr. Judah P. Hopkins of Skaneateles, N. Y.   Child :
4073.   Harriet⁷, m. Dr. Bartlett of Skaneateles.   Child:
    4074.   Edward T⁸. Bartlett of New York City.

## 4075 = 4071. LUTHER[6] MARSH

b. at Walpole, N. H., son of Capt. Elisha[5] Marsh, (Rev. Elisha[4], Cornet Ebenezer[3], Daniel[2], John[1]) ; m. No. 4075.

**4075.** Emma Rawson, dau. of Thomas Hooker Rawson at one time state superintendent of the Salina salt works and afterwards doctor at Canandaigua, N. Y. where he is buried. He was descended from Edward Rawson who came to Newburyport, Mass., in 1636 and was in Boston in 1650 and secretary of the colony there 36 years. Mr. Marsh's great-grandfather Rev. Grindal Rawson m. in 1798 Dorothy, great-grand-daughter of Rev. Charles Chauncey, second president of Harvard college, whose lineage is traced back to the ancient crowns of England, France and Germany. Luther[6] Marsh removed from Walpole to Onondaga Co., N. Y. On his way perhaps was awhile editor at Elizabethtown, N. Y. The New York state *Gazetteer* gives "The *Reveille*, the first paper in the county (Essex) was started at Elizabethtown, about 1810, by Luther Marsh." He seems to have been as eccentric as his grandfather for while high sheriff of Onondaga Co., in riding through what was ironically called "Christian Hollow," seeing a man suddenly drop his hoe and make for the woods, in his exuberant strength, activity and vitality he dismounted and after hot pursuit grasped the panting fugitive and explained, "Well, I have no process against you now, but I thought I would let you know that if I ever did have any, it wouldn't do you any good to run." We get a glimpse of Gov. DeWitt Clinton slapping on the knee the senator who asked him to reappoint Sheriff Marsh and saying "Squire Birdseye, I wish you to understand that the good people of Pompey Hill cannot have all the offices in the state of New York."

The son of Emma Rawson had "lost his own mother on the anniversary of his seventh birthday." That seventh anniversary came April 4, 1820. Luther[6] Marsh m. (2) No. 4076.

**4076.** Margaret Leonard, dau. of Rev. Joshua who graduated at Brown university in 1788 and after preaching at Ellington, Ct., settled in Cazenovia, N. Y., and in May, 1799 formed the first Presbyterian church and has published that then from Cazenovia to the Pacific ocean and in New York state to the north and south of him there was not one Congregational church or Presbyterian pastor. From 1814 to 1822 he was principal of Pompey academy. Margaret Leonard was descended from James Leonard who came from Pontypool, Wales, in 1652, to Taunton, Mass., and set up the first iron works established in this country. Luther[6] Marsh d. at Chicago, Ill., Nov. 14, 1859. Child:

4077. Luther Rawson[7], b. April 4, 1813; m. J. E. Stewart, 4078.

### 4078 = 4077. LUTHER RAWSON[7] MARSH

b. at Pompey, Onondaga Co., N. Y., April 4, 1813, son of Luther[6] and Emma (Rawson) Marsh, (Capt. Elisha[5], Rev. Elisha[4], Cornet Ebenezer[3], Daniel[2], John[1]) ; a remarkable man, by heredity charged, 100 years before he was born, with somewhat of the erratic, independent tendencies of the clergyman and judge, his great-grand-father ; by environment in constant association from boyhood with not a few of America's foremost men, the intimate companion of Gov. Horatio Seymour and a partner of Webster ; in student life at Capt. Partridge's celebrated military academy in Connecticut among splendid competitors gaining a medal for the second best English oration and commended therefor by no less a judge than Aaron Burr; a profound admirer of eloquence, going to Bunker Hill to hear Webster's address, eagerly seeking to know and hear every great man, thrilled and captivated by Theodore Dwight Weld, "the grand-est platform orator of that or perhaps of any time ;" by choice a lawyer and public speaker, delighted with literary refinement and culture, an intimate friend of Lester, author of the "Glory and Shame of England" and guest of Willis at Glen Mary, rising in New York City to rank among those at the very front, brimfull and bubbling over with wit and fun, meeting safely the keenest at the bar ; chosen by the New York Historical society to attend Webster's funeral at Marshfield and giving the society an address on return, selected by Raymond to write for the New York *Times* a four column article on Webster's death, which was included by the Appletons in their Memo-rials of Webster, chosen by the N. Y. legislature in 1882–3 on the commission to locate grounds for public parks which shall meet the future needs of the city of New York; helping wisely in care of Central Park and suggesting provision for the public at Niagara, his

*Luther R. Marsh*

life has been too full and brilliant to be given here with any completeness. As to opinions in which he chooses to differ from the world at large this is not the place to state or discuss them and the great future has time enough to test and finally judge them.

He spent several years in various places before settling in New York City, first at Pompey, then at Middletown, Ct., then clerk at Onondaga Hill, next at Skaneateles 1830-36, then in New York City, then at Utica 1837-42 where he conducted in 1840 a campaign paper called *The Sledge Hammer.* While at Utica he joined Horatio Seymour, No. 150, in a campaign tour through the Boonville region advocating the democratic faith.

There at Utica came a turning point. Theo. D. Weld in 16 lectures without a note before him, rounded out his great argument for the abolition of slavery. That remarkable man Alvan Stewart gave up most of his time to anti-slavery and temperance movements and did more than any other man to unite whigs and abolitionists and form the republican party. Mr. Marsh was gradually weaned from being an ardent democrat to free soil sentiments, and when the extension of slavery into new territory assumed importance he joined the republican party. Stewart's words in 1841, "These states must necessarily be in eternal conflict until liberty conquers slavery, or slavery overturns the liberty of all," preceded Senator Seward's historic expression, the "irrepressible conflict," and Lincoln's aphorism. "these states can never remain half slave and half free." After about five years at Utica, Mr. Marsh returned to New York and made that the headquarters of all his brilliant business life.

I cannot give dates after long effort but from an encyclopedia I read what may help explain the modification of his political views. " As soon as Mr. Marsh was fairly established in his profession he consummated an engagement he had formed." He m. No. 4078.

**4078.** Jeannie E. Stewart, daughter of Alvan Stewart, a lady to whom Mrs. Fanny Osgood dedicated a poem and of whom Gen.. Geo. P. Morris sang some years after :

> Jeannie Marsh of Cherry Valley,
> In whose name the muses rally,
> Of all the nine, none so divine
> As Jeannie Marsh of Cherry Valley.
> A sylvan nymph of queenly grace,
> A goddess she in form and feature,
> The sweet expression of the place,
> A dimple in the smile of nature.

Not long after, Mr. Marsh took a house in 15th St., New York, near Dr. Cheever's church, where his father-in-law lived with him until the death of Mr. Stewart in 1849. About 1883 Mr. Marsh was accustomed to spend his summers partly at Newport and at the beautiful village of Charlestown, N. H., and the rest on his farm at Brockton, Lake Erie, amid his orchards and vineyards. Of recent years he has retired from business and lives at 10 Barton St., Middletown, Orange Co., N. Y.

I will give of many, a single example of his wit. A case was suffering from the "law's delay" owing to the many engagements of the Judge. Finally Mr. Marsh inquired "Have you settled the case of Col. Sheep?" "Col. Sheep," said the Judge, "I do not remember any such case." "Perhaps your Honor will remember it better by the name it had when it came into your custody, that of Colonel Lamb." The case was settled within a week.

### 4080 = 4065.2.   REUBEN[6] MARSH

b. at Chesterfield, N. H., 1790–1800, son of Benjamin[5] and Hannah (Graves) Marsh, (Rev. Elisha[4] and Susannah (Wilder) Marsh, Cornet Ebenezer[3], Daniel[2], John[1]) ; m. about 1823, No. 4080.

**4080.** Mary Wetherbee.   Resided at Chesterfield.   Children :

    4081.  Benjamin L[7]., b. 1824 ; m. Annie Smith, 4083.
    4082.  Charles, b. 1829 ; m. Julia M. Barrett, 4088.

### 4083 = 4081.   BENJAMIN L[7].  MARSH

b. at Chesterfield, N. H., 1824, son of Reuben[6] and Mary (Wetherbee) Marsh, (Benjamin[5], Rev. and Judge Elisha[4], Cornet Ebenezer[3], Daniel[2], John[1] of Hadley and Hartford) ; m. Oct. 18, 1854, No. 4083.

**4083.** Annie Smith of Boston.   He resided in Boston and was a prominent merchant of the well-known firm of Jordan, Marsh & Co.   He died in New York June 13, 1865, æ. 41 years.   She m. (2) a Mr. Pearl who has since died.   She resides with her dau. Mrs. Hawes.   Children :

4084. Anna Cora[8], b. June 3, 1856 in Boston; m. Oct. 16, 1877, Joseph P. Hawes of Boston; his office 54 Kilby St., residence 182 Savin Hill Ave. Children:

4085. Arthur Prince[9], b. Sept. 12, 1878.
4086. Hazel[9], b. Nov. 8, 1880.
4087. Mary Louise, b. Sept. 20, 1861: d. Oct. 11, 1889.

4088 = 4082. CHARLES[7] MARSH

b. at Chesterfield, N. H., 1829, son of Reuben[6] and Mary (Wetherbee) Marsh, (Benjamin[5], Rev. Elisha[4], Cornet Ebenezer[3] Daniel[2], John[1]); m. Dec. 21, 1858. No. 4088.

4088. Julia Maria Barrett of Brighton, Mass., b. May 11, 1832, and he d. July 9, 1886. He was brother of Benjamin L. Marsh and a very successful merchant of the firm of Jordan, Marsh & Co. Children:

4089. Edith Barrett[8], b. March 24, 1863 ; m. Geo. H. Binney, 4092.
4090. Mabel Minot, b. March 4, 1867 ; m. June 9, 1888, Arthur N. Milliken of Boston, attorney at law, 82 Devonshire St., resides No. 7, Otis Place, Boston.
4091. Charles R[8]., b. in Boston, March 2, 1872 : resides with his mother, 35 Commonwealth Ave.

4092 = 4089. EDITH BARRETT[8] MARSH

b. March 24, 1863, dau. of Charles[7] and Julia M. (Barrett) Marsh of Boston, (Reuben[6], Benjamin[5], Rev. Elisha[4], Cornet Ebenezer[3], Daniel[2], John[1]) ; m. Oct. 21, 1884, No. 4092.

4092. George H. Binney of Boston. Children :

4093. George H[9]., b. Jan. 20, 1886.
4094. Edith M., b. Jan. 10, 1888.

We are indebted to Col. L. B. Marsh of Boston, President of the Marsh Family Association, 1887 to 1893, for the following sketch of the Marsh brothers of the firm Jordan, Marsh & Co.

Benjamin L[7]. Marsh and his junior brother Charles[7] Marsh, sons of Reuben[6] and Mary Marsh of Chesterfield, N. H., came to Boston and each entered stores as salesmen previous to 1850. Benjamin was not a novice in business experience when, with Mr. Eben D. Jordan, the house of Jordan, Marsh & Co., was established in 1851. He had received a most excellent business education with one of the largest and most respectable dry goods importing and jobbing houses in our city. He was one of those young men who at once win confidence and esteem. The firm of Jordan, Marsh & Co., commenced business under very favorable circumstances, being supplied very considerably by one of the largest commission houses in England that had connections with manufacturers who sought an outlet for their surplus goods. With these and other advantages, including his large acquaintance with the trade, their ability was sufficient to win from the start a large share of business. In a short time their credit was firmly established and they had the confidence and good will of the public.

In 1865 Benjamin died. He was regarded as a most excellent business man. For fourteen years of active business he enjoyed the confidence and respect of the mercantile community. In social life he was kind-hearted, benevolent, a true friend and an esteemed citizen. He was ambitious, courageous and successful. He lived to see the business that he and his partners had created and developed, become one of the largest in our city.

His brother Charles was admitted a partner about 1852. He too had experience in business in the house of Pearl, Smith & Co., as a salesman. As such he had shown marked ability and was very popular. He well sustained his brother in his particular department of the business. At his brother's death he took his place and his executive ability and courage as well as business knowledge, were manifest in the increase and development of the immense business they were then doing.

It is very seldom that three partners are so suitably associated in business as were Mr. Eben D. Jordan, Benjamin L. Marsh and Charles Marsh. Each had his peculiar and distinctive traits of character. No wonder that the junior partners of such men are distinguished for great mercantile ability. Mr. Jordan, still in active business, is enjoying the fruits of the united labor, energy and success of their well developed mercantile capacity.

Without doubt hard work and an overtaxed brain caused the death of Benjamin L. Marsh at the age of 41 ; and the same causes may also have contributed to the death of his brother Charles at the age of 57.

# THE WETHERSFIELD, LYME, NORWICH, CT., LINE.

## 4095 = 4044. MARY[4] MARSH

b. at Hadley, Mass,, March 3, 1715, dau. of Cornet Ebenezer[3] and Mary (Parsons) Marsh, (Daniel[2], John[1]) ; m. Nov. 6, 1735, No. 4095.

**4095.** Dr. Ezekiel Porter, b. about 1706, son of Dr. Samuel Porter of Farmington, Ct. He settled in Wethersfield, Ct., and on the family table in the burying yard there we read, " In memory of Dr. Ezekiel Porter a very eminent and celebrated surgeon, a sincere lover of mankind, a warm and steady friend of the civil and religious liberties of the country. An upright and charitable man, an exemplary Christian. Who departed this life greatly lamented by all who knew him, Oct. 3, 1775, in the 69th year of his age." " Mrs. Mary Marsh Porter, relict of Dr. Ezekiel Porter, who died Nov. 17, 1796, æ. 80." At her age of 77 President Stiles of Yale, a zealous early reporter, sought interview with her May 25, 1792 as to the Hadley regicide Judges, and called her " a sensible and judicious woman." (See his pleasing report of her ; History of Hadley, pp. 219 and 220.) Skillful in medicine and a daring horse-woman, after Dr. Porter's death, Widow Mary continued his practice and had patients for some distance in neighboring towns. Her marriage to Dr. Porter may

24

have had connection with Dr. Hezekiah Porter's short residence in Hadley at her father's door and it no doubt led to the removal of her two brothers Jonathan and John to Wethersfield, and to Dr. Jonathan's choice of profession and also his son's choice and his daughter's marriage to Dr. Lee who studied with his uncle Dr. Ezekiel Porter. Dr. Samuel Lee's mother was sister of Dr. Ezekiel and dau. of Dr. Samuel Porter. Children :

4096.    Abigail[5], b. about 1737 ; m. (1) Col. Thomas Belden, b. about 1732, who d. in 1782, æ. 50 and she m. (2) Rev. Dr. Dana of New Haven. She d. in 1798, æ. 61. Child :

4097.    Col. Ezekiel Porter[6] Belden, was a captain in the revolutionary army and for a time attached to the staff of George Washington.


4098 = 4047.   HANNAH[4] MARSH


b. at Hadley, Mass., abt. 1724, dau of Cornet Ebenezer[3] and Mary (Parsons) Marsh, (Daniel[2], John[1]) ; m. May 20, 1739, No. 4098.

**4098.**   Samuel Ely of Lyme, Ct., b. about 1713. He d. Feb. 11, 1784, and was descended from Richard Ely who came to this country and settled in 1660 at Lyme, Ct., where he and his two sons William and Richard soon had over 4000 acres and he paid one sixth of the town tax. He d. there 1684, 100 years before Samuel. The gravestone of Mrs. Hannah (Marsh) Ely reads " who departed this life April 7th A. D. 1787, in ye 63d year of her age." She had some illustrious descendants. Children :

4099.    Samuel[5], b. Nov. 6, 1740.
4100.    Elijah, b. May 8, 1743 ; m. Mrs. Catherine Lee, 4109.
4101.    Hannah, b. May 26, 1745.
4102.    Mary, b. about 1746 ; " d. Dec. 10, 1751, æ. 5."
4103.    Abner, m. Dorcas Brockway, dau. of Semilius and Dorcas (Giddings) Brockway.
4104.    Elizabeth, m. Abram Perkins.
4105.    Lois, m. Ezra Selden.
4106.    Mary, m. Thomas Anderson.
4107.    Jerusha, m. Williams.
4108.    Marsh.

## 4109 = 4100.  ELIJAH[5] ELY

b. Lyme, Ct., May 8, 1743, son of Hannah[4] (Marsh) Ely, (Ebenezer[3] Marsh, Daniel[2], John[1]) ; m. Feb. 14, 1765, No. 4109.

**4109.** Mrs. Catherine Lee, b. Sept. 8, 1749 ; d. Nov. 15, 1787 ; dau. of Elisha and Hepzibah Lee. Mr. Elijah[5] Ely was drowned near Saybrook ferry with his son-in-law, March 24, 1799. Children :

    4110.  Phebe[6], b. May 10, 1766; m. Calvin Selden; 4116.
    4111.  Elijah, b. April 10, 1769.
    4112.  Samuel, b. April 26, 1770.
    4113.  Cate, b. May 5, 1774.
    4114.  Hannah, b. May 12, 1776.
    4115.  Hepzibah, b. July 22, 1780.

## 4116 = 4110.  PHEBE[6] ELY

b. at Lyme, Ct., May 10, 1766, dau. of Elijah[5], son of Hannah[4] (Marsh) Ely, (Ebenezer[3] Marsh, Daniel[2], John[1]) ; m. Sept. 20, 1790, No. 4116.

**4116.** Calvin Selden, b. at Lyme, Ct., March 14, 1763. (Was he son of Ezra and Lois [Ely] Selden, No. 4105, as his son Ezra's name might hint?)  He d. at Lyme, Oct. 28, 1820 and she at New Haven, Oct. 15, 1853.  Children, (all b. at Lyme):

    4117.  Roxana[7], b. May 19, 1791.
    4118.  Ezra, b. Aug. 17, 1793 ; d. Aug. 16, 1814.
    4119.  Elizabeth, b. April 18, 1796 ; m. (1) Joseph Spencer, 4123.
    4120.  Samuel Lee, b. Oct. 12, 1800; Hon. Judge N. Y. State Court
        of Appeals, resided Rochester, N. Y.
    4121.  Almira, b. Sept. 20, 1803.
    4122.  Henry Rodgers, Hon. Lt. Gov. N. Y. and Judge N. Y. State
        Court of Appeals, resided Rochester, N. Y.

## 4123 = 4119.  ELIZABETH[7] SELDEN

b. at Lyme, Ct., April 18, 1796, dau. of Calvin Selden and Phebe[6] (Ely) Selden, dau. of Elijah[5] Ely, son of Hannah[4] (Marsh) Ely, (Ebenezer[3] Marsh, Daniel[2], John[1]) ; m. (1) Sept. 24, 1818, No. 4123.

**4123.** Joseph Spencer, son of Isaac and Lucretia (Colt) Spencer of Hartford, who d. at Albany, N. Y., May 2, 1823. She m. (2) April 21, 1831, at Rochester, N. Y., No. 4124.

**4124.** Lieut. afterwards Major Gen. Amos B. Eaton, son of Prof. Amos and Sally (Cady) Eaton. Mrs. Eaton d. Washington, D. C., May 8, 1868. Gen. Eaton m. (2) Sept. 10, 1870, Mrs. Mary (Jerome) Smith, widow of Col. E. Kirby Smith of U. S. A. He d. at New Haven, Feb. 21, 1877. Children :

> 4125. Elizabeth Selden[8], b. Dec. 5, 1819, at Rochester, N. Y.
>
> By second husband.
>
> 4126. Ellen Dwight, b. March 19, 1832, at Fort Niagara.
> 4127. Daniel Cady, b. Sept. 12, 1834; m. Caroline Ketcham, 4129.
> 4128. Frances Spencer, b. July 18, 1836, at Fort Gratiot, Mich.

4129 = 4127.   PROF. DANIEL CADY[8] EATON

b. at Fort Gratiot, Mich., Sept. 12, 1834, son of Maj. Gen. A. B. and Elizabeth[7] (Selden) Eaton ; m. Feb. 13, 1866, No. 4129.

**4129.** Caroline Ketcham, dau. of Tredwell and Mary (Van Winkle) Ketcham of N. Y. City. They reside in New Haven, Ct. Children :

> 4130. Elizabeth Selden[9], b. Aug. 25, 1867.
> 4131. Henry Ketcham, b. Aug. 12, 1870 ; d. at Lyme, Ct., accidentally from his own gun, July 17, 1885.
> 4132. George Francis, b. May 30, 1872.

---

## THE NORWICH, CT. LINE.

4133 = 4045.   DR. JONATHAN[4] MARSH

b. at Hadley, Mass., about 1720, son of Cornet Ebenezer[3] and Mary (Parsons) Marsh, (Daniel[2], John[1]) ; probably studied at Wethersfield,

Ct., with his sister's husband, Dr. Ezekiel Porter or her father-in-law, Dr. Samuel Porter of Farmington, Ct. This led him to settle for a time at Wethersfield, but eventually at Norwich, Ct. During the French war he was in the northern army, 1755-7, a skillful surgeon. In the Colonial Records of Connecticut he is called " army surgeon in the expedition to Crown Point." "March 13, 1746, he received deed of land in Norwich, Ct., describing him 'of Weathersfield in the county of Hartford, Colony of Connecticut.'" He m. Nov. 5, 1747, No. 4133.

**4133.** Sarah Hart of Farmington, Ct., great-grand-daughter of Stephen Hart of Farmington. He owned land at the foot of Mt. Holyoke in Hockanum, Hadley, probably a part of the land recorded in 1674 as given by Hadley town to his great-grandfather "John[1] Marsh his heirs, executors and assigns forever." The record of that "parcell" Dec. 19, 1674 reads "alsoe in the meddow called Hockanum. One parcell containing ffour akars one rood and thirty-three poles more or less," "abutting on the river norwest and the lotts running up the mountain southeast in bredth ffive rod and $\frac{4}{10}$ of a rod." His two sons held this land up to Nov. 30, 1791. Dr. Marsh's death was due to his profession, from the absorption of virus in treating a wound caused by an explosion at Hartford in celebrating the repeal of the stamp act in 1766. He d. June 3, 1766 in the 47th year of his age and was buried in the church yard at Wethersfield. His family remained at Norwich but his brother and sister lived at Wethersfield, almost a part of Hartford. The malignity of the disease may account for burial near by. The explosion above mentioned took place in the upper room of a school building where many young men of Hartford were making cartridges and other fireworks. Children :

4134.  Sarah[5], b. July 27, 1749; m. Dr. Samuel Lee, 4140.
4135.  Abigail, b. April 8, 1751 ; m. Maj. John Ripley, 4152.
4136.  Jonathan, b. June 15, 1754 ; m. Mrs. Alice Fitch, 4176.
4137.  Hannah, b. Nov. 19, 1757; m. Dr. Summer of Westfield, Mass.
4138.  Mary, b. Nov. 11, 1759; m. Benjamin Dyer of Windham, Ct., son of Col. Dyer of "Bull Frog" fame.
4139.  Joseph, b. March 6, 1762 ; m. Eunice Huxley, 4180.

## 4140 = 4134.    SARAH⁵ MARSH

b. at Norwich, Ct., July 27, 1749, dau. of Dr. Jonathan⁴ and Sarah
(Hart) Marsh, (Cornet Ebenezer³, Daniel², John¹) ; m. March 23,
1769, No. 4140.

**4140.** Dr. Samuel⁴ Lee of Windham, Ct., who studied medicine
with his mother's brother Dr. Ezekiel Porter whose wife was Mary
Marsh, sister of Dr. Jonathan Marsh. Dr. Lee⁴ was son of Capt.
Hezekiah³ and Sarah (Porter) Lee, John² and Elizabeth (Loomis),
John¹ of Farmington and Mary Hart, dau. of Stephen.    Sarah Porter
was dau. of Dr. Samuel Porter of Farmington.    Birds of medical
feather flock together.    Dr. Samuel Porter had son Dr. Ezekiel
Porter, whose wife's brother became Dr. Jonathan Marsh and his
student and nephew Dr. Samuel Lee m. Dr. Jonathan Marsh's
daughter.    Dr. Lee was social, skillful and of extensive practice.
Of great agility and muscular strength he once hopped 40 feet at
three bounds, and once lifted a cart with nine men in it by getting
under it.    He entered into the revolutionary struggle with great zeal,
was on committee to examine applicants for service as army surgeons
and served himself until the war closed.    He became intimate with
Maj. Gen. Charles Lee, the English officer who served under Washington and named one of his sons after him.    He d. at Windham,
Dec. 7, 1805.    The historian of the John Lee Family, Sarah Marsh⁷
Lee, writes of the grandmother Sarah⁵ (Marsh) Lee after whom she
was named, " My grandmother must have been very much like her
Aunt Mary (Mary [Marsh] Porter, 4095).    She certainly inherited a
skill in surgery, even setting bones.    Her husband used to say that
she could perform all these operations as well, if not better than he
could and he was a very skillful surgeon."    Children :

4141.    Sarah⁶, b. Jan. 29, 1771 ; m. Aug. 2, 1794, Capt. John Lathrop
of Windham, descended from Rev. John the 1st Inde-
pendent Min. in England, came to N. E. 1634, also
descended from Gov. Wm. Bradford of the Mayflower.
She had eight children, thirteen grandchildren and five
great-grandchildren, mentioned in the Lee Book.

4142.    Samuel, b. Jan. 17, 1773; m. March, 1794, Lucy Gray, dau.
of Dr. Thomas Gray. Dr. S. Lee was physician and
surgeon and George Washington signed his patent for
his medicine still used, the first of its kind ever patented
in this country. He d. Dec. 22, 1815 and his widow m.

Dr. Thomas Hubbard, later Prof. of Surgery at Yale. Four children. He had three grandsons who gave their lives in the late civil war.

4143. Jonathan, b. June 26, 1775, bap. Jan. 27, 1776; m. April 9, 1795, Jerusha Frink; d. Jan. 5, 1822. She d. Jan. 8, 1852. Eight children.

4144. Clarissa, b. July 6, 1777; d. Medina, O., 1859.

4145. Mary, b. Sept. 7, 1779; m. Geo. W. Webb of Windham, had two children and d. in 1863.

4146. Frances, b. April 20, 1783, bap. May 23, 1783; m. March 7, 1812, Thomas Mather, b. Sept. 25, 1780, son of Dr. Samuel Mather, of Westfield, Mass. He d. May 17, 1845, she Oct. 14, 1847. Three children.

4147. William, b. March 30, 1786, bap. May 27, 1786; d. Oct. 15, 1790.

4148. Infant, d. July 1, 1788.

4149. Charles, b. March 14, 1790, bap. Aug. 1, 1790; m. (1) Oct. 28, 1817, Bethia Fitch, b. Feb. 3, 1792, dau. of Zenas Howes. She d. Jan. 17, 1828. He m. (2) Dec. 15, 1828, Harriet Gordon, b. Nov. 2, 1802, dau. of Alexander Gordon. He was extensively engaged in manufacturing in Willimantic and in drugs at Norwich, Ct. See Hist. John Lee and Descendants, 1634—1878 for a beautiful tribute to his character by his dau. He d. Norwich, Oct. 25, 1865. Child:

4150. Sarah Marsh[7] Lee, b. Sept. 28, 1819. Historian John Lee Family.

4151. Almyra, b. Feb. 13, 1793; m. David King of Westfield, Mass., resided at Medina, O. and d. there Jan. 24, 1875. [For 114 descendants of Sarah (Marsh) Lee see Hist. John Lee.]

## 4152 = 4135. ABIGAIL[5] MARSH

b. at Norwich, Ct., April 8, 1751, dau. of Dr. Jonathan[4] and Sarah (Hart) Marsh, (Cornet Ebenezer[3], Daniel[2], John[1]); m. June 7, 1769, No. 4152.

**4152.** Major John[3] Ripley, b. March 31, 1738, son of Joshua[2], b. May 10, 1688, d. Nov. 18, 1773, m. [both of Windham,] Dec. 3, 1712, Mary Backus, d. Oct., 1770; Joshua[1] of Hingham, Mass., b. May 9, 1658, d. May 18, 1739, m. Nov. 28, 1682, Hannah Bradford, b. May 9, 1662, d. May 28, 1738, dau. of William Bradford,

Jr. of Plymouth.    Maj. John Ripley served in the old French and in the revolutionary wars and was "a thorough gentleman, Christian and patriot." Abigail (Marsh) Ripley d. July 27, 1805, æ. 54. He d. June 27, 1823. Child :

> 4153.  Julia[6], b. May 16, 1792 ; m. Judge Henry Terry, 4154.    There were probably other children.

4154 = 4153.    JULIA[6] RIPLEY

b. at Windham, Ct., May 16, 1792, dau. of Maj. John and Abigail[5] (Marsh) Ripley, (Dr. Jonathan[4] Marsh, Ebenezer[3], Daniel[2], John[1] of Hartford, Ct.) ; m. April 29, 1810, No. 4154.

**4154.** Judge Henry Terry, b. Jan. 12, 1771, son of Gen. Nathaniel and Catherine (Wadsworth) Terry.    Catherine's father Col. Jeremiah Wadsworth was the intimate friend of George Washington, was Commissary General for nearly all the revolutionary war and Washington when in Hartford always made his house his home.    Gen. Nathaniel Terry was Judge county court 1807–9, member of congress 1817–19, helped form state constitution 1818, Mayor of Hartford and presiding Judge of the city court 1824–31.    He was son of Col. Nathaniel Terry and Abiah Dwight.    [For extended notice of her ancestry and all these parties see Dwight Book passim.]    Judge Henry Terry was a lawyer at Enfield and Hartford, for many years member of Connecticut legislature and Judge of probate.    He d. at Enfield, Sept. 22, 1827, æ. 66.    His widow resided at Framingham, Mass.    Children :

> 4155.  Julia Maria[7], b. Feb. 17, 1811 ; d. Dec. 26, 1813.
> 4156.  Henry Dwight, b. Hartford, March 16, 1812 ; a lawyer of Detroit, Mich., entered the late war as Col. of Mich. 5th, was promoted Brig. Gen. by President Lincoln for his great bravery in the battles of Williamsburg and Fair Oaks.    Led by Terry the 5th advanced within 50 feet of the enemy, fought for four hours, made two splendid charges and drove the confederates out of their rifle pits.    Gen. Terry m. Louisa Marion Clemens, dau. of Judge Clemens of Mt. Clemens, Mich. Children :
> 4157.  Henry Clemens[8].
> 4158.  Julia Ripley.
> 4159.  Dwight.

4160. Caroline, b. Enfield, Ct., Sept. 12, 1813; d. Oct. 22, 1813.
4161. Julia Maria, b. Oct. 2, 1814; m. Lothrop Wight, 4168.
4162. Lucy Ripley, b. Enfield, July 15, 1816; m. June 8, 1854, Daniel McFarland, Jr., of Framingham; d. at Hartford, June 9, 1861.
4163. Elizabeth Taylor, b. June 7, 1818; m. June 28, 1848, Amasa Fiske Dwight, b. March 20, 1821, son of William Dwight of Sturbridge, Mass., a lumber merchant at Detroit, Mich. Children:
    4164. Alfred Taylor[8], b. Sept. 26, 1850; lumber merchant at Detroit, Mich.
    4165. Walter Terry, b. Aug. 25, 1855.
4166. William Bradford, b. Enfield, Dec. 2, 1820, bookbinder, Hartford, wounded before Richmond and d. Nov. 1, 1864 in hospital at Point of Rocks, Va.
4167. Horace Hall, b. Enfield, March 1, 1825; was in the 32d Wis. Reg. at the taking of Atlanta.


## 4168 = 4161. JULIA MARIA[7] TERRY

b. at Enfield, Ct., Oct. 2, 1814, dau. of Judge Henry and Julia[6] (Ripley) Terry, Maj. John and Abigail[5] (Marsh) Ripley, (Dr. Jonathan[4] Marsh, Cornet Ebenezer[3], Daniel[2], John[1]); m. Oct. 27, 1834, No. 4168.

**4168.** Lothrop Wight, b. at Sturbridge, Mass., Aug. 13, 1811, son of Alpheus and Miriam (Belknap) Wight, a wholesale dry goods merchant, Boston, who d. at Framingham, Feb. 2, 1855. Children:

4169. Julia Maria,[8] b. Boston, July 28, 1835; m. 1851, Alexander R. Esty, a Boston architect; she d. Feb. 26, 1862. Children:
    4170. Annie[9], b. 1856.
    4171. Fanny, b. 1858.
    4172. Harry, b. 1859; d. Dec., 1862.
4173. Lothrop, b. Boston, March, 29, 1839; bookkeeper, Chicago; m. Mary Warren of Framingham, Mass.; entered navy, 1862; on Admiral Wilkes' staff 1863, was watch officer on "The Vanderbilt" after the Alabama and Georgia, for a time in command of the Mendota, honorably discharged Aug. 19, 1865.
4174. Lawrence Terry, b. Framingham, July 12, 1848; bookkeeper in Boston.
4175. William Henry, b. Framingham, Aug. 1, 1852.

## 4176 = 4136.  DR. JONATHAN⁵ MARSH, JR.

b. at Norwich, Ct., June 15, 1754, son of Dr. Jonathan⁴ and Sarah
(Hart) Marsh, (Cornet Ebenezer³, Daniel², John¹); m. May 29, 1776,
No. 4176.

**4176.** Mrs. Alice Fitch of Windham, Ct. The English Stamp
Act was the strange occasion of his father's death. Americans at
Hartford in 1766 were enthusiastic in celebrating its repeal. An explosion wounded many and in treating one of those wounds, Dr. Marsh
absorbed virus that caused his death. Jonathan, Jr., was then but
12 years old, but under his mother's skillful tuition he became so
expert and famous in bone setting that his early death April 18, 1798,
in his 44th year was esteemed a public calamity. (See History Norwich, Ct. and also "John Lee and Descendants.")  Children :

> 4177.  Lucy⁶, b. Nov. 12, 1776.
> 4178.  Sally, b. Sept. 28, 1781.
> 4179.  Polly, b. July 14, 1784 ; m. Bela B. Hyde, b. at Norwich,
> Oct., 1784.  They settled at Rome, N. Y., where he d.
> Nov. 17, 1853 and she in 1854.

## 4180 = 4139.  JOSEPH⁵ MARSH

b. at Norwich, Ct., March 6, 1762, son of Dr. Jonathan⁴ Marsh of
Norwich and Sarah (Hart) Marsh, (Cornet Ebenezer³, Daniel²,
John¹); m. Dec. 16, 1790, No. 4180.

**4180.** Eunice Huxley, b. at Norwich, Jan., 1769, dau. of Phinehas Huxley. He was a joiner as appears from Massachusetts
Hampshire County Records of Deeds : "Nov. 30, 1791, Jonathan
Marsh, Physician, and Joseph Marsh, Shop Joiner of Norwich, Ct.
sell lands in Hockanum to Ebenezer Marsh, Jr., as heirs of Jonathan
Marsh deceased." He d. Sept. 30, 1829, and his widow April 13,
1844.  Children :

> 4181.  Fanny⁶, b. April 17, 1792 ; d. unm. 1870.
> 4182.  Jonathan, b. Oct. 8, 1794; left home when about 10, studied
> medicine with his uncle Dr. Sumner of Westfield,
> Mass., went west, m. lived and died.
> 4183.  Hart Lee, b. Oct. 4, 1796, went to western New York ; m. at
> the age of 21, Bediva Marble, and d. at Irving, Chau-
> tauqua Co., about 1872.  He left a widow and several
> children :

4184. Daniel[7].
4185. Nathan. Both, 1887, "living a few years ago."
4186. Joseph, b. Nov. 15, 1799; m. Lora Fitch, 4194.
4187. Phinehas, b. Jan. 15, 1801 ; d. Feb. 4, 1803.
4188. Julia Sumner, b. March 1, 1803 ; m. George A. Harriot, 4207.
4189. Abby R., b. April 21, 1805; res. and d. (1887) unm. in Sprague, Ct.
4190. Phinehas, b. April 21, 1807; unm. and was in 1846 on a wrecked steamboat near New Orleans.
4191. Eunice Huxley, b. Sept. 24, 1811 ; m. Joseph A. Griffing, 4217.
4192. Hannah S., b. Nov. 8, 1813 ; m. Laurens Brewster, 4228.
4193. Oliver Ripley, b. April 9, 1816 ; m. Miss Mainor, 4244.


## 4194 = 4186. JOSEPH[6] MARSH

b. at Norwich, Ct., Nov. 15, 1799, son of Joseph[5] and Eunice (Huxley) Marsh, (Dr. Jonathan[4], Cornet Ebenezer[3], Daniel[2], John[1]) ; m. No. 4194.

**4194.** Lora Fitch of Windham, Ct. He d. in 1843. Children :

4195. Charles Henry[7], m. Martha Roath, 4201.
4196. Oliver, d. y.
4197. Abby A., d. y.
4198. Emily, m. —— Nash, had three children, res. Mass.
4199. Mary, d. y.
4200. Elizabeth, d. y.


## 4201 = 4195. CHARLES HENRY[7] MARSH

b. at Norwich, Ct., son of Joseph[6] and Lora (Fitch) Marsh, (Joseph[5], Dr. Jonathan[4], Cornet Ebenezer[3], Daniel[2], John[1]) ; m. No. 4201.

**4201.** Martha Roath of Greenville, Ct. They had five sons. He d. leaving his widow and sons all living in Greenville. Children :

4202. Albert[8].
4203. George.
4204. Joseph.
4205. ————.
4206. ————.

4207 = 4188. JULIA SUMNER[6] MARSH

b. at Norwich, Ct., March 1, 1803, dau. of Joseph[5] and Eunice (Huxley) Marsh, (Dr. Jonathan[4], Ebenezer[3], Daniel[2], John[1]); m. in 1830, No. 4207.

**4207.** George A. Harriott. His widow now (1887) resides in New York City. Children :

 4208. Elizabeth A[7]., m. John Gardner of New York City; d. leaving one son :
  4209. Herman[8] of N. Y. City.
 4210. Abby Frances, res. Middletown, Ct., unm.
 4211. Georgianna, res. with mother in New York, unm.
 4212. Mary, m. Frank D. Brewster of Middletown, Ct. She d. leaving two boys :
  4213. Frank[8], with father in Middletown.
  4214. Frederick, with father in Middletown.
 4215. James A., m. and lives in Mich.
 4216. Susan R., res. with mother in New York, unm.


4217 = 4191. EUNICE HUXLEY[6] MARSH

b. Sept. 24, 1812, in Norwich, Ct., dau. of Joseph[5] and Eunice (Huxley) Marsh, (Dr. Jonathan[4], Cornet Ebenezer[3], Daniel[2], John[1]); m. March 31, 1839, No. 4217.

**4217.** Joseph A. Griffing. Resides now a widow in Franklin, Ct. Children :

 4218. James A[7]., b. Sept. 4, 1843; m. May 17, 1871, Anna M. Bowlsby of Brooklyn, N. Y. Children :
  4219. Eunice E[8].
  4220. Edith W.
 4221. Samuel, d. y.
 4222. Arthur, d. y.
 4223. Alfred, d. y.
 4224. Eunice, d. æ. 4.
 4225. George H., b. Sept. 20, 1850; m. Oct. 17, 1883, Gertrude V. Malona of Waterford, Ct. They res. at Franklin, Ct. Children :
  4226. Joseph M[8].
  4227. Hattie Marsh.

## 4228 = 4192. HANNAH S⁶. MARSH

b. at Norwich, Ct., Nov. 8, 1813, dau. of Joseph⁵ and Eunice (Huxley) Marsh, (Dr. Jonathan⁴, Cornet Ebenezer³, Daniel², John¹); m. March 3, 1839, No. 4228.

**4228.** Laurens Brewster. She is now (1887) living in Sprague, Ct. a widow. She has five children all living in 1887. Children :

    4229. Eldridge D⁷., m. Mrs. Drusilla Ward; res. in Lebanon, Ct. Children :
        4230. Nettie⁸.
        4231. George.
    4232. Julia H., m. Edwin Mulkin. Children :
        4233. Elmer⁸.
        4234. Hannah.
        4235. Lily.
        4236. Lottie.
    4237. Darius D., m. Sarah Cory; res. Sprague. Child :
        4238. Sarah F⁸.
    4239. Elizabeth, m. Earl Marsh Holbrook, res. Columbia. Child :
        4240. Laurens⁸.
    4241. Georgianna, m. Thomas Lillibridge of Norwich. Children :
        4242. Frank⁸.
        4243. Florence.

## 4244 = 4193. OLIVER RIPLEY⁶ MARSH

b. at Norwich, Ct., April 19, 1816, son of Joseph⁵ and Eunice (Huxley) Marsh, (Dr. Jonathan⁴, Cornet Ebenezer³, Daniel², John¹); " left Connecticut when only 18 years of age " writes his son J. W. Marsh, who gives the following account and list of his descendants. He m. (1) in Alabama [where he stayed about four years] when near the age of 26, about 1842 No. 4244.

**4244.** Miss Mainor, who d. about 1843–4 and he soon m. (2) No. 4245.

**4245.** Elizabeth McGaw. He removed about 1846 to Winston Co., Miss. and was one of the first settlers of Louisville, Miss. and remained there several years, then removed to Noxubee Co. and remained there " until I [his son J. W.] was about 14 years of age " (1862) when he returned and followed teaching in Winston Co. and " erected the first steam saw-mill that was ever heard whistle in Win-

ston Co." Mrs. Elizabeth Marsh d. about 1860 or 61, and he m.
(3) No. 4246.

**4246.** Nancy Lovern, who d. not having had any children. He
m. (4) about 1878, No. 4247.

**4247.** Sarah Myers, who d. March 2, 1881. Children, (all but
first by second wife) :

    4248. Miriam A[7]., b. about 1843; m. Wm. Fulcher, 4256.
                By second wife.
    4249. Philomela, b. about 1845; m. (1) Wm. Moore, 4263.
    4250. J. W., b. Dec. 22, 1848; m. Sallie Murphy, 4268.
    4251. Oliver Ripley, b. April 21, 1851; m. Jan., 1892, Mary Hag-
           gard. No children.
    4252. Fannie, b. 1853; m. S. E. Layne, 4275.
    4253. Eunice, b. 1855; m. B. Ashmore, 4279.
    4254. Georgia, b. 1858; m. G. F. Milegan, res. in Texas. Had
           three children.
    4255. Hannah, b. 1860; m. A. Skeen, res. Texas. Had four
           children.

### 4256 = 4248.   MIRIAM[7] MARSH

b. in Alabama, about 1843, dau. of Oliver Ripley[6] and —— (Mainor)
Marsh, (Joseph[5], Dr. Jonathan[4], Cornet Ebenezer[3]. Daniel[2], John[1]) ;
m. No. 4256.

**4256.** William Fulcher.  Children :

    4257. Rianza[8].
    4258. William H.
    4259. Jane.
    4260. Walter.
    4261. Dona.
    4262. George.

### 4263 = 4249.   PHILOMELA[7] MARSH

b. in Alabama, about 1845, dau. of Oliver Ripley[6] and Elizabeth
(McGaw) Marsh, (Joseph[5], Dr. Jonathan[4], Cornet Ebenezer[3], Daniel[2],
John[1]) ; m. (1) No. 4263.

**4263.** William Moore.  They resided in Texas where he d. in
March, 1887 and she m. (2) sometime in 1889, No. 4264.

**4264.** John Williams. Her three children were by her first husband. Children :

    4265. Willie, (a daughter).

    4266. Ino, (or Jno. for John).

    4267. Jessie.

$$4268 = 4250. \quad \text{J. W}^7. \text{ MARSH}$$

b. at Louisville, Miss., Dec. 22, 1848, son of George Ripley[6] and Elizabeth Marsh, (Joseph[5] of Norwich, Ct., Dr. Jonathan[4] of Hadley, Mass. and of Wethersfield and Norwich, Ct., Cornet Ebenezer[3] of Hadley, Daniel[2], John[1] both of Hartford and Hadley, Mass.); m. about 1876 No. 4268.

**4268.** Sallie Murphy. He is a farmer and owns 700 acres of good land. Children :

    4269. L. W$^s$., b. Feb. 23, 1877.

    4270. A. M., b. June 4, 1879.

    4271. J. O., b. Feb. 8, 1882.

    4272. L. F., b. Feb. 15, 1885.

    4273. Carrie, b. March 20, 1888; d. Sept. 22, 1888.

    4274. C. E., b. Sept. 23, 1890.

$$4275 = 4252. \quad \text{FANNIE}^7 \text{ MARSH}$$

b. at Winston Co., Miss., 1853, dau of Oliver Ripley[6] and Elizabeth Marsh, (Joseph[5], Dr. Jonathan[4], Cornet Ebenezer[3], Daniel[2], John[1]) ; m. No. 4275.

**4275.** S. E. Layne of Texas. Children :

    4276. Sallie[8].

    4277. ————.

    4278. ————.

$$4279 = 4253. \quad \text{EUNICE}^7 \text{ MARSH}$$

b. in Winston Co., Miss., 1855, dau. of Oliver Ripley[6] and Elizabeth Marsh, (Joseph[5], Dr. Jonathan[4], Cornet Ebenezer[3], Daniel[2], John[1]); m. March 9, 1871, No. 4279.

**4279.** B. Ashmoore.   Children :

4280.  Lilla⁸.
4281.  Lula.
4282.  Della.
4283.  Anna.
4284.  Sallie.
4285.  Vernettie. }
4286.  Ornettie.  } Twins.

---

## THE HOME LINE.

---

4287 = 4046.   EBENEZER⁴ MARSH

b. at Hadley, Mass.. in 1723 or 1721, son of Cornet Ebenezer³
Marsh, (Daniel², John¹); was born and lived his early life on the
Lewis lot east side of Hadley Broad St., but removed as early as
1770 to the original John¹ Marsh lot on the west side with his aged
father and spent there the rest of his days.  J. Pierce's diary reads,
" Dec. 9, 1742, begin to instruct Eben Marsh in Arithmetic Monday
and Thursday evenings."  He was then 19 or 21.  He was field
driver 1743 and 1744.  He m. Dec. 4, 1746, No. 4287.

**4287.** Sarah⁴ Eastman, dau. of Timothy³, Timothy², Roger¹).
He was 1748 highway surveyor, 1749 fence viewer.  Jan. 7, 1750,
the town voted to Capt. Moses Marsh, Ebenezer Marsh, Jr., Samuel
Marsh and seven others the liberty of erecting a grist mill on Fort
river near Lawrence's bridge with the use of said stream so long as
they shall keep a grist mill there in good repair.  He was 1752,
hogreave, 1755 and 58, fence viewer, 1763 had "fees for service ",
1764 to seat meeting house, 1770 highway surveyor and fence

viewer, 1771, 72 and 73, sealer of leather. In 1773, while living himself at the original John[1] Marsh lot, Cornet Ebenezer bought of the town an addition to his son Timothy's home lot, which was the south half of the original William Lewis lot. William Lewis was Timothy Marsh's grandfather's grandfather. This addition was on the east, eight rods square and towards Pine Plain St. He was on committee 1773 to set bounds of street, 1774 to repair wharf of north end of the town, and on " correspondence " Jan. 4, 1775 to receive donations for Boston and Charlestown, chosen selectman, refused to serve, 1776 fence viewer, 1778 highway surveyor, 1779 on town money, on committee with militia officers, delegate to convention at Northampton, to examine war services, on transfer of credit. Voted June 28, 1779, transfer of Timothy Marsh's service to his father's account. He was moderator of four town meetings that year, Aug. 23, Sept. 13, Oct. 19 and 20. In 1780 by town vote, corn was estimated at $20 a bushel. He was on committee for clothing and to procure soldiers, to give opinion against Mr. Strong and to seat meeting house, 1781 to collect minister's salary, to build pews and estimate their dignity and to seat the meeting house, on purchasing for the army and to meet delegates, 1782 sealer of leather, 1783 to see Mr. Hopkins, 1784 to seat meeting house and about soldiers, 1785 sealer of leather and on wearing of river bank, 1786 delegate to Hatfield convention, 1791 about town land. He d. May 29, 1795 æ. by family record 74, or by gravestone, (both in good preservation) 72. His gravestone stands near the north end of his grandfather Daniel's lot and also his wife's, who d. Jan. 31, 1794. Distribution of his estate gave to Timothy the homestead on which he lives, with buildings on same. To Sarah four acres and one hundred and forty-six rods on south side of homestead on which he lived, the original John[1] Marsh lot. To Ebenezer north side of homestead one acre and ninety-four rods and liberty of ingress and egress to buildings partly on Sarah's land.

Inventory taken June 23, 1795 :

| | |
|---|---|
| To homestead on which he lived, | £230. |
| To homestead where Timothy lives, | £130. |
| Total real and personal estate. | £668, 6s. |

Children :

4288. Timothy[5], b. July 6, 1747 ; d. May 12, 1751.
4289. Daniel, b. June 26, 1749; d. April 30, 1751.
4290. Timothy, b. Oct. 5, 1751 ; m. Mercy Smith, 4297.

4291.   Sarah, b. July 20, 1754 ; m. Nath. Dickinson, 4345.
4292.   Ebenezer, b. Sept. 8, 1757 ; d. Jan. 25, 1761.
4293.   Elijah, b. Dec. 25, 1760; d. Jan. 11, 1761.
4294.   Ebenezer, b. Jan. 5, 1762; d. unm. about 1818.
4295.   Mary, b, May 9, 1765 ; d. May 9, 1765.
4296.   Susanna, b. Jan. 26, 1766; d. Feb. 26, 1766.

$$4297 = 4290. \quad \text{TIMOTHY}^5 \text{ MARSH}$$

b. at Hadley, Mass., Oct. 5, 1751, son of Ebenezer[4] and Sarah
(Eastman) Marsh, (Cornet Ebenezer[3], Daniel[2], John[1]); resided at
Hadley, inherited south half of the William Lewis lot, field driver
1774 and 1776, revolutionary soldier, four months of his service by
town vote June 28, 1779 transferred to his father ; m. Sept. 23, 1779,
No. 4297.

**4297.**   Mercy Smith[5], b. Oct. 26, 1756, dau. of Windsor[4] Smith,
shop-keeper, Chileab[3], Chileab[2], Lieut. Samuel[1] of Hadley, from
England 1634.   Timothy was in 1781 tythingman, 1782 hogreave, in
1785 Ensign Timothy was collector.   He d. Oct. 18, 1796, the next
year after his father.   Widow Mercy and " Spinster Sarah Marsh "
sold for £160, March 14, 1806, their home lot to Samuel Woodard,
shoemaker.   She m. (2) Josiah[5] Cowles, b. March 20, 1744, son of
Jonathan[4], Jonathan[3], John[2], John[1]); removed to Leverett, Mass.
and d. Aug. 31, 1851, æ. 95.   Children :

4298.   Infant[6], b. Oct. 25, 1780; d. same day.
4299.   Mary, b. Nov., 1781 ; m. Thomas Baker, 4306.
4300.   Sarah, bap. Oct. 26, 1783 ; m. Eleazer Wright; d. about 1832.
4301.   Clarissa, bap. April 9, 1786; m. April 25, 1805, Oliver War-
          ren.   She d. about one year after m. and he m. (2) March,
          1808, Esther Dickinson of Hatfield.
4302.   Lois, b. June, 1788 ; m. Feb., 1807, Elisha Dickinson b. Jan.
          30, 1781 ; lived and d. at Whitingham, Vt.   Children :
      4303.   Harrison[7].
      4304.   Emily.
4305.   Jonathan, b. Jan. 19, 1793 : m. Harriet Warner, 4318.

$$4306 = 4299. \quad \text{MARY}^6 \text{ MARSH}$$

b. at Hadley, Mass., Nov., 1781, dau. of Timothy[5] and Mercy (Smith)

Marsh, (Ebenezer⁴, Ebenezer³, Daniel², John¹); m. Jan. 22, 1800, No. 4306.

**4306.** Thomas Baker of Chesterfield, Mass.; removed to La Fayette, N. Y., about 1803 and d. Dec. 8, 1840. Children:

4307. King⁷, b. Nov. 11, 1800; m. Nov. 12, 1821, Catherine Cramer of La Fayette; d. May 18, 1841, had ten children.

4308. Anson, b. Nov. 5, 1802; d. Nov. 20, 1802.

4309. Timothy, b. Oct. 11, 1803; m. Jan. 22, 1828, Lucy Bardwell of Williamstown; rem. 1832 to La Fayette. in 1855 to Waupaca, Wis. Had seven children.

4310. Clarissa, b. Jan. 18, 1806; m. James Abbott, res. in La Fayette; d. March 1, 1861. Had five children.

4311. Electa, b. Aug. 23, 1808; m. Hiram Abbott. No children.

4312. Lyman, b. Aug. 16, 1810; m. Sarah Beach. Had four children.

4313. Thomas E., b. July 31, 1812; m. Jan. 17, 1833, Samantha Baker. Had six children.

4314. Mary, b. Sept. 24, 1814; d. April 18, 1816.

4315. Ansel, b. Aug. 4, 1818; m. April 6, 1847, Martha L. Foster, res. Norwalk, O. Had five children.

4316. Martha M., b. Dec. 28, 1821; m. Wm. Otterbourne.

4317. Rufus, b. July 7, 1825 d. June 30, 1839.

## 4318 = 4305. JONATHAN⁶ MARSH

b. Jan. 19, 1793, Hadley, Mass., son of Timothy⁵ and Mercy (Smith) Marsh, (Ebenezer⁴, Ebenezer³, Daniel², John¹); his parents living on the south half of the Lewis lot. When he was three years old his father d. Oct. 18, 1796, leaving his mother a widow with five children. When seven he saw Sammy Sumner (age 6) drowned and long after would not allow his own children to play at the river. In 1806 his mother sold the place, and m. Josiah Cowles and removed to Leverett. He was early apprenticed to a shoemaker, but disliked the trade and was bound out to Silas Ball of Townsend, Vt., and when 21 took certificate that he had learned the carpenters and joiners trade. With a large muscular frame he would surpass the other apprentices in feats of strength and skill. He worked, his first free year in Westfield, Mass., and joined a military company, the only one thereabouts not ordered to Boston in 1814. He worked one season at Pompey, N. Y. and visited Niagara Falls and the battle field of Lundy's Lane.

In the "great revival" of 1816 he joined the church as did his after
wife Harriet Warner.   He is described at this time as full of humor
and fond of a joke, but withal a very religious man.   Having made
his home in Hadley or Leverett in 1820, Dec. 26 he bought of
Elihu Warner for $240 two and one-half acres on Middle St. the east
end of a lot sold by Capt. Moses Marsh in 1782, built a one and
one-half story house and m. Oct. 25, 1821, No. 4318.

**4318.**   Harriet[6] Warner, dau. of Elihu[5], Orange[4], Jacob[3], Jacob[2],
Andrew[1] of Cambridge, 1632, Hartford 1639 and of Hadley first
settlers.   Jonathan[6] Marsh in 1821 was taxed on the old Marsh lot.
Warner and Marsh families had lived on West St. side by side for
160 years, just where the main highway now passes out toward
Northampton.   At the death of his uncle Ebenezer[5] his house had
come into possession of Jonathan[6] who tore it down, using some of
the timber in his new home.   His father-in-law also in 1822 sold the
old Warner homestead and built a two-story house next south of his
dau. on Middle St. so that the Marsh and Warner families were still
side by side.   At one time with other carpenters Jonathan[5] Marsh did
work on the south college at Amherst and in 1841 he helped move
the old Hadley meeting house from West to Middle St. opposite his
home and the next year he helped finish it off in its present shape.
He also added a half story to his house.   He d. May 3, 1843, leaving his widow and five children.   She d. Sept. 24, 1864.   The
*Hampshire Gazette* May 11, 1843 has: " Died, in Hadley, May 3,
after a short but exceedingly painful sickness  Mr. Jonathan Marsh,
aged fifty, whose memory will be long and fondly cherished not only
by his widow, children, aged mother and other family connections to
whom he was inexpressibly dear, but by the people of the town of
which he was a valuable citizen, and the church whereof for many
years he was an exemplary member."   Children :

4319.   John Warner[7], b. Feb. 1, 1824; m. Harriet E. Cook, 4324.
4320.   Timothy Smith, b. Sept.18, 1826; m. (1) M. P. Bartlett, 4332.
4321.   Josiah Dwight, b. March 6, 1829; m. (1) S. L. Ingram, 4337.
4322.   Harriet Sophia, b. Sept. 4, 1832.
4323.   Sarah Elizabeth, b. Oct. 12, 1835.


4324 = 4319.   JOHN WARNER[7] MARSH

b. at Hadley, Mass., Feb. 1, 1824, son of Jonathan[6] and Harriet

J. D. Marsh

*To face page 373.*

(Warner) Marsh, (Timothy⁵, Ebenezer⁴, Cornet Ebenezer³, Daniel²,
John¹); carpenter, resides at Hadley, m. Oct. 29, 1845, No. 4324.

    **4324.** Harriet Elizabeth Cook. Children :

        4325. William Dwight⁸, b. Sept. 12, 1852 ; m. May 23, 1878, Bertha
            Belle Bryant. b. June 22, 1852.

        4326. Mary Lester, b. April 13, 1855 ; m. May 19, 1885, George
            Perkins Metcalf of Orange, Mass., son of Eli Perkins
            of Worthington. Child: George Warner, b. April 5,
            1893.

        4327. Lucy Russell, b. April 3, 1857.

        4328. John Warner, b. July 21, 1859; m. Feb. 14, 1889, Mrs. Lilla
            Frances Wilson, dau. of Francis Smith of New Haven,
            Ct. They left Hadley for California, Feb. 20, 1889,
            but returned. Child: Harold B., b. Jan. 7, 1890; d.
            May 21, 1891.

        4329. George Cook, b. Nov. 21, 1861.

        4330. Henry Rindge, b. Dec. 12. 1864 ; d. Jan. 18, 1865.

        4331. Fred Smith, b. Oct. 16, 1869.

---

### 4332 = 4320. TIMOTHY SMITH⁷ MARSH

b. at Hadley, Mass., Sept. 18, 1826, son of Jonathan⁶ and Harriet
(Warner) Marsh, (Timothy⁵, Ebenezer⁴, Cornet Ebenezer³, Daniel²,
John¹); farmer, resides at Hadley, m. (1) April 25, 1855, No. 4332.

    **4332.** Maria Pomeroy Bartlett, dau. of Capt. Lewis. He m.
(2) June 8, 1870, No. 4332.1.

    **4332.1.** Eliza Ann³ Cook, dau. of Samuel P². Cook, Samuel¹.
Children :

        4333. Nellie Smith⁸, b. March 8, 1856; m. April 9, 1885, Thomas
            A. Palmer of Monticello, Fla., b. Feb. 26, 1859.

        4334. Hattie Maria, b. Feb. 28, 1863 ; d. Sept. 17, 1863.

        4335. Jennie Maria, b. Feb. 9, 1865 ; d. May 14, 1865.

        4336. Edward Smith, b. March 31, 1874.

---

### 4337 = 4321. JOSIAH DWIGHT⁷ MARSH

b. at Hadley, Mass., March 6, 1829, son of Jonathan⁶ and Harriet
(Warner) Marsh, (Timothy⁵, Ebenezer⁴, Cornet Ebenezer³, Daniel²,
John¹), (all lived at Hadley) is a carpenter by trade, has given his

children a fine education, the son being a graduate of Amherst and professor at Ripon, his dau. a graduate of Mt. Holyoke and a teacher in Canada and at the west. He himself has been a teacher of elegant penmanship, with remarkable samples of skill, and the Marsh family is deeply indebted to him for unwearied researches in the town records of Hadley and the county records of Northampton and Springfield. He m. (1) Nov. 30, 1854, No. 4337.

**4337.** Sarah Lucretia Ingram, dau. of Peter Ingram of Fond du Lac, Wis. She d. Dec. 14, 1888 and he m. (2) Nov. 6, 1889, No. 4338.

**4338.** Lucy Ann Hayward, b. Nov. 15, 1839. dau. of E. E. Hayward. Children :

> 4339. Charles Dwight[8], b. Dec. 20, 1855 ; m. F. L. Wilder, 4342.
> 4340. Carrie Barnard, b. May 11, 1859; d. April 10, 1863.
> 4341. Emily Roberts, b. Dec. 24, 1864. Teacher.

### 4342 = 4339. PROF. CHARLES DWIGHT[8] MARSH

b. at Hadley, Mass., Dec. 20, 1855, son of Josiah Dwight[7] and Sarah Lucretia (Ingram) Marsh, (Jonathan[6], Timothy[5], Ebenezer[4], Cornet Ebenezer[3], Daniel[2], John[1]); m. Dec. 27, 1883, No. 4342.

**4342.** Florence Lee Wilder, b. Aug. 17, 1856, dau. of Charles Wilder of Holliston, Mass. He graduated at Amherst college 1877, M. A. 1880, professor of chemistry and biology, Ripon college, Wis. Children :

> 4343. Hadleigh, b. Nov. 21, 1888.
> 4344. Charles Wilder, b. Feb. 1, 1890.

### 4345 = 4291. SARAH[5] MARSH

b. at Hadley, Mass., July 20, 1754, dau. of Ebenezer[4] and Sarah (Eastman) Marsh, (Cornet Ebenezer[3], Daniel[2], John[1]); m. Dec. 9, 1779, No. 4345.

**4345.** Nathaniel[5] Dickinson of Amherst, Nathaniel[4], Samuel[3] and (Hannah[3] Marsh, No. 3769, Jonathan[2], John[1] Marsh) Nehemiah[2], Nathaniel[1] of Wethersfield 1637 and Hadley 1659. Nathaniel[5]

Dickinson, Jr., Esq., was a somewhat distinguished man.  He was b. Sept. 1, 1750, graduated at Harvard college 1771 studied law three years with the celebrated Maj. Hawley of Northampton, was town delegate to the first provincial congress in 1774, to that at Cambridge in 1775 and to the third at Watertown.  He was representative to general court in 1778, '80 and '83.  Once when the tory minister of Amherst, Mr. Parsons, to the concluding words of the proclamation from the pulpit "God save the commonwealth of Massachusetts," added, "But I say God save the king," lawyer Dickinson sprang up in his pew and cried out "I say you are a ———— rascal." He was author of a large part of Amherst revolutionary papers.  Gov. Hancock in 1781 appointed him justice of the peace.  Sarah (Marsh) Dickinson, d. Dec. 9, 1801, æ. 47.  He d. Nov. 10, 1802, æ. 51.  Children:

4346.  Susanna⁶, b. Sept. 6, 1781; m. May 29, 1803, Chester Dickinson, both were great-grandchildren of Samuel³ and Hannah³ (Marsh) Dickinson.  He d. in Amherst, May 10, 1850; she d. Oct. 8, 1836.

4347.  Walter, b. May 2, 1784; m. Lydia Dickinson, 4348.

## 4348 = 4347. WALTER⁶ DICKINSON

b. at Amherst, Mass., May 2, 1784, son of Hon. Nathaniel and Sarah⁵ (Marsh) Dickinson, dau. of Ebenezer⁴ Marsh, (Cornet Ebenezer³, Daniel², John¹); m. Nov. 7, 1806, No. 4348.

4348. Lydia Dickinson, b. July 9, 1791, whose brother Chester had m. his sister Susanna.  Chester⁶ and Lydia⁶ were children of John⁵ Dickinson, son of Nehemiah⁴, son of Samuel³ and Hannah³ (Marsh) Dickinson; while Susanna⁶ and Walter⁶ were children of Nathaniel⁵ son of Nathaniel⁴, son of Samuel³ and Hannah³ (Marsh) Dickinson, Jonathan² Marsh, John¹.  Thus both Walter and his wife were of the sixth generation from John Marsh through Jonathan², John¹ and Walter was also of the sixth generation from John Marsh through Daniel², John¹ and their children could trace their descent in three ways from John¹ Marsh; whether they would ever think of it is another matter, or care for it if told!  Both lived and died in Amherst, Lydia, March 21, 1827, æ. 35, and Walter, April 9, 1851, æ. 66.  Children:

4349.  Sylvester[7], b. Nov. 23, 1809; m. Harriet Cutler; d. July 24, 1856. Had three children.
4350.  Frederick Ely, b. Oct. 25, 1811 ; m. Elmira Brown. Children :
    4351.  Ely Othman[8].
    4352.  Henry.
    4353.  Julia, b. Oct., 1839.
4354.  Marquis Fayette, b. Jan. 4, 1814 ; m. H. Williams, 4366.
4355.  Nathaniel Albert, b. Dec. 1, 1815 ; d. Nov. 4, 1884.
4356.  Lydia Eastman, b. Sept. 17, 1817 ; unm.
4357.  Nehemiah Othman, b. July 25, 1819; d. April 13, 1833.
4358.  Leander Melancthon, b. Aug. 20, 1821 ; m. L. Adams, 4381.
4359.  Amy Stoughton, b. Oct. 22, 1823 ; m. Avery Douglas Hubbard. Children :
    4360.  Emma Dickinson[8].
    4361.  Alice Abby, b. March 31, 1850.
    4362.  Frederick Avery.
    4363.  Charles Elijah.
4364.  Walter Mason, b. Feb. 27, 1826 ; m. Margaret Shaw. Children :
    4364.1.  Lydia Wilson, b. May 11, 1869.
    4364.2.  Carrie Belle, b. Jan. 24, 1871 ; d. April 4, 1871.
    4364.3.  Fannie Elizabeth. b. Jan. 23, 1873 ; d. Jan. 3, 1877.
    4364.4.  Jane Elsworth, b. Feb. 24, 1876 ; d. Nov. 26, 1876.
    4364.5.  John, b. Sept. 30, 1877.
4365.  Sarah Marsh, b. March 3, 1828 , m. J. Cowls, 4387.


4366 = 4354.  MARQUIS FAYETTE[7] DICKINSON


b. at Amherst, Mass., Jan. 4, 1814, son of Walter[6] and Lydia[6] (Dickinson) Dickinson, Sarah[5] (Marsh) Dickinson, (Ebenezer[4] Marsh, Cornet Ebenezer[3], Daniel[2], John[1]) ; m. about 1839, No. 4366.

**4366.**  Hannah Williams, dau. of Asa Williams.  Mr. Dickinson has long been one of the most prominent citizens of Amherst and has with the aid of a noble wife, brought up a remarkable family. The homestead is just north of the Agricultural college grounds. Children :

    4367.  Marquis Fayette[8], b. Jan. 16, 1840; m. No. 4377.
    4368.  Walter Nehemiah, b. Oct. 30, 1843 ; d. April 17, 1845.
    4369.  Lydia Jane, b. July 17, 1846; m. Rev. Henry N. Couden. Had four children and d. Feb. 13, 1884.

4370. Sarah Amelia, b. Oct. 8, 1848; m. in Amherst, Aug. 6, 1873, F. L. Pope, son of Ebenezer Pope, b. in Great Barrington, Mass., Dec. 2, 1840. He is a distinguished electrician of N. Y. City; was telegraph operator in Great Barrington, Springfield and Providence, R. I., from 1857 to 1862; assistant engineer of American Telegraph Co. in New York until 1864; assistant engineer of Russo-American telegraph from Washington Territory to Siberia and Behring's Straits (partially completed and abandoned in 1867), in which capacity he made the first exploration of the region lying about the sources of the Skeena, Stickeen and Yukon rivers in British Columbia and Alaska. In 1867 settled in Union township, near Elizabeth, N. J. and remained there till 1894, when he returned to his ascestral home in Great Barrington. Is an electrical engineer and author, place of business in New York. Children :

4370.1. Son[9], b. and d. 1874.
4370.2. Hannah Dickinson, b. May 3, 1876.
4370.3. Amy Stoughton, b. Aug. 9, 1878.
4370.4. Franklin Leonard Wainwright, b. July 29, 1880.
4370.5. Seth Willard, b. Oct. 23, 1883; d. Nov. 13, 1883.

4371. Roxie Elizabeth, b. April 3, 1851; m. E. A. Holbrook, Esq., of Holbrook, Mass.

4372. Asa Williams, b. Oct. 24, 1853; a lawyer in Jersey City, N.J.; m. Dec. 21, 1882, in Easton, Penn., Anna W. Hay.

4373. Walter Mason, b. April 3, 1856; grad. West Point, U. S. army, Prof. Mass. Agricultural college; m. Feb. 3, 1885, at St. Paul, Minn., Martha E. Otis.

4374. Julia Cowles, b. June 7, 1859; m. June 23, 1886, Rev. C. S. Nickerson, Beverly, Mass. Children :

4374.1. George Payne[9], b. March 31, 1890.
4374.2. Francis Lindsey, b. Sept. 20, 1892.

4375. Hannah Frances, b. Sept. 28, 1861 ; m. June 20, 1888, Prof. J. B. Lindsey, Mass. State Agricultural Experiment Station. Child :

4375.1. Amy Blaney[9], b. April 13, 1893.

4376. Mary Underhill, b. July 3, 1864; d. June 28, 1870.

4377 = 4367. MARQUIS FAYETTE[8] DICKINSON, JR.

b. at Amherst, Mass., Jan. 16, 1840, son of M. F[7]. and Hannah (Williams) Dickinson, (Walter[6] Dickinson, Sarah[5] [Marsh] Dickinson, Ebenezer[4] Marsh, Cornet Ebenezer[3], Daniel[2], John[1]) ; m. Nov. 23, 1864, No. 4377.

**4377.** Cecilia R., adopted dau. of Samuel Williston of Easthampton, Mass. He graduated at Amherst college 1862, M. A. 1865, overseer charitable fund, trustee · Williston seminary, a prominent · lawyer in Boston, Mass. They have had three children.

4381 = 4358.  LEANDER MELANCTHON[7] DICKINSON

b. at Amherst, Mass., Aug. 20, 1821, son of Walter[6] and Lydia[6] (Dickinson) Dickinson, (Sarah[5] [Marsh] Dickinson, Ebenezer[4] Marsh, Cornet Ebenezer[3], Daniel[2], John[1]) ; m. No. 4381.

**4381.** Laura Adams. Children :

4382.  Lydia Thankful[8], b. Sept. 21, 1852 ; m. C. E. Wilson.
4383.  Julia, b. Oct. 14, 1857; d. Feb. 13, 1858.
4384.  Edward Leander, b. April 2, 1860.
4385.  Mason Adams, b. Jan. 23, 1863; m. Jan. 18, 1888, Susie M. Strickland, b. Dec. 18, 1862. Children :
    4385.1.  Edith A[9]., b. March 16, 1890.
    4385.2.  Freeman N., b. Dec. 22, 1891.
4386.  Frank Nims, b. Jan. 15, 1866.

4387 = 4365.  SARAH MARSH[7] DICKINSON

b. at Amherst, Mass., March 3, 1828, dau. of Walter[6] and Lydia[6] (Dickinson) Dickinson, (Sarah[5] [Marsh] Dickinson, Ebenezer[4] Marsh, Cornet Ebenezer[3], Daniel[2], John[1]) ; m. No. 4387.

**4387.** Jonathan[7] Cowls, son of Jonathan[6] and Esther (Graves) Cowls, (David[5], Jonathan[4], Jonathan[3], John[2], John[1] of Farmington, Ct., 1662 and Hatfield, Mass. 1664.) They reside at Amherst. Children :

4388.  Walter Dickinson[8], b. June 30, 1852.
4389.  Newton Erastus, b. April 1, 1854.
4390.  Abbie Grace, b. Aug. 21, 1856.
4391.  S. Jeannette, b. Dec. 17, 1858; m. Francis L. Frary, merchant in Minneapolis, Minn. Children :
    4391.1.  Francis Cowls[9], b. July 9, 1884.
    4391.2.  Hobart Dickinson, b. April 28, 1887.
    4391.3.  Ralph Thomas, b. March 18, 1889; d. Nov. 16, 1890.
    4391.4.  Louise Grace, b. May 11, 1891.
4392.  Nellie Graves, b. Dec. 31, 1866; m. Edwin Harris Dickinson, 3806.

# THE WETHERSFIELD, CT., ROCKY HILL LINE.

## 4393 = 4048.  JOHN⁴ MARSH

b. at Hadley, Mass., in 1726, son of Cornet Ebenezer³ and Mary (Parsons) Marsh, (Daniel², John¹), "intentions of m. posted in Hadley Nov. 6, 1748 with Abigail Buckley of Weathersfield, Ct."; m. Jan. 17, 1749, No. 4393.

**4393.** Abigail Bulkley, b. 1720, "lineal descendant of Rev. Peter Bulkley, D. D. of Concord, Mass., which town he founded." John⁴ Marsh removed to Wethersfield and settled in Rocky Hill, there building a substantial and comfortable house a short distance south east of the Congregational church. This house July 4, 1883, after sheltering five generations was burned by careless boys exploding fire crackers in the vicinity and thus old time records and relics of over a century were lost. John⁴ Marsh was a baker and supplied boats with ship bread. Children :

4394.  Mary⁵, b. Sept. 2, 1749; m. John Morton.
4395.  Martha, b. Nov. 10, 1751; m. Stephen Bulkley, 4401.
4396.  John, b. Sept. 27, 1753; m. Miss Goodrich, 4462.
4397.  Rebecca, b. Nov. 2, 1755; m. Josiah Carter or Curtis?
4398.  Abigail, b. Oct. 16, 1756; m. Charles Wright. It is said, "she lived near a hundred years!"
4399.  Anna, m. Simeon Butler.
4400.  Ely, b. April 25, 1764; m. Azubah Butler, 4476.

## 4401 = 4395.  MARTHA⁵ MARSH

b. at Rocky Hill, Wethersfield, Ct., Nov. 10, 1751, dau. of John⁴ and Abigail (Bulkley) Marsh, (Cornet Ebenezer³, Daniel², John¹); m. about 1773, No. 4401.

**4401.** Stephen Bulkley, b. Nov. 19, 1749, son of Jonathan and Abigail (Williams) Bulkley, whose contract of marriage was confirmed at Wethersfield, Nov. 13, 1746. Martha (Marsh) Bulkley d. April 6, 1804. Stephen d. May, 1813. Their house at Rocky Hill still belongs to the family and is in good order. Children :

4402.  Honor⁶, b. May 5, 1774; m. Daniel Edwards, 4411.
4403.  Stephen, b. April 18, 1776; d. y.
4404.  Catherine, b. Oct. 15, 1778; d. y.
4405.  Caty, b. Sept. 2, 1780; m. Zenas Edwards, 4422.
4406.  Stephen, b. March 21, 1783; unm. lived to great age.
4407.  Allen, b. July 19, 1786; m. Eliza Ann Riley, 4434.
4408.  Patty, b. Jan. 31, 1790; d. May 4, 1790.
4409.  Frederick, b. June 1, 1792 ; m. Nancy Riley, 4443.
4410.  Daughter, b. Dec. 18, 1796; lived one hour.


4411 = 4402.  HONOR⁶ BULKLEY

b. at Wethersfield, Ct., May 5, 1774, dau. of Martha⁵ (Marsh) and
Stephen Bulkley, (John⁴, Cornet Ebenezer³, Daniel², John¹); m. Nov.
16, 1795, No. 4411.
4411.  Daniel Edwards of Middletown, who d. æ. 27, Sept. 23,
1798.  Child :

4412.  Martha⁷, b. Sept. 2, 1796; m. Aaron R. Savage, 4413.


4413 = 4412.  MARTHA⁷ EDWARDS

b. Sept. 2, 1796, dau. of Honor⁶ (Bulkley) Edwards, (Martha⁵ [Marsh]
Bulkley, John⁴ Marsh, Cornet Ebenezer³, Daniel², John¹) ; m. July 21,
1817, No. 4413.
4413.  Aaron R. Savage, Mate Brig Commerce, who d. May 6,
1831.  She d. Sept. 11, 1877, æ. 81 years and nine days, in Cromwell, Ct.  Children :

4414.  Louisa Willshire⁸, b. March 25, 1819; d. July 12, 1822.
4415.  Margarete Randolph, b. April 9, 1821 ; m. Wm. W. Riley,
          4419.
4416.  Sarah Louisa Willshire, b. May 25, 1823 ; d. April 28, 1863.
4417.  Ruth Roberts, b. Dec. 17, 1824 ; d. Dec. 27, 1824.
4418.  Martha Edwards, b. Nov. 26, 1828; lived 12 hours.


4419 = 4415.  MARGARETE RANDOLPH⁸ SAVAGE

b. at Middletown, Ct., April 9, 1821, dau. of Martha⁷ (Edwards)
Savage, (Honor⁶ [Bulkley] Edwards, Martha⁵ [Marsh] Bulkley, John⁴

Marsh, Cornet Ebenezer[3], Daniel[2], John[1]) ; m. at Middletown, Ct., Oct. 18, 1842, No. 4419.

**4419.** William Willshire Riley, inventor, honorary member of the Parisienne Academie des Invention, Paris, France, awarded diploma and medal. His father Capt. James Riley of the Brig Commerce, was shipwrecked on the African coast, captured and enslaved by wandering Arabs and after starvation and untold sufferings, ransomed by William Willshire, the British Consul at Magadore. Capt. James Riley published in 1817 " Riley's Narrative " which had a large sale and led to the ransom of several hundred shipwrecked sailors from barbarian slavery, mainly through William Willshire's efforts in whose honor Capt. James changed the name of his boy born, and named during his absence, Asher Miller, after his two grandfathers, to William Willshire Riley. Capt. James Riley left the sea and was appointed deputy surveyor for northwestern Ohio and took his family there in covered wagons in 1820 and entered the first land in that section and called the town which he laid out, Willshire. It is in Van Wert Co., O. and there was then no white settlement west nearer than St. Louis. Young Willshire had six years experience with buckskin clothes and Indian boys. Allen G. Thurman was a schoolmate in 1820 while the family was delayed there, and such men as William Henry Harrison and Henry Clay were guests in his father's cabin, half way from Fort St. Mary to Fort Wayne and the only cabin within 30 miles of either place. William Willshire returned to Connecticut when 13 and was apprenticed to a jeweler in Hartford nearly seven years. He has resided in New York City and in Lima, Mansfield and Columbus, O. He has shaken hands with every president of the United States from Monroe to Benjamin Harrison and has eaten mush with a gold spoon in the executive mansion with General Jackson when he was president of the United States. Mrs. Riley's father as mate, was captive with her husband's father the captain. " A fellow feeling makes us wondrous kind." They reside at Cromwell, Ct. Children :

 4420. Sarah Willshire[9], b. Mansfield, O., July 29, 1843 ; d. Cromwell, Ct., Oct. 5, 1844.

 4421. Martha Willshire, b. Cromwell, Ct., Nov. 29, 1844 ; d. Columbus, O., Jan. 30, 1872. Both buried in Cromwell, Ct.

## 4422 = 4405.  CATHERINE[6] BULKLEY

b. at Rocky Hill, Wethersfield, Ct., Sept. 2, 1780, dau. of Stephen and Martha[5] (Marsh) Bulkley, (John[4], Cornet Ebenezer[3], Daniel[2], John[1]) ; m. Dec. 1, 1800 or 1801, No. 4422.

**4422.** Zenas Edwards of Middletown, Ct., now Cromwell. Children :

    4423.  A son[7], b. May 19, 1807.
    4424.  Bulkley, b. May 29, 1811 ; m. Abigail Topliff, 4428.
    4425.  Catherine, b. March 6, 1813 ; m. (1) Joseph Edwards, who d.
        Sept. 3, 1849; had son who d. at 18 months and dau.:
    4426.  Mrs. Crombie, resides at Lincoln, Neb. and has children and grandchildren.
    4427.  Mary, b. March 23, 1820; d. Aug. 17, 1872, æ. 52 years, one month and nineteen days.

## 4428 = 4424.  BULKLEY[7] EDWARDS

b. at Middletown (Cromwell), Ct.. May 29, 1811, son of Zenas and Catherine[6] (Bulkley) Edwards, (Martha[5] [Marsh] Bulkley, John[4], Cornet Ebenezer[3], Daniel[2], John[1]); m. No. 4428.

**4428.** Abigail Topliff. He is a prominent man, selectman for years, and member of legislature several terms. Children :

    4429.  Charles[8], b. 1835 ; m. Emily Allison and d. Aug. 20, 1860, æ. 25 years, and left son and dau. who d. y.
    4430.  John Marsh, b. 1836; d. May 6, 1864, æ. 27 years and six months.
    4431.  Frances Augusta, b. Jan., 1838; m. George Wilcox, son of Ebenezer Wilcox. She d. March 14, 1882, æ. 44 years, one and one-half months. Child :
    4432.  Sarah, only dau.
    4433.  Sarah, b. 1843 ; d. April 1. 1862, æ. 18 years and eight months.

## 4434 = 4407.  ALLEN[6] BULKLEY

b. at Wethersfield, Ct., July 19, 1786, son of Stephen and Martha[5] (Marsh) Bulkley, (John[4] Marsh, Cornet Ebenezer[3], Daniel[2], John[1]); m. No. 4434.

**4434.** Eliza Ann Riley, niece or grand-daughter of Justus Riley of Wethersfield where they both resided. Children:

    4435. Harriet Abbott[7], d. y.

    4436. Harriet Abbott, m. Mr. Roberts of Hartford. Children:

        4437. Thomas.

        4438. Grace Chetwood; m.

    4439. Ebenezer Riley, mòved west, has sons and daus.

    4440. Joseph, lived in Cal. during gold excitement.

    4441. John Marsh, d. y.

    4442. Mary Jane, m. Mr. Spere ; res. in Boston.

## 4443 = 4409. FREDERICK[6] BULKLEY

b. at Wethersfield, Ct., June 1, 1792, son of Stephen and Martha[5] (Marsh) Bulkley, (John[4] Marsh, Cornet Ebenezer[3], Daniel[2], John[1]); resided at Wethersfield; m. Oct. 6, 1814, No. 4443.

**4443.** Nancy Riley of Rocky Hill. He d. Sept. 28, 1860. She d. Dec. 24, 1857. Children:

    4444. Martha Marsh[7], b. Feb. 16, 1816; d. aged about 6 years.

    4445. Julia, b. Jan. 2, 1819. Twin of Jane.

    4446. Jane, b. Jan. 2, 1819; m. Walter Edwards[7], son of Abel and Elizabeth[6] (Marsh) Edwards.

    4447. Nancy, b. Dec. 10, 1822; m. Ben. Tower of Ft. Wayne, Ind.ʼ

    4448. Stephen, b. May 5, 1825; m. Prudence Warner, 4453.

    4449. Catherine, b. April 23, 1834; m. John Warner, Nov. 20, 1872. Children:

        4450. Kittie.

        4451. Gertrude. ⎱ Twins.
        4452. Grace. ⎰

## 4453 = 4448. STEPHEN[7] BULKLEY

b. at Wethersfield, Ct., May 5, 1825, son of Frederick[6] and Nancy (Riley) Bulkley, (Martha[5] [Marsh] Bulkley, John[4] Marsh, Cornet Ebenezer[3], Daniel[2], John[1]); m. Jan. 23, 1850, No. 4453.

**4453.** Prudence Warner, dau. of John Warner. Children:

    4454. Fannie[8], b. Nov. 2, 1850; m. and has children.

    4455. Alice, b. April 9, 1852.

    4456. Prudence, b. Jan. 2, 1854.

    4457. Frederick, b. Feb. 8, 1856.

4458.   Stephen, b. Jan. 4, 1861.
4459.   Charles, b. March 25, 1864. }
4460.   Chester, b. March 25, 1864. }
4461.   Robert Riley, b. Sept. 6, 1866.


### 4462 = 4396.  JOHN[5] MARSH.

b. at Wethersfield, Ct., Rocky Hill, Sept. 27, 1753, son of John[4] and Abigail (Bulkley) Marsh, (Cornet Ebenezer[3], Daniel[2], John[1]); m. No. 4462.

**4462.**  Miss Goodrich.  Children :

4463.   Elizabeth[6], m. Abel Edwards, 4467.
4464.   Axey, m. Aaron McKee.
4465.   Polly, m. John Burkett.
4466.   Daniel, d. at manhood.


### 4467 = 4463.  ELIZABETH[6] MARSH

b. at Wethersfield, Ct., dau. of John[5] and —— (Goodrich) Marsh, (John[4], Cornet Ebenezer[3], Daniel[2], John[1]) ; m. No. 4467.

**4467.**  Abel Edwards.  Child :

4468.   Walter[7], m. Jane Bulkley, 4469.


### 4469 = 4468.  WALTER[7] EDWARDS

b. at Wethersfield, Ct., son of Abel and Elizabeth[6] (Marsh) Edwards, (John[5] Marsh, John[4], Cornet Ebenezer[3], Daniel[2], John[1]) ; m. Nov. 15, 1843, No. 4469.

**4469.**  Jane[7] Bulkley, No. 4446, dau. of Fred[6] and grand-dau. of Stephen and Martha[5] (Marsh) Bulkley.  Walter Edwards d. May, 1874 in Wethersfield.  Children :

4470.   Elizabeth[8], b. Oct. 29, 1844; m. Edward M. Francis.
          Children :
4471.   Everett[9], b. Sept. 26, 1872.
4472.   Bernice, b. Jan. 14, 1874.  They reside in Hartford, Ct.
4473.   Fannie, b. May 28, 1846; d. æ. 4.
4474.   Frederic, b. Oct. 14, 1850.
4475.   Frank, b. Feb. 12, 1853 ; lives in Cromwell, Ct.

## 4476 = 4400.  ELY⁵ MARSH

b. at Wethersfield, Ct., April 25, 1764, son of John⁴ and Abigail (Bulkley) Marsh, (Cornet Ebenezer³, Daniel², John¹), called "a tall fine looking man"; m. in 1787, No. 4476.

4476.  Azubah Butler, and in 1797 removed to Sherburne, N. Y. He was a carpenter and farmer. Trustee of the Congregational church. His wife d. April 8, 1809. He d. June 1, 1839. Four of the children were born at Wethersfield, the fifth at Sherburne. Children:

> 4477.  Norman⁶, b. Jan. 27, 1788; m. Hannah Smith, 4482.
> 4478.  Lathrop, b. June 28, 1790; m. Eliza Sheffield of New York; d. 1847.
> 4479.  Marilla, b. Nov. 24, 1792; m. 1812, Lewis Lathrop of Sherburne and had four children and d. Dec. 28, 1856. Child :
>> 4479.1.  G. W. Lathrop.
> 4480.  Anne, b. Nov. 23, 1795; d. unm. March 19, 1880.
> 4481.  Simeon Butler, b. June 1, 1798; m. Eliza Carrier, 4492.

## 4482 = 4477.  NORMAN⁶ MARSH

b. at Wethersfield, Ct., Jan. 27, 1788, son of Ely⁵ and Azubah (Butler) Marsh, (John⁴, Cornet Ebenezer³, Daniel², John¹); a sash and blind manufacturer ; m. (1) at Sherburne, N. Y., May 9, 1808, No. 4482.

4482.  Hannah Smith.  She d. Sept. 29, 1825.  He m. (2) No. 4482.1.

4482.1.  Fannie M. Ford.  Children :

> 4483.  Emily Azubah⁷, b. June 27, 1809; m. Oct. 2, 1832, Rev. Francis Janes. She d. Oct. 15, 1874. They had three children, now living, clergymen in N. Y. state.
> 4484.  Charles Lathrop, b. June 6, 1811 ; d. Aug. 7, 1816.
> 4485.  Sarah Ann, b. Jan. 12, 1814 ; m. May 5, 1835, Rev. Frederic Ayres. She now resides at Long Ridge, Ct. Had nine children, six are living.
> 4486.  George Dwight, b. Aug. 2, 1818; m. April 26, 1842, Harriet Smith, and d. Feb. 21, 1846. She is also d. Child :
>> 4487.  Harriet Louisa⁸, b. Newark Valley, N. Y., May 2, 1843; d. July 13, 1854.
> 4488.  Mary, b. Lisle, N. Y., June 10, 1820 ; d. March 19, 1861.
> 4489.  Elizabeth, b. at Lisle, N. Y., April 26, 1824 ; d. June 8, 1863.

26

By second wife.

4490.  Hannah, b. Lisle, Oct. 15, 1829; d. Jan. 30, 1884.

4491.  Fanny, b. Lisle, Oct. 15, 1829; twin, res. at Binghamton, N. Y.

ɪ

## 4492 = 4481.  SIMEON BUTLER⁶ MARSH

b. at Sherburne, New York, June 1, 1798, son of Ely⁵ and Azubah (Butler) Marsh, (John⁴, Cornet Ebenezer³, Daniel², John); composer in 1834 of the tune " Martyn " found in all the tune books and universally sung by Christian people; m. June 1, 1820, No. 4492.

**4492.**  Eliza Carrier of Hamilton, N. Y., who d. Feb. 28, 1873⁐ He d. at Albany, N. Y., July 14, 1875.  Children:

> 4493.  Jane Eliza⁷, b. Dec. 29, 1827; m. May 14, 1844, John Watts Van Derveer of Amsterdam, N. Y. She d. Nov. 18, 1863.  Children now living:
>> 4494.  Maria⁸, wife of A. T. Van Heusen of Amsterdam, N. Y.
>> 4495.  Emily, wife of John N. Hubbard of Chicago, Ill.
> 4496.  John Bulkley, b. July 30, 1830; m. F. M. Van Vorst, 4497.

## 4497 = 4496.  PROF. JOHN BULKLEY⁷ MARSH

b. July 30, 1830, son of Simeon Butler⁶ and Eliza (Carrier) Marsh, (Ely⁵, John⁴, Ebenezer³, Daniel², John¹); m. May 8, 1855, No. 4497.

**4497.**  Frances M. Van Vorst of Schenectady, N. Y.  Resided in Albany, N. Y., 28 years, present residence Elmira, N. Y.  He is] professor of voice culture and organ instruction in Elmira female college and organist at the Park church.  Child :

> 4498.  Walter Van Vorst⁸, b. Dec. 15, 1858; m. E. M. Ottman, 4499

## 4499 = 4498.  WALTER VAN VORST⁸ MARSH

b. Dec. 15, 1858, son of Prof. John Bulkley⁷ and Frances M. (Van Vorst) Marsh, (Simeon Butler⁶, Ely⁵, John⁴, Ebenezer³, Daniel² John¹); m. Oct. 24, 1883, No. 4499.

**4499.**  Ella May Ottman of Albany, N. Y.  Present residence Kingston, N. Y.  He is route agent of western division of Nationat express.  Child :

> 4500.  Elinor Hess⁹, b. May 12, 1885.

# THE HOME AND NEW YORK CITY LINE.

4501 = 4052. CAPT. MOSES[4] MARSH

b. at Hadley. Mass., March 20, 1718, son of Capt. Job[3] and Mehitable (Porter) Marsh, (Daniel[2], John[1]) ; m. Nov. 2, 1739, No. 4501.

**4501.** Hannah[4] Cook, b. Oct. 16, 1719, dau. of Capt. Moses[3] and Mary (Barnard) Cook, son of Capt. Aaron[2] and Sarah[2] (Westwood) the dau. William[1] Westwood and her son Maj. Aaron[1] Cooke of Northampton. Mehitable[4] (Porter) Marsh, was dau. Joanna[3] (Cook) Porter who was dau. Capt. Aaron[2] Cook and Sarah Westwood. Thus Capt. Moses[4] Marsh's mother and wife were own cousins. He was in the Louisburg expedition in 1745, as appears from a letter in possession of Josiah Dwight[7] Marsh (No. 4337) of Hadley. Jan. 7, 1750, as "Capt." and one of the proprietors, was granted leave by Hadley to build a gristmill (see No. 4287) ; 1751, chosen selectman, refused to serve ; 1752, fence viewer and on committee about bridge. In 1757 Capt. Moses Marsh led his company 90 miles west, 1753 and 1758 selectman, 1759 moderator of town meetings, Jan. 12 and March 5, on committee for repairing meeting house clock and fence viewer and to proportion land ; 1760, assessor, selectman, deer reaf, moderator town meetings, May 12 and June 16, committee to seat meeting house, to repair or rebuild Fort bridge and permanent committee to seat meeting house, 1762 selectman, assessor, deer reef and moderator Dec. 6. In 1763 on committee to build pews, 1764 moderator, selectman, assessor, committee to seat meeting house, 1765 moderator, 1766 assessor, 1767 moderator, 1768 to seat meeting house and prepare letter to Boston, 1770 committee of inquiry, selectman, assessor, to lease land at lower end of the street, and Aug. 3, moderator, 1771 and 1772 moderator, 1773 to sell part of the back street, constable, refused to serve, selectman. Granted to east end of lot, 5 rods, four feet by 16 rods, 10 feet, May 14 moderator, Oct. 7 on correspondence, Nov. 4 moderator, and to sett street bounds, 1774 moderator, June 9 and on correspondence, 1775 on correspondence. (That year a committee to bring cannon from Williamstown.) Selectman 1776, on provision committee on pest house, moderator, Jan. 30, May 3, May 30, July 8.

That the town was in earnest J. Pierce's diary shows: "April 20, 1775. We receive the news of the battle of Lexington at 9 A. M.! At one, fifty men march from Hadley." J. Pierce town clerk in 1776 administers the salt petre oath to Capt. Moses Marsh, " you do solemnly swear that the whole process of the manufacture of the salt petre now presented by you was begun, carried on and finished within the limits of this colony, and that no foreign salt petre is mixed therewith. So help you God."

At a meeting of the inhabitants of Hadley at the meeting house May 30, 1776, at 3 P. M. warned and assembled to instruct their representative, they voted that " *If the American congress should for the safety of the* United Colonies declare them independent of the kingdom of Great Britain, we the inhabitants of said Hadley will engage with our lives and fortunes to support them in the measure. Capt. Moses Marsh, Moderator."

J. Pierce's diary reads on, " Nov. 3. Fifteen men innoculated at Capt. Marsh's to the great disturbance of the day as sabbath and sacrament. Nov. 7. Innoculating hospital burnt."

In 1778 he was moderator and constable; in 1779 delegate to county convention; 1780 to give opinion against Mr. Strong. March 12, 1782 he sold his place, the original Andrew Bacon lot, with the easterly addition for £425, to John Chester Williams, nine acres more or less, with house, barn and all buildings. He then removed to Worthington, Mass., and d. there Oct. 4, 1796, æ. 78. Children :

4502. Moses[5], b. Oct. 22, 1740; d. Aug. 16, 1746.
4503. Hannah, b. Oct. 2, 1744; d. Aug. 12, 1746.
4504. Moses, b. June 11, 1747; d. Nov. 16, 1757.
4505. Hannah, b. Feb. 2, 1749; d. Sept. 15, 1753.
4506. Job, b. May 4, 1752; d. Jan. 26, 1754.
4507. Joseph, b. Oct. 26, 1754; m. Mindwell Pomeroy, 4511.
4508. Job, b. about 1756; m. Elizabeth Smith, 4514.
4509. Mehitable, b. about 1758-61; m. Judge Samuel Cook, 4521.
4510. Hannah, b. 1763; m. Daniel Marsh, 4601.

## 4511 = 4507.  JOSEPH[5] MARSH

b. at Hadley, Mass., Oct. 26, 1754, son of Capt. Moses[4] and Hannah

(Cook) Marsh, (Capt. Job[3], Daniel[2], John[1]); m. about 1781, No. 4511.

**4511.**   Mindwell[4] Pomeroy, bap. April 11, 1756, dau. of Ebenezer[3], Ebenezer[2] Jr., Ebenezer[1]. He removed to Brookfield, Vt. and was there killed by the falling of a tree, Aug., 1783, æ. 28. His widow m. (2) in 1784, Ebenezer Clark of Lunenburgh, Vt., widower of her sister Eunice. Children :

4512.   Sally[6], b. June 10, 1782 ; m. 1800, Lemuel Jones of Lunenburgh, Vt.; removed to Malone, N. Y.; alive there 1853.
4513.   Joannah, b. Jan., 1784; m. Daniel Clark of Lunenburgh and
removed to Huntsburg, O.; resided there 1853.

### 4514 = 4507.   DR. JOB[5] MARSH

b. at Hadley, Mass., about 1756, son of Capt. Moses[4] and Hannah (Cook) Marsh, (Capt. Job[3], Daniel[2], John[1]); graduated at Yale college 1777, settled as physician at Worthington, Mass.; m. Sept. 10, 1783, No. 4514.

**4514.**   Elizabeth[6] Smith, b. Dec. 29, 1758, dau. of Oliver[5], Jonathan[4], Luke[3], Chileab[2], Lieut. Samuel[1]. He returned to Hadley and d. July 26, 1797. He introduced innoculation at Worthington, advertising it in the *Hampshire Gazette*, March 28, 1793. Widow Elizabeth d. June 7, 1823 and gravestones of both are in the lot of Daniel[2] Marsh in the Hadley burial ground. Children:

4515.   Elizabeth[6], b. March 22, 1784; m. William Smith, 4522.
4516.   Joseph, b. Feb. 16, 1786 ; m. (1) Roxa Johnson, 4531.
4517.   Timothy, d. y.
4518.   Moses, d. y.
4519.   Moses, b. Aug. 29, 1792; m. (1) Elizabeth M. Johnson, 4550.
4520.   Ethelinda, m. Ebenezer Harrington of Worcester and d. in
Hadley, Aug. 5, 1840.

### 4521 = 4509.   MEHITABLE[5] MARSH

b. at Hadley, Mass., about 1758–61, dau. of Capt. Moses[4] and Hannah (Cook) Marsh, (Capt. Job[3], Daniel[2], John[1]); m. May 11, 1781, No. 4521.

**4521.** Judge Samuel[1] Cook, b. at Hadley, March 18, 1755, son of Jonathan[4] and Ruth (Goodman), Samuel[3] and Ann[3] (Marsh), [dau. Jonathan[2], John[1] Marsh] Capt. Aaron[2] Cook, Maj. Aaron[1]. Ruth (Goodman) Cook was ̈dau. of Thomas son of Thomas and Grace[3] (Marsh) Goodman, dau. of Samuel[2] Marsh, John[1]. Judge Cook removed first to Worthington, as did his father-in-law, and afterwards to Morristown, Vt.

## 4522 = 4515.   ELIZABETH[6] MARSH

b. probably at Worthington, March 22, 1784, dau. of Dr. Job[5] and Elizabeth (Smith) Marsh, (Capt. Moses[4], Capt. Job[3], Daniel[2], John[1]) ; m. Dec. 17, 1805, No. 4522.

**4522.** William[6] Smith, b. March 5, 1782, son of Enos[5], Jonathan[4], Luke[3], Chileab[2], Lieut. Samuel[1].  He d. June 12, 1840, æ. 58.  She d. Dec. 18, 1856, æ. 72.  Children :

    4523.  Elizabeth Marsh[7], b. Oct. 15, 1806 ; d. unm.
    4524.  William Dickinson, b. Sept. 5, 1808; m. Louisa Taylor and had four children, one named Job Marsh.
    4525.  Julia, b. July 17, 1810; d. unm. May 23, 1829, æ. 18.
    4526.  Charles, b. May 17, 1812; m. Dec. 6, 1838, Eliza Maria French.  Two children.
    4527.  Ethelinda, b. March 11, 1814 ; m. Nov. 2, 1842, Stephen Lawrence.  Three children.
    4528.  Theodore, b. Feb. 15, 1817 ; d. Jan. 16, 1819.
    4529.  Sarah Ann, b. Jan. 10, 1820.
    4530.  Caroline, b. Feb. 13, 1823.

## 4531 = 4516.   JOSEPH[6] MARSH

b. probably at Worthington, Feb. 16, 1786, son of Dr. Job[5] and Elizabeth (Smith) Marsh, (Capt. Moses[4], Capt. Job[3], Daniel[2], John[1]) ; m. (1) Jan. 26, 1814, No. 4531.

**4531.** Roxa Johnson, dau. of Stephen Johnson.  She d. Nov. 20, 1828, and he m. (2) Oct. 13, 1829, No. 4532.

**4532.** Roxanna Wright, b. March 30, 1798 and d. April 29, 1836; he m. (3) Feb. 13, 1839, No. 4533.

**4533.** Catherine Cooledge. She d. Aug. 20, 1842 and he m. (4) April 7, 1844, No. 4534.

**4534.** Harriet (Boltwood) Newhall, b. Jan. 24, 1800, widow of George Newhall. Harriet[6] Boltwood was dau. of William[5], William[4], Solomon[3], Samuel[2], Robert[1]. She d. Aug. 23, 1865. Joseph[6] Marsh, d. Jan. 26, 1871, æ. 84. He was a wagon-maker and then farmer. Children :

    4535. Elvira Minerva[7], b. Sept. 5, 1814; m. 1834, Willard M. Kellogg of Amherst.

    4536. Mary Lyman, b. Feb. 18, 1818; m. 1840, William Watson Dickinson of Amherst.

    4537. Margaret, b. July 28, 1820; m. Lucius Nash, 4542.

    4538. Henry Martyn, b. Dec. 21, 1827 ; m. Almira S. Morton, 4546.

        By fourth wife.

    4539. Charles Cooledge, b. Nov. 24, 1845; m. Sept. 7, 1870, Mary Foster of Brooklyn, N. Y. Children:

        4540. Edward Graves[8], b. Feb. 15, 1873.

        4541. Harrison Boltwood, b. June 7, 1875.

## 4542 = 4537. MARGARET[7] MARSH

b. at Hadley, Mass., July 28, 1820, dau. of Joseph[6] and Roxa (Johnson) Marsh, (Dr. Job[5], Capt. Moses[4], Capt. Job[3], Daniel[2], John[1]) ; m. May, 1844, No. 4542.

**4542.** Lucius Nash, b. Oct. 25, 1814, son of Erastus[5] and Penelope (Gaylord) Nash, Enos[4], Enos[3], John[2], Timothy[1] and Rebekah, dau. of Rev. Samuel Stone of Hartford. She d. May 30, 1846 and Mr. Nash m. (2) Nov. 14, 1846, No. 4543.

**4543.** Elizabeth Marsh, (No. 4552), dau. of Moses[6], Dr. Job[5], Capt. Moses[4], Capt. Job[3], Daniel[2], John[1]. She d. Feb. 28, 1856, æ. 38, and he m. (3) Cornelia Johnson. He d. Aug. 5, 1879 in Bowensburg, Ill. Children:

    4544. George Williams[8], b. May 10, 1845.

        By second wife.

    4545. Henry Barnard, b. Dec. 8, 1847 ; d. June 14, 1849.

## 4546 = 4538. HENRY MARTYN[7] MARSH

b. at Hadley, Dec. 21, 1827, son of Joseph[6] and Roxa (Johnson)

Marsh, (Dr. Job[5], Capt. Moses[4], Capt. Job[3], Daniel[2], John[1]) ; m. May 10, 1854, No. 4546.

**4546.** Almira Sophronia Morton, dau. of John Alden Morton. Resides in Hadley. Children :

    4547. Edgar Henry[8], b. Sept. 26, 1855.
    4548. Sara Morton, b. Oct. 16, 1857.
    4549. Carrie Graves, b. Oct. 12, 1861.

### 4550 = 4519.  MOSES[6] MARSH

b. at Worthington or Hadley, Aug. 29, 1792, son of Dr. Job[5] and Elizabeth (Smith) Marsh, (Capt. Moses[4], Capt. Job[3], Daniel[2], John[1]) ; m. (1) 1817, No. 4550.

**4550.** Elizabeth M. Johnson, b. 1790, who d. Dec. 2, 1825, æ. 34. She is called on her gravestone " Betsey J." He m. (2) Oct., 1827, No. 4551.

**4551.** Elizabeth Merrill, b. July, 1796 ; d. May 12, 1850, æ. 55. Moses[6] Marsh, d. May 31, 1851. Children :

    4552. Elizabeth Smith[7], b. Jan. 24, 1818 ; m. Lucius Nash, 4543.
    4553. An infant son, mentioned on gravestone of Betsey J., wife of Moses.
    4554. Edward Henry, b. June 8, 1829; m. (1) Mary Harris, 4556.
    4555. George Francis, b. Dec. 22, 1832 ; d. Minneapolis, July 27, 1859, æ. 27.

### 4556 = 4554.  EDWARD HENRY[7] MARSH

b. at Hadley, Mass., June 8, 1829, son of Moses[6] and Elizabeth (Merrill) Marsh, (Dr. Job[5], Capt. Moses[4], Capt. Job[3], Daniel[2], John[1]) ; m. (1) about 1853, No. 4556.

**4556.** Mary Harris, who d. July 1, 1854.  He m. (2) March 19, 1856, No. 4557.

**4557.** Harriet Hubbard Wells, b. May 25, 1832, who d. Dec. 1, 1866. He m. (3) Jan. 27, 1869, No. 4558.

**4558.** Adeline Hull Hyde, b. Feb. 20, 1842.  He d. in New York City March 23, 1884.  The drug house which he helped form in New York was the third in size in the city.  His fellow merchants took action and the *N. Y. Oil, Paint and Drug Reporter* of March 26, 1884, gave extended report, here much abridged.

"Mr. Edward H. Marsh, of the firm of Lazell, Marsh & Gardner, d. suddenly Sunday morning at his residence in Brooklyn. He was well Saturday and at business as usual and in the evening with wife and sister visited the art exhibition; retired well, woke at 2 A. M. and d. in 20 minutes. He was born at Hadley, Mass., in 1829; at 16 entered employ of C. A. Harrington & Co., of Worcester; next spent five years with L. T. Lazell druggist and then went into business for himself at Worcester. Removed to Bellows Falls; Mr. Lazell, going to New York and finding he could buy the jobbing business of Haskell, Merrick & Bull, telegraphed to Mr. Marsh, for whom he had a strong personal liking, and in whose business capacity he placed great confidence, to see if he would join him. In result March 1, 1855, the firm of Lazell, Marsh & Hunn was formed, continuing till 1860 when the style was changed to Lazell, Marsh & Gardiner. Mr. Marsh and Mr. Lazell were partners 29 years and associates in business 35 years. Mr. Lazell called their partnership something more than a business relation, a warm personal friendship intensified by time. He knew Mr. Marsh thoroughly. At times impetuous, partly due to physical suffering he was a man of ingrain truthfulness and justice and could always be depended upon to do unflinchingly what he believed to be right. He left a wife and four children, the youngest 14. The oldest was obliged to retire from connection with the house on account of ill health. The second, a graduate of the School of Mines is now pursuing his studies under Prof. Hoffman at Berlin. A third after graduating at Amherst last year entered the employ of his father's firm."

As soon as Mr. Marsh's death was generally known a meeting of the Drug, Paint and Chemical exchange organization was called and resolutions were passed of heartfelt sympathy with the family with these strong words as to his character. "Endowed by nature with deliberate judgment and a keen perception of and devotion to, the principles of justice; trained from youth to the calling to which his years of manhood have been untiringly devoted, he has been a living example of the best type of the merchant and the citizen."

In moving the adoption of the minute Mr. D. C. Robbins recollected very well the honorable beginning of this firm. It succeeded the old firm of Haskell & Merrick and sustained its reputation; always honorable in its dealings, always the representative of the highest mark in the trade. The firm located in New York City and made a most important change in the system of credits instituting for the first time in our midst the rule that settlements should be made at the end of six months. I was so struck with the scheme that in my next statements I gave notice to the trade that I should pursue the same course.

Mr. Gellatly indorsed every word and added "I desire for the sake of the religion which he professed to add my testimony as to the sincerity with which he was a follower of the Lord Jesus Christ. Prominent as a business man, he was equally prominent influential and useful as a member of the church with which he was connected."
Mrs. Marsh now resides at Lee, Mass. Children :

4559.   Edward Merrill[8], b. Jan. 17, 1854.
       By second wife.
4560.   Charles Wells, b. July 12, 1858; graduated from Columbia
       college, School of Mines in 1879. Received the degree
       of Ph. D. from that institution and has studied chemis-
       try in Germany for nearly two years.
4561.   Frank Ballard, b. July 20, 1860; m. Marion Bolton, 4563.
       By third wife.
4562.   Harriette Cornelia, b. June 18, 1871.


## 4563 = 4561.   FRANK BALLARD[8] MARSH

b. at Brooklyn, N. Y., July 20, 1860, son of Edward Henry[7] and Harriet Hubbard (Wells) Marsh, (Moses[6], Dr. Job[5], Capt. Moses[4], Capt. Job[3], Daniel[2], John[1]); m. Oct. 3, 1888, No. 4563.
**4563.** Marion Bolton, of Brooklyn. He graduated at Amherst college 1883, resided for a time in Springfield, Mass. Resides at Brooklyn, N. Y. Child:

4564.   Edward Henry[9], b. Brooklyn, Nov. 23, 1889.


## 4565 = 4053.   SAMUEL[4] MARSH

b. at Hadley, Mass., April 19, 1721, son of Capt. Job[3], and Mehit-able (Porter) Marsh, (Daniel[2], John[1]); m. Dec. 5, 1745, his cousin, No. 4565.

**4565.** Phebe[4] Porter, b. Jan. 19, 1720, dau. of Samuel[3] and Anna (Colton) Porter, Hon. Samuel[2], Samuel[1] of Windsor, Ct. and Hadley, Mass. One of the proprietors of the lower grist mill. He d. Oct. 2, 1760. She d. Oct. 1, 1779, æ. 60. Her will divided her property about equally, giving the house to Samuel but more land to Phebe and Rebecca. Children :

4566. Daughter[5], b. Aug. 23, 1746; d. same day.
4567. Phebe, b. about 1753; m. Benoni Dickinson, 4570.
4568. Rebecca, m. Eleazar[6] Cook, b. Feb. 11, 1755, son of Lieut. Noah[5], Noah[4], Westwood[3], Capt. Aaron[2], Maj. Aaron[1]. He removed to St. Albans, Vt. d. 1800. After m. they remained in her home till after the mother's will Nov. 6, 1779.
4569. Samuel, m. Abigail Briggs, 4589.

## 4570 = 4567. PHEBE[5] MARSH

b. at Hadley, Mass., at the Stanley lot, about 1753, dau. of Samuel[4] and Phebe (Porter) Marsh, (Capt. Job[3], Daniel[2], John[1]); m. Feb. 23, 1774, No. 4570.

**4570.** Benoni[5] Dickinson, b. Dec. 12, 1747, son of Nathaniel[4], Nathaniel[3], Nathaniel[2], Nathaniel[1]. He was a soldier in 1776. He resided in Northfield, Mass. on the Connecticut river and Vermont border. She d. Nov. 23, 1835, æ. 82. According to History of Northfield. He d. July 17, 1839. For 45 grandchildren see History Northfield, Mass. Children :

4571. Samuel[6], b. Jan. 20, 1775; m. Susanna Barton. Nine children.
4572. Ethelinda, b. Dec. 3, 1776; m. June 21, 1801, Heman Dickinson.
4573. Polly, b. Jan. 12, 1781; m. Feb. 7, 1803, Horace Holton. She was alive in 1875.
4574. Job Marsh, b. June 30, 1783 ; m. (1) Rhoda Holton, 4579.
4575. Betsey, b. Dec. 25, 1785; m. March 4, 1812, Gideon D. Stebbins of Vernon, Vt.
4576. Nathaniel Porter, b. April 9, 1788; m. Ardelia T. Williams. Ten children.
4577. Roswell, b. Sept. 5, 1792; d. April 28, 1803.
4578. Asahel, b. June 25, 1795 ; m. Maria Gold. Thirteen children.

### 4579 = 4574.  CAPT. JOB MARSH[6] DICKINSON

b. at Northfield, Mass., June 20, 1783, son of Benoni and Phebe[5] (Marsh) Dickinson, (Samuel[4] Marsh, Capt. Job[3], Daniel[2], John[1]) ; m. (1) June 18, 1810, No. 4579.

**4579.** Rhoda Holton, b. Nov. 27, 1782, dau. of Elijah Holton. He m. (2) her sister, No. 4580.

**4580.** Widow Ruth (Holton) Field, who had m. (1) Martin Scott, and (2) George Field. She was b. Feb. 7, 1792 and d. Nov. 21, 1869, æ. 77. Capt. Job Marsh Dickinson had nine children. For details see History of Northfield. Children :

> 4581.  Lydia Stebbins[7], b. April 18, 1811; m. Joel[4] Brigham of Marlboro, Mass., son of Maj. Jedediah[3], Lieut. Jedediah[2], Samuel[1], living on the homestead of five generations. They had dau.:
>> 4582.  Henrietta Marsh[8] Brigham, who sent to the Marsh Family Historian a piece of silk from one of 18 silk dresses that were handed down to various Marsh descendants from Mehitable (Porter) Marsh, who d. in 1739, wife of Capt. Job. Marsh. Her father's estate was over £10,000 and £196 of goods were on the way from London when he d. July 29, 1722.
> 4583.  Elijah Marsh, b. Aug. 1, 1816; m. Maria A. Belding, 4584.

### 4584 = 4583.  ELIJAH MARSH[7] DICKINSON

b. at Northfield, Mass., Aug. 1, 1816, son of Capt. Job Marsh[6], (Phebe[5] [Marsh] Dickinson, Samuel[4] Marsh, Capt. Job[3], Daniel[2], John[1]) ; m. June 1, 1843, No. 4584.

**4584.** Maria A. Belding, b. in Vermont Oct. 2, 1820, dau. of Elijah Belding. E. M. Dickinson settled in Marlboro, but removed in 1854 to Fitchburg, Mass., where with his son Charles P. he is manufacturing shoes. He also sent for the historian's inspection, silk from a dress worn far back in the last century. Children :

> 4585.  Mary M[8]., b. July 5, 1844; m. June 8, 1870, Henry Allison.
> 4586.  Anna S., b. March 31, 1846; m. June 8, 1870, Fred F. Woodward.
> 4587.  Charles P., b. March 8, 1854.
> 4588.  Edward M., b. March 14, 1860; d. Dec. 2, 1860.

## 4589 = 4569. SAMUEL[5] MARSH

b. at Hadley, perhaps not far from 1751, son of Samuel[4] and Phebe- (Porter) Marsh, (Capt. Job[3], Daniel[2], John[1]) ; m. Dec. 28, 1775, No. 4589.

**4589.** Abigail Briggs. He made his will Jan. 21, 1798, giving to his widow half his house and garden and in all, one-third of the estate ; to his son Augustus one-half his house, and the other one-half after his mother's death and the rest to his four children. The inventory was : "House and three and one-half acres of land, $468.34. Total, $514.25." He d. 1798, between time of the will Jan. 21 and the inventory March 29, 1798. Augustus Marsh sold his right to home place to Jonathan E. Porter, March 17, 1802. His mother, Widow Abigail m. (2) published Sept. 12, 1801, Zephaniah Ross of Spring-field, Mass. Children :

    4590. Augustus[6].
    4591. Phebe Porter, m. June 12, 1799, Benjamin Buell of Spring-
            field.
    4592. Samuel.
    4593. Lucinda.

## 4594 = 4054. DANIEL[4] MARSH

b. at Hadley, Mass., Jan. 28, 1725, son of Capt. Job[3] and Mehitable- (Porter) Marsh, (Daniel[2], John[1]) ; m. published Dec. 17, 1750, No.. 4594.

**4594.** Hannah Parsons, dau. of Timothy of Durham, Ct., lived. in Hadley ; resided on south half of original Stanley lot. He d. Jan. 4, 1810, æ. 85. She d. Feb. 9, 1800, æ. 74. Children :

    4595. Mehitable[5], b. Dec. 3, 1751; d. Aug. 30, 1752.
    4596. William, b. Oct. 21, 1753; soldier at capture of Cornwallis at.
            Yorktown, Va., Oct. 19, 1781. He d. unm. in Warren..
    4597. Daniel, b. Jan. 6, 1756; m. (No. 4510) Hannah Marsh, 4601.
    4598. Mary, b. Sept. 9, 1758; m. Dec. 11, 1781, Joseph Field and
            d. March 6, 1832.
    4599. Eliphalet, b. Feb. 2, 1761; m. pub. Jan. 21, 1800, Lucy
            Magoon of Ware, Mass.
    4600. Timothy Parsons, b. Sept. 9, 1766; m. Easter Dunbar, 4640..

## 4601 = 4597.   DANIEL⁵ MARSH

b. at Hadley, Mass., Jan. 6, 1756, son of Daniel⁴ and Hannah
(Parsons) Marsh, (Capt. Job³, Daniel², John¹); m. Dec., 1781, his
cousin, No. 4601.

**4601.** Hannah⁵ Marsh, b. 1763, dau. of Capt. Moses⁴ and Hannah (Cook) Marsh, (Capt. Job³, Daniel², John¹). They lived upon
the original Stanley lot which had been in possession of their ancestry
Marsh, Porter and Stanley from the first settlement of Hadley; first
Thomas Stanley owned it and was buried Jan. 30, 1663 in Hadley.
His dau. Hannah m. Samuel Porter before 1660, and their son, Hon.
Samuel Porter on marriage to Joanna Cooke, Feb. 22, 1783, went to
live on this lot and they remained there all their lives and after their
death Capt. Job Marsh, who had married their dau. Mehitable, came
into possession and so it came down to his children's children and
their children.   When Daniel⁴ and Hannah (Parsons) lived there, it
was for a time used as a tavern, and boys covered the top of a chimney to smoke out a tory, but Hannah made them undo their work and
protected her guest.   Daniel⁵ d. Jan. 12, 1812, and his cousin-widow,
Hannah, with her children Lucretia⁶, Lewis⁶ and Joseph⁶, sold the
homestead April 12, 1820, to Benjamin Lombard, Jr., five acres more
or less.   The widow then removed to Belchertown, where she d. Jan.
19, 1837.   Children:

    4602.  Mehitable⁶, b. June 19, 1783; d. Sept. 3, 1784.
    4603.  Lucretia, b. March 6, 1785; d. unm. Feb. 24, 1840.
    4604.  Lewis, b. March 1, 1787; m. Sophia Barton, 4613.
    4605.  Joseph, b. Jan. 1, 1789; d. unm. Sept. 17, 1859.
    4606.  Mary, b. Feb. 1, 1791; m. Daniel Hitchcock, 4623.
    4607.  Henry, b. Aug. 24, 1793; d. May 15, 1794.
    4608.  Hannah, b. April 29, 1795; m. S. D. Fuller, 4627.
    4609.  Mehitable, b. Sept. 5, 1798; d. Dec. 13, 1798.
    4610.  Phebe Parsons, b. Nov. 15, 1800; d. unm. Feb. 25, 1856.
    4611.  Eliza, b. May 19, 1803; d. Sept. 12, 1804.
    4612.  Laura, b. Dec. 22, 1810; m. Eliab Washburn of Belchertown;
          d. Nov. 5, 1873, had two children, both d. y.

## 4613 = 4604.   LEWIS⁶ MARSH

b. at Hadley, Mass., March 1, 1787, son of Daniel⁵ and Hannah⁵
(Marsh) Marsh, son of Daniel⁴, dau. of Capt. Moses⁴, sons of Capt.

Job[3] and Mehitable (Porter) Marsh, Daniel[2] and Hannah (Lewis) Marsh, John[1] and Anne (Webster) Marsh, all of Hadley, was a carpenter and worked on the Hadley meeting house in 1808. He m. Feb. 1, 1810, No. 4613.

**4613.** Sophia Barton, b. June 13, 1789, dau. of Daniel Barton of Ludlow. He removed to Belchertown about 1815; was about 1828-9 for about two years in Rochester, N. Y. and then removed to Ashtabula Co., O., where he d. July 8, 1864. Widow Sophia d. March 27, 1879, æ. 89 years, 3 months and 14 days. Children:

4614. Chauncey[7], b. June 14, 1811; m. Nov. 3, 1831, Huldah Rhodes and lives (1886) in Wis.

4615. Daniel B., b. May 2, 1813; m. (1) Dec. 31, 1834, Charlotte Rawson of Andover, O. He m. (2) Emily Heath of Andover, O. and resided (1886) in Nebraska.

4616. Lewis D., b. March 5, 1816; m. Mariette Oatman, Cherry Valley, O. and d. Oct. 5, 1883.

4617. Rodney, b. Aug. 24, 1819; m. July 3, 1839, Phila Payne, Colebrook, O.; res. 1886, Hartsgrove, Ashtabula Co., O.

4618. Emeline, b. Jan. 4, 1821; d. March 13, 1821.

4619. Sophia, b. Jan. 16, 1822; m. May 7, 1840, O. B. Groves, Windsor, O.

4620. Maria, b. July 9, 1826; d. Aug. 17, 1826.

4621. Clarissa M., b. Jan. 14, 1828; m. (1) April 1, 1850, Truman Wildman, Windsor, O.; m. (2) Ancil Hill, Windsor, O.

4622. Olive, b. Aug. 15, 1830; res. (1886) Arthur, Ill.


**4623 = 4606.  MARY[6] MARSH**

b. at Hadley, Feb. 1, 1891, dau. of Daniel[5] and Hannah[5] (Marsh) Marsh, (Daniel[4], Job[3], Daniel[2], John[1]); m. Oct. 12, 1812, No. 4623.

**4623.**  Daniel Hitchcock of Warren, Mass.  Children:

4624. Harriet[7], b. July 20, 1813; d. Sept. 9, 1813.

4625. Joseph Field, b. July 27, 1815; d. Dec. 20, 1880.

4626. Mary, b. April 14, 1818.


**4627 = 4608.  HANNAH[6] MARSH**

b. at Hadley, April 29, 1795; dau. of Daniel[5] and Hannah[5] (Marsh) Marsh, (Daniel[4], Job[3], Daniel[2], John[1]); m. April 10, 1821, No. 4627.

**4627.** Sylvanus D. Fuller of Ware, Mass.   Children :

- 4628.  Laura[7], b. Feb. 6, 1822 ; d. July 15, 1878.
- 4629.  Charles W., b. May 10, 1824 ; d. July 28, 1861.
- 4630.  James R., b. March 3, 1826; m. Aug., 1850; res. Victory Mills, Saratoga Co., N. Y.
- 4631.  Mary, b. Nov. 8, 1829; m. Aug., 1850, Calvin W. Hastings, Palmer and d. Sept. 24, 1878.
- 4632.  Martha, b. May 5, 1833; d. Nov. 18, 1861.
- 4633.  Francis D., b. Feb. 8, 1837.
- 4634.  Carrie J., b. June 10, 1839 ; m. H. E. W. Clark, 4635.

4635 = 4634.   CARRIE J[7]. FULLER

b. at Ware, Mass., June 10, 1839, dau. of Hannah[6] (Marsh) Fuller, (Daniel[5] Marsh, Daniel[4], Job[3], Daniel[2], John[1]) ; m. Jan. 9, 1864, No. 4635.

**4635.** Capt. H. E. W. Clark of Alvarado, Cal., and the 5th Mass. cavalry.   Resided 1886, in Thorndyke, Mass.   Children :

- 4636.  Charles H[8]., b. Dec. 11, 1866.
- 4637.  Henry C., b. Oct. 26, 1868 ; d. Sept. 10, 1874.
- 4638.  F. Granger, b. July 21, 1871.
- 4639.  Genevea F., b. Sept. 3, 1873.

4640 = 4600.   TIMOTHY PARSONS' MARSH

b. at Hadley, Mass., Sept. 9, 1766, son· of Daniel[4] and Hannah (Parsons) Marsh, she was the dau. of Timothy Parsons and he son of Capt. Job[3], Daniel[2], John[1] ; published Oct. 11, 1799, m. Nov., 1799, No. 4640.

**4640.** Easter Dunbar of Palmer, b. March 14, 1774.   He d. Oct. 19, 1829 and she d. March 3, 1854 or '44.   Children :

- 4641.  Luther[6], b. March 30, 1800 ; m. and resided at Breckville, O.; d. Sept. 13, 1876.
- 4642.  Daniel, b. April 16, 1801 ; d. y.
- 4643.  Estes, b. July 23, 1802 ; m. Mary Ames, 4651.
- 4644.  Daniel, b. March 1, 1804 ; m. Minerva Cowles, 4663.
- 4645.  Laura, b. Sept. 30, 1805 ; d. y.
- 4646.  Asenath, b. Aug. 20, 1807 ; m. Jacob Norris, 4668.
- 4647.  Laura, b. July 30, 1809 ; d. Oct. 4, 1829.
- 4648.  Esther, b. Oct. 14, 1811 ; m. Samuel T. Ames, 4675.

4649. Mary Field, b. Nov. 6, 1813; m. Dec. 1, 1836, Willard G. Andrews of Ware. He d. June, 1880.

4650. Samuel Parsons, b. July 17, 1815; d. y.

## 4651 = 4643. ESTES⁶ MARSH

b. July 23, 1802, son of Timothy Parsons⁵ and Easter (Dunbar) Marsh, (Daniel⁴, Capt. Job³, Daniel², John¹) ; m. No. 4651.

**4651.** Mary Ames of Belchertown. Removed to Kentucky in 1839 and d. Aug. 23, 1884. Children :

4652. Laura Irene⁷, b. June 14, 1833; m. John Faulkner, 4658.
4653. Estes, b. July, 1834; d. y.
4654. Susan Juliette, d. y.
4655. Estes Parsons, b. Feb., 1839; d. y.
4656. Sarah Ames, b. June, 1845; d. y.
4657. Mary Chapman, b. Dec., 1847; d. y.

## 4658 = 4652. LAURA IRENE⁷ MARSH

b. June 14, 1833, dau. of Estes⁶ and Mary (Ames) Marsh, (Timothy Parsons⁵, Daniel⁴, Capt. Job³, Daniel², John¹) ; m. No. 4658.

**4658.** John Faulkner of Kentucky who d. 1850. Mrs. Laura I. Faulkner resides at Point Pleasant, Ky. Children :

4659. Mary A., m. lives in Kentucky.
4660. Sallie C., m. lives in Kentucky.
4661. Albert G., m. and lives in Kentucky.
4662. Eugene C., m. lives in Kentucky.

## 4663 = 4644. DANIEL⁶ MARSH

b. March 1, 1804, son of Timothy Parsons⁵ and Easter (Dunbar) Marsh, (Daniel⁴, Capt. Job³, Daniel², John¹); m. No. 4663.

**4663.** Minerva Cowles of Belchertown. He resided there most of his life and d. Feb. 7, 1887. Children :

4664. Ellen M⁷., b. June 11, 1835; m. Jan. 5, 1859, J. E. Bowdoin of Ware. Children :
4665. Jennie M⁸., b. Dec. 8, 1859; d. June 26, 1887.

27

4666.   Mary E., b. April 21, 1863; m. Feb. 27, 1884, Henry B.
    Addison of Ware.
4667.   Daniel Henry, b. July 7, 1841; d. y.


4668 = 4646.   ASENATH[6] MARSH

b. Aug. 20, 1807, dau. of Timothy Parsons[5] and Easter (Dunbar)
Marsh, (Daniel[4], Capt. Job[3], Daniel[2], John[1]); m. March, 1835, No.
4668.

**4668.**  Jacob Norris.   Removed to Rock Island, Ill. and d. May
11, 1849.   Children:

    4669.   Charles K[7]., not living.
    4670.   Iowa Jane, m. Mr. Warren; res. Rock Island.
    4671.   George, m. and res. in Kansas.
    4672.   Laura, not living.
    4673.   Martha, m. H. M. Stacy; res. at Springeld, Mass.
    4674.   Mary, m. Samuel Wallace; res. San Bernardino, Cal.


4675 = 4648.   ESTHER[6] MARSH

b. Oct. 14, 1811, dau. of Timothy Parsons[5] and Easter (Dunbar)
Marsh, (Daniel[4], Capt. Job[3], Daniel[2], John[1]); m. April 13, 1836,
No. 4675.

**4675,**  Samuel T. Ames of Belchertown.   Removed Sept., 1839,
to Kentucky and was living 1887, in Berea, Ky.   Children:

    4676.   George Parsons[7], b. March 31, 1838; d. Sept. 17, 1839.
    4677.   George, b. June 18, 1842; m. and res. Berea, Ky.
    4678.   Benjamin Franklin, b. July 26, 1847.
    4679.   Mary Field, b. March 27, 1850; m. Charles F. Smith of
        Palmer, Mass. where they now live.

# THE BERKSHIRE LINE. JUDGE PEREZ MARSH AND HIS DESCENDANTS OF DALTON AND PITTSFIELD, BERKSHIRE COUNTY, MASS.

## 4680 = 4055. DR. AND JUDGE PEREZ[4] MARSH

b. at Hadley, Mass., Oct. 25, 1729, son of Capt. Job[3] and Mehitable (Porter) Marsh, (Daniel[2], John[1].) J. Pierce's diary gives hints as to early education of Perez: "Sept. 9, 1841. Received of Mr. Job Marsh £1, 4s. in order for buying of several books." "Aug. 15, 1744. Go to Cambridge and offer Perez Marsh to college (accepted)." Josiah Pierce was a graduate of Harvard college 1735 and a notable man. (See No. 3746.) Perez graduated at Harvard college, 1748, was A. M. 1754 at both Harvard and Yale. He probably studied with Dr. Thomas Williams, at any rate he was his surgeon's mate in the French and Indian war of 1755, and made report of the entire loss, American and English, in the different regiments at the battle of Lake George, Sept. 8, 1755, when Col. Ephraim Williams, the founder of Williams college, was killed. The following paragraph is from the account of that battle in the History of the Williams Family.

"According to a return made by Dr. Perez Marsh, surgeon's mate in Col. Williams' regiment, the loss on the part of the English and Americans in both the engagements, was 216 killed and 96 wounded, making a total of 312 and a few missing. Col. Williams' regiment suffered the most, 46 were killed, 20 wounded and several missing." Dr. Perez is also spoken of as "attending to divers sick men at Fort Lyman."

He had been brought into contact with the Williams family by the fact that his uncle John[3] Marsh No. 3996 had married Sarah Williams No. 3998, who was sister of Rev. William Williams of Hatfield and aunt of his surgeon, Dr. Thomas Williams and of Col. Ephraim in whose regiment he was surgeon's mate.  This also led on to his relation to Sarah Williams, who was dau. of Col. Israel, son of Rev. William Williams.

The tradition in the Marsh family, handed down from the fair Sarah[5], is that the gallant Colonel Ephraim[4] who was over 40, desired to marry Sarah[5] who was 19 and dau. of his half cousin Col. Israel[4]. Isaac[2] Williams (son of Robert[1]) had, by first wife, Martha Park, a son, Rev. William[3] and by second wife Judith Cooper, had children Sarah[3] (who m. John[3] Marsh) and Ephraim[3] of Stockbridge, Mass., father of Col. Ephraim[4] and Dr. Thomas[4].  Col. Ephraim[4] sought Sarah[5].  Sarah declined.  He offered to make his will giving all his property to her before starting for Lake George.  She still preferred the surgeon's mate aged 25, to the Colonel of 40 and at Albany the will was made which gave his property to Williams college.

We find, soon after the battle of Lake George, that Dr. Perez Marsh settled on the eastern edge of Pittsfield, the date is uncertain although said to be 1755.  He is always spoken of as first of the settlers in what is now Dalton.  It was called the Ashuelot Equivalent being given in exchange for lands in New Hampshire.  This led the Hadley book to state p. 534, that Perez Marsh "was a physician in Pittsfield," and p. 603, "Sarah (Williams) m. —— Marsh and resided in Ashuelot, N. H.," which was not the case.  Dr. Perez Marsh m. about 1759, No. 4680.

**4680.**  Sarah Williams, b. 1736, he aged 30 and she 23, dau. of Col. Israel Williams and Sarah Chester.  The children of these parents will be interested in the parentage of their foremother Sarah Williams.  Through her mother, Sarah Chester, we all are descended from :

1.  William[1] Chester of London and of Bornet, Hertford Co.
2.  Leonard[2] Chester and Bridget[2] Sharpe, dau. John[1].
3.  John[3] Chester and Dorothy[2] Hooker of Hartford, sister of the famous Rev. Thomas[2] and dau. Thomas[1] of England.
4.  Leonard[4] Chester of England, b. 1609, of Watertown 1633, of Wethersfield later, d. 1648, æ. 39, and his wife Mary Wade Sharpe, dau. Nicholas.
5.  Capt. John[5] Chester, lived 1635–1697 and Sarah Welles 1631–1698, dau. Hon. Thomas Welles, Colonial Governor Connecticut and Elizabeth Hunt.

6. Major John[6] Chester, 1656–1711, Judge and Speaker and Hannah Talcott, 1666–1741, dau. Capt. Samuel Talcott and Hannah Holyoke, b. 1644, dau. Elizur Holyoke and Mary Pynchon, dau. William Pynchon founder of Springfield. Elizur was son of Edward Holyoke at Lynn, 1639 who m. 1612 our ancestor, Prudence Stockton, dau. Rev. John of Kinholt, England.

7. Sarah[7] Chester, 1707–1770, m. Col. Israel Williams, 1709–1789. Through Sarah (Willlams) Marsh's father, Col. Israel, we all come from his mother, Christian Stoddard, who lived 1676–1764, and her ancestry. She was dau. of Rev. Solomon, 1643–1729, Harvard college ﬂ662, minister at Northampton 56 years and the remarkable Esther Warham who lived 92 years, 1644–1736, dau. of Rev. John Warham, first minister of Windsor, Ct. and Jane, widow of Thomas Newbury. Rev. Solomon was son of Hon. Anthony Stoddard, 1618–1686, to Boston 1639, and Mary Downing (sister Sir George afterwards Lord Downing) dau. Hon. Emanuel and Lucy[5] Winthrop, b. Jan. 9, 1600, (they both joined Salem church Nov. 4, 1638) sister Gov. John and dau. Adam[3] Winthrop, b. London, Aug. 10, 1548, m. 1579, Anne Brown, *who had a French Bible*, d. 1629, dau. of Henry of Edwardston, clothier and Agnes Brown, d. Dec. 17, 1590, son of Adam[2] Winthrop, 1498–1562, Lord of the Manor Groton and Patron of the living, (m. 1534 Agnes Sharpe, 1616–1665, dau. of Robert,) son of Adam[1] Winthrop and Joanna Burton. (Those who wish can trace in the Stoddard book their ancestry back from Hon. Anthony b. 1618 to William Stoddard, Knight who came, 1066, with his cousin William the Conqueror from Normandy to England.)

The Williams descent is from Robert[1], d. Sept. 1, 1693 and Elizabeth Stratton d. July 28, 1674. (They came over 1638.) Capt. Isaac[2], 1638–1708 and Martha Park, Rev. William[3] Williams 1665 to 1741, a minister 56 years at Hatfield, Mass., called by his nephew, Jonathan Edwards, son of Esther Stoddard, "a great divine of very comprehensive knowledge;" "Christ was the great subject of his preaching;" and Dr. Chauncey in his sketch of eminent men in New England calls him "a greater man" than his father-in-law, Rev. Sol-. omon Stoddard, who, Elliott says, "has always been considered one of the greatest divines in New England". Chauncey also thinks him greater than any of his sons who were all men of mark. His son

Col. Israel[4] Williams, living 1709–1789, Harvard college 1729,
active in French and Indian wars 1744 and 1755, commissary under
Col. John Stoddard of Northampton (one of the three so called
" river gods " who m. Prudence Chester sister of Col. Israel's wife)
and upon Col. Stoddard's death, succeeded him and was charged
with the plan of the entire system of works to protect all Western
Massachusetts and Western New Hampshire. He had command of
all the forces and garrisons from the Connecticut to the Housatonic
and the Hudson. " Probably no man in the country during the war
of 1755 rendered more efficient aid than Col. Williams." That was
a school for the revolution. It makes us sad to say that his very
loyalty to King and old England and the flag he had served under,
made him a tory. " While confined in the jail at Northampton for
his political sentiments, his dau. a girl of 17, (about 1770) carried
him his daily food from Hatfield, submitting to the greatest indignities
from suspicious opposers." To day of her death in Pittsfield, æ. 81,
Dec. 11, 1834, she spoke of the revolutionary war as rebellion and of
herself as a subject of the English crown. She was a woman of great
wit and brilliancy, became wife of John Chandler Williams and in
her dying room, taking the communion bread with the rector's words
" Take and eat this in remembrance that Christ died for thee," irre-
pressibly replied, " That I will ! " The people of Hatfield after the
revolution grew more lenient, and being cured of their hostility to Col.
Williams they were accustomed as for the minister when he entered or
left church, so also to rise and continue standing while Col. Israel
passed to his seat or the open air.

On the way to and from French and Indian battle fields, men of
Hampshire found out the beauty and promise of the Housatonic
valley and Berkshire Hills. There four of Col. Israel Williams' eight
children settled, two at Pittsfield Center, and two, three miles east,
in Ashuelot Equivalent, afterwards Dalton. At the center were
Eunice, wife of Maj. Israel Stoddard, and Lucretia, who had cared
for her father in Northampton jail, now the wife of John Chandler
Williams, Esq., Harvard college 1778, whose three children m. one,
Hon. Edward Newton ; another, Moses Hayden, member of congress ;
a third, Harris Seymour of Canandaigua, N. Y.

Dea. William Williams and Dr. Perez and Sarah (Williams) Marsh
settled as neighbors close by the eastern Pittsfield border, in full

sight of Pittsfield, on the slope whose ridge a little higher up commands a view of Greylock on the north and westward all the Housatonic valley, and the scalloped Taconic range toward wonderful sunsets, and through the gap where the Boston & Albany railway passes out of New England into New York, a glorious view of the mighty Catskill mountains.

At the age of 35 in 1764 Dr. Perez Marsh was appointed Judge of the Court of Common Pleas for Berkshire county and held the office for 16 years until 1781. Judge Perez and Sarah (Williams) Marsh joined the Pittsfield church in 1765, the next year after it was formed. Rev. Thomas Allen was their pastor and their daughter m. the famous parson's son. Five daughters married very prominent citizens of Pittsfield, and they could not have asked more pleasant surroundings or prospects.

The town of Dalton was "detached from Pittsfield" and incorporated in 1784 and the first meeting for its organization was held April 19th at the house of Judge Perez Marsh. Of the first warrants (four in all) one was posted in his dwelling house. Nathaniel Kellogg who had been with him one of the three first settlers about 1755, had m. No. 4008, Hannah Barnard Hastings, dau. of Abigail (Marsh) Hastings, who was cousin of Perez Marsh. Dea. William Williams did not move into Dalton till some years after 1755. He was a trustee of Williams college and for several years state senator, called in History of Dalton "a leader and guide, an ornament and glory to the town." Dr. Perez d. in his 55th year, May 20, 1784. Sarah (Williams) Marsh d. June 2, 1817, æ. about 81. Children :

4681. Chester[5], b. Oct. 1, 1760; m. Hannah Burnham, 4692.
4682. Sarah, b. March 28, 1762 ; m. Israel Peck, 4701.
4683. Lucretia, b. March 20, 1764 ; d. Feb. 15, 1768.
4684. Martha, b. Nov. 5, 1765 ; m. Thomas Gold, 4858.
4685. Eunice, b. Sept. 9, 1767 ; m. Darius Larned, 4925.
4686. Henry, b. July 18, 1769; d. June 13, 1770.
4687. Henry, b. Sept. 11, 1771 ; m. Betsy Lawrence, 5245.
4688. Lucretia, b. Jan. 9, 1774 ; m, William Mellen, 4948.
4689. Elizabeth, b. Sept. 8, 1776 ; m. Jonathan Allen, 5201.
4690. Harriet, b. July 31, 1779: d. Oct., 1781.
4691. Christopher, b. Aug. 31, 1782 ; d. unm. Feb., 1806, of small pox caught from a patient of his father.

4692 = 4681.   CHESTER⁵ MARSH

b. (probably at Ashuelot Equivalent, Dalton) Oct. 1, 1760, son of
Dr. Perez⁴ and Sarah (Williams) Marsh, (Capt. Job³, Daniel², John¹);
resided at Dalton; m. Jan. 30, 1785, No. 4692.

**4692.**   Hannah Burnham of Wethersfield, dau. of Peter Burnham,
b. Dec. 6, 1761.   " She belonged to a family of wealth and prominence."   Chester⁵ d. in Dalton at the Dorrance house about 1830.
Widow Hannah resided in Pittsfield with her daughter and d. there.
Children :

> 4693.   Harriet⁶, b. 1786; d. 1843; m. Wm. C. Jarvis, Esq. of Pitts-
>         field, b. Boston, Mass., adm. to bar 1811, member Mass.
>         legislature and also its speaker, representing Pittsfield
>         in 1821, '22, '23 and '24.
> 4694.   Sophia, m. Fordyce Merrick, Esq., of Pittsfield.   Child:
>         4695.   Infant, d. y.
> 4696.   Elizabeth, b. 1795; d. 1855; m. Benj. Watson, 4697.

4697 = 4696.   ELIZABETH⁶ MARSH

b. at Dalton, Mass., dau. of Chester⁵ and Hannah (Burnham) Marsh,
(Judge Perez⁴, Capt. Job³, Daniel², John¹); m. No. 4697.

**4697.**   Major Benjamin Watson of Pittsfield.   Children :

> 4698.   Elizabeth⁷, b. 1822; m. (1) ————.   Children:
>         4699.   Rev. Joab Brace⁸, valedictorian Yale college 1837, A.
>                 M. 1841; d. 1845.
> 4700.   ————, m. (2) Charles A. Hopkins of Buffalo, who d.
>         Mrs. Hopkins was for several years matron at Smith
>         college.   No children.   Resided 1894 at Northamp-
>         ton, Mass.

4701 = 4682.   SARAH⁵ MARSH

b. at Dalton, Berkshire Co., Mass., Ashuelot Equivalent, March 28,
1762, dau. of Dr. Perez⁴ and Sarah (Williams) Marsh, (Capt. Job³,
Daniel², John¹); m. Sept. 11, 1784, No. 4701.

**4701.**   Israel Peck of Pittsfield.   She d. March 8, 1813, æ. 51.
Children :

4702. Laura Adeline[6], b. Oct. 12, 1785 ; m. David Bush, 4711.
4703. Henry, b. May 16, 1787 ; m. Lucy Miles, 4757.
4704. Perez Porter, b. March 12, 1790 ; m. Clarissa Goodman, 4778.
4705. Julia, b. March 4, 1792 ; m. Theodore Hinsdale, 4792.
4706. Otis, b. Oct. 11, 1795 ; m. Martha C. Dickinson, 4809.
4707. Eunice Stoddard, b. Sept. 17, 1796 ; m. S. P. Patterson, 4817.
4708. Elizabeth, b. July 25, 1798 ; m. Leonard Morse, 4832.
4709. Harriet, b. March 30, 1800 ; m. J. M. Goodman, 4853.
4710. George Adams, b. Dec. 11, 1805 ; d. June 17, 1876.

## 4711 = 4702. LAURA ADELINE[6] PECK

b. at Pittsfield, Mass., Oct. 12, 1785, dau. of Sarah[5] Marsh, (Dr. Perez[4], Capt. Job[3], Daniel[2], John[1]) ; m. April 7, 1807, No. 4711.

**4711.** David Bush of Pittsfield, son of Capt. David, who was on Pittsfield's committee of Safety and Correspondence, June 30, 1774. Children ‹

4712. Caroline Augusta[7], b. May 5, 1809 ; m. Joseph B. Bloss, 4724.
4713. John Brown, b. July 29, 1810 ; d. Dec. 19, 1825.
4714. Charles Peck, b. Nov. 11, 1813 ; m. (1) Phillippa Call, 4740.
4715. George Clinton, b. Sept. 4, 1815 ; m. (1) M. A. Provost, 4749.
4716. David, b. Jan. 10, 1817 ; m. July 25, 1843, Susan Lockwood ; had son[8], res. in New York and dau. d. y.
4717. Sarah Theresa, b. July 19, 1818 ; m. Nov. 24, 1841, Edward H. Thompson. Children :
4718. Edward Hughes[8], b. Jan. 25, 1848.
4719. Sarah Theresa, b. Dec. 26, 1858 ; d. Aug. 19, 1859.
4720. Benjamin Franklin, b. Jan. 21, 1821 ; m. Caroline K. Sawyer, Jan. 21, 1855. Children :
4721. Winifred Theresa[8], b. April 3, 1856 ; d. June 13, 1856.
4722. Edward Frank, b. May 1, 1860.
4723. Mary Almira, b. June 13, 1865.

## 4724 = 4712. CAROLINE AUGUSTA[7] BUSH

b. May 5, 1809, dau. of Laura A[6]. (Peck) Bush, Sarah[5] (Marsh) Peck, (Dr. Perez[4], Capt. Job[3], Daniel[2], John[1]) ; m. April 2, 1828, No. 4724.

**4724.** Joseph B. Bloss. Children :

4725. Caroline Louisa[8], b. June 14, 1829; d. y.
4726. John Brown, b. Dec. 31, 1831 ; m. Sarah R. Gilbert, 4732.
4727. Theodore Chauncey, b. March 12, 1833; d. y.
4728. Charles Edward, b. Oct. 22, 1834; res. 1885, unm. in Detroit, Mich.
4729. Harriet Wentworth, b. Aug. 20, 1837 ; d. y.
4730. Caroline Frances, b. Aug. 25, 1839; m. Sept. 23, 1869, Wm. H. McCourtie of Kalamazoo, Mich.  Child:
    4731. William M[9]., b. Dec. 12, 1875.


4732 = 4726.   JOHN BROWN[5] BLOSS

son of Caroline Augusta[7] (Bush) Bloss, dau. of Laura A[6]. (Peck) Bush, Sarah[5] (Marsh) Peck, (Dr. Perez[4], Capt. Job[3], Daniel[2], John[1]) ; m. No. 4732.
**4732.** Sarah R. Gilbert of Washington.   Children :
    4733. Caroline Amanda[9], b. June 29, 1860; m. Sept. 4, 1882, Luther S. Fristoe.
    4734. Joseph Bayard, b. Oct. 13, 1867.
    4735. Gilbert, b. Dec. 18, 1873.
    4736. Amy, d. y.
    4737. John G., d. y.
    4738. Frederick, d. y.
    4739. Mary, d. y.


4740 = 4714.   REV. CHARLES PECK[7] BUSH, D. D.

b. Nov. 11, 1813, son of David Bush and Laura Adeline[6] Peck, dau. of Sarah[5] (Marsh) Peck, (Dr. Perez[4] Marsh, Capt. Job[3], Daniel[2], John[1]); m. (1) No. 4740.
**4740.** Philippa Call.  He was pastor at Norwich, Ct., A. M. Yale 1850, was district secretary of the American Board at Rochester, N. Y. and afterwards at N. Y. City.  He m. (2) No. 4741.
**4741.** Elizabeth B. Homer of Boston.  He d. 1880.  Children :
    4742. Walter Griffen[8], d. y.
    4743. Julia Philippa, d. y.
    4744. Mary Payson, d. y.
    4745. Caroline E., unm. missionary to Harput, Turkey.
    4746. Anna.

By second wife.

4747. Everett, d. y.
4748. Charles Homer.


4749 = 4715. GEORGE C[7]. BUSH

b. Sept. 4, 1815, son of Laura A[6]. (Peck) Bush, Sarah[5] (Marsh) Peck, (Dr. Perez[4] Marsh, Capt. Job[3], Daniel[2], John[1]); m. (1) No. 4749.

**4749.** Mary A. Provost. He m. (2) No. 4750.
**4750.** Ulyssa A. Savage. Children all by first wife :

    4751. George Provost[8], b. June 25, 1853; m. July 10, 1879, Jennie Mickle. Children :
        4752. George Mickle[9], b. Oct. 12, 1880.
        4753. Alice Paul, b. Oct. 29, 1884.
    4754. Mary Clinton, b. Dec. 13, 1854.
    4755. David Chauncey, b. April 27, 1856.
    4756. Charles M., b. May 17, 1858.


4757 = 4703. HENRY[6] PECK

b. at Pittsfield, Mass., May 6, 1787, son of Sarah[5] (Marsh) Peck,. Dr. Perez[4] Marsh, (Capt. Job[3], Daniel[2], John[1]); m. Nov. 20, 1814, No. 4757.

**4757.** Lucy Miles. He d. Sept. 28, 1867. Children :

    4758. Julia Elizabeth[7], b. Nov. 27, 1815 ; m. Jan. 12, 1840, Horace Aplin.
    4759. Sarah Esther, b. May 18, 1817 ; d. y.
    4760. George Henry, b. Feb. 5, 1819; m. Sept. 19, 1848, Maria C. Roberts. Children :
        4761. Katherine Roberts[8], b. Sept. 10, 1849.
        4762. George Henry, b. Sept. 3, 1858; d. Oct. 12, 1882.
    4763. Otis Lyman, b. April 15, 1822 ; m. M. J. Clarke, 4765.
    4764. Harriet Maria, b. June 18, 1825 ; m. John G. Pool, 4774.


4765 = 4763. OTIS LYMAN[7] PECK

b. April 15, 1822, son of Henry[6] and Lucy (Miles) Peck, (Sarah[5.

[Marsh] Peck, Dr. Perez[4] Marsh, Capt. Job[3], Daniel[2], John[1]) ; m. Nov. 12, 1849, No. 4765.

**4765.** Martha J. Clarke. After living awhile at Sandusky City, Ohio, they have resided long at Toledo, O., where Mr. Peck has had charge of large railroad interests. Children :

4766. Harriet Lucy[8], b. Oct. 17, 1850 ; m. June 10, 1873, William R. M. Burgess. Children :
   4767. Mattie Milne[9], b. Oct. 10, 1877.   .
   4768. Marjorie, b. Jan. 14, 1881.
4769. Fannie, b. Nov. 3, 1854.   }
4770. Elizabeth Miles, b. Nov. 3, 1854.   }
4771. George Lyman, b. July 10, 1858 ; m. Nov. 9, 1886, Harriet May Stannard of Westbrook, Ct. Children :
   4772. Eloise Kirtland[9], b. Sept. 29, 1888.
   4773. Lyman Stannard, b. March 30, 1892.

4774 = 4764.   HARRIET MARIA[7] PECK

b. June 18, 1825, dau. of Henry[6] and Lucy (Miles) Peck, (Dr. Perez[4] Marsh, Capt. Job[3], Daniel[2], John[1]) ; m. Sept. 10, 1846, No. 4774.

**4774.** John G. Pool. She d. March 15, 1851. Children :

4775. Julia Eliza[8], b. Dec. 11, 1847 ; m. Dec. 31, 1878, William Hamilton. Child :
   4776. Jessie Mitchell[9], b. Jan. 12, 1880.
4777. Harriet Maria, b. Feb. 2, 1851.

4778 = 4704.   PEREZ PORTER[6] PECK

b. March 12, 1790, son of Sarah[5] (Marsh) Peck, (Dr. Perez[4] Marsh, Capt. Job[3], Daniel[2], John[1]) ; m. about 1816, No. 4778.

**4778.** Clarissa Goodman. Resided at Rochester, N. Y. and at Sandusky, O. He d. June 16, 1871 and she Feb. 24, 1874. Children :

4779. Clarissa Maria[7], b. July 31, 1817 ; m. Angus Smith and d. Aug., 1858.
4780. Frederick, b. May 20. 1819; d. in the army.
4781. Benjamin Franklin, b. Feb. 8, 1821 ; d. Amherst college, 1840.
4782. Henry, b. Oct. 6, 1823 ; d. Rochester, N. Y., 1840.
4783. James Sidney, m. Nellie Hayes. Child :

4784. Katie[8].
4785. Charles Fox, m. Bessie Hill. Child:
 4786. Mary[8].
4787. Catherine Edwards, m. (2d wife) Angus Smith a prominent merchant in Milwaukee, Wis. Child:
 4788. Jesse Hoyt[8].
4789. Mary, d. y.
4790. Ann Janette, d. y.
4791. Mary L., m. Nov., 1872, Charles O. Brigham.

## 4792 = 4705. JULIA[6] PECK

b. at Pittsfield, Mass., March 4, 1792, (another record " April, 1793 ") dau. of Sarah[5] (Marsh) Peck, (Dr. Perez[4] Marsh, Capt. Job[3], Daniel[2], John[1]) ; m. Sept. 23, 1815, pub. Sept. 2, second wife, No. 4792.

 **4792.** Theodore Hinsdale, Jr. of Pittsfield. She d. June 19, 1842. They resided on South St. Children :

 4793. Henry[7], b. Oct. 3, 1818; d. April 20, 1819.
 4794. Fanny Pomeroy, b. April 20, 1820; m. David E. Bartlett, 4799.
 4795. Mary, b. Feb. 10, 1822 ; res. 1884, unm. at North Wilbraham.
 4796. George Peck, b. April 6, 1824; m. Lucretia Pratt, 4806.
 4797. Edward Ruthven, b. April 3, 1833.
 4798. Caroline Elizabeth, b. April 24, 1837 ; d. Oct. 21, 1837.

## 4799 = 4794. FANNY POMEROY[7] HINSDALE

b. at Pittsfield, Mass., April 20, 1820, dau. of Julia[6] (Peck) Hinsdale, Sarah[5] (Marsh) Peck, (Dr. Perez[4] Marsh, Capt. Job[3], Daniel[2], John[1]) ; m. July 16, 1846, No. 4799.

 **4799.** Prof. David Ely Bartlett of the New York City and Hartford, Ct. deaf and dumb asylums, b. Sept. 29, 1805, Yale college, 1828, son of Rev. Shubael Bartlett, b. April 2, 1778, Yale college, 1800, 50 years pastor of Congregational church, East Windsor, Ct., (descended from Robert Bartlett at Plymouth in ship Ann, 1623 and on mother's side from Warrens and Brewsters) m. Feb. 19, 1803, Fanny Leffingwell of Hartford, dau. of John and Lois. Mr. Bartlett d. 1879. Children :

4800.  Fanny Hinsdale[8], b. June 9, 1847 ; d. March 9, 1848.
4801.  Theodore Hinsdale, b. Jan. 7, 1849 ; d. July 15, 1849.
4802.  Mary Leeds, b. Sept. 14, 1850 ; res. 1884 Hartford with mother.
4803.  Margaret Wyatt, b. May 21, 1852 ; res. 1884 Hartford with mother.
4804.  Charles Leffingwell, b. Nov. 13, 1853 ; m. June 7, 1880, Clara Crouse ; res. (1884) in Utica, N. Y.
4805.  Louise Leffingwell, b. Nov. 9, 1859.  Teaching in 1884 in Vt.


4806 = 4796.  GEORGE PECK[7] HINSDALE


b. at Pittsfield, Mass., April 6, 1824, son of Julia[6] (Peck) Hins-dale, Sarah[5] (Marsh) Peck, (Dr. Perez[4] Marsh, Capt. Job[3], Daniel[2], John[1]) ; m. No. 4806.
4806.  Lucretia Pratt.  Resides at Toledo, O.  Children :
    4807.  Helen Mar[8], b. April 4, 1864 ; d. Sept. 30, 1874.
    4808.  Grace, d. y.


4809 = 4706.  OTIS[6] PECK


b. at Pittsfield, Mass., Oct. 11, 1795, son of Israel and Sarah[5] (Marsh) Peck, (Dr. Perez[4] Marsh, Capt. Job[3], Daniel[2], John[1]) ; m. Oct. 30, 1824, pub. April 11, 1824, No. 4809.
4809.  Martha Chapman Dickinson, b. Jan. 22, 1800, d. May 8. 1872.  He d. Aug. 4, 1874.  They lived and d. in Pittsfield, Children :
    4810.  Maria E[7]., b. July 30, 1825 ; res. at homestead, Pittsfield.
    4811.  Oliver Dickinson, b. July 15, 1827 ; d. Feb. 17, 1831.
    4812.  Frederick Center, b. Aug. 30, 1829 ; m. Nov. 6, 1862, Catha-rine A. Goodrich who d. Nov. 11, 1875.  Children :
        4813.  Caroline Bailey[8], b. March 17, 1866.
        4814.  Anna Williams, b. Jan. 9, 1870.
        4815.  Allen, b. Oct. 31, 1875.
    4816.  Martha Austin, b. May 13, 1834.  The sisters and brother and his children live at the homestead, Pittsfield.

## 4817 = 4707. EUNICE STODDARD[6] PECK

b. at Pittsfield, Mass., Sept. 17, 1796, dau. of Israel and Sarah[5] (Marsh) Peck, (Dr. Perez[4] Marsh, Capt. Job[3], Daniel[2], John[1]); m. No. 4817.

    **4817.** Samuel Putnam Patterson of Albany, N. Y. Children :

        4818. Harriet[7].
        4819. Mary, m. J. A. Barker, 4821.
        4820. George P., m. Helena Watrous, 4828.


## 4821 = 4819. MARY[7] PATTERSON

b. ———, dau. of Eunice Stoddard[6] (Peck) Patterson, Sarah[5] (Marsh) Peck, (Dr. Perez[4] Marsh, Capt. Job[3], Daniel[2], John[1]); m. Nov. 22, 1847, No. 4821.

    **4821.** Jacob Andrews Barker. Children :

        4822. Mary Ella[8], b. Feb. 2, 1849; d. May 22, 1850
        4823. George Putnam, b. May 18, 1852 ; m. Aug. 7, 1879, Alice
                Helen Lyman. Child :
            4824. Helen[9], b. April 9, 1880.
        4825. Jacob Andrews, b. Nov. 2, 1856.
        4826. Frank Sidnor, b. June 14, 1860 ; m. Dec., 1886, Laura Cook
            of Sandusky, O.
        4827. Henry Kip, b. Feb. 4, 1862.


## 4828 = 4820. GEORGE P[7]. PATTERSON

b. May 18, 1852, son of Eunice Stoddard[6] (Peck) Patterson, Sarah[5] (Marsh) Peck, (Dr. Perez[4] Marsh, Capt. Job[3], Daniel[2], John[1]) ; m. No. 4828.

    **4828.** Helena Watrous of Norwalk, O. Child :

        4829. Helena[8], b. April 29, 1861 ; m. Wm. Howard Oatman, Dec.
            24, 1879. Children :
            4830. Daniel Howard[9], b. Dec., 1880; d. July 3, 1881.
            4831. George Howard, b. March 5, 1884.

## 4832 = 4708.  ELIZABETH[6] PECK

b. at Pittsfield, Mass., July 25, 1798, dau. Sarah[5] (Marsh) Peck, (Dr. Perez[4] Marsh, Capt. Job[3], Daniel[2], John[1]); m. (1) Jan. 27, 1824, No. 4832.

**4832.** Leonard Morse, who d. June 18, 1828 and she m. (2) May 10, 1836, No. 4832.1.

**4832.1.** William R. Hoyt.  She d. Jan. 26, 1882.  Children:

    4833.  Lafayette[7], b. Oct. 30, 1824; d. Jan. 19, 1825.
    4834.  Mary J., b. Oct. 11, 1828; m. J. B. Monroe, 4849.

               By second husband.

    4835.  William Leonard, b. May 9, 1837.
    4836.  George Samuel, b. Dec. 5, 1838; m. F. Adams, 4845.
    4837.  LaFayette H., b. Sept. 26, 1840; d. July 31, 1845.
    4838.  Sarah, b. Sept. 6, 1842; m. Ransom B. Thomas, Nov. 18, 1862.  Children:
        4839.  Margaret[8], b. July 6, 1864; d. Aug. 10, 1864.
        4840.  Mary Elizabeth, b. March 1, 1869; d. April 23, 1874.
        4841.  Frederick James, b. Aug. 26, 1871.
        4842.  Allen Carey, b. Feb. 28, 1875.
        4843.  William Ransom, b. Jan. 28, 1877.
        4844.  Sarah Elizabeth, b. Feb. 4, 1883.


## 4845 = 4836.  GEORGE SAMUEL[7] HOYT

b. Dec. 5, 1838, son of Elizabeth[6] (Peck) Hoyt, Sarah[5] (Marsh) Peck, (Dr. Perez[4] Marsh, Capt. Job[3], Daniel[2], John[1]); m. March 25, 1867, No. 4845.

**4845.** Fannie Adams.  Children:

    4846.  Augusta T[8]., b. July 16, 1868; d. Feb. 18, 1874.
    4847.  Harry B., b. April 21, 1870.
    4848.  Mary E., b. Aug. 26, 1872.


## 4849 = 4834.  MARY J[7]. MORSE

b. Oct. 11, 1828, dau. of Leonard and Elizabeth[6] (Peck) Morse, Sarah[5] (Marsh) Peck, (Dr. Perez[4] Marsh, Capt. Job[3], Daniel[2], John[1]); m. July 24, 1849, No. 4849.

**4849.** James B. Monroe.  Children:

4850. Minnie[8], b. June 23, 1851; m. Dec. 28, 1875, Lieut. J. J. Hunter, U. S. navy. Child:
    4851. James B. Monroe[9], b. Nov. 26, 1876.
4852. Clara, b. Sept. 13, 1856; d. April 6, 1858.


## 4853 = 4709. HARRIET[6] PECK

b. at Pittsfield, March 30, 1800, dau. of Israel and Sarah[5] (Marsh) Peck, (Dr. Perez[4] Marsh, Capt. Job[3], Daniel[2], John[1]); m. No. 4853.
    **4853.** Josiah M. Goodman of Pittsfield, Mass. Children:
        4854. Theodore Henry[7], m. Sarah Hosmer of Sandusky, O.
        4855. Frances, m. Charles Bangs of LaFayette, Ind. Child:
            4856. Callie[8].
        4857. Louisa, m. Thomas Green.


## 4858 = 4684. MARTHA[5] MARSH

b. "Ashuelot Equivalent," afterwards Dalton, Mass., Nov. 5, 1765, dau. of Judge Perez[4] and Sarah (Williams) Marsh, (Capt. Job[3], Daniel[2], John[1]); m. about 1785, No. 4858.
    **4858.** Thomas Gold, Esq., of Pittsfield, b. 1760. They lived on East St., Pittsfield.

> " Somewhat back from the village street
> Stands the old fashioned country-seat."

There Longfellow came in 1843 with his bride, the grand-daughter of Martha Marsh, and not long after wrote of "The Old Clock on the Stairs," " Half way up the stairs it stands, and points and beckons with its hands "; and of the house itself, which came to be a summer home of the Appletons, he wrote:

> " In that mansion used to be
> Free hearted hospitality:
> His great fires up the chimney roared."
> " There groups of merry children played,
> There youths and maidens dreaming strayed."
> " From that chamber, clothed in white,
> The bride came forth on her wedding night."

Esquire Gold was a lawyer of considerable prominence in Pittsfield and by the five sisters, daughters of Perez Marsh, the Peck, Gold,

28

Allen, Larned and Mellen families were brought into closest relationship with the families of Williams and Marsh, making a very broad and intimate cousinship. Mr. Gold d. Feb. 13, 1827, æ. 67. Widow Martha (Marsh) Gold lived for many years longer in the fine old homestead with her youngest daughter Martha. Her son Thomas Augustus Gold lived in a very pleasant residence on the next lot. Children :

4859.  Maria Theresa[6], b. Nov. 7, 1786; m. Nathan Appleton, 4872.
4860.  Thomas Augustus, b. May 18, 1788; m. Dorothy Gardiner, 4892.
4861.  Elizabeth Sedgwick, b. May 6, 1790; m. Charles Lee and d. in Rochester, N. Y., Sept. 27, 1822. Child:
    4862.  Charles Gold[7].
4863.  Sarah Williams, b. March 5, 1793 ; m. William Darling, Esq. of Hudson, N. Y., and d. Nov. 6, 1822. Child :
    4864.  Sarah Gold[7], b. Oct. 27, 1822; d. March 17, 1823.
4865.  Caroline Wolcott. b. July 18, 1795 ; pub. June 6, 1818; m. William Gardiner, brother of Dorothy (Gardiner) Gold and of Judge Gardiner of Rochester, N. Y. Child :
    4865.1.  Caroline Rebecca[8], b. Oct. 27, 1821.
4866.  Frances Jeannette, b. Aug. 19, 1797 ; m. Dr. Orrin Wright, 4897.
4867.  William Erskine, b. July 10, 1799 ; m. Caroline Handy, 4913.
4868.  Martha Washington, b. Oct. 5, 1801 ; m. Charles Benjamin, merchant of Pittsfield, brother of the missionary and uncle of S. G. W. Benjamin our late minister to Persia,
4869.  Theodore Egbert, b. Feb. 15, 1805 ; d. Vicksburg, Miss. Oct. 27, 1841.
4870.  Charles Ruggles, b. Nov. 2, 1808; m. went to California. Child :
    4871.  California[7].

4872 = 4859.    MARIA THERESA[6] GOLD

b. at Pittsfield, Mass., Nov. 7, 1786, dau. of Martha[5] (Marsh) Gold, (Judge Perez[4] Marsh, Capt. Job[3], Daniel[2], John[1]) ; m. at Pittsfield, April 13, 1806, No. 4872.

4872.  Nathan Appleton of Boston, Mass. She d. at Boston, Feb. 10, 1833. Children :

4873. Thomas Gold[7], b. March 31, 1812; Harvard college, 1831, classmate of Motley and Wendell Philips and warm friend of O. W. Holmes and Longfellow; "himself no mean poet," author of "Faded Leaves," founder of the Boston Literary Club, distinguished for wit and humor; d. unm. in New York City, April 17, 1884.

4874. Mary, m. Robert James Mackintosh, son of Sir James the eminent statesman and historian; res. London, Eng. Children:

    4875. Ronald[8].

    4876. Eva.

    4877. Angus.

4878. Charles Sedgwick, b. Oct. 9, 1815; d. Oct. 25, 1835.

4879. Fanny Elizabeth, b. Boston, 1817; m. H. W. Longfellow, 4880.

## 4880 = 4879. FRANCES ELIZABETH[7] APPLETON

b. at Boston, Mass., 1817, dau. of Maria Theresa[6] (Gold) Appleton, Martha[5] (Marsh) Gold, (Judge Perez[4] Marsh, Capt. Job[3], Daniel[2], John[1]); m. at Boston, 1843, No. 4880.

**4880.** Henry Wadsworth Longfellow, b. at Portland, Me., Feb. 27, 1807, son of Hon. Stephen Longfellow, member of congress and, Zilpah (Wadsworth) Longfellow, descended from John Alden and Priscilla. This Pilgrim descent did not interest Longfellow much till rather late in life. No young person can be expected to care much for either of his eight great-great-grandmothers. But Longfellow came to look deeper than mere ancestral record and to read between the lines. By poetic power he came to live with and love his foremother Priscilla and to hear her pop the question that meant so much for John and for John's descendant two centuries later, 'Why don't you speak for yourself, John?"

The poet graduated with Hawthorne at Bowdoin college in 1825. He is proof that the highest style of man can love truly more than once. He had m. in 1831, Mary S. Potter, who d. in Rotterdam, Holland, Nov. 29, 1835. He could never forget this first wife,

      "Who to (his) youth was given,
      More than all things else to love him,"

nor cease to hear her

      "Soft rebukes in blessings ended,
      Breathing from her lips of air."

Hyperion shows the play of a true soul in passing from a past to a present. Crude, and not yet developed into the finish of his later song, it is young manhood looking backward and downward to a morning splendor receding and seeming lost in inconceivable depths and also it is an awakening to look onward and upward. It is absurd to say that "who has truly loved one, can never truly love another." Substitute Frances for "Mary" and Appleton for "Ashburton" and America for "England," and it is plain enough who led "Paul Flemming" sunsetward into new Eden.

When in 1843, Longfellow with his fair bride came to the two Gold homesteads in Pittsfield, the homes, side by side, of mother and son, your historian's father, Henry Marsh, Esq., Williams college 1815, the third graduate of Harvard law school, 1819, was living just across East St., opposite the Gold places. He was the only Marsh grandson of Judge Perez, whose seven married children were five daus. and Chester who had only three daus. and Henry Senior, who had two daus. and but one son, the only grandson of Marsh name. And yet of the many who assembled to greet the newly wedded pair, half or more were of Marsh descent. The scarlet tie of cousinship with each other and with the bride, was from Judge Perez and Sarah (Williams) Marsh, in the veins of Golds, Pecks, Marshes, Allens, Larneds, Westons, Kittredges, Watsons, Humphreys, Bushes, Hinsdales and others.

The writer, not out of his teens, nor long out of college was only too happy to be there. Here was a living poet! Some of us knew by heart half the "Voices of the Night." "Potnia, Potnia Nux," Holy, Holy Night, has been a talisman in this and other lands. That Longfellow had married a kinswoman, was honor enough; to be introduced, to touch the hand of each and have a pleasant word was added delight.

We have loved and honored Longfellow from that hour. Writing much he has no words to blot. At home in Harvard, having the ear of all the Englands, living in the fine old Cambridge mansion where Washington had his headquarters, his was an ideal home. There children came and sometimes

> "Grave Alice, laughing Allegra,
> And Edith with golden hair"

would try to storm his castle wall, only to be put deeper down into the dungeon of his heart.

There tragedy came. Oh the horror of it ! when the drop of burning sealing wax fell upon the muslin dress and the cruel flame ended in agony the mother's life ! Mrs. Longfellow was burned to death in 1861.

The poet grew on in love and honor and into wider fame. His "Morituri Salutamus" is a most noble approach to closing scenes. He d. March 24, 1882. Westminster Abbey honors his memory.

As in the prelude to "Voices of the Night" he sings of his delight to go into the thick wood and lie down

"Beneath some patriarchal tree,"

where all

"His hoary arms uplifted he "

and then look up and listen pleased to hear

"A slumberous sound, a sound that brings
The feelings of a dream,
As of innumerable wings."

So, not dreaming, in blessed transition, he finds himself, whether awake he can hardly tell, beyond all realms of death, lying under the wonderful tree of life, that stretches up and out into all the eons and spaces, and around him are all the most glorious forms of life, and the day is a day of heaven, and above him are wings innumerable and in his ears a continuous sound of perfect joy and at his side the smiling one who promised, " Because I live ye shall live also," and he lives forevermore. Children :

4881. Charles[8], m. Harriet Spellman of Cambridge.
4882. Ernest.
4883. Fanny, d. y.
4884. Alice Mary.
4885. Edith, b. Oct. 22, 1853; m. Richard H. Dana, 4887.
4886. Anne, m. 1885, Joseph G. Thorpe of Cambridge.

## 4887 = 4885.  EDITH[8] LONGFELLOW

b. Oct. 22, 1853, dau. of Frances E[7]. (Appleton) Longfellow, Maria Theresa[6] (Gold) Appleton, Martha[5] (Marsh) Gold, (Perez[4] Marsh, Job[3], Daniel[2], John[1]) ; m. Jan. 10, 1878, No. 4887.

**4887.** Richard Henry Dana, b. at Cambridge, Jan. 3, 1851, Harvard college 1874, son of Richard Henry[3] Dana, b. at Cambridge,

Aug. 1, 1815, author of the book we all read " Two years before the Mast," Harvard college 1837, defender of Shadrach and Anthony Burns, one of Free Soil Party founders ; d. Rome, Jan. 7, 1882, son of Richard Henry[2], poet, b. May 15, 1787 ; d. Feb. 12,1879, in his 92d year, son of Chief Justice Francis[1] Dana. Resides at Boston. Children :

4888. Richard Henry[9], b. Sept. 1, 1879.
4889. Henry Wadsworth Longellow, b. Jan. 26, 1881.
4890. Frances Appleton, b. May 26, 1883.
4891. Allston, b. Sept. 29, 1884.
    (These children are descended on the father's side from George[1] Marsh of Hingham, 1635; 2, Onesiphorus[2]; 3, John[3].; 4, David[4]; 5, Rev. John[5]; 6, Mary[6] (Marsh) Watson; 7, Sarah[7] (Watson) Dana; 8, Richard[8] H. Dana.)

### 4892 = 4860. THOMAS AUGUSTUS[6] GOLD

b. at Pittsfield, Mass., May 18, 1788, son of Martha[5] (Marsh) Gold, (Dr. Perez[4] Marsh, Capt. Job[3], Daniel[2], John[1]) ; m. pub. March 6, 1818, No. 4892.

**4892.** Dorothy Gardiner, of Manlius, N. Y. He was a lawyer and resided in Pittsfield. Children :

4893. Thomas Gardiner[7], b. April 24, 1819.
4894. William Augustus, b. May 20, 1821.
4895. Nathan Appleton, b. Aug. 20, 1827 ; d. Dec. 8, 1830.
4896. Maria Theresa, b. Oct. 28, 1835 ; d. Sept., 1864 in Rochester, N. Y.

### 4897 = 4866. FRANCES JEANNETTE[6] GOLD

b. at Pittsfield, Aug. 19, 1797, dau. of Martha[5] (Marsh) Gold, (Dr. Perez[4] Marsh, Capt. Job[3], Daniel[2], John[1]) ; m. pub. Nov. 21, 1818, No. 4897.

**4897.** Dr. Orrin Wright of Pittsfield and d. Dec. 9, 1826. He d. Oct. 28, 1836. Children :

4898. Charles Gold[7], b. Jan. 11, 1820 ; m. in New Orleans and d. in 1863. Children :

4899.  Fanny[8].

4900.  Oliver.

4901.  Frances Jeannette, b. July 29, 1821 ; m. George F. Danforth, 4903.

4902;  Thomas, b. May 20, 1823 ; d. unm. in 1858.

## 4903 = 4901.  FRANCES JEANNETTE[7] WRIGHT

b. at Pittsfield, Mass., dau. of Frances J[6]. (Gold) Wright, Martha[5] (Marsh) Gold, (Dr. Perez[4] Marsh, Capt. Job[3], Daniel[2], John[1]) ; m. April 27, 1846, No. 4903.

**4903.**  Judge George Franklin Danforth of Rochester, N. Y., b. July 5, 1819, son of Isaac Danforth of Boston and Dolly (Hutchins) Danforth of Concord, N. H.   Judge Danforth was freshman Amherst college 1836—7, graduated Union college 1840.   Associate Judge N. Y. court of appeals since Jan. 1, 1879.   Mrs. Danforth d. Jan. 25, 1885.   Children :

> 4904.  Fanny Wright[8], m. Henry Fitch Huntington, banker of Rochester, N. Y.   Children :
>> 4905.  Jeannette[9].
>> 4906.  George Danforth.
>> 4907.  Elizabeth.
> 4908.  Herbert.
> 4909.  Charles.
> 4910.  Henry Gold.
> 4911.  Mary Celina.
> 4912.  Jessie Appleton.

## 4913 = 4867.  WILLIAM ERSKINE[8] GOLD

b. at Pittsfield, Mass., July 10, 1799, son of Martha[5] (Marsh) Gold, (Dr. Perez[4] Marsh, Capt. Job[3], Daniel[2], John[1]) ; m. No. 4913.

**4913.**  Caroline Handy.   Children :

> 4914.  Fanny[7], m. David Worcester.   Children :
>> 4915.  Mary[8].
>> 4916.  Caroline.
>> 4917.  Elwood.
>> 4918.  Elizabeth.

4919. Elizabeth, m. (1) Isaac R. Elwood; (2) John B. Scholey.
Children (Elwoods):
 4920. Frank[8], m. Mrs. Frederika (Pumpelly) Raymond.
 4921. Agnes.
 4922. Elizabeth.
 4923. William, d. unm.
 4924. Caroline, m. Harry J. MacDonald.


4925 = 4685.  EUNICE[5] MARSH

b. at Dalton, Berkshire Co., Mass., Sept. 9, 1767, dau. of Judge Perez[4] Marsh, (Capt. Job[3], Daniel[2], John[1]); m. about 1790, No. 4925.

4925. Darius[6] Larned (Learned) of Thompson, Ct. and Pittsfield, Mass., son of Simon[5], William[4], Isaac[3], Isaac[2], William[1]; resided at Pittsfield. He d. Widow Larned d. Aug. 12, 1843. Children all born in Pittsfield:

 4926. Eunice Williams[6], b. Aug. 9, 1791; m. Jonathan Allen, 5202.
 4927. Frederick Sylvester, b. Dec. 8, 1792; d. unm. in Augusta, Ga., 4947.
 4928. Benjamin Franklin, b. Sept. 6, 1794; m. Mrs. Lucy F. Watson, 4930.
 4929. Mary Stoddard, b. April 4, 1797; m. Gad Humphreys, 4935.


4930 = 4928.  MAJOR GENERAL BENJAMIN F[6]. LARNED

b. Pittsfield, Mass., Sept. 6, 1794, son of Eunice[5] (Marsh) Larned, (Judge Perez[4] Marsh, Capt. Job[3], Daniel[2], John[1]); he was of military descent.  His grandfather Marsh was surgeon's mate at the battle of Lake George (see No. 4680.)  His grandfather, Col. Simon Larned, b. 1756, at Thompson, Ct., was an officer in the revolutionary war, came to Pittsfield, 1784, was Berkshire county sheriff many years and member of congress of the district 1807-8, served through the war of 1812 as Colonel 9th regiment U. S. infantry and d. Nov. 16, 1817, æ. 61.  He m. 4930.

4930.  "Pittsfield town records show that Major Benjamin F. Larned of U. S. army and Mrs. Lucy F. Watson were pub. Sept. 27, 1823, and married at Lenox, Oct. 14, 1823."  He was long at Detroit, active in the Presbyterian church of which Dr. Duffield was pastor, and in command of the U. S. forces in Ft. Gratiot. The writer remembers well spending a week in the pleasant family there in 1843. In the civil war he was promoted to be Paymaster General of the U. S. army, with residence at Washington, with the title by Brevet, of Major General. Children:

4931. Frederick[7], m. Louisa.
4932. Frank.
4933. Edward.
4934. Charles T. He was major and paymaster in Rosecrans' army in Tenn. and was very highly endorsed by Rosecrans who urged his stay as "faithful, indefatigable and efficient " and bewailed his transfer to Cincinnati.

## 4935 = 4929. MARY STODDARD[6] LARNED

b. at Pittsfield, April 4, 1797, dau. of Eunice[5] (Marsh) Larned, (Judge Perez[4] Marsh, Capt. Job[3], Daniel[2], John[1]) ; m. about 1818, No. 4935.

**4935.** Gad Humphreys. Resided at Pittsfield, Mass. and St. Augustine, Fla. Children :

4936. Mary S[7]., b. May 17, 1819; m. Thomas J. Hulbert, 4943.
4937. Ann Eliza, b. Jan. 25, 1821.
4938. Frederic C., b. Oct. 6, 1823 ; m. Sarah Drysdale.
4939. Frances Smith, b. April 13, 1827, in St. Augustine; m. Mr. Hopkins.
4940. Catharine Larned, b. Jan. 5, 1829.
4941. Edward, b. April 1, 1835.
4942. Charles, b. May 1, 1837.

## 4943 = 4936. MARY S[7]. HUMPHREYS

b. at Bridport, Vt,, May 17, 1819, dau. of Mary Stoddard[6] (Larned) Humphreys, Eunice[5] (Marsh) Larned, (Judge Perez[4] Marsh, Capt, Job[3], Daniel[2], John[1]) ; m. No. 4943.

**4943.** Thomas J. Hulbert. Resided at Detroit, Mich. and in Washington, D. C., where Aug. 31, 1882, he was in the treasury department. Children:

4944.  Fanny[8].
4945.  Kellogg.
4946.  Annie.

## 4947 = 4927.   FREDERICK SYLVESTER[6] LARNED

b. Dec. 8, 1792, son of Eunice[5] (Marsh) Larned, (Judge Perez[4] Marsh, Capt. Job[3], Daniel[2], John[1]); d. unm. in Augusta, Ga.

## MARSH—MELLENS.

## 4948 = 4688.   LUCRETIA[5] MARSH

b. at Dalton, Mass., Jan. 9, 1774, dau. of Judge Perez[4] Marsh, (Capt. Job[3], Daniel[2], John[1]); m. at Dalton, Nov. 8, 1791, No. 4948.
**4948.** Capt. William Henry[2] Mellen, b. Hopkinton, Mass., May 20, 1766, son of Lieut. Col. James[1] Mellen; d. Hudson, N. Y., Jan. 11, 1826. She resided long with her dau. Mrs. Leeds in N. Y. City and d. with her children in Brooklyn, N. Y., Dec. 21, 1851. Children :

4949.  Betsy[6], b. May 18, 1793; m. Timothy Kellogg, 4959.
4950.  Lovett Russell, b. April 17, 1795; m. Lucretia D. Taylor, 5055.
4951.  Louisa Billings, b. Pittsfield, July 28, 1797; d. Hudson, N. Y., June 17, 1814.
4952.  Mary Warren, b. Sept. 2, 1800; m. Samuel Leeds, 5080.
4953.  Martha Marsh, b. Jan. 12, 1803; m. Joseph Benjamin, 5132.
4954.  Harriet Lucretia, b. Pittsfield, Jan. 15, 1805; d. there Aug. 3, 1805.
4955.  Christopher Marsh, b. Pittsfield, July. 23, 1806; m. Catherine A. Villee, 5152.
4956.  William Henry, b. Athens, N. Y., Oct. 10, 1810; m. Catherine T. Ostrander, 5162.
4957.  Charlotte Sophia, b. Athens, N. Y. Dec. 17, 1812; m. Wm. W. Pinneo, 5168.

4958. John Stoddard, b. Hudson, N. Y., July 27, 1815; m. Sarah. C. Thorpe, 5186.

---

## MARSH—MELLEN—KELLOGGS.

---

### 4959 = 4949. BETSY[6] MELLEN

b. Pittsfield, Mass., May 18, 1793, dau. of Lucretia[5] (Marsh) Mellen,. (Judge Perez[4] Marsh, Capt. Job[3], Daniel[2], John[1]) ; m. July 4, 1810, at Athens, N. Y., No. 4959.

4959. Timothy Kellogg, b. at Stillwater, N. Y., July 20, 1786. He d. at Brooklyn, N. Y., April 7, 1855. She d. there Oct. 6, 1873. They resided at New York City and Brooklyn. Children :

4960. Sarah Williams[7], b. Hudson, Aug. 11, 1811; d. New York City, Nov., 1812.
4961. Robert Ransom, b. May 18, 1813; m. Mary E. Morse, 4971.
4962. Charles, b. Hudson, N. Y., March 31, 1816; m. Walden, N. Y.. May 5, 1842, Catherine Ann Neafie. Studied for the ministry, became judge. No children. Adopted Kate Harman, child of his sister.
4963. DeWitt Clinton, b. Feb. 6, 1818; d. N. Y. City, Jan. 6, 1826..
4964. Louisa Isabella, b. March 31, 1820; m. L. W. Gilbert, 4993.
4965. Sarah Williams, b. June 1, 1822 ; m. Charles F. Burckett, 5001.
4966. Mary Elizabeth, b. May 28, 1824; m. Herbert M. Harman,. 5007.
4967. Martha Benjamin, b. Sept. 4, 1826; m. James R. Van Brunt,. 5014.
4968. Walter Lawrence, b. Jan. 6, 1829; m. Ruth Francis, 5027.
4969. Sophia Lucretia, b. Nov. 8, 1831 ; m. Edward Orr, 5029.
4970. Josephine Maria, b. March 10, 1834; m. Geo. W. Harman,. 5046.

---

### 4971 = 4961. REV. ROBERT RANSOM[7] KELLOGG

b. at Hudson, N. Y., May 18, 1813, son of Betsey[6] (Mellen) Kellogg,.

Lucretia[5] (Marsh) Mellen, (Dr. Perez[4] Marsh, Capt. Job[3], Daniel[2], John[1]); m. at New York City, June 21, 1837, No. 4971.

4971. Mary Elizabeth Morse, b. at New York City, Jan. 22, 1814. He d. at Milford, Pa., Sept. 25, 1866. She resides with oldest daughter. Children :

4972. Mary Theodosia[8], b. April 17, 1838; m. F. A. Thompson, 4975.
4973. Robert Morse, b. July 17, 1840; m. Martha E. Royce, 4984.
4974. Sarah Josephine, b. May 2, 1846; m. M. Van Inwegen, 4988.

4975 = 4972.    MARY THEODOSIA[8] KELLOGG

b. at New York City, April 17, 1838, dau. of Rev. Robert R[7]. Kellogg ; m. at LeRoy, N. Y., April 28, 1857, No. 4975.

4975. Frederick Augustus Thompson, b. at Stamford, N. Y., Oct. 1, 1830. Children :

4976. Mary Theodosia[9], b. LeRoy, Dec. 11, 1857 ; d. there Jan. 11, 1858.
4977. Lillie Augusta, b. LeRoy, Dec. 29, 1858.
4978. Leonard Kellogg, b. LeRoy, Jan. 10, 1861 ; m. Brooklyn, June 2, 1881, Eva Hester Geraghty.
4979. Mary Morse, b. Milford, Pa., April 10, 1863.
4980. Grace Theodosia, b. Brooklyn, N. Y., Oct. 15, 1867.
4981. Josephine Kellogg, b. Brooklyn, March 1, 1870.
4982. Frederick Robert, b. Brooklyn, July 28, 1871 ; d. there Nov. 12, 1875.
4983. Burton, b. Brooklyn, June 26, 1879.

4984 = 4973.    ROBERT MORSE[8] KELLOGG

b. at Brooklyn, N. Y., July 17, 1840, son of Rev. Robert R[7]. Kellogg ; m. at Milford, Pa., Aug. 5, 1873, No. 4984.

4984. Martha Elizabeth Royce, b. there Oct. 12, 1841. Children all b. at Port Jervis, N. Y. He was killed on the railroad, Jersey City, N. J., March 16, 1870. Children :

4985. Lucy Morse[9], b. July 12, 1864.
4986. Mary Josephine, b. Aug. 20, 1866.
4987. Martha Robertine, b. June 10, 1869.

## 4988 = 4974. SARAH JOSEPHINE[8] KELLOGG

b. at Romeo, Mich., May 2, 1846, dau. of Rev. Robert R[7]. Kellogg; m. Port Jervis, N. Y., Oct. 7, 1874, No. 4988.

**4988.** Moses Van Inwegen, b. at Cuddlebackville, N. Y., July 29, 1851. Children, all b. at Port Jervis, N. Y.:

4989. Clara Josephine[9], b. June 22, 1875; d. July 12, 1875.
4990. Robert Kellogg, b. July 14, 1876.
4991. Clarence Wellington, b. May 7, 1878.
4992. Alberta, b. Nov. 2, 1880.

## 4993 = 4964. LOUISA ISABELLA[7] KELLOGG

b. at Hudson, N. Y., March 31, 1820, dau. of Betsey[6] (Mellen) Kellogg, Lucretia[5] (Marsh) Mellen, (Judge Perez[4] Marsh, Capt. Job[3], Daniel[2], John[1]); m. at N. Y. City, Sept. 20, 1838, No. 4993.

**4993.** Lyman Washburn Gilbert, b. at Bristol, Vt., July 20, 1808; d. at New Brighton, N. Y., March 8, 1871. Children:

4994. Mary Elizabeth Mills[8], b. N. Y. City, March 16, 1842; d. Brooklyn, Dec. 14, 1853.
4995. Adelaide Sophia Louisa, b. N. Y. City, March 19, 1845; d. Brooklyn, July 15, 1848.
4996. Agnes Josephine Isabella, b. Philadelphia, Pa., Jan. 29, 1847; d. Brooklyn, Aug. 15, 1849.
4997. Helen Augusta Leeds, b. N. Y. City, Aug. 14, 1848; d. Brooklyn, Aug. 15, 1849.
4998. Louisa Isabella Augusta, b. Brooklyn, Oct. 22, 1853; d. N. Y., May 29, 1861.
4999. Anna Louisa Myers, b. Brooklyn, Oct. 27, 1861.
5000. Ida Isabella Kendall, b. Brooklyn, Dec. 25, 1862.

## 5001 = 4965. SARAH WILLIAMS[7] KELLOGG

b. at New York City, June 1, 1822, dau. of Betsey[6] (Mellen) Kellogg, Lucretia[5] (Marsh) Mellen, (Judge Perez[4] Marsh, Capt. Job[3], Daniel[2], John[1]); m. at Brooklyn, N. Y., Dec. 13, 1852, No. 5001.

**5001.** Charles Frederick Burckett, b. at Wertheim, Ger., July 14, 1821. Children:

5002.  Frederick Kellogg[8], b. Brooklyn, July 25, 1854.
5003.  Charles Henry, b. New Orleans, La., March 30, 1856.
5004.  Walter Latting, b. New Orleans, Jan. 23, 1858.
5005.  William Mellen, b. Brooklyn, April 9, 1860.
5006.  Timothy Kellogg, b. Brooklyn, Jan. 27, 1862; d. there Feb. 13, 1862.

5007 = 4966.  MARY ELIZABETH[7] KELLOGG

b. in New York City, May 28, 1824, dau. of Betsey[6] (Mellen) Kellogg, Lucretia[5] (Marsh) Mellen, (Judge Perez[4] Marsh, Capt. Job[3], Daniel[2], John[1]); m. at Brooklyn, Dec. 25, 1851, No. 5007.
5007.  Herbert Manuel Harman, b. at Pulaski, N. Y., Oct. 28, 1823.  She d. at Oswego, N. Y., where all her children were born, Feb. 12, 1868.  Children:

5008.  Mary Gertrude[8], b. March 17, 1856.
5009.  Ella Lucretia, b. Jan. 9, 1859; d. Jan. 10, 1865.
5010.  Anna Louisa, b. Oct. 29, 1860.
5011.  Milton Herbert, b. Aug. 4, 1863.
5012.  Charles Kellogg, b. Oct. 9. 1865.
5013.  Kate, b. Feb. 3, 1868, adopted by Charles Kellogg, 4962.

5014 = 4967.  MARTHA BENJAMIN[7] KELLOGG

b. at New York City, Sept. 24, 1826, dau. of Betsey[6] (Mellen) Kellogg, Lucretia[5] (Marsh) Mellen, (Judge Perez[4] Marsh, Capt. Job[3], Daniel[2], John[1]); m. at Brooklyn, Dec. 29, 1847, No. 5014.
5014.  James Rider Van Brunt, b. in Brooklyn, Sept. 20, 1820. Children b., m. and d. in Brooklyn.  Children:

5015.  James Kellogg[8], b. Dec. 25, 1849; m. Oct. 29, 1877, Ella Florence Stevens, b. N. Y. City, Jan. 8, 1858.  No children.
5016.  Martha Elizabeth, b. Aug. 19, 1851; m. Brooklyn, Nov. 27, 1873, Daniel Futhill Rouk, b. N. Y. City, March 27, 1852.  Children all b. in Brooklyn:
5017.  George Albert[9], b. Nov. 18, 1874.
5018.  Jennie, b. June 6, 1876.
5019.  Mary, b. Feb. 27, 1878.
5020.  Elsie Norwood, b. Sept. 7, 1880.

5021. Sarah Burckett, b. Nov. 11, 1853.

5022. Jane Adriance, b. Oct. 27, 1855.

5023. Caroline Henshaw, b. Nov. 23, 1857.

5024. Louisa Gilbert, b. Aug. 13, 1860.

5025. Albert Cropsey, b. Oct. 30, 1862 ; d. May 2, 1875.

5026. Mary Garetta, b. March 5, 1865 ; d. Sept. 24, 1865.

5026.1. Mary Garetta, b. July 9, 1867 ; d. June 6, 1868.


5027 = 4968. WALTER LAWRENCE[7] KELLOGG

b. at New York City, Jan. 6, 1829, son of Betsey[6] (Mellen) Kellogg, Lucretia[5] (Marsh) Mellen, (Dr. Perez[4] Marsh, Capt. Job[3], Daniel[2], John[1]) ; m. at Lexington, Mich., Dec. 30, 1851, No. 5027.

**5027.** Ruth Francis, b. at Wales, N. Y., March 23, 1831. Child :

> 5028. Walter Bostwick[8], b. Lexington, Oct. 17, 1866.


5029 = 4969. SOPHIA LUCRETIA[7] KELLOGG

b. at Brooklyn, N. Y., Nov. 8, 1831, dau. of Betsey[6] (Mellen) Kellogg, Lucretia[5] (Marsh) Mellen, Dr. Perez[4] Marsh, Capt. Job[3], Daniel[2], John[1]) ; m. Brooklyn, March 3, 1851. No. 5029.

**5029.** Edward Orr, b. at New Bedford, Mass., Feb. 26, 1826. He d. at Detroit, Mich. Children b. and d. at Detroit, except Edward Trumbull d. in Brooklyn. Children :

> 5030. Henry Kellogg[8], b. March 21, 1852; d. April 25, 1857.
> 5031. Elizabeth Kidder, b. March 28, 1853; m. Detroit, July 4, 1876, James Edward Dickinson, b. Mt. Clemens, Mich., Oct. 31, 1849. Children all b. in Detroit:
>> 5032. Howard Orr[8], b. Aug. 21, 1877.
>> 5033. Paul Clemens, b. Jan. 7, 1879.
>> 5034. Julia Theodora, b. July 31, 1881.
> 5035. Edward Trumbull, b. May 14, 1854; d. Sept. 7, 1854.
> 5036. Frank Howard, b. May 14, 1855; d. July 4, 1855.
> 5037. Mary Louisa, b. Oct. 14, 1856.
> 5038. Charles Morris, b. Feb. 18, 1858.
> 5039. Sophia Estelle, b. Jan. 26, 1861 ; d. Nov. 26, 1862.
> 5040. Virginia Lincoln, b. May 24, 1863.
> 5041. Charlotte Page, b. Feb. 14, 1865.

5042.  Grace Lucretia, b. May 31, 1867 ; d. July 6, 1868.
5043.  Wendall Prime, b. June 16, 1868 ; d. July 11, 1868.
5044.  Edward Kellogg, b. March 30, 1870.
5045.  Florence Maud, b. Oct. 17, 1872.


5046 = 4970.   JOSEPHINE MARIA[7] KELLOGG

b. at New York City, March 10, 1834, dau. of Betsey[6] (Mellen) Kellogg, Lucretia[5] (Marsh) Mellen, (Dr. Perez[4] Marsh, Capt. Job[3], Daniel[2], John[1]) ; m. at Brooklyn, Jan. 24, 1854, No. 5046.

**5046.**  George Wales Harman, b. at Oswego, N. Y., Feb. 15, 1833. Children b. at Oswego :

> 5047.  William Wales[8], b, Aug. 20, 1855 ; m. at Oswego, Sept. 10, 1877, Ida May Adelaide Whitman, b. Morrisville, N. Y., May 18, 1857.  Child :
>> 5048.  Grace Alice[9], b. at Oswego, Oct. 23, 1878 ; d. at Camden, N. Y., April 9, 1880.
> 5049.  Herbert Percy, b. Dec. 3, 1857.
> 5050.  Edwin Bronson, b. April 9, 1859.
> 5051.  Frances Althea, b. April 8, 1862 ; d. Oswego, Aug. 11, 1862.
> 5052.  Lucretia Mellen, b. July 23, 1863.
> 5053.  Josephine Kellogg, b. Dec. 22, 1866.
> 5054.  Albert Mannister, b. Nov. 11, 1869.


### MELLENS.


5055 = 4950.   LOVETT RUSSELL[6] MELLEN

b. at Pittsfield, Mass., April 17, 1795, son of Lucretia[5] (Marsh) Mellen, (Judge Perez[4] Marsh, Capt. Job[3], Daniel[2], John[1]) ; m. at Hudson, N. Y., Oct. 17, 1827, No. 5055.

**5055.**  Lucretia Douglas Taylor, b. at Hudson, April 24, 1795 ; d. there Oct. 9, 1880.  Children :

5056. Martha Taylor⁷, b. Hudson, Aug. 4, 1828; d. Nov. 7, 1828.
5057. Mary Warren Leeds, b. April 14, 1830; m. J. M. Punderson, 5061.
5058. Lovett Russell, b. at Hudson, Dec. 7, 1831; d. there Oct. 22, 1832.
5059. Martha Taylor, b. Nov. 6, 1833; m. S. P. Barnard, 5069.
5060. Louisa Billings, b. at Hudson, Oct. 27, 1837; m. at Hudson, June 2, 1880, second wife, Abraham Underhill of N. Y. City, b. at Yorktown, N. Y., Dec. 25, 1804.

5061 = 5057. MARY WARREN LEEDS⁷ MELLEN

b. at Hudson, N. Y., April 14, 1830, dau. of Lovett R⁶. Mellen, Lucretia⁵ (Marsh) Mellen, (Judge Perez⁴ Marsh, Capt. Job³, Daniel², John¹); m. at Hudson, N. Y., Jan. 26, 1852, No. 5061.
5061. James Mellen Punderson, b. at Hudson, Aug. 9, 1822.
Children :

5062. Russell Mellen⁸, b. at Buffalo, N. Y., April 29, 1853.
5063. Frank Talman, b. at Hudson, July 16, 1854.
5064. Mary Eleanor, b. at Hudson, Dec. 25, 1856; d. there Aug. 1, 1858.
5065. James Hyatt, b. at Hudson, Jan. 19, 1859.
5066. Louise Mellen, b. at Hudson, Nov. 4, 1860.
5067. John Whitney, b. at Hudson, Nov. 13, 1862.
5068. Robert Fitzhugh, b. at Hudson, Nov. 13, 1862; d. Aug. 8, 1863.

5069 = 5059. MARTHA TAYLOR⁷ MELLEN

b. at Hudson, N. Y., Nov. 6, 1833, dau. of Lovett R⁶. Mellen, Lucretia⁵ (Marsh) Mellen, (Judge Perez⁴ Marsh, Capt. Job³, Daniel², John¹); m. at Hudson, No. 5069.
5069. Stephen Paddock Barnard, b. at Hudson, April 11, 1831. He d. at Grand Rapids, Mich., May 5, 1875. She d. there Dec. 13, 1879. Children :

5070. Robert Alexander⁸, b. Hudson, Aug. 28, 1855.
5071. Edmund Marcy, b. Hudson, May 29, 1860.
5072. Stephen Paddock, b. Hudson, Sept. 1, 1862.

29

5073.  Anna Burchsted, b. Hudson, July 20, 1864; m. Grand Rapids,
        Mich, Nov. 12, 1884, Addison Spencer Goodman.
5074.  Katherine Mellen, b. Hudson, March 27, 1867; d. Grand
        Rapids, July 5, 1877.
5075.  Henry Burchsted, b. Grand Rapids, Sept. 3, 1869.
5076.  William Van Vleck, b. Grand Rapids, Sept. 3, 1869.
5077.  Florence, b. Grand Rapids, Dec. 31, 1870.
5078.  Frederic, b. Grand Rapids, Feb. 19, 1873; d. there Aug., 1873.
5079.  Maud, b. Grand Rapids, Oct. 24, 1875.

---

MARSH—MELLEN—LEEDS.

---

5080 = 4952.   MARY WARREN[6] MELLEN

b. at Pittsfield, Mass., Sept. 2, 1800, dau. of Lucretia[5] (Marsh) Mellen, (Judge Perez[4] Marsh, Capt. Job[3], Daniel[2], John[1]); m. in New
York City, Nov. 12, 1823, No. 5080.

5080.   Samuel Leeds, merchant, b. at Dorchester, Mass., May
11, 1796; resided at New York City and d. there Sept. 22, 1868.
Mrs. Leeds d. there Jan. 31, 1878.   Children b. and if dead d. in
New York City:

5081.  Samuel Penniman[7], b. Nov. 15, 1824; m. Julia Lockwood,
        5091.
5082.  Mary Lucretia, b. Aug. 16, 1826; d. March 8, 1828.
5083.  Daniel Webster, b. Feb. 29, 1828; m. M. C. Wheelwright,
        5092.
5084.  William Mellen, b. Nov. 12, 1829; m. N. Y. City, Jan. 9, 1856,
        Catherine Yonge Lochwood, b. N. Y. City, Aug. 31,
        1825, dau. Roe Lockwood, bookseller.   No children.
5085.  Robert, b. Nov. 26, 1831; d. Dec. 25, 1838.
5086.  Charles Henry, b. Jan. 9, 1834; m. S. P. Lambert, 5103.
5087.  Lovett Russell, b. Nov. 1, 1835; d. Sept. 14, 1860.
5088.  James Mellen, b. Feb. 13, 1838; d. Jan. 28, 1873.
5089.  Mary Ingersoll, b. Jan. 9, 1840; m. W. H. VanKleeck, 5111.
5090.  Robert, b. Oct. 28, 1842; m. R. B. Dwight, 5124.

5091 = 5081.   REV. SAMUEL PENNIMAN[7] LEEDS, D. D.

b. in New York City, Nov. 15, 1824, son of Samuel and Mary Warren[6] (Mellen) Leeds, Lucretia[5] (Marsh) Mellen, (Judge Perez[4] Marsh, Capt. Job[3], Daniel[2], John[1]) ; m. (1) in New York City, Oct. 3, 1849, No. 5091.

**5091.**   Julia Lockwood, b. in New York City, Jan. 19, 1828, dau. of Roe Lockwood, Esq., publisher and bookseller, Broadway, N. Y. They resided at Cuyahoga Falls, O., 1849 and onwards, and for many years 1860 and on at Hanover, N. H., where Mrs. Leeds d. Oct. 29, 1874. A very beautiful private memorial has been written of her, describing faithfully one of the loveliest of characters " of grace etherial and rare." She gives this hint to young converts, " Never pick and choose among the commandments of God." Mr. Leeds is well known to all Dartmouth graduates having for more than 30 years been pastor of the united village and college church. He was on the committee of 25 provided for at the National Council at St. Louis to prepare a creed to be suggested to the Congregational churches. He m. (2) July 20, 1882, at Springfield, Mass., No. 5091.1.

**5091.1.**   Mrs. Emily H. Barnes (née Wells).   No children.

5092 = 5083.   DANIEL WEBSTER[7] LEEDS

b. in New York City, Feb. 29, 1828, son of Samuel and Mary Warren[6] (Mellen) Leeds, Lucretia[5] (Marsh) Mellen, (Judge Perez[4] Marsh, Capt. Job[3], Daniel[2], John[1]) ; m. in Brooklyn, N. Y., April 3, 1850, No. 5092.

**5092.**   Maria Chamberlain Wheelwright, b. at Dorchester, Mass., Sept. 1, 1830.   Children :

> 5093.   Anna Gardner[8], b. in Brooklyn, Dec. 12, 1850 ; d. there March 8, 1851.
> 5094.   Julia Penniman, b. in Brooklyn, Jan. 13, 1852 ; m. at Elizabeth, N. J., Nov. 14, 1877, Charles Edward Brown, b. at Boston, Mass., Dec. 12, 1845.   Children :
>> 5095.   Charles Edward[9], b. at Elizabeth, Nov. 1, 1878.
>> 5096.   Harold Webster, b. at Elizabeth, April 20, 1882.
> 5097.   Helen Maria, b. in Brooklyn, March 6, 1854 ; d. there March 27, 1854.

5098.  Gardner Wheelwright, b. June 8, 1855, in Brooklyn.
5099.  James Ingersoll, b. in New York City, Dec. 25, 1857 ; m. at
        Elizabeth, N. J., Nov. 20, 1883, Nellie Moore.   Child :
    5100.  Russell Ingersoll⁸, b. at Elizabeth, Sept. 26, 1884.
    5101.  Lovett Russell, b. in New York City, Nov. 15, 1861.
5102.  George Wheelwright, b. at Englewood, N. J., Sept. 30, 1863.

5103 = 5086.   CHARLES HENRY⁷ LEEDS

b. in New York City, Jan. 9, 1834, son of Samuel and Mary Warren⁶
(Mellen) Leeds, Lucretia⁵ (Marsh) Mellen, (Judge Perez⁴ Marsh,
Capt. Job³, Daniel², John¹) ; m. in New York City, Dec. 21, 1865,
No. 5103.
5103.  Sarah Perley Lambert, b. in Brookline, Mass., May 20,
1834.  He resides (1894) in Stamford, Ct., and is Mayor of that
city.  Children b. in New York :

    5104.  Edward Lambert⁸, b. Sept. 14, 1866.
    5105.  Alfred, b. Oct. 20, 1867 ; Yale college 1887 ; m. at Spring-
            field, Oct. 24, 1894, Louise Morgan, dau. of Elisha
            Morgan.
    5106.  Ellen, b. April 1, 1869.
    5107.  Norman, b. Nov. 15, 1871.
    5108.  Mary Warren, b. Jan. 14, 1874.
    5109.  Howard, b. Feb. 18, 1876; d. at Chappaqua, N. Y., Aug.
            10, 1882.
    5110,  Arthur Russell, b. April 8, 1879.

5111 = 5089.   MARY INGERSOLL⁷ LEEDS

b. in New York City, Jan. 9, 1840, dau. of Mary Warren⁶ (Mellen)
Leeds, Lucretia⁵ (Marsh) Mellen, (Judge Perez⁴ Marsh, Capt. Job³,
Daniel², John¹) ; m. in New York City, May 25, 1859, No. 5111.
5111.  William Henry Van Kleeck, wholesale merchant of New
York City, b. at Syracuse, N. Y., Jan. 17, 1838.  Children all b. in
New York City :

    5112.  Mary Leeds⁸, b. May 30, 1860; m. R. M. Shepard, 5121.
    5113.  William Henry, b. May 2, 1862 ; m. at Brooklyn, N. Y., Oct.
            8, 1884, Lilly Gunderson Knight, b. Jan. 1, 1861.

5114. Warren, b. Jan. 31, 1864.
5115. Camilla, b. Sept. 26, 1866.
5116. Laura, b. Nov. 11, 1871; d. in New York City, Feb. 26, 1873.
5117. Bertha, b. June 17, 1875.
5118. Helen, b. Aug. 1, 1877.
5119. Chester Marsh, b. Feb. 29, 1880.
5120. Nelson Roe, b. Feb. 5, 1882.

5121 = 5112. MARY LEEDS[8] VAN KLEECK

b. in New York City, May 30, 1860, dau. of Mary I[7]. (Leeds) Van Kleeck; m. in N. Y. City, May 25, 1882, No. 5121.

**5121.** Robert Mellen Shepard, b. at New Orleans, La., May 17, 1851; resides at Hudson, N. Y. She has prepared for this work with surpassing neatness and accuracy a list of all the descendants of her great-grandmother Lucretia[5] (Marsh) Mellen (No. 4948) whose fine portrait in her New York home she had been familiar with from childhood. Children:

5122. Mary Warren[9], b. at Hudson, N. Y., April 13, 1883.
5123. William Van Kleeck, b. at Hudson, Dec. 15, 1884.

5124 = 5090. ROBERT[7] LEEDS

b. in New York City, Oct. 28, 1842, son of Mary Warren[6] (Mellen) Leeds; m. at Brooklyn, N. Y., May 19, 1864, No. 5124.

**5124.** Rebecca Bunnoch Dwight, b. in New York City, Oct. 17, 1841, (see Dwight Book p. 455). Children b. except LeRoy, in Brooklyn. Children:

5125. Mary Louise[8], b. Oct. 18, 1865.
5126. Rebecca Dwight, b. Feb. 8, 1870.
5127. Robert Russell, b. June 22, 1871.
5128. William Dwight, b. Feb. 3, 1873; d. at Georgetown, Ct.,
        Aug. 11, 1874.
5129. Edna Dwight, b. Sept. 28, 1874.
5130. Mabel, b. Oct. 24, 1875.
5131. LeRoy, b. Dec. 3, 1880, at Providence, R. I.

## MARSH—MELLEN—BENJAMINS.

### 5132 = 4953.   MARTHA MARSH[6] MELLEN

b. in Pittsfield, Mass., Jan. 12, 1803, dau. of Lucretia[5] (Marsh) Mellen, (Judge Perez[4] Marsh, Capt. Job[3], Daniel[2], John[1]) ; m. at Hudson, N. Y., Jan. 7, 1822, No. 5132.

**5132.** Joseph Benjamin, b. at Egremont, Mass., June 20, 1796; d. at New York City, May 25, 1872.   Children b. at Carbondale, Pa.:

5133.  Lucretia Marsh[7], b. Jan. 28, 1833; m. S. E. Dimmock, 5136.
5134.  Susan Sophia, b. Aug. 21, 1836; d. at Carbondale, Aug. 14, 1843.
5135.  Joseph Ritner, b. July 25, 1839; m. Abbie B. Sabin.

### 5136 = 5133.   LUCRETIA MARSH[7] BENJAMIN

b. at Carbondale, Pa., Jan. 28, 1833, dau. of Martha M[6]. (Mellen) Benjamin, Lucretia[5] (Marsh) Mellen, (Judge Perez[4] Marsh, Capt. Job[3], Daniel[2], John[1]) ; m. in Elizabeth, N. J., March 1, 1854, No. 5136.

**5136.** Hon. Samuel Erskine Dimmock, b. at Bloomingburg, N. Y., Dec. 24, 1822, d. at Harrisburgh, Pa., Oct. 12, 1875.   She d. at Honesdale, Pa., Feb. 14, 1880 and there were born all her children :

5137.  Walter Erskine[8], b. July 4, 1856 ; m. at Scranton, Pa., Oct. 22, 1881, Mary Scott Lord.   He d. in New York City, Jan. 16, 1882.
5138.  Joseph Benjamin, b. Oct. 15, 1858; m. at Hartford, Ct., Nov. 9, 1881, Louise B. Hunt.   Child:
  5139.  Jeannette[9], b. at Honesdale, Pa.
5140.  George Du Bois, b. Nov. 29, 1859 ; m. at Scranton, Pa., June 8, 1881, Frances Byington Boyd.
5141.  Charles Hunter, b. Jan. 3, 1862 ; d. at Honesdale, Sept. 21, 1862.
5142.  John Carr, b. Aug. 13, 1865 ; d. at Honesdale, Nov. 24, 1865.
5143.  Edward or Frederick Marsh, b. June 8, 1867 ; d. at Honesdale, Aug. 21, 1867.
5144.  Martha Mellen, b. Nov. 7, 1868.
5145.  Maud, b. June 4, 1871.

## 5146 = 5135. JOSEPH RITNER[7] BENJAMIN

b. at Carbondale, Pa., July 25, 1839, son of Martha M[6]. (Mellen) Benjamin, Lucretia[5] (Marsh) Mellen, (Judge Perez[4] Marsh, Capt. Job[3], Daniel[2], John[1]); m. in New York City, Nov. 23, 1871, No. 5146.

**5146.** Abbie Benjamin Sabin, b. at Williamstown, Mass., April 26, 1847. Children b. and d. in New York City:

> 5147. Infant[8], b. Nov. 1, 1872; d. Nov. 6, 1872.
> 5148. Bessie, b. Oct. 6, 1873; d. Jan. 9, 1874.
> 5149. Martha Sabin, b. Nov. 15, 1874.
> 5150. Lucy Seymour, b. Feb. 22, 1877.
> 5151. Bessie Harriet, b. April 5, 1883.

### MARSH—MELLENS.

## 5152 = 4955. CHRISTOPHER MARSH[6] MELLEN

b. at Pittsfield, Mass., July 23, 1806, son of Lucretia[5] (Marsh) Mellen, (Judge Perez[4] Marsh, Capt. Job[3], Daniel[2], John[1]); m. at Hudson, N. Y., Jan. 2, 1839, No. 5152.

**5152.** Catharine Ann Villee, b. at Hudson, Dec. 10, 1809 and d. there Sept. 26, 1850. He d. there July 6, 1852. Children b. and d. there:

> 5153. James Lovett[7], b. Oct. 31, 1840; d. March 27, 1878.
> 5154. Charles Otis, b. March 17, 1842; m. at Carbondale, Pa., Oct. 11, 1864, Maggie Ottman, b. at Greene, N. Y., Nov. 12, 1844. Children b. and d. at Carbondale:
>> 5155. Florence[8], b. March 10, 1866; d. Aug. 6, 1866.
>> 5156. Charles Winthrop, b. Aug. 1, 1868.
> 5157. Cornelia Villee, b. Oct. 1, 1843; m. Carbondale, Oct. 18, 1871, Edward Clarkson, b. at Carbondale, Dec. 6, 1831. Child:
>> 5158. Maggie Jemima[8], b. at Carbondale, Feb. 27, 1874.
> 5159. Samuel Leeds, b. March 7, 1845.
> 5160. Christopher Marsh, b. May 22, 1847.
> 5161. Cornelius Villee, b. and d. Sept., 1850.

## 5162 = 4956.   WILLIAM HENRY[6] MELLEN

b. at Athens, N. Y., Oct. 10, 1810, son of Lucretia[5] (Marsh) Mellen, (Judge Perez[4] Marsh, Capt. Job[3], Daniel[2], John[1]); m. at Hudson, N. Y., Dec. 30, 1832, No. 5162.

**5162.** Catherine Taylor Ostrander, b. at Hudson, June 26, 1812, and d. there Nov. 14, 1881.   Children all b. at Hudson :

5163.  Harriet Sophia[7], b. Feb. 5, 1834 ; d. April 28, 1834.
5164.  Louisa, b. Nov. 23, 1835 ; d. Feb. 16, 1836.
5165.  Isabel, b. Nov. 18, 1837.
5166.  Kate, b. July 2, 1840 ; d. May 13, 1864.
5167.  Harriet Augusta, b. Aug. 4, 1844 ; m. at Hudson, Oct. 2, 1867, Samuel Edwards, b. at Schenectady, April 24, 1839.  No children.


PINNEOS.


## 5168 = 4957.   CHARLOTTE SOPHIA[6] MELLEN

b. at Athens, N. Y., Dec. 17, 1812, dau. of Lucretia[5] (Marsh) Mellen, (Judge Perez[4] Marsh, Capt. Job[3], Daniel[2], John[1]) ; m. at Hudson, N. Y., Dec. 11, 1834, No. 5168.

**5168.** William Williams[5] Pinneo, b. at Milford, Ct., March 16, 1808, son of Beza[4], James[3], James[2], James[1], who came to America in 1685 at time of revocation of the edict of Nantes which had given liberty to Huguenots.  William W. Pinneo was a merchant in New York City and resided in New York City and in Brooklyn and later in Elizabeth, N. J., where he d. Nov. 22, 1873.   Children :

5169.  William Walter[7], b. in New York City, Oct. 28, 1835 ; m. M. S. Montgomery, 5181.
5170.  Mary Sophia, b. in New York City, Dec. 21, 1837 ; d. in Brooklyn, Oct. 30, 1842.
5171.  Sarah, b. in New York City, Oct. 8, 1839.

5172. Joseph Otis, b. in Brooklyn, March 29, 1842; m. in Elizabeth, N. J., Oct. 20, 1869, Esther King Halsey, b. in Sing Sing, N. Y., Jan. 1, 1845. He was M. D. No children.

5173. Susan Sophia, b. in Brooklyn, April 25, 1844; d. in Hudson, Aug. 24, 1844.

5174. Edward Fiske, b. in Brooklyn, July 25, 1845.

5175. James Beza, b. in Brooklyn, Feb. 25, 1848; d. in Elizabeth, N. J., Sept. 14, 1873.

5176. Charles Henry, b. in Brooklyn, Jan. 28, 1850; d. in Brooklyn, April 20, 1851.

5177. Caroline Norton, b. in Brooklyn, March 23, 1852; d. at Elizabeth, March 22, 1879.

5178. Frederick Stedman, b. in Elizabeth, April 2, 1854; m. there May 12, 1881, Katherine Harriott Miller. He was killed on a railroad in New Jersey, Dec. 26, 1883. Child:

5179. Edgar Harriott[8], b. at Elizabeth, Feb. 16, 1882.

5180. Russell Leeds, b. in Elizabeth, Oct. 31, 1856; m. there Dec. 13, 1882, Frederika A. Miller, sister of above.


5181 = 5169. WILLIAM WALTER[7] PINNEO

b. in New York City, Oct. 28, 1835, son of Charlotte Sophia[6] (Mellen) Pinneo, Lucretia[5] (Marsh) Mellen, (Dr. Perez[4] Marsh, Capt. Job[3], Daniel[2], John[1]); m. at Elizabeth, N. J., Dec. 2, 1858, No. 5181.

5181. Maggie Strawbridge Montgomery, b. May 11, 1835; d. at Danville, Pa., April 17, 1865. He d. at New Iberia, La., April 4, 1871. Children:

5182. Helen Montgomery[5], b. in New York City, Nov. 22, 1859.

5183. William Williams, b. in New York City, April 17, 1861; d. at Elizabeth, N. J., Aug. 15, 1884.

5184. Daniel Montgomery, b. in Danville, Nov. 5, 1863; d. there July 12, 1864.

5185. Charlotte Sophia, b. Danville, March 19, 1865.


5186 = 4958. JOHN STODDARD[6] MELLEN

b. at Hudson, N. Y., July 27, 1815, son of Capt. William Henry and Lucretia[5] (Marsh) Mellen, (Judge Perez[4] Marsh, Capt. Job[3], Daniel[2], John[1]); m. at Hudson, Dec. 19, 1838, No. 5186.

**5186.** Sarah Cornelia Thorpe, b. at Hudson, May 19, 1819. He d. there Jan. 24, 1883. Children:

5187. Edwin Stoddard[7], b. at Hudson, Aug, 25, 1840; m. there Jan. 30, 1862, Mary Elizabeth Payne, b. at Chatham, N. Y., July 27, 1842. No children.

5188. William Henry, b. at Greenport, N. Y., May 9, 1843; m. Emeline Merck, (?) b. at St. Johns, N. F., July 27, 1845. Children:

5189. Arthur William[8], b. at Berlin, Wis., Feb. 27, 1872.

5190. Antoinette Louise, b. at New York City, May 23, 1876.

5191. Sophia Pinneo, b. at Hudson, Sept. 28, 1845.

5192. Sarah Cornelia, b. at Hudson, April 26, 1848; m. there Dec. 26, 1867, Norman Henry Niver, b. at Greenport, N. Y., June 17, 1845. Child b. in N. Y. City:

5193. Frederick Mellen[8], b. Jan. 1, 1869.

5194. John Stoddard, b. in Hudson, Sept. 22, 1850, m. at Glencoe, N. Y., Feb. 17, 1875, Charlotte Hoffman, b. at Claverack, N. Y., Sept. 14, 1850. Child:

5195. Charles Ernest[8], b. at Hudson, July 2, 1880.

5196. Caroline Abrams, b. at Hudson, Feb. 9, 1853; m. there Oct. 12, 1876, Henry Etting, b. there May 15, 1846. No children.

5197. Mary Leeds, b. at Hudson, March 12, 1855; m. there Sept. 26, 1878, Amiel Folger, b. there Dec. 17, 1856. No children.

5198. Martha Benjamin, b. at Greenport, N. Y., Aug. 21, 1857.

5199. Louise Billings, b. at Claverack, N. Y., Oct. 16, 1859.

5200. Antoinette, b. at Claverack, Feb. 2, 1863; d. there Oct. 2, 1865.

---

**MARSH—ALLENS.**

---

**5201 = 4689. ELIZABETH[5] MARSH**

b. at Dalton, Mass., Sept. 9, 1776, dau. of Judge Perez[4] Marsh, (Capt. Job[3], Daniel[2], John[1]); m. pub. Aug. 4, 1800, No. 5201.

**5201.** Hon. Jonathan[3] Allen, b. at Pittsfield, Mass., March 23, 1773, son of Rev. Thomas[2] Allen, the "fighting parson" of the battle of Bennington, Joseph[1] Allen of Northampton. The mother of Jonathan[3] was Elizabeth[4] Lee, dau. of Rev. Jonathan[3], David[2], John[1] Lee of ¿Hartford 1635. Hon. Jonathan Allen was town clerk, Pittsfield, 1798–1804, and for some time merchant, partner of Stalham Williams, his wife's cousin, son of Dea. William Williams of Dalton. In 1804–1809 he had banking experience in Boston, and with scores of others was left almost penniless " by the stupendous swindling of Dexter."

Mrs. Elizabeth (Marsh) Allen d. 1805. Her early death, æ. 28, made a profound sensation in Pittsfield where every person knew every other. He m. (2) in Nov., 1807, his niece, No. 5202.

**5202.** Elizabeth Williams[6] Larned, No. 4926, b. Aug. 9, 1791, dau. of Eunice (Marsh) Larned, sister of his first wife. She d. March 17, 1868, æ. 76. His banking failure brought out the man. He went in 1811 to Lisbon and of 6000 sheep of Count Monaca's flocks, confiscated by Napoleon, purchased 100 of the celebrated Merino breed and from Lisbon, Europe's only unblockaded port, brought them to Boston and sold 60 for all expenses and profits. His 40 sheep multiplied (as your historian well knows, from his father's purchases of fine Merinos) on a farm of 200 acres which Mr. Allen bought in 1819 and sold in 1833 ; returned to the village and was postmaster 1837 till his death in 1845. He was selectman 1817–18, in Massachusetts House 1816, 1817, 1821 and 1830, in Massachusetts Senate 1822 and 1823 and in 1825 chosen to give Pittsfield's address of welcome to LaFayette. He was a president of the Berkshire agricultural society and trustee of the Berkshire medical institute. He d. May 26, 1845. Children :

> 5203. George Washington[6], b. about 1801 or 2 ; Colonel in U. S. army, in command of Jefferson Barracks near St. Louis, before the Mexican war ; d. unm. at Vera Cruz, Mex., 1848.
>
> 5204. Charles James Fox, b. about 1803 or 4 ; appraiser U. S. Custom House, Boston ; m. Marie Antoinette Willis of Pittsfield ; d. at Boston in 1861. Children :
>
> > 5205. Marie[7], m. Richard Monks of Boston. One child.
> > 5206. Charles James Fox, m. Miss Belnap of Louisville, Ky. One child.
> > 5207. Lucy Willis, m. Charles Stevens, resides in Chicago. One child.

## By second wife.

5208.  Robert[7], b. Feb. 20, 1810; d. March 21, 1817.
5209.  Frederic William, b. about 1811; d. at Baltsville, Md. in
        1840, æ. 29.
5210.  Thomas, b. Aug. 29, 1813; m. A. C. Russell, 5224.
5211.  Frances Sedgwick, b. July 15, 1815; d. at Pittsfield about
        1839, æ. 24.
5212.  Mary Larned, b. June 3, 1822; m. May 23, 1844, Thomas S.
        O'Sullivan, brother of John, our minister to Spain;
        engineer on Missouri Pacific railroad; killed with
        many others of St. Louis at Gasconade Bridge, Nov. 1,
        1855.  Mrs. O'Sullivan resides at Pittsfield, Mass.
        Children:
    5213.  Herbert[8], b. Feb., 1848; d. June 14, 1852.
    5214.  Louis, b. Oct., 1854; d. Sept. 14, 1859.
5215.  Elizabeth Love, b. Oct. 9, 1826; m. May 20, 1851, H. G.
        Marquand, 5234.
5216.  William, b. at Pittsfield, Mass., Aug. 24, 1824; d. Oct. 23,
        1875 at Davenport, Iowa; graduated at Union college
        1844; m. Nov. 26, 1850, Augusta B. Dorrance of Port-
        land, Me.; colonel in war of 1861, was paymaster Vols.
        U. S. A. and in the ambulance department.  Children:
    5217.  Jennie Allen[8], b. Nov. 12, 1851; m. Josiah A. Crawford,
           June 19, 1871.
    5217.1. Richard, b. July 13, 1853; d. May 7, 1856.
    5217.2. Mary Larned, b. June 24, 1857; d. 1857.
    5218.  William Larned, b. June 7, 1858; m. A. Van Patten,
           5223.3.
    5219.  Thomas, b. Feb. 16, 1860; d. Aug. 9, 1861.
    5219.1. Louis Lee, b. Feb. 2, 1863; d. Aug. 2, 1865.
    5219.2. Ernest Dorrance, b. Aug. 26, 1865.
5220.  Maria Malleville, b. March 16, 1831; m. Aug. 29, 1861, Judge
        Benjamin R. Curtis of Boston of the superior court.
        Children:
    5221.  Allen[8], b. Aug. 14, 1862; m. E. Weston, 5223.1.
    5222.  Edwin Stoughton, b. May 23, 1864; d. in 1871.
    5222.1. Isabella Cochran, b. Oct. 16, 1866; d. in 1867.
    5222.2. Amy Hope, b. July, 1869; d. May 4, 1871.
5223.  Robert, b. in 1835; d. in 1872.  Was employed on the Iron
        Mt. railroad.  Resided at St. Louis; unm.


### 5223.1 = 5221.  ALLEN[8] CURTIS

b. Aug. 14, 1862, son of Judge Benjamin R. and Maria Malleville[7]
(Allen) Curtis, Eunice W[6]. (Larned) Allen, Eunice[5] (Marsh) Larned,

(Judge Perez[4] Marsh, Capt. Job[3], Daniel[2], John[1]) ; m. No. 5223.1.

**5223.1.** Evelyn Weston. Child :

    5223.2. Evelyn[9], b. June 30, 1891.


5223.3 = 5218. WILLIAM LARNED[8] ALLEN

son of William Allen ; m. Oct. 1, 1885, No. 5223.3.

**5223.3.** Alice Van Patten. Children :

    5223.4. Larned Van Patten[9], b. Feb. 21, 1887.
    5223.5. Elizabeth Marian, b. March 23, 1892.
    5223.6. William Seabury, b. Aug. 8, 1894.


5224 = 5209. HON. THOMAS[7] ALLEN, M. C., LL. D.

b. at Pittsfield, Mass., Aug. 29, 1813, son of Jonathan and Eunice Williams[6] (Larned) Allen, grand-son Eunice[5], (Marsh) Larned, (Judge Perez[4] Marsh, Capt. Job[3], Daniel[2], John[1]) ; graduated at Union college 1832, admitted to the bar in New York City when 22, went to Washington in winter of 1836–7, was made editor of the *Madisonian*, and I take these words from the eulogy of Senator Dawes in the U. S. senate chamber, June 23, 1882 : "At the opening of congress (1837) Mr. Allen, then only 23, was elected by the house of representatives public printer and two years later was elected to the same office by the senate. Our history furnishes no parallel to this bestowal by the house of representatives and the senate of the U. S. successively of such power and responsibility upon one so young." He m. July 12, 1842, No. 5224.

**5224.** Ann Clementina Russell, dau. of Judge William Russell of St. Louis who went to St. Louis in 1803, before the Spanish flag was taken down, on Napoleon's transfer of Louisiana to the U. S.

Mr. Allen removed to St. Louis and more than any other man finally stirred slow-going Missouri and St. Louis to enter upon their grand railroad destiny. It was like Cyrus Field's ups and downs in laying the Atlantic cable. But Mr. Allen pulled through. He became first president of the Missouri Pacific railroad 1850–54, president of the St. Louis & Terre Haute railroad, 1857–8 ; president of the Iron

Mountain railroad.  He was four years state senator in Missouri and finally member of congress.  He spent summers in Pittsfield, erecting an elegant homestead at the old place by the public square.  He bought for $20,000, the farm where his father had lived for a time. He gave the " Berkshire Athenaeum," a stately free library and museum, to his native town.  He was a life long democrat and an ardent Union man.  The Pittsfield company for the war of the Union was named for him the Allen Guards.  After his election in Nov., 1880 to the 47th congress by the second district of Missouri he traveled extensively in Europe to regain health, took his seat at Washington in Dec., 1881, but on April 8, 1882 at Washington, as Senator Dawes expresses it, having been true to the motto of his fathers, " Fortiter geret crucem," he gave up doing as he longed to do, something more for Missouri and died in the Christian faith. Children :

5225.  Elizabeth Larned[8], b. Aug. 12, 1843; m. William R. Donalson of St. Louis.

5226.  Frances Mary, b. June 6, 1845; d. April 1, 1846.

5227.  William Russell, b. Jan. 19, 1847; m. May 20, 1874, Louisa Billings Woodward.

5228.  Thomas, b. Oct. 19, 1849; artist; m. (1) at Northampton, Mass., June 30, 1880, Eleanor Goddard Whitney, b. at Northampton, Nov. 29, 1856, dau. of Prof. Josiah Dwight Whitney, LL. D. of Cambridge, Mass., and Eleanor Goddard, dau. of Samuel of Brookline, Mass. Prof. Whitney was nephew of Sarah (Whitney) Marsh, No. 5249.  Mrs. Allen d. at Ècouen, France, near Paris, May 14, 1882.  Mr. Allen m. (2) Oct. 23, 1884, Alice Ranney.  Children :

5228.1.  Eleanor Whitney[9], b. April 18, 1882, at Ècouen, France.

5228.2.  Thomas, b. Feb. 24, 1887.

5228.3.  Eric, b. Jan. 17, 1890; d. June 21, 1890.

5228.4.  Robert Fletcher, b. Nov. 17, 1892.

5229.  George Washington, b. March 31, 1852.

5230.  Bradford, b. Aug. 27, 1854; d. at St. Louis in 1884, leaving a wife and dau. 7 years old.

5231.  Annie Lee, b. Oct. 6, 1857.

5232.  Grace, b. June 27, 1860; d. Jan. 30, 1864.

5233.  Alice Maude, b. Jan. 2, 1864; m. June 20, 1888, Charles L. Atwater.

## 5234 = 5215.  ELIZABETH LOVE[7] ALLEN

b. at Pittsfield, Mass., Oct. 9, 1826, dau. of Jonathan and Eunice Williams[6] (Larned) Allen, Eunice[5] (Marsh) Larned, (Judge Perez[4] Marsh, Capt. Job[3], Daniel[2], John[1]) ; m. at Pittsfield, Mass., May 20, 1851, No. 5234.

**5234.** Henry Gurdon[3] Marquand, b. April 11, 1819, son of Isaac[2], who d. Nov. 24, 1838 and Mabel Perry of Fairfield, Ct., son of Henry[1], b. Island of Guernsey, July 8, 1737 ; m. Lucretia Jennings of Fairfield, Ct., and d. there July 12, 1772. The family have given largely to Yale and Princeton colleges. Mr. H. G. Marquand is well known in New York and St. Louis as connected with the Iron Mountain and other railroad interests as banker and financier. They resided in New York City. She died Feb. 3, 1895. Children :

    5235. Linda[8], b. at Rome, Italy, May 1, 1852 ; m. Sept.. 1875, Roderick Terry. Children :

        5236. Roderick[9].

        5237. Eunice.

    5238. Allan, b. in New York, Dec. 10, 1853 ; professor at Princeton, N. J.

    5239. Frederick Alexander, b. at Southport, Ct., Sept. 26, 1855 ; m. in 1881, Alice Oyston ; d. at Lawrence, L. I., Dec. 20, 1885. Children :

        5240. Alice Oyston[9].

        5241. Elizabeth Love.

    5242. Henry, b. in New York, April 5, 1857.

    5243. Mabel, b. in New York, Oct. 29, 1860.

    5244. Elizabeth Love, b. in New York, June 16, 1862 ; m. Harold Godwin.

## 5245 = 4687.  HENRY[5] MARSH, SR.

b. at Dalton, Mass., Sept. 11, 1771, son of Judge Perez[4] and Sarah (Williams) Marsh, (Capt. Job[3] of Hadley, Mass., Daniel[2] of Hadley, John[1] of England, Hartford and Hadley) ; m. April, 1796, No. 5245.

**5245.** Betsey Lawrence of notable descent, b. March 27, 1777, dau. of Rev. Micah, Harvard college, 1759 and Eunice (Willard) Lawrence. Her mother was descended from Richard[1] Willard of Kent, England ; d. 1617 and from his son the distinguished Kentish

soldier of our early history, Major Simon[2] Willard, b. May, 1605 who
m. Mary Dunster, sister of the first president of. Harvard college.
The line came down through Henry[3] and Dorcas Cutler, Josiah[4] and
Hannah Wilder, Col. Josiah[5] and Hannah[5] Hubbard of George[1]
Hubbard, John[2] of Hadley, Jonathan[3], Major Jonathan[4], Hannah[5]
and Colonel Josiah[5] Willard, Eunice[6] (Willard) and Rev. Micah
Lawrence to Betsey[7] (Lawrence) Marsh. On the father's side the
descent being the same with that of Abbott Lawrence, minister to
England in 1849, is definitely traced from Robert Lawrence of Lan-
cashire who attended Richard I. to Palestine in 1191 and for distinguished service in the siege of Acre was knighted " Sir Robert of
Ashton Hall." Those who wish can trace this descent for 16 generations in England to Henry[16] Lawrence b. at Wisset, England 1609
and of Charlestown, Mass., 1635. See " Family of John Lawrence,
1636–1869." The American line is Henry's son John[1], Nathaniel[2],
John[3], John[4], Rev. Micah[5], Betsey[6] (Lawrence) Marsh. Henry Marsh,
Sen., although not a churchmember, as a magistrate had enough of
the Puritan to sometimes stop highway travelers and not allow them
to go forward on Sunday. He removed his residence and built a
pleasant new residence, with ample hall and with cheerful fireplaces
in both stories. I remember well the marble hearth, brass andirons
and fender. He had five sisters married in Pittsfield with troops of
children and being the head of the Dalton household he made his
home cheerful with a marked hospitality. Frequent welcomes made
glad times. They had only three children. He d. in his new home
in Dalton Sept. 8, 1824, æ. 55, like his father æ. 54 and grandfather
æ. 56, not having attained to the 70 years of John[1] or the 72 of
Daniel[2]. His widow lived generally with her son, but always where
she could best serve her children. She d. at the home of her dau.
Harriet, Mrs. Dr. Kittredge, in Hinsdale, Mass., Feb. 26, 1847, æ.
70. Children all b. at Dalton :

> 5246. Henry[6], b. Feb. 9, 1797 ; m. Sarah Whitney, 5249.
> 5247. Sarah Williams, b. Aug. 2, 1799 ; m. Col. G. D. Weston, 5258.
> 5248. Harriet, b. Oct. 22, 1809 ; m. Dr. B. F. Kittredge, 5268.

### 5249 = 5246. HENRY[6] MARSH, ESQ.

b. at Dalton, Mass., Feb. 9, 1797 ; son of Henry[5] of Dalton, (Judge
Perez[4], Capt. Job[3] of Hadley, Daniel[2], John[1] of Hartford) ; graduated

at Williams college, 1815, Harvard law school, one of the first three, in 1818, admitted to bar 1819. He represented Dalton in the Massachusetts legislature in 1819, 1833 and 1835. He m. at Northampton, Mass., Sept. 5, 1821, No. 5249.

**5249.** Sarah Whitney, b. at Westfield, Mass., July 8, 1796. Herself a teacher and of a highly educated lineage, her grandfather Rev. Aaron Whitney was of Harvard College 1737, her father Major Abel Whitney, Harvard college 1777, her mother's father, Judge and Col. Josiah Dwight, Yale college 1736, her mother's brothers graduated both at Harvard college, Thomas Dwight in 1778 and Josiah in 1786. Her brother's sons are now 1893, professors in Harvard, Yale and Beloit. She taught in New Haven and in Maryland and at Hopkins academy, Hadley, as assistant of Daniel Huntington, father of the Bishop, where her brother's wife, Sarah Williston, had preceded her ; both of them teaching only before marriage, except their children.. Having such a wife and both of his own grandfathers having graduated at Harvard College, it was not strange perhaps that Henry[8] Marsh should have three sons at one time in his Alma Mater, Williams college. He was an active business man, having in his day the finest sheep barn in Berkshire county and over 2000 sheep, some from Mr. Jonathan Allen's, his cousin's imported flock. But when prospered he told his children that he meant to give them a good education and that very likely the education might be all. In 1839–43 he spent three years in Pittsfield. The Ashuelot Manufacturing Co., in which he had been most concerned failed and in the autumn of 1843 he went west and entered with two of his sons into mercantile and shipping business on the lakes at Racine, Wis. and in 1846 at Sandusky City, O., from which place in 1850 with his son Calvin Waldo he went to St. Louis and was extensively engaged in purchases of wheat and other produce when his oldest son, Henry Lawrence, was taken with cholera at Lasalle, Ill. and the father going to care for him was himself taken down and d. June 4, 1852, æ. 55. The son d. June 10, æ. 30. Henry[6] Marsh, Esq., was a fascinating man, an eloquent speaker, a successful Sunday school superintendent, an active Christian. His Saviour knew best what discipline was necessary for him. An only son, and among the very numerous descendants of his grandfather, Judge Perez[4], the only grandson of Marsh name, his father could not bear to have him go, as he wished, to New

30

York City and carry on his profession of law.   How different might
have been his life !   But it is well !

Sarah Whitney was dau. of Major Abel, who was aid of Gen. Shep-
ard at Springfield in the Shay's rebellion.   Her mother's father, Col.
Josiah Dwight, was judge of Hampshire County (then all western
Massachusetts) 1750–1768, time of his death, and his father Capt.
Henry Dwight, judge from 1727–1731 ; d. March 26, 1732.   Her
father d. March 2, 1807, when she was ten and her brother Josiah
Dwight Whitney then twenty, afterwards merchant and banker of
Northampton, promised and kept his promise to be a father to her.
He was unspeakably kind to her and her children.   Her mother m.
(2) July 4, 1809 Calvin Waldo, Esq., b. at Mansfield, Ct., March 12,
1759, son of Shubael and Abigail (Allen) Waldo, graduated at Dartmouth college 1785, a lawyer of Dalton, Mass.   Mrs. Waldo lived
there till his death Aug. 25, 1815, and after that with her son J. D.
and d. at his house in Northampton, Aug. 22, 1820.   Sarah Whitney
showed her character by standing up all alone in the very large old
church at Northampton, as the old records quaintly say, " April 18,
1819, Sarah Whitney received to communion by vote of ye church."
After marriage 1821, and death of her husband 1852, she lived with
her children in St. Louis, Mo., Batavia, Ill., Pittsfield, Mass. and
from her 75th to her 86th year, eleven years of most healthy and
happy old age in the family of her son Dwight W. at Owego, N. Y.
and at Amherst and Haydenville, Mass., close by the scenes of her
early days.   In 1882 her dau. Mrs. Eager of Racine, Wis., persuaded
her to return from Amherst and spend her closing days at her home.
She grew feebler, yet enjoying life and March 11, 1883 having lived
a beautiful Christian life of 86 years and 8 months, she passed on to
the land where she was ready and glad to go.   Her grave is in
Racine cemetery near that of her eldest son.   Children :

> 5250.  Henry Lawrence[7], b. July 9, 1822 ; m. Clara E. Canfield,
> 5285.
> 5251.  Dwight Whitney, b. Nov. 5, 1823 ; m. (1) Julia W. Peck,
> 5289.
> 5252.  Calvin Waldo, b. April 8, 1825 ; m. Anna W. King, 5296.
> 5253.  Robert, b. April 25, 1828 ; d. Dec. 18, 1828.
> 5254.  Elizabeth Willard, b. Nov. 28, 1829, see No. 5298.1
> 5255.  Clarissa Dwight, b. Feb. 4, 1834 ; m. S. W. Eager, 5299.
> 5256.  Sarah Williams, b. May 24, 1836 ; d. at Pittsfield, Mass.,
> May 14, 1841, æ. 5.

5257. Charles Francis, b. at Pittsfield, Oct. 11, 1842, after boyhood resided mainly at Barre and Northampton, unm.

## 5258 = 5247. SARAH WILLIAMS[6] MARSH

b. at Dalton, Mass., Aug. 2, 1799, dau. of Henry[5] Marsh, Sr. and Betsey (Lawrence) Marsh, Judge Perez[4] and Sarah (Williams) Marsh, (Capt. Job[3], Daniel[2], John[1]); m. Nov. 2, 1820, No. 5258.

**5258.** Col. Grenville Dean[2] Weston of Dalton, b. at New Bedford, Mass., Nov. 16, 1797, son of Isaiah and uncle of Gov. Byron Weston. He was a man of fine presence, often marshal at the Berkshire county gatherings, a singer of wonderful bass voice, a merchant. Mrs. Weston d. in March, 1841. Col. Weston d. Dec. 1, 1866, both in Dalton. Children:

> 5259. Sarah Dean[7], b. Aug. 11, 1822; m. Oct., 1855, Orson Dayton and resided in Hudson, Mich. Children:
>> 5260. Grenville Weston[8].
>> 5261. Hattie Louise.
>> 5262. Willard B.
> 5263. Grenville M., b. Feb. 25, 1829; m. Nov. 24, 1858, Helen M. Norris of Sandusky, O. Mrs. Weston d. at Toledo, O., Oct. 4, 1868. He m. (2) Aug. 30, 1871, Elizabeth Reeve McLaren, who d. Sept. 2, 1876. He resided at Memphis, Tenn. and at St. James, Minn. and d. at St. Paul, Minn., Jan. 29, 1890. Children:
>> 5264. Grenville Norris[8], b. Jan. 28, 1860; m. Dec. 25, 1884, Lulu B. Hammond who d. in Florida, probably in 1889. Child:
>>> 5264.1. Grenville Heman[9], b. Dec. 10, 1885.
>> 5265. Gracia Marston, b. Dec. 18, 1861; d. unm.
>> 5266. Bessie, b. Aug. 15, 1867.
>> 5266.1. Grace Marsh, b. Nov. 22, 1872.
>> 5266.2. William McLaren, b. Nov. 17, 1874.
> 5267. Harriet, b. Nov. 30, 1831; m. Oct. 15, 1857, Samuel Mills Smead, M. D., grad. Feb. 22, 1854, Western Reserve Medical college; resided at Madison, O.; Deputy U. S. Marshal 14 years, 1873-1887; d. at Madison, O., June 30, 1888.

## 5268 = 5248. HARRIET[6] MARSH

b. at Dalton, Mass., Oct. 22, 1809, dau. of Henry[5], Sr. and Betsey

(Lawrence) Marsh, (Judge Perez[4], Capt. Job[3], Daniel[2], John[1]); m.
May 19, 1829, at Dalton, No. 5268.

5268.    Benjamin F. Kittredge, M. D., b. July 11, 1802, in Dalton,
resided at Hinsdale, Mass.  He was b. in Dalton only as that part
of Hinsdale where he always lived was not taken from Dalton until
1804.  " Dr. Frank," as he was generally called to distinguish him
from his father, Dr. Abel, was one of the most prominent men in
Hinsdale, as were his father and his brother Hon. Charles J. Kittredge.  He took his M. D. 1828, became member of the Massachusetts medical society, 1838 and practiced extensively in several towns.
He was a man of much humor and used often to call his eighth daughter "Capt. Jim."  " A true friend and a good citizen, both his family
and the town met with great loss in his death."  He d. April 18,
1862, in his 60th year.  Mrs. Kittredge was a model mother and a
noble Christian.  She d. Apr. 21, 1886.  Children :

5269.    Harriet Cornelia[7], b. April 16, 1830; m. Hon. James White
        5279.
5270.    Elizabeth Payson, b. Jan. 20, 1833 ; resides unm. in 1895, in
        Hinsdale.
5271.    Julia Root, b. March 12, 1835 ; m. May 17, 1865, Mr. Ira S.
        Johnson of Canaan, N. Y.; farmer and stockraiser.  He
        d. at Washington, D. C., April 6, 1890.  At his funeral
        in Canaan, the presence of men of note from Washing-
        ton, New York City, Albany, Hudson, N. Y. and Berk-
        shire, Mass., testified strongly to his worth, more marked
        at Canaan was the closing of hotel, post office and stores
        and suspension of all business.  The front of the Pres-
        byterian church of which he had been a consistent
        member was heavily draped in mourning and it was
        manifest as testified that " He was one of Nature's
        noblemen, whom all delighted to honor."  " He loved
        Canaan and its people and they in turn loved him."
        Mrs. Johnson resided at Canaan.  She d. Aug. 15, 1893.
        Child :
5272.    Jason Franklin[8], b. April 22, 1868; d. April 15, 1869.
5273.    Frances Janette, b. Nov. 21, 1837 ; m. James Hosmer, Esq.,
        5282.
5274.    Eunice Chamberlain, b. May 5, 1840 ; d. Sept. 2, 1861.
5275.    Sarah Marsh, b. July 22, 1842 ; resides in 1895, unm. at
        Hinsdale.
5276.    Mary Worthington, b. Sept. 22, 1843 ; d. Aug. 25, 1864.
5277.    Katherine Waldo, b. Aug. 14, 1846 ; d. May 19, 1882.
5278.    Infant daughter, b. and d. Oct. 11, 1849.

5279 = 5269. HARRIET CORNELIA[7] KITTREDGE

b. at Hinsdale, Mass., April 16, 1830, dau. of Harriet[6] (Marsh) Kittredge, (Henry[5] Marsh, Judge Perez[4], Capt. Job[3], Daniel[2], John[1]) ; m. Jan. 22, 1856, No. 5279.

**5279.** Hon. James White of Boston, b. at Hinsdale, Mass., July 9, 1828, graduated at Williams college 1851, teacher two years at Williston seminary, Easthampton, Mass., left study for ministry in his second year at Andover owing to trouble with eyes, entered upon business in Boston in firm of White, Browne & Co., importers, and prospered. He was elected a trustee of Williams college in 1881 and its treasurer in 1886, when he removed to Williamstown. While in Boston he was an officer of the Central church and very efficient as an officer of the Home missionary, City missionary and other benevolent societies. Children:

5280. Lizzie Davis[8], b. Nov. 25, 1859.
5281. Franklin Kittredge, b. Dec. 3, 1866, Williams college, 1890.

5282 = 5273. FRANCES J[7]. KITTREDGE

b. at Hinsdale, Mass., Nov. 21, 1837, dau. of Harriet[6] (Marsh) Kittredge, (Henry[5] Marsh, Judge Perez[4], Capt. Job[3], Daniel[2], John[1]) ; m. Dec. 14, 1859, No. 5282.

**5282.** James Hosmer, Esq. He was for a time in business with his father in Boston and later removed to Hinsdale as accountant in the Plunkett Woolen Co., and now (1893) in the Gov. Byron Weston paper mills. He has been an indispensable aid in the Hinsdale creamery. His services in the Congregational church have been invaluable. He was son of Zelotes Hosmer, Esq., of Cambridge who had as early as 1849 one of the most pleasant residences and finest private libraries in Cambridge, who "kept on his counting room desk for purposes of business the last *Edinburgh, London Quarterly* or *North American Review*" and was "so well read in English history and topography as to have almost a tourist's familiarity with Stratford-on-Avon, the Bodleian Library and the British Museum." Zelotes Hosmer was for 12 years superintendent of the Shepard Sunday school, Cambridge. He was son of Charles and

Lydia Hosmer and descended from James Hosmer of Concord, 1637.
The line of Mrs. Zelotes Hosmer, whose maiden name was Louisa
Lawrence, and was from Rev. Micah Lawrence, through Hubbard
and Mary, dau. of Major Phillip Goss.    See Betsey Lawrence, No.
5245, sister of Hubbard, for Rev. Micah, their father and see the
John Lawrence Book for line unbroken from Sir Robert Lawrence,
crusader, 1191 with King Richard I. of England, James and Frances
(Kittredge) Hosmer, second cousins and both of Lawrence descent,
the same family with Abbott Lawrence of Boston our former minister
to England.    Reside in Hinsdale.    Children:

> 5283.    Mary Kittredge[8], b. Oct. 4, 1864; d. Sept. 9, 1867.
> 5284.    Harriet Louisa, b. March 27, 1867 ; d. Sept. 28, 1868.

## 5285 = 5250.    HENRY LAWRENCE[7] MARSH

b. at Dalton, Mass., July 9, 1822, son of Henry[6] and Sarah (Whitney)
Marsh, Henry[5] and Betsey (Lawrence) Marsh, Judge Perez[4] and
Sarah (Williams) Marsh, Capt. Job[3] and Mehitable (Porter) Marsh,
Daniel[2] and Hannah (Lewis) Marsh, John[1] and Annie (Webster)
Marsh; Williams college 1841 ; m. at Racine, Wis., Sept. 25, 1845,
No. 5285.

**5285.**    Clara Ellis Canfield of Racine, b. at Sandisfield, Berkshire
County, Mass., Feb. 13, 1825, dau. of Roswell and Deborah Canfield.

Except a short time Sandusky, Ohio, Henry L. and family resided
at Racine, Wis., where at very early age he became an elder in the
Presbyterian church.    While at Sandusky he contributed able articles
to the *City Press* in advocacy of the public schools and was a liberal
donor to Western Reserve college.    He was a merchant at Racine
and also engaged in lumber business.    While at Lasalle, Ill., he was
taken with cholera and d. there July 10, 1852, æ. 30.

Roswell Canfield and his sons were greatly prospered in business,
but Mr. Canfield and his oldest son died and also his two daughters
lost their husbands very early and the three widows Mrs. Canfield,
Mrs. Smith and Mrs. Marsh lived long together bringing up the grand-
children as one family in their pleasant home on Main St., Racine,
where Mrs. Smith and Mrs. Marsh are (1895) living still.    Children:

> 5286.    Henry Whitney[8], b. Feb. 8, 1847 ; m. C. Ramsdell, 5306.
> 5287.    Maria Canfield, b. Jan. 8, 1849 ; m. J. M. Clark, 5312.
> 5288.    Lizzie Dwight, b. Nov. 3, 1851 ; d. Sept. 21, 1852.

5289 = 5251. REV. DWIGHT WHITNEY[7] MARSH, D. D.

b. at Dalton, Mass., Nov. 5, 1823, son of Henry,[6] Jr. and Sarah (Whitney) Marsh, (Henry[5], Judge Perez[4], Capt. Job[3], Daniel[2], John[1]); Williams College 1842, A. M. 1845, at Andover Theological Seminary 1842–3, teacher at St. Louis, Mo. 1843–7, graduated at Union Theological Seminary, N. Y. City 1849; m. (1) Oct. 19, 1852, by Dr. Cheever at New York City to No. 5289.

**5289.** Julia White Peck, b. at Hartford, Ct., June 10, 1829, dau. of Elisha and Mary Jane (Averill) Peck of Hartford, Ct. and New York City. Mr. Marsh was ten and one-half years a missionary at Mosul, Turkey. Layard gave to him and he sent from that place to Williams college the first Nineveh slabs that were ever sent to this country. He went out engaged but unmarried in 1849 and returned in 1852 and was married spending only five months in this country.

Julia White Peck was named with reference to Bishop White. Her mother d. in N. Y. City at the house of Augustine Averill, Esq. at the early age of 29 years and 10 months. She then came under the care and teaching for a time of Miss Sarah McLean in the family of Rev. Allen McLean, A. M., graduated at Yale College, 1805, the famous blind clergyman so long at Simsbury, Ct. Her teacher became her father's second wife and these new relations were to Miss Peck of inestimable value. After completing her education in Hartford and at the Spingler Institute, N. Y., she taught both in N. Y. City, her parent's home, and in New Haven, that of her only sister, Mrs. Charles Allen, who d. at the early age of her mother, 29 years and 10 months. She sailed from Boston, Jan. 7, 1853, with her husband, and did a valuable missionary work, very much beloved by her missionary associates, one of whom, Mrs. Walker, now of Auburndale, wrote, "when I go to heaven I expect to see her in the midst of a group of angels and they listening to her!" She closed her beautiful life at Mosul, Aug. 12, 1859.

Mr. Marsh returned to our country, Aug. 19, 1860 and spent a year in making missionary addresses under direction of the American Board and at their request, the war coming on, another year and more preaching at Hinsdale, Mass. Then responsibilities in connection with his father's family, decided him with the approval of Dr. Anderson and Secretary Treat, to remain in this country. He m. (2) at Rochester, N. Y., Aug. 21, 1862, No. 5290.

**5290.** Elizabeth Le Baron Clarke, b. at Winchendon, Mass., Aug. 24, 1833, dau. of Rev. Eber Liscom Clarke, Williams college 1811, and Sarah Lawrence, descended from 1, Lawyer Daniel[1] Clarke, b. 1623, who came to Windsor, Ct., 1639, with his uncle Rev. Ephraim Huit, magistrate and secretary Hartford colony 1644 and on, m. March 13, 1644, Mary Newberry, dau. of Thomas of Windsor, Ct., 1636 and d. Aug. 12, 1710, æ. 87 ; she d. Oct. 13, 1719 ; 2, Daniel[2] Clarke, Jr., b. April 5, 1654 ; d. 1710, æ. 56 ; m. 1678, Hannah[3] Pratt, Daniel[2], John[1] of Hartford, d. 1655 ; 3, Aaron[3] Clarke, bap. Hartford, Nov. 17, 1687 ; m. Susannah ; 4, Lemuel[4] Clarke, b. Nov. 24, 1731, d. June 25, 1801, æ. 70 ; m. Mercy Bridges, dau. of Edward of Colchester, Ct., d. May 7, 1762 ; 5, Eliphalet[5] Clarke, b. Jan. 7, 1761, d. June 2, 1840, æ. 79 ; m. Hepzibah Fay, b. 1763, d. 1814, æ. 51, dau. of Capt. Jedediah ; 6, Rev. Eber Liscom[6] Clarke, b. March 23, 1786, d. 1857, æ. 71 ; m. Sept. 19, 1832, Sarah[4] Lawrence, b. July 17, 1798, d. April 17, 1886 ; 7, Elizabeth Le Baron[7] Clarke. Her mother was dau. of Grove[3] and Elizabeth[6] (Robbins) Lawrence, son of Ariel[2] and Lucy Wilcox, Samuel[1] Lawrence. Her grandmother Elizabeth Robbins[6] was dau. of Rev. Ammi Ruhamah[5] Robbins and Elizabeth Le Baron, Rev. Philemon[4] Robbins of Brantford, Ct., and Hannah[4] Foote, Dr. Isaac[3] Foote and Rebecca Dickerman, Robert[2] and Sarah, Nathaniel[1] Foote, b. in England, about 1593, freeman Watertown, Mass. 1634, Wethersfield 1636, d. 1644, æ. about 51 ; m. Elizabeth Deming, b. about 1693. She m. (2) Gov. Thomas Welles and d. July 28, 1683, æ. about 88. Rev. Philemon[4] Robbins, Harvard college 1729, was son of Nathaniel[3], b. in Cambridge 1678, Nathaniel[2], b. in Cambridge 1649, Richard[1] of Cambridge, Mass., emigrated as early as 1639. Elizabeth[3] Le Baron, great grandmother of Elizabeth Le Baron (Clarke) Marsh, was dau. of Lazarus[2] Le Baron and Lydia Bradford, Surgeon Francis[1] Le Baron and Mary Wilder, dau. of Edward Wilder and Elizabeth Eames, dau. of Anthony Eames. Lydia[4] Bradford, great great grandmother of Elizabeth Le Baron (Clarke) Marsh, was dau. of David[3] Bradford and Elizabeth Finney ; son of William[2] and Mary Holmes (Atwood) Bradford, son of Gov. William[1] Bradford of the Mayflower. Elizabeth Finney was dau of Josiah Finney and Elizabeth Warren, son of John Finney and Elizabeth Bailey. Elizabeth[3] Warren, was dau. of Priscilla Farmer and Joseph[2] Warren, son of Richard[1] Warren of the Mayflower. Rebecca[3] Dickerman above, b. 1679, d. Oct. 15, 1757, was dau. of

Lieut. Abraham² Dickerman, b. Jan. 3, 1658 and Mary dau. of John Cooper, Thomas¹ Dickerman, of Dorchester, Mass., 1636 and New Haven later; m. Ellen. Thus Mrs. Marsh had a double descent from the Mayflower and her Le Baron ancestor was a surgeon on a French privateer that was captured at the upper end of Buzzards Bay in 1694, when Dr. Le Baron joined the Plymouth colony.

Mr. and Mrs. Marsh resided in 1862–69 at Rochester, N. Y., associate principals with Miss Sara C. Eaton in Rochester Seminary for young ladies, except one year at Godfrey, Ill., 1867–8, Monticello Station. While at Monticello Mr. Marsh wrote "The Tennessean in Persia," pub. by Presbyterian Board at Philadelphia. Success in teaching at Rochester was so manifest that Mr. Marsh was by the trustees unanimously elected in 1869 president of the Rogersville university, Tenn., which after a journey to Tennessee and careful inspection he declined, preferring pastoral work; 1869–71 at Whitneys Point, N. Y.; 1871–76 at Owego, N. Y.; 1876–78 at Amherst, Mass.; 1878–82 Haydenville, Mass. He was made D. D. by Williams college in 1873. Since 1882 they have resided in Amherst, Mass. Children :

5291.  Henry⁸, b. at Mosul, Turkey, July 19, 1854; d. Aug. 1, 1854.
5292.  Waldo, b. at Mosul, Turkey, Dec. 15, 1856; d. May 5, 1859.
       By second wife.
5293.  William Dwight, b. at Bernardston, Mass., Nov. 21, 1865; Amherst College 1888, now (1895) preaching at Schroon Lake, N. Y.
5294.  Elizabeth Lawrence, b. Sept. 8, 1869, at Bernardston; d. Sept. 3, 1884, at Amherst, Mass.
5295.  Helen Whitney, b. Sept. 9, 1871, at Owego, N. Y.; d. there July 18, 1872.


5296 = 5252. COL. CALVIN WALDO⁷ MARSH

b. at Dalton, Mass., April 8, 1825, son of Henry⁶ Jr. and Sarah (Whitney) Marsh, (Henry⁵, Judge Perez⁴, Capt. Job³, Daniel², John¹) ; was in Williams college one year, was in shipping business and a vessel owner on the great lakes at Sandusky, O., 1846–50, when he removed to St. Louis, Mo. and was commission merchant there. He m. Dec. 26, 1860, at Roxbury, Mass., No. 5296.

**5296.** Anna Ward King, dau. of John King, artist of Boston, and Mary (Luke) King. He became a member of company A, 7th Missouri militia, National Guard. When the war began, that company was composed mostly of southern sympathizers and at a regular meeting it was resolved to expel from its ranks all Union men. Mr. Marsh received written notice of his expulsion and pasted it on his desk, thinking it honor that his loyalty was thus noticed. That company went with the rebel Gen. Price into the Confederate army. He was then made Major of the 5th Missouri Volunteers, was present at taking of Camp Jackson and went to Springfield, Mo., under Gen. Lyon. He was then promoted to rank of Lieut. Col. and placed on Gen. Schofield's staff as Assistant Adjutant General. The " Rebellion Record " of the war shows that he was generally in charge of Gen. Schofield's headquarters office at St. Louis where general orders required all correspondence to be directed to Lieut. Col. Marsh. But about the time of the battle of Pea Ridge he was at the front in Arkansas, as appears in one of Maj. Gen. Schofield's letters dated Osage Spring, Arkansas, Oct. 1, 1862 : "Col. Marsh has arrived." After the war he remained at St. Louis, and d. June 25, 1873. The children reside with their mother in Denver, Col. Children :

> 5297.  Waldo King[S], b. Sept. 19, 1861; in national bank, Denver.
> 5298.  Mary Gordon, b. June 8, 1864.

### 5298.1.   ELIZABETH WILLARD[7] MARSH

b. in Dalton, Mass., Nov. 28, 1829, was educated at Maplewood, Pittsfield, Mt. Holyoke and Bradford Seminaries, and spent her life in teaching. She had a school in St. Louis, and at Batavia, Ill., and afterwards taught in private families in Pittsfield, Mass., Batavia, N. Y. and Hudson, Wis. At the latter place on Lake St. Croix she made her home with her life-long friend, Mrs. Charles W. Porter, dau. of Judge Lockwood of Batavia, Ill. Western people have warm hearts. The love of that family to her was a beautiful thing, brightening and blessing her life. She died at Hudson, Wis., April 23, 1882.

## 5299 = 5255. CLARISSA DWIGHT[7] MARSH

b. in Dalton, Mass., Feb. 4, 1834, dau. of Henry[6], Jr. and Sarah (Whitney) Marsh, grand-daughter of Clarissa (Dwight) Whitney, (Henry[5], Judge Perez[4], Capt. Job[3], Daniel[2], John[1]) ; m. May 7, 1857, No. 5299.

**5299.** Capt. Samuel Watkins Eager, Jr., b. Nov. 19, 1827, son of Hon. Samuel W. Eager, member of congress of Newburg, Orange Co., N. Y. and Catherine Macaulay. He is a lawyer and member of the Grand Army. He went to St. Louis in 1845 and remained till 1868 when he removed to Racine, Wis., where he now resides (1895). He was clerk in the court house, St. Louis for 18 years, 1849–67 ; and for six years was clerk of St. Louis city and county, a very important office. Having been so long in the court house he knew loyal men and rebels by heart. Having charge of that noblest building in St. Louis, he kept flying over its dome the flag of the Union (one 37 feet by 70 and hoisted some 200 feet high) visible for 10 to 20 miles around, a joy to every patriot eye. He was Assistant Adjutant General on General Edward's staff. Thoroughly honest and patriotic, he was the right man in the right place. He is very well known in Wisconsin and is the author of the fine hymn, " The unknown Graves of the Loyal Dead." Children :

> 5300. Catherine Macaulay[8], b. Aug. 20, 1859; m. May 18, 1892,. Eugene W. Leach of Racine, Wis.
>
> 5301. Henry Marsh, b. Jan. 10, 1862 ; d. Jan. 26, 1864.
>
> 5302. Robert Whitney, b. Sept. 19, 1865 ; unm. 1895 ; resides at Mason City, Iowa.
>
> 5303. Sarah Marsh, b. March 21, 1868, at St. Louis, as the three above.
>
> 5304. Mary Dwight, b. April 20, 1870, in Racine, Wis.
>
> 5305. Elizabeth Willard, b. Sept. 4, 1877 ; d. Aug. 26, 1878.

## 5306 = 5286. HENRY WHITNEY[8] MARSH

b. at Racine, Wis., Feb. 8, 1847, son of Henry Lawrence[7] and Clara Ellis (Canfield) Marsh, (Henry[6], Jr., Henry[5], Judge Perez[4], Capt. Job[3], Daniel[2], John[1]) ; m. Nov. 13, 1877, No. 5306.

**5306.** Caroline Ramsdell. b. April 5, 1852, dau. of Jonathan.

Gannett and Eliza Ann Ramsdell.   They reside at Manistee, Mich.
He is engaged in the lumber business.   Children :

5307.   Jessie Edna[9], b. Dec. 5, 1878.
5308.   Clara Belle, b. July 22, 1882.
5309.   Bertha, b. Sept. 25, 1883.
5310.   Henry Lawrence, b. Dec. 30, 1884.
5311.   Irene, b. Feb. 7, 1886.
5312.   Lida Ramsdell, b. June 30, 1891.

.

5313 = 5287.   MARIA CANFIELD[8] MARSH      ●

b. at Racine, Wis., Jan. 8, 1849, dau. of Henry Lawrence[7] and Clara
Ellis (Canfield) Marsh, (Henry[6], Jr., Henry[5], Judge Perez[4], Capt.
Job[3], Daniel[2], John[1]); m. at Racine, Oct. 17, 1878, No. 5313.

**5313.**   John Miller Clark, Esq., Broker, N. Y. City.   He has a
seat in the New York Stock Exchange, and they reside at Plainfield,
N. J.   Child :

5314.   Clara Marsh[9], b. at Plainfield, N. J., Dec. 20, 1889.

# PLEASE ADD.

---

To account of John[3] Marsh, page 27.

In his wise and touching address at Hartford, Feb. 5, 1895, as to the long time desecration and much needed improvement of the oldest burial ground located in the heart of that city, Dr. George Leon Walker mentions that of the great company gathered into that ground between 1698 and 1752, "only scattered names are recoverable. But among them are men filling a large place in the affairs of the Hartford of the two generations in question." Then he gives the names of 16 men and one is " Capt. John Marsh." Then he gives the following town act :

On December 18, 1730, the town appointed " Nathan Stanley, Ozias Pitkin, Captain John Marsh[3], Captain Thomas Steele and Captain John Whiting, a committee in behalf of the town to consider and determine " on a petition of the " First Church or Society in Hartford," for " liberty to set a meeting house either in part or in whole on the burying lott."

To No. 145 page 33, for Morris W. Seymour, Esq., Bridgeport, Ct.

My father was the late Hon. Origen Storrs Seymour, Chief Justice of this state, who was a son of Ozias, for many years the Sheriff of Litchfield County, who was a son of Major Moses Seymour and Molly (not Mary) Marsh, who was the daughter of Col. Ebenezer Marsh. My mother was Lucy Morris Woodruff, daughter of Major-General Morris Woodruff and Candace Catlin.

To page 37, No. 201.1.

Ormond Marsh, born at Litchfield, Ct., Nov. 5, 1787, died in 1854. Ann Whistler, born at Fort Washington now Cincinnati, Ohio, Sept. 1, 1794, died at Litchfield, Ct., March 29, 1829.

Ormond Marsh and Ann Whistler were married at Detroit, Jan. 6, 1812. Children :

John Whistler Shethar Marsh, born at Litchfield, Ct., April 6, 1814, died at Litchfield, Feb. 11, 1815.

Mary Rachel Jones Marsh, born at Litchfield, Oct. 4, 1816, died at Litchfield, Feb. 4, 1817.

Harriet Ann Marsh, born at Litchfield, March 2, 1818, married William Robert Wood, at Detroit, Mich., Jan., 1844.

Sarah Jane Marsh, born at Litchfield, Dec. 23, 1819, married John A. Rucker, 1861, died without children in 1862.

George Marsh born at Litchfield, Dec. 6, 1821, married (1) Mary Russell Loring née Adams, born Oct. 31, 1819, died June 18, 1860; (2) Sarah Ann Ritchie, born Oct. 30, 1834. Died off the coast of Peru, S. A., Feb. 16, 1867.

James Ormond Marsh, born at Litchfield, March 29, 1824, married Minerva Louise Atwood.

William Bishop Marsh, born at Litchfield, March 8, 1829, died March 29, 1829.

### Children of George and Mary Marsh :

George Whistler Marsh, born in Boston, Mass., Dec. 21, 1848, d. at Townsend Harbor, Mass., April 17, 1864.

Charles Sumner Marsh, born in Boston, Mass., April 1, 1850, married Anna F. Remington née Beals.

Sibbie Horne Marsh, born in South Boston, Mass., Jan. 9, 1853.

Mary Loring Marsh, born in Watertown, Mass., April 30, 1855, married Albert A. Faunce, born in 1843, died Oct. 26, 1884. She died at East Cambridge, Oct. 24, 1882.

### Children of George and Sarah Marsh :

Luella Maud Marsh, born at East Cambridge, Mass., Sept. 27, 1863.

Edward Livingstone Marsh, born at East Cambridge, Feb. 28, 1865, married Mary Hormel.

### Child of Charles S. and Anna F. Marsh :

George Marsh, born Dec. 4, 1867, at East Cambridge, Mass.

Child of Albert A. and Mary Loring Faunce :

Mary Faunce, born at East Cambridge, Oct. 15, 1882.

Children of Edward L. and Mary Marsh :

Harold Hormel Marsh, born at East Cambridge, March 4, 1891.
Wilbur Atwell Marsh, born at East Cambridge, July, 1893.

To No. 252, page 45.

James[6] Baldwin, m. Abigail Dickinson. Their child, Susan[7], m.
Alfred Peck. Their son William Guy[8] Peck, m. Ida Dayton. Their
son Guy Dayton[9] Peck, lives in New York City, place of business,
280 Broadway.

To No. 465 page 61.

Lewis[7] Marsh d. in Burlington, Ct., Dec. 14, 1894. He was a
member of the Connecticut General Assembly in 1872.

To No. 735, page 82.

Mr. Porter was born Aug. 28, 1855, at Hartford, son of James
Timothy and Elizabeth Ann Porter ; 1867–1871, student at Hartford
public high school, but left before graduation ; 1871–1876. clerk with
William L. Matson, banker, and his successor in business, the Secur-
ity Company ; 1877–1880, student at Sheffield Scientific school of
Yale college, graduating with the usual degree of Ph. B.; 1880–1883,
special expert agent, 10th U. S. census, to examine and report upon
water power of U. S. See Reports 10th Census of U. S., Vols.
XVI and XVII.; 1883, to date engaged in teaching, first in the
Mathematical and afterwards in the Civil Engineering Department of
the Massachusetts Institute of Technology, Boston. At present
Associate Professor of Hydraulic Engineering. Member of the
Boston Society of Civil Engineers, the American Society of Civil
Engineers, the New England Water Works Association, etc. Dwight
Porter had :

Kate Elizabeth, born July 9, 1882.
Annie Alice, born Feb. 16, 1884.
James Marsh, born Jan. 27, 1886.
Helen Margerie, born Dec. 19, 1887.

## To No. 868, page 93.

"Young Mr. Samuel Marsh of Hartford married a Miss Jones."
Letter of Rev. Roger Viets, dated Oct. 30, 1799.

## To No. 1824, page 123.

Miss Pamelia Barber, b. June 24, 1828, m. Jan. 7, 1851, Oliver
Wellman.

## To No. 1993.48, page 145.

Children, " all born at the Manior de Monte Belle ":
Louis Joseph¹¹, b. Aug., 1881.
Talbot Mercer, b. March 25, 1883.
James Randall Westcott, b. Sept. 14, 1884.
Philippe Bruneau Montigny, b. May 19, 1887.

## To No. 2291.1, page 180.

John Worthington Marsh, married Annie Silsby Porter, daughter
of Frederick W. and Caroline (Silsby) Porter, Oct. 9, 1872. Annie
Silsby Porter was born June 22, 1851, at Springfield, Vt. Children :
John Porter Marsh, born Feb. 24, 1874 at Chicago, Ill.
Miriam Elizabeth Marsh, born Aug. 7, 1875, at Springfield, Vt.

## To No. 2712, page 214.

### AN INTERESTING HISTORY.

*From a Winsted, Ct., Paper.*

The *National Exponent* is a newspaper published weekly at Chicago,
in the interest of the deaf.

The issue of Jan. 31, contains a full account of the 55th anniversary of the marriage of Mr. and Mrs. Jonathan P. Marsh, in that
city, with portraits of both Mr. and Mrs. Marsh. The celebration
took place on Washington Boulevard at the house of a son-in-law,
Edwin Bowes, with whom they reside.

Mr. and Mrs. Marsh (then Paulina Bowditch) were among the
early pupils of the American Asylum for the Deaf and Dumb, at
Hartford, established in 1817, and the first one in America. Its

first principal was Rev. Thomas H. Gallaudet, a graduate of Yale college in 1805, who went abroad to perfect himself as a teacher of the deaf mutes and spent some time in France under the instruction of the Abbe Sicard.

Mr. Marsh is a native of this town, born April 26, 1814, and is an elder brother of the esteemed Edward F. Marsh, who died Feb. 4, 1895 in New Hartford. Their father Rev. Frederick Marsh, was ordained pastor of the church in Winchester Feb. 1, 1809, and continued to reside there until his death in 1873.

Rev. Mr. Marsh was a college classmate of Dr. Gallaudet and was visited by him at Winchester soon after the opening of the asylum. Tradition tells that after Dr. Gallaudet had seen the bright eyed dumb boy for a few minutes, he turned to Mrs. Marsh, the boy's mother, and said, " your son tells me that you keep a horse, two cows and many sheep." "Why how is that possible?" asked Mrs. Marsh, and burst into tears, for up to that time there was no hope of educating mutes and they were considered hopelessly unfortunate.

Mr. Jonathan Marsh has filled a long life with usefulness and has been specially happy in his home. His only son died in boyhood. His two daughters both mutes, married mutes. One has four children who speak, now men and women; and the other three mute children.

Edward F. Marsh of New Hartford, whose critical illness was announced in Monday's *Herald*, died that day at the age of 78 years. He was a son of the Rev. Frederick Marsh, who for 50 years was pastor of the Winchester Center church, and father of Fred. W. Marsh of Winsted. Mr. Marsh was well known here by our older townspeople and has many relatives hereabout, among his nephews being Judge Carrington and Henry F. and Joseph Marsh. He is Frederick Edward No. 2710.4, p. 215.

## No. 2951, page 237.

The dates of birth for children of Jonathan[5], were:

Jacob, b. Dec. 24, 1778 in Ware.
Jonathan, b. Oct. 24, 1781 in Ware.
Infant daughter, b. Sept. 22, 1780, died next day.
Sewell, b. May 24, 1784, in Ware.
Eunice, b. June 8, 1786, in Ware.

31

Foster, b. Aug. 25, 1788, in Ware.

Infant son, b. May 30, 1791, died June 9, 1791.

Sophia, b. May 30, 1794, in Ware.

### No. 3082, page 250.

Jacob[6], m. Abigail Howard, March 24, 1801.

### No. 3085, page 250.

Foster[6], farmer, m. (1) May 7, 1815, Lucy Thompson. He m. (2) Catherine H. Fish, b. at Hardwick, Mass., in 1809. He d. in Ware, Mass., Nov. 11, 1860 and she d. there Oct. 18, 1873. Children :

Rev. Loring Bradlee[7], b. Feb. 12, 1816.

Rev. Samuel Dexter, Yale college 1844, went in 1848 missionary of the American Board to the Zulus in South Africa and d. there Dec. 11, 1853. He m. Aug. 25, 1847, Mary Sherman Skinner, dau. of Roger Sherman Skinner, descended from Roger Sherman, signer of the Declaration of Independence. Child : Helen.

Lewis Augustine, painter and paper hanger, m. Jane N. Smith. He had a son and a dau. and d. at Springfield, Mass. His widow lives at Ware.

George Thompson, now living in Boston, a painter ; m. Margaret Bullen and had a dau. who died.

Saphira J., unm. living in Boston.

### By second wife.

Dwight Foster, b. July 10, 1851, living in Ware, Mass., a lumber merchant. He m. (1) Sept. 10, 1873, Adda E. W. Rugg, who d. in Ware, April 18, 1874. He m. (2) March 30, 1876, Clara N. Ayres of Northampton. Children :

Ernest Foster, b. July 23, 1878.

Errol Dwight, b. July 19, 1889.

To No. 4377, page 377.

Family record of M. F. Dickinson. Jr., Counsellor at Law, Boston, Mass., made up March 4, 1895.

Marquis F. Dickinson, Jr., born Jan. 16, 1840, at Amherst, Mass. Cecilia Risk Williston, his wife, daughter of Henry Risk, for 17 years in the English army in which he is said to have held a commission. He participated in the battle of Waterloo. After quitting the service he married Cecilia Brett (or Fox) and at one time resided at Birmingham, England, where his two oldest children were born. Removing to Canada he became Imigration Agent and later, Inspector General of Weights and Measures. The daughter Cecilia was born in Canada, Nov., 1838, but whether at Montreal, Hamilton or Toronto is uncertain. Her mother died at the age of about 37, probably in Montreal ; and her father died in the Mass. General Hospital at Boston about 1850. She was adopted and reared by Hon. Samuel Williston of Easthampton, Mass., and was married there to Mr. Dickinson, Nov. 23, 1864, by Rev. Samuel T. Seelye, D. D. Children :

Williston Dickinson, b. at Boston, Feb. 16, 1869, d. at Amherst, Aug. 22, 1872.

Charles Dickinson, b. at Boston, July 17, 1872. At present a member of the class of '96, Harvard College.

Florence Dickinson, b. at Boston, Feb. 10, 1875, d. at Boston, Aug. 27, 1875.

Jennie Couden Dickinson, adopted daughter, b. at Chatham, Mass., Jan. 22, 1884. Daughter of Rev. Henry N. Couden and Lydia Jane (Dickinson) Couden, deceased, sister of M. F. Dickinson, Jr., who d. in Chatham, Mass., Feb., 1884.

To No. 3026, page 244.

Children of Lorin L. Ball and Augusta Jane (Marsh) Ball :

Isabelle Augusta, b. Feb. 16, 1857, m. Oscar A. Barron, Dec. 3, 1878. Child : Ella Melissa, b. March 22, 1880.

Nettie Addie, b. Jan. 28, 1859.

Ella J., b. Nov. 16, 1860, d. Sept. 17, 1873.

Minnie Lucretia, b. Jan. 12, 1862.

John Henry, b. Feb. 23, 1864, m. Lizzie A. Haskins, June 17, 1885. Child : Elwyn Haskins, b. April 25, 1893.

Leonard Lafontaine, b. Sept. 28, 1866, m. Jennie E. Fales, June 5, 1889. Children : Clara E., b. July 8, 1890 ; Herbert LeRoy, b. Nov. 7, 1892.

William Monroe, b. Jan. 20, 1868, m. Nettie M. Hayes, Nov. 27, 1892.

Alyn St. Clare, b. Sept. 20, 1869.

Bertha Lois, b. Oct. 5, 1876.

## To No. 1991.2, page 139.

C. Ellis Stevens, LL. D., D. C. L., F. S. A. (Edinburgh) the very learned author of " Sources of the Constitution of the United States " has recently been " knighted by the Queen Regent of Spain with the Order of Isabella of Castile, the historic patroness of American discovery."

## To No. 5249, page 449.

The mother of Sarah Whitney was Clarissa Dwight of Springfield, Mass., dau. of Col. Josiah Dwight and Elizabeth[5] Buckminster, Col. Thomas[4], Joseph[3], Joseph[2], and Thomas[1]. Capt. Henry Dwight, father or Col. Josiah, m. Lydia[3] Hawley of Northampton, Joseph[2], Harvard College 1674, Thomas[1]. Timothy Dwight, grandfather of Col. Josiah, m. in 1664 Anne Flynt, dau. of Rev. Henry Flynt and Margaret Hoar, sister of President Hoar of Harvard College. Timothy was son of John Dwight, who d. in 1660.

## To No. 132, page 31.

The following are extracts from a pleasant letter of Hon. E. J. Phelps our late Minister to England, now Professor at Yale University, dated "New Haven, Conn., Jan. 20, 1895." "Have been breaking up at Burlington and removed here for the winter."

" Samuel Shethar Phelps was my father." " I was born July 11, 1822. Married Mary, daughter of Stephen Haight of Vermont long time Sergeant at Arms of the U. S. Senate.

Have had four children :

Edward Haight, deceased.

Frances Shurtleff, deceased.

Mary Haight, wife of Prof. Horatio Loomis of the University of Vermont.

Charles Pierpont, now living in Boston."

# INDEX.

33

# INDEX.

35